5
YEAR

Classwork

Literacy

Eileen Jones

Acknowledgements

The author and publishers wish to thank the following for permission to use copyright material:

Curtis Brown Ltd on behalf of the authors for an extract from Nina Bawden, *Carrie's War*, Victor Gollancz, 1973, copyright © 1973 Nina Bawden; and Anthony Thwaite, 'The Fly', copyright © Anthony Thwaite.

Faber and Faber Ltd for an excerpt from T S Eliot, 'Macavity: The Mystery Cat', from *Old Possum's Book of Practical Cats*, by T S Eliot; and Ted Hughes 'Amulet' from *Under the North Star* by Ted Hughes.

Martin Glynn for 'Genius'.

David Higham Associates on behalf of the authors for an extract from Roald Dahl and Richard George, *James and the Giant Peach – A Play*, Penguin, 1982; and extracts from Jamila Gavin, *The Temple by the Sea* and Jamila Gavin, *Coram Boy*.

The Christopher Little Agency on behalf of the author for an extract from J K Rowling, *Harry Potter & the Prisoner of Azkaban*, 1999, pages 20–1. Copyright © J K Rowling 1999.

Jennifer Luithlen Agency on behalf of the author for an extract from Robert Swindells, *The World's Only English Commanche*, included in BBC Children in Need Collection, BBC Worldwide (2002). Copyright © 2002 Robert Swindells.

Maggie Noach Literary Agency on behalf of the author for material from Jean Ure, 'The Winner', included in *BBC Children in Need Collection*, BBC Worldwide (2002). Copyright © 2002 Jean Ure.

The Orion Publishing Group for extracts from Lucy Coats, *The Magic Head* and *The Volcano Monster*, from *Atticus the Storyteller's 100 Greek Myths*, by Lucy Coats, Orion Children's Books.

Roger Stevens for 'Louder'.

Jill Townsend for 'Tortoise and Hare Race'.

A P Watt Ltd on behalf of The National Trust for Places of Historical Interest or Natural Beauty for an extract from Rudyard Kipling, 'Mowgli's Brothers', from *The Jungle Book*, by Rudyard Kipling.

Kit Wright for 'Rabbiting On'.

Scholastic Ltd. for an extract from Philip Pullman, *Northern Lights* (1995) part 1 of *His Dark Materials*, Scholastic Children's Books. © Philip Pullman 1995.

Walker Books Ltd. for an extract from Marcia Williams, *King Arthur and the Knights of the Round Table*. © Marcia Williams 1996.

Cover photo by Corbis E1170 (NT).

Every effort has been made to trace the copyright holders but if any have been inadvertently overlooked the publishers will be pleased to make the necessary arrangement at the first opportunity.

Contents

Introduction

How Classworks works

What this book contains

- Chunks of text, both annotated and 'blank' for your own annotations.
- Checklists (or toolkits), planning frames, storyboards, scaffolds and other writing aids.
- Examples of modelled, supported and demonstration writing.
- Lesson ideas including key questions and plenary support.
- Marking ladders for structured self-assessment.
- Blocked unit planning with suggested texts, objectives and outcomes.
- Word-level starter ideas to complement the daily teaching of phonics, handwriting and other skills.
- There are no scripts, no worksheets and nothing you can't change to suit your needs.

How this book is organised

- There are blocked units of work (see previous page) lasting between one week and several, depending on the text type.
- Each blocked unit is organised into a series of chunks of teaching content.
- Each 'chunk' has accompanying checklists and other photocopiable resources.
- For every text we *suggest* annotations, checklists and marking ladders.
- Every unit follows the *teaching sequence for writing* found in *Grammar for Writing* (DfES 2000).
- You can mix and match teaching ideas, units and checklists as you see fit.

How you can use *Classworks* with your medium-term plan

- Refer to your medium-term planning for the blocking of NLS objectives.
- Find the text-type you want to teach (or just the objectives).
- Use the contents page to locate the relevant unit.
- Familiarise yourself with the text and language features using Classworks checklists and exemplar analysis pages, and other DfES or QCA resources such as *Grammar for Writing*.
- Browse the lesson ideas and photocopiables to find what you want to use.
- You can just use the text pages ... photocopy and adapt the checklists ... use or change some of the teaching ideas ... take whatever you want and adapt it to fit your class.

Planning a blocked unit of work with Classworks

Classworks units exemplify a blocked unit approach to planning the teaching of Literacy. What follows is an outline of this method of planning and teaching, and how *Classworks* can help you

You need: *Classworks* Literacy Year 5, medium-term planning; OHT (optional).
Optional resources: your own choice of texts for extra analysis; *Grammar for Writing*.

Method

- From the medium-term planning, identify the **outcome**, **texts** and **objectives** you want to teach.
- *Classworks* units **exemplify** how some units could be planned, resourced and taught.
- Decide how to 'chunk' the text you are analysing, for example, introductory paragraph, paragraph 1, paragraph 2, closing paragraph.
- *Classworks* units give an example of **chunking** with accompanying resources and exemplar analysis. Texts for pupil analysis (labelled 'Pupil copymaster') are intended for whole class display on OHT.
- **Whatever you think of the checklists provided, analyse the text with *your* class and build *your own* checklist for the whole text, and for each chunk.**
- Plan your blocked unit based on the following teaching sequence for writing.
- *Classworks* units outline one way of planning a **blocked unit**, with exemplifications of some days, and suggestions for teaching content on others.

Shared Reading – analysing the text – create 'checklist' or writer's toolkit	The children analyse another of that text type and add to checklist	Review checklist
Shared Writing – demonstrate application of 'checklist' to a small piece of writing	The children write independently based on your demonstration	Use examples on OHT to check against the 'checklist'

- This model is only a guideline, allowing the writing process to be scaffolded. You would want to build in opportunities for planning for writing, talking for writing, teaching explicit word-level and sentence-level objectives that would then be modelled in the shared writing, and so on. There are ideas for word-level and sentence-level starters on pages 184–185.
- Allow opportunities for the children to be familiar with the text type. This might include reading plenty of examples, drama, role play, video, and so on.

Assessment

- Make sure that 'checklists' are displayed around the room and referred to before writing and when assessing writing in the **plenary**.
- One or two children could work on an OHT and this could be the focus of the plenary.
- Use a **marking ladder** for the children to evaluate their writing. This is based on the checklist your class has built up. We give you an example of how it might look for each blocked unit. There's a blank copy on page 186.

What each page does

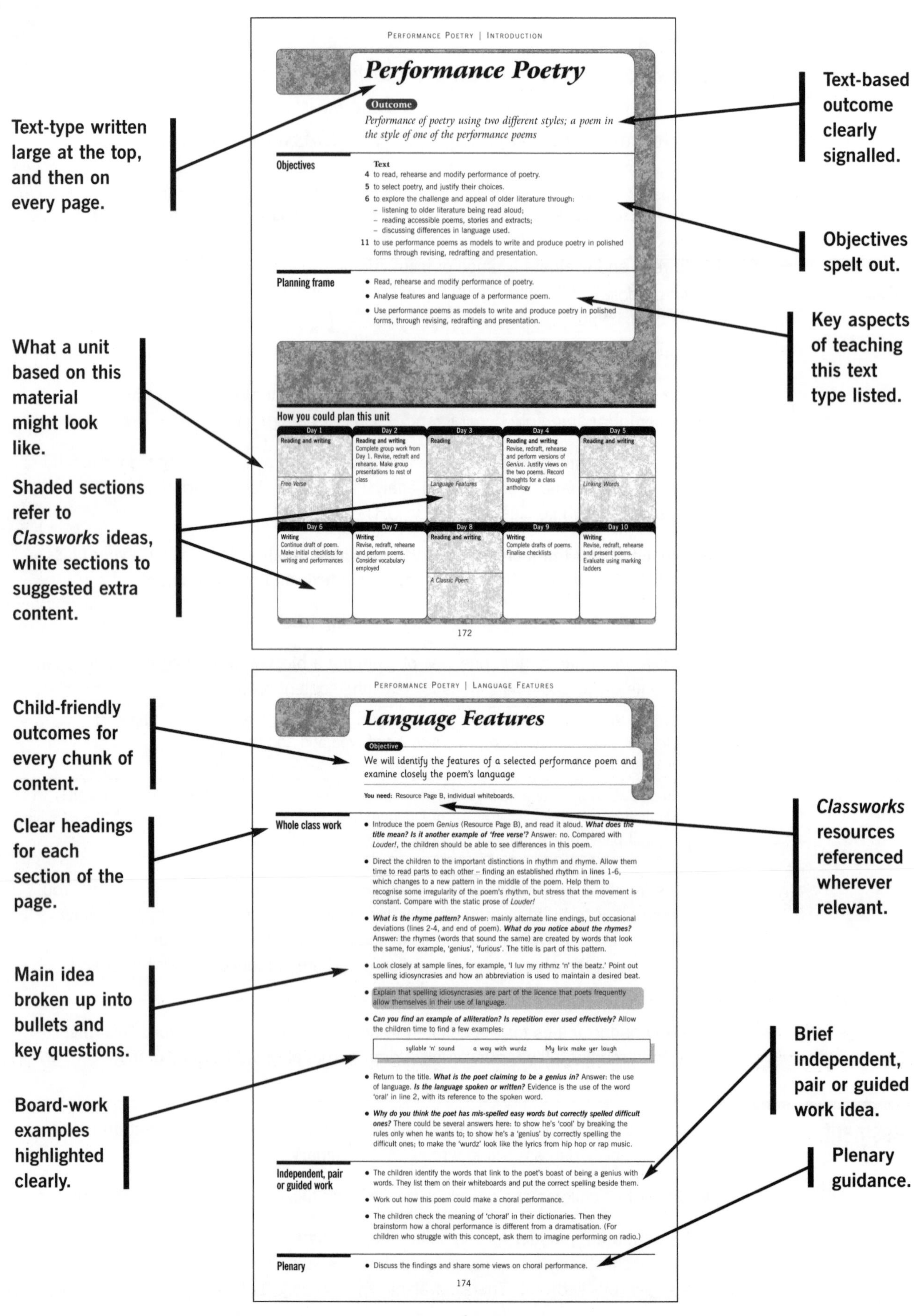

PERFORMANCE POETRY | INTRODUCTION

Performance Poetry

Outcome

Performance of poetry using two different styles; a poem in the style of one of the performance poems

Objectives

Text

4 to read, rehearse and modify performance of poetry.
5 to select poetry, and justify their choices.
6 to explore the challenge and appeal of older literature through:
– listening to older literature being read aloud;
– reading accessible poems, stories and extracts;
– discussing differences in language used.
11 to use performance poems as models to write and produce poetry in polished forms through revising, redrafting and presentation.

Planning frame

- Read, rehearse and modify performance of poetry.
- Analyse features and language of a performance poem.
- Use performance poems as models to write and produce poetry in polished forms, through revising, redrafting and presentation.

How you could plan this unit

Day 1	Day 2	Day 3	Day 4	Day 5
Reading and writing *Free Verse*	**Reading and writing** Complete group work from Day 1. Revise, redraft and rehearse. Make group presentations to rest of class	**Reading** *Language Features*	**Reading and writing** Revise, redraft, rehearse and perform versions of *Genius*. Justify views on the two poems. Record thoughts for a class anthology	**Reading and writing** *Linking Words*

Day 6	Day 7	Day 8	Day 9	Day 10
Writing Continue draft of poem. Make initial checklists for writing and performances	**Writing** Revise, redraft, rehearse and perform poems. Consider vocabulary employed	**Reading and writing** *A Classic Poem*	**Writing** Complete drafts of poems. Finalise checklists	**Writing** Revise, redraft, rehearse and present poems. Evaluate using marking ladders

172

PERFORMANCE POETRY | LANGUAGE FEATURES

Language Features

Objective

We will identify the features of a selected performance poem and examine closely the poem's language

You need: Resource Page B, individual whiteboards.

Whole class work

- Introduce the poem *Genius* (Resource Page B), and read it aloud. ***What does the title mean? Is it another example of 'free verse'?*** Answer: no. Compared with *Louder!*, the children should be able to see differences in this poem.
- Direct the children to the important distinctions in rhythm and rhyme. Allow them time to read parts to each other – finding an established rhythm in lines 1-6, which changes to a new pattern in the middle of the poem. Help them to recognise some irregularity of the poem's rhythm, but stress that the movement is constant. Compare with the static prose of *Louder!*
- ***What is the rhyme pattern?*** Answer: mainly alternate line endings, but occasional deviations (lines 2-4, and end of poem). ***What do you notice about the rhymes?*** Answer: the rhymes (words that sound the same) are created by words that look the same, for example, 'genius', 'furious'. The title is part of this pattern.
- Look closely at sample lines, for example, 'I luv my rithmz 'n' the beatz.' Point out spelling idiosyncrasies and how an abbreviation is used to maintain a desired beat.
- Explain that spelling idiosyncrasies are part of the licence that poets frequently allow themselves in their use of language.
- ***Can you find an example of alliteration? Is repetition ever used effectively?*** Allow the children time to find a few examples:

syllable 'n' sound   a way with wurdz   My lirix make yer laugh

- Return to the title. ***What is the poet claiming to be a genius in?*** Answer: the use of language. ***Is the language spoken or written?*** Evidence is the use of the word 'oral' in line 2, with its reference to the spoken word.
- ***Why do you think the poet has mis-spelled easy words but correctly spelled difficult ones?*** There could be several answers here: to show he's 'cool' by breaking the rules only when he wants to; to show he's a 'genius' by correctly spelling the difficult ones; to make the 'wurdz' look like the lyrics from hip hop or rap music.

Independent, pair or guided work

- The children identify the words that link to the poet's boast of being a genius with words. They list them on their whiteboards and put the correct spelling beside them.
- Work out how this poem could make a choral performance.
- The children check the meaning of 'choral' in their dictionaries. Then they brainstorm how a choral performance is different from a dramatisation. (For children who struggle with this concept, ask them to imagine performing on radio.)

Plenary

- Discuss the findings and share some views on choral performance.

174

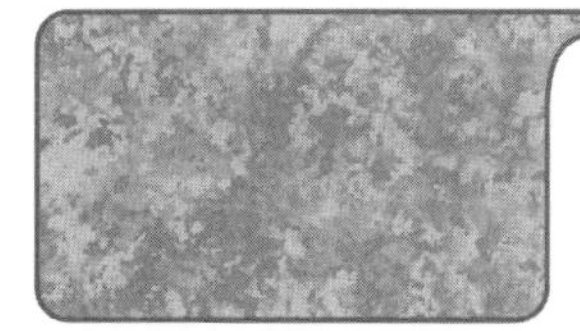

Instruction Writing

Outcome

A set of instructions

Objectives

Sentence

3 to discuss, proof-read and edit their own writing for clarity and correctness.

9 to identify the imperative form in instructional writing ... and use this awareness when writing for this purpose.

Text

22 to read and evaluate a range of instructional texts in terms of their:
- purpose
- organisation and layout
- clarity and usefulness.

25 to write instructional texts and test them out.

Planning frame

- Read and analyse the features of instructional writing.
- Evaluate a range of instructional texts.
- Recognise and use appropriately imperative verb forms.
- Present a series of instructions in chronological order.
- Identify and use time connectives.

How you could plan this unit

Day 1	Day 2	Day 3	Day 4	Day 5
Reading Read a range of different instructions. What do they have in common? Begin to identify some features of instruction writing	**Reading** *Effective Instructions*	**Writing** *Creating a Draft*	**Writing** Continue writing instructions that can be tested. Discuss, proof-read and edit. Review checklist	**Writing** Polish own writing. Test instructions. Evaluate using marking ladder (Resource Page E)

Effective Instructions

Objective

We will identify and understand the key features of an instructional text, including imperatives, and evaluate its effectiveness

You need: Resource Pages A and B; a range of instructions from different areas of the school; Post-it™ notes.

Whole class work

- Introduce the unit by using some imperative forms in your instructions to the class, for example: '*Find* your copy of the text about the photocopier. *Have* that ready to use. *Listen* to my next three sentences.'
- Ask the children to identify the verb in each. ***What does the verb always do?*** Answer: issue commands. Explain that the meaning of the word 'imperative' relates to that.
- Point out the absence of a pronoun. ***What do you notice about the position of the verb?*** Answer: it's at the beginning.
- Read the instructions on using the school photocopier (Resource Page A). Focus on the simplicity of the construction of the sentences, picking out some examples. ***How does this help the text?*** Answer: clarity.
- Consider instructions 7 and 8. Use questions to prompt the children to recognise a greater complexity in the sentence structure:
  - ***What is the effect?***
  - ***Is there confusion?***
  - ***What has happened to the imperative verb?***
- ***Find 'after', 'now', 'finally' in the text. Why are they used? Are they important? What is the benefit from them? How do they help the audience?*** Ask the children to identify their roles in the sentences; guide them towards the labels 'linking words' and 'connectives'. An exemplar analysis is given on Resource Page B.
- Discuss the layout, reminding the children that clarity is important. ***Could the layout be improved?*** For example, using different positioning of text, the use of colour, more effective organisational devices and so on.

Independent, pair or guided work

- In pairs, the children recall the instructional writing within the school environment, for example, classroom instructions written next to the computer; cloakroom rules written outside; instructions for lunchtime arrangements outside the dining hall.
- Ask the children to list what they can find (within the classroom) or can remember. ***How effective is the instructional writing? Why do you think that?***
- Record on Post-it™ notes what features matter most.

Plenary

- Share some of the findings. Discuss and list what the most effective texts have in common.
- Make a display of the Post-it™ notes for compiling checklists later in the week.

Creating a Draft

Objective

We will write our own instructions for an activity

You need: Resource Pages C and D.

Whole class work

- Review the purpose of instructional writing – to teach how to do or make something.
- Explain that the most effective instructional writing avoids confusion by presenting information clearly and in the correct chronological order.
- Demonstrate how to write an instructional text (Resource Page C). Discuss what the writing is trying to achieve: in this case, how to cook a fresh pizza.
  - ***What needs to come first?*** Remind the children that the title must convey the aim.
  - ***How much detail should there be?*** Remember that too much or unnecessary detail can be confusing.
  - ***Are imperative verb forms being used?***
  - ***Is the chronology right?***
- Read through the finished draft together and analyse its effectiveness.
  - ***Where do imperatives normally appear in a sentence?***
  - ***What is distinctive about the imperative form?*** Answer: it requires no pronoun.
  - ***Would the occasional use of time-linking words be beneficial?***
  - ***Can the layout be improved?***
- List the ways in which the instructions could have been improved, for example, use of a diagram or picture, clearer instructions and so on.

Independent, pair or guided work

- In pairs, the children brainstorm topics for their writing, for example:

  Saving/retrieving computer work
  How to send an email
  Playing short tennis/other sport
  Planning a new layout for the classroom
  How to design a simple work folder
  Sending computer attachments

  Remind them that they need to choose a set of instructions that can be tested in the school or by email to someone else.
- Discuss ideas and display checklists (Resource Page D).
- Independently, the children draft their set of instructions.

Plenary

- Select three or four children to share their ideas. ***Are their instructions straightforward to follow?***
- ***Are any common pitfalls emerging with this text type?*** For example, two or three instructions need to happen simultaneously – how could you write this? How do you avoid getting bogged down in too much detail? (Use appendices, bullets, boxes.)
- List and display suggestions.

Pupil copymaster

How to use the school photocopier

Requirements

- Proper photocopying paper
- A document no thicker than 50mm

Instructions

1 Place your work face down in Slot A.
2 Make sure there is blank paper in Slot B.
3 Switch the photocopier on (Switch C).
4 Wait for the red light to stop blinking.
5 After the light has changed to green, press 'Clear'.
6 Now key in the number of copies you want.
7 Choose the size you want, pressing either 'A4' or 'A5' on the left of the machine.
8 If you go wrong, press 'Clear' and begin again.
9 Now press the key marked 'Start'.
10 Collect your copies from the exit tray.
11 Finally, remember to remove your work.

Troubleshooting

Were you using the correct paper?

Is your work too thick?

Check for jammed paper inside the machine.

Have one more try.

Get advice – **this is an expensive machine!**

Exemplar analysis

Example of analysis of *How to use the school photocopier*

How to use the school photocopier	*The title states the aim or purpose of the text.*
Requirements • Proper photocopying paper • A document no thicker than 50mm	*Any equipment needed is listed prominently.*
Instructions	*Sub-headings and other organisational devices offer clarity.*
1 Place your work face down in Slot A.	*Diagrams/illustrations are also common; they are useful when references such as these are made.*
2 Make sure there is blank paper in Slot B.	
3 Switch the photocopier on (Switch C).	
4 Wait for the red light to stop blinking.	*Chronological order in the text is essential.*
5 After the light has changed to green, press 'Clear'.	
6 Now key in the number of copies you want.	
7 Choose the size you want, pressing either 'A4' or 'A5' on the left of the machine.	*Verbs in the imperative usually start the sentence.*
8 If you go wrong, press 'Clear' and begin again.	
9 Now press the key marked 'Start'.	*Time reference words reinforce the chronology of the instructions.*
10 Collect your copies from the exit tray.	
11 Finally, remember to remove your work.	
Troubleshooting	*The final part is the least important, yet it remains helpful. It often deals with possible problems or frequently asked questions.*
Were you using the correct paper?	
Is your work too thick?	
Check for jammed paper inside the machine.	
Have one more try.	
Get advice – **this is an expensive machine!**	*The final words are highlighted. They are not necessary for using the photocopier, but they are important to the writer.*

Exemplar material

Making pizza

Serves 4
Preparation time: *15 mins*
Cooking time: *15 mins*
Oven temperature: *Gas Mark 6; Electricity 175°C/350°F*

Ingredients
Ready-made pizza base
Tinned chopped tomatoes
1 small onion
50g grated Cheshire cheese

What to do
Fry onion gently until soft. Add tomatoes and heat for 2 mins.
Spread mixture over base, cover with cheese and place in oven.

To serve
Add salad and crusty bread.

Exemplar material

Checklists for instruction writing

Example of a checklist for the title

- State what the instructions are for
- Avoid confusion by using correct names
- Do not write in full sentences
- Highlight important words in **bold letters** or CAPITALS

Example of a checklist for the text

- Include a list at the start of any requirements or equipment needed
- Use imperative verbs (usually at the beginning of sentences)
- Use the present tense
- Follow chronological steps
- Support the chronology with time words when needed, for example, 'before', 'now', 'next', 'afterwards'

Example of a checklist for the layout

- Make it clear and easy to follow
- Use short lines or bullet points to divide chronological stages
- Use subheadings to divide the text (pointing to sections of information)
- Use numbers and/or letters to emphasise correct order
- Use organisational devices such as boxes, bullet points and symbols
- Use illustrations/diagrams

Marking ladder

Name: ______________________

Pupil	Objective	Teacher
	My set of instructions includes a title to catch the eye.	
	The title says what the instructions are for.	
	I used correct names in the text.	
	I included a list of requirements/equipment at the beginning.	
	I used verbs in the imperative.	
	I used the present tense.	
	I listed all the steps in chronological order.	
	I included diagrams/illustrations.	
	I used time words.	
	I used a helpful layout.	
	What could I do to improve my instruction writing next time?	

Narrative Structure

Outcome

A review for a book or narrative opening

Objectives

Sentence

3 to discuss, proof-read and edit their own writing for clarity and correctness.

6 to understand the need for punctuation as an aid to the reader.

Text

1 to analyse the features of a good opening and compare a number of story openings.

2 to compare the structure of different stories, to discover how they differ in pace, build-up, sequence, complication and resolution.

4 to consider how texts can be rooted in the writer's experience.

9 to develop an active attitude towards reading: seeking answers, anticipating events, empathising with characters and imagining events that are described.

14 to map out texts showing development and structure.

Planning frame

- Learn about the need for a story to have structure.
- Look at ways in which a story's structure may be planned or mapped, and produce own maps.
- Compare a number of story openings, identifying important features.

How you could plan this unit

Day 1	Day 2	Day 3	Day 4	Day 5
Reading Study the opening of *The Winner* (Resource Page A). What genre is it? Use text annotation (Resource Page B) to identify key points	**Reading/Writing** Study the ending of *The Winner* (Resource Page C). Consider the plot links with the opening. The children attempt own text annotation (see Resource Page D)	**Reading and writing** *Connectives and Reporting Verbs*	**Reading and writing** *Structure Maps*	**Writing** Complete checklist for narrative maps (Resource Page H). Recount the plot of *The Winner* (Resource Page H) and do individual maps. Marking ladder
Day 6	**Day 7**	**Day 8**	**Day 9**	**Day 10**
Writing *Book Reviews*	**Writing** Compile a class checklist for a review (Resource Page H). Work on reading journals for *The Winner*	**Writing** Complete review for *The Winner.* Use marking ladder (Resource Page I)	**Reading** *Story Openings*	**Writing** Discuss, proof-read and edit reviews. Use marking ladder

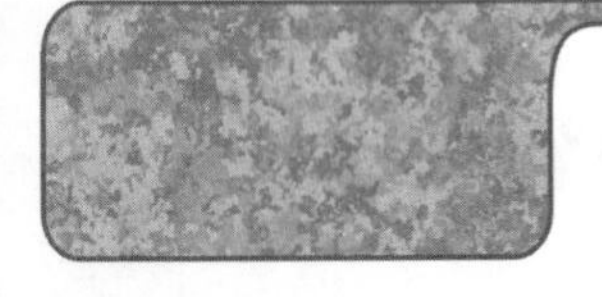

Connectives and Reporting Verbs

Objective

We will see how punctuation helps the reader, and will use it in creating complex sentences with connectives

You need: Resource Pages A and C.

Whole class work

- Reread *The Winner* (Resource Pages A and C). Consider the emotional appeal of the text. ***How do you react to the final paragraph? Does everyone respond in the same way?*** Ask the children what is likely to determine differences in their reactions.
- ***Could there be links with the author's own experiences as a child? Was she a slow learner, poor at sport, bullied, always felt different, always asked questions?***
- Ask two children to read the dialogue aloud. ***Which words should be left out so it sounds like a play?***
- ***What is the function of the words they have omitted?*** (Use the term 'reporting verbs'.) ***Could the author manage without some of the reporting verbs? How? What powerful verbs could be used instead?***
- ***Do all the characters speak in an equally complex way?*** (Sixer's speech is babyish.)
- Cover up the text. Ask the children what punctuation is needed to write a dialogue. Elicit that using new paragraphs for different people makes it clear who is speaking.
- Look at the paragraphs with no dialogue. Focus on their punctuation rules. ***When is a new paragraph used?*** Answer: to start a new idea.
- Which character(s) do the children empathise with? Are any of the experiences relevant to them?
- The children identify and highlight connectives. Brainstorm and display a less common range of connectives, for example:

whereas whenever since in case while although as long as if

Independent, pair or guided work

- Ask the children to continue to write a new version of the rest of the text, focusing on creating compound sentences, using a wide range of connectives. Connectives can be used at the beginning of a sentence.
- It may help some children to read their work aloud to help 'hear' where commas are needed.

Plenary

- Select a few pairs to speak some of their new dialogue.
- ***Are you less sympathetic to a more literate Sixer? Does it change how Ms Steelman comes across to the reader?***
- The children use a response sandwich to evaluate others' work: one good comment; one area for improvement; another good comment.

Structure Maps

Objective

We will learn about the structure of stories and map out a text

You need: Resource Pages A–E and H.

Whole class work

- Reread the opening and ending of *The Winner* (Resource Pages A and C).
- Focus on the structure of the story (see Resource Pages B and D).
  - ***Was the ending predictable from the start?***
  - ***Why is the title important?***
  - ***What does it tell us about how the story might progress?***
- ***How does Sixer feel at the beginning?*** Answer: not a winner. This frustration is likely to be resolved by the end. ***Why?***
- Draw out the concept of a writer developing the story and leading towards an ending, for example, making a situation worse before it improves; dropping hints/signposts of the conclusion; subtle references to the title and so on.
- A story is likely to give its main character happy/high moments and low/sad ones. ***Which sort of moments are the beginning and end?***
- Talk about the need for parallel and sub-plots as well as a main plot. A reader is likely to become bored by too simple or obvious a plot.
- Using a familiar story, for example, *Cinderella*, demonstrate plotting a narrative structure map (Resource Page E).

Independent, pair or guided work

- Explain that narrative structure maps can be used by an author to plan their story. Ask the children to think again about the beginning and end of *The Winner*. ***What might have happened in between?***
- The children plan a middle section, retaining this beginning and ending.
- Remind the children of the need for the plan to show the order of events.

Plenary

- Discuss some of the ideas for the story line using a response sandwich: one good comment; one area for improvement; another good comment.
- Begin to compile a class checklist for a narrative structure map (see checklist 1, Resource Page H for ideas).

Book Reviews

Objective

We will write a book review, paying special attention to our use of punctuation

You need: Resource Pages A, C, F and H.

Whole class work

- Brainstorm some ideas about book reviews:

> Who writes reviews?
> Where are they published?
> What are they for?
> Why do people use them?

Explain that all writers try to have their books reviewed either in newspapers and magazines or on the Internet and that reviewers are paid to read books and write their opinions.

- Ask the children to suggest how a review should be set out. ***Does the layout matter?*** Answer: no set format, but author, title and so on, must be included. Start to compile a class checklist (see checklist 2, Resource Page H for ideas).
- Stress that a review is an opinion. You can say whether you like or dislike something, but you must say why.

Independent, pair or guided work

- The children write a 100-word review of *The Winner* (Resource Pages A and C) or the opening page of *The World's Only English Comanche* (Resource Page F) for a particular audience (their peers, younger children, their parents and so on).
- While writing, or using the computer, the children should also focus on punctuation. Remind them that commas mark grammatical boundaries, colons signal what follows and so on.

> Ask yourself: Is this sentence too simple? How can I join these two simple sentences? Have I used powerful verbs?

- Select some examples to be read aloud. ***Does it make sense? Is it clear to someone who hasn't read the book? Are some constructions too confusing/too simple?*** Encourage the children to edit and polish their work to ensure clarity.
- Some children may have time to consider the ways in which book blurbs (on the back cover) are different from reviews.

Plenary

- Share some of the ideas about the new story.
- Select one or two children to read out their reviews.

Story Openings

Objective

We will compare a number of story openings and analyse the features of a good opening

You need: Resource Pages A and F–H.

Whole class work

- Revisit the story openings you have studied (Resource Pages A and F). Talk about the variation in feelings they have provoked in the class. ***Why do we differ? Is age/gender/family situation a factor?*** (Someone who has a small brother, or is the youngest of a big family, may be familiar with Sixer's frustrations.) ***Is the language too simple/complex? How much does all this matter – does it encourage/discourage you to move past the first page of a story?***
- Draw out the most important consideration: namely, if the writer wants the reader to carry on reading, attention must be grabbed early on and held.
- Brainstorm requirements for an effective narrative opening (see checklist 3, Resource Page H for ideas). Encourage the children's contributions by asking them to think about books they have enjoyed as opposed to ones they abandoned after the first page or two.

Independent, pair or guided work

- Ask the children to read the opening of *Harry Potter and the Prisoner of Azkaban* (Resource Page G).
- The children compare and 'rate' all three openings, using the checklist.
- Ask the children to try to work out reasons for their grading.

Plenary

- Discuss the results. ***Which opening was the most popular/least popular?*** Ask the children to explain their rating.
- ***Is there anything else we can add to our checklist?***

Pupil copymaster

The Winner – opening

His name was Sixth of Six.

Sixth of Six, Batch B.

His fellow Batch Bs called him Sixie, or Sixer. His teacher called him 6B. There were four other batches in the class. Batch K, Batch L, Batch M, Batch P. They all had a Sixth of Six.

Batch B was a boy batch. So was Batch K. The rest were all girls. You never had a batch that was mixed. Sixer had sometimes wondered about this. He had once asked his teacher, Ms Steelman, why it was. Ms Steelman had seemed taken aback.

"That's a very strange thing to be thinking about," she had said.

It was as if she didn't expect batch kids to think.

"It's just the way things are. Don't worry about it!"

Sixer wasn't worried; he was just puzzled, that was all. There were lots of things that puzzled Sixer. What, for instance, was the difference between batch people and real people? Sixer felt like a real person! He knew he wasn't, though. Sometimes boys from outside ganged up against the batch boys and called them names.

"Clones!" "Drones!" "Reps!"

He had asked Ms Steelman what a rep was but she had told him it wasn't anything that need concern him.

"Those boys were extremely rude. They ought to know better. Don't take any notice of them!"

Ms Steelman never answered any of his questions. He was the only one who ever asked them, so you would have thought that she would have had the time. But maybe Ms Steelman didn't know herself? That was something else that Sixer sometimes wondered about.

from The Winner, *by Jean Ure*

Exemplar analysis

Example of analysis of *The Winner* – opening

His name was Sixth of Six.

Sixth of Six, Batch B.

His fellow Batch Bs called him Sixie, or Sixer. His teacher called him 6B. There were four other batches in the class. Batch K, Batch L, Batch M, Batch P. They all had a Sixth of Six.

Batch B was a boy batch. So was Batch K. The rest were all girls. You never had a batch that was mixed. Sixer had sometimes wondered about this. He had once asked his teacher, Ms Steelman, why it was. Ms Steelman had seemed taken aback.

"That's a very strange thing to be thinking about," she had said.

It was as if she didn't expect batch kids to think.

"It's just the way things are. Don't worry about it!"

Sixer wasn't worried; he was just puzzled, that was all. There were lots of things that puzzled Sixer. What, for instance, was the difference between batch people and real people? Sixer felt like a real person! He knew he wasn't, though. Sometimes boys from outside ganged up against the batch boys and called them names.

"Clones!" "Drones!" "Reps!"

He had asked Ms Steelman what a rep was but she had told him it wasn't anything that need concern him.

"Those boys were extremely rude. They ought to know better. Don't take any notice of them!"

Ms Steelman never answered any of his questions. He was the only one who ever asked them, so you would have thought that she would have had the time. But maybe Ms Steelman didn't know herself? That was something else that Sixer sometimes wondered about.

from The Winner, *by Jean Ure*

The main character is immediately introduced.

The story is written in the third person. An alternative telling for this story would be to allow Sixer to tell his own story (writing in the first person).

A story must have a setting: the words 'teacher' and 'class' immediately indicate that this one is set in a school.

Early on in the story, supporting characters are introduced. A writer is unlikely to try to sustain a narrative plot with just one character – many characters, sub-plots or even parallel plots are likely to be present.

A reader will probably always presume that the time is the present day, unless informed otherwise. However, the names 'Batch K', 'Batch L' are strange, and could cause the reader to wonder if the time setting is a future time, or the place setting an alien planet. The story should eventually clear up any confusion.

References here to 'like a real person' and 'Clones!' and 'Drones!' confirm that there is something 'different' about this character and his setting; this makes the reader curious.

Many questions have been posed in the story. By doing this, the writer is capturing interest – she can now build the plot around resolving the problems facing her character, and answer the questions the reader is asking.

Pupil copymaster

The Winner – ending

"Winston Churchill was born in 1874. He was greatly beloved of the British people and became a great statesman and a great war leader, known affectionately as Winnie. At school he was not regarded as particularly bright, but in spite of that – ."

Sixer listened, intently. Sometimes there were words he hadn't heard before and didn't understand, but all the same, it was exciting! Jolee-Ann was telling this whole story from the marks on the page!

"I like do that," said Sixer, when she'd finished.

"What, read?" said Jolee-Ann. She almost laughed. The idea of a dr– a replicated person being able to read! But she stopped herself, just in time. "Shall I try and teach you?" she said.

"Yes, please!" said Sixer.

All the other kids were running about with their balloons, or flying their kites, but Sixer went on sitting there with Jolee-Ann the whole afternoon. By the time Ms Steelman came looking for him, to take him back to school, he could write the first ten letters of the alphabet and spell the words 'big', 'fig' and 'jig'. He could hardly wait to tell Ms Steelman!

"I write words," he said. "Look!"

Ms Steelman looked. "Good gracious me!" she said. "Who taught you that?"

"Jolee-Ann. She read my book."

And he told Ms Steelman what the book was about. A great man called Winston Churchill who was no good at school but went on to be prime minister and win a big war and everybody loved him and called him Winnie.

"Why did they do that, I wonder?" said Ms Steelman. "Was it because his name was Winston, do you think?"

But Sixer said no. They called him Winnie because he had won. Because he was a winner.

"This what I going be," said Sixer. "I going be like Winston Churchill." He clutched his book: his precious book. "I going be a WINNER!"

from The Winner, *by Jean Ure*

Exemplar material

Example of analysis of *The Winner – ending*

"Winston Churchill was born in 1874. He was greatly beloved of the British people and became a great statesman and a great war leader, known affectionately as Winnie. At school he was not regarded as particularly bright, but in spite of that – ."

Sixer listened, intently. Sometimes there were words he hadn't heard before and didn't understand, but all the same, it was exciting! Jolee-Ann was telling this whole story from the marks on the page!

"I like do that," said Sixer, when she'd finished.

"What, read?" said Jolee-Ann. She almost laughed. The idea of a dr– a replicated person being able to read! But she stopped herself, just in time.

"Shall I try and teach you?" she said.

"Yes, please!" said Sixer.

All the other kids were running about with their balloons, or flying their kites, but Sixer went on sitting there with Jolee-Ann the whole afternoon. By the time Ms Steelman came looking for him, to take him back to school, he could write the first ten letters of the alphabet and spell the words 'big', 'fig' and 'jig'. He could hardly wait to tell Ms Steelman!

"I write words," he said. "Look!"

Ms Steelman looked. "Good gracious me!" she said. "Who taught you that?"

"Jolee-Ann. She read my book."

And he told Ms Steelman what the book was about. A great man called Winston Churchill who was no good at school but went on to be prime minister and win a big war and everybody loved him and called him Winnie.

"Why did they do that, I wonder?" said Ms Steelman. "Was it because his name was Winston, do you think?"

But Sixer said no. They called him Winnie because he had won. Because he was a winner.

"This what I going be," said Sixer. "I going be like Winston Churchill." He clutched his book: his precious book. "I going be a WINNER!"

from The Winner, *by Jean Ure*

The story is still written in the third person, but dialogue is now frequent.

Jolee-Ann's actions resolve the problems and conflicts that have arisen in the story. A plot structure is cumulative, with one action leading to the next.

The function of this section is to bring together different strands of the main plot or sub-plots, and complete them.

This is a typical happy, 'tidy' ending to a story: problems set out at the start (frustration and unhappiness) have been resolved. A story requires a good ending, although a writer may deliberately leave questions unanswered.

A new character is introduced.

She is obviously a character of significance as she is willing to adopt a different attitude towards Sixer. (Compare with the attitude of Ms Steelman.) Jolee-Ann's attitude is essential to the end of the story.

The changed attitude of Ms Steelman from the beginning of the story indicates a parallel plot in which she (not just Sixer) has been changing.

Readers like to identify why a book or story has been given a particular title. The link between the story and its title is sometimes not apparent until the very end – there may be subtle allusions throughout.

Pupil copymaster

Narrative structure map

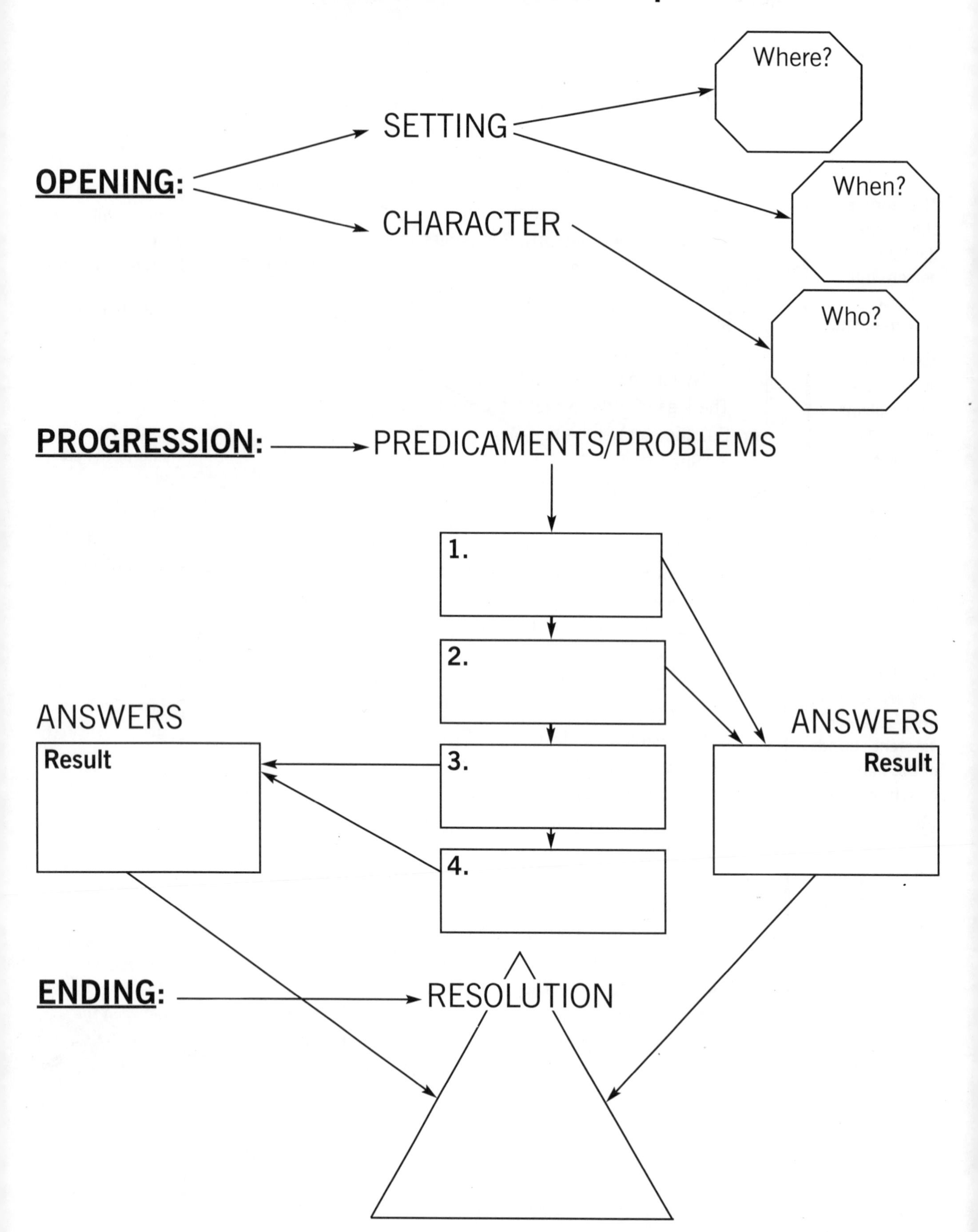

Pupil copymaster

The World's Only English Comanche

Hello. My name's Florence and I want to tell you a story. It's about something that happened to me a very long time ago, when I was a little girl.

It was wartime, the second world war, and I was staying with my great aunt Laura in Tiverton. Mum and Dad lived in London, but the city was being bombed every night so they'd sent me to Devon where I'd be safe. Well I was safe, but I wasn't happy.

You see, this wasn't a holiday for me. I might be at my great aunt's for a long time, so I had to go to school, and that was the trouble. The children of Tiverton had never met anyone from London before. "Cor," one of them said, the first time I opened my mouth, "don't she talk queer?" It was in the playground, my first morning. Kids gathered round, poking me and laughing.

"Say something," they jeered, "go on, say anything." Mum had told me to be polite to everyone so I said, "Good morning, my name's Florence, what's yours?"

"Mickey Mouse," says one. "Minnie Mouse," says another. "Rumplestiltskin," says someone else. They're all laughing, pushing me round the ring.

After a minute the teacher came out. "What on earth is going on?" she snapped, barging into the middle. "It's like a bear garden out here. Oh," she said when she saw me, "you must be the girl from London. You haven't made a very good start here, have you Florence?"

It wasn't fair. I hadn't started it. I tried to tell her but she said, "Never mind that now, you'd better come to the cloakroom and tidy yourself: we're not used to slum dwellers in Tiverton."

from The World's Only English Comanche, *by Robert Swindells*

Pupil copymaster

Harry Potter and the Prisoner of Azkaban

Harry Potter was a highly unusual boy in many ways. For one thing, he hated the summer holidays more than any other time of year. For another, he really wanted to do his homework, but was forced to do it in secret, in the dead of night. And he also happened to be a wizard.

It was nearly midnight, and he was lying on his front in bed, the blankets drawn right over his head like a tent, a torch in one hand and a large leather-bound book (*A History of Magic*, by Bathilda Bagshot) propped open against the pillow. Harry moved the tip of his eagle-feather quill down the page, frowning as he looked for something that would help him write his essay, 'Witch-Burning in the Fourteenth Century Was Completely Pointless – discuss'.

The quill paused at the top of a likely-looking paragraph. Harry pushed his round glasses up his nose, moved his torch closer to the book and read:

Non-magic people (more commonly known as Muggles) were particularly afraid of magic in medieval times, but not very good at recognising it. On the rare occasion that they did catch a real witch or wizard, burning had no effect whatsoever. The witch or wizard would perform a basic Flame-Freezing Charm and then pretend to shriek with pain while enjoying a gentle, tickling sensation. Indeed, Wendelin the Weird enjoyed being burnt so much that she allowed herself to be caught no fewer than forty-seven times in various disguises.

Harry put his quill between his teeth and reached underneath his pillow for his ink bottle and a roll of parchment. Slowly and very carefully he unscrewed the ink bottle, dipped his quill into it and began to write, pausing every now and then to listen, because if any of the Dursleys heard the scratching of his quill on their way to the bathroom, he'd probably find himself locked in the cupboard under the stairs for the rest of the summer.

The Dursley family of number four, Privet Drive, was the reason that Harry never enjoyed his summer holidays. Uncle Vernon, Aunt Petunia and their son, Dudley, were Harry's only living relatives. They were Muggles, and they had a very medieval attitude towards magic. Harry's dead parents, who had been a witch and a wizard themselves, were never mentioned under the Dursleys' roof. For years, Aunt Petunia and Uncle Vernon had hoped that if they kept Harry as downtrodden as possible, they would be able to squash the magic out of him. To their fury, they had been unsuccessful, and now lived in terror of anyone finding out that Harry had spent most of the last two years at Hogwarts School of Witchcraft and Wizardry. The most the Dursleys could do these days was to lock away Harry's spellbooks, wand, cauldron and broomstick at the start of the summer holidays, and forbid him to talk to the neighbours.

This separation from his spellbooks had been a real problem for Harry, because his teachers at Hogwarts had given him a lot of holiday work. One of the essays, a particularly nasty one about Shrinking Potions, was for Harry's least favourite teacher, Professor Snape, who would be delighted to have an excuse to give Harry detention for a month. Harry had therefore seized his chance in the first week of the holidays. Whilst Uncle Vernon, Aunt Petunia and Dudley had gone out into the front garden to admire Uncle Vernon's new company car (in very loud voices, so that the rest of the street would notice it too), Harry had crept downstairs, picked the lock on the cupboard under the stairs, grabbed some of his books and hidden them in his bedroom. As long as he didn't leave spots of ink on the sheets, the Dursleys need never know that he was studying magic by night.

Harry was keen to avoid trouble with his aunt and uncle at the moment, as they were already in a bad mood with him, all because he'd received a telephone call from a fellow wizard one week into the school holidays.

from Harry Potter and the Prisoner of Azkaban *Copyright © J.K. Rowling*

Exemplar material

Checklists for writing about narrative structure

Example of a checklist for mapping narrative structure ①

- Use general headings
- Use an easy-to-follow layout
- Use helpful labels, e.g. 'difficulties', 'predicaments', 'answers', 'resolution'
- Write in notes and phrases, not sentences
- Include setting – time and place
- Include character
- Follow a clear story sequence
- Use organisational devices such as boxes/shapes
- Show chronology of plot (using numbers or arrows)
- Include link with title

Example of a checklist for a review/journal entry

- Include title of book
- Include author's name
- Include date of entry (if a journal)
- State your first impression
- Say how the story progresses
- Is the ending predictable?
- Describe your reactions to characters
- Are there any memorable descriptions?
- Describe changes in your feelings
- Do you recommend the story?

Example of a checklist for an effective narrative opening

- Set the right pace
- Introduce character early on
- Evoke sympathy or interest in character
- Introduce plot/sub-plots
- Use humour
- Use good, yet comprehensible, language
- Aim for immediate impact
- Include curiosity factor or X-factor

Example of a plot summary of *The Winner*

- Refusals by Ms Steelman to answer questions
- Incidents of teasing by 'real' boy
- Growing awareness of being the only one in the batch to be interested in answers
- Increasing frustration of Sixer coupled with increasing irritation of Ms Steelman, as Sixer keeps wanting to know about the world
- Sixer looked after by a girl called Jolee-Ann
- Final success and happiness for Sixer

Marking ladder

Name: ______________________________

Pupil	Objective	Teacher
	My narrative structure map is written in notes and phrases, rather than sentences.	
	I included important headings.	
	I showed the chronology of events – using numbers or arrows, for example.	
	My setting and characters are clear.	
	I included helpful labels: 'difficulties', 'predicaments', 'answers', 'resolution'.	
	I included clear links with the title.	
	I used an easy-to-follow layout.	
	I followed a chronological story sequence.	
	I used organisational devices to separate events – for example, boxes/shapes.	
	What could I do to improve my narrative map next time?	

Story Openings

Outcome

Two story beginnings; a reading journal entry; example of a new character being written into a story

Objectives

Sentence

4 to adapt writing for different readers and purposes by changing vocabulary, tone and sentence structures to suit.

5 to understand the difference between direct and reported speech.

7 from reading, to understand how dialogue is set out.

Text

3 to investigate how characters are presented, referring to the text.

10 to evaluate a book by referring to details and examples in the text.

11 to experiment with alternative ways of opening a story.

12 to discuss the enduring appeal of established authors and 'classic' texts.

13 to record their ideas, reflections and predictions about a book, e.g. through a reading log or journal.

15 to write new scenes or characters into a story, in the manner of the writer, maintaining consistency of character and style, using paragraphs to organise and develop detail.

Planning frame

- Experiment with alternative ways of opening a story.
- Investigate how characters are presented, referring to the text.
- Adapt writing for different readers and purposes.
- Discuss the enduring appeal of established authors/'classic' texts.
- Record reflections and ideas through a reading log/journal.
- Evaluate a book by referring to details and examples in the text.

How you could plan this unit

Day 1	Day 2	Day 3	Day 4	Day 5
Reading and writing *Use of Dialogue*	**Writing** Revise the rules of direct speech. Work on the new story opening	**Writing** Proof-read, edit and complete writing. Start a class checklist on story openings (see Resource Page F, or revisit checklist 4 from previous unit)	**Reading and writing** *Strong Characters*	**Reading and writing** Use Day 4 as model for investigation of the character Pantalaimon, referring to the text

Day 6	Day 7	Day 8	Day 9	Day 10
Reading *Writing Styles*	**Writing** Review points from Day 6. Begin writing a new character into the story. Emphasise style consistency	**Writing** Discuss, proof-read and edit writing. Polish final versions	**Reading** *Classic Texts*	**Writing** Make new reading journal entries for class novel. Stress character presentation and textual detail. Evaluate using marking ladder (Resource Page G)

Use of Dialogue

Objective

We will look at the difference between direct and reported speech and experiment with alternative ways of opening a story

You need: Resource Pages A, C and F and page 20; individual whiteboards.

Whole class work

- Read the opening of *Northern Lights* (Resource Page A). Discuss the make-up of the opening. ***Is it all description?*** Elicit the extent to which dialogue is used.
- Focus on the use of dialogue. ***How does this affect the appearance/layout of the second half of the text?*** Answer: speech marks and number of paragraphs. Point out that with more reported speech, so many new paragraphs would not be necessary.
- Explain the difference between direct and reported speech: direct speech quotes the actual words said; reported speech explains or reports the message.
- Demonstrate changing a piece of direct speech into reported speech:

Direct speech:	"There's no one there," he whispered. "But we must be quick."
Reported speech:	He whispered that there was no one there, but that they must be quick.

  Ask the children to identify the changes involved.

- Brainstorm what needs to go in a reading journal (see checklist 1, Resource Page F). Review the purpose: an ongoing, personal reaction to a piece of literature. There is no set layout for a journal and regular entries for a long class novel may look different from a single entry for a short story completed in one reading.

Individual, pair or guided work

- The children use whiteboards to rewrite examples of direct speech (Resource Page C). Take some feedback and focus on the changes that are occurring.
- Now look briefly at the beginning of *Harry Potter and the Prisoner of Azkaban* from the previous unit (page 20). ***Why hasn't the writer used any dialogue?*** Possible answer: Harry was alone, although he could have been talking to himself …
- ***What other style features can be identified in the opening?*** For example:
  - intriguing chapter heading, 'Owl Post'
  - description of 'muggles'
  - list of things that make Harry different from other boys.
- In pairs, the children brainstorm a new beginning for *Harry Potter and the Prisoner of Azkaban*, referring to the checklist. Ideas could include:
  - there is somebody else in the room (who and why)
  - an earlier arrival of Ron
  - Harry's owl sneaked in with a message – who from
  - an audible family argument.
- The new beginnings should contain some examples of direct speech.

Plenary

- Share ideas, and look at a few early drafts of direct speech sentences.
- Remind the children of the need for a consistent style.

Strong Characters

Objective

We will investigate how characters are presented in a story, and learn how to evaluate a book by referring to the text

You need: Resource Pages A and D.

Whole class work

- Discuss the importance of strong characters: ones that attract interest. To establish a strong character, an author needs to reveal that character's personality. Discuss examples from stories with which your class are familiar. For example, ***How can you tell that Charlie in* Charlie and the Chocolate Factory *is generous?*** Answer: he shares his bar of chocolate. ***How do you know Scrooge in* A Christmas Carol *is mean?*** Answer: he won't let his clerk have a decent fire; the words he uses about Christmas.
- Discuss how an author can simply 'label' his characters. Encourage the children to think about books for younger readers, for example, the Mister Men series, where the writer begins by stating the key characteristic, 'Mr Clumsy was always clumsy', and then describes an event that proves he is clumsy.
- ***What is the drawback of this approach for an older audience?*** Help the children to identify that this promotes stereotypes and can be boring. The writer must be more subtle, supplying information gradually so the character is revealed by things s/he says or does, or doesn't say or do. For example, Harry disobeys the Dursleys by doing his homework under the covers, but he doesn't argue with them.

Independent, pair or guided work

- Now focus on Lyra, introduced at the beginning of *Northern Lights* (Resource Page A). Explain that you want to discover what you can about her, just by looking at the dialogue. Explain that these pieces of text are called 'quotes' even if they are not just reporting what characters said. Refer to Resource Page D.
- In pairs, the children identify other characteristics of Lyra, then look for examples of speech that support their theories.
- Some children can also consider description and action. ***What can you find out about Lyra from these?*** Again, the children list the characteristics and find the action sequence that proves it, using a quote from the text.

Plenary

- Discuss the characteristics that the children have identified.
- Talk about how the children react to Lyra.
  - ***Is this what the author intended?***
  - ***Why do you think that?***
  - ***What evidence is there in the text to support this – can you find a quote?***

Writing Styles

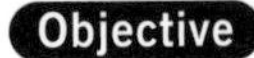

Objective

We will adapt writing for different readers and purposes

You need: Resource Pages A and B.

Whole class work

- Introduce the word 'style' in relation to a piece of writing. Explain that it is the way a writer expresses him/herself, and puts together a text. Some writers have such a strong style that you can identify their writing even if it doesn't have their name on it.
- Write and display a few sentences about the weather, making the structure and vocabulary very simple and obvious, for example:

  > It isn't sunny today. There are lots of clouds.

  What sort of audience is the writing intended for? Does it suit a young reader? Ask the children to work out why. Answers could include:
  - use of short, simple sentences
  - low level and breadth of vocabulary
  - lack of complicated, descriptive detail
  - use of straightforward statements that are readily understood.
- Together, rewrite the work for an older, more sophisticated reader. Include:
  - more difficult vocabulary
  - a mixture of sentence types: simple/compound/complex
  - variety in sentence structure, for example, conjunctions not always in the same place, more difficult punctuation marks
  - hints/thought-provoking comments
  - more detailed/complicated descriptions.

  > The sun appears to be hidden behind low-lying cumulus nimbus cloud, therefore the temperature is only just reaching the low double figures.

Independent, pair or guided work

- Ask the children to focus on the second part of *Northern Lights* from 'But she put her palm over the ringing crystal' (Resource Page A), thinking about the author Philip Pullman's style.
- The children record their observations in note form, referring to the text for detailed description, for example, 'oval table of polished rosewood'.

Plenary

- Referring to Resource Page B, discuss some of the ideas about the author's style. ***How do we know it's set in the past? What can we tell about the two characters from what they say and what they do? How does the author move the story along?***
- ***How might a new character be introduced into the opening of this book? What style techniques do you think Philip Pullman would use?***
- Brainstorm some character types, names, role in the novel and so on.
- Make the point that any change to the first part of the book would still need to adhere to this style.

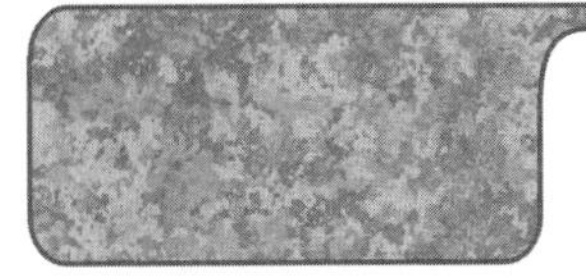

Classic Texts

Objectives

We will discuss the enduring appeal of established authors and classic texts. We will also analyse the features of a good opening

You need: Resource Pages E, F and H.

Whole class work

- Read the opening of *The Railway Children* (Resource Page E).
- ***What do you think of this writer's style?*** Identify:

> 'old-fashioned' labels of 'father' and 'mother'
> references to toys, and interests
> unusual job titles such as 'nursemaid'

- All of the above make the book sound 'old-fashioned' and suggest it could be for a young audience. ***It is not really aimed at a very young audience. What clues can you find in the text to support this?***

> sophisticated sentence structure
> complex detail
> difficult vocabulary: 'modern convenience', 'extremely dull', 'tiled passage', 'great occasions', 'unjust', 'excellent reason', 'refurnishing'

- Ask the children when they think the story takes place. Then discuss the fact that it is nearly a hundred years old. Some books are modern but set in the past, but this was a 'modern' novel when it was written. Explain that it is recommended for older children, and still sells very well. ***Why do you think this might be the case?***

> Children always like stories about other children
> The opening is complicated - going back to before they were railway children
> There is an immediate connection with the title
> There is an early build-up to a dramatic sentence: 'The dreadful change came quite suddenly'
> The reader wants to carry on and find out what the change is
> Their parents or grandparents might have read it and enjoyed it.

- Now look at the checklist of features for a good story opening (Resource Page F). Amend your class checklist as appropriate, adding the need for a consistent style.

Independent, pair or guided work

- Ask the children to share the new story openings they have written in this unit.
- In pairs, evaluate them, using the marking ladder (Resource Page H).

Plenary

- ***What were the common pitfalls when introducing a new character?***
- Share some of the new characters from the previous lesson, using a response sandwich to evaluate their success: one good comment, one idea for improvement, another good comment.

Pupil copymaster

Northern Lights

Chapter 1 – The Decanter of Tokay

Lyra and her daemon moved through the darkening Hall, taking care to keep to one side, out of sight of the kitchen. The three great tables that ran the length of the Hall were laid already, the silver and the glass catching what little light there was, and the long benches were pulled out ready for the guests. Portraits of former Masters hung high up in the gloom along the walls.

Lyra reached the dais and looked back at the open kitchen door and, seeing no one, stepped up beside the high table. The places here were laid with gold, not silver, and the fourteen seats were not oak benches but mahogany chairs with velvet cushions.

Lyra stopped beside the Master's chair and flicked the biggest glass gently with a fingernail. The sound rang clearly through the Hall.

"You're not taking this seriously," whispered her daemon. "Behave yourself."

Her daemon's name was Pantalaimon, and he was currently in the form of a moth, a dark brown one so as not to show up in the darkness of the Hall.

"They're making too much noise to hear from the kitchen," Lyra whispered back. "And the Steward doesn't come in till the first bell. Stop fussing."

But she put her palm over the ringing crystal anyway, and Pantalaimon fluttered ahead and through the slightly open door of the Retiring Room at the other end of the dais. After a moment he appeared again.

"There's no one there," he whispered. "But we must be quick."

Crouching behind the high table, Lyra darted along and through the door into the Retiring Room, where she stood up and looked around. The only light in here came from the fireplace, where a bright blaze of logs settled slightly as she looked, sending a fountain of sparks up into the chimney. She had lived most of her life in the College, but had never seen the Retiring Room before: only Scholars and their guests were allowed in here, and never females. Even the maidservants didn't clean in here. That was the Butler's job alone.

Pantalaimon settled on her shoulder.

"Happy now? Can we go?" he whispered.

"Don't be silly! I want to look around!"

It was a large room, with an oval table of polished rosewood on which stood various decanters and glasses, and a silver smoking-mill with a rack of pipes. On a sideboard nearby there was a little chafing-dish and a basket of poppy-heads.

"They do themselves well, don't they, Pan?" she said under her breath.

She sat in one of the green leather armchairs. It was so deep she found herself nearly lying down, but she sat up again and tucked her legs under her to look at the portraits on the walls. More old Scholars, probably: robed, bearded and gloomy, they stared out of their frames in solemn disapproval.

"What d'you think they talk about?" Lyra said, or began to say, because before she'd finished the question she heard voices outside the door.

"Behind the chair – quick!" whispered Pantalaimon ...

from Northern Lights *by Philip Pullman*

Exemplar analysis

Example of analysis of *Northern Lights*

Pullman uses *a* balance between dialogue and description. It allows a character to have a voice, as opposed to the writer always telling us about them.

This is a compound sentence; the two halves are joined by the conjunction 'but'. A mixture of sentence constructions and punctuation is evident throughout.

Varied sentence lengths stop the reader getting bored. A short simple sentence finishing or starting a paragraph is often very effective.

Interesting, informative verbs supply strong visual images.

Descriptions are detailed. The audience can visualise in detail the room and contents.

A short, simple sentence is followed by a more complex sentence or clause.

But she put her palm over the ringing crystal anyway, and Pantalaimon fluttered ahead and through the slightly open door of the Retiring Room at the other end of the dais. After a moment he appeared again.

"There's no one there," he whispered. "But we must be quick."

Crouching behind the high table, Lyra darted along and through the door into the Retiring Room, where she stood up and looked around. The only light in here came from the fireplace, where a bright blaze of logs settled slightly as she looked, sending a fountain of sparks up into the chimney. She had lived most of her life in the College, but had never seen the Retiring Room before: only Scholars and their guests were allowed in here, and never females. Even the maidservants didn't clean in here. That was the Butler's job alone.

Pantalaimon settled on her shoulder.

"Happy now? Can we go?" he whispered.

"Don't be silly! I want to look around!"

It was a large room, with an oval table of polished rosewood on which stood various decanters and glasses, and a silver smoking-mill with a rack of pipes. On a sideboard nearby there was a little chafing-dish and a basket of poppy-heads.

"They do themselves well, don't they, Pan?" she said under her breath.

She sat in one of the green leather armchairs. It was so deep she found herself nearly lying down, but she sat up again and tucked her legs under her to look at the portraits on the walls. More old Scholars, probably: robed, bearded and gloomy, they stared out of their frames in solemn disapproval.

"What d'you think they talk about?" Lyra said, or began to say, because before she'd finished the question she heard voices outside the door.

"Behind the chair – quick!" whispered Pantalaimon ...

from Northern Lights *by Philip Pullman*

Notice the use of a colon to introduce a part of the sentence that logically follows. Its use here is a signpost that more information is going to be given about the Scholars. (Look also at the long paragraph, 'Crouching ... alone'. Here the colon advises that further explanation about the Retiring Room is coming.)

Commas are used here as a pair to separate 'or began to say' from the main sentence. The fact that Pullman varies his sentence types is bound to lead to varied punctuation.

Pupil copymaster

Turning direct speech into reported speech

Rewrite the following examples of direct speech as reported speech.

1 "Happy now? Can we go?" he whispered.

2 "Don't be silly! I want to look around!"

3 "They do themselves well, don't they, Pan?" she said under her breath.

4 "What d'you think the Scholars talk about?" Lyra said.

5 "Behind the chair – quick!" whispered Pantalaimon.

Answers

1 He asked her in a whisper if she was happy, and could they go.

2 Lyra told him not to be silly. She said that she wanted to look around.

3 Under her breath, she asked Pan if he agreed that they did themselves well.

4 Lyra asked Pan what he thought the Scholars talked about.

5 Pantalaimon whispered to Lyra to get behind the chair quickly.

Pupil copymaster

Speech plans for characters

About Lyra	Spoken words that prove it
Inquisitive	What d'you think they talk about?
Daring	Stop fussing
Observant	
Jealous	

About Pantalaimon	Spoken words that prove it

Pupil copymaster

The Railway Children

Chapter 1 – The Beginning of Things

They were not railway children to begin with. I don't suppose they had ever thought about railways except as a means of getting to Maskelyne and Cook's,* the Pantomime, Zoological Gardens, and Madam Tussaud's. They were just ordinary suburban children, and they lived with their Father and Mother in an ordinary red-brick-fronted villa, with coloured glass in the front door, a tiled passage that was called a hall, a bath-room with hot and cold water, electric bells, French windows, and a good deal of white paint, and 'every modern convenience', as the house-agents would say.

There were three of them. Roberta was the eldest. Of course, Mothers never have favourites, but if their Mother had had a favourite, it might have been Roberta. Next came Peter, who wished to be an Engineer when he grew up; and the youngest was Phyllis, who meant extremely well.

Mother did not spend all her time in paying dull calls to dull ladies, and sitting dully at home waiting for dull ladies to pay calls to her. She was almost always there, ready to play with the children, and read to them, and help them to do their home-lessons. Besides this she used to write stories for them while they were at school, and read them aloud after tea, and she always made up funny pieces of poetry for their birthdays and for other great occasions, such as the christening of the new kittens, or the refurnishing of the doll's house, or the time when they were getting over the mumps.

These three lucky children always had everything they needed: pretty clothes, good fires, a lovely nursery with heaps of toys, and a Mother Goose wall-paper. They had a kind and merry nursemaid and a dog who was called James, and who was their very own. They also had a Father who was just perfect – never cross, never unjust, and always ready for a game – at least, if at any time he was not ready, he always had an excellent reason for it, and explained the reason to the children so interestingly and funnily that they felt sure he couldn't help himself.

You will see that they ought to have been very happy. And so they were, but they did not know how happy till the pretty life in Edgecombe Villa was over and done with, and they had to live a very different life indeed.

The dreadful change came quite suddenly.

* Famous magic show

from The Railway Children, *by E. Nesbit*

Exemplar material

Checklists for story openings and journals

Example of a checklist for a reading journal ①

- Include the title of the story
- Include the author's name
- Use an interesting, clear layout
- Give your first impressions of the story (including from the cover)
- Anticipate how the story will progress and end
- Describe the progression/change in your reactions
- Discuss the effectiveness of the images and the language
- Make references to the text
- Describe your thoughts on finishing the story
- Include your message/recommendation to others

Example of a checklist for a story opening

- Introduce character(s), with some revelations about them
- Describe the setting: where and when
- Introduce problems/questions/ complications to be resolved later
- Use appropriate language style and sentence structure
- Use a balance of sentence types and paragraphs
- Use expressive vocabulary
- Ensure that your style is consistent
- Use descriptions that can be visualised
- Have you seized and held the reader's interest?

Marking ladder

Marking ladder for a reading journal

Name: ____________________

Pupil	Objective	Teacher
	My journal entry includes the title of the story.	
	It includes the author's name.	
	I used an interesting, clear layout.	
	I gave my first impressions of the story (including from the cover).	
	I included a prediction, particularly about the ending.	
	I described any progression/change in my opinion.	
	I described my thoughts during reading and afterwards.	
	I quoted memorable words (referring to text).	
	I included a message/recommendation to others.	
	What could I do to improve my journal entry next time?	

Marking ladder

Marking ladder for a story opening

Name: ______________________________

Pupil	Objective	Teacher
	My story opening seizes and holds the reader's interest.	
	The audience learns where, when and who.	
	The characters reveal something about themselves.	
	I used a balance of sentence types and paragraphs.	
	I varied the sentence structure and punctuation.	
	I used sufficiently complex vocabulary.	
	My descriptions can be visualised.	
	I kept the style consistent.	
	I included a promise of later action.	
	My story opening will hold the reader's attention.	
	What could I do to improve my story opening next time?	

Modern and Classic Poems

Outcome

Two contrasting poems

Objectives

Sentence

1 investigate word order by examining how far the order of words in sentences can be changed:
- which words are essential to meaning
- which can be deleted without damaging the basic meaning
- which words or groups of words can be moved into a different order.

Text

6 to read a number of poems by significant poets and identify what is distinctive about the style or content of their poems.

7 to analyse and compare poetic style, use of forms and the themes of significant poets; to respond to shades of meaning; to explain and justify personal tastes; to consider the impact of full rhymes, half rhymes, internal rhymes and other sound patterns.

8 to investigate and collect different examples of word play, relating form to meaning.

16 to convey feelings, reflections or moods in a poem through the careful choice of words and phrases.

Planning frame

- Analyse and compare poetic forms and style, considering the impact of rhymes and other sound patterns.
- Investigate word order in poems, and experiment with making changes.
- Recognise how feelings, reflections or moods in a poem are conveyed through the careful choice of words and phrases.
- Produce poems conveying feelings, making careful choice of words.

How you could plan this unit

Day 1	Day 2	Day 3	Day 4	Day 5
Reading Blake's *The Fly*	**Reading and writing** Thwaite's *The Fly*	**Writing** Analyse Thwaite's poetic style and form. Compare the two poems. Explain and justify personal tastes	**Writing** Begin writing own poem entitled *The Fly*, using rhyme. Discuss, proof-read and edit	**Writing** Make an initial checklist for writing a poem (see Resource Page I). Edit and complete poems

Day 6	Day 7	Day 8	Day 9	Day 10
Reading and writing *The Tyger*	**Writing** Reread *The Tyger* (Resource Page A). Investigate word selection and word order, as Day 2	**Reading** *Two Different Poems*	**Writing** Revise task. Emphasise careful selection of words. Draft own poems. Finalise checklist (see Resource Page I)	**Reading and writing** Discuss, proof-read, edit and complete poems. Evaluate poems using marking ladder

Blake's The Fly

Objective

We will analyse a poem to understand form and style, and how feelings and moods are conveyed

You need: Resource Pages A, D and I.

Whole class work

- Display Blake's poem *The Fly* (Resource Page A). ***What made you immediately label this as a poem? Do all poems have to look like this?***
- Review poetic terms: 'verse', 'rhyme', 'pattern', 'rhythm'. Review terms the children use in analysis: 'alliteration', 'simile' and 'metaphor' (see revision sheet, Resource Page D), 'powerful verbs', 'onomatopoeia' and so on.
- Ask individual children to read different verses of *The Fly*. Encourage the others to listen rather than read. Before taking feedback, the children read the poem again to themselves.
- Ask simple, observational questions first: ***What is the pattern of the poem?*** Guide the children towards thinking about: the regular beat of the lines; the consistent length of verses; the rhyme pattern.
- ***What is different about verse 5?*** Answer: shorter lines; rhyme of verse 1 and 2; opposites of 'live' and 'die' in last couplet.
- Discuss how poetry is open to interpretations as long as one can find 'evidence' in the text. ***What do you think this poem is about?*** Discuss how it is an extended metaphor, comparing a man with a fly, and a fly with a man. Brainstorm other ideas.
- Briefly discuss the language and use of 'thee' and 'thou'. Explain that the poem was written over 200 years ago. Some children may find religious overtones both in language use and considerations of life and death and happiness.

Independent, pair or guided work

- Ask the children to consider the mood of this poem. Ask them to note first impressions of the mood, before looking closely and quoting from the poem.
- Model answering the questions below. Emphasise again that people respond differently to poetry: not everyone will think the same things about the same poem.

> My first impression of the poem's mood was ...
> Later I thought ...
> Important words or phrases ...
> The message they give ...

Plenary

- Share some of the ideas, taking particular notice of the words the children quoted.
- Give your ideas, perhaps suggesting that an apparently simple poem has a deeply reflective element, as Blake compares a man's life and death to that of a fly. ***Does he think we are uncaring about everyone and everything except ourselves?***
- ***What does he say about the importance of 'thought'? Why do you think he said this?***
- Begin to build up a checklist that can later be used when the children write their own poetry (see checklist 1, Resource Page I).

Thwaite's The Fly

Objective

We will compare poetic style and investigate word order

You need: Resource Pages B, C and I; whiteboards; scissors.

Whole class work

- Read Thwaite's poem *The Fly* (Resource Page B). Sit quietly for a few moments. Ask the children to listen very carefully. ***What can you hear?*** Answer: shuffling of feet, voices in other classrooms, cars outside and so on. Build up empathy for the situation of the poet by brainstorming when you and your class have been in a similar situation – annoyed by a persistent noise.
- Comment on the fact that although this poem has the same title as Blake's, the message and mood is very different. ***What is the mood of his poem?*** In pairs, the children make notes on their whiteboards.
- ***How have you come to these conclusions?*** Elicit points such as:

> Being anti the fly
> Putting himself first
> Lacking sympathy for another creature (until towards the end)
> Finding it an annoyance
> Wanting to destroy it

- Look closely at the language (see exemplar analysis on Resource Page C). ***Which words are essential for conveying the poet's mood?*** Answer: 'sick whining', 'quietly'.
- Experiment orally by leaving out one or two words. ***Does it matter? Is the meaning still the same?***
- ***What about word order?*** If you write 'whining sick buzz' the inference becomes that the fly is ill and not that it is annoying the poet.

Independent, pair or guided work

- The children work in pairs or small groups to experiment with this poem, retaining its basic meaning, focusing on word order.
- The children select one verse and cut up the words so they can be re-ordered. (Leave the full poem on display for the children to refer to.) The children then move words or groups of words; leave some words out; decide which words must be kept.
- Each pair or group decides whether they want to create a new 'Fly' poem or keep the meaning of Thwaite's poem.

Plenary

- Listen to and discuss some versions of different parts of the poem.
- Produce a class chart with these headings:

> Words essential to meaning of poem
> Words that can be deleted without damaging the basic meaning
> Words/groups of words that can be moved into a different order

- Add any new ideas to the class checklist (see Resource Page I).

The Tyger

Objective

We will see how a poet shows feelings or moods in a poem through the choice of words

You need: Resource Pages A, E and F; a tape recording of you reading Blake's *The Tyger* (Resource Page E).

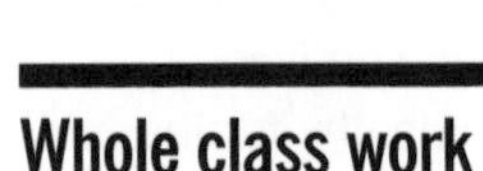

Whole class work

- Play the recording. ***Is there anything that immediately strikes you?*** Be patient, and replay parts, stopping when appropriate, in order to elicit the answers 'repetition' and 'use of questioning'. ***Is* The Fly *similar?***
- Allow the children to reread *The Fly* (Resource Page A) for their answers. ***What does this tell us about the poet William Blake?*** Help the children to identify that Blake does not always keep to one style or format.
- Now focus on rhyme. Play the tape again. ***What is the rhyming pattern? How does it differ from that of* The Fly*?*** Answer: rhyming couplets, as opposed to rhyming alternate lines. ***What differences are there between the first and last verses?*** Answer: 'could' is changed to 'dare'. ***Why might this be?***
- Talk about other sound patterns such as alliteration. Using Resource Page E, the children underline examples in the first three verses.
- ***How does the vocabulary of* The Tyger *differ from that of* The Fly*?*** Answers should include complexity and level of difficulty. Ask the children to supply reasons why Blake may have done this, for example:
  - targeting a different audience
  - wanting to convey a different feeling
  - trying to show the two animals very differently.
- ***Which type of language suits a small, easily killed animal? How is the tiger made to seem? What about the fly?***
- Reread verse 5 of *The Tyger*. ***What is the tiger contrasted with? Why?*** Answer: a lamb is a symbol of meekness. Blake is emphasising the difference between the two.
- Point out the word 'He' in verse 5. Some children may associate this with God or a Creator. Discuss what this suggests about Blake. Discuss that both poems touch on the big issues of life, death and a Creator.

Independent, pair or guided work

- Ask the children to record an 'evidence' sheet of what they have learned about Blake (content of poems, his style, attitudes) from these two poems, referring to the text when appropriate (Resource Page F).

Plenary

- Share and discuss the children's findings.

Two Different Poems

Objective

We will compare and contrast the style and content of poems by different poets

You need: Resource Pages G and H.

Whole class work

- In pairs, the children read *Rabbiting On* (Resource Page G). Ask them to read the poem aloud together to discover its form.
- ***What have you found out?*** Answer: it's a conversation between two people with the second person reluctant to answer the first person's questions, so little content or progression is made during the conversation. The poem is made up entirely of question and answer. ***What might be the relationship between the two people? Why do you think that?***
- ***How is rhyme used in this poem?*** Point out that it is used differently from the previous poems studied. ***Do you think the words have been carefully chosen as in the other poems?*** Introduce the idea that they could be purposely ordinary to emphasise how mundane the vocabulary is, or to show that the second person doesn't feel like talking.
- ***What about the title? How is it linked to the poem?*** Explain that the title is an example of 'double entendre' (double meaning) or a pun. Discuss how this play on words adds meaning to the poem and makes this a cleverer poem than the audience first realises. Discuss how the title is part of the poem and gives the reader a clue as to what the poem will be about. Alternatively, the poem will explain the meaning of the title.
- Now display *Amulet* (Resource Page H). ***Do you know what the title means?*** Challenge the children to look the word up in a dictionary if they do not know.
- Read the poem aloud. ***How is its form different from the other poems studied?*** Answer: the absence of rhyme, only one verse. ***What else do you notice about its construction? Is it simple? How is it clear that the end has been reached?***
- Reread the poem to allow time for its message to be absorbed.

Independent, pair or guided work

- Ask the children to focus on vocabulary.
- Model searching for words that play a strong part in the poem's descriptions. Then ask the children to list the words or phrases that they think have been chosen with particular care. The children then record the effect of the words, and the images and feelings they convey. For example, 'The doe's tears make us feel pity for the doe'.

Plenary

- Share ideas, focusing on the words that seem essential to the poem's meaning.
- Talk again about the poem's form, particularly its use of repetition and lack of rhyme.
- The children use the repetitive format to write their own poem set at a particular time of year. Each line should start with, 'Inside the ... '

Pupil copymaster

The Fly, by William Blake

Little Fly,
Thy summer's play
My thoughtless hand
Has brushed away.

Am not I
A fly like thee?
Or art not thou
A man like me?

For I dance,
And drink, and sing,
Till some blind hand
Shall brush my wing.

If thought is life
And strength and breath,
And the want
Of thought is death;

Then am I
A happy fly,
If I live
Or if I die.

Pupil copymaster

The Fly by Anthony Thwaite

The fly's sick whining buzz
Appals me as I sit
Alone and quietly,
Reading and hearing it
Banging against the pane,
Bruised, falling, then again
Starting its lariat tour
Round and round my head
Ceiling to wall to floor.

But I equip myself
To send him on his way,
Newspaper clutched in hand
Vigilant, since he may
Settle, shut off his shriek
And there lie mild and weak
Who thirty seconds ago
Drove air and ears mad
With shunting to and fro.

Exemplar analysis

Example of analysis of Thwaite's *The Fly*

The fly's sick whining buzz
Appals me as I sit
Alone and quietly,
Reading and hearing it
Banging against the pane,
Bruised, falling, then again
Starting its lariat tour
Round and round my head
Ceiling to wall to floor.

But I equip myself
To send him on his way,
Newspaper clutched in hand
Vigilant, since he may
Settle, shut off his shriek
And there lie mild and weak
Who thirty seconds ago
Drove air and ears mad
With shunting to and fro.

This is strong language for a very small insect.

An immediate contrast is drawn between the noisy, intrusive fly and the quiet, peaceful writer.

The list of places constantly re-visited makes the audience, and not just the writer, feel dizzy. All of this makes the audience sympathise with the writer, not the fly.

Powerful verbs are a feature of this poem.

This is an effective choice of word. It refers to the constant changes of direction, thereby reinforcing sympathy for the writer, and justifying his actions.

The alliteration emphasises the sound and its effect as the insect crashes against the window.

The writer probably intends this to be a metaphor, painting a vivid picture as the fly's journeying turns into a lariat, or a lasso.

This phrase introduces an annoying pattern of repetitive movement.

These words form another metaphor, turning the writer into a soldier or guard, keeping watch with his weapon.

Interesting use of alliteration.

Deliberate contrast with the noisy, fast-moving creature of earlier lines.

Pupil copymaster

Similes and metaphors

A simile

A simile is when the writer compares one thing to another of a different category, usually introduced by 'as' or 'like'.

SIMILE = something similar (Latin)
It's 'smile' with an extra 'i'.

I am ready and armed like a soldier.
The fly is like a crackling radio.
He was as white as a sheet.
She sang like a bird.

A metaphor

A metaphor is when the writer writes about something as if it is something else.

META = with (Greek)

PHEREIN = to bear, to carry (Greek)

I am a soldier, ready and armed.
The fly is a crackling radio.
He was so hungry he wolfed the food down.

Pupil copymaster

The Tyger

Tyger! Tyger! burning bright
In the forests of the night,
What immortal hand or eye
Could frame thy fearful symmetry?

In what distant deeps or skies
Burnt the fire of thine eyes?
On what wings dare he aspire?
What the hand dare seize the fire?

And what shoulder, and what art,
Could twist the sinews of thy heart?
And when thy heart began to beat,
What dread hand? and what dread feet?

What the hammer? what the chain?
In what furnace was thy brain?
What the anvil? what dread grasp
Dare its deadly terrors clasp?

When the stars threw down their spears,
And watered Heaven with their tears,
Did he smile his work to see?
Did He who made the Lamb make thee?

Tyger! Tyger! burning bright
In the forests of the night,
What immortal hand or eye
Dare frame thy fearful symmetry?

William Blake

Pupil copymaster

Evidence sheet

Poet's name:	
Characteristic	Evidence (quotes from poem)
Writes about animal life	
Writes about life	

Pupil copymaster

Rabbiting On

Where did you go?
Oh ... nowhere much.

What did you see?
Oh ... rabbits and such.

Rabbits? What else?
Oh ... a rabbit hutch.

What sort of hutch?
Just a hutch, that's all.

But what did it look like?
Like a rabbit hutch.

Well what was in it?
Small rabbits and such.

I worried about you
While you were gone.

Why don't you stop
Rabbiting on?

Kit Wright

Pupil copymaster

Amulet

Inside the Wolf's fang, the mountain of heather.
Inside the mountain of heather, the Wolf's fur.
Inside the Wolf's fur, the ragged forest.
Inside the ragged forest, the Wolf's foot.
Inside the Wolf's foot, the stony horizon.
Inside the stony horizon, the Wolf's tongue.
Inside the Wolf's tongue, the Doe's tears.
Inside the Doe's tears, the frozen swamp.
Inside the frozen swamp, the Wolf's blood.
Inside the Wolf's blood, the snow wind.
Inside the snow wind, the Wolf's eye.
Inside the Wolf's eye, the North Star.
Inside the North Star, the Wolf's fang.

Ted Hughes

Exemplar material

Checklist for writing a poem

- Use an interesting, poetic form
- Use a distinctive, memorable style
- Aim for a text that bears rereading
- Convey feelings and mood
- Decide about rhymes and sound patterns
- Include possible word play and shades of meaning
- Show awareness of the effectiveness of repetition
- Make careful choice of words
- Deliberately position words and phrases
- Include a message to the reader
- Include a link between poem and title

Marking ladder

Name: ____________________

Pupil	Objective	Teacher
	I have used an interesting form for my poem.	
	The style is distinctive and memorable.	
	I used repetition or word play to effect.	
	I thought about rhyme and sound patterns.	
	I chose words carefully	
	I deliberately positioned words and phrases.	
	I showed feelings and mood.	
	I included a message to the reader.	
	I made a link between the poem and title.	
	My poem could be enjoyed more than once.	
	What could I do to improve my poem next time?	

Plays

Outcome

A scene or short play to be performed

Objectives

Sentence

2 to understand the basic conventions of standard English and consider when and why standard English is used: agreement between nouns and verbs; consistency of tense and subject; avoidance of double negatives; avoidance of non-standard dialect words.

5 to understand the difference between direct and reported speech, e.g. through: finding and comparing examples from reading; discussing contexts and reasons for using particular forms and their effects; transforming direct into reported speech and vice versa, noting changes in punctuation and words that have to be changed or added.

7 from reading, to understand how dialogue is set out.

Text

5 to understand dramatic conventions including: the conventions of scripting; how character can be communicated in words and gesture; how tension can be built up through pace, silences and delivery.

18 write own playscript, applying conventions learned from reading; include production notes.

19 to annotate a section of playscript as a preparation for performance, taking into account pace, movement, gesture and delivery of lines and the needs of the audience.

20 to evaluate the script and the performance for their dramatic interest and impact.

Planning frame

- Understand dramatic conventions.
- Transform direct into reported speech, and vice versa.
- Write own playscript; include production notes.
- Annotate a section of play script as a preparation for performance, taking into account pace, movement, gesture and delivery of lines and the needs of the audience.
- Understand the basic conventions of standard English and consider when and why it is used.

How you could plan this unit

Day 1	Day 2	Day 3	Day 4	Day 5
Reading Read the playscript extract from *James and the Giant Peach* (Resource Page A). Highlight dramatic conventions. Write extra production notes	**Reading and writing** *Direct and Reported Speech 1*	**Reading and writing** *Direct and Reported Speech 2*	**Writing** Begin writing new scenes. Focus on dialogue and character, thinking of audience needs	**Writing** Begin class checklist (see Resource Page E for ideas). Discuss, proof-read, edit and complete scenes. Add production notes

Day 6	Day 7	Day 8	Day 9	Day 10
Reading and writing *Standard English*	**Reading and writing** *Writing Dialogue*	**Writing** Revise writing task. Plan and write initial drafts of play	**Writing** Complete checklists. Discuss, proof-read, edit and complete plays	**Perform plays** Evaluate using marking ladder (Resource Page F)

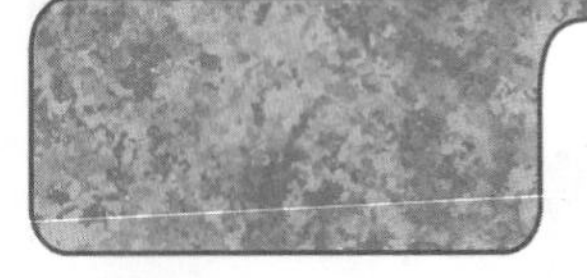

Direct and Reported Speech 1

Objective

We will learn to understand the difference between direct and reported speech and how to change direct into reported speech, noting the changes that take place

You need: Resource Page A; individual whiteboards.

Whole class work

- Reread the first part of *James and the Giant Peach* (Resource Page A), allocating individual parts. Now ask the children to cover their scripts, and listen while one person reads everything. ***Why is it difficult to understand? How would the text be better written now?*** Answer: a narrative with indications of who is speaking, but still containing dialogue.
- ***What words would you need to add?*** Answer: 'said', 'answered' and so on.
- Discuss the terms 'dialogue' and 'direct speech'.
- Model an example of direct speech:

  The centipede said, "We've been waiting for you."

- Ask the children if too much direct speech – which would involve constant new paragraphs – would be a good idea. ***Would the style become repetitive? How could you have a balanced narrative, yet still report what was said?*** Help the children towards the label 'reported speech'.
- Model a reported speech version of your example:

  The centipede said that they had been waiting for him.

- Ask the children to record on whiteboards the differences they can spot. Focus on:

  The changes of person – 'we' has become 'they'
  Changes in punctuation – a comma has disappeared
  Introduction of words – 'that'

Independent, pair or guided work

- Convert selected speeches from *James and the Giant Peach* into direct speech.
- Transform new direct speech sentences into reported speech.
- Underline the changes made between the first and second versions.

Plenary

- Go through the work together, displaying both versions of speech. (Keep this work for a later lesson.)
- ***What problems did you encounter when changing direct to reported speech?*** For example, length of sentences, repetition of 'said', having to indicate who is speaking and so on.

Direct and Reported Speech 2

Objective

We will change reported speech into direct speech, noticing punctuation and word changes. We will also consider the needs of the audience

You need: Resource Pages A and E; individual whiteboards.

Whole class work

- Revise yesterday's independent task of changing direct speech into reported speech. Explore one or two examples:

> Direct speech: The Centipede said, "We've been waiting for you."
> Reported speech: The Centipede said that they had been waiting for him.

- Ask the children to comment again on the necessary changes between the two, encouraging them to focus on the verb. ***What has happened to the verb?***
- Identify that the verb in the reported speech has had to move into the past tense. Reinforce this with another example:

> Direct speech: The old-green grasshopper said, "You look positively ill!"
> Reported speech: The old-green grasshopper said that he looked positively ill.

- Ask the children to supply you with examples of reported speech from their reading books. As you write one on your board, the children transform it into direct speech on their whiteboards. Give help where needed, paying particular attention to verbs.
- Now return to the play text (Resource Page A), and ask a single group to read it aloud. ***What are the requirements of the rest of us? How is our interest kept?***
- Encourage a wide-ranging discussion, moving towards the concept of the audience having needs. Work together on producing a list of ways to satisfy those needs: clear delivery of lines; pace; and so on (see checklist 1, Resource Page E).

Independent, pair or guided work

- In pairs or small groups, the children brainstorm adding another scene to the play.
- Ask them to look at where the text starts and stops – their scene will precede or follow it. Their task today is to plan the scene:

> who will be in it
> where it will take place
> the events
> how to retain dramatic interest
> casting parts

Plenary

- Share some of the groups' ideas.
- Ask each group to justify how their plan will meet the audience's needs.

Standard English

Objectives

We will explore the standard ways of speaking and writing English. We will discover that complex words and sentences can be clarified through stage directions

You need: Resource Page C; Post-it™ notes.

Whole class work

- Read *The Trick* (Resource Page C). Ask the children to find a word they do not understand, for example: 'snap' [lunch]; 'daps' [trainers]; 'lardied' [faded]. ***What sort of word do you think it is? Is it in a different language?***
- Introduce the term 'dialect words'. Discuss any dialect words for your area. Consider the extent of their usage. ***Who uses them – and when?***
- Briefly discuss the difference between accent and dialect.

accent = local mode of pronunciation
dialect = non-standard vocabulary, pronunciation or idioms

- Be aware that discussing accent and dialect can be a sensitive subject. Try to avoid using labels such as 'correct' and 'incorrect'. Instead discuss when it is 'appropriate' and 'inappropriate'. Many children will correctly move between types of speaking when necessary.
- ***Can you identify changes in grammar (the way the rules of English are applied)?*** Encourage the children to reread the script together, before sharing results.
- Discuss that non-standard grammar is usually acceptable when spoken but not when written. ***Why might this be?***
- Divide your board into four sections:

non-agreement between nouns and verbs	inconsistency of tense and subject	double negatives	non-standard dialect words

Explain what the terms mean. Now ask the children to find one example of each in the text, write it on a Post-it™ note and stick in the right section. Discuss findings.

- Talk about the common misuse of adjectives and adverbs. Remind them of their different roles; make sure that they are secure in their grasp of the fact that an adjective only modifies a noun (or pronoun).

Independent, pair or guided work

- Ask the children to rewrite *The Trick* in standard English. They must make sure that any audience will comprehend it.

Plenary

- Listen to some of the changed speeches.
- Discuss the need for standard English. ***Why do we need to bother with it? What problems result from an absence of it? When can non-standard English be appropriate?*** Answer: when a character is recognised as speaking in that way.

Writing Dialogue

Objective

We will learn how dialogue is set out

You need: Resource Pages C and D.

Whole class work

- Study the extract from *Treasure Island* (Resource Page D) – or you could use an extract from your class novel.
- Ask the children to focus on the appearance of the dialogue. ***What do you immediately notice about the layout? What are the rules to remember?***
- Revise the rules for dialogue: when to begin new paragraphs, punctuation and so on. Emphasise that alternate speakers require separate paragraphs.
- Now focus on commas, and the positioning of them in direct speech. For example:

  > The Centipede said, "We've been waiting for you."

  Why is there a comma after 'said'? Which two parts of the sentence must be separated? Guide the children towards the rule that spoken words must be kept distinct from unspoken: a comma usually takes this role.
- Now reverse the sentence:

  > "We've been waiting for you," said the Centipede.

  Identify that a comma still separates spoken and unspoken parts; this time it is placed when the speech marks are going to close, rather than when they are going to open.
- Now rewrite the sentence in reported speech:

  > The Centipede said that they had been waiting for him.

  Which of these words is often left out? Answer: 'that'. Practise the reversing of reported and direct speech in a few more examples.
- Look again at *The Trick* (Resource Page C). ***What type of writing is this? How do you know it is a play not a narrative? What is the plot?***

Independent, pair or guided work

- Ask the children to add dialogue to the example narrative for *Treasure Island* (Resource Page D). ***What might the pirates have been saying to each other?***
- Now ask the children to add dialogue to the plot of *The Trick*, but in narrative form. Remind them to keep to the rules of direct speech.

Plenary

- Share some of the children's sentences, asking the children to write them up for display. ***Is the punctuation correct? Is it helpful?***
- Talk about a new task for the rest of the week: to write a play to be performed, based on a fairy tale (or you could use your class novel). The children could work in small groups, writing different scenes and liaising with each other to ensure continuity between scenes.

Pupil copymaster

James and the Giant Peach

Scene 2

OLD-GREEN-GRASSHOPPER:	Look who's here!
CENTIPEDE:	We've been waiting for you!
JAMES:	Oh no! No! *[James acts scared to death and frozen with fear as the curtain opens slowly to reveal* OLD-GREEN-GRASSHOPPER, SPIDER, LADYBIRD, CENTIPEDE, *and* EARTHWORM *sitting comfortably.* SILKWORM *is curled up asleep in a corner]*
SPIDER:	I'm hungry!
OLD-GREEN-GRASSHOPPER:	I'm famished!
LADYBIRD:	So am I!
CENTIPEDE:	Everyone's famished! We need food! *[Pause, as all look at* JAMES*]*
SPIDER:	*[Leaning toward* JAMES*]* Aren't you hungry? *[*JAMES *is still petrified with fear]*
OLD-GREEN-GRASSHOPPER:	*[To* JAMES*]* What's the matter with you? You look positively ill!
CENTIPEDE:	He looks as though he's going to faint any second.
LADYBIRD:	Oh, my goodness, the poor thing! I do believe he thinks it's *him* we are wanting to eat! *[Everyone roars with laughter]*
ALL:	Oh, dear, oh dear! What an awful thought!
LADYBIRD:	You mustn't be frightened. We wouldn't *dream* of hurting you. You are one of us now, didn't you know that? You are one of the crew. We're all in the same boat.
OLD-GREEN-GRASSHOPPER:	We've been waiting for you all day long. We thought you were never going to turn up. I'm glad you made it.
CENTIPEDE:	So, cheer up, my boy, cheer up! And meanwhile I wish you'd come over here and give me a hand with these boots. It takes me hours to get them all off by myself. *[*JAMES *crosses the room and kneels beside* CENTIPEDE*]*
CENTIPEDE:	Thank you so much. You are very kind.
JAMES:	Well ... uh ... you have a lot of boots.
CENTIPEDE:	I do have a lot of legs and a lot of feet. One hundred to be exact. *[Proudly]* I am a centipede, you know.
EARTHWORM:	*There* he goes again! He simply cannot stop telling lies about his legs! He's only got forty-two! The trouble is that most people don't bother to count them. And anyway, there is nothing *marvellous*, you know, Centipede, about having a lot of legs.
CENTIPEDE:	Poor Earthworm. *[Whispering in* JAMES'S *ear]* He's blind, you know. He can't see how splendid I look.
EARTHWORM:	In my opinion, the *really* marvellous thing is to have no legs at all and to be able to walk just the same.
CENTIPEDE:	You call that *walking*! You're a *slitherer*, that's all you are! You just *slither* along.
EARTHWORM:	I *glide*.
CENTIPEDE:	You are a slimy beast.
EARTHWORM:	I am *not* a slimy beast. I am a useful and much-loved creature. Ask any gardener you like. And as for you ...
CENTIPEDE:	I am a *pest*! *[Grinning proudly and looking around the room for approval]*
LADYBIRD:	He is so proud of that, though for the life of me I cannot understand why. Oh ... please excuse me ... my name is Ladybird.

Adapted by Richard George from James and the Giant Peach, *by Roald Dahl*

Exemplar analysis

Example of analysis of *James and the Giant Peach*

In the stage directions, the playwright communicates how the play is to be staged. These production notes are very important to the director.

The name of each speaking character is put on the left-hand side.

The name of the speaker is clearly differentiated from the words he/she speaks – capital letters and a colon are commonly used.

This is an important direction to maintain pace. The audience is likely to be young: regular movement and change are needed, therefore.

No speech marks are used in a playscript.

Production notes are needed here as the action/manner of delivery are not obvious.

<u>*Scene 2*</u>

OLD-GREEN-GRASSHOPPER:	Look who's here!
CENTIPEDE:	We've been waiting for you!
JAMES:	Oh no! No! *[James acts scared to death and frozen with fear as the curtain opens slowly to reveal* OLD-GREEN-GRASSHOPPER, SPIDER, LADYBIRD, CENTIPEDE, *and* EARTHWORM *sitting comfortably.* SILKWORM *is curled up asleep in a corner]*
SPIDER:	I'm hungry!
OLD-GREEN-GRASSHOPPER:	I'm famished!
LADYBIRD:	So am I!
CENTIPEDE:	Everyone's famished! We need food! *[Pause, as all look at* JAMES*]*
SPIDER:	*[Leaning toward* JAMES*]* Aren't you hungry? *[*JAMES *is still petrified with fear]*
OLD-GREEN-GRASSHOPPER:	*[To* JAMES*]* What's the matter with you? You look positively ill!
CENTIPEDE:	He looks as though he's going to faint any second.
LADYBIRD:	Oh, my goodness, the poor thing! I do believe he thinks it's *him* we are wanting to eat! *[Everyone roars with laughter]*
ALL:	Oh, dear, oh dear! What an awful thought!
LADYBIRD:	You mustn't be frightened. We wouldn't *dream* of hurting you. You are one of us now, didn't you know that? You are one of the crew. We're all in the same boat.
OLD-GREEN-GRASSHOPPER:	We've been waiting for you all day long. We thought you were never going to turn up. I'm glad you made it.
CENTIPEDE:	So, cheer up, my boy, cheer up! And meanwhile I wish you'd come over here and give me a hand with these boots. It takes me hours to get them all off by myself. *[*JAMES *crosses the room and kneels beside* CENTIPEDE*]*
CENTIPEDE:	Thank you so much. You are very kind.
JAMES:	Well ... uh ... you have a lot of boots.
CENTIPEDE:	I do have a lot of legs and a lot of feet. One hundred to be exact. *[Proudly]* I am a centipede, you know.
EARTHWORM:	*There* he goes again! He simply cannot stop telling lies about his legs! He's only got forty-two! The trouble is that most people don't bother to count them. And anyway, there is nothing *marvellous*, you know, Centipede, about having a lot of legs.
CENTIPEDE:	Poor Earthworm. *[Whispering in* JAMES'S *ear]* He's blind, you know. He can't see how splendid I look.
EARTHWORM:	In my opinion, the *really* marvellous thing is to have no legs at all and to be able to walk just the same.
CENTIPEDE:	You call that *walking*! You're a *slitherer*, that's all you are! You just *slither* along.
EARTHWORM:	I *glide*.
CENTIPEDE:	You are a slimy beast.
EARTHWORM:	I am *not* a slimy beast. I am a useful and much-loved creature. Ask any gardener you like. And as for you ...
CENTIPEDE:	I am a *pest*! *[Grinning proudly and looking around the room for approval]*
LADYBIRD:	He is so proud of that, though for the life of me I cannot understand why. Oh ... please excuse me ... my name is Ladybird.

Adapted by Richard George from James and the Giant Peach, *by Roald Dahl*

The use of brackets and italics for the stage directions makes it obvious that they are not part of the dialogue.

This instruction for a pause shows that the writer wants to build up tension.

Stage directions are often required because the dialogue does not explain the playwright's intentions.

Further stage directions. The laughter is important as it reveals the harmless character of creatures.

It is essential this speech is delivered correctly, as it reveals more about the character.

This is an important direction: the Centipede is revealing his character in movements, not just words.

Pupil copymaster

The Trick

[Set in a crowded classroom, as the children get changed for games lessons]

HARRY:	Fancy a laugh? Let's try a trick on Goody-goody.
JOE:	Okay, I'm game.
HARRY:	Right, here's the plot ... *[He and* JOE *go into a whispering huddle]*
SARAH:	What's you talkin' quiet about?
EMILY:	They'll be just acting real nasty as usual. Ignore 'em, Sarah. Get your daps on so us was first in line for netball.
JOE:	*[*JOE *suddenly raises his voice]* Oh no! I haven't got no shorts! That's my favourite lesson done for. [A small boy on the next table looks up]
JAMES:	*[In a very proper voice]* Well, actually, I have a spare pair, Joe. They are somewhat lardied, but you're welcome to borrow them.
JOE:	Cor, you're a star, James. I've not got no other friends like you. *[*JAMES *beams with pride as he walks to* JOE's *place with the shorts. In the meantime,* HARRY *swoops on* JAMES's *empty table, grabs a pair of football boots, and dashes away with them]*
MR PHEASANT:	*[Enters the room dressed in a tracksuit]* Are you boys going to be all day? *[Silence as everyone rushes to dress and line up]* James as usual. Busy trying to learn how to tie your laces, I suppose. *[Sniggers from the other children]*
JAMES:	Actually, Mr Pheasant, I seem to have mislaid my footwear. I'm sure my boots were here a moment ago. I er ... er ... er ...
MR PHEASANT:	Help him! *[There's a general rushing around and shouts of* Not here *and* No. *Then HARRY's voice is heard above the rest]*
HARRY:	*[Holding boots aloft]* Got them, sir. In with the snap boxes!
MR PHEASANT:	*[sarcastic tone]* Presumably he was planning to eat them – he might as well, he can't play properly in them. *[Hoots of laughter from other children]*
EMILY:	Us can tidy the classroom, Mr Pheasant.
MR PHEASANT:	No, he can do it on his own. Come on, let's leave him to it. *[The class leaves;* HARRY *and* JOE *exchange smug looks]*

Pupil copymaster

Dialogue and narrative

Treasure Island – dialogue

"Well then," said he, "this is the berth for me. Here you matey," he cried to the man who trundled the barrow; "bring up alongside and help up my chest. I'll stay here a bit," he continued. "I'm a plain man; rum and bacon and eggs is what I want, and that head up there for to watch ships off. What you mought call me? You mought call me captain. Oh I see what you're at there;" and he threw down three or four gold pieces on the threshold. "You can tell me when I've worked through that," says he, looking as fierce as a commander.

Treasure Island – narrative

In I got bodily into the apple barrel, and found there was scarce an apple left; but sitting down there in the dark, what with the sound of the waters and the rocking movement of the ship, I had either fallen asleep or was on the point of doing so when a heavy man sat down with rather a clash close by. The barrel shook as he leaned his shoulders against it, and I was just about to jump up when the man began to speak. It was Silver's voice, and before I had heard a dozen words, I would not have shown myself for all the world, but lay there, trembling and listening, in the extreme of fear and curiosity, for from these dozen words I understood that the lives of all the honest men aboard depended upon me alone.

from Treasure Island, *by Robert Louis Stevenson*

Exemplar material

Checklists for plays

Example of a checklist for play layout

- Make it clear and easy to use
- Distinguish between name of character and his/her words
- Clearly distinguish stage directions from dialogue
- Start a new line for different speeches
- Do not use speech marks

Example of a checklist for stage directions

- Include guidelines for director and actor
- Use brackets (and italics if possible)
- Make them easy to follow
- Clear up any possible confusion
- Keep stage directions to a minimum

Example of a checklist for the audience's needs

- Use widely understood words
- Keep up the pace
- Include movement or gesture
- Provide impact in plot

Example of a checklist for a playscript

- Follow the usual pattern of scripting
- Use the correct layout
- Provide stage directions
- Use technical terms
- Think about performance
- Match the words to the characters
- Use standard and non-standard English as appropriate to character
- Develop characters and relationships
- Use punctuation effectively
- Remember the audience's needs
- Ensure that the play has dramatic interest

Marking ladder

Name: ______________________________

Pupil	Objective	Teacher
	My playscript follows the usual pattern of scripting.	
	I used the correct layout.	
	I did not use speech marks.	
	I have thought about performance.	
	I have remembered the audience's needs.	
	My script includes: • stage directions • technical terms • good match between character and dialogue • development of characters and relationships.	
	I used standard and non-standard English appropriately.	
	I used effective punctuation.	
	My playscript has dramatic interest.	
	What could I do to improve my playscript next time?	

Note-taking and Recounts

Outcome

Notes for recounts; two recounts of same event for different readers

Objectives

Sentence

1 investigate word order by examining how far the order of words in sentences can be changed:
- which words are essential to meaning
- which can be deleted without damaging the basic meaning
- which words or groups of words can be moved into a different order.

3 to discuss, proof-read and edit their own writing for clarity and correctness, e.g. by creating more complex sentences, using a range of connectives, simplifying clumsy constructions.

4 to adapt writing for different readers and purposes by changing vocabulary, tone and sentence structures to suit, e.g. simplifying for younger readers.

5 to understand the difference between direct and reported speech, e.g. through
- finding and comparing examples from reading
- discussing contexts and reasons for using particular forms and their effects.

Text

21 to identify the features of recounted texts such as sports reports, diaries, police reports.

23 to discuss the purpose of note-taking and how this influences the nature of notes made.

24 to write recounts based on subject, topic or personal experiences for (a) a close friend and (b) an unknown reader, e.g. an account of a field trip, a march, an historical event.

26 to make notes for different purposes, e.g. listing cues for a talk, and to build on these notes in their own writing or speaking.

27 to use simple abbreviations in note-taking.

Planning frame

- Identify the features of recounted texts.
- Understand the purpose of note-taking and how purpose influences type of notes.
- Make and use notes as cues for a talk and use simple abbreviations.
- Simplify a recount for younger readers.
- Examine which words can be deleted or moved and which are essential to to meaning.
- Write recounts from personal experiences for a close friend and an unknown reader.

How you could plan this unit

Day 1	Day 2	Day 3	Day 4	Day 5
Reading *Recount Features*	**Reading and writing** *Chronology and Connectives*	**Reading** Use checklist 2, Resource Page G to identify other features of recounts. Consider other recount sources	**Reading and writing** *Notes*	**Writing** Explore other purposes for note-making. Make a set of cue cards for a two-minute talk

Day 6	Day 7	Day 8	Day 9	Day 10
Writing Use notes/cues to give talk. How effective are the notes?	**Reading and writing** *Adapting for the Reader*	**Writing** Review Day 7. Rewrite text for a younger reader	**Reading and writing** *Preparing Notes*	**Reading and writing** Read new text, identify features. Recognise links with notes. Add to class checklist (see Resource Page G)

Day 11	Day 12	Day 13	Day 14	Day 15
Reading and writing *Simplifying a Text*	**Writing** Revise task. Work on notes for recounts	**Writing** Draft recounts. Finalise checklists	**Writing** Work on recounts. Discuss, proof-read and edit	**Writing** Complete recounts. Evaluate using marking ladders (see Resource Pages H and I)

Recount Features

Objective

We will identify features of a recount text, focusing on the introduction

You need: Resource Pages A and G; scissors; glue; Post-it™ notes (one per child).

Whole class work

- ***Do you know what a 'recount text' is? What do you think its function is?*** Answer: to retell something.
- Read Resource Page A. Explain that this is a recount. ***What does it recount?*** Answer: a football match.
- Focus on the first paragraph. Discuss why the opening paragraph is of key importance. Brainstorm ideas on what this paragraph sets out to do. Use the label 'introduction'.
- List the 5 W questions: what, where, when, why and who. ***Why is this information included? Does this information help the reader? Why?*** Answer: it sums up what the writing is going to be about.
- Introduce the word 'orientate'. Ask the children to try defining it or to use a dictionary.
- Ask them to try to apply the definition to this context. ***How can writing orientate a reader?*** Answer: it can put the reader on the right course in terms of expectations about the writing.
- Now ask simple questions about the first paragraph, such as ***Who is playing? Which stadium are they in? When... ?*** and so on. Explain that all that information is there to orientate the reader and that this is the purpose of the introduction.

Independent, pair or guided work

- Ask the children to work individually, cutting the text into separate paragraphs.
- The children re-arrange the paragraphs in a new order, and glue them on to paper.
- The children swap texts with a work partner. The children record on a Post-it™ note a comment or two about their partner's text, for example:

> Difficult to follow. Didn't know what was coming next. Confused at the beginning.

Plenary

- Listen to one or two texts, but focus on the comments, making a display of them.
- ***Is there a common complaint from readers? Does one paragraph matter more than others?***
- Stress the importance of the introduction. Emphasise that a recount text must always begin with an introduction to orientate the reader, as it has essential information for the rest of the text. Start a class checklist (see Resource Page G for ideas).
- Some children may have noted that the chronology or sequence is important (this will make a good starting point for another lesson).
- Keep the display of comments for future reference.

Chronology and Connectives

Objective

We will identify features of a recount text, focusing on chronological sequence

You need: Resource Pages A, B and G.

Whole class work

- Use the independent work from the previous lesson as a starting point, looking again at the collected list of comments. Direct the children's attention to sequential order. Can you see anything similar in these comments? ***Can you identify a common theme?*** Answer: chronological order. Accept the children's vocabulary before introducing this term.

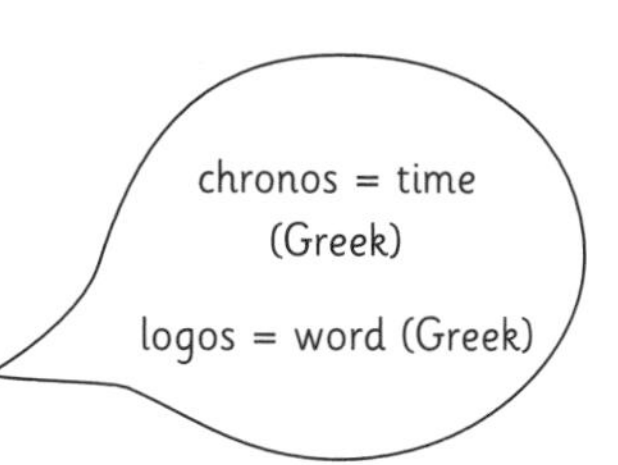

- ***How do you know what is the correct chronological order of this text?*** Direct the children towards the facts of the text, for example,
  - the 'second goal' can't be mentioned before the first goal
  - there can't be 'less than 10 minutes to play' (paragraph 5) until most of the second half has been played.
- Ensure that the children recognise that the choice of words has confirmed the sequential order.
- Review connectives. Explain that you will focus on connectives associated with time, such as 'while', 'once', 'in the end'.
- Model two paragraphs about your morning. Start both paragraphs with time connectives. Make sure that your paragraphs have to stay in sequence in order to make sense, and that the chosen connectives reinforce this.

> Initially, I thought today was going to go well. Little did I know! As soon as I set foot out of ...
>
> Afterwards I realised I had been stupid ...

- Experiment orally with leaving out one or two words. ***Does it matter? Is the meaning still the same?*** Go over your text with your class, making sure that they understand the value and role of the connectives.

Independent, pair or guided work

- Independently, the children underline time connectives in Resource Page A.
- In pairs, the children discuss the effect of using these words.

Plenary

- Work through the paragraphs together, identifying the connectives (Resource Page B).
- Discuss the merit and effect of different words. ***Can you think of any other words that could be used instead?***
- Re-emphasise the chronological sequence connectives bring to a text. Explain that they are a very common feature of a recount. Start a class checklist (see checklist 2, Resource Page G for ideas).

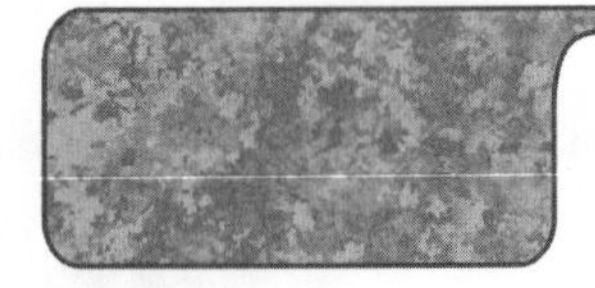

Notes

Objective

We will discuss the purpose of note-taking and how this influences the nature of notes made

You need: Resource Pages A, C and G.

Whole class work

- Ask the children to define the term 'notes'. (Short letters to friends, reminders to themselves to do something, lists of what they want to buy.) Emphasise the word 'short'.
- Now ask the children to think about taking notes. ***What does this mean?*** For example, journalists recording their thoughts about an event, or a secretary recording formal proceedings such as the Annual Governors' Meeting. Their parents probably receive a report. ***What is the report?*** Answer: a recount of what was said and done at the meeting. ***How could someone remember everything that was said?***
- Guide them towards understanding that someone took notes in order to write the recount later. ***What do you think the notes would be like?*** Brainstorm ideas on the format: headings, asterisks, bullet points, abbreviated words, possibly small diagrams. Draw a spidergram on the board of all the ideas.
- Encourage the children to recognise that not all notes will be identical. ***What might shape the format?*** Answers could include:

> personal style
> what the notes are needed for
> how accurate the recount is going to have to be
> who will read the recount

- Now look at the notes on Resource Page C. Encourage free discussion on the layout. ***Why might the notes be difficult for someone other than the writer to read?***
- ***Who do you think wrote these notes?*** Answer: the reporter, because only the person who wrote them could really understand them.

Independent, pair or guided work

- Ask the children to list any abbreviations used, and say what they think they mean.
- List helpful organisational devices that are used, for example, headings.
- Choose one or two paragraphs of the football recount (Resource Page A) and match the note to the finished text. 'Nervy goalie' ➤ 'the goalkeeper became edgy'

Plenary

- Share and discuss the children's findings. Begin a class checklist for note-taking (see Resource Page G for ideas).
- Clear up any unresolved problems with abbreviations.

Adapting for the Reader

Objective

We will adapt writing for different readers and simplify writing for younger readers

You need: Resource Pages A and B.

Whole class work

- Reread Resource Page A. Ask the children to think about the style of the text. ***What does style mean?*** Answer: the manner in which a text is written: length of sentences; powerful verbs; descriptions; first or third person and so on. Refer to Resource Page B.
- ***What is the style of this recount?*** Encourage a wide-ranging discussion.
- Now focus on specific areas, beginning with the vocabulary. ***How complicated are the words?***
- Focus on paragraph 3. ***Which words would probably not be understood by a younger reader?*** Point out that even if the children are unsure of a particular word, they probably still know the general meaning. A younger reader probably wouldn't.
- Move on to tone. Explain that this is the way the reader is addressed. ***Who might read this recount?*** Answer: somebody who knows and likes football. ***How can you tell?*** Answer: technical terms and details about the game.
- Consider sentence structure. Read aloud the final sentence of paragraph 4. ***Is this a simple sentence?*** Answer: no. Point out that its use of commas and a subordinate clause makes it too complex for a younger reader.
- List the main facts contained in paragraph 2. ***Can these be written more simply, in a chattier style?***
- Model a revised version:

> Straightaway one person looked better than the rest. His name was McKinley, and he was the centre-forward. He scored a goal all on his own in just a minute! Then the score was 1–0 and Kantford were winning.

Independent, pair or guided work

- Ask the children to read paragraph 3 and list the main facts in note form.
- Independently, the children write a new version of the paragraph, in a style suitable for a younger reader (but not boring!).

Plenary

- Listen to some of the new versions.
- Hold a constructive debate about which words and phrases work best and why.
- Produce a co-operative effort on the board, incorporating the best ideas and examples of style, vocabulary, tone and sentence structure.

Preparing Notes

Objective

We will understand the purpose of note-taking and see how this affects the type of notes made

You need: Resource Page D; science exercise books.

Whole class work

- Look together at Resource Page D. ***What are these? Is this a proper text? What do you think they might be for?***
- Allow plenty of time for the children to unearth information. Eventually they should identify this writing as:
  - a set of notes
  - about an event
  - preparation for a recount the writer will have to write (because of individual use of personal abbreviations)
- Discuss the abbreviations used. Explain that abbreviations are often only of help to the writer, as he or she makes their own up. Some are standard: eg. / v. Some are non-standard or made up: 'grps' means 'groups' (made up for speed).
- Identify common symbols, such as &, =, >, ?. Discuss what > probably means. Answer: 'to/in the direction of'. ***Why has the writer used a question mark?*** Answer: uncertainty about the exact number of shops.
- Discuss the layout and the organisational devices used, including: punctuation; underlining; CAPITALS to show importance; numbers.
- ***Why are numbers particularly helpful?*** Answer: for showing chronological sequence. ***Who will eventually read the final recount?*** Answers could include a teacher; readers of the school magazine. Emphasise that these notes are obviously for a formal recount.
- ***How can we tell that the recount will be quite formal?*** Brainstorm ideas:

> detailed description
>
> accuracy about order of events
>
> restrained, formal language, for example, 'delicious' rather than 'yummy', 'horribly dressed' rather than 'FOUL!!'

- Now suggest how the notes could be different if the recount was for a friend. Discuss briefly what might stay (proper names), and what would go/change/be moved (some of the vocabulary).

Independent, pair or guided work

- Ask the children to prepare a set of notes for a recount for a best friend who missed a recent science lesson. The recount will need the correct facts, but only the friend will read the recount. Emphasise that they are writing notes for this recount.

Plenary

- Share some of the sets of notes. ***Could your friend write a recount of the lesson from them, or have you left out important facts? Might your friend mis-spell some of the technical terms?***
- Emphasise that the purpose of the notes influences the way they look/are written.

Simplifying a Text

Objectives

We will simplify writing for younger readers. We will also examine which words in a text can be deleted or moved, and which are essential

You need: Resource Pages E and F; whiteboards.

Whole class work

- Read Resource Page E (and see Resource Page F). ***What level of reading difficulty do you think this is?*** Encourage an exchange of ideas, with reasons for opinions.
- ***Is the recount suitable for younger readers?*** Answers may be varied, but direct the children's focus towards vocabulary. ***Which words are difficult?***
- Ask the children to record simplified synonyms on their whiteboards.
- Brainstorm lists of words that can be deleted ('particularly') as opposed to being essential to meaning ('Victorian').
- ***Does moving words make the text easier?*** For example: 'We were split into two mixed groups as soon as we arrived', would be a simpler construction than the one in the recount.
- Focus on sentence structure. Talk about younger readers requiring straightforward sentence structure. Read aloud sentence 3, paragraph 2. Comment on its complex structure, length and punctuation.
- Together write a simplified version, for example:

> George was the guide of my group. He told us about his clothes and his boot pick. It was for getting stones out.

- Discuss introducing a 'chattier' tone, suitable for younger readers, for example:

> I really liked the pill machine.
> The time went rushing past.

Independent, pair or guided work

- In pairs, the children rewrite a section of the recount, making it easier for a younger reader to understand.
- Encourage the children to read sections to each other to test out phrases and constructions.

Plenary

- Listen to some of the new versions.
- Encourage your class to discuss and criticise constructively using a response sandwich: one good comment, one idea for improvement, another good comment.
- Talk to your class about their task for the rest of the week: two sets of notes and the recounts, linked to another subject, for example, a field trip. The writing should be based on personal experience, and be for two different types of readers: a friend who couldn't go and an unknown reader of the local newspaper.

Pupil copymaster

A Fitting Final

MIDLANDS CUP GOES TO KANTFORD
by Tom Marsh

The Under 16s Hetherington Cup final was held last Saturday. In appalling weather conditions, Kantford School, Brinsworth played Aidan School, Olmington at the world-famous 'Stadium of Wonder' in Manchester. These boys probably had not just their opposition, but also their own nerves, to do battle with, but they entertained the maximum crowd for the full 90 minutes.

First there was a display of individual brilliance: McKinley, Kantford's centre forward, was given too much space by a yet-to-settle Aidan. His sole advance on goal and successful shot were staggering displays of confidence. A deficit of 1–0 after a minute and a half was the worst of starts for Aidan.

After that, Aidan struggled for ball control. Then the battle for mid-field possession became increasingly one-sided, and their defence was under constant assault. Next, the goalkeeper became edgy, and finally Kantford's second goal – this time from Thompson, but set up by McKinley – was all too predictable. Perhaps the frantic gestures and signals from the side helped Aidan to retain the semblance of a formation, but they seemed grateful for the half-time whistle.

What on earth was said to them? Aidan re-emerged from that tunnel a new team! First their defence was tight, and they made every pass count, rather than squandering hard-won possession. Then there was their mid-field. It was this group that really changed Aidan's game: first they were winning balls, next they were passing them accurately, then they were getting them to their two strikers. A first goal by Dixon from a set piece was well deserved. Their second goal, from a movement first started by Dunn, who then crossed to Whyles, for it to be finally headed home by Beecham, was proof of what teamwork brings.

Now, with less than 10 minutes to play, came the real excitement. A whole season of football had led up to this, and neither side felt ready to give up easily. End-to-end play followed with both sides thrilling their supporters with shots on goal which never quite saw the back of the net. At last it all finished as it had started: in the last minute, McKinley began a searing run from mid-field. He scythed through the opposition, and finally the game was decided: his shot through the goalie's legs was never in doubt.

Alan Sharpe in the BBC commentary box said, "I think we may just have a future United and England star there, Ron."

He was right. It was a commendable performance by two teams, but one person dominated and many of us watching felt that we had just witnessed two memorable individual goals by a future star. McKinley gave Kantford their winning score of 3–2.

Exemplar analysis

Example of analysis of *A Fitting Final*

Introduction orientates reader, setting scene. It tells 'who', 'where' and 'when' – it is a necessary part of this text type.

Time connective giving immediate chronological order to text.

Time connectives provide a useful link between paragraphs, and emphasise chronological order.

Two connectives that follow one another in meaning.

Time connective at start of paragraph is likely feature of a recount.

Recount adopts tone of formality to match reader: here, person interested in sport.

MIDLANDS CUP GOES TO KANTFORD
by Tom Marsh

The Under 16s Hetherington Cup final was held last Saturday. In appalling weather conditions, Kantford School, Brinsworth played Aidan School, Olmington at the world-famous 'Stadium of Wonder' in Manchester. These boys probably had not just their opposition, but also their own nerves, to do battle with, but they entertained the maximum crowd for the full 90 minutes.

First there was a display of individual brilliance: McKinley, Kantford's centre forward, was given too much space by a yet-to-settle Aidan. His sole advance on goal and successful shot were staggering displays of confidence. A deficit of 1–0 after a minute and a half was the worst of starts for Aidan.

After that, Aidan struggled for ball control. Then the battle for mid-field possession became increasingly one-sided, and their defence was under constant assault. Next, the goalkeeper became edgy, and finally Kantford's second goal – this time from Thompson, but set up by McKinley – was all too predictable. Perhaps the frantic gestures and signals from the side helped Aidan to retain the semblance of a formation, but they seemed grateful for the half time whistle.

What on earth was said to them? Aidan re-emerged from that tunnel a new team! First their defence was tight, and they made every pass count, rather than squandering hard-won possession. Then there was their mid-field. It was this group that really changed Aidan's game: first they were winning balls, next they were passing them accurately, then they were getting them to their two strikers. A first goal by Dixon from a set piece was well deserved. Their second goal, from a movement first started by Dunn, who then crossed to Whyles, for it to be finally headed home by Beecham, was proof of what teamwork brings.

Now, with less than 10 minutes to play, came the real excitement. A whole season of football had led up to this, and neither side felt ready to give up easily. End-to-end play followed with both sides thrilling their supporters with shots on goal which never quite saw the back of the net. At last it all finished as it had started: in the last minute, McKinley began a searing run from mid-field. He scythed through the opposition and finally the game was decided: his shot through the goalie's legs was never in doubt.

Alan Sharpe in the BBC commentary box said, "I think we may just have a future United and England star there, Ron."

He was right. It was a commendable performance by two teams, but one person dominated and many of us watching felt that we had just witnessed two memorable individual goals by a future star. McKinley gave Kantford their winning score of 3–2.

Connectives working together to show sequential order of events.

Other vocabulary, such as this adjective, is often employed to confirm a fact – in this case, that there has already been one goal.

Recounts are written in the past tense: they retell events.

These connectives are co-operating, thereby stressing sequence of footballers' movements.

Single words employed for chronology.

Choice of adverb makes it clear the contest is over.

Closing statement finishes recount; this is a common feature.

Quote adds interest and authenticity. Notice layout of direct speech.

Recounts focus not just on specific occasions, but also specific people.

Pupil copymaster

Notes for football recount

Under 16

Saturday – Wonder, Manch.
Kantford School, Brinsworth v Aidan School, Olmington
Capacity crowd

Soaking wet!

1st half

AID

- Rocked by early goal
- Messy midfielders
- Bad ball control
- Defence pushed
- Nervy goalie
- Desperate coach on line – arm waving

KAN

v.confident McKinley gl 70 secs

dominate play

gl 2 32 min Thompson (McKinley set up)

2nd half

- Total change!
- Improve defence & pass
- More possess.
- Set piece gl 57 min Dixon
- 68min gl Beecham (gd 3 way wk)

Less of own way

x Dunn → x Whyles → x Beecham

Last 10 mins

- tempo
- end to end
- pace
- near misses

50 secs left - brill. Solo run+gl Mc Kinley
final win Kant 3-2

* Quote re. McK. Alan S to Ron P:

– I think we may just have a future United and England star there Ron

Pupil copymaster

Notes for Black Country Museum visit

Wed. 3/6/02

- Vict. History topic
- Us + J6
- Museum nr Dudley
- 2 grps
- Our guide – George: Vict. Clothes & boot pick for stones

1. tram > village
2. look – bridge, canal, post box (VR)
3. shops – 6? Inside, talks from shopkeepers showing things. Best thing: pill cutter in chemist's.
4. Sweet shop last, jars sweets – FREE SWEETS! – delicious!
5. School:
   - much smaller than ours
   - had go on their slates
   - horribly dressed teacher
   - stern, with cane
6. little church (last place) called CHAPEL
   - lady talked
   - said Victs v. religious
   - sang Vict. Hymn (blessed ye who come)
7. back

Pupil copymaster

Our History Trip

On Wednesday 3rd June, J5 and J6 visited the Black Country Museum, which is situated near the town of Dudley. The purpose of the visit was to extend our knowledge of the Victorian Age: how people lived, what they wore and what their buildings looked like.

As soon as we arrived, we were split into two mixed groups, in order to make the sizes manageable. Each group was given a guide, who was dressed in Victorian clothes. My group's guide, George, immediately described his items of clothing, and explained why he was carrying certain items – such as a boot pick to remove the bits of stone that got trapped in the soles of boots.

After that, he took us on a tram down into the centre of the village. Once off the tram, he gave us a talk on the important sights, such as a Victorian post box with the letters VR on it. Then we had a guided tour of the shops – these were proper Victorian shops. Once we got inside each, the shopkeeper explained what he sold, which was often a variety of items, and showed us special items. I was particularly impressed by a machine for cutting pills. The last shop was my favourite: it had wonderful jars of sweets, and we were allowed to taste some. They were delicious!

Next we visited the old school, which was surprisingly tiny. We sat at the desks and wrote on slate boards, with a stern teacher, dressed in black and white, holding a cane, standing over us. I definitely prefer our school and teachers! Finally, we had a short look at the chapel, which was their word for church. We went inside, and a lady first talked to us about how religious the Victorians were, and then we sang a Victorian hymn that we knew.

At last we had to leave. The time had passed too quickly, but I felt that I had learnt a great deal about Victorian life in just one day. This was certainly a visit worth making.

Exemplar analysis

Example of analysis of *Our History Trip*

Introduction orientates reader, setting a scene. It tells 'who' went on the trip, 'where' and 'when'.

Time connective gives immediate chronological order.

Time connectives are a useful link between paragraphs, and emphasise chronological order.

Again a time connective provides a useful time link between paragraphs.

Further example of connectives co-operating, as they stress sequence of events.

Time connective begins short, concluding paragraph.

On Wednesday 3rd June, J5 and J6 visited the Black Country Museum, which is situated near the town of Dudley. The purpose of the visit was to extend our knowledge of the Victorian Age: how people lived, what they wore and what their buildings looked like.

As soon as we arrived, we were split into two mixed groups, in order to make the sizes manageable. Each group was given a guide, who was dressed in Victorian clothes. My group's guide, George, immediately described his items of clothing, and explained why he was carrying certain items – such as a boot pick to remove the bits of stone that got trapped in the soles of boots.

After that, he took us on a tram down into the centre of the village. Once off the tram, he gave us a talk on the important sights, such as a Victorian post box with the letters VR on it. Then we had a guided tour of the shops – these were proper Victorian shops. Once we got inside each, the shopkeeper explained what he sold, which was often a variety of items, and showed us special items. I was particularly impressed by a machine for cutting pills. The last shop was my favourite: it had wonderful jars of sweets, and we were allowed to taste some. They were delicious!

Next we visited the old school, which was surprisingly tiny. We sat at the desks and wrote on slate boards, with a stern teacher, dressed in black and white, holding a cane, standing over us. I definitely prefer our school and teachers! Finally, we had a short look at the chapel, which was their word for church. We went inside, and a lady first talked to us about how religious the Victorians were, and then we sang a Victorian hymn that we knew.

At last we had to leave. The time had passed too quickly, but I felt that I had learnt a great deal about Victorian life in just one day. This was certainly a visit worth making.

Recount written in past tense; it retells an event.

These connectives work together, establishing chronological order.

Adjective conveys information relating to sequential order: sweet shop is last on tour.

Recount written in first person. This is often the case.

Choice of adverb makes it clear the chapel was last place visited.

Text is supported by illustration or photo of key moment.

Closing statement finishes the recount.

Recount adopts tone of formality to match its reader: in this case, the teacher.

Exemplar material

Checklists for note-taking and recounts

Example of a checklist for introduction of a recount ①

- Set the scene
- Orientate the reader
- Say who and when involved
- State where happened

Example of a checklist for a recount

- Include an introduction
- Include supporting illustrations (if helpful)
- Write in 1st or 3rd person
- Use the past tense
- Use essential words
- Make frequent use of connectives (particularly time connectives)
- Show chronological sequence
- Use appropriate style and tone for the reader
- Use appropriate vocabulary and sentence structure
- Include closing statement

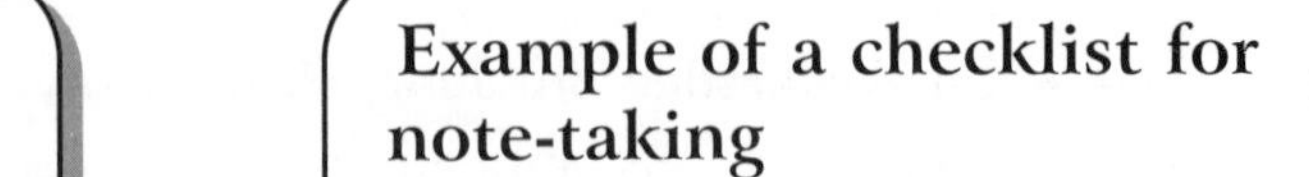

Example of a checklist for note-taking

- Write so they can be understood by writer
- Include correct facts
- Include correct 'technical' words/proper names
- Show chronological order of events
- Demonstrate awareness of reader of eventual recount
- Use appropriate style
- Use abbreviations
- Use helpful layout
- Use organisational devices
- Use signs/symbols

Marking ladder

Marking ladder for a recount

Name: ______________________________

Pupil	Objective	Teacher
	My recount includes an introduction.	
	I included time connectives.	
	I included illustrations (if helpful).	
	I included essential words.	
	I used the past tense.	
	I used appropriate style and tone for the reader.	
	I made the right choice of vocabulary and sentences.	
	I showed chronological order.	
	I wrote in 1st or 3rd person.	
	I included a closing statement.	
	What could I do to improve my recount next time?	

Marking ladder

Marking ladder for note-taking

Name: ______________________________

Pupil	Objective	Teacher
	I can understand my notes.	
	I included correct facts.	
	I included correct 'technical' words/proper names.	
	I showed chronological order of events.	
	I used a helpful layout.	
	I used organisational devices.	
	I thought about whom I was writing the recount for.	
	I used a helpful style.	
	I used abbreviations.	
	I used signs/symbols.	
	What could I do to improve my notes next time?	

Fables

Outcome

Written version of a fable; oral retelling of fables

Objectives

Sentence

6 to be aware of the differences between spoken and written language, including: conventions to guide reader; the use of punctuation to replace intonation, pauses, gestures.

Text

1 to identify and classify the features of myths, legends and fables, e.g. the moral in a fable, fantastical beasts in legends.

2 to investigate different versions of the same story in print or on film, identifying similarities and differences.

3 to explore similarities and differences between oral and written storytelling.

11 to write own versions of legends, myths and fables, using structures and themes identified in reading.

14 to make notes of story outline as preparation for oral storytelling.

Planning frame

- Identify and classify the features of fables.
- Make notes of story outline as preparation for oral storytelling.
- Retell stories and make tape recordings of them.
- Explore similarities and differences between oral and written storytelling.
- Be aware of differences between spoken and written language.
- Investigate different versions of a story on film, identifying similarities and differences.
- Write own fable, using structures and themes identified.

How you could plan this unit

Day 1	Day 2	Day 3	Day 4	Day 5
Reading *The Hare and the Tortoise*	**Reading and writing** Make notes on story as preparation for oral retelling	**Reading and writing** Use notes to retell stories. Make tape recording	**Reading and writing** *Oral Storytelling*	**Reading** Revise points from Day 4. Listen to recordings from Day 3. Compile a checklist for oral storytelling (see Resource Page E). Retell oral versions of familiar traditional tale

Day 6	Day 7	Day 8	Day 9	Day 10
Reading and writing *A Fox and a Sick Lion*	**Reading and writing** *Film Versions*	**Writing** Plan and begin task of writing own fables. Compile a checklist (see Resource Page E)	**Writing** Discuss, proof-read and edit writing. Finalise checklists	**Writing** Complete fables. Evaluate using marking ladder

The Hare and the Tortoise

Objective

We will identify the features of fables

You need: Resource Pages A and B; whiteboards; postcard-size pieces of card.

Whole class work

- Read *The Hare and the Tortoise* (Resource Page A). Ask the children to classify it as fiction or non-fiction, giving reasons.
- Identify different features of the story. ***What immediately strikes you about the characters?*** Answer: they are all animals.
- Point out the use of capital letters and the use of common nouns as proper nouns. ***What is unusual about these?*** Answer: the writer is treating the animals as people. ***In what other way are the animals treated as people?*** Answer: the animals speak.
- Ask the children to turn over their texts while you read the story. ***Are you surprised at how short the story is? Why might a story be so short?*** The children may put forward the idea of reading it aloud, but your prompting should bring the discussion around to the notion of oral storytelling. (NB Storytelling in other genres or from other cultures is not necessarily so short.)
- ***What is the name of this genre?*** Answer: fable. ***What do you know about fables?*** Encourage the children to consider the following:

> the use of animals
>
> they are short
>
> they are clever/amusing
>
> a teaching mesage called a moral is written after them

- Explain that fables are simply fictitious tales but have long been associated with a moral as the denouement. This fable is from Aesop, a Greek story-teller who lived in the 6th century BC. The stories were only written down hundreds of years after they were first told.
- Emphasise that the moral advises people how to live; it is not about animals (see Resource Page B).

Independent, pair or guided work

- The children read *The Hare and the Tortoise* to each other and discuss with their partner the moral (or teaching message) of the story.
- On whiteboards, the children draft the moral that would follow this fable. The moral should be about three lines long and should not mention animals.
- The children edit their writing before producing a final 'neat' copy on card.

Plenary

- Listen to and discuss some of the morals.
- Make a display of them.
- ***Which ones best sum up the message of the fable?***

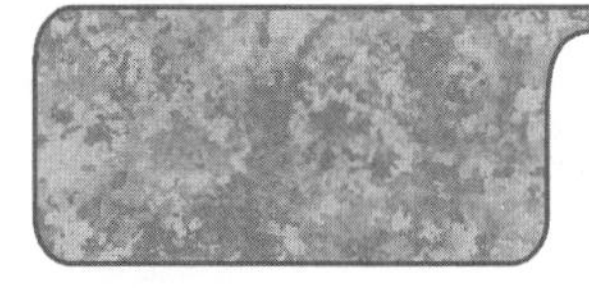

Oral Storytelling

Objective

We will discover the similarities and differences between oral and written storytelling

You need: Resource Pages A and E; a recording by you of an oral retelling of the story; whiteboards.

Whole class work

- Look again at *The Hare and the Tortoise* (Resource Page A). Ask the children to explain the meaning of the first sentence. Then ask them to suggest interesting, meaningful ways to read it.
- Help lead them to the discovery that meanings of words can be linked to voice: therefore, a slow, precise tone emphasises the characteristics of the Tortoise.
- Talk about the importance of voice (as opposed to just the choice of words) in oral storytelling. ***How would you read the Hare's words in the third paragraph?***
- ***Which words in the written story describe how the Hare speaks?*** Answer: 'bragged' and 'sneered'. In the oral version, the storyteller's voice has to actually brag and sneer.
- Ask one person to read aloud the final sentence of the second paragraph. ***Do you agree with the way this was read? What feelings should you try to bring out?*** Answer: the gloating feelings/behaviour of the Hare.
- ***How does the written form emphasise this?*** The children should identify the importance of the exclamation mark. Ask them to find another exclamation mark (final paragraph). ***What feelings does this one emphasise?*** Answer: the Hare's horror and surprise.
- ***What effect does the exclamation mark after 'again' have?*** Answer: it reinforces the sneering tone of the Hare.

Independent, pair or guided work

- Explain to the children that they will be thinking about the similarities and differences between oral and written storytelling.
- The children listen again to your oral version, making notes on their whiteboards while it is playing. (You may need to play it more than once.)
- Then the children compare notes with a partner.
- In pairs, the children work together to produce a list of the similarities and differences they have found between the oral and written storytelling versions.

Plenary

- Brainstorm a list of the children's ideas. Add to the class checklist (see Resource Page E for ideas).
- Replay your recording, drawing attention to the parts where you have made good use of voice, pauses and intonation.

A Fox and a Sick Lion

Objective

We will identify the features of fables

You need: Resource Pages C and D.

Whole class work

- Read *A Fox and A Sick Lion* (Resource Page C). Ask the children to confirm its genre.
- ***Can you remember how fables first started?*** Remind the children of their origin in an oral form. ***How does this affect the length of this story?*** Answer: it is short, so it can be remembered and retold.
- ***Who is this fable about? Why have I just used the word 'who' rather than 'what'?*** Answer: the animals are treated as people.
- ***In what way are the animals treated as people?*** Answer: writing letters, living in a palace, speaking, and so on.
- Encourage the children to explore the text more deeply in response to the last question. Can they recognise that 'offer their sympathy', and 'wished ... a speedy recovery' are expressions commonly applied to people?
- Now use questions to focus on the moral. ***What is the part after the story called? What is a moral's purpose?***
- Allow the children a few minutes' discussion in pairs or small groups, before collecting class ideas on the meaning of this moral. ***How does the moral relate to the fable?***
- Re-emphasise:

> Fables are usually about animals with human characteristics.
>
> A moral is about people and how we ought to live our lives (and should not refer to animals).

Independent, pair or guided work

- Ask the children to reread this fable, and to identify and list the main events.
- Using their lists, the children put the events into chronological order. Warn the children that the written order may not always be the order in which the events take place.

Plenary

- Review the main events and discuss any queries.
- Agree the correct chronological order (see Resource Page D).

Film Versions

Objective

We will investigate a different version of the same moral on film

You need: Resource Pages C and D; large sheets of paper (for storyboards).

Whole class work

- Review the different forms of storytelling from this unit: reading the written word and listening to the spoken word.
- ***Can you suggest some other ways that we tell each other stories?*** Answer: TV, comics, books and e-books, computer games, films, radio and so on.
- ***How many of you know the story of the latest Harry Potter film? Have you all read the book?*** The answer to the second question could be 'no'. Discuss how they have still managed to gain detailed knowledge of the story from watching the film/video.
- Help the children to recognise that the film storyteller uses a strong visual element.
- Now explore how *A Fox and A Sick Lion* could be presented through film. Display Resource Page C.
- ***How would the oral storyteller read the first sentence?*** Answer: perhaps in a frail/hoarse voice.
- ***How could a film maker demonstrate to the audience that the Lion is ill?*** Answer: visually. Encourage the children to brainstorm ideas, for example, the Lion sitting in bed, clutching a hot water bottle; the Lion surrounded by cough medicine bottles, cold cures and boxes of tissues.
- ***How will the audience know that the Lion is King? Will it be obvious he lives in a palace?*** Suggestions about crowns, robes, types of buildings, will reinforce the point about seeing a fact, rather than hearing or reading about it.
- Make the point that there will still be connections with the other storytelling forms. ***Why would it be useful to show some of the words the Lion writes? How does a film use any spoken words?*** Answer: dialogue or narrator.

Independent, pair or guided work

- Ask the children to plan a film version of this fable using storyboards – one brief sketch for each of the main events. (Resource Page D, the chronological order of events, will help.) Some children may wish to work in pairs.
- The cartoon film version of the fable will differ from the written one, but the basic story must remain.
- Draw the scenes in a series of frames. Add 'director's notes' about sounds and words.

Plenary

- The children present their work, explaining the sounds and words that would accompany the scenes.

Pupil copymaster

Aesop's Fable: The Hare and the Tortoise

The Tortoise was a slow, plain animal. Strangely, however, the Tortoise waged a bet with the Hare that he could beat him in a race, an animal who was known for his speed! The Hare quickly accepted the bet, and both agreed that the Fox would be the judge.

The route was marked out, and the two animals set off from the starting line together. Immediately, the Hare moved ahead, jogging easily, building up a greater and greater lead on the poor Tortoise. At the half-way point the gloating Hare could not even see the other animal!

"What is the point of tiring myself on a hot day?" bragged the Hare to the Rabbit who was watching from the sidelines. "I can have a rest, wait for that snail-like creature to catch me up, and then just overtake him again!" he sneered.

However, the Hare had forgotten the effects of a mid-day sun, and he fell into a deep sleep. The Tortoise crawled past the sleeping Hare. By the time the Hare awoke, the Tortoise was in the lead! The hare raced to catch up, but he had left it too late. The slow, dependable Tortoise beat the fast Hare.

Exemplar material

Morals

1 *We all depend on the help of one another, and even the great can have need of the most ordinary people. Kindnesses will be repaid.*

Story about Lion getting trapped in a net. Lion had let the Mouse go instead of eating her, so Mouse freed the Lion by nibbling through the net.

2 *People cannot rely solely on natural advantages. If people don't continue to work and use their skills, they will end up behind others.*

Story of the Hare and the Tortoise.

Pupil copymaster

Aesop's Fable: A Fox and a Sick Lion

The Lion grew sick. All the animals of the forest came to visit their King in his Palace to offer their sympathy. The Lion noticed that the Fox did not bother coming. He sent him an invitation, saying how ill he was and that he would enjoy his company.

On receiving the letter, the Fox sent back a reply. The reply wished the Lion a speedy recovery, but said that he could not accept the invitation, as he had seen many animals enter the Lion's Palace but none come out.

When people who are usually threatening and dangerous, suddenly seem kind and friendly, think carefully before trusting them.

Pupil copymaster

Chronological order of events

1. Lion gets ill.
2. One animal after another enters the Palace.
3. The Fox watches them going in.
4. Something happens to the visitors: Captured? Eaten? Used as servants? (The audience isn't told.)
5. Lion works out that the Fox hasn't visited. (Maybe he has a list.)
6. Lion writes an invitation.
7. Sends it. (How?)
8. Fox receives it.
9. Fox writes his reply and sends it.

Exemplar material

Checklists for fables

Example of a checklist for oral storytelling

- Make effective use of your voice
- Include changes in tone and speed
- Match voice to meaning
- Use emphasis
- Use dramatic pauses

Example of a checklist for a moral

- Give a clear message
- Advise on living
- Talk to people
- Make no mention of animals
- Make a clear link with the meaning of the story

Example of a checklist for a fable

- Make it a complete story
- Don't make it too long
- Make it clever and/or amusing
- Make sure that the plot can be understood
- Write mainly about animals
- Treat animals as people
- Use a capital letter to start animal's name
- Include a moral underneath

Marking ladder

Name: ______________________

Pupil	Objective	Teacher
	My fable is a complete story.	
	I made it clever/amusing.	
	I made it quite short.	
	I used animals as main characters.	
	I treated animals as people.	
	I used capital letters.	
	My story can be understood.	
	I included a moral underneath.	
	How could I improve my fable next time?	

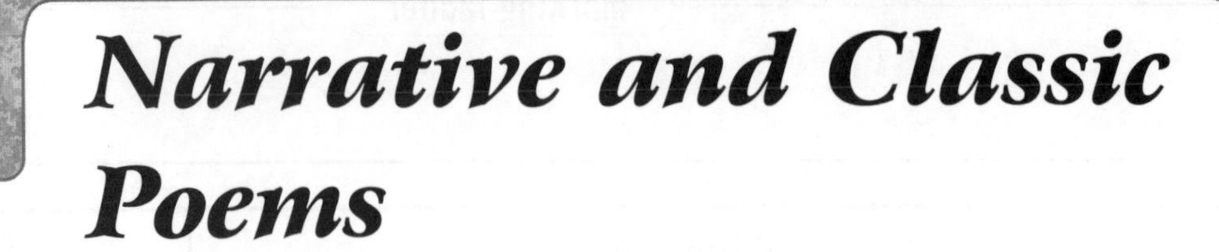

Narrative and Classic Poems

Outcome

Choral performance; additional verse of a poem

Objectives

Sentence

4 to revise from Y4 ... the different kinds of noun.

Text

4 to read a range of narrative poems;

5 to perform poems in a variety of ways;

6 to understand terms which describe kinds of poems and to identify typical features;

7 to compile a class anthology of favourite poems with commentaries which illuminate the choice;

12 to use the structures of poems read to write extensions of these, e.g. additional verses, or substituting own words and ideas.

Planning frame

- Read a range of narrative and classic poems.
- Become familiar with terms that describe kinds of poems.
- Perform poems in a variety of ways.
- Begin compilation of a class anthology, with commentaries, of favourite poems.
- Use the structure of a poem to substitute own words and ideas and to write an extension of it.

Note

- This unit can be linked with the previous unit on Fables.

How you could plan this unit

Day 1	Day 2	Day 3	Day 4	Day 5
Reading *Narrative Poems*	**Reading and writing** *Tortoise and Hare Race.* Analyse poem's structure and language	**Reading** Review Day 1. Group performances. Discuss problems. Make checklist (see Resource Page H)	**Reading and writing** *Performance*	**Reading** *From a Railway Carriage.* Analyse poem's structure and language

Day 6	Day 7	Day 8	Day 9	Day 10
Reading and writing *Word Choice*	**Writing** *Adding Verses*	**Writing** Finalise checklist. Discuss, proof-read, edit and complete writing. Evaluate using marking ladder	**Reading** Develop a class choral performance of *From a Railway Carriage*. Discuss views on the poems read and record in a class anthology	**Reading** Class choral performance of *From a Railway Carriage*. Evaluate using marking ladder (Resource Page J)

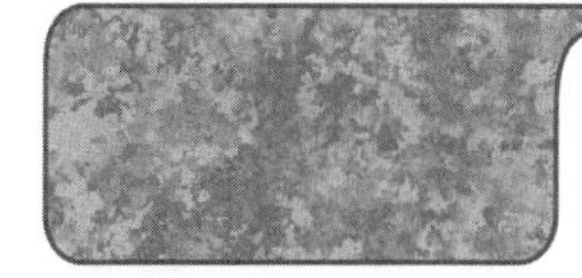

Narrative Poems

Objectives

We will perform poems in a variety of ways. We will also learn terms that describe kinds of poems

You need: Resource Pages A–C; Post-it™ notes.

Whole class work

- ***What does a narrator do?*** Answer: tells a story. ***So what is a narrative?*** Answer: a story.
- Remind the children of the fable *The Hare and the Tortoise* and review the plot (Resource Page A).
- Introduce the concept of telling a story in the form of a poem. This is known as a 'narrative poem' (as opposed to most poems they will meet which reflect a feeling, mood or brief moment in time). Now read the poem *Tortoise and Hare Race* (Resource Page B). Explain that this is an example of a narrative poem.
- Focus on the sound and beat of the poem while you read it aloud. Read the poem more than once, emphasising effective parts. For example, emphasise the line 'And still he slept', reading it in an appropriate tone.
- Then move to the story line of the poem, analysing the different parts of the plot, and identifying which verses deal with them – the first four verses describe the build-up to the race, for example (see Resource Page C).
- ***How long are most of the verses?*** The children will soon recognise the irregularity of the poem, and the random length of verses. Point out that this helps dramatise the function of telling a story.
- Ask individuals to read different lines, deliberately choosing lines of varying lengths. ***Is there a set rhythm (the same number of beats per line)?*** With the children, count or clap the syllables/beats in lines 1 and 3 so that they recognise the changes.

Independent, pair or guided work

- The children work in small groups, deciding how lines should be read for appropriate dramatic effect.
- Ask them to plan a group reading of the poem, reminding them that they do not all have to read at once (although this may be appropriate in places).
- Talk about the need to retain the audience's interest in the story through variety of:
  - volume (or number of readers)
  - tone
  - emphasis
  - pace.

Plenary

- ***Has working on a dramatic reading altered your understanding of/interest in the poem?*** Encourage them to provide evidence from group work to support their answers.
- ***Do you think it makes a good oral performance poem? Why do you think that?***
- ***Do you like the poem? Why?*** Give the children a few minutes to note their thoughts on Post-it™ notes. These can be used later for a booklet of commentaries or an anthology of poems.

Performance

Objective

We will perform poems in a variety of ways

You need: Resource Pages D and E; a selection of percussion instruments.

Whole class work

- Display *From a Railway Carriage* (Resource Page D). Ask the children to read the poem quietly to themselves.
- Now ask a group to read it together, without any practice. Do the same with a different group.
- ***What do you notice about their reading?*** Answers may focus on speed or volume or clarity. Widen the discussion to the question of whether they have read it with the tone/feeling that is appropriate for this poem.
- ***What is this poem about?*** Allow the children to talk about this in pairs, before holding a general discussion (see Resource Page E for ideas). Make sure that they understand the poem's basic subject matter: a list of sights seen from a fast-moving train.
- ***Should it be read quickly or slowly?*** Answer: quickly, because this fits in with the rhythm of the poem which mimics the movement of the train.
- ***Why is this poem easier to read aloud than* The Tortoise and the Hare*?*** Answer: it has an obvious and regular rhythm that the first poem did not have.
- Put this to the test by asking a new group to perform part of the poem while the rest of the class tap out the beat. Identify the number of beats to a line. Investigate whether there are any exceptions or problem areas (for example, the last part of the first verse may prove awkward). ***Why do you think the poet didn't stick strictly to the rhythm created?***

Independent, pair or guided work

- Ask the children to work in small groups to plan a performance of a verse/verses of the poem.
- Consider the use of background sound effects and percussion instruments where they would be effective.

Plenary

- Share the performances with the class.
- Evaluate using a response sandwich: one good comment, one idea for improvement, another good comment.

Word Choice

Objective

We will focus on the language and images in a poem

You need: Resource Pages D–F; whiteboards (one between two).

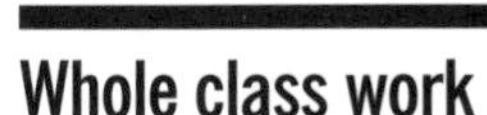

Whole class work

- Read *From a Railway Carriage* (Resource Page D) again. ***What sights are seen from the train in the first four lines of the poem?*** Answer: bridges, houses, hedges, ditches, horses, cattle.
- ***What simile describes the horses and cattle?*** Answer: troops in a battle. Talk to the children about the effect of this simile: it emphasises the animals' speed and strong movements (see Resource Page E). ***What mood is the poet trying to create by comparing animals to men in battle?***
- Discuss the images created by the use of 'fairies' and 'witches'. ***What is the effect on the audience?*** Suggest that the poet uses these words to create a picture of magically fast movement, because these are magical/fairy-tale creatures. Discuss the idea that the poet is comparing everyday objects to very unusual ones. ***Why do you think he does this?***
- Revise the definition of a noun – a word that names a thing or feeling. Revise the different kinds of nouns (Resource Page F).
- Model substituting a collective noun for 'troops' – for example, 'armies' or 'units'. ***What effect does this have on the rest of the line?*** Answer: there is now an extra syllable, so the poet would need to change 'a battle' to 'battle'.
- Emphasise the care that goes into word selection. ***What is effective about the selection of words in the first two lines?*** Answers could focus on the alliteration of 'f'; the closeness of 'ch' and 'dg' sounds as well as their similar appearance; the choice and repetition of 'faster', a word to match the train's movements.

Independent, pair or guided work

- In pairs, the children read the rest of the poem.
- Ask them to:

> Highlight any words that you find particularly effective (and be prepared to say why).
>
> Note on your whiteboard any images that are created by different parts of the poem.
>
> Discuss any changes you would make to particular words or pairs of lines and write these on your whiteboard.

Plenary

- Share some of the views, and listen to new pairs of lines that have been created. ***Has the rhythm been maintained? Where it has been deliberately altered, what effect does this have?***
- Photocopy the whiteboards to record opinions to add to commentaries for your class anthology.

Adding Verses

Objective

We will look at how to write an extension to a poem

You need: Resource Pages D, G and H.

Whole class work

- Reread *From a Railway Carriage* (Resource Page D). Comment on the length of the poem. ***How could the poet extend this poem, yet still keep the verse format?***
- During the ensuing discussion, ask the children to consider the poem's last words. ***Why are these relevant?*** Answer: they suggest finality, and therefore any extra verses need to precede this.
- ***How long is each verse? How is each verse constructed?*** Answer: a structure of four rhyming couplets.
- ***What else must be taken into account when extending the poem?*** List ideas, for example:

> the definite rhythm of the poem
>
> similar length lines
>
> use of capital letters and favoured punctuation (colons and semi-colons are common)
>
> frequent division of lines into two halves, e.g. 'Faster than fairies, faster then witches'; 'And here is a mill, and there is a river'
>
> little use of adjectives and adverbs – therefore increased importance of powerful verbs

- Model working on some ideas for an additional verse. Discuss appropriate openings, for example, 'Look ...', 'Now ...', 'Here/There ...'
- ***What other sights might you see from a train window that could be mentioned?*** Display a list of the children's nouns, encouraging them to think of powerful verbs to accompany them, and meaningful rhymes (see Resource Page G). (It is important that you steer the children away from 'forced' rhymes that do not make sense, but do rhyme.)

Independent, pair or guided work

- Ask the children to plan an additional verse for this poem, either to open the poem or as a middle verse. Some children may wish to work in pairs.
- The children need to list what/who will be mentioned, and then to compose rhyming line endings.
- Remind them of the need for powerful verbs and sounds.
- The children begin to draft four rhyming couplets.

Plenary

- Share some ideas.
- Work together on an initial class checklist for writing an extension of a poem (see Resource Page H for ideas).

Pupil copymaster

Aesop's Fable: The Hare and the Tortoise

The Tortoise was a slow, plain animal. Strangely, however, the Tortoise waged a bet with the Hare that he could beat him in a race, an animal who was known for his speed! The Hare quickly accepted the bet, and both agreed that the Fox would be the judge.

The route was marked out, and the two animals set off from the starting line together. Immediately, the Hare moved ahead, jogging easily, building up a greater and greater lead on the poor Tortoise. At the half-way point the gloating Hare could not even see the other animal!

"What is the point of tiring myself on a hot day?" bragged the Hare to the Rabbit who was watching from the sidelines. "I can have a rest, wait for that snail-like creature to catch me up, and then just overtake him again!" he sneered.

However, the Hare had forgotten the effects of a mid-day sun, and he fell into a deep sleep. The Tortoise crawled past the sleeping Hare. By the time the Hare awoke, the Tortoise was in the lead! The hare raced to catch up, but he had left it too late. The slow, dependable Tortoise beat the fast Hare.

Pupil copymaster

Tortoise and Hare Race

'Tortoise, you're very slow you know.
No wonder. Your legs are so short.'

'I get to where I want to go,'
said Tortoise with a snort.

Hare
was everywhere,
light and springy,
pinging past
fast,
all over the place.

'Besides I'd beat you in a race
if we were having one.'
'All right, we'll let Fox choose the place,
and see it's fairly run.'

The race began.
Off Hare ran.
'I'll probably win
before you begin,'
he jeered
as he disappeared.

And Tortoise was slow getting away
but he said as he jogged along,
'Little by little wins the day.
And Hare will get bored before long.'

Hare
was so sure
he'd be there
before

the Tortoise,
he thought
he'd take
a short break
and fell deep
asleep
in the sun.

He slept
and slept
while the minutes
kept on ticking away
through the heat of the day.

And still he slept

as Tortoise crept up and passed
on his way to the Finishing Post.
The end of the race was in sight at last.
He expected Hare there to boast.
But Hare woke
with a shock.
His body-clock
said he'd overslept.
So up he leapt
and started to run –
but there was someone already ahead
and at this minute
about to win.
'It can't be Tortoise.'
But it was.

Yes, there ahead with Fox was Tortoise –
winner of the race
and that despite his legs' shortness
and his slow pace.

Jill Townsend

Exemplar analysis

Example of analysis of *Tortoise and Hare Race*

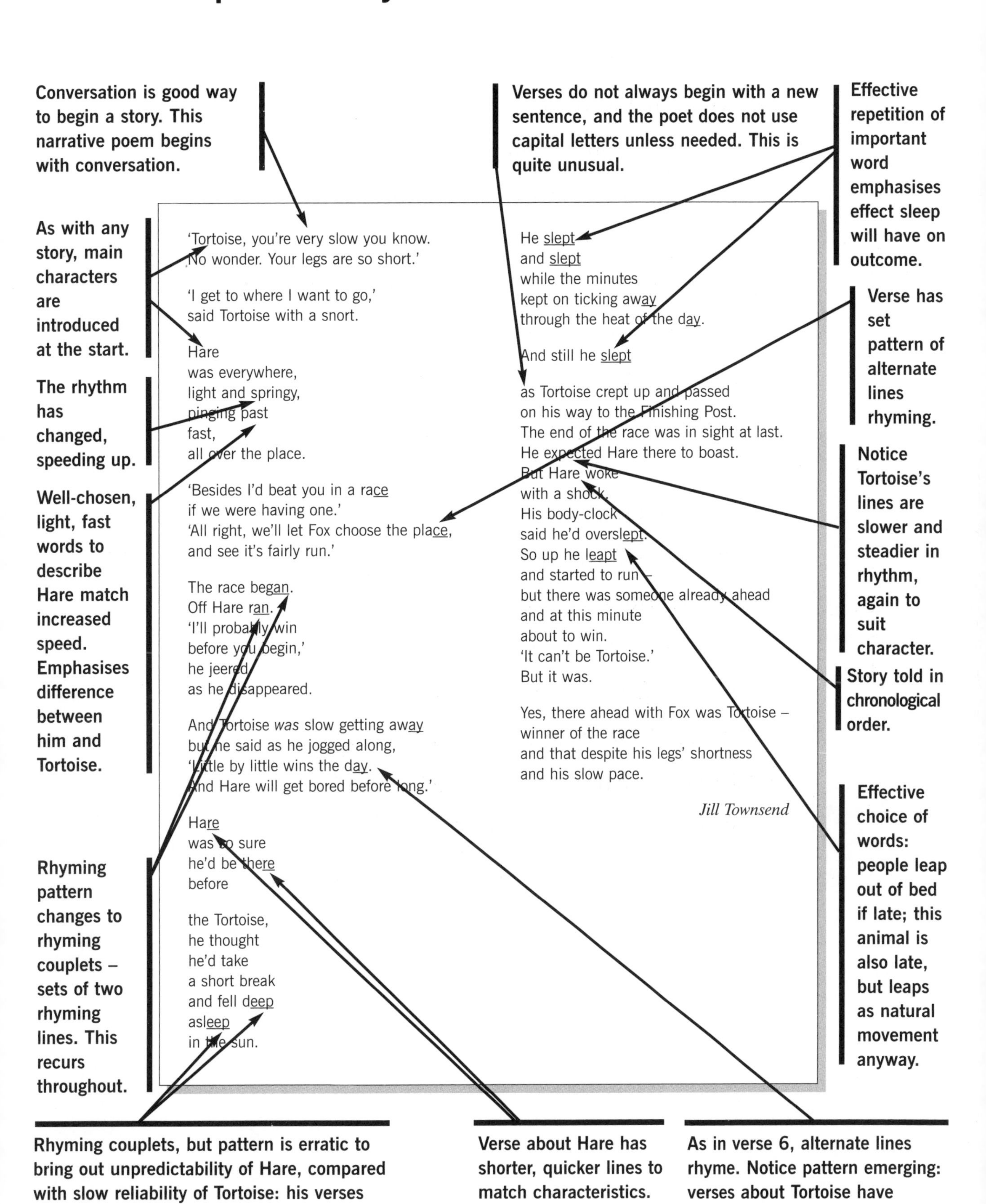

'Tortoise, you're very slow you know.
No wonder. Your legs are so short.'

'I get to where I want to go,'
said Tortoise with a snort.

Hare
was everywhere,
light and springy,
pinging past
fast,
all over the place.

'Besides I'd beat you in a race
if we were having one.'
'All right, we'll let Fox choose the place,
and see it's fairly run.'

The race began.
Off Hare ran.
'I'll probably win
before you begin,'
he jeered
as he disappeared.

And Tortoise *was* slow getting away
but he said as he jogged along,
'Little by little wins the day.
And Hare will get bored before long.'

Hare
was so sure
he'd be there
before

the Tortoise,
he thought
he'd take
a short break
and fell deep
asleep
in the sun.

He slept
and slept
while the minutes
kept on ticking away
through the heat of the day.

And still he slept

as Tortoise crept up and passed
on his way to the Finishing Post.
The end of the race was in sight at last.
He expected Hare there to boast.
But Hare woke
with a shock.
His body-clock
said he'd overslept.
So up he leapt
and started to run –
but there was someone already ahead
and at this minute
about to win.
'It can't be Tortoise.'
But it was.

Yes, there ahead with Fox was Tortoise –
winner of the race
and that despite his legs' shortness
and his slow pace.

Jill Townsend

Pupil copymaster

From a Railway Carriage

Faster than fairies, faster than witches,
Bridges and houses, hedges and ditches;
And charging along like troops in a battle,
All through the meadows the horses and cattle:
All of the sights of the hill and the plain
Fly as thick as driving rain;
And ever again, in the wink of an eye,
Painted stations whistle by.

Here is a child who clambers and scrambles,
All by himself and gathering brambles;
Here is a tramp who stands and gazes;
And there is the green for stringing the daisies!
Here is a cart run away in the road
Lumping along with man and load;
And here is a mill and there is a river:
Each a glimpse and gone for ever!

Robert Louis Stevenson

Exemplar analysis

Example of analysis of *From a Railway Carriage*

Faster than fairies, faster than witches,
Bridges and houses, hedges and ditches;
And charging along like troops in a battle,
All through the meadows the horses and cattle:
All of the sights of the hill and the plain
Fly as thick as driving rain;
And ever again, in the wink of an eye,
Painted stations whistle by.

Here is a child who clambers and scrambles,
All by himself and gathering brambles;
Here is a tramp who stands and gazes;
And there is the green for stringing the daisies!
Here is a cart run away in the road
Lumping along with man and load;
And here is a mill and there is a river:
Each a glimpse and gone for ever!

Robert Louis Stevenson

Repetition helps audience to immediately identify poem's pace.

Appropriate, strong verbs evident throughout – necessary as poet has made little use of adverbs or adjectives.

Poet wants audience to make two associations: speed of movement and sound of guard signalling train on with whistle.

Pronouns referring to 'child'. Writers always need to make clear to what or whom pronouns refer.

Verb presents the image of children making daisy chains: just using the right verb paints the picture.

Poem's clear, steady rhythm is established.

Simile – horses and cattle compared to troops going into battle.

Poem written in pairs of rhyming couplets.

Verse is one long sentence, split up by colons and semi-colons. Notice set length of eight lines.

Carefully structured: exclamation mark at end of line 4 is balanced by same in line 8.

Repetition of one sound is effective, emphasising the train's movement.

Powerful verb suggests awkward, over-loaded movement.

Good choice of common noun, as everything has only been seen very quickly.

A pronoun referring to 'tramp'.

Words suggest ending of poem and of places/people glimpsed.

This poet favours use of semi-colons and colons; punctuation is often a matter of personal preference in poetry.

Pupil copymaster

Nouns

A noun is a word naming a person, thing or feeling. Nouns can be singular (one) or plural (more than one). There are four main types:

Proper noun = a specifically named person/place/thing, beginning with a capital letter.

Robert
Banbury Park
May

Common noun = a non-specific reference to a thing/person/place.

man
town park
month

Collective noun = a noun that names a group/collection of people/things.

crowd
herd
shoal

A collective noun is treated as a singular noun, and therefore needs a singular verb, for example:

The herd of cows **is** seen from the train.

Similarly, a collective noun needs a singular pronoun, for example:

The crowd **pushes its** way to the barrier.

Abstract noun = a noun that names an idea/feeling/concept, which has to be visualised in the mind, rather than physically seen.

excitement
friendship
love

Exemplar material

Modelled writing

NOUNS:

ducks, geese, hens, lambs, and various animals
family, school children, farmer, driver, baby, boy, girl, man, woman, fisherman
pond/duck pond, lake, canal, boat, boathouse, stream
tree, flowers, bushes, field, crops, tools, harvest, lane, path, track
tractor, car, school bus,
church, farm, farmhouse, cottage, houses
garden, school, playground, park, swing, seesaw, pram, picnic
kite, clouds

VERBS:

waving, playing, steering, heaves, works, toils, labours, pushing/pulling
splashes, wades, gambolling, frolicking
clucking, shooing, wading
munches, relaxes, laughs and plays, pushes and pulls

SOUNDS:

squelching, squirming, shouting and shooing, shivering and shaking,
shoves ... shouts ... pushes
waving ... braving.

RHYMES:

tree ...bee ... see
park ... lark ...
cries ... tries ...
church ... lurch ...
swinging ... winging ... bringing

school ... rule
lane ... train ... crane
food ... mood ...
look ... book ... rook ... crook
wait ... gate ... late

RHYMING COUPLETS:

There is a train on the way back,
Huffing and puffing, on the next track;

Here is a church, bearing its steeple;
And there is a bus, jostling the people.

A stream and a pond, splashing on meeting;
A duck and a swan, paddling in greeting.

Now comes a lane, swinging and swaying;
And there is a girl, dawdling and playing.

All of the birds, flying and soaring,
Watching a boat, slipping its mooring;

Exemplar material

Checklists for narrative and classic poems

Example of a checklist for writing an additional verse ①

- Match rest of poem
- Use correct rhythm pattern
- Rhymes – when used – should make sense
- Use powerful words
- Consider sounds of words
- Use repetition where effective
- Use surprising/witty word combinations
- Portray images with words

Example of a checklist for a choral performance

- Make it clear
- Use expression and feeling
- Use correct rhythm
- Use appropriate pace
- Consider use of sound effects/music
- Vary delivery
- Consider volume – not necessarily constant
- Use appropriate tone – to fit meaning

Marking ladder

Marking ladder for an additional verse

Name: ______________________________

Pupil	Objective	Teacher
	My new verse fits in with the rest of the poem.	
	I used correct rhythm pattern.	
	I used appropriate rhymes.	
	I used powerful words.	
	I used effective images.	
	I used repetition.	
	I used surprising/witty word combinations.	
	I considered sounds of words.	
	What could I do to improve my verse next time?	

Marking ladder

Marking ladder for a choral performance

Name: ______________________________

Pupil	Objective	Teacher
	My delivery was clear.	
	I used feeling and expression.	
	I followed correct rhythm.	
	I considered volume.	
	I used the right speed.	
	My tone of voice suited the words' meaning.	
	I used variety in my delivery.	
	I considered background sound or music.	
	What could I do to improve my performance next time?	

Myths and Legends

Outcome

A myth and a legend

Objectives

Sentence

3 to understand how writing can be adapted for different audiences and purposes, e.g. by changing vocabulary and sentence structures.

Text

1 to identify and classify the features of myths, legends and fables.

2 to investigate different versions of the same story in print or on film, identifying similarities and differences.

8 to distinguish between the author and the narrator, investigating narrative viewpoint and the treatment of different characters.

10 to understand the differences between literal and figurative language.

11 to write own versions of legends, myths and fables, using structures and themes identified in reading.

13 to review and edit writing to produce a final form matched to the needs of an identified reader.

Planning frame

- Read and analyse examples of myths.
- Read different versions of one myth and analyse differences.
- Identify and classify the features of legends.
- Understand the differences between literal and figurative language.
- Write own versions of myths and legends based on own analysis.

Note

- You may wish to illustrate myths and legends with famous paintings. This will demonstrate to your class how influential Greek myths have been throughout the centuries. For example, *George and the Dragon* by Ucello is in The National Gallery, as is Titian's *Death of Acteon* (showing Diana the huntress).

How you could plan this unit

Day 1	Day 2	Day 3	Day 4	Day 5
Reading *Introducing Myths*	**Reading and writing** *Presenting Characters*	**Reading and writing** Use annotation (Resource Page B) to revise structure and features of *The Magic Head*. Complete plot revisions from Day 2. Draw out a 'film version' of the revised myth	**Reading and writing** *Features of Myths*	**Reading** Use computer web sites to research identities of Greek gods. Identify typical themes of myths

Day 6	Day 7	Day 8	Day 9	Day 10
Reading Reread *The Volcano Monster* (Resource Page D). Use exemplar analysis (Resource Page E) to analyse structure and features	**Reading and writing** *Effective Imagery*	**Writing** Plan and begin task of writing own myth. Compile a checklist (see Resource Page J)	**Writing** Discuss, proof-read and edit writing	**Reading and writing** Complete and polish writing. Evaluate using marking ladder (Resource Page K)

Day 11	Day 12	Day 13	Day 14	Day 15
Reading and writing *Features of Legends*	**Reading** *Literal and Figurative Language*	**Writing** Set task of writing own legend, using Arthur and Merlin as starting points. Compile checklist (see Resource Page J). Draft legends	**Writing** Finalise checklist. Discuss, proof-read and edit work	**Evaluation** Shared reading of legends. Evaluate using marking ladders (Resource Page L)

Introducing Myths

Objectives

We will identify and classify the features of myths and legends. We will also investigate how a character is treated

You need: Resource Pages A and J; storyboard blanks; individual whiteboards.

Whole class work

- ***What is a myth?*** Debate ideas with the class. Then ask them to refer to their dictionaries. Finally agree on a definition.
- Now display a class list of features that you would expect a myth to have (see also Resource Page J for ideas):

a fictitious narrative
an ancient, traditional story
supernatural beings

  Depending on your discussion, you may decide to omit some features at this stage.

- Supply some information about Greek myths, and their abundance. Search for a well-known myth subject on http://www.google.com – there are thousands of sites dedicated to mythology.
- Explain that myths are set in ancient times, in a different culture, and began as an oral form.
- Now move on to *The Magic Head* (Resource Page A). ***What does the title immediately tell you? Is this going to be a fictional text?*** Make sure that the children have identified the relevance of the word 'magic'.
- Read the text more than once, to ensure that the children have followed the story. Ask the children to name characters in the story. ***Who is the hero of the story?***
- The children reread the myth in pairs to search for the three possessions Perseus has that prove he is no ordinary human being. The children write or draw their answers on whiteboards and hold them up on a given signal. (Answers: his bag of invisibility; his magic sword; the head of Medusa.)
- ***What else is exceptional about Perseus?*** Answer: he can fly. ***Therefore, what sort of being is he?*** Answers could include: imaginary; magical; supernatural; a god.

Independent, pair or guided work

- Ask the children to list at least four different ways Perseus is presented and to record their thoughts about the way he is described by the storyteller.
- The children storyboard Perseus's role in the story (no more than six sketches).

Plenary

- Share ideas. ***What did you feel about Perseus?*** Bravery is likely to be the most common impression.
- Discuss the parts of the text that support their views. ***Has the storyteller favoured Perseus in the way the story is told?***
- Save the storyboards and the list of features for later work.

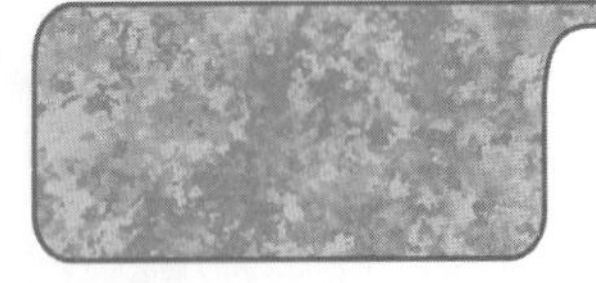

Presenting Characters

Objective

We will compare different versions of the same story in print and on film, and look at the treatment of different characters

You need: Resource Pages A and C; children's storyboards from previous lesson.

Whole class work

- Using the storyboards from the previous lesson, allow the children time to share ideas and view one another's pictures. Point out particularly effective ones.
- Make comparisons between the 'film frames' and the written text. ***Would a film version of the myth offer obvious advantages over words?*** A film could supply a stronger message, for example, the size of Perseus's sword could be seen.
- Ask the children to read the last few lines of paragraph 5 (Resource Page A) to themselves. ***Is there one piece of information about the sword that a picture would probably not bring?*** Possible answer: that it is magic (although a skilled illustrator could convey this). But reading the word 'magic' gives information before the sword's powers are seen.
- Ask the children to identify particularly powerful words used to describe the monster. ***How are its teeth made terrifying? Does this simile – the comparison with a man's arm – work as well as your pictures?*** Allow the children time to exchange views with response partners, as well as to refer back to their pictures.
- Now read paragraph 6 together and list the events, pointing out that they are all presented in one, average-length paragraph. ***How many film frames would be needed? Can the written word sometimes be the better option? Why?*** Allowing the plot to progress more quickly could be one reason. What effect does listing all the events have (rather than describing them in detail)?
- Remind the children of the importance given to Perseus in the story. ***How is Andromeda presented? What sort of character is she?***
- In pairs, the children list references to Andromeda and how this affects the reader's opinion of her (Resource Page C).

Independent, pair or guided work

- Ask the children to work out ways in which they can present Andromeda more positively. For example, instead of screaming, she could behave calmly or bravely. Brainstorm some suggestions.
- The children rewrite or amend one part (or sentence) so that Andromeda becomes a stronger character.

Plenary

- Discuss some of the new characteristics that Andromeda has been given.
- Listen to some of the revised descriptions.
- ***Have the changes affected the other characters?***

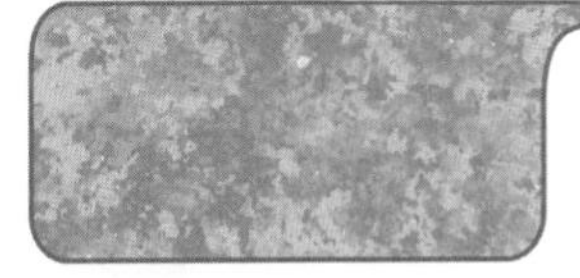

Features of Myths

Objective

We will identify and classify the features of myths

You need: Resource Pages A, D and F.

Whole class work

- Display Resource Page A. Reread the first paragraph. Bring attention to the word 'prayed'. ***What do you associate with this word?*** School assembly; Church; Temple and so on.
- ***What does this tell the reader about Zeus?*** Answer: he is a god and has far greater powers than Perseus.
- ***Can you work out what else Zeus was the god of?*** If necessary, direct them towards the beginning and end of the paragraph. They need to identify the relevance of these words:

> The wind blew and the lightning flashed.
>
> Zeus had sent the storm on purpose.

- Explain that in addition to being the chief of the gods, Zeus was also the god of thunder and lightning. Natural phenomena, particularly if they were violent or frightening ones, were often explained by references to gods. Myths frequently give these explanations.
- Tell the children the title of the next myth you are going to read: *The Volcano Monster* (Resource Page D). ***What does the title suggest might happen?*** Answers will vary, but most children will predict:
  - The importance of a monster in the story
  - A connection between a volcano and a monster.

Independent, pair or guided work

- Explain about the beliefs of Greek mythology, and its multitude of gods and goddesses and that each was associated with a different human/earthly characteristic. In pairs, the children research one Greek god or goddess on http://www.mythweb.com to find out five facts about them. This will build up a useful database for the children to use throughout the unit.
- Ask the children to read the new myth to each other.
- List the similarities that they can find (Resource Page F).
- ***Can you work out what the myth is trying to explain using references from the text?***

Plenary

- Share the lists of similarities and listen to the explanations.
- Add to your class checklist of features.

Effective Imagery

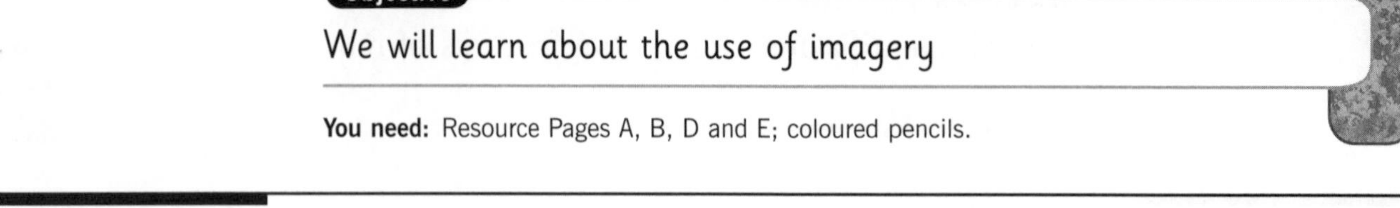

Objective

We will learn about the use of imagery

You need: Resource Pages A, B, D and E; coloured pencils.

Whole class work

- Talk about the role of a storyteller, in both the oral and written form. ***What are the 'tools' of the trade? What must be achieved to make storytelling successful?*** Answer: to bring a story to life with words.
- Discuss how words can achieve this. Read the first two paragraphs of *The Magic Head* (see Resource Pages A and B). ***Are any words particularly memorable?***
- Discuss the words that the children have selected and ask them to justify their choices. ***What image came into your mind? Was one of your senses appealed to? Was it always your sight?***
- Introduce the word 'imagery' and define it: the use of language to create a vivid picture – often visual.
- Discuss how this can be achieved:
  - vocabulary – powerful, evocative words
  - simile – writing that something is like something else
  - metaphor – writing about something as if it is something else.
- Ask the children to search for an example of a simile in *The Magic Head*. Answer: 'as long as a man's arm'. Discuss the effect of this imagery on our sense of sight, and our feelings about Perseus and his task.
- Look at paragraph 6 of the text:

> He was furious at the king and queen's decision, and rushed at Perseus with his sword raised.

- The words underlined are strong, with each word reinforcing the other, because someone greatly angered is likely to take quick decisions and make quick movements. A sword ready poised completes the picture.

Independent, pair or guided work

- Ask the children to read *The Volcano Monster* (see Resource Pages D and E).
- The children highlight in different colours places where they think language is used effectively, including:
  - imagery: similes and metaphors
  - powerful verbs
  - a direct appeal to the reader/reader's senses.

Plenary

- Share findings, stressing that everyone reacts to a piece of language differently.
- Remind the children of the message behind this myth: namely, an explanation for the existence of the volcano, Mount Etna.
- Ask them to start thinking about writing a myth – perhaps to explain the existence of a waterfall or iceberg, or an event such as an earthquake/hurricane/flood.

Features of Legends

Objective

We will identify the features of a legend

You need: Resource Pages G, H and J; individual whiteboards.

Whole class work

- Explain that the final shared text is a legend. ***What do you think that means?*** Debate their ideas.
- Use the story of Saint George and the Dragon as an example. ***Do you think Saint George existed?*** Answer: Yes. ***Do you think a dragon existed?*** Answer: No! Explain that the dragon could have been a metaphor for evil.
- Explain that this is a typical legend: a story that started about a true person – a hero – with the facts and the character becoming exaggerated over time.
- The children refer to dictionaries, before agreeing on a definition.
- Display a class list of features that you would expect a legend to have (see also Resource Page J for ideas):

> a traditional story
>
> a setting in olden times
>
> heroes as characters
>
> good overcoming bad

- Read *Excalibur* (Resource Page G). Ask questions to ensure that the children understand the dominance and virtue of one character. ***What happens in the plot? Who is the hero? Who are the minor/major characters? How does good overcome bad?***
- Emphasise that in a legend, this concept of good always winning in the end is essential. ***Where does this happen in this story?*** Answer: when Arthur wins the battle against Pellinore.

Independent, pair or guided work

- The children read the legend again by themselves, identifying the aspects that make this story similar to the myths they have read (see Resource Page H).
- Finally, the children pick out some of the words and events that emphasise that Arthur is a hero, giving reasons for their choices.

Plenary

- Discuss the findings.
- Confirm that the genres of myth and legend are very closely linked, with the legend's probable basis of truth forming the main distinction.
- ***Are there any clear differences?***

Literal and Figurative Language

Objective

We will look at the differences between literal and figurative language

You need: Resource Pages G and I.

Whole class work

- Review the meaning of the word 'imagery'. Ask the children to identify examples of powerful imagery expressed in *Excalibur* (Resource Page G). (For example, the detailed description of the sword; the strong adjectives used to describe the dragons.)
- ***Can you find an example of a simile?*** ('swords clashing like blasts of thunder') Discuss who/what is being compared to what and the simile's effectiveness.
- Reread these words from the second paragraph: 'Arthur was lion of his jungle, and no stray animal could be allowed to attack. He roared his anger, and sought out and pounced on his prey.' ***What do the words mean?*** Arthur was a strong leader, determined to free his people of this threat. Furious, he immediately attacked Sir Pellinore.
- Make certain that the children do not think that the text is saying that Arthur is a lion, or that he roars. Stress that the language of the text is being used figuratively; your explanation is literal (it uses the words in their usual sense).
- Supply the word 'metaphor', and revise its definition from earlier in the unit. ***Who is the lion?*** Answer: Arthur. ***Who is the stray animal?*** Answer: Pellinore.
- Point out the way in which the metaphor to describe Arthur is continued and strengthened with the use of 'roared' and 'pounced'.
  - ***Why is the metaphor used?*** Answer: to create a particular impression of Arthur.
  - ***What is that impression?*** Answer: of a courageous, fearless leader.
  - ***What image comes to mind? Which word involves the reader's hearing, not just sight?*** Answer: 'roared'.
- Spend some time ensuring that the difference between figurative and literal language is understood. Work together with some examples of similes or metaphors that the children may know, turning them into literal language.

> The Coach is a slave-driver, forcing us to work until we drop.
> The Coach forces us to work hard, until we can't manage any more.
>
> "You need to be as fit as a fiddle if you want a seat in my orchestra!" roared the conductor.
> "If you want to be in this team, you have to be fit!" shouted the conductor.

Independent, pair or guided work

- Display Resource Page I. Ask the children to discuss the sentences with a partner, working out what they mean and whether a simile or a metaphor has been used.
- Translate the sentences into simple, literal language.

Plenary

- Work together through the sentences, listening to the literal versions.
- Stress again the reasons for figurative language – to make imagery more powerful.

Pupil copymaster

The Magic Head

The wind blew and the lightning flashed, and Perseus was blown this way and that, through thunder and clouds and rain, till he didn't know which way was up. He clutched his precious bag with one hand and his cap of invisibility with the other, and prayed to Zeus to save him. But Zeus had sent the storm on purpose.

As soon as Perseus was over the coast of Ethiopia, the wind died, and the rain came out in a sky as blue as delphiniums. Looking down, he saw a great rock. Something was moving on the top of it, and Perseus flew down to have a closer look. There, chained to a post, was the loveliest girl he had ever seen.

"Who are you, and what are you doing here?" he asked as he landed, and took off his cap. The girl screamed as he appeared, but when he had calmed her down, she told him that she was Andromeda, the daughter of the king and queen, and that she had been left as a sacrifice to Poseidon, the god of the sea, whom her mother had offended.

"Run for your life," she said. "A monster is coming to eat me up, and if you stay here you will be killed as well!" But Perseus had fallen in love with Andromeda, and was determined to save her if he could. So he hid behind a rock and waited.

Soon a great roiling and broiling in the sea started, and a huge warty head appeared, with trails of seaweed and slime hanging from it. The monster opened its mouth, and showed its teeth, each one as long as a man's arm. As Andromeda cowered away, Perseus ran forward with his magic sword and plunged it into the creature's throat. It nearly bit his arm off as it reared away, roaring and pouring blood into the water.

With the monster dead, Perseus cut through Andromeda's chains, and they flew to her father's palace. The king and queen were surprised and delighted to see their daughter alive, and agreed that Perseus could marry her at once. But just then in came the man who had been engaged to Andromeda before she had gone off to be sacrificed. He was furious at the king and queen's decision, and rushed at Perseus with his sword raised. Perseus whipped Medusa's head out of his bag, and in a trice the man was turned to stone.

Andromeda and Perseus returned to Seriphos, but Danäe was nowhere to be found. The king of Seriphos had tried to marry her again, and she had gone into hiding.

"How dare he annoy my mother!" roared Perseus. And he marched into the throne room and thrust Medusa's head into the king's surprised face, turning him to stone at once.

The people of Seriphos were happy, because the king had been cruel to all of them. His stone body was thrown into the harbour, and Perseus and Andromeda were crowned king and queen in his place. Danäe came out of hiding, and the joyful hugging and feasting and laughter went on for weeks and weeks. Perseus soon gave Medusa's head and the other magical things back to the gods. And he was so happy that he vowed never to go on any adventures again.

Adapted by Lucy Coats, from the Greek myths of Atticus

Exemplar analysis

Example of analysis of *The Magic Head*

A violent beginning – events or weather – is typical of this genre. A myth is often used to explain a climatic/ environmental condition.

Title 'The Magic Head' immediately places story in realm of fantasy.

Two Greek gods are mentioned at start. Myths began as an oral storytelling form, and audience would be familiar with names.

Superlative descriptions are another common feature of myths.

Greek myths belong in an ancient time and different culture where belief in a multitude of gods was common, as in Hinduism today.

Magical properties and powers are normally attached to both characters and objects.

Real place names, belonging to part of world known to the Greeks of this time, commonly feature in Greek myths (America and Australia had yet to be discovered).

A monster or horrifying creature is not essential to a myth, but is common. Descriptions of such creatures are usually made as gruesome as possible.

The wind blew and the lightning flashed, and Perseus was blown this way and that, through thunder and clouds and rain, till he didn't know which way was up. He clutched his precious bag with one hand and his cap of invisibility with the other, and prayed to Zeus to save him. But Zeus had sent the storm on purpose.

As soon as Perseus was over the coast of Ethiopia, the wind died, and the rain came out in a sky as blue as delphiniums. Looking down, he saw a great rock. Something was moving on the top of it, and Perseus flew down to have a closer look. There, chained to a post, was the loveliest girl he had ever seen.

"Who are you, and what are you doing here?" he asked as he landed, and took off his cap. The girl screamed as he appeared, but when he had calmed her down, she told him that she was Andromeda, the daughter of the king and queen, and that she had been left as a sacrifice to Poseidon, the god of the sea, whom her mother had offended.

"Run for your life," she said. "A monster is coming to eat me up, and if you stay here you will be killed as well!" But Perseus had fallen in love with Andromeda, and was determined to save her if he could. So he hid behind a rock and waited.

Soon a great roiling and broiling in the sea started, and a huge warty head appeared, with trails of seaweed and slime hanging from it. The monster opened its mouth, and showed its teeth, each one as long as a man's arm. As Andromeda cowered away, Perseus ran forward with his magic sword and plunged it into the creature's throat. It nearly bit his arm off as it reared away, roaring and pouring blood into the water.

With the monster dead, Perseus cut through Andromeda's chains, and they flew to her father's palace. The king and queen were surprised and delighted to see their daughter alive, and agreed that Perseus could marry her at once. But just then in came the man who had been engaged to Andromeda before she had gone off to be sacrificed. He was furious at the king and queen's decision, and rushed at Perseus with his sword raised. Perseus whipped Medusa's head out of his bag, and in a trice the man was turned to stone.

Andromeda and Perseus returned to Seriphos, but Danäe was nowhere to be found. The king of Seriphos had tried to marry her again, and she had gone into hiding.

"How dare he annoy my mother!" roared Perseus. And he marched into the throne room and thrust Medusa's head into the king's surprised face, turning him to stone at once.

The people of Seriphos were happy, because the king had been cruel to all of them. His stone body was thrown into the harbour, and Perseus and Andromeda were crowned king and queen in his place. Danäe came out of hiding, and the joyful hugging and feasting and laughter went on for weeks and weeks. Perseus soon gave Medusa's head and the other magical things back to the gods. And he was so happy that he vowed never to go on any adventures again.

Adapted by Lucy Coats, from the Greek myths of Atticus

Good usually prevails, and is rewarded. This ending is very traditional: hero is to marry beautiful woman; enemies are defeated.

Certain characters (here Perseus) are usually presented in an obviously favourable way. Perseus's courage is emphasised by description of size of monster's teeth.

Punishment or defeat is commonly presented as eternal.

Pupil copymaster

References to Andromeda

Text reference	Resulting impression on reader
The loveliest girl he had ever seen	Beautiful
The girl screamed	Quick to panic
When he had calmed her down	Needs someone else to take charge
"Run for your life"	Thinks of others
Determined to save her	Inspires loyalty
Andromeda cowered away	Timid
Had been engaged	Quick to change her mind

Pupil copymaster

The Volcano Monster

When Gaia learnt that Zeus had trapped her Titan children in Tartarus, she shook with rage. And out of her raging body there appeared two great and horrible monsters called Typhon and Echidna.

Echidna had a woman's head and arms, but her body was like an enormous fat snake, covered in warty spots and spines.

Typhon had a hundred heads, each one dripping with venom and slime. When he roared like a hundred lions or trumpeted like a herd of elephants, great rivers of boiling mud and fiery stones poured out of his mouths.

When the gods saw him, they were so frightened that they turned themselves into animals and ran far away to hide in the woods.

Typhon tore up enormous mountains by the roots and he hurled them at Zeus and his brothers and sisters, hissing like a thousand snakes. But Zeus was brave, and he called to the other gods to come and help him defeat the monster.

Soon a fierce battle raged over the earth, and everything was destroyed. The gods were tired out and nearly beaten. But as Typhon lifted Mount Etna to throw at Zeus's head, Zeus let fly one of his thunderbolts, and knocked the mountain down on Typhon's heads, trapping him forever.

Echidna fled to a cave in southern Greece when she saw how Zeus had destroyed her mate. There she had many children, all as hideous as herself, and Zeus allowed them to live in peace, so that future heroes of Greece could fight them when the time was right.

As for Typhon, he lies wriggling and struggling under Mount Etna to this day, spewing smoke and flames out of the top, and raining down boiling stones on the poor people of Sicily.

Adapted by Lucy Coats, from the Greek myths of Attticus

Exemplar analysis

Example of analysis of *The Volcano Monster*

Title 'The Volcano Monster' immediately makes this a piece of fiction, with its mention of imaginary creature.

When Gaia learnt that Zeus had trapped her Titan children in Tartarus, she shook with rage. And out of her raging body there appeared two great and horrible monsters called Typhon and Echidna.

Echidna had a woman's head and arms, but her body was like an enormous fat snake, covered in warty spots and spines.

Typhon had a hundred heads, each one dripping with venom and slime. When he roared like a hundred lions or trumpeted like a herd of elephants, great rivers of boiling mud and fiery stones poured out of his mouths.

When the gods saw him, they were so frightened that they turned themselves into animals and ran far away to hide in the woods.

Typhon tore up enormous mountains by the roots and he hurled them at Zeus and his brothers and sisters, hissing like a thousand snakes. But Zeus was brave, and he called to the other gods to come and help him defeat the monster.

Soon a fierce battle raged over the earth, and everything was destroyed. The gods were tired out and nearly beaten. But as Typhon lifted Mount Etna to throw at Zeus's head, Zeus let fly one of his thunderbolts, and knocked the mountain down on Typhon's heads, trapping him forever.

Echidna fled to a cave in southern Greece when she saw how Zeus had destroyed her mate. There she had many children, all as hideous as herself, and Zeus allowed them to live in peace, so that future heroes of Greece could fight them when the time was right.

As for Typhon, he lies wriggling and struggling under Mount Etna to this day, spewing smoke and flames out of the top, and raining down boiling stones on the poor people of Sicily.

Adapted by Lucy Coats, from the Greek myths of Attticus

Annotations:

- An evil act by a god is typical myth beginning.
- Zeus is most important of fictional Greek gods and very well known: the story is instantly recognisable as a myth.
- Shaking with rage can be related to natural phenomenon of earth shaking in earthquake.
- Fearsome creatures are not necessary for a myth, but often appear.
- Magical events such as this are common features of myths.
- Name of real volcano is mixed with imaginary, fantastic happenings.
- Explains the frightening physical phenomenon of a volcano. Such explanations through myths were part of an ancient culture.
- Myths were a familiar part of Ancient Greek culture.
- References to heroes abound. Notice that Zeus is presented as a just and right god; his enemies, such as Echidna, are often ugly.
- An explanation for the rumblings of Mount Etna, Italy (erupting for half a million years and one of the world's most active volcanoes).

Pupil copymaster

Similarities between two myths

Both myths mention Zeus, making clear his importance.

Both feature ugly, dangerous monsters.

Both feature magical properties: can turn into animals (The Volcano Monster); invisibility cap (The Magic Head).

Both include references to violent, extreme weather.

Both feature battles.

Both feature terrible, final fates for the losers.

Both include mention of real, geographical places - frequently in or close to Greece.

Pupil copymaster

Excalibur

King Arthur made his court at Camelot. He was a brave and just King, who, with the help of his magician, Merlin, ruled over a prosperous land. Arthur was as brave as any other knight, ready to slay the fearsome, fire-breathing dragons that still roamed the country. He was always ready to risk his life in the cause of justice.

One day, he heard that Sir Pellinore was attacking innocent travellers on the road to Camelot. Immediately, he mounted his charger, hid his head behind a visor, and galloped off. Arthur was lion of his jungle, and no stray animal could be allowed to attack. He roared his anger, and sought out and pounced on his prey.

The battle between Arthur and Pellinore was desperate, as both men struck each other so fiercely that they fell from their horses. They fought hand to hand, their gleaming swords clashing like blasts of thunder. Arthur was knocked to the ground, and just when all seemed lost, Merlin appeared. His magical wand touched Pellinore, and Pellinore fell down in a trance.

However, Arthur and Merlin now had more work: Arthur needed another sword. Merlin told him of the wondrous sword, Excalibur, crafted on a mystical isle. The pair rode and rode until they reached a lake – the Lake of Avalon. Out of the lake they saw rise up an arm, clothed in the finest, softest silk, and holding aloft the finest sword ever seen. Its handle was covered with a million jewels, of amazing brightness, glittering and dazzling in the sun; its scabbard was decorated with a pattern of gold and silver, made from a mosaic of marbled fragments. Arthur and Merlin gasped!

Then from the mist drifted the Lady of the Lake. Like a swan she glided towards Arthur and helped him into a boat. Together they floated towards the sword. As Arthur grasped the sword, the Lady of the Lake mysteriously vanished. Alone, Arthur returned to the bank. It was then that Merlin told him of the sword's powerful secret: the sword might break, but it was the scabbard that would keep him safe. With the scabbard at his side, not a drop of his blood would ever be shed.

So Arthur and Merlin returned to Camelot, where everyone cheered their courageous King, and gave thanks for his safe return.

Marcia Williams

Pupil copymaster

Comparing myth and legend

Similarities	Differences	
	Legends	Myths
Magical elements	Stories about people	Stories about gods and goddesses
Set in the past	Usually based on truth	Explanations of strange or important happenings in nature (for example, a volcano)
Powerful imagery	Emphasis on strong heroes and heroic deeds	
Beasts/monsters mentioned	Strong contrast between honour (Arthur) and dishonour (Pellinore)	
Battles/danger		
Brave deeds		
Attack/revenge		
Traditional endings		

Pupil copymaster

Simile or metaphor?

1. Merlin was a fox, slyly tricking any hunters.
2. Sir Pellinore was like a shivering mouse that could be eaten.
3. Merlin's wand was like a box of tricks, always ready to be opened.
4. This time, Merlin got a sleeping pill out of his box.
5. Arthur the lion roared his approval.
6. Pellinore lay on the ground, caught by the brave lion and the cunning fox.

Answers

1. *(Metaphor)* Merlin was sly and cunning, always able to beat an enemy.
2. *(Simile)* Sir Pellinore was a timid opponent who could be defeated.
3. *(Simile)* Merlin always carried his wand, and it could do anything.
4. *(Metaphor)* This time, Merlin used the wand to cast a sleeping spell.
5. *(Metaphor)* King Arthur cheered in support.
6. *(Metaphor)* Pellinore was on the ground, beaten by Arthur and Merlin.

Exemplar material

Checklists for myths and legends

Example of a checklist for a myth ①

- Story about gods and goddesses
- Includes magical elements and powers
- Features heroic characters
- May explain a strange/important happening in nature
- Features danger and violent acts
- Includes attack/revenge
- Set in ancient times
- Uses powerful imagery
- May mention strange creatures

Example of a checklist for a legend ②

- Story about people
- Little mention of gods/goddesses
- Possible basis of truth
- Features heroic characters
- Emphasis on bravery and daring deeds
- Battles/fights likely
- Distinction made between honour and dishonour
- Good defeats evil
- Features a traditional ending

Marking ladder

Marking ladder for a myth

Name: ______________________

Pupil	Objective	Teacher
	My myth is about gods and goddesses.	
	It is set in ancient times.	
	It features danger/revenge.	
	It includes use of magical powers.	
	I used powerful imagery.	
	My characters are heroes.	
	My myth explains a strange/important happening.	
	It features strange, frightening creatures.	
	What could I do to improve my myth next time?	

Marking ladder

Marking ladder for a legend

Name: ______________________________

Pupil	Objective	Teacher
	My legend is about people.	
	It has a possible basis of truth.	
	It features monsters/strange beasts.	
	It features some magical powers.	
	It makes little mention of gods/goddesses.	
	It includes brave heroic characters.	
	It places emphasis on brave heroes and daring deeds.	
	It may feature battles/fights/struggles.	
	It makes a distinction between honour and dishonour.	
	Good defeats evil.	
	My legend includes a traditional ending.	
	What could I do to improve my legend next time?	

Explanation Texts

Outcome

Notes; an explanatory text for a younger audience

Objectives

Sentence

8 to construct sentences in different ways, while retaining meaning, through: combining two or more sentences; re-ordering them; deleting or substituting words; writing them in more telegraphic ways.

9 to secure the use of the comma in embedding clauses within sentences.

Text

15 to read a range of explanatory texts, investigating and noting features of impersonal style.

16 to prepare for reading by identifying what they already know and what they need to find out.

17 to locate information confidently and efficiently.

21 to convert personal notes into notes for others to read, paying attention to appropriateness of style, vocabulary and presentation.

22 to plan, compose, edit and refine short non-chronological reports and explanatory texts using reading as a source, focusing on clarity, conciseness and impersonal style.

24 to evaluate their work.

Planning frame

- Read a range of explanatory texts, investigating and noting features of impersonal style.
- Convert personal notes into notes for others to read.
- Plan, compose, edit and refine an explanatory text.

How you could plan this unit

Day 1	Day 2	Day 3	Day 4	Day 5
Reading Read a range of different explanations. What do they have in common? Begin to identify some features of explanatory texts	**Reading and writing** *Commas and Clauses*	**Reading and writing** Review simplifications from Day 2. Consider different ways of constructing the text's sentences while retaining meaning. Look for ways to combine sentences and shorten them	**Reading and writing** *Writing Notes*	**Reading and writing** Revise previous lesson. Convert personal notes into notes for another to use. Test them out

Day 6	Day 7	Day 8	Day 9	Day 10
Reading and writing *Using the Passive*	**Reading and writing** *Causal Connectives*	**Writing** Do reading research. Make notes. Begin text	**Reading** Continue writing explanations. Finalise checklist	**Reading** Edit and refine writing. Evaluate using marking ladders (Resource Pages G and H)

Commas and Clauses

Objectives

We will look at details of the style of explanatory texts. We will also learn about the use of commas in sentences

You need: Resource Pages A and C.

Whole class work

- Look again at the guitar text (Resource Page A). Ask the children for comments.
- Now display and read Resource Page C. ***Is there a difference in style between these two?*** Focus on the main point: the new text is far more casual, personal in style.
- Now return to the guitar text, labelling its style as formal or impersonal. ***What do you think that means?*** Answer: having no personal reference/not concerned with a specific individual. Brainstorm further ideas, before focusing on the relevance of:
  - the level of complexity of the sentences
  - the frequent use of the passive voice – when the action is done to the subject, rather than by the subject, for example, 'The strings are stretched'. Explain briefly but for detailed work see 'Using the Passive' later in this unit.
- Now focus on the sentences. ***What are they like?*** The children may label many as 'hard'; 'long'; 'complicated'; 'too many commas'. Introduce the word 'complex', and explain that this means containing a main clause and subordinate clause(s).
- Ask the children to look at sentence 1 in paragraph 2 and try to work out its main clause (the clause that would make a complete sentence on its own). If necessary, supply the clue that it is only 12 words. Answer: 'The strings are played by a pulling movement of the player's fingers.'
- ***Can you pick out a subordinate (dependent) clause? It 'depends' on the main clause and cannot be a sentence on its own.*** Answer: 'which is known as plucking' or 'commonly made from nylon'.
- Read the sentence aloud, while the children shut their eyes. ***Put your hand up when you 'hear' a comma. Can you spot where a pair of commas works together?***
- Emphasise that a pair of commas is often used in this way to hold a clause in its place in the sentence.

Independent, pair or guided work

- Ask the children to locate three other places where a pair of commas works together.
- Reading aloud to each other will help in 'hearing' the link of one comma with another.
- In pairs, the children rewrite these sentences more simply, so that they are suitable for younger readers. The main facts must still be there, but a sentence may be shortened, or words substituted or left out, but key technical words should be used.

Plenary

- As a class, identify pairs of commas that hold clauses within sentences.
- Listen to and discuss some of the children's simplifications.
- ***Have correct facts and some technical vocabulary been retained?*** Evaluate using a response sandwich: one good comment; one idea for improvement; another good comment.

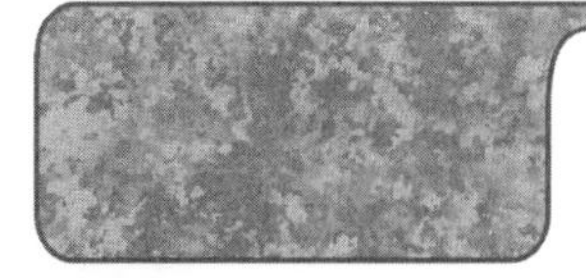

Writing Notes

Objectives

We will learn how to find written information more quickly, and look at making notes

You need: Resource Pages A and C; individual whiteboards.

Whole class work

- Hold up a page of writing. ***How do you find out what this is about if you are in a hurry?*** Answers should include: quick reading; just get main sense; find main subject. Explain that the children have just described the process of skimming.
- Hold up an open history book (with headings/sub-headings/highlighted words). ***How do you find a piece of information you need?*** Answers: try to spot right place; notice word; see a key word; use headings/highlighted words. Explain that this is scanning. Stress the value of skimming and scanning.
- Display Resource Page C. ***Can you quickly find out what a satellite is for?*** Answer: to make long distance phone calls. Time how long it takes for most children to display it on their 'show-me' boards. Discuss if and how they scanned the text.
- Look at the whole of Resource Page C. ***What type of text is it? Does it make sense? Is it a finished text? Why are abbreviations used?*** Answer: notes.
- Identify details of the notes, for example,
  - layout: spaces and new headings
  - quick abbreviations, e.g. 'elec'.
  - careful focus on correct spelling of technical words, for example, 'satellite'.
- Demonstrate writing notes for the first paragraph of the guitar text (Resource Page A):

Guitar – mus. instr.

Construction: wd, hollow,

Parts: long neck, pegs, STRINGS, bridge (str. tighter/looser)
– held all way up guit. by pegs (top) + bridge (bottom)

- Point out the use of capital letters and underlining to emphasise importance; the retention of technical words; the use of quick abbreviations, for example, 'wd' for 'wood'. ***Could there be a problem with this type of explanation?*** Answer: only the writer can understand it; the notes would not be usable by someone else.

Independent, pair or guided work

- The children make their own notes for paragraphs 2 and 3 of the guitar text.
- Emphasise that all the information must be there, especially new, technical words.
- Remind the children that they should imagine that they will be writing in detail from these notes at a later time.

Plenary

- Ask for volunteers to show their notes.
- Would the notes help in writing an impersonal, explanatory text?

Using the Passive

Objectives

We will focus on the use of the passive form. We will also look some more at clauses within sentences

You need: Resource Pages A and D.

Whole class work

- Display Resource Page A. ***There are many examples of passive forms in this text. Can you remember what this means?*** Supply the example of the fourth sentence in paragraph 1: 'These strings ... are stretched along the length of the guitar.'
- Pick out other examples:

> The strings ... are played ...
> The string is plucked ...
> ... another part of the string is held.

- ***Why is the passive used so frequently?*** Answer: it makes an explanation text sound more authoritative; it gives it an appropriate formal tone or style. The reader does not need to know how someone felt when the guitar was played to understand an explanation for the production of sound.
- ***What is the opposite of 'passive'?*** Answer: active. This is the usual construction of a sentence, in which the subject does the action, for example, 'the string moves'.
- Try changing some of your passive examples into active forms. Do some together, and then the children try on their whiteboards. Take feedback.

> You stretch the strings.
> You pluck the string.
> You have to pluck the string ...
> ... while you hold another part of the string.

- Point out that 'you' has usually been added in order for it to make sense. ***What is the effect?*** Answer: the tone is now too casual; it is not appropriate for an explanatory text. Explain that an explanatory text is normally in the third person.
- Display Resource Page D. Revise findings from the earlier lesson 'Commas and Clauses'. ***What punctuation frequently held the clause within a sentence?*** Answer: a pair of commas.

Independent, pair or guided work

- The children identify and write out examples of commas used for embedding clauses within sentences on Resource Page D.
- If time allows, rewrite some of these sentences, so that they suit a younger audience, retaining the meaning but simplifying the construction.

Plenary

- Share findings.
- Display and discuss some of the revised sentences.

Causal Connectives

Objectives

We will learn about causal connectives. We will then plan an explanatory text for a younger audience

You need: Resource Pages D and F.

Whole class work

- ***What is a connective?*** Answer: a linking word or phrase between different parts of a text. Explain that an explanatory text makes particular use of causal connectives.
- Give everyday examples of causal connectives:

> He fouled – that meant the end of their hopes.
> As a result they lost.

- Point out that the causal connectives deal with cause and effect.
- Give the children a few minutes to search for an example in each paragraph of Resource Page D:

> in order to ... [paragraph 1]
> because of ... [paragraph 2]
> so that ... [paragraph 3]

- Read Resource Page D. Talk about the writer having assumed a level of knowledge. ***What knowledge of the subject has this writer assumed?*** Answer: understanding of what sound is and what sound waves are; understanding of the word 'vibration'.
- ***How can you tell this?*** Answer: no definitions of these words/phrases are given.
- Stress that when using explanation texts, a reader needs to locate information confidently: therefore, the text must be at the right level. ***What would be a problem for a younger reader in the style of this text?*** Discussion should lead to:
  - more appropriate sentence constructions
  - simpler vocabulary (for example, 'needed' instead of 'required')
  - the right amount of essential technical vocabulary (for example, omit intricate details of inner ear).
- Now set the task of writing an explanatory text for a younger reader, linked to your class science work. Talk about those children's likely current level of knowledge and the need to check information by reading and making notes.
- Brainstorm ideas for the topics.

Independent, pair or guided work

- In pairs or independently, the children choose a specific area of a topic for their text. They need to decide what they think their audience will already know, and what they are likely to want to find out.
- Decide on reading sources or other reference sources and find reading material.

Plenary

- Share some ideas for titles and areas of work.
- Make initial class checklists for notes and explanations (see Resource Page F).

Pupil copymaster

The Guitar

How does a guitar make its sound?

A guitar is a musical instrument. It is made of wood, usually, and is hollow. The neck is long, with **pegs** at the top for holding **strings** in place. These strings, which can be tightened or slackened, are stretched along the length of the guitar. In order that the strings stay in place, there is a bridge at the bottom for securing them.

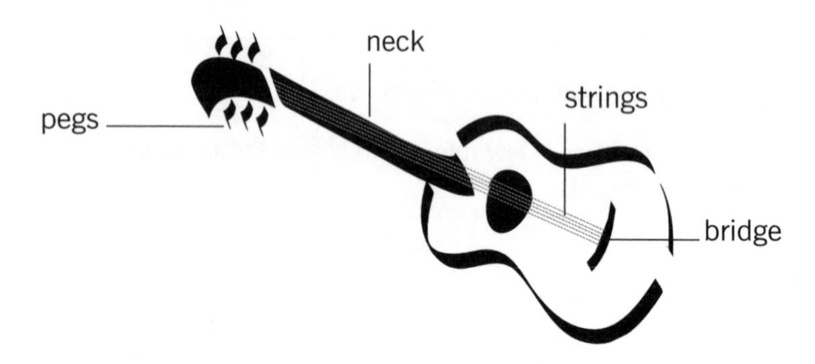

The strings, commonly made from nylon, are played by a pulling movement of the player's fingers, which is known as **plucking**, as it involves this light pulling or 'twitching' movement of the fingertips across one part of a string. First the string is plucked, while another part of the string is held. Then, as a result, the string moves or **vibrates**. Finally, because the string vibrates, so the air around it moves. When this movement of air, called a **vibration**, takes place, the sound is produced.

A guitar's strings, which are normally six in number, can alter the **pitch** of the sound: in order to make the pitch of the sound higher, the string can be tightened. Similarly, when one part of a string is held down, so the string becomes shorter: if a shorter string is plucked, then it produces a higher sound.

Exemplar analysis

Example of analysis of *The Guitar*

Explanations tell us how or why something works or happens. The title is often a question beginning 'How' or 'Why'.

Begins with a short statement, introducing the topic.

Correct, technical terms are an essential part, and are often highlighted.

The passive form is frequently found in explanations. It gives a formal, impersonal tone.

A causal connective emphasises the logic of what is being explained.

How does a guitar make its sound?

A guitar is a musical instrument. It is made of wood, usually, and is hollow. The neck is long, with **pegs** at the top for holding **strings** in place. These strings, which can be tightened or slackened, are stretched along the length of the guitar. In order that the strings stay in place, there is a bridge at the bottom for securing them.

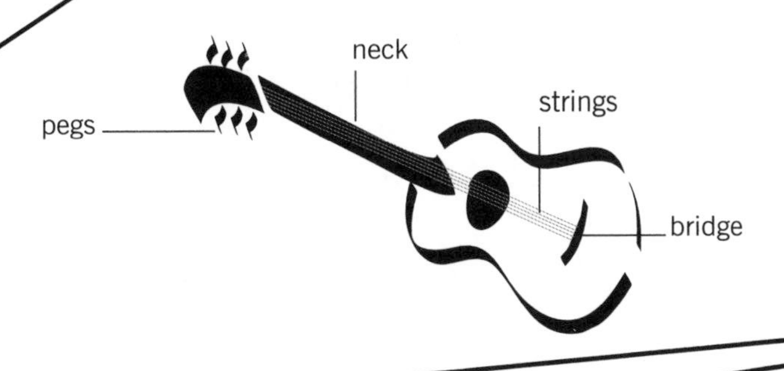

Sentences are often complex, with a pair of commas used to embed a subordinate clause.

An explanation must give information in a series of steps: sequential connections emphasise chronology.

A pair of commas holds the clause within the sentence.

Logical connections are also common.

Hypothetical language ('if' followed by its logical conclusion, using the connection 'then') is usual in an explanation.

Causal connection.

The strings, commonly made from nylon, are played by a pulling movement of the player's fingers, which is known as **plucking**, as it involves this light pulling or 'twitching' movement of the fingertips across one part of a string. First the string is plucked, while another part of the string is held. Then, as a result, the string moves or **vibrates**. Finally, because the string vibrates, so the air around it moves. When this movement of air, called a **vibration**, takes place, the sound is produced.

A guitar's strings, which are normally six in number, can alter the **pitch** of the sound: in order to make the pitch of the sound higher, the string can be tightened. Similarly, when one part of a string is held down, so the string becomes shorter: if a shorter string is plucked, then it produces a higher sound.

Pupil copymaster

Notes

1. Numbers
2. Electrical signal
3. Travel – cable – tl.exchange (+others)
   – elec cables
4. Rch phone B = ring

Voice = vibrations
sound waves = elec. impulses
NB cable of optical fibre

SATELLITE:
Space
Why? L. dist.calls
E.g. Eng. – Aust.

Pupil copymaster

The human ear

How does the human ear hear sounds?

The purpose of the human ear is to detect **sounds**. In order to do this, a complicated construction is required. The ear is composed of three sections: outer, middle and inner parts. **Sound waves**, first collected by the outer ear, have to be channelled through the middle ear, before they are received by the inner ear.

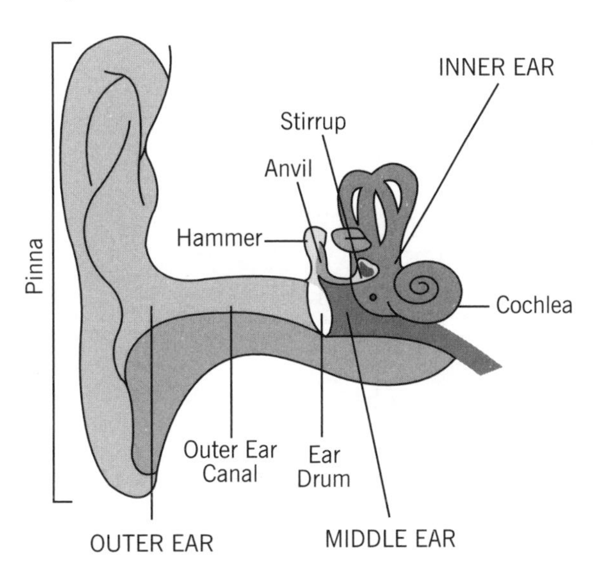

As the **vibrations** from the sound waves make contact with the eardrum, which is a membrsane within the ear, it is made to vibrate. These vibrations are **amplified** because of the presence of the hammer, anvil and stirrup, three small bones, which are in the middle ear. After that, the vibrations reach the inner ear.

The cochlea, a coiled tube that is filled with fluid, is contained in the inner ear. So that vibrations can be received, a membrane, which contains tiny receptor cells, is located in the inner ear. The translation of the vibrations into nerve impulses is performed by these receptor cells, which send the **nerve impulses** to the brain, so that they may be finally interpreted in the brain as sound.

Exemplar analysis

Example of analysis of *The human ear*

The correct chronological order of events is emphasised by sequential connections.

Title is in the form of a question beginning 'How…?', typical of an explanatory text. The text then answers the question.

How does the human ear hear sounds?

The purpose of the human ear is to detect **sounds**. In order to do this, a complicated construction is required. The ear is composed of three sections: outer, middle and inner parts. **Sound waves**, first collected by the outer ear, have to be channelled through the middle ear, before they are received by the inner ear.

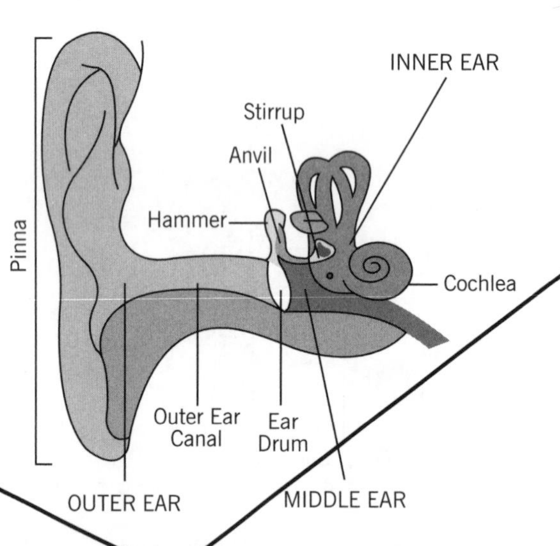

Pair of commas used to embed a subordinate clause.

A sequential connection is emphasised.

Another pair of commas embedding a subordinate clause. The main clause could function as a sentence without it.

A pair of commas is used to hold the clause within this complex sentence.

As the **vibrations** from the sound waves make contact with the eardrum, which is a membrane within the ear, it is made to vibrate. These vibrations are **amplified** because of the presence of the hammer, anvil and stirrup, three small bones, which are in the middle ear. After that, the vibrations reach the inner ear.

The cochlea, a coiled tube that is filled with fluid, is contained in the inner ear. So that vibrations can be received, a membrane, which contains tiny receptor cells, is located in the inner ear. The translation of the vibrations into nerve impulses is performed by these receptor cells, which send the **nerve impulses** to the brain, so that they may be finally interpreted in the brain as sound.

Notice how complex the sentence is.

Providing information as a series of steps is an essential feature of explanatory texts. The use of this word in the final line stresses this.

Relevance of explanation to title question is emphasised by use of this connective.

Exemplar material

Checklists for explanation texts

Example of a checklist for notes

- Make them clear
- Use helpful layout
- Use organisational devices
- Use symbols/signs/abbreviations
- Use abbreviations that can be understood by writer/eventual reader
- Ensure facts are correct
- Use chronological order
- Use correct ‘technical’ words/proper names
- Ensure they are suitable for eventual purpose

Example of a checklist for style features of an explanatory text

- Use formal tone
- Use correct ‘technical’ words/proper names
- Possibly use passive form
- Use time connectives
- Use cause and effect connections
- Use verbs in present tense
- Ensure sentence constructions are appropriate to audience

Example of a checklist for an explanatory text

- Tell how/why something works or happens
- Title may be a question beginning ‘How’ or ’Why’
- Include an introductory opening statement
- Feature information in a series of steps
- Use correct chronological order
- Use diagrams when helpful
- Use appropriate language style
- Show awareness of vocabulary and sentence construction
- Answer title question

Marking ladder for notes

Name: ____________________

Pupil	Objective	Teacher
	My notes are clear.	
	They are appropriate for the purpose.	
	The layout is helpful.	
	The facts are correct.	
	I used chronological order.	
	I used organisational devices.	
	I used symbols/signs/abbreviations.	
	The abbreviations will be understood by their eventual reader.	
	I used correct 'technical' words/proper names.	
	How could I improve my notes next time?	

Marking ladder

Marking ladder for an explanatory text

Name: ______________________________

Pupil	Objective	Teacher
	My text deals with how/why something works or happens.	
	The title may be a question.	
	My text may begin 'How' or 'Why'.	
	I used an introductory opening statement.	
	I gave information in a series of steps.	
	I used helpful diagrams.	
	I used chronological order.	
	I used verbs in present tense.	
	I used technical words.	
	I used time and causal connectives.	
	My text answers the title question.	
	How could I improve my explanation next time?	

Non-chronological Reports

Outcome

Notes; a non-chronological report related to other curriculum areas

Objectives

Sentence

5 to use punctuation effectively to signpost meaning in longer and more complex sentences.

9 to secure the use of the comma in embedding clauses within sentences.

Text

16 to prepare for reading by identifying what they already know and what they need to find out.

17 to locate information confidently and efficiently.

18 [be taught] how authors record and acknowledge their sources.

20 note-making: to discuss what is meant by 'in your own words' and when it is appropriate to copy, quote and adapt.

22 to plan, compose, edit and refine short non-chronological reports and explanatory texts, using reading as a source, focusing on clarity, conciseness and impersonal style.

23 to record and acknowledge sources in their own writing.

24 to evaluate their work.

Planning frame

- Read a range of non-chronological reports and note features of style.
- Plan, compose, edit and refine short non-chronological reports, using reading as a source.

How you could plan this unit

Day 1	Day 2	Day 3	Day 4	Day 5
Reading *Locating Information*	**Reading** *Making Notes*	**Writing** Review children's notes from Day 2. They write a new text, in own words, from notes. Compare results	**Reading and writing** *Using Colons*	**Reading** Read example texts. Use annotations (Resource Pages B and D) to identify features

Day 6	Day 7	Day 8	Day 9	Day 10
Reading and writing *Using Clauses*	**Reading and writing** Research, using books and CD-ROMs. Make notes	**Reading and writing** Compile a checklist for notes. Complete notes. Begin writing text	**Writing** Compile a checklist for a non-chronological report. Plan and compose report	**Writing** Edit and refine writing. Evaluate notes and report, using marking ladders

Locating Information

Objective

We will identify the main features of non-chronological reports and locate information within a report

You need: Resource Page A; individual whiteboards.

Whole class work

- Display Resource Page A. ***What type of text does it look like?*** Answers: non-fiction; reference; factual; informative.
- Provide the label 'non-chronological report'. Explain that a report describes the way things are. ***Why is it called non-chronological?*** Answer: there is no need for the information to have a particular sequence.

chronos = time (Greek)

logos = word (Greek)

- Demonstrate this by moving the section 'Fresh Food' to the end. ***Which section needs to have a particular place?*** Answer: the introductory paragraph. ***Why?*** Answer: it introduces the whole report with the first sentence.
- Allow the children only a short time to think before displaying the answers to the following on 'show me' boards. ***Quickly find out how long it is safe to keep frozen food.*** Answer: as long as one year. ***When did canning start?*** Answer: 1810.
- ***How did you find your answers?*** Discuss the methods used to locate information, for example, making use of headings (skimming and scanning).
- Ask the children to find the heading 'Frozen Food'. ***What does the text warn needs to be remembered once frozen food has thawed?*** Answer: it must be used.
- Demonstrate locating the word 'thaw' and then reading the text near it to find the answer. Explain that this is scanning, which involves looking over a text very quickly, trying to locate a key word.

Independent, pair or guided work

- Independently, the children set five questions about storing food. (All the answers must be available in the text.)
- The children swap with their partner and answer their questions, locating information as efficiently as possible.
- Compare the methods used.

Plenary

- Use some of the questions as a general exercise.
- Stress the need to use helpful 'signposts', such as headings/key words when locating information.

Making Notes

Objective

We will practise our reading and note-making skills

You need: Resource Page A.

Whole class work

- Review work from the previous lesson. ***What does 'scanning' mean? Does anyone know what 'skimming' means?*** Answer: reading quickly to get an initial overview of the subject matter and the main ideas of a text. (See also Explanation Texts, page 127.)
- ***What would you do if you needed to understand a text more fully?*** Discuss this, helping the children to reach the conclusion that more careful reading would be needed. Explain that this is close reading.
- Talk about the use made by the reader of an informative text: to find out what you want to know. ***If you were doing research for a topic, why could close reading of some of this text be a waste of time?*** Encourage the children to put forward ideas, and suggest that some of this information may already be known.
- Talk about the importance of preparing for reading by identifying what you already know and what you need to find out. For example, 'fresh food has a short life' may already be known; therefore, that sentence will be skimmed over.
- Discuss further using a text for research. ***How should you write down what you find out?*** Brainstorm possibilities:

> – Copy text - only suitable for short parts.
>
> – Quote words - put a short extract in quotation marks to show they are not your own words. Only suitable for short parts. This is a good idea when the idea or words are unusual.
>
> – Adapt text – keep the same basic ideas, but make minor changes. (See the acknowledgement, 'Adapted from How Things Work by Claire Llewellyn'.)
>
> – Use your own words – read and absorb information, then produce a piece of original writing.

- Point out that for the first three points above, acknowledgement of writer and text is needed, for the fourth no acknowledgement is required.

Independent, pair or guided work

- The children read closely the sections 'Frozen foods' and 'Canned and dried foods' on Resource Page A.
- They make brief notes – in their own words – on what they find out.
- They plan how they will use these notes in a new text (entitled, for example, 'Long term storage of food').

Plenary

- Display some of the notes.
- In pairs, look at possible improvements using a response sandwich: one good comment; an idea for improvement; another good comment.

Using Colons

Objectives

We will find information efficiently. We will see how punctuation and meaning work together, and further practise our note-making

You need: Resource Pages C and E.

Whole class work

- Review work on reading skills. Revise skimming, scanning and close reading. Talk about when different approaches are most suitable.
- ***Which is your preferred choice for a new text?*** Discuss answers, finally suggesting that skimming is probably the best choice as they need a general sense of the text.
- Display Resource Page C. Allow the children one or two minutes to skim the text. ***What is it about?*** Ask them to use their own words. Answers might include:
  - Explaining which foods are best.
  - Food types and what they provide.
  - Mixing modern life with the right diet.
- Remind the children about acknowledging sources. Revise the differences between copying, quoting and adapting. Point out the quoted words/the acknowledgement. Emphasise that the source's exact words must be used and put in quotation marks.
- ***Why do you think these quoted words have been used?*** Answer: they provide a good ending. They may also sum up the message this writer wants to put across.
- Pick out this sentence from the third paragraph: 'Modern, snatched lunchtime eating habits are seen in most of the UK's workplaces: this is dangerous.'
- ***Why is a colon used?*** Answer: it introduces the result of what has just been said. Discuss this, and point out another example: 'Protein, which is essential ... supplies energy to the brain.'
- Talk about punctuation being an aid to understanding. This sentence is long and complicated; the colon signposts to the reader that an explanation is following.

Independent, pair or guided work

- Working in pairs, the children make a close reading of the text.
- Ask them to find out about and make notes on ten (or more) pieces of information given in the report (see Resource Page E). Stress the need to use their own words, apart from technical vocabulary.
- The pairs draw up four columns, headed with their own names, 'Both' and 'New'. Then they list their ten pieces of information and indicate (tick or cross) whether the item was already known by either or both.

  BEN ✓ SARAH ✓ BOTH ✓ NEW ✗

Plenary

- Share some of the results and ideas.
- Display some of the notes made. ***Would they be useful for writing your own report? Were most of the facts already known to you?***
- Point out the need to prepare for research by identifying what you already know and what you need to find out.

Using Clauses

Objectives

We will find information efficiently. We will see how punctuation and meaning work together and further practise our note-making

You need: Resource Pages C and F.

Whole class work

- Display Resource Page C, focusing on sentence structure. Reread the second paragraph. ***What are your initial impressions of the sentences?*** Encourage the children to think about their length and their complexity.
- Introduce the term 'complex sentence' and define it: a sentence containing a main clause and a subordinate clause. Explain that subordinate means lower.
- Sentences 1 and 3 in the second paragraph are both complex sentences with subordinate clauses. Complex sentences are common in this text type.
- Identify the subordinate clauses:

  'which is essential for growth and sustained health of bones'

  'such as those found in mackerel'

- The children practise identifying some others, for example:

  'such as provided by chicken'

  'the sugar contained in fresh fruit'

- ***Most of these clauses have commas before and after them. Why?*** Discuss the children's ideas, helping them to recognise that the commas hold the subordinate clause in place within the sentence by separating it from the main clause.
- Explain that punctuation often 'signposts' meaning. ***Look at sentence 1, in the second paragraph. What punctuation would you pick out? Why?*** Answer: the colon. Revise its function from earlier in the unit. Here, it signals that more information about the brain is coming.

Independent, pair or guided work

- Ask the children to choose a topic (Geography/History/Science are good areas) for their own non-chronological report (see Resource Page F for ideas). Brainstorm a preparation checklist.
- The children decide on the specific area and focus of their report.
- The children identify:
  - What I already know.
  - What I need to find out.
- Decide on resources to be used. List book(s), CD-ROMs, IT programs, local and national newspapers/magazines, and web sites.

Plenary

- Discuss ideas and plans. Assist with any problems.
- Are all the topics suitable? Are the children aware of all the resources?

Pupil copymaster

A non-chronological report

STORING FOOD

Food must be stored safely. Care must be taken that the cooking area, as well as the utensils used, are kept clean. Scrupulous cleaning ensures that a hygienic environment is maintained.

Fresh food

Fresh food has a short life. After a week or two in the fresh air, a fresh red apple has started to rot and turn brown. With storage in a dark, cool, covered place, its life may be greatly extended. In the case of meat and dairy products, cool storage is even more important, for the process of going bad and producing bacteria is quicker.

Refrigeration

The life of fresh food can be extended by a cooler environment. Fresh food deteriorates most quickly when it is allowed to become warm. The use of a refrigerator to keep food cold allows food to last a few days longer.

Frozen foods

In a freezer, food undergoes a process whereby all the water inside the food is turned into ice. By this, the food's life is greatly increased, and foods can safely be kept for up to one year. However, once allowed to thaw, the food must be used, not refrozen.

Canned and dried foods

Food sealed in a tin is kept in a healthy state for several years; it is essential that the tin is airtight. Food was first stored in this way in 1810.

Drying foods is another convenient way of preserving them. Astronauts, for example, are supplied with food that is like powder. Water is added to eat the food. Fruits such as raisins and dried apricots are the result of this process of drying, allowing them to be kept in an edible condition for months.

Adapted from How Things Work, *by Claire Llewellyn*

Exemplar analysis

Example of analysis of a non-chronological report

A short introductory statement usually opens the report; this is more general than the rest.

Sub-headings are a frequently used device, helping to signpost specific areas of information.

A report's verbs should be in the present tense.

Reports should be non-chronological. There is no reason why this section may not swap order with the preceding section.

STORING FOOD

Food must be stored safely. Care must be taken that the cooking area, as well as the utensils used, are kept clean. Scrupulous cleaning ensures that a hygienic environment is maintained.

Fresh food
Fresh food has a short life. After a week or two in the fresh air, a fresh red apple has started to rot and turn brown. With storage in a dark, cool, covered place, its life may be greatly extended. In the case of meat and dairy products, cool storage is even more important, for the process of going bad and producing bacteria is quicker.

Refrigeration
The life of fresh food can be extended by a cooler environment. Fresh food deteriorates most quickly when it is allowed to become warm. The use of a refrigerator to keep food cold allows food to last a few days longer.

Frozen foods
In a freezer, food undergoes a process whereby all the water inside the food is turned into ice. By this, the food's life is greatly increased, and foods can safely be kept for up to one year. However, once allowed to thaw, the food must be used, not refrozen.

Canned and dried foods
Food sealed in a tin is kept in a healthy state for several years; it is essential that the tin is airtight. Food was first stored in this way in 1810.

Drying foods is another convenient way of preserving them. Astronauts, for example, are supplied with food that is like powder. Water is added to eat the food. Fruits such as raisins and dried apricots are the result of this process of drying, allowing them to be kept in an edible condition for months.

Adapted from How Things Work, *by Claire Llewellyn*

A report describes the way things are – here, of different ways to store food.

This text type is impersonal. Use of the passive voice (where something is done to the subject) helps achieve impersonal style.

Technical vocabulary is essential.

Clarity is important, so an explanation such as this will often feature in a report.

Notice the subordinate clause embedded within the sentence by commas. Sentence structure may be complex, and commas are important guides to meaning.

Acknowledgements are made after the text. The writer of this text is acknowledging a dependence on the work and ideas of another writer.

Pupil copymaster

Health report

KEEPING HEALTHY

Eating habits are developed by environmental and social factors. Climate, land and customs all contribute, but the diet must still meet health-giving requirements. With modern living and convenience foods, the body's need for a necessary balance of fats, proteins and carbohydrates may be overlooked, if the quick, fast-taken food has little nutritional value.

Brain power

Protein, which is essential for growth and sustained health of bones, affects the brain: a portion of protein-rich meat, such as provided by chicken, supplies energy to the brain. Thinking power and concentration is improved after receiving this source of energy. However, a variety of sources should be considered: white meat, for example, has been shown to be preferable to red meat; the nutrients found in oily fish, such as those found in mackerel, not only improve the use of the brain, but are also identified as a valuable source of essential fats.

Living in the UK

Modern, snatched lunchtime eating habits are seen in most of the UK's workplaces: this is dangerous. Instead of fast release carbohydrates, fructose, the sugar contained in fresh fruit, is a better source of slow, longer-lasting energy. Many fruits contain important minerals, also providing energy which is slowly released. Combining modern eating with these essential nutrients can "stimulate our mind, rev up our metabolism and protect against the effects of stress."*

*Cooking *by Raymond Blanc and Amanda Ursell*
The Sunday Times, *19/01/03*

Exemplar analysis

Example of analysis of the health report

Introductory statement opens the report; it is expected that this is more general than the rest.

The title is a clear description of the subject matter.

KEEPING HEALTHY

Eating habits are developed by environmental and social factors. Climate, land and customs all contribute, but the diet must still meet health-giving requirements. With modern living and convenience foods, the body's need for a necessary balance of fats, proteins and carbohydrates may be overlooked, if the quick, fast-taken food has little nutritional value.

Brain power

Protein, which is essential for growth and sustained health of bones, affects the brain: a portion of protein-rich meat, such as provided by chicken, supplies energy to the brain. Thinking power and concentration is improved after receiving this source of energy. However, a variety of sources should be considered: white meat, for example, has been shown to be preferable to red meat; the nutrients found in oily fish, such as those found in mackerel, not only improve the use of the brain, but are also identified as a valuable source of essential fats.

Living in the UK

Modern, snatched lunchtime eating habits are seen in most of the UK's workplaces: this is dangerous. Instead of fast release carbohydrates, fructose, the sugar contained in fresh fruit, is a better source of slow, longer-lasting energy. Many fruits contain important minerals, also providing energy which is slowly released. Combining modern eating with these essential nutrients can "stimulate our mind, rev up our metabolism and protect against the effects of stress."*

*Cooking *by Raymond Blanc and Amanda Ursell*
The Sunday Times, *19/01/03*

A long complex sentence, in which punctuation acts as an aid to the reader's understanding.

Subtitles are a frequently used device, helping to signpost specific areas of information. They make a report more accessible.

Frequent use of the passive gives a strong impersonal style.

Long, complex sentences appear frequently. Notice the use of commas to hold clauses in place, as well as other punctuation (e.g. colons) to signpost meaning.

There is no set order to the paragraphs: the text is non-chronological.

A report's verbs should be in the present tense.

Technical vocabulary is essential.

Quotation marks are used to show that these are the exact words of someone else.

Acknowledgements are made after the text. Here, the text containing the quotation and its authors are mentioned.

Exemplar material

Information notes

1. Human body needs balanced diet.
2. Balance = protein + fats + carbohydrates.
3. Protein keeps bones healthy.
4. Fruit's sugar = fructose.
5. Mackerel: an oily fish.
6. Oily fish helps mental ability.
7. Protein of benefit to brain.
8. Better to eat white meat v. red meat.
9. Fructose gives energy that is released slowly.
10. Carbohydrates give energy, but quickly.
11. Slower energy - like fructose - better.
12. Protein needed for growing.
13. Fats, carbohydrates, protein all necessary for health.

Exemplar material

Checklists for non-chronological reports

Example of a checklist for preparation

- Decide on topic and specific area
- Identify current knowledge
- Identify what you need to find out
- Select resources

Example of a checklist for notes

- Locate information
- Use appropriate methods of reading
- Make your notes clear
- Use quick methods of recording (e.g. abbreviations)
- Use your own words – unless copying
- Quote speech precisely
- Use correct technical words
- Ensure planned information can be found
- List sources

Example of a checklist for a non-chronological report

- Describe the way things are
- Include an opening statement
- Feature text in paragraphs
- Order is non-chronological
- Use verbs in present tense
- Make some use of passive voice
- Use impersonal style
- Use correct technical words
- Include clear explanations
- Make possible use of headings
- Include some longer/complex sentences
- Use appropriate, helpful punctuation
- Use quotation marks correctly
- Include acknowledgement of sources

Marking ladder

Marking ladder for notes

Name: ______________________________

Pupil	Objective	Teacher
	I can understand my notes.	
	I used my reading skills well.	
	I found what I planned.	
	I used quick methods of recording (e.g. abbreviations).	
	I used my own words – unless copying.	
	I used precise quoted words.	
	I used correct technical words.	
	I listed my sources.	
	What could I do to improve my notes next time?	

Marking ladder

Marking ladder for a non-chronological report

Name: ______________________________

Pupil	Objective	Teacher
	My report describes the way things are.	
	I wrote an opening statement.	
	I used paragraphs.	
	I used an impersonal tone.	
	My report is non-chronological.	
	I used verbs in the present tense.	
	I made some use of the passive voice.	
	I used correct technical words.	
	I gave clear explanations when needed.	
	I used some longer/complex sentences.	
	I used appropriate and helpful punctuation.	
	I included headings.	
	I used quotation marks correctly.	
	I acknowledged my sources.	
	What could I do to improve my report next time?	

Narrative: Empathy and Point of View

Outcome

A short story written from the point of view of a different character; a reading journal

Objectives

Sentence

2 to understand how writing can be adapted for different audiences and purposes.
5 to revise use of apostrophes for possession (from Yr 4, term 1).

Text

1 to investigate a range of texts from different cultures, considering patterns of relationships, social customs, attitudes and beliefs: identify these features by reference to the text; consider and evaluate these features in relation to their own experience.
2 to identify the point of view from which a story is told and how this affects the reader's response.
3 to change point of view, e.g. tell incident or describe a situation from the point of view of another character or perspective.
7 to write from another character's point of view.
8 to record predictions, questions, reflections while reading, e.g. through the use of a reading journal.

Planning frame

- Read a range of texts from a different culture and identify their features.
- Consider and evaluate these features in relation to their own experiences.
- Analyse how the point of view is communicated by the author.
- Rewrite a story from a different point of view.

How you could plan this unit

Day 1	Day 2	Day 3	Day 4	Day 5
Reading and writing *Rewriting an Extract*	**Reading** Read, analyse and annotate cultural features of text (Resource Pages C and D). Discuss which characters are most sympathetic	**Reading and writing** *Creating Empathy*	**Writing** Complete class checklist for a reading journal entry (Resource Page K). The children make an entry for current stage of class novel, using Day 3 model	**Reading and writing** *Cultural References*

Day 6	Day 7	Day 8	Day 9	Day 10
Reading Investigate and annotate further features of the text, using Resource Pages H and I. Evaluate features in relation to personal experience. Discuss reactions to story	**Reading and writing** *A Different Viewpoint*	**Writing** Begin initial draft of short story. Finalise checklist. Work on writing	**Writing** Write text. Edit and refine writing	**Reading** Polish and complete writing. Evaluate reading journal and short story using marking ladders (Resource Pages L and M)

Rewriting an Extract

Objectives

We will read a text from a different culture and identify the point of view from which a story is told, and how this affects the reader's response. We will also learn how writing can be adapted for different purposes

You need: Resource Pages A, B and K.

Whole class work

- Read aloud the introduction to *Clever Anaeet* (Resource Pages A and B). ***Why is the introduction important?*** The children should easily identify that it places the whole story. Direct their attention to the geographical references of story origins, and traditions surrounding carpets. The fact that the story is from a different culture is important.
- ***How do you, a modern UK reader, react to this traditional, cultural text?*** Encourage the children to express their feelings. ***Is too much emphasis placed on the weaving of a carpet? Do attitudes seem strange?***
- Read the sentence 'A servant announced the arrival of the priest.' Point out how this differs from our culture, where there is no access to royalty. ***Do the names add any clues about the setting?***
- Consider language. ***Has the writer used words you have never heard?*** The answer is probably no. Point out that this is achieved by not using words that could only be understood in that part of the world, or adopting a style of English with dialect words (such as Cockney rhyming slang).
- Focus on the description of the carpet. Ask the children to comment on the style the writer has used. Answers could include 'fussy', 'old-fashioned', 'elaborate'.
- Work together on rewriting the extract in more straightforward language (see example 3, Resource Page K).
- Point out changes to vocabulary and sentence structure: 'difficult' is a less mysterious word than 'complex'; 'dark' is far more ordinary than 'richly coloured'. The first sentence has a simpler construction, no longer needing commas to hold a phrase in place. The construction of the second sentence is also much simpler, with the active form 'wove' replacing the passive form 'were woven'.
- ***What is the effect of the changes?*** Answer: the carpet has lost some of its mystery and beauty, but the text is easier for a younger audience.

Independent, pair or guided work

- Ask the children to read the paragraph: 'But Queen Anaeet gave the carpet ... as wise a one as yourself.'
- Independently or in pairs, the children work on drafting, refining and rewriting the paragraph in a simpler, more straightforward style for a younger audience, substituting or omitting vocabulary and altering sentence structure as they wish.

Plenary

- Listen to and discuss new versions. Evaluate using a response sandwich: one good comment; one area for improvement; another good comment.

Creating Empathy

Objectives

We will identify the point of view from which a story is told, how this affects the reader's response and how points of view may be changed. We will record our feelings through a reading journal

You need: Resource Pages A, B, E and K.

Whole class work

- Remind the children of their earlier discussion about characters. ***Did most of you feel that Vachagan was a good person? Why?*** Favourable comments may include his bravery/leadership qualities/cleverness.
- Consider how views are formed about characters. ***What does the writer depend on?*** Answer: the words he/she uses, and the point(s) of view from which a situation is described.
- Display these examples from *Clever Anaeet* (Resource Pages A and B):

> Vachagan stepped boldly forward.
>
> Vachagan instructed them.

- ***What does the first extract make you think about Vachagan?*** Answer: he is courageous and confident. ***What does the second extract make you think about him?*** Answer: he is a strong leader and knows that people will follow his directions.
- ***Which words make us view Vachagan favourably?*** Answer: 'boldly' and 'instructed'. Stress the positive effect of both words: they help to create empathy between reader and character.
- Empathy = identifying with a character in a story, seeing the situation from that point of view and feeling what they feel.
- ***What words could you use instead of 'instructed' to encourage the reader to feel empathy only with the men, not Vachagan?*** Ideas could include: 'ordered'; 'shouted at'.
- The change in vocabulary would affect the way the story was told: not liking the way Vachagan makes the men work so hard, or gives instructions, you might only feel empathy with the men, seeing the situation from their point of view.

Independent, pair or guided work

- Ask the children to hold a discussion about the class novel, finding out which characters they feel empathy with.
- ***Do your feelings about the characters change? Does the story change, gradually including different points of view? How does the writer achieve these results?***
- Make notes on situations/incidents and textual references.
- In pairs or small groups, the children brainstorm how to set out a reading journal entry, showing which characters are sympathetic at this stage (see Resource Page E).

Plenary

- Share ideas on the format of the reading journals, emphasising that different formats are equally valid.
- Begin a class checklist for a reading journal entry (see Resource Page K for ideas).

Cultural References

Objectives

We will identify cultural features found in a text and compare customs and attitudes among cultures. We will also revise the use of possessive apostrophes

You need: Resource Pages F, G and J; individual whiteboards.

Whole class work

- Display Resource Pages F and G. Ask the children to skim the text. ***What does it seem to have in common with* Clever Anaeet?** Answer: an emphasis on its cultural roots. ***What clues tell you this?*** Answer: place and people names.
- Now make a close reading of the text. ***What is the chief distinction between this story and* Clever Anaeet?** Answers may involve geography, but guide the children towards thinking about time period. ***When is this story set? Is it modern or an old traditional tale?*** Answer: modern.
- ***Where is it set?*** Answer: references prove it is not set in India (for example, 'on our last visit to India'). The story is set in modern England.
- ***Are any local language/dialect words used?*** Give the children time to identify 'sarees' (Indian dresses) and 'salvar kameez' (Indian tunic and pyjamas). Discuss that the author includes these words in her glossary.
- Use the text to revise use of apostrophes for possession. The children identify examples:

Rani's birthday (singular)	the Shankars' large house (plural)
Rani's birthday invitation (singular)	the Mahajans' party (plural)
Shanta's mother/father (singular)	

- Go over the rules as necessary (Resource Page J).
- Demonstrate the long forms of writing, in order to emphasise the convenience of an apostrophe: 'the birthday of Rani'; 'the large house of the Shankars'; 'the birthday invitation from Rani'; 'the party thrown by the Mahajans'; 'the mother/father of Shanta'.

Independent, pair or guided work

- Ask the children to study the text, finding references to social customs/attitudes.
- The children list customs with references on their whiteboards.
- Compare them with traditional English customs:

> Custom A teenage girl dancing as the main entertainer at her birthday party.
>
> Text 'Rani herself would be the star performer'
>
> Traditional English 'Alexi would have music, but all the guests would dance.' Or 'Elisa did this when she was younger'.

Plenary

- Share findings and discuss the variety in the children's own experiences.
- Discuss how some customs cross countries and cultures, for example, the American high school prom is now often held in UK schools. Some customs do not travel, for example, no tossing of pancakes on Shrove Tuesday in a non-Christian country.

A Different Viewpoint

Objectives

We will identify the point of view from which a story is told, and how this affects the reader's response, and we will write from another character's point of view

You need: Resource Pages F, G and K.

Whole class work

- Read Resource Pages F and G again. Focus on empathy and revise the definition from earlier in the unit. ***Which character do you feel most empathy with?***
- ***Why is it easy to emphasise/feel sympathy with Shanta?*** Answer: her mother's behaviour towards her. Ask the children to search the text for references, for example,
  - 'She looked at her daughter and couldn't help showing her irritation.'
  - 'She thought of her niece, Rani, with her fair skin ...'
  - 'Shanta's skin was too dark ...'
- Ask the children to consider other characters. ***How does the writer want us to view Mr Biswas?*** Point out the words 'pained voice', and how they make the reader feel sorry for him and present his point of view.
- ***What shows that Mr Biswas is as generous as he can afford to be?*** Answer: he bought Mrs Biswas a silk saree when they were in India.
- ***What about Rani? Does the writer deal favourably with her?*** Answer: too little is known about her at this stage, as this extract is taken from the beginning of the story.
- ***Are Rani's parents presented favourably?*** Answer: they enjoy 'showing off' Rani, but they were 'very generous' and 'everyone' came to their parties. Emphasise that a single word, for example 'generous', can alter the reader's response to a character.
- Point out the words 'pouted her mother'. ***What effect do they have on the reader's feelings about Mrs Biswas? Do you empathise with her?***

Independent, pair or guided work

- The children examine how the writer presents the character Mrs Biswas.
- The children retell the story, so that Mrs Biswas becomes a more sympathetic character. For example, she could recognise that Shanta isn't as pretty as Rani, but try to boost her self-confidence.
- ***The main facts that move the story on remain, but you, the writer, will try to make the reader feel empathy with Mrs Biswas, and see her point of view.***
- The children make a plan for their new version of the story.

Plenary

- Discuss the plans.
- Compile an initial checklist for a story supporting the point of view of a particular character (see Resource Page K for ideas).

Pupil copymaster

Clever Anaeet

The weaving of fine rugs and carpets is one of Armenia's traditional crafts. The carpets are famed for their elaborate garden designs and their dazzling colours – often provided by dyes made from natural plant sources.

The gardens are linked to the beliefs of the cultural religion, Islam, and represent the Garden of Paradise.

At that moment a priest approached, escorted by armed guards. He pushed the guide roughly to one side and addressed the men.

"Which of you here has a trade?"

Vachagan stepped boldly forward and spoke: "We all do, for we can weave carpets the like of which you will have never seen before. They are more valuable than gold and as fine as the down on a bird's breast."

The priest's eyes narrowed as he gave orders for the necessary materials to be brought. "If your boast proves to be untrue, then you will all be skinned alive," he snarled.

At once the team were set to work and Vachagan instructed them. The men's backs were bent hour after hour over the loom as their shuttles flew back and forth. Their eyes ached from following the fine pattern in the gloom, their skin paled and they grew thin and gaunt. But slowly, under the guidance of Vachagan, the most beautiful carpet began to emerge. Its richly coloured threads were woven into intricate patterns, while gold thread formed sacred symbols and signs of good fortune. And embroidered into the complex tapestry was a message. It told of Vachagan's imprisonment and his whereabouts, but it was visible only to the most discerning eye.

Finally the carpet was completed. The priest was indeed impressed.

continued ...

Pupil copymaster

Clever Anaeet (continued)

"This carpet is fit for royalty," Vachagan hinted, "for there are ancient signs and symbols woven into the cloth that would not be understood by common folk. And I am sure that even Queen Anaeet would marvel at its beauty. I warrant she would pay you handsomely for it."

That very night the priest set off for the palace.

Queen Anaeet had ruled wisely in Vachagan's absence. But now, as the year was drawing to a close, she worried for her husband's safety. Whenever merchants, minstrels and other travellers visited the palace, she listened closely to their stories, hoping for news of Vachagan.

One morning, as Queen Anaeet sat in the palace garden, a servant announced the arrival of a priest.

"Your Majesty," the servant said, "this visitor boasts of a woven carpet fit only for the eyes of a queen."

When the priest was admitted, he bowed and proceeded to unroll the carpet with a flourish. Anaeet's attendants gasped with amazement as the light caught the golden threads of the carpet.

But Queen Anaeet gave the carpet hardly a second look. Her heart was heavy and she was constantly distracted now by the fear that some misfortune had befallen her husband. The priest, sensing her lack of interest, began to praise every detail of the carpet. "Your Majesty, there is no other carpet like this one. It outshines the stars and is more delicate to the touch than the petals of a rose. But what is more, O Majesty, it is endowed with magical properties. It has signs and symbols that may be understood only by one as wise as yourself."

Anaeet's attention was caught at last. Holding a corner of the carpet in her hands, she saw letters woven cleverly into the design.

Retold by Tanya Robyn Batt, in The Fabrics of Fairy Tale

Exemplar analysis

Example of analysis of *Clever Anaeet*

Introduction establishes this as a text from a culture likely to be different from that of most of the readers.

The weaving of fine rugs and carpets is one of Armenia's traditional crafts. The carpets are famed for their elaborate garden designs and their dazzling colours – often provided by dyes made from natural plant sources.

The gardens are linked to the beliefs of the cultural religion, Islam, and represent the Garden of Paradise.

Religious beliefs are important in most cultures.

It is unusual to depict a priest as a 'baddie'.

At that moment a priest approached, escorted by armed guards. He pushed the guide roughly to one side and addressed the men.

"Which of you here has a trade?"

This culture's attitude to work is stressed here: a trade will always be of use, and hard work will bring reward.

Vachagan stepped boldly forward and spoke: "We all do, for we can weave carpets the like of which you will have never seen before. They are more valuable than gold and as fine as the down on a bird's breast."

The priest's eyes narrowed as he gave orders for the necessary materials to be brought. "If your boast proves to be untrue, then you will all be skinned alive," he snarled.

At once the team were set to work and Vachagan instructed them. The men's backs were bent hour after hour over the loom as their shuttles flew back and forth.

The attitude to hard work is reinforced, with the men willing to work agonisingly hard. Notice also their unquestioning obedience of their leader.

Their eyes ached from following the fine pattern in the gloom, their skin paled and they grew thin and gaunt. But slowly, under the guidance of Vachagan, the most beautiful carpet began to emerge. Its richly coloured threads were woven into intricate patterns, while gold thread formed sacred symbols and signs of good fortune.

The part that religious beliefs play in the society is stressed – certain holy signs and symbols are supposed to show good luck. It is unusual for any culture not to set some store by certain omens.

And embroidered into the complex tapestry was a message. It told of Vachagan's imprisonment and his whereabouts, but it was visible only to the most discerning eye.

Finally the carpet was completed. The priest was indeed impressed.

continued ...

Exemplar analysis

Example of analysis of *Clever Anaeet* (continued)

"This carpet is fit for royalty," Vachagan hinted, "for there are ancient signs and symbols woven into the cloth that would not be understood by common folk. And I am sure that even Queen Anaeet would marvel at its beauty. I warrant she would pay you handsomely for it."

That very night the priest set off for the palace.

Queen Anaeet had ruled wisely in Vachagan's absence. But now, as the year was drawing to a close, she worried for her husband's safety. Whenever merchants, minstrels and other travellers visited the palace, she listened closely to their stories, hoping for news of Vachagan.

One morning, as Queen Anaeet sat in the palace garden, a servant announced the arrival of a priest.

"Your Majesty," the servant said, "this visitor boasts of a woven carpet fit only for the eyes of a queen."

When the priest was admitted, he bowed and proceeded to unroll the carpet with a flourish. Anaeet's attendants gasped with amazement as the light caught the golden threads of the carpet.

But Queen Anaeet gave the carpet hardly a second look. Her heart was heavy and she was constantly distracted now by the fear that some misfortune had befallen her husband. The priest, sensing her lack of interest, began to praise every detail of the carpet. "Your Majesty, there is no other carpet like this one. It outshines the stars and is more delicate to the touch than the petals of a rose. But what is more, O Majesty, it is endowed with magical properties. It has signs and symbols that may be understood only by one as wise as yourself."

Anaeet's attention was caught at last. Holding a corner of the carpet in her hands, she saw letters woven cleverly into the design.

Retold by Tanya Robyn Batt, in The Fabrics of Fairy Tale

This seems strange for most modern cultures and relationships. Here a priest is assuming he will have – and does gain – easy access to a queen.

The flamboyant description of the carpet expresses Armenian pride in its traditional skill of carpet making.

The phrase shows that supernatural beliefs were acceptable.

A narrative which focuses on its cultural links often contains a moral: here, it is that the people will always need their traditional skill, particularly in times of difficulty.

Pupil copymaster

Frame for a reading journal

Title	
Author	
Point in story	
Feelings about characters: First impressions	
Now	
As story progressed	
By the end?	
Significant incidents	
Telling behaviour	
Revealing words	

I feel most empathy with ______________________ because I can sympathise with this point of view: ______________________

____

Pupil copymaster

The Temple by the Sea

Excitement is mounting as the celebration draws nearer ...

Rani's birthday was always considered a very special occasion. People looked forward to it because everyone came, from the youngest to the oldest. Cousins and aunts and uncles and grannies and grandpas, and all Rani's friends from school – they all came. There would be mountains of food and rivers of wine and fruit juices; and a constant caravan of dishes would parade through with all sorts of savouries and titbits and delicious sweets. Although the Shankars always brought in the finest entertainers to amuse their many party guests, it was Rani herself who would be the star performer, rounding off the evening with a brilliant demonstration of her dancing.

Ever since Rani's birthday invitation had arrived, Shanta's mother, Mrs Biswas, had been fretting about what to wear. Mrs Biswas often wore an expression of annoyance. She was mostly annoyed because she felt her parents had made her marry beneath her. Mr Biswas was a teacher and would never be rich – not like Mr Shankar, Rani's father, who was in business. Mrs Biswas envied the Shankars' large house and big cars; and she especially envied the beautiful sarees Mr Shankar brought back for his wife whenever he went off on a business trip.

However, every party invitation was received eagerly – for it would be terrible not to be included on the Shankar party list, even though it meant terrible anxiety about what to wear. Mrs Biswas dreaded looking poorer than the rest. She would flick through the sarees which hung in her wardrobe and then conclude in a very loud voice, for the benefit of her husband, "I have nothing to wear. I'll just have to go shopping."

continued ...

Pupil copymaster

The Temple by the Sea (continued)

"Why can't you wear that one of Banarasi silk which I bought you on our last visit to India?" asked Shanta's father in a pained voice.

"Because I wore that at the Mahajans' party, and everyone would remember it," retorted his wife who could never be seen at a party in the same saree twice.

"I think you should wear that beautiful turquoise blue one with the peacock border," murmured Shanta.

"Don't be silly, child," pouted her mother, annoyed. "That's not good enough for a party at the Shankars'." She looked at her daughter and couldn't help showing her irritation. The girl was so awkward, so nondescript; so unpretty. Shanta's mother had never forgotten overhearing one of her sisters-in-law making the comment that if one must have daughters, at least they should be pretty.

"It's too bad," Shanta's mother often groaned. "Why should the Shankars have wealth as well as beauty?" She thought of her niece, Rani, with her fair skin, slender figure and face like a goddess, and compared her to Shanta. In her opinion, Shanta's skin was too dark, her forehead too broad, her feet too big and her figure rather stumpy. True, she had large glowing eyes, and people said of Shanta that her eyes and her rich black hair were her most beautiful features; but where would eyes get you in this world? Who would want to marry her? Shanta's mother gave a discontented sigh. "I suppose we had better decide what you are going to wear, too," she said to her daughter.

"I shall wear the salvar kameez which Dad brought me back from India," said Shanta. "It's really lovely."

Jamila Gavin

Exemplar analysis

Example of analysis of *The Temple by the Sea*

The title 'The Temple by the Sea' sets a mystical tone, away from story's immediate setting.

Excitement is mounting as the celebration draws nearer ...

Rani's birthday was always considered a very special occasion. People looked forward to it because everyone came, from the youngest to the oldest. Cousins and aunts and uncles and grannies and grandpas, and all Rani's friends from school – they all came. There would be mountains of food and rivers of wine and fruit juices; and a constant caravan of dishes would parade through with all sorts of savouries and titbits and delicious sweets. Although the Shankars always brought in the finest entertainers to amuse their many party guests, it was Rani herself who would be the star performer, rounding off the evening with a brilliant demonstration of her dancing.

Ever since Rani's birthday invitation had arrived, Shanta's mother, Mrs Biswas, had been fretting about what to wear. Mrs Biswas often wore an expression of annoyance. She was mostly annoyed because she felt her parents had made her marry beneath her. Mr Biswas was a teacher and would never be rich – not like Mr Shankar, Rani's father, who was in business. Mrs Biswas envied the Shankars' large house and big cars; and she especially envied the beautiful sarees Mr Shankar brought back for his wife whenever he went off on a business trip.

However, every party invitation was received eagerly – for it would be terrible not to be included on the Shankar party list, even though it meant terrible anxiety about what to wear. Mrs Biswas dreaded looking poorer than the rest. She would flick through the sarees which hung in her wardrobe and then conclude in a very loud voice, for the benefit of her husband, "I have nothing to wear. I'll just have to go shopping."

continued ...

Commonplace mention of a forthcoming birthday contrasts with mystery of the title.

The description, particularly of the food, conveys the importance of the event. Particular dishes are part of every culture, but in modern times, one country increasingly adopts from another.

In modern, multicultural societies Indian names in an English setting are not unusual.

Traditional dance is an important and admired skill in many cultures.

The two cultures – where the family live, and where they are from – meet here: wearing the saree from her Indian roots, while living in England, is important to Mrs Biswas.

Exemplar analysis

Example of analysis of *The Temple by the Sea (continued)*

"Why can't you wear that one of Banarasi silk which I bought you on our last visit to India?" asked Shanta's father in a pained voice.

"Because I wore that at the Mahajans' party, and everyone would remember it," retorted his wife who could never be seen at a party in the same saree twice.

"I think you should wear that beautiful turquoise blue one with the peacock border," murmured Shanta.

"Don't be silly, child," pouted her mother, annoyed. "That's not good enough for a party at the Shankars'." She looked at her daughter and couldn't help showing her irritation. The girl was so awkward, so nondescript; so unpretty. Shanta's mother had never forgotten overhearing one of her sisters-in-law making the comment that if one must have daughters, at least they should be pretty.

"It's too bad," Shanta's mother often groaned. "Why should the Shankars have wealth as well as beauty?" She thought of her niece, Rani, with her fair skin, slender figure and face like a goddess, and compared her to Shanta. In her opinion, Shanta's skin was too dark, her forehead too broad, her feet too big and her figure rather stumpy. True, she had large glowing eyes, and people said of Shanta that her eyes and her rich black hair were her most beautiful features; but where would eyes get you in this world? Who would want to marry her? Shanta's mother gave a discontented sigh. "I suppose we had better decide what you are going to wear, too," she said to her daughter.

"I shall wear the salvar kameez which Dad brought me back from India," said Shanta. "It's really lovely."

Jamila Gavin

Religious beliefs are shown by the use of this word.

The extract has dwelt on Mrs Biswas's dissatisfaction with Shanta: later parts of the story reveal the qualities of Shanta. The moral is: do not forget where you are from, and be grateful for what you have.

That young women marry is important in many cultures; not to find a husband can be seen as a disgrace. It may often be decided by not just the girl's looks, but her family's wealth and position in society.

Shanta, attending school in England, still wants to retain cultural roots with her family's home.

Pupil copymaster

Possessive apostrophes

An apostrophe can tell you who owns something. It is a quick way to explain ownership. There are three rules:

- When the owner is **singular**, add **'s**
- When the owner is **plural and ends in s**, just add an **'**
- When the owner is **plural and does not end in s**, add **'s**

● *Remember this rule:* Ask yourself ***Who is the owner?*** Then put the apostrophe straight after the answer.

Exemplar material

Checklists for narratives

Example of a checklist for a reading journal

- Include title of story
- Include author's name
- Use interesting, clear layout
- Give first impressions of character/s
- Say who you felt empathy with
- Describe changes in your feelings
- Make references to the book
- Quote specific words
- Make predictions about characters/point of view
- Anticipate how the story will progress and end

Example of a checklist for a narrative supporting a character's point of view

- Think about character descriptions
- Decide who you support
- Decide which point of view you want the reader to respond well to
- Decide how characters speak
- Describe incidents from appropriate point of view
- Use verbs/adverbs skilfully
- Think about audience response
- Consider whether the reader will feel empathy

Example of modelling a rewritten extract

Vachagan guided the others, and slowly a beautiful carpet began to appear. They wove dark threads into patterns, and gold and silver ones into religious symbols and good omens. The difficult tapestry also contained a hidden message.

Marking ladder

Marking ladder for a reading journal

Name: ____________________

Pupil	Objective	Teacher
	I included the title of the story.	
	I included the author's name.	
	I used an interesting, clear layout.	
	I gave my first impressions of the character(s).	
	I said who I felt empathy with.	
	I described progression/changes in feelings.	
	I made references to incidents/descriptions.	
	I quoted words from the book.	
	I considered how the story's point of view might progress.	
	I made predictions, particularly about the ending.	
	What could I do to improve my journal entry next time?	

Marking ladder

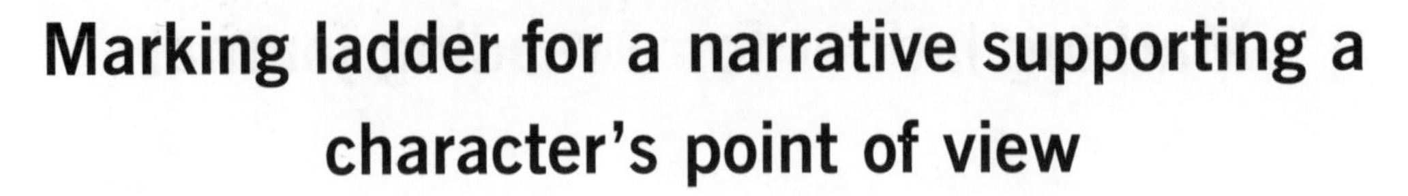

Marking ladder for a narrative supporting a character's point of view

Name: ______________________________

Pupil	Objective	Teacher
	I described characters carefully.	
	I decided on a point of view.	
	I supported these characters ____________.	
	I was aware of the reader's response to words.	
	I considered how characters spoke.	
	I described incidents from an appropriate point of view.	
	I used verbs/adverbs skilfully.	
	I considered whether the reader would feel empathy.	
	What could I do to improve my story next time?	

Performance Poetry

Outcome

Performance of poetry using two different styles; a poem in the style of one of the performance poems

Objectives

Text

4 to read, rehearse and modify performance of poetry.

5 to select poetry, and justify their choices.

6 to explore the challenge and appeal of older literature through:
- listening to older literature being read aloud;
- reading accessible poems, stories and extracts;
- discussing differences in language used.

11 to use performance poems as models to write and produce poetry in polished forms through revising, redrafting and presentation.

Planning frame

- Read, rehearse and modify performance of poetry.
- Analyse features and language of a performance poem.
- Use performance poems as models to write and produce poetry in polished forms, through revising, redrafting and presentation.

How you could plan this unit

Day 1	Day 2	Day 3	Day 4	Day 5
Reading and writing *Free Verse*	**Reading and writing** Complete group work from Day 1. Revise, redraft and rehearse. Make group presentations to rest of class	**Reading** *Language Features*	**Reading and writing** Revise, redraft, rehearse and perform versions of *Genius*. Justify views on the two poems. Record thoughts for a class anthology	**Reading and writing** *Linking Words*

Day 6	Day 7	Day 8	Day 9	Day 10
Writing Continue draft of poem. Make initial checklists for writing and performances	**Writing** Revise, redraft, rehearse and perform poems. Consider vocabulary employed	**Reading and writing** *A Classic Poem*	**Writing** Complete drafts of poems. Finalise checklists	**Writing** Revise, redraft, rehearse and present poems. Evaluate using marking ladders (Resource Pages G and H)

Free Verse

Objective

We will read, rehearse and perform poems, and use a performance poem as a model for further writing

You need: Resource Page A.

Whole class work

- Read the poem *Louder!* (Resource Page A). ***Is this text difficult to understand?*** (Don't mention the word 'poem' at this stage.) Read it again, allowing more time for the children to absorb the words.
- ***What would make the message of this text clearer?*** Reread it, this time making a pronounced change between the teacher's voice and Andrew's voice. By now the children should have identified the need for a different voice to help you read the poem.
- Now display the poem. ***What type of text does it look like?*** Answers may include:
  - an ordinary piece of writing
  - an advertisement (as these overuse capital letters and exclamation marks)
  - a joke (because of the mixture of large and small print).
- Identify the text as a poem. ***Why doesn't this text seem like a poem?*** Answer: it uses everyday, straightforward language, there is no set construction of lines/rhythm/rhyme.
- Point out the infinite variety of poetry. Explain that this poem is an example of free verse, which follows no pattern of rhyme or rhythm.
- ***Did you immediately know that this was a poem? How?*** Discussion should lead to the conclusion that the way you read helped them. Emphasise that poems are written to be spoken and listened to, not just read. Some poems, such as this one (which needs more than one voice), are specifically written for performance.
- ***How would you perform it? What do you notice about the size of the print for Andrew's part?*** Answer: it gets bigger every time he speaks. ***What about his final speech?*** Discuss the use of bold, large capital letters (and an exclamation mark) to denote deafening volume.
- Experiment with some readings, for example, splitting the class into four groups and two groups.

Independent, pair or guided work

- Ask the children to work on writing a second half to this poem.
- The poem could be a symmetrical half to match the first half, with Andrew's voice gradually growing quiet again.
- Brainstorm ideas within the group for the teacher's new lines, testing how they sound.

Plenary

- Share some of the vocabulary being used.
- Point out the need for helpful punctuation as well as print size.

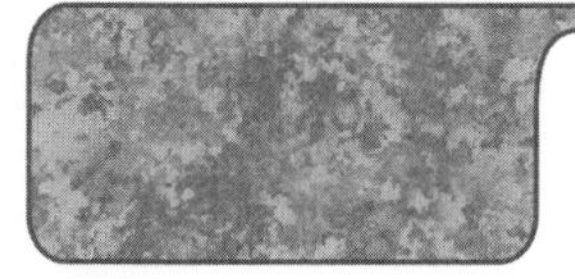

Language Features

Objective

We will identify the features of a selected performance poem and examine closely the poem's language

You need: Resource Page B, individual whiteboards.

Whole class work

- Introduce the poem *Genius* (Resource Page B), and read it aloud. ***What does the title mean? Is it another example of 'free verse'?*** Answer: no. Compared with *Louder!*, the children should be able to see differences in this poem.
- Direct the children to the important distinctions in rhythm and rhyme. Allow them time to read parts to each other – finding an established rhythm in lines 1-6, which changes to a new pattern in the middle of the poem. Help them to recognise some irregularity of the poem's rhythm, but stress that the movement is constant. Compare with the static prose of *Louder!*
- ***What is the rhyme pattern?*** Answer: mainly alternate line endings, but occasional deviations (lines 2-4, and end of poem). ***What do you notice about the rhymes?*** Answer: the rhymes (words that sound the same) are created by words that look the same, for example, 'genius', 'furious'. The title is part of this pattern.
- Look closely at sample lines, for example, 'I luv my rithmz 'n' the beatz.' Point out spelling idiosyncrasies and how an abbreviation is used to maintain a desired beat.
- Explain that spelling idiosyncrasies are part of the licence that poets frequently allow themselves in their use of language.
- ***Can you find an example of alliteration? Is repetition ever used effectively?*** Allow the children time to find a few examples:

syllable 'n' sound   a way with wurdz   My lirix make yer laugh

- Return to the title. ***What is the poet claiming to be a genius in?*** Answer: the use of language. ***Is the language spoken or written?*** Evidence is the use of the word 'oral' in line 2, with its reference to the spoken word.
- ***Why do you think the poet has mis-spelled easy words but correctly spelled difficult ones?*** There could be several answers here: to show he's 'cool' by breaking the rules only when he wants to; to show he's a 'genius' by correctly spelling the difficult ones; to make the 'wurdz' look like the lyrics from hip hop or rap music.

Independent, pair or guided work

- The children identify the words that link to the poet's boast of being a genius with words. They list them on their whiteboards and put the correct spelling beside them.
- Work out how this poem could make a choral performance.
- The children check the meaning of 'choral' in their dictionaries. Then they brainstorm how a choral performance is different from a dramatisation. (For children who struggle with this concept, ask them to imagine performing on radio.)

Plenary

- Discuss the findings and share some views on choral performance.

Linking Words

Objective

We will use a poem as a model for our own poetry writing

You need: Resource Pages B and C.

Whole class work

- Reread *Genius* (Resource Page B). Remind the children of its subject matter, their independent work on it previously, and the link between the words identified and the poem's theme.
- Now focus on the rhymes the writer has used. ***Is there a similar link between the meanings of all of these words and the poem's subject matter?*** Answer: no. For example, 'odorous' means producing a smell, which has nothing to do with being a gifted speaker.
- ***Why has the poet chosen these '-us' words?*** Exchange ideas, there being no 'correct' answer, but put forward the concept of choosing them at random because they end with the same digrapheme. ***What is the evidence for this?*** Answer: it is very hard to think of 20 or more words, ending in '-us', plus the poem is about language.
- Read out these two lines: 'I know I'm going on and on, But I certainly ain't MONOTONOUS'. Point out the link in meaning between 'monotonous' and 'going on and on'. Similarly, 'odorous' is fitted into the poem by the nearby word 'smell'.
- Work together, identifying further examples of places where seemingly irrelevant '-us' adjectives have been linked to the poem by another word.

'-us' adjective	Link
'devious'	'sneaky'
'miraculous'	'astounded'
'delirious'	'round 'n' round the bend'

- Emphasise that in this way the '-us' adjectives have been forced to fit the poem.
- Discuss with the children how they can write their own poems, using *Genius* as a model. The same basic concept could be retained (being brilliant at something), using the same format.
- Choose a popular ending for the rhymes, for example '-ble' or '-ful' and brainstorm a list (see Resource Page C for ideas).

Independent, pair or guided work

- The children decide what their poem will be about (for example, being a whizz with computers/being a sporting natural/having a flair for numbers).
- Choose rhyming words (about 15–20), perhaps finding some of their own.
- Decide on a title, for example, *Infallible!* or *Wonderful!*
- Begin to draft the lines.

Plenary

- Share ideas and some lines.
- Remind the children of how to link a possibly irrelevant word with the rest of the poem: for example, in a poem about number skills, 'endurable' can be made to fit by a mention of the 'long-lasting' effects of getting the right answer.

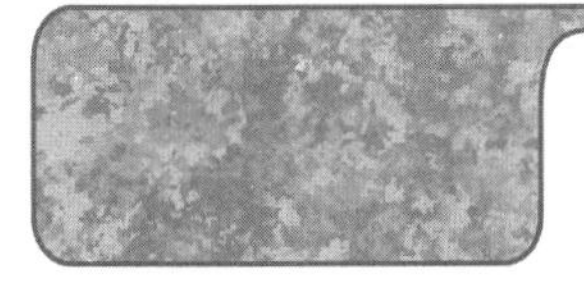

A Classic Poem

Objective

We will listen to older literature being read aloud and read an extract from a poem, then discuss differences in the language used

You need: Resource Pages D–F.

Whole class work

- Display the extract from *Macavity: The Mystery Cat* (Resource Page D). Read the poem to the class. ***Is this free verse? Why not?*** Answer: the set pattern of the poem prevents it from being free verse.
- Investigate the rhyming pattern: namely, rhyming couplets. Point out the complete regularity. Investigate the poem's rhythm, encouraging the children to tap out the beat as you read sample parts. ***Does background sound improve the oral presentation?***
- Point out the beat changes in line 3, as a new pattern is established. Consider whether verses are all the same length. ***Why do they always consist of an even number of lines?*** Answer: to maintain the pattern of rhyming couplets.
- Explain that this is a classic poem: that is, written by a well-known poet from the past that, although old, remains highly thought of. Point out that this is an extract from a poem (the other poems read have been complete).
- Ask if anyone has seen the musical *Cats*. Explain that it consists of poems by the same author set to music. This emphasises the 'performance' element to Macavity.
- Look closely at the language. ***Has the poet used effective language techniques? Are there examples of alliteration?*** Answer: verse 4, line 2; verse 5, line 2.
- ***Is repetition used effectively?***
  - Verse 2: 'once and once again'
  - Verse 3: 'his eyes'; 'his brow'; 'his head'; 'his coat'
  - Verse 4: 'you may meet'; 'you may'.
- Discuss some of the difficult vocabulary: 'gravity'; 'fakir'; 'levitation'; 'depravity'; 'feline'. ***Does using polysyllabic words affect the way the poem is read or how the audience think about Macavity?***
- ***How could you add a new verse to this poem? What would you write about?*** Talk about the necessity of retaining the same style: rhyme pattern, rhythm, and type of punctuation, as well as keeping to the topic of an amazing cat, able to do anything and not get caught. Brainstorm ideas (see Resource Page E for starting points).

Independent, pair or guided work

- Ask the children to plan a new verse of about 8 lines.
- Work on an early draft.

Plenary

- Listen to ideas and offer help and suggestions.
- Compile a class checklist for writing in a particular style (see Resource Page F for ideas).

Pupil copymaster

Louder!

OK, Andrew, nice and clearly – off you go.

Welcome everybody to our school concert ...

Louder, please, Andrew. Mums and dads won't hear you at the back, will they?

Welcome everybody to our school concert...

Louder, Andrew. You're not trying.
Pro – ject – your – voice.
Take a b i g b r e a t h and louder!

Welcome everybody to our school concert...

For goodness sake, Andrew. LOUDER! LOUDER!

Welcome every
body to our
school concert!

Now, Andrew, there's no need to be silly.

Roger Stevens

Pupil copymaster

Genius

I am a liric maniac
An Urban Oral GENIUS
My style iz fast 'n' FURIOUS
My manna iz SPONTANEOUS
My lirix make yer laugh sometimes
As well as bein' SERIOUS
I'll send yer round 'n' round the bend
I'll make yer act DELERIOUS
Each word is hot, and can't be held
I suppose you'd say I'm DANGEROUS
I know I have a way with wurdz
The wurd I'd use iz NOTORIOUS
For those who want to challenge me
I find it quite RIDICULOUS
When critics try and put me down
Can't see them. They're ANONYMOUS
The only thing I have ter say
I see them all as ODIOUS
I luv my rithmz 'n' the beatz
Smell my wurdz, they're ODOROUS
I love my lirix to the max
Evry syllable 'n' sound iz MARVELLOUS
I execute my wurdz so well
I suppose you'd call it MURDEROUS
To work so hard on all these wurdz
Some say it is LABORIOUS
There's double meaning in my style
Four syllables ter you. AM … BIG … U … OUS
I know I'm going on and on
But I certainly ain't MONOTONOUS
You have ter chill 'n' agree with me
The feeling is UNANIMOUS
Ter get inside yer head like this
I know that I am DEVIOUS
I do it in a sneaky way
I suppose I'd say MISCHEVIOUS
When pepul think about my rimez,
I know that they are CURIOUS
Don't understand the resun why
Becuze the cluez R OBVIOUS
Okay you're right, my wurdz 'R' good
I suppose they are MIRACULOUS
Astounded by this type of rime
I know you 'R' OBLIVIOUS
There'z only one thing left ter say
I'm bad 'n' cool
'N' INFAMOUS.

Martin Glynn

Pupil copymaster

Words rhyming with '-ble'

Horrible; terrible; laughable; sensible; contemptible; regrettable; fallible; infallible; reliable; inflatable; washable; curable; pliable; potable; edible; audible; breakable; (in)flammable; gullible; noticeable; manageable; portable; excitable; tangible; (il)legible; traceable

Pupil copymaster

An extract from *Macavity: The Mystery Cat*

Macavity's a Mystery Cat: he's called the Hidden Paw –
For he's the master criminal who can defy the Law.
He's the bafflement of Scotland Yard, the Flying Squad's despair:
For when they reach the scene of crime – *Macavity's not there!*

Macavity, Macavity, there's no one like Macavity,
He's broken every human law, he breaks the law of gravity.
His powers of levitation would make a fakir stare,
And when you reach the scene of crime – *Macavity's not there!*
You may seek him in the basement, you may look up in the air –
But I tell you once and once again, *Macavity's not there!*

Macavity's a ginger cat, he's very tall and thin;
You would know him if you saw him, for his eyes are sunken in.
His brow is deeply lined with thought, his head is highly domed;
His coat is dusty from neglect, his whiskers are uncombed.
He sways his head from side to side, with movements like a snake;
And when you think he's half asleep, he's always wide awake.

Macavity, Macavity, there's no one like Macavity,
For he's a fiend in feline shape, a monster of depravity.
You may meet him in a by-street, you may see him in the square –
But when a crime's discovered, then *Macavity's not there!*

He's outwardly respectable. (They say he cheats at cards.)
And his footprints are not found in any file of Scotland Yard's.
And when the larder's looted, or the jewel-case is rifled,
Or when the milk is missing, or another Peke's been stifled,
Or the greenhouse glass is broken, and the trellis past repair –
Ay, there's the wonder of the thing! *Macavity's not there!*

Thomas Stearns Eliot (1888–1965)

Exemplar material

Modelled writing

And when the rich and famous find their jewels have gone astray,

____ on his way,

And when the Cabinet Minister finds his document leaked today,

or ______________________________________ sent astray,

And when the King discovers that his crown has gone astray, or

the Queen ______________________________________

Macavity's no common cat, who delights in idle play, __________

____ each day,

Macavity has wondrous powers, the like you've never seen, ______

____ has been,

Macavity is always scheming, his brain a fearsome force, _______

____ of course,

Themes

Tricking of rich and powerful

Mysterious moving of objects/documents/maps from one place to another

Details of his background - countries/cities he has been

Comparisons to clever/heroic figures of the past: Plato, Socrates, Napoleon, Nelson

Exemplar material

Checklists for performance poetry

Example of a checklist for writing an additional verse in the same style

- Choose a theme that matches or extends rest of poem
- Use correct rhythm pattern
- Ensure that rhymes make sense
- Use an effective choice of words
- Use language techniques
- Use helpful punctuation and font
- Consider sounds of words

Example of a checklist for a choral performance of a poem

- Ensure clarity
- Use expression and feeling
- Use a balance of voices
- Use correct rhythm
- Use appropriate pace
- Use background sound/sound effects
- Include variation in delivery
- Consider volume – not necessarily constant
- Use appropriate tone of voice – to fit meaning

Marking ladder

Marking ladder for writing an additional verse

Name: ____________________

Pupil	Objective	Teacher
	My verse fits in with the rest of the poem.	
	I used correct rhyme pattern.	
	My rhymes make sense.	
	I used an appropriate rhythm pattern.	
	I used an effective choice of words.	
	I used language techniques.	
	I used helpful punctuation and font size.	
	I considered sounds of words.	
	What could I do to improve my poetry writing next time?	

Marking ladder

Marking ladder for a choral performance

Name: ______________________________

Pupil	Objective	Teacher
	I gave a clear delivery.	
	I used a good balance of voices.	
	I used feeling and expression.	
	I used the correct rhythm.	
	I considered volume.	
	I used the right speed.	
	My tone of voice suited the words' meaning.	
	There was variety in the delivery.	
	I considered background sound/sound effects.	
	What could I do to improve my performance next time?	

Word- and sentence-level starter activities

Pluralisation

- Have a quick brainstorming session of sample singular nouns, keeping to ones with '-s'/'-es' plurals. Give the children whiteboards or cards with 's' and 'es' on them. Point to a displayed word: ***Does this have an 's' plural or an 'es' plural?*** The children hold up the chosen card or write the answer on their whiteboards.

Give me more of ...

- A variation of the game above. Point to a singular word on display, and check the children's whiteboard answers. Ask them to work in groups: allow two minutes to come up with two rules for pluralisation. Check and repeat.

Spot the errors

- Use an error-strewn passage of text (example given below). ***Can you list 13 corrected spellings? Be ready to justify your correction with a rule.***

  'The photoes shook on the pianoes and the crys and barks and howls were heard. The babeys and puppeys played at the partys: they ate the jellys and pitzas, loafs and all the lunchs, while the oxes were out in the daireys, and the deers were dreaming of dishs.'

Who's the teacher?

- Allow short sessions for the children to test a partner on words in their spelling log, or other words. They then swap roles. Let them devise ways of testing one another, for example: 'Write the word that is the 't' 'which'. Answer: 'witch'. Remember 'together' is out to 'get' you! ***Have you taught and learned five words today?***

I'm a Dalek

- Speak robotically for division into syllables. For example, 'I be/lieve in a/li/ens. Do you be/lieve? Are you an ... a/li/en? Do you ... be/lieve?' Point to a child for them to write up the word correctly. Celebrate correct spellings. Continue for two- and three-syllable words related to literacy texts or other curriculum areas, for example, 'mon/ster'; 'hap/py'; 'pers/on'; 'treas/ure'; 'com/put/er'.

String them together

- Use similar/awkward/confusing letter strings, for example, 'uff', 'ough', 'ought', and ask 'mystery word' questions. Provide clues, for example, 'The opposite of smooth.' The children display the answer: 'rough'. Let the children play in groups, with one of them acting as quizmaster. Continue with a prefix such as 'dis-', or a suffix such as '-al-. Maintain a snappy pace.

Taking it literally

- Talk about idiomatic expressions with the class. Display quick sketches in the style of *Catchphrase*, for example, 'A man under snow, rain or sun. What's the expression?' Answer: 'under the weather'. Select ones the children are likely to know. Teach some new idioms and ask the children to match them to a picture. Encourage them to try to catch one another out with their own drawings on white boards. Use dictionaries: ***Can you identify origins of the idioms?***

Breaking the rule

- Provide a list of words. Ask the children to (i) identify a spelling rule (ii) think of an exception. Examples: 'believe', 'sieve', 'grieve' but 'receive'; 'laziness', 'heaviness', 'happiness' but 'dryness'; 'breakable', 'laughable', 'irritable' but 'changeable'.

I Spy

- Play 'I Spy' focusing on a recently met sound or letter string. The clue must have the first letter and one other numbered letter, for example, "I spy ... something beginning with 'p', and the third letter is 'o'." Make constant rule changes to the clue, for example, stating the first letter and last two, the initial letter and the last letter, the initial letter and the number of syllables, and so on.

Snakes and Ladders Scrabble

- In this game the children have to convert a start word at the top of a 'ladder' into a finish word at the bottom, but they are only allowed to change one letter at a time. Every rung of the ladder must be a real word. Work as a class for some, moving on to small groups. ***Who can use the fewest rungs of the ladder?*** For example: 'late' → 'fate' → 'fare' → 'farm' → 'harm' = 5 rungs; 'hint' → 'tint' → 'tilt' → 'till' 'tell' → 'sell' = 6 rungs. Other possibilities: 'ring' → 'barn'; 'pray' → 'tear'; 'reach' → 'lunch'; 'lane' → 'some'; 'wait' → 'pine'.

Building blocks

- ***Who is in on the act?*** Give pairs of children the two-minute challenge of writing as many words as they can containing 'act', for example, 'react'; 'actor'; 'activate'; 'activity'; 'action'; 'reaction'. Repeat the process with other simple words that appear in other words, for example: 'do'; 'take'; 'hand'; 'hero'; 'call'. ***Are any spelling rules coming into play?*** (for example, 'take' in 'overtaking'). Encourage the use of dictionaries.

Looking the part

- Supply a list of adverbs linked to a manner of speaking or acting, for example, 'timidly'; 'nervously'; 'excitedly'; 'furiously'; 'boldly'; 'confidently'; 'sulkily'. Ask the children to write an accompanying verb on their whiteboards. Challenge the children to produce sketches on their whiteboards of likely people to fit verb and adverb (for example, a picture of a football team manager who bellows furiously into the face of the player who has just missed a penalty). Can others guess which verb/adverb is shown?

Sounding the part

- This uses the list of adverbs in a similar way to the activity above. The children must give you an appropriate sentence in the appropriate voice and an appropriate pose. The children can then use thesauruses to find synonyms for adverbs. Award a score for the most apt.

Simply similar

- Ask for three or four quick synonyms for everyday adjectives, for example, 'happy'; 'easy'; 'small'; 'quick'; 'large'; 'angry'. Write the words suggested on the board, and ask the children to order them alphabetically. Debate differences of opinion, encouraging the children to use dictionaries for their final verdict. Set team challenges, for example: 'Find three synonyms to fit here: "The time was awkward for me." "Her expression was miserable." "The new gallery was magnificent." "She had a competitive attitude to everything." "The jewellery was exquisite."' Ask each team to display its results. Which word do they think is most appropriate? Why? Make sure that the children are learning to identify shades of meaning.

Lost my letter?

- Brainstorm words ending in a vowel. Look for common connections in meaning: for example, music, food, other languages, animals and so on. Ask the children (in pairs or small teams) to group the words, using dictionaries and reference books. What can they find out? Are some letter endings common to a particular subject/language?

One a day

- Focus on prefixes, working with one of these daily: 'auto-' (self); 'tele-' (distant); 'trans-' (across); 'bi-' (two/twice); 'circum-' (about/round). ***How many words with the prefix can you think of in two minutes? What does the prefix mean?*** Set team challenges, such as extending the list of words (dictionaries and textbooks such as Science/Maths will help), or asking if the children know words from another language using this prefix (there has got to be a link in meaning). Compare team results. Award points and keep a running total for the week.

Root causes

- Supply a simple verb, for example, 'act'. Ask the children for a word derived from it. Reverse the process: for example, supply the word 'approval' for the children to identify the root 'prove'. Point out typical spelling patterns, for example, -pp-.

Marking ladder

Name: ______________________

Pupil	Objective	Teacher
	What could I do to improve my work next time?	

AA

Complete Test

Practical, Theory Test and The Highway Code for car drivers

AA Publishing

Produced by AA Publishing.

First edition published 2005, reprinted 2005
Second edition with revised questions published August 2005
Third edition with revised questions published 2006
Reprinted 2006
Fourth edition with revised questions published 2007
Fifth edition with updated Highway Code published 2007

ISBN: 978-0-7495-5616-7

Published by AA Publishing (a trading name of Automobile Association Developments Limited, whose registered office is Fanum House, Basing View, Basingstoke, Hampshire RG21 4EA; registered number 1878835). A3395

Visit the AA website ***www.theAA.com***

Colour separation by Keene Group, Andover
Printed in Italy by Printer Trento

Visit **www.highwaycode.gov.uk** for all the latest information on *The Highway Code*

While every effort has been made to include the widest possible range of questions available at the time of printing, the Government may from time to time change, add or remove questions, and the publisher cannot be held responsible for questions that may appear on a question paper which were not available for inclusion in this book.

Contents

Introduction

You want to pass the driving test and take advantage of the freedom and mobility that driving a car can give you. Do the following three things and you will achieve your goal of passing the driving test.

Acquire **knowledge** of the rules through your instructor and by studying *The Highway Code*. A key element is to test and reinforce your knowledge.

Take the right **attitude**. Be careful, courteous and considerate to all other road users.

Learn and understand the **skills** of driving by taking lessons from a trained and fully qualified driving instructor.

We're here to help you become a careful and safe driver and we've designed this book to help you take the first steps towards achieving your goal – preparing for your **Theory Test**.

Six essential steps to getting your licence

1. Get your Provisional licence

You can apply online for your provisional licence at www.direct.gov.uk/motoring or use form D1, available from any Post Office. The driving licence is issued in the form of a two-part document: a photo card and paper counterpart. So that you can legally begin learning to drive, at the appropriate date, you must be in possession of the correct licence documents. Take care when completing all the forms. Many licences cannot be issued for the required date because of errors or omissions on the application forms. You will have to provide proof of identity such as a current UK passport; make sure you have all the documents needed.

2. Learn *The Highway Code*

The Highway Code is essential reading for all drivers, not just those learning to drive. It sets out all the rules for good driving, as well as the rules for other road users such as pedestrians and motorcycle riders. When you have learned the rules you will be able to answer most of the questions in the Theory Test and be ready to start learning the driving skills you will need to pass your Practical Test.

3. Apply for and take the Theory Test

The driving test is in two parts: the Theory Test and the Practical Test.

Once you have a valid provisional licence you may take the Theory Test at any time, but you must pass it before you are allowed to apply for the Practical Test. However, it is important that you should not take your Theory Test too early in your course of practical lessons. This is because you need the experience of meeting real hazards while you are learning to drive, to help you pass the Hazard Perception element of the Theory Test.

You can book your Theory Test by post, by phone or online. Visa, MasterCard, Delta, Visa Electron, Switch/Maestro and Solo cards are all accepted. Application forms are available from test centres, Approved Driving Instructors or by calling the booking number below. Forms need to be sent with a cheque, postal order or credit

or debit card details.
By Post DSA (Driving Standards Agency), Booking Department, PO Box 381, Manchester M50 3UW
By Phone 0870 0101 372
Online www.dsa.gov.uk

4. Start to learn to drive

We recommended that you learn with an Approved Driving Instructor (ADI). Only an ADI may legally charge for providing tuition.

Choose an instructor or driving school by asking friends or relatives who they recommend. Price is important, so find out whether the school offers any discounts for blocks or courses of lessons paid in advance; if you decide to pay in advance, make sure the driving school is reputable. If lesson prices are very low, ask yourself 'why?' Check how long the lesson will last. And don't forget to ask about the car you'll be learning to drive in. Is it modern and reliable? Is it insured? Does it have dual controls?

The most efficient and cost-effective way to learn to drive is to accept that there is no short-cut approach to learning the necessary skills. Agree with your instructor on a planned course of tuition suited to your needs, take regular lessons, and don't skip weeks and expect to pick up where you left off. Ensure the full official syllabus is covered and, as your skills develop, get as much practice as possible with a relative or friend – but make sure they are legally able to supervise your practice. They must be over 21 years of age and have held a full driving licence for at least three years.

5. Apply for and take the Practical Test

Once you have passed the Theory Test, and with your instructor's guidance based on your progress, you can plan ahead for a suitable test date for the Practical Test.

You can book your Test by calling 0870 0101 372 between 8am and 6pm Monday to Friday. You can pay for your test using a credit or debit card. The person who books the test must be the cardholder. You can change your practical test appointment by calling the same number or at www.direct.gov.uk/motoring.

Make sure you have the following details to hand when booking your Practical Test.

- Theory Test pass certificate number
- driver number shown on your licence
- driving school code number (if known)
- your preferred date
- unacceptable days or periods
- if you can accept a test at short notice
- details of any disability or any special circumstances
- your credit/debit card details

Saturday and weekday evening tests are available at some driving test centres. The fee is higher than for a driving test during normal working hours on weekdays and evening tests are available during the summer months only.

Telephone bookings and enquiries
0870 0101 372

Facsimile
0870 0102 372

Welsh speakers
0870 0100 372

Minicom
0870 0107 372

6. Apply for your full driver's licence

To obtain a full licence you need to send your Pass Certificate and your provisional licence to the DVLA in Swansea, within two years of passing your Practical Test.

After the Practical Test

The Driving Standards Agency and the insurance industry recognise and seek to reward those drivers who enhance their basic skills and widen their experience by taking further training in the form of the Pass Plus scheme.

This is a six-module syllabus which covers town and rural driving, night driving, driving in adverse weather conditions, and on dual carriageways and motorways. It offers you the opportunity to gain more driving experience with the help of an instructor to hand. An increasing number of insurance companies are prepared to offer discounts to new drivers who have completed the course. There is no test to take at the end of the course.

More information

For more practical information on learning to drive including the Theory Test, Hazard Perception and the Practical Test visit www.theAA.com and www.dsa.gov.uk
For information on the Pass Plus scheme visit www.passplus.org.uk

How to use this book

This book is arranged in seven sections.

Part 1 explains what to expect and how to prepare for each part of the Test: Theory, Hazard Perception and Practical.

This section explains how to take the Theory Test using a touch-screen computer and gives details of the video clips used in the Hazard Perception part of the test. In the Practical section we have included information about the Driver's Record which your instructor will complete after each lesson.

We tell you what to expect on the day you take your test, details of the documents you must have with you, and tell you what the examiner will be looking for in your general driving.

We have also included information on the new Vehicle Safety Check questions which now form part of the Practical Test.

Part 2 contains questions and answers for learner drivers set by the experts at the AA driving school as an aid to help you pass your Practical Test. They are designed to test your knowledge of what is required before you even sit in the driver's seat. Topics include parallel parking, reversing and motorway driving.

Part 3 is designed to help you understand each of the 14 topics in the Theory Test. This section will tell you what type of questions you can expect in each section and we've included lots of helpful tips. Each topic is colour coded to its

Learn to drive in a modern car with a reputable driving school

relevant section in Part 4 of this book, which contains all the official Theory Questions. Experience has taught us that learner drivers find particular questions difficult and are often confused when they see questions which are similar. Reading through the background to each topic, before looking at the questions, will help you to avoid the pitfalls and help you to group questions together as you will often find several questions are asking the same thing but in a slightly different way.

Part 4 contains all the official Theory Test questions for car drivers which appear in the question bank of the DSA. You could be tested on any of these questions when you take your touch-screen Theory Test.

The questions are arranged in topics, such as Safety Margins and Rules of the Road. Each theme has its own colour band to help you find your way around. However, as you start to work through the questions you will soon discover that similar questions on the same topic may appear in different sections. Don't be put off by this, but read each question and the choice of answers very carefully. Similar questions may be asked in a slightly different way to test your knowledge.

Most of the Theory Test questions can be answered if you learn *The Highway Code*. However, you will only find the answers to some questions by talking to your driving instructor and learning about good driving practice on the road.

You'll find all the correct answers to the Theory Test questions in Part 6 at the back of the book, that way, you can easily test yourself to see what you are getting right and what you still need to work on.

Part 5 is a short glossary, which explains some of the more difficult words and terms used in the theory questions and *The Highway Code*. It's in alphabetical order and you can use this to check if you're not sure what a chicane is, for example, or what brake fade means.

Part 6 has all the answers to the Theory Test questions.

Part 7 contains *The Highway Code* with its own index.

Part 1
The Tests: What to Expect

You have to pass two driving tests before you can apply for a full driving licence – the Theory Test, including Hazard Perception, and the Practical Test. The Theory Test was introduced in 1996 to check that drivers know more than just how to operate a car, and the Hazard Perception element was introduced in 2001 to test learner drivers on their hazard awareness skills.

You are strongly recommended to prepare for the Theory Test and Hazard Perception at the same time as you develop your skills behind the wheel for the Practical Test. Obviously, there are many similarities between the two tests and you need the experience of meeting real hazards in order to pass the Hazard Perception element of the Theory Test.

It is all about making you a safer driver on today's busy roads. By preparing for both tests at the same time, you will reinforce your knowledge and understanding of all aspects of driving and you will improve your chances of passing both tests first time.

The Practical Test was extended in September 2003 to include Vehicle Safety Check questions that test the driver's ability to carry out basic procedures to ensure that the vehicle is safe to drive. Checks include the tyre tread and oil level.

You have to pass both the Hazard Perception test and the Theory Test questions. At the end of the test they will tell you your scores for both parts. Even if you only failed on one part of the Theory Test, you still have to take both parts again next time.

What to expect in the multiple-choice test

You will have 40 minutes to complete the questions in the test, using a touch-screen to select your answers. The test is a set of 35 questions drawn from a bank of almost 1,000, all of which have multiple-choice answers. In order to pass the test you must answer a minimum of 30 questions correctly within the given time. The Government may change the pass mark from time to time. Your driving school or the DSA will be able to tell you if there has been a change. The questions appear on the screen one at a time and you can return to any of the questions within the 40 minutes to re-check or alter your answers. The system will prompt you to return to any questions you have not answered fully.

Preparing for the Theory Test

Read and get to know *The Highway Code*. You'll find that many of the theory questions relate directly to it. Look at the list of Theory Test topics, then read through the topic summary. Now turn to the section containing the questions. Read through the questions and tick your choice of answer(s). Now check your answer(s) against those at the back of the book. If you don't understand the answer(s), look up the subject in *The Highway Code* or take a note of the question and discuss it with your instructor.

Questions marked with an **NI** symbol are those NOT found in Theory Test papers in Northern Ireland.

Remember

- Don't try too many questions at once.
- Don't try to learn the answers by heart.
- The order of the questions in this book may be different from how they are arranged in the test – so don't try to memorise the order.

How to answer the questions

Each question has four, five or six possible answers. You must mark the boxes with the correct answer(s). Each question tells you how many answers to mark.

Study each question carefully, making sure you understand what it is asking you. Look carefully at any diagram, drawing or photograph. Before you look at the answers given, decide what you think the correct answer(s) might be. You can then select the answer(s) that matches the one you had decided on. If you follow this system, you will avoid being confused by answers that appear to be similar.

What to expect in the Hazard Perception Test

After a break of up to three minutes you will begin the Hazard Perception part of the test.

The Hazard Perception test lasts for about 20 minutes. Before you start you will be given some instructions explaining how the test works; you'll also get a chance to practise with the computer and mouse before you start. Next you will see 14 film or video clips of real street scenes with traffic such as cars, pedestrians, cyclists etc. The scenes are shot from the point of view of a driver in a car. You have to notice potential hazards that are developing on the road ahead – that is, problems that could lead to an accident. As soon as you notice a hazard developing, click the mouse. You will have plenty of time to see

Left: Real road scenes feature in the video clips in the Hazard Perception test
Above: Click the mouse when you spot potential hazards – the pedestrian crossing the side road and the cyclist approaching a parked vehicle (ringed in yellow). Click again as the hazard develops when the cyclist (ringed in red) moves out to overtake the parked vehicle.

the hazard – but the sooner you notice it, the more marks you score.

Each clip has at least one hazard in it – some clips may have more than one hazard. You currently have to score a minimum of 44 out of 75 to pass, but the pass mark may change so check with your instructor or the DSA before sitting your test. (Note that the computer has checks built in to show anyone trying to cheat – for example someone who keeps clicking the mouse all the time.) Be aware that, unlike the Theory Test questions, you will not have an opportunity to go back to an earlier clip and change your response, so you need to concentrate throughout the test.

Preparing for the Hazard Perception Test

Who do you think have the most accidents – new or experienced drivers? New drivers have just had lessons, so they should remember how to drive safely, but in fact new drivers have the most accidents.

Learner drivers need training in how to spot hazards because they are often so busy thinking about the car's controls that they forget to watch the road and traffic – and losing concentration for even a second could prove fatal to you or another road user. Proper training can help you to recognise more of the hazards that you will meet when driving and to spot those hazards earlier so you are less likely to have an accident. Your driving instructor has been trained to help you learn hazard perception skills and can give you plenty of practice in what to look out for when driving, how to anticipate hazards, and what action to take to deal with hazards of all kinds.

You won't be able to practise with the real video clips used in the test, of course, but training books and practice videos and DVDs are available.

What to expect in the Practical Test

Once you have passed both parts of your Theory Test, you can apply for the Practical Test. The Practical Test is all about making sure that those who pass are competent and safe in the basic skills of driving.

The requirements for passing your test are a combination of practical skills and mental understanding. The open road can be a risky environment, and your test result will show whether you're ready to go out there alone or whether you need a little more practice first.

You'll be asked to sign a declaration that the insurance of your car is in order. Without this, the test can't proceed.

The paperwork

You'll need to have with you:

- your signed provisional driving licence (both parts if you've got a photo licence). If your licence doesn't have a photo you'll need additional photographic identity (ID) Acceptable ID, such as a current passport, must have your photograph and signature. See the DSA website for an up-to-date list of acceptable photo ID.
- your Theory Test pass certificate
- your appointment letter
- your completed Driver's Record (if you have one) signed by your instructor

Eyesight test

Your driving test begins with an eyesight test. You have to be able to read a normal number plate at a minimum distance of 20.5 metres (about 67.5 feet). If you fail the eyesight test your driving test will stop at that point and you will have failed.

Vehicle safety checks

You will have to answer two vehicle safety check questions. The questions fall into three categories:

- identify
- tell me how you would check...
- show me how you would check...

These questions are designed to make sure that you know how to check that your vehicle is safe to drive.

If you turn up for your test in an unsuitable vehicle, you will forfeit your test fee.

Although some checks may require you to identify where fluid levels should be checked you will not be asked to touch a hot engine or physically check fluid levels. You may refer to vehicle information systems (if fitted) when answering questions on fluid levels and tyre pressures.

All vehicles differ slightly so it is important that you get to know all the safety systems and engine layout in the vehicle in which you plan to take your practical test.

Don't worry about making a few mistakes. You can still pass your test as long as the mistakes are only minor driving faults.

The Driving Test

During the test you will be expected to drive for about 40 minutes along normal roads following the directions of the examiner. The roads are selected so as to provide a range of different conditions and road situations and a varied density of traffic.

Your examiner will select suitable areas for you to carry out the set exercises. He or she will tell you to pull up and stop, and will then explain the exercise to you before you do it:

- you *may* or *may not* be asked to perform an emergency stop
- you *will* be asked to perform two reversing exercises selected by the examiner from:
  reversing round a corner;
  reverse parking (behind a parked car, or into a marked bay);
  turning in the road

Driving test standards are monitored so that whatever examiner you get, or whatever test centre you go to, you should get the same result. You might find a senior officer in the car as well as the examiner; he or she is not watching you, but checking that the examiner is doing his or her job properly.

Throughout the test, the examiner will be assessing:

- whether you are competent at controlling the car
- whether you are making normal progress for the roads you are on
- how you react to any hazards that occur in the course of the test
- whether you are noticing all traffic signs and signals and road markings, and reacting to them in the correct manner.

In order to pass the driving test, you must

- not commit any serious fault and
- commit fewer than 15 driving errors of a less serious nature

If, during the test, you do not understand what the examiner says to you, ask him or her to repeat the instruction.

If you are faced with an unusually difficult or hazardous situation in the course of your test that results in you making a driving fault, the examiner will take the circumstances into account when marking you for that part of the test.

How to prepare for the Practical Test

Be sure that you are ready to take the test. This is where choosing a reliable qualified driving instructor is vital.

You should feel confident:

- about driving in all conditions
- that you know *The Highway Code*

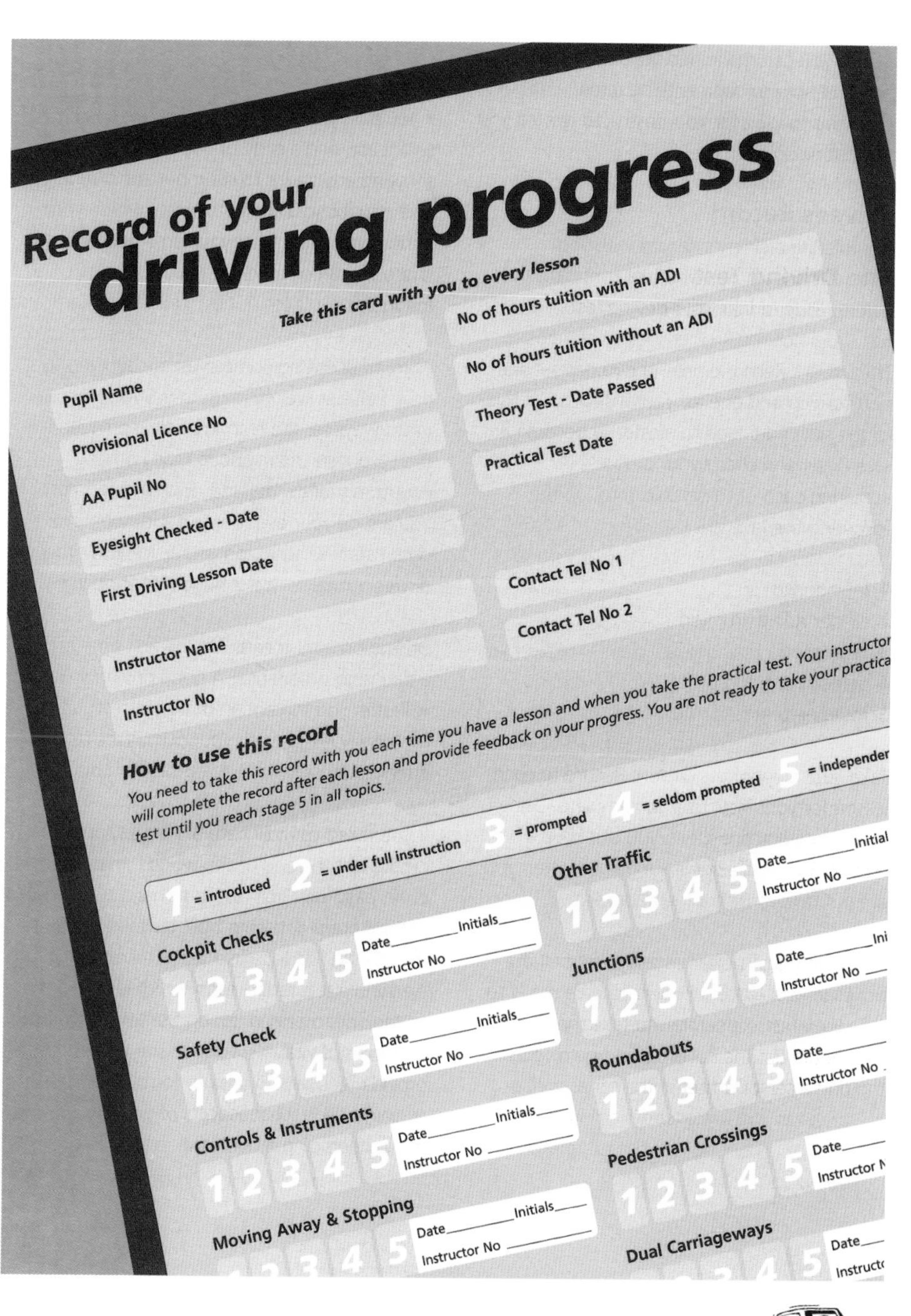

Record of your
driving progress

Take this card with you to every lesson

Pupil Name

Provisional Licence No

AA Pupil No

Eyesight Checked - Date

First Driving Lesson Date

Instructor Name

Instructor No

No of hours tuition with an ADI

No of hours tuition without an ADI

Theory Test - Date Passed

Practical Test Date

Contact Tel No 1

Contact Tel No 2

How to use this record

You need to take this record with you each time you have a lesson and when you take the practical test. Your instructor will complete the record after each lesson and provide feedback on your progress. You are not ready to take your practica test until you reach stage 5 in all topics.

1 = introduced 2 = under full instruction 3 = prompted 4 = seldom prompted 5 = independen

Cockpit Checks
1 2 3 4 5 Date________ Initials____ Instructor No ________

Safety Check
1 2 3 4 5 Date________ Initials____ Instructor No ________

Controls & Instruments
1 2 3 4 5 Date________ Initials____ Instructor No ________

Moving Away & Stopping
1 2 3 4 5 Date________ Initials____ Instructor No ________

Other Traffic
1 2 3 4 5 Date________ Initial Instructor No ____

Junctions
1 2 3 4 5 Date________ Ini Instructor No ____

Roundabouts
1 2 3 4 5 Date________ Instructor No

Pedestrian Crossings
1 2 3 4 5 Date________ Instructor N

Dual Carriageways
1 2 3 4 5 Date____ Instruct

- that you can make decisions on your own about how to cope with hazards, without having to wait for your instructor to tell you what to do.

Driver's Record

Completing a Driver's Record with your instructor should help you feel confident that you're ready to take your driving test.

The Driver's Record comes in two parts – one part for you and one for your instructor. It lists all the skills you need to master to become a safe driver and charts your progress in acquiring each of these skills through the following five levels:

1 Introduced
2 Under full instruction
3 Prompted
4 Seldom prompted
5 Independent

Take your copy of the Driver's Record to each lesson for your instructor to complete. Using the Private Practice sheet, you can keep a record of driving experience gained when you are out driving with a friend or relative.

When your instructor has completed all the boxes in your Driver's Record you are ready to take your test. Remember to take the completed Driver's Record along with you to the driving test centre.

After the Test

If you pass your test you'll be given a pass certificate, and a copy of the examiner's report showing any minor faults you made during your test. You'll find it useful to know where your weaknesses lie, so that you can concentrate on improving those aspects of your driving in the future.

With a full driving licence you are allowed to drive vehicles weighing up to 3.5 tonnes, use motorways for the first time, drive anywhere in the European Union and in many other countries worldwide, and tow a small trailer. You are on your own dealing with whatever circumstances arise: fog, snow, ice and other drivers' mistakes. It is a huge responsibility.

Driving on a motorway for the first time can be a daunting experience. A good driving school will offer you the option of a post-test motorway lesson with your own instructor, and it makes sense to take advantage of this.

If you failed you will naturally be disappointed, but it's not the end of the world – many people don't pass their first test, but then sail through a second or third, having built on the experience of what it's like to take a test. The examiner will give you a test report form which is a record of all the skills assessed during the test, identifying any areas of weakness. He or she will also provide feedback in spoken form, and will explain to you what aspects of your driving are still in need of improvement.

Part 2
The Practical Test Questions and Answers

The Practical Test

Section 1

Section 2

Section 3

Section 4

Section 5

Section 6

Section 7

Section 8

Section 9

Section 10

Section 11

Section 12

Section 13

Section 14

Section 15

Section 16

Section 17

Good defensive driving depends on adopting the right attitude from the start. These questions will test your knowledge of what is required before you even sit in the driver's seat.

1

What do you need before you can drive on a public road?

Fill in the missing words

P_ _ _ _ _ _ _ _ _ _

_ _ _ _ _ _ _

2

The best way to learn is to have regular planned tuition with an ADI (Approved Driving Instructor).

An ADI is someone who has taken and passed all three driving instructor's e _ _ _ _ _ _ _ _ _ _ _ and is on the official r_ _ _ _ _ _ _

Complete the sentence

Answers on page 92

HINTS & TIPS

A fully qualified ADI should display a green certificate on the windscreen of their car. Ask to see it.

3

Anyone supervising a learner must be at least _ _ years old and must have held (and still hold) a full driving licence (motor car) for at least t_ _ _ _ years

Complete the sentence

4

Your tuition vehicle must display L-plates. Where should they be placed?

Answer____________________

____

____

5

Young and inexperienced drivers are more vulnerable. Is this true or false?

Tick the correct box **True** ☐ **False** ☐

6

Showing responsibility to yourself and others is the key to being a safe driver. Ask yourself, would you ...

Tick the correct box

1 Want to drive with someone who has been drinking? **YES** ☐ **NO** ☐

2 Want to drive with someone who takes risks and puts other lives at risk? **YES** ☐ **NO** ☐

3 Want to drive with someone who does not concentrate? **YES** ☐ **NO** ☐

4 Want to drive with someone who drives too fast? **YES** ☐ **NO** ☐

7

Do you want to be a safe and responsible driver?

Tick the correct box **YES** ☐ **NO** ☐

8

You must pass a theory test before you can take the practical test. When would be the best time to sit this test?

Mark two answers

1 Before applying for a provisional licence ☐

2 Just before taking the practical test ☐

3 Some time during the early weeks of your driving lessons ☐

4 After full study of available training materials ☐

9

To use the controls safely you need to adopt a suitable driving position. There are a number of checks you should make.

Fill in the missing words

1 Check the h _ _ _ _ _ _ _ _ is on.

2 Check the d _ _ _ _ are shut.

3 Check your s _ _ _ is in the correct position.

4 Check the h _ _ _ r _ _ _ _ _ _ _ _ is adjusted to give maximum protection.

5 Check the driving m _ _ _ _ _ _ are adjusted to give maximum rear view.

6 Check your s _ _ _ b _ _ _ is securely fastened.

10

Here is a list of functions and a list of controls.

Match each function to its control by placing the appropriate letter in the box

THE FUNCTIONS	THE CONTROLS
A To control the direction in which you want to travel	☐ The handbrake
B To slow or stop the vehicle	☐ The driving mirrors
C To increase or decrease the engine's speed	☐ The gear lever
D To give you a clear view behind	☐ The clutch
E To hold the vehicle still when it is stationary	☐ The steering wheel
F To enable you to change gear	☐ The foot-brake
G To enable you to make or break contact between the engine and the wheels	☐ The accelerator

Fill in the missing word

The accelerator can also be called the g _ _ pedal

Answers on page 92

11

Which foot should you use for each of these controls (in cars with a manual gearbox)?

R = Right foot **L** = Left foot

The foot-brake ☐

The clutch ☐

The accelerator ☐

12

Are the following statements about steering true or false?

Tick the appropriate boxes	**True**	**False**
1 I must keep both hands on the wheel at all times.	☐	☐
2 To keep good control I should feed the wheel through my hands.	☐	☐
3 I can place my hands at any position as long as I am comfortable.	☐	☐
4 When going round corners, it is best to cross my hands (hand over hand).	☐	☐
5 I should never take both hands off the wheel when the vehicle is moving.	☐	☐
6 To straighten up I should feed the wheel back through my hands.	☐	☐

Answers on page 92

13

Match each of the following functions to its control.

THE FUNCTIONS	**THE CONTROLS**
A To enable you to see the road ahead and other road users to see you without causing dazzle	☐ The direction indicators
B To show other road users which way you intend to turn	☐ Dipped beam
C To use only when visibility is 100 metres/yards or less	☐ Main beam
D To enable you to see further, but not to be used when there is oncoming traffic	☐ Rear fog lamp
E To warn other road users of your presence	☐ Horn
F To warn other road users when you are temporarily obstructing traffic	☐ Hazard lights

1

The following is a list of actions involved in moving off from rest. Number the boxes 1 to 9 to show the correct sequence

The first box has been filled in to give you a start

[1] **A** Press the clutch down fully

[ ] **B** Check your mirrors

[ ] **C** Set the accelerator pedal

[ ] **D** Move the gear lever into 1st gear

[ ] **E** Decide whether you need to give a signal

[ ] **F** Let the clutch come to biting point and hold it steady

[ ] **G** Check your blind spot

[ ] **H** If safe, release the handbrake and let the clutch up a little more

[ ] **I** Press the accelerator pedal a little more and let the clutch up fully

Answers on page 93

2

The following is a list of actions required for stopping normally. Number the boxes 1 to 9 to show the correct sequence.

The first box has been filled in to give you a start

[1] **A** Check your mirrors

[ ] **B** Take your foot off the accelerator pedal

[ ] **C** Decide whether you need to signal and, if necessary, do so

[ ] **D** Press the brake pedal, lightly at first and then more firmly

[ ] **E** As the car stops, ease the pressure off the foot-brake (except when you are on a slope)

[ ] **F** Just before the car stops, press the clutch pedal right down

[ ] **G** Put the gear lever into neutral

[ ] **H** Apply the handbrake fully

[ ] **I** Take both feet off the pedals

Answers on page 93

Gears enable you to select the power you need from the engine to perform a particular task.

3

Which gear gives you the most power?

Answer ☐

1 3 5
2 4 R

4

If you were travelling at 60mph on a clear road, which gear would you most likely select?

Answer ☐

5

When approaching and turning a corner, as shown in the diagram, which gear would you most likely use?

Answer ☐

6

You need to change gear to match your e_ _ _ _ _ _ speed to the speed at which your v_ _ _ _ _ _ _ is travelling. The s_ _ _ _ _ the engine is making will help you know w_ _ _ _ to change gear.

Complete the sentences

7

Number the boxes to show the correct sequence of actions required when changing up.

The first box has been filled in for you

[1] **A** Place your left hand on the gear lever

☐ **B** Move the gear lever to the next highest position

☐ **C** Press the clutch pedal down fully and ease off the accelerator pedal

☐ **D** Let the clutch pedal come up fully and, at the same time, press the accelerator pedal

☐ **E** Put your left hand back on the steering wheel

Answers on page 93

8

Are the following statements about changing down true or false?

Tick the appropriate boxes

	True	False
1 I would stay in the highest gear as long as possible, even if my engine started to labour	☐	☐
2 I would change down early so that the engine helps to slow the car down	☐	☐
3 I would avoid using the foot-brake as much as possible	☐	☐
4 I would usually slow the car down by using the foot-brake first. Then, when I am at the required speed, I would change down to the appropriate gear	☐	☐
5 I would always change down through the gears so that I do not miss out any intermediate gears	☐	☐

Answers on page 94

HINTS & TIPS

In your driving test, you will be expected to show that you can control the car smoothly.
If you should stall, put the gears in neutral and the handbrake on, and start again.

9

When changing gear, I should look ...

1 Ahead ☐

2 At the gear lever ☐

3 At my feet ☐

Which is correct?

10

Do's and don'ts

Tick the appropriate boxes

	Do	Don't
1 Force the gear lever if there is any resistance	☐	☐
2 Rush the gear changes	☐	☐
3 Match your speed with the correct gear	☐	☐
4 Use the brakes, where necessary, to reduce speed before changing down	☐	☐
5 Listen to the sound of the engine	☐	☐
6 Take your eyes off the road when changing gear	☐	☐
7 Hold the gear lever longer than necessary	☐	☐
8 Coast with the clutch down or the gear lever in neutral	☐	☐

11

Which wheels turn when you turn the steering wheel?

A The front wheels

B The back wheels

Answer ☐

12

When you turn your steering wheel to the right, which way do your wheels turn?

A To the right

B To the left

Answer ☐

13

The steering lock is ...

A The locking mechanism that stops the steering wheel from moving when the ignition key is removed

B The angle through which the wheels turn when the steering wheel is turned

Answer ☐

14

Which wheels follow the shorter pathway?

A The front wheels

B The back wheels

Answer ☐

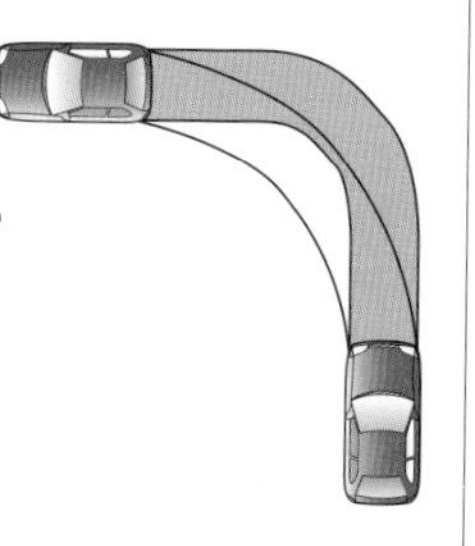

15

Which is the correct position for normal driving?

Put letter A, B or C in the box

Answer ☐

A B C

16

Which diagram shows the correct pathway when driving normally?

Put a letter A or B in the box

Answer ☐

A B

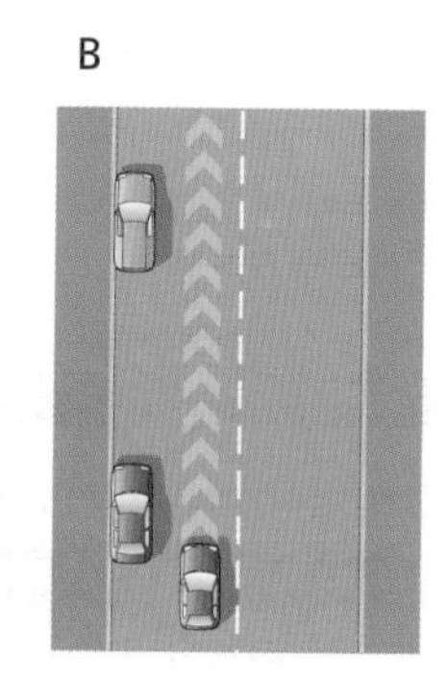

Answers on page 94

17

Pushing the clutch pedal down ...

A Releases the engine from the wheels

B Engages the engine with the wheels

Answer ☐

18

The point where the clutch plates meet is called the b__ __ __ __ __ point.

Fill in the missing word

19

By controlling the amount of contact between the clutch plates, it is possible to control the speed of the car.

Would you use this control ...

Tick the appropriate boxes	**True**	**False**
1 When moving away from rest?	☐	☐
2 When manoeuvring the car in reverse gear?	☐	☐
3 When slowing down to turn a corner?	☐	☐
4 In very slow moving traffic?	☐	☐
5 To slow the car down?	☐	☐

HINTS & TIPS

Remember:
MSM stands for Mirror, Signal, Manoeuvre. Always use this routine when moving off, turning or overtaking.

Answers on page 94

1

A junction is a point where t__ __ o__ m__ __ __ r__ __ __ __ meet.

Complete the sentence

2

Here are five types of junction. Name them

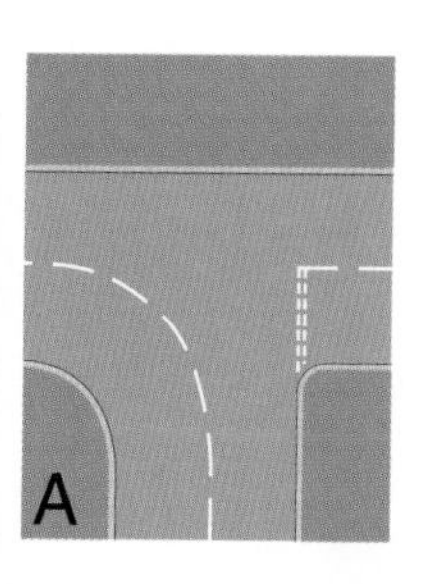

____

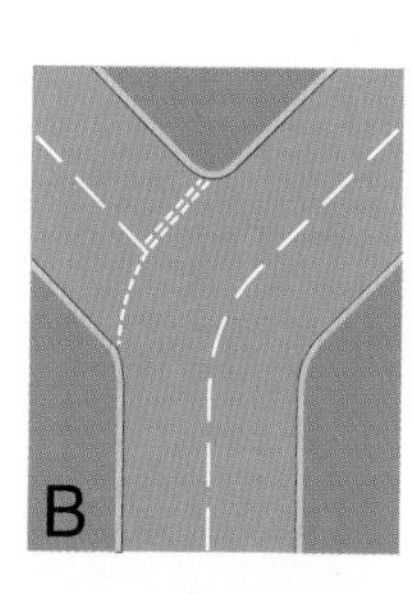

____

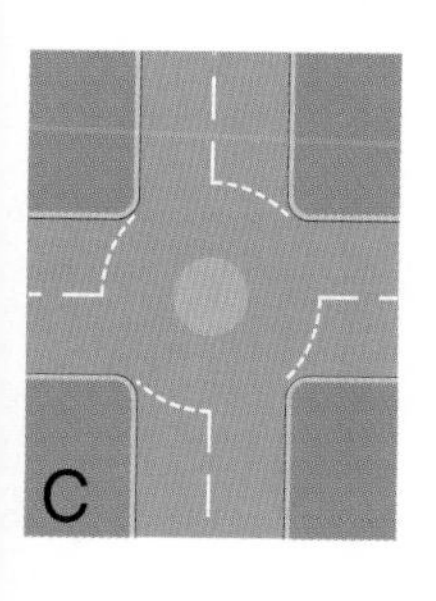

____

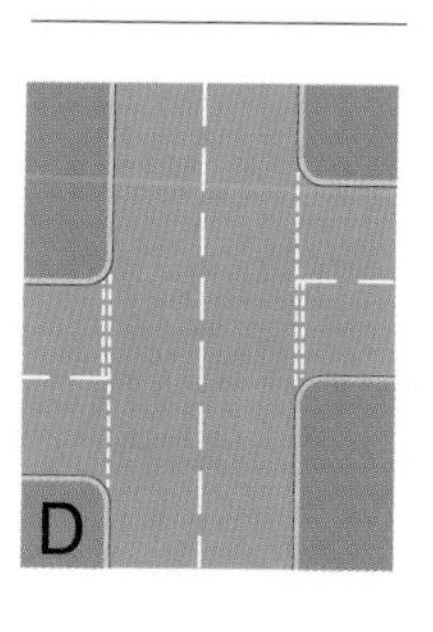

____

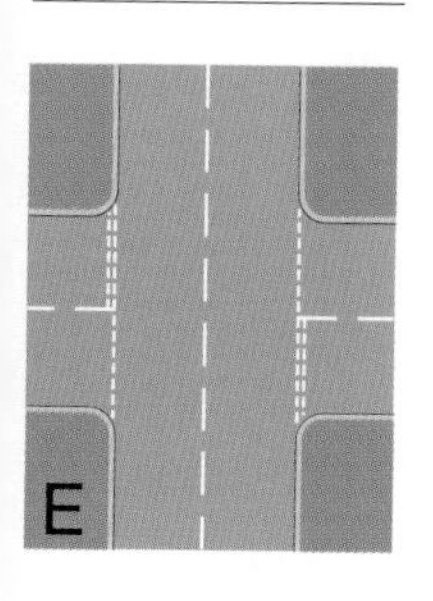

____

Answers on page 95

3

Match these road signs to the junctions shown opposite.

Put letters A, B, C, D and E in the boxes

1 ☐

2 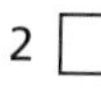

3 ☐

4 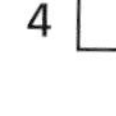

5 ☐

4

What do these signs mean?

1 Stop and give way

2 Slow down, look, and proceed if safe

3 Give way to traffic on the major road

Put a number in each box

A ☐

B ☐

5

At every junction you should follow a safe routine.

Put the following into the correct order by numbering the boxes 1 to 5

Signal ☐ Speed ☐ Position ☐
Mirrors ☐ Look ☐

6

The diagram below shows a car turning right into a minor road. The boxes are numbered to show the correct sequence of actions.

Complete the sentence

At point 5 you should look and
a _ _ _ _ _ the situation,
d _ _ _ _ _ to go or wait,
and a _ _ accordingly.

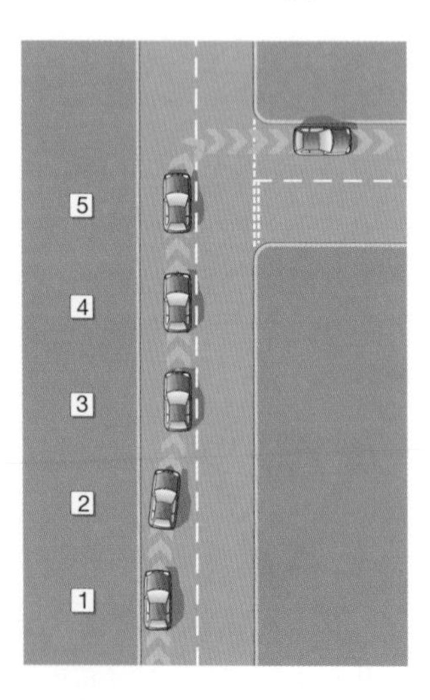

Answers on page 95

7

**Turning left into a minor road.
Which diagram below shows the best path to follow when driving a motor car A, B, C or D?**

Answer ☐

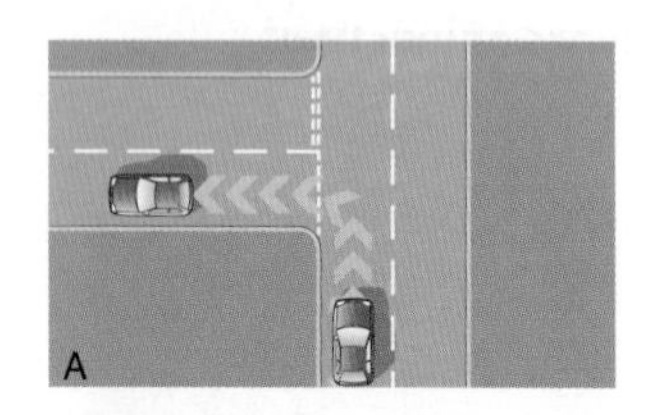

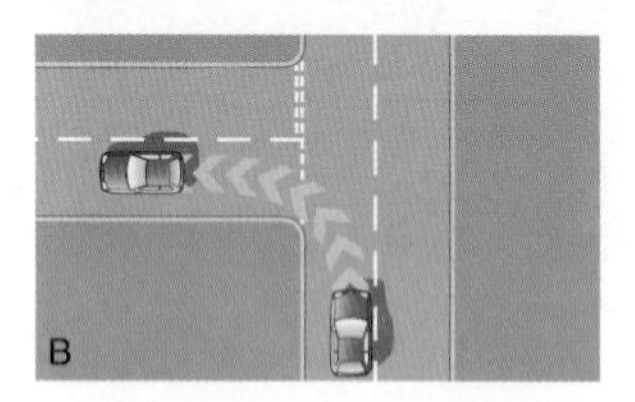

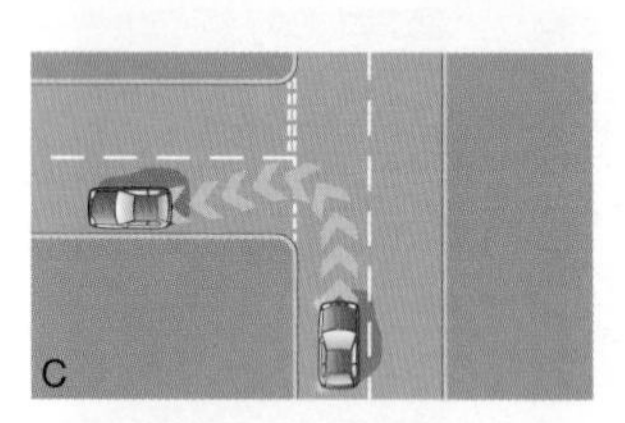

8

You turn into a side road. Pedestrians are already crossing it. Should you ...

Tick the appropriate box

A Sound your horn ☐
B Slow down and give way ☐
C Flash your lights ☐
D Wave them across ☐

9

Turning right into a minor road.
Which diagram shows the best path to follow: A, B, C or D?

Answer ☐

A

B

C

D

10

These are the golden rules for emerging from junctions.

Complete the sentences

1 Always use your m_ _ _ _ _ _ to check the speed and p_ _ _ _ _ _ _ of vehicles behind.

2 Always cancel your s_ _ _ _ _ _ .

3 Speed up to a s_ _ _ speed after joining the new road.

4 Keep a s_ _ _ d_ _ _ _ _ _ _ between you and the vehicle ahead.

5 Do not attempt to o_ _ _ _ _ _ _ until you can assess the new road.

Answers on page 95

11

All crossroads must be approached with caution.

Match actions 1, 2 and 3 listed below with these diagrams

Actions

1 Approach with caution, look well ahead and be prepared to stop. Remember other drivers may assume they have priority.

2 Look well ahead, slow down and be prepared to give way to traffic on the major road.

3 Look well ahead and into the side roads for approaching vehicles. Remember other drivers may not give you priority.

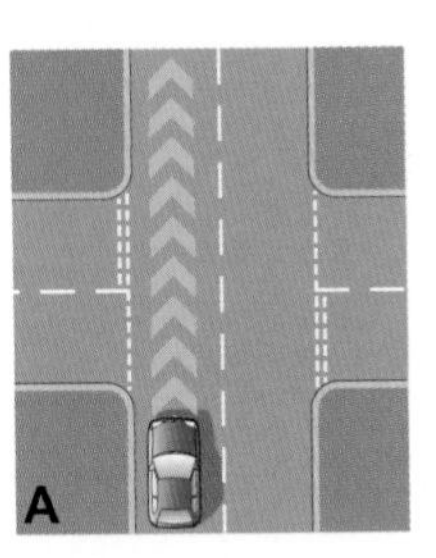

Answer ☐

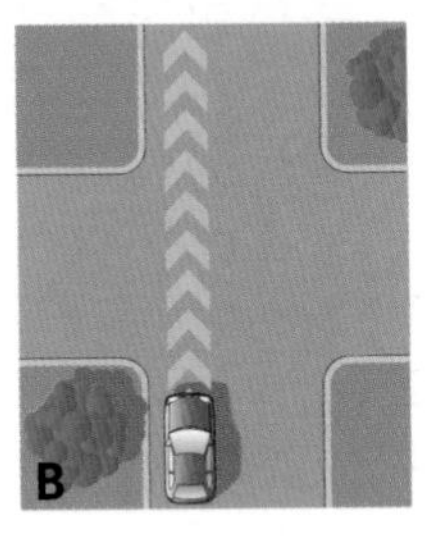

Answer ☐

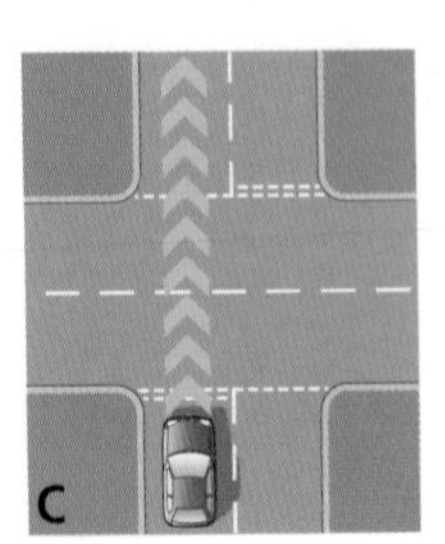

Answer ☐

12

Which of the following statements describes the correct procedure when approaching a roundabout?

Put letter A, B or C in the box

A The broken white line at a roundabout means I must stop and give way to traffic already on the roundabout.

B The broken white line at a roundabout means I must give priority to traffic already on the roundabout.

C The broken white line means I should give way to any traffic approaching from my immediate right.

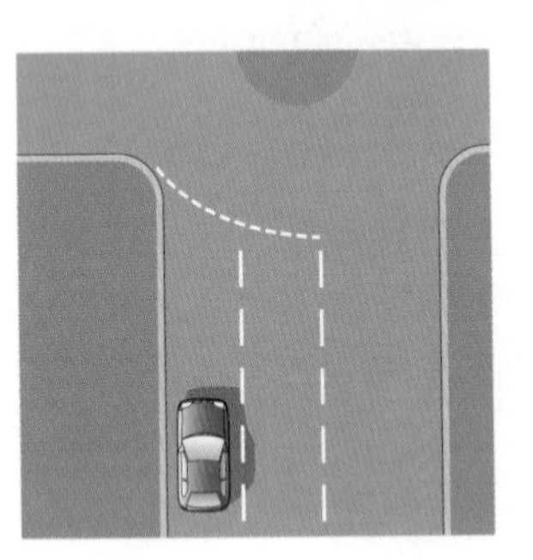

Answer ☐

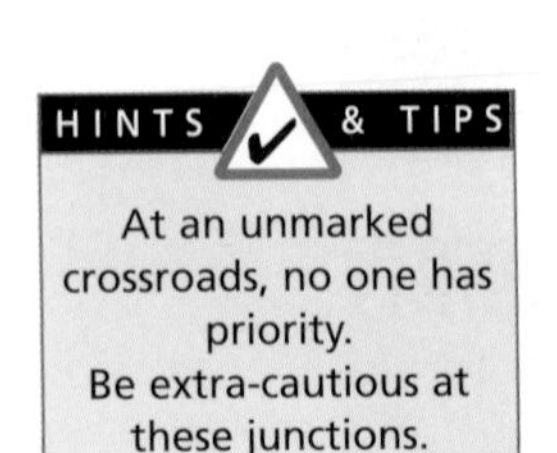

Answers on page 95

13

The following sentences give guidance on lane discipline on a roundabout.

Fill in the missing words

1 When turning left at a roundabout, I should stay in the _ _ _ _ hand lane and should stay in that lane throughout.

2 When going ahead at a roundabout, I should be in the _ _ _ _ hand lane, and should stay in that lane throughout, unless conditions dictate otherwise.

3 When turning right at a roundabout, I should approach in the r_ _ _ _ hand lane, or approach as if turning right at a junction, and stay in that lane throughout.

14

The letters A, B and C in the diagram mark places where you should signal.

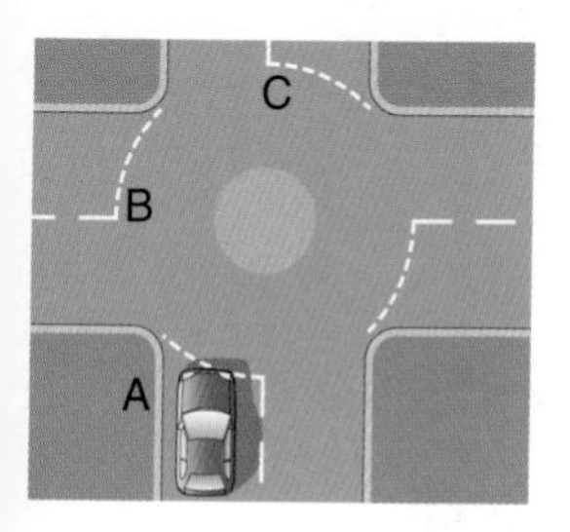

Complete the sentences

1 I would signal at **A** when turning _ _ _ _.

2 I would signal at **B** when g_ _ _ _ _ _ _ _ _ _.

3 I would signal at **A** and at **C** when turning _ _ _ _ _.

15

At a roundabout you should always use a safe routine.

Fill in the missing words

M_ _ _ _ _ _ _, s_ _ _ _ _ _,
p_ _ _ _ _ _ _ _, s_ _ _ _ _,
l_ _ _.

16

What does this sign mean?

Write 1, 2 or 3 in the box

1 Roundabout

2 Mini-roundabout

3 Vehicles may pass either side.

Answer ☐

HINTS & TIPS

Be careful at roundabouts where destinations are marked for each lane. Make sure you are in the correct lane for your destination.

Answers on page 95

1

It is safest to park off the road or in a car park whenever possible. If you have to park on the road, think ...

Fill in the missing words

1 Is it s__ __ __ ?

2 Is it c__ __ __ __ __ __ __ __ __ __ __ __ __?

3 Is it l__ __ __ __ ?

2

In this diagram four of the cars are parked illegally or without consideration of others.

Put the numbers of these cars in the boxes

☐ ☐ ☐ ☐

For reverse parallel parking manoeuvres, see pages 52–4.

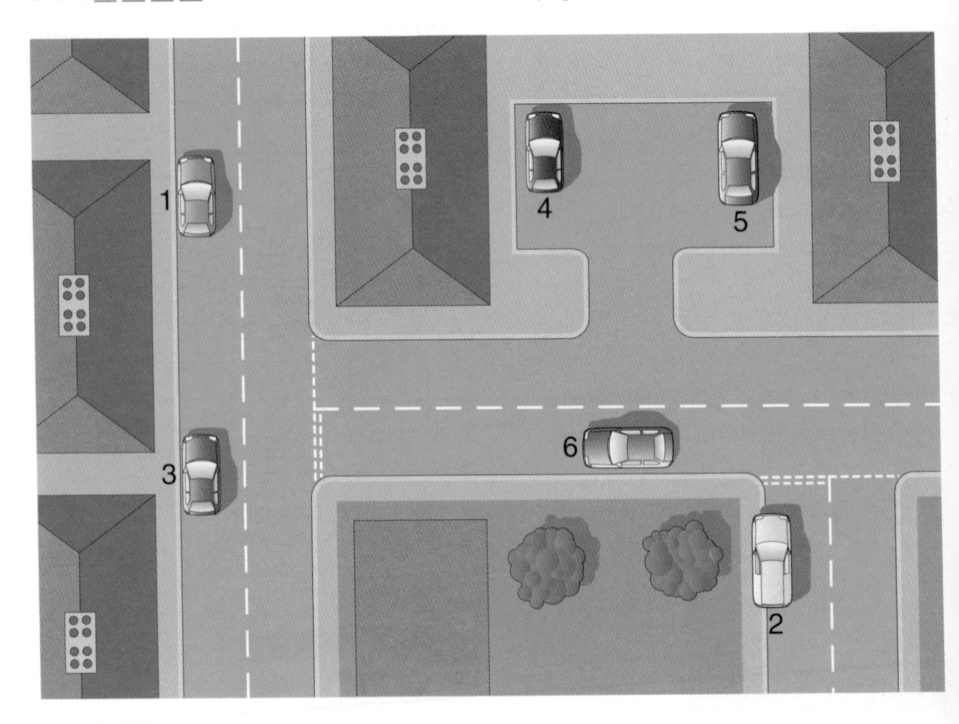

Answers on page 96

3

Check how well you know the rules about where you may and may not park. Are the following statements true or false?

Tick the correct boxes

	True	False
1 In a narrow street, I should park with two wheels up on the pavement to leave more room for other traffic.	☐	☐
2 I am allowed to park in a 'Disabled' space if all other spaces are full.	☐	☐
3 I should not park on the zig-zag lines near a zebra crossing.	☐	☐
4 Red lines painted on the road mean 'No Stopping'.	☐	☐

4

List three places not mentioned in Question 3 where you should *not* park.

1 ______________________________

2 ______________________________

3 ______________________________

HINTS & TIPS

Use your *Highway Code* to find out more about parking regulations

Answers on page 96

1

The diagram shows a stationary vehicle on the left-hand side of the road. Which should have priority, vehicle 1 or vehicle 2?

Answer ☐

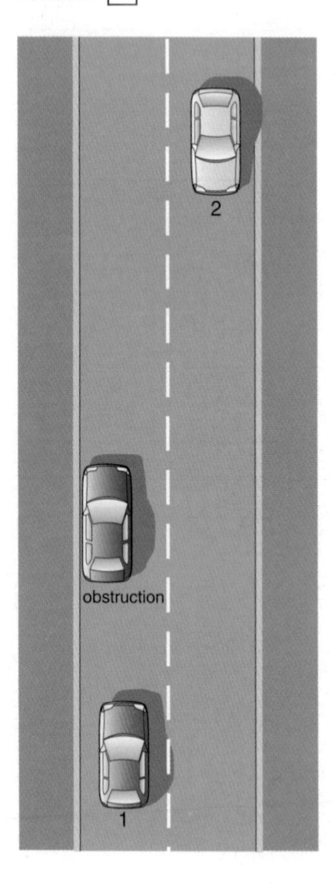

Answers on page 96

2

This diagram shows a steep downward hill with an obstruction on the right-hand side of the road. Which vehicle should be given priority, vehicle 1 or vehicle 2?

Answer ☐

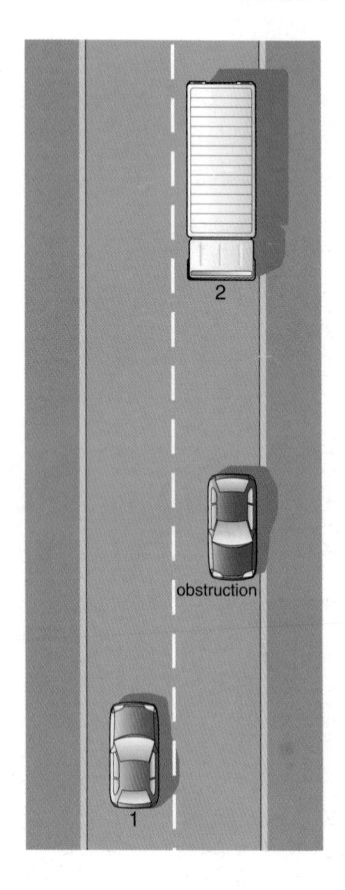

3

The diagram shows two vehicles, travelling in opposite directions, turning right at a crossroads.

Are these statements true or false?

Tick the appropriate boxes

	True	False
1 The safest route is to pass each other offside to offside.	☐	☐
2 If the approaching vehicle flashes its headlamps, I should turn as quickly as possible.	☐	☐
3 I should always try to get eye-to-eye contact with the driver of the other vehicle to determine which course to take.	☐	☐

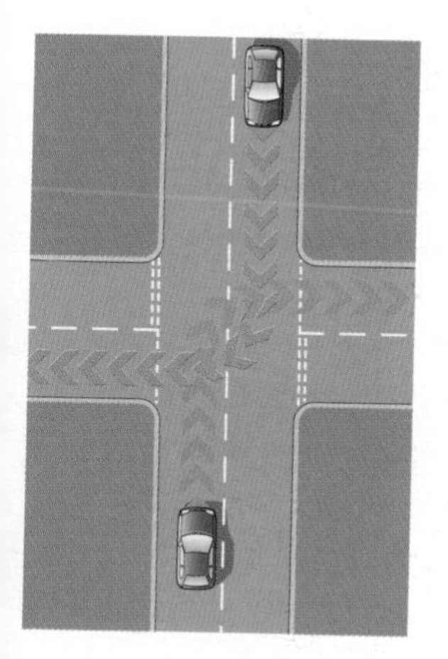

4

Which of the following factors, illustrated in the diagram, should be taken into consideration when turning right into a side road?

Tick the appropriate boxes

	YES	NO
1 The speed of the approaching vehicle (**A**)	☐	☐
2 The roadworks	☐	☐
3 The speed of vehicle **B**	☐	☐
4 The cyclist	☐	☐
5 Your speed (vehicle **C**)	☐	☐
6 The pedestrians	☐	☐
7 The car waiting to turn right (**D**)	☐	☐

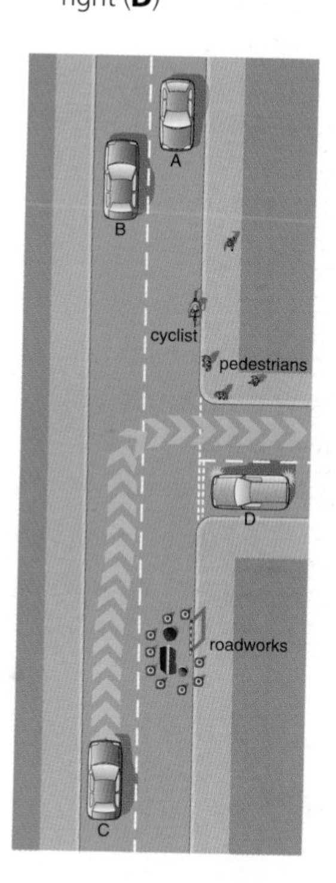

Answers on page 96

1

Are the following statements true or false when stopping in an emergency?

Tick the correct boxes

	True	False
1 Stopping in an emergency increases the risk of skidding.	☐	☐
2 I should push the brake pedal down harder as I slow down.	☐	☐
3 It is important to react quickly.	☐	☐
4 I should always remember to look in my mirrors as I slow down.	☐	☐
5 I should signal left to tell other road users what I am doing.	☐	☐
6 I should keep both hands on the wheel.	☐	☐
7 I should always check my mirrors and look round before moving off.	☐	☐

2

Is the following statement true or false? An emergency stop will be carried out on every driving test

Tick the correct box **True** ☐ **False** ☐

Answers on page 97

3

Cadence braking is a technique which can be used in very slippery conditions in an emergency.

Fill in the missing words

The technique requires you to p_ _ _ the brake pedal.

The procedure to follow is:

1 Apply m_ _ _ _ _ _ _ pressure.

2 Release the brake pedal just as the wheels are about to l_ _ _.

3 Then q_ _ _ _ _ _ _ apply the brakes again. Apply and release the brakes until the vehicle has stopped. This technique should only be used in emergency situations.

4

Anti-lock braking systems (ABS)* work in a similar way to cadence braking.

Fill in the missing words

When braking in an emergency, ABS brakes allow you to s_ _ _ _ and b_ _ _ _ at the same time. You do not have to p_ _ _ the brakes as you would in cadence braking. When using ABS you keep the p_ _ _ _ _ _ _ applied.

HINTS & TIPS

If a vehicle is travelling too close behind you, then increase the gap you have ahead. Always think for the driver behind.

Are these statements about ABS braking true or false?

Tick the correct boxes

	True	False
1 Cars fitted with ABS braking cannot skid.	☐	☐
2 I do not need to leave as much room between me and the car in front if I have ABS brakes because I know I can stop in a shorter distance.	☐	☐

**ABS is a registered trade mark of Bosch (Germany). ABS stands for Anti-Blockiersystem*

The distance taken for a car to reach stopping point divides into thinking distance and braking distance.

5

Could these factors affect thinking distance?

Tick the appropriate boxes

	YES	NO
1 The condition of your tyres	☐	☐
2 Feeling tired or unwell	☐	☐
3 Speed of reaction	☐	☐
4 Going downhill	☐	☐

6

Most drivers' reaction time is well over ...

Tick the appropriate box

½ second ☐

1 second ☐

5 seconds ☐

7

Stopping distance depends partly on the speed at which the car is travelling.

Complete the sentences

1 At 30mph your overall stopping distance will be __ __ metres or __ __ feet.

2 At 50mph your thinking distance will be __ __ metres or __ __ feet.

3 At 70mph your overall stopping distance will be __ __ metres or __ __ __feet.

8

Stopping distance also varies according to road conditions.

Complete the sentences

In wet weather your vehicle will take l __ __ __ __ __ to stop. You should therefore allow m __ __ __ time.

9

Too many accidents are caused by drivers driving too close to the vehicle in front. A safe gap between you and the vehicle in front can be measured by noting a stationary object and counting in seconds the time that lapses between the vehicle in front passing that object and your own vehicle passing that object.

Complete the sentence

Only a fool b __ __ __ __ __ the t __ __ s __ __ __ __ __ rule.

Answers on page 97

1

Are these statements about moving off at an angle true or false?

Tick the correct boxes

	True	False
1 I should check my mirrors as I am pulling out.	☐	☐
2 I should check my mirrors and blindspot before I pull out.	☐	☐
3 I should move out as quickly as possible.	☐	☐
4 The amount of steering required will depend on how close I am to the vehicle in front.	☐	☐
5 I should look for oncoming traffic.	☐	☐
6 As long as I am signalling, people will know what I am doing. I will be able to pull out because somebody will let me in.	☐	☐

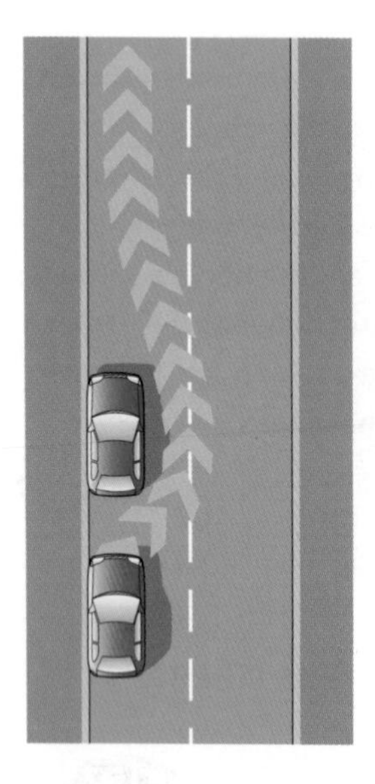

2

Are these statements about moving off uphill true or false?

Tick the correct boxes

	True	False
1 On an uphill gradient the car will tend to roll back.	☐	☐
2 To stop the car rolling back I need to use more acceleration.	☐	☐
3 I do not need to use the handbrake.	☐	☐
4 The biting point may be slightly higher.	☐	☐
5 I need to press the accelerator pedal further down than when moving off on the level.	☐	☐
6 I need to allow more time to pull away.	☐	☐
7 The main controls I use will be the clutch pedal, the accelerator pedal and the handbrake.	☐	☐

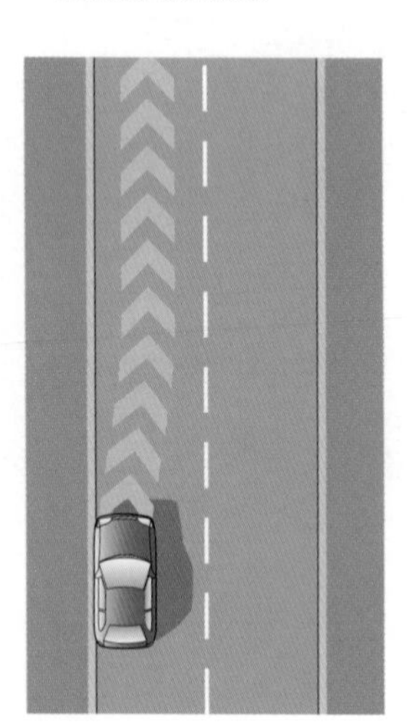

Answers on page 98

3

Are these statements about moving off downhill true or false?

Tick the correct boxes

	True	False
1 The car will tend to roll forwards.	☐	☐
2 The main controls I use will be the handbrake, the clutch pedal and the accelerator pedal.	☐	☐
3 The only gear I can move off in is 1st gear.	☐	☐
4 I should release the handbrake while keeping the foot-brake applied.	☐	☐
5 I should look round just before moving off.	☐	☐
6 I must not have my foot on the foot-brake as I start to release the clutch.	☐	☐

Answers on page 98

4

The following statements are about approaching a junction when going uphill or downhill. With which do you agree?

When going downhill ... **YES NO**

1 It is more difficult to slow down ☐ ☐

2 Putting the clutch down will help slow the car down ☐ ☐

3 The higher the gear, the greater the control ☐ ☐

4 When changing gear you may need to use the foot-brake at the same time as the clutch ☐ ☐

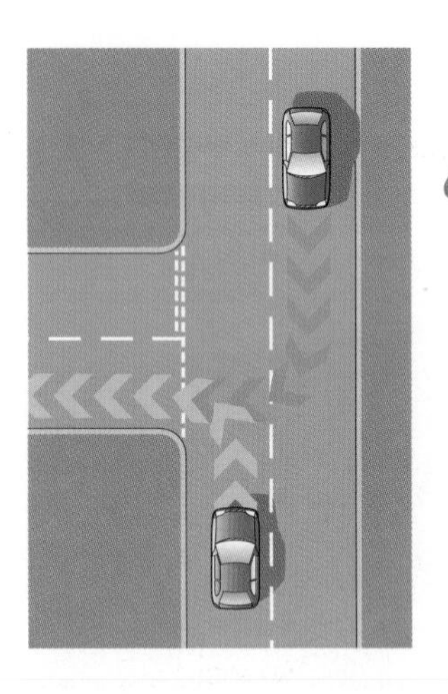

When going uphill ... **YES NO**

5 Early use of mirrors, signals, brakes, gears and steering will help to position the car correctly ☐ ☐

6 You may need to use your handbrake more often ☐ ☐

7 When you change gear, the car tends to slow down ☐ ☐

Answers on page 98

1

Before reversing there are three things to consider.

Fill in the missing words

1 Is it s__ __ __?

2 Is it c__ __ __ __ __ __ __ __ __ __?

3 Is it within the l__ __?

2

Are the following statements about reversing true or false?

Tick the appropriate boxes

	True	False
1 Other road users should see what I am doing and wait for me.	☐	☐
2 I should wave pedestrians on, so that I can get on with the manoeuvre more quickly.	☐	☐
3 I should avoid being too hesitant.	☐	☐
4 I should avoid making other road users slow down or change course.	☐	☐

3

How should you hold the steering wheel when reversing left?

Which is correct? Answer ☐

A B C

4

These statements are all about reversing.

Tick those which you think are correct

	True	False
1 My car will respond differently in reverse gear.	☐	☐
2 My car will feel no different.	☐	☐
3 Steering is not affected. The car responds the same as when going forward.	☐	☐
4 The steering will feel different. I will have to wait for the steering to take effect.	☐	☐

5

Which way will the rear of the car go when it is reversed? Left or right?

A B

Answer ___________ Answer___________

Answers on page 99

6

It is important to move the vehicle slowly when reversing.

Complete the sentence

Moving the vehicle slowly is safer because I have control and it allows me to carry out good o__ __ __ __ __ __ __ __ __ __ checks.

7

When reversing, good observation is vital. Where should you look?

Tick the correct answer

1 At the kerb ☐
2 Ahead ☐
3 Where your car is going ☐
4 Out of the back window ☐

8

Are these statements about reversing round a corner true or false?

Tick the correct boxes

	True	False
1 If the corner is sharp, I need to be further away from the kerb.	☐	☐
2 The distance from the kerb makes no difference.	☐	☐
3 I should try to stay reasonably close to the kerb all the way round.	☐	☐

Answers on page 99

9

Before reversing I should check ...

Tick the correct box

1 Behind me ☐
2 Ahead and to the rear ☐
3 My door mirrors ☐
4 All round ☐

10

Which position is the correct one in which to start steering?

A, B, C or D? Answer ☐

11

Which way should you steer?

Answer________________

12

What will happen to the front of the car?

Answer________________

13

Are these statements about steering when reversing round a corner true or false?

Tick the correct boxes **True False**

1 The more gradual the corner, the less I have to steer. ☐ ☐

2 I need to steer the same for every corner. ☐ ☐

3 The sharper the corner, the more I have to steer. ☐ ☐

14

As I enter the new road, I should continue to keep a look-out for p__ __ __ __ __ __ __ __ __ __ and other r__ __ __ u__ __ __ __.

I should s__ __ __ if necessary.

Complete the sentences

15

True or false? When reversing from a major road into a side road on the right, I have to move to the wrong side of the road.

Tick the correct box **True** ☐ **False** ☐

16

Which diagram shows the correct path to follow when moving to the right-hand side of the road? A or B?

Answer ☐

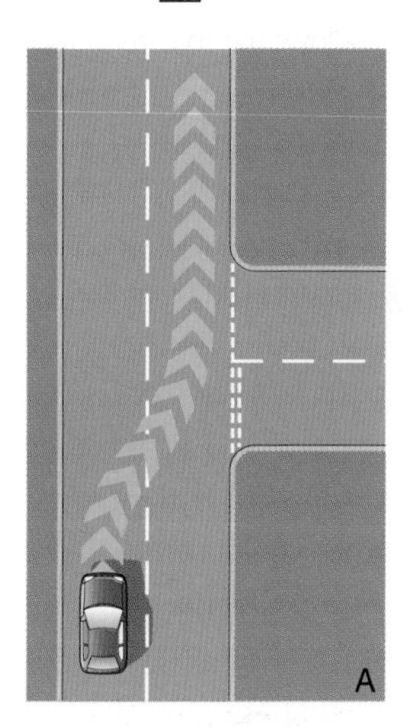

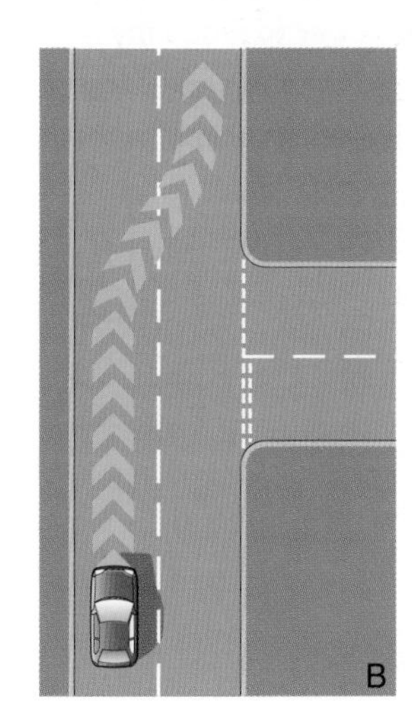

Answers on page 99

17

Which of the following correctly describes your sitting position for reversing to the right?

1 I will need to sit so that I can see over my right shoulder.

2 I will need to sit so that I can see over my right shoulder, ahead and to the left.

3 My position is the same as when reversing to the left.

Which statement is correct? 1, 2 or 3

Answer ☐

18

True or false? I may need to change my hand position on the wheel.

Tick the correct box **True** ☐ **False** ☐

19

True or false? It is easier to judge my position from the kerb when reversing to the right than when reversing to the left.

Tick the correct box **True** ☐ **False** ☐

Answers on page 99

20

Reversing to the right is more dangerous than reversing to the left because ...

1 I cannot see as well

2 I am on the wrong side of the road

3 I might get in the way of vehicles emerging from the side road

Which statement is correct – 1, 2 or 3?

Answer ☐

21

How far down the side road would you reverse before moving over to the left-hand side?

Which diagram is correct? A or B?

Answer ☐

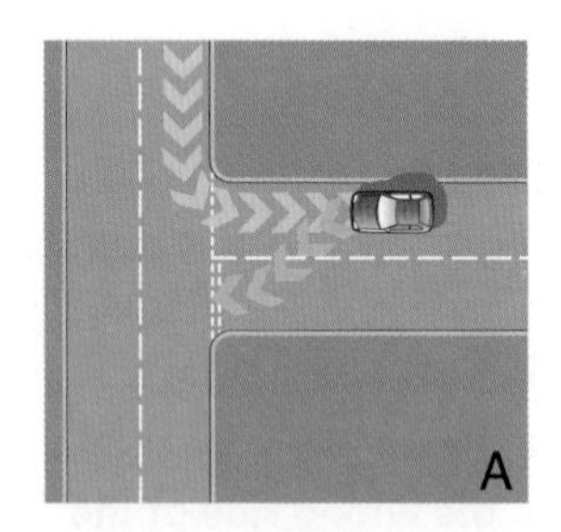

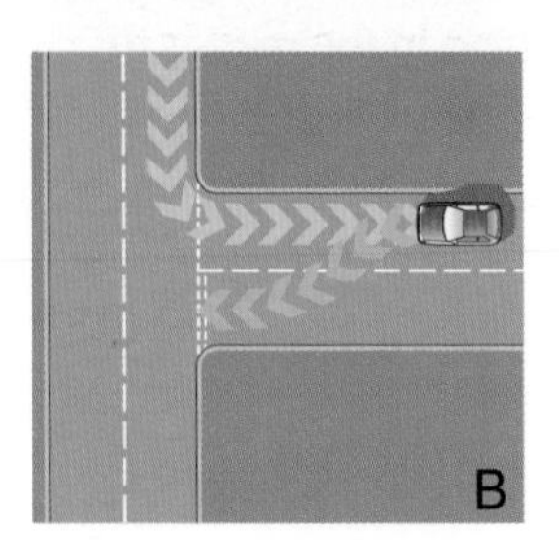

22

Look at the diagrams and decide which is safer.

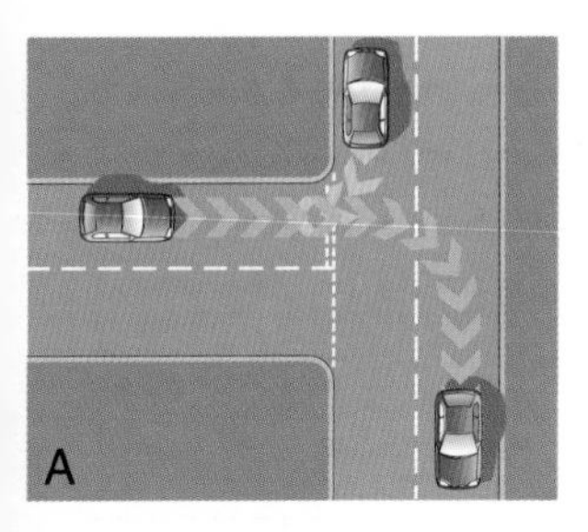

A Reversing into a side road

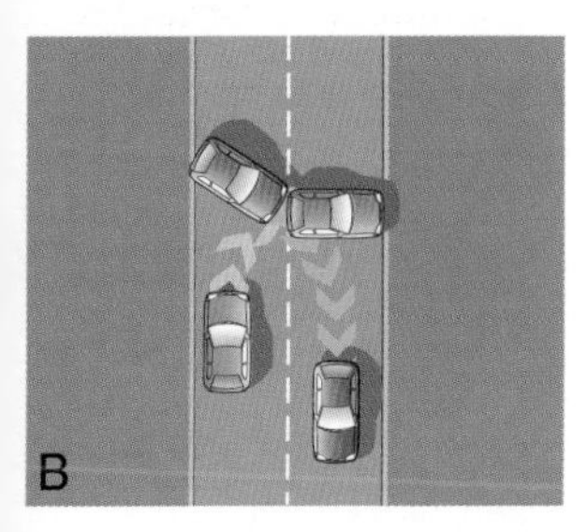

B Turning round in the road

Answer ☐

23

The secret of turning in the road is to move the vehicle s__ __ __ __ __ and steer b__ __ __ __ __ __.

Complete the sentence

24

I must be able to complete the manoeuvre in three moves: 1 forward, 2 reverse, 3 forward. True or false?

Tick the correct box **True** ☐ **False** ☐

25

Before manoeuvring what should you take into consideration?

Tick the correct boxes

1 The size of your engine ☐

2 The width of the road ☐

3 The road camber ☐

4 The steering circle of your vehicle ☐

5 Parking restrictions ☐

26

Before moving forward, it is important to check a__ __ r__ __ __ __ __ for other road users.

Complete the sentence

HINTS & TIPS

When taking your test, you will be assessed on how well you can control the car; so don't rush your manoeuvres.

Answers on page 100

27

Turning in the road requires proper use of the steering wheel.

Answer the following questions…

1 When going forwards, which way should you steer?

Answer ______________________

2 Before you reach the kerb ahead, what should you do?

Answer ______________________

3 When reversing, which way should you steer?

Answer ______________________

4 Before you reach the kerb behind you, what should you do?

Answer ______________________

5 As you move forward again, which way should you steer to straighten up?

Answer ______________________

28

Reversing is a potentially dangerous manoeuvre. Good observation is essential.

Answer the following questions

1 If you are steering left when reversing, which shoulder should you look over?

Answer ______________________

2 As you begin to steer to the right, where should you look?

Answer ______________________

29

When parking between two cars …

1 The car is more manoeuvrable when driving forwards

2 The car is more manoeuvrable when reversing

3 There is no difference between going into the space forwards or reversing into it

Which statement is correct? 1, 2 or 3?

Answer ☐

HINTS & TIPS

In your driving test you may be asked to reverse into a parking bay at the test centre, or to park behind another car, using reverse gear. So make sure you practise these manoeuvres.

Answers on page 100

30

The diagram shows a car preparing to reverse into a parking space. Which position is the correct one in which to start steering left, A, B, C or D?

Answer ☐

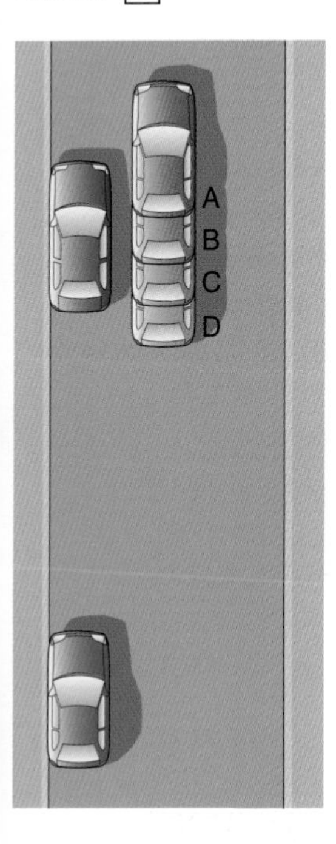

31

With practice you should be able to park in a gap ...

1 Your own car length

2 1½ times your own car length

3 2 times your own car length

4 2½ times your own car length

Answer ☐

32

Use the diagram to help you answer the following questions.

1 Which way would you steer?

Answer ______________________

2 At this point what would you try to line up with the offside (right-hand side) of your vehicle?

Answer ______________________

3 As you straighten up what do you have to be careful of?

Answer ______________________

4 What do you need to do to straighten up?

Answer ______________________

5 What would you need to do in order to position the vehicle parallel to the kerb?

Answer ______________________

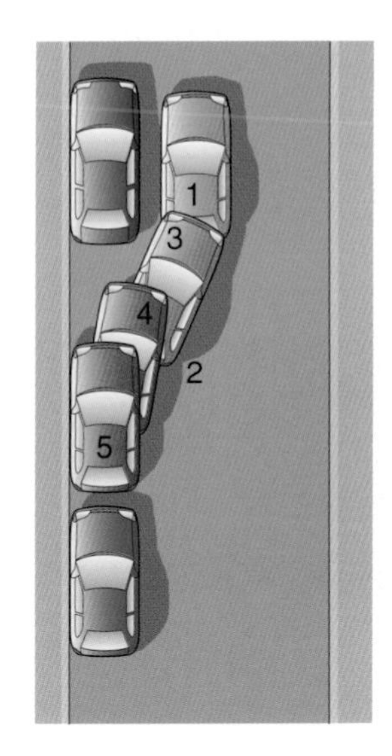

Answers on page 100

33

True or false? During my driving test ...

Tick the correct boxes

	True	False
1 I will certainly be asked to perform the manoeuvre in Question 32	☐	☐
2 I have to be able to park in a tight space between two cars	☐	☐
3 It may be that only the lead car is present	☐	☐

34

When carrying out this manoeuvre, where is it important to look?

Answer ______________________________

35

Look at the diagram and answer the following question.

Which bay should you use and why?

Answer ______________________________

____

____

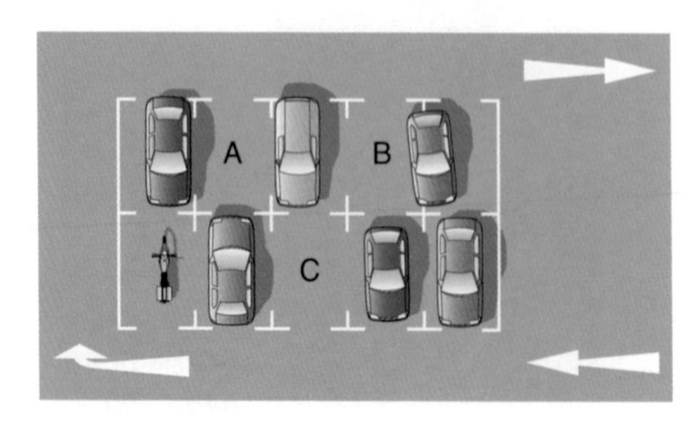

36

Why, wherever possible, should you choose to reverse into a parking bay?

Answer ______________________________

____

____

____

37

As well as being very aware of how c_ _ _ _ I am to the parked cars on either side, I should also be alert for cars moving near me from all d_ _ _ _ _ _ _ _ _ _, as well as the possibility of p_ _ _ _ _ _ _ _ _ _ _ walking around my car.

Complete the sentence

Answers on page 100

1

Traffic lights have three lights, red, amber, and green, which change from one to the other in a set order. Number the boxes 1 to 5 to show the correct order. The first answer has been filled in to give you a start.

☐ Amber [1] Red ☐ Red and amber

☐ Red ☐ Green

2

What do the colours mean?

Fill in the correct colour for each of the following

1 Go ahead if the way is clear.

Colour ____________

2 Stop and wait.

Colour ____________

3 Stop unless you have crossed the stop line or you are so close to it that stopping might cause an accident.

Colour ____________

4 Stop and wait at the stop line.

Colour ____________

3

Which of the following statements are true?

On approach to traffic lights you should ...

Tick the appropriate boxes

1 Speed up to get through before they change ☐

2 Be ready to stop ☐

3 Look for pedestrians ☐

4 Sound your horn to urge pedestrians to cross quickly ☐

4

Some traffic lights have green filters. Do they mean ...

1 You can filter in the direction of the arrow only when the main light is showing green?

2 You can filter even when the main light is not showing green?

Answer ☐

5

The diagram shows the three lanes at a set of traffic lights.

Which lane would you use for ...

1 Going ahead Answer ____________

2 Turning right Answer ____________

3 Turning left Answer ____________

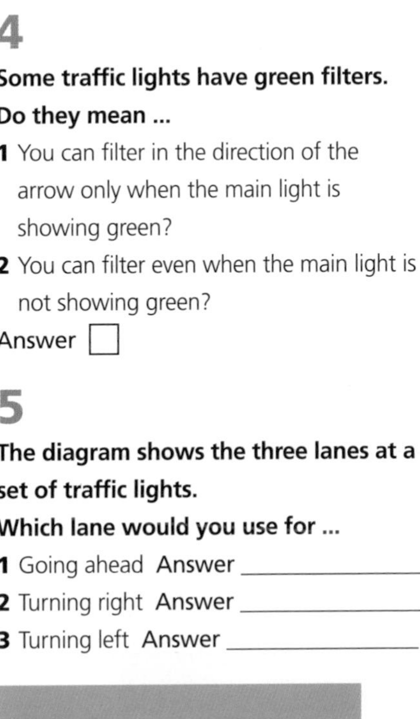

Answers on page 101

6

At some traffic lights and junctions you will see yellow criss-cross lines (box junctions). Can you ...

Tick the correct boxes

	YES	NO
1 Wait within them when going ahead if your exit is not clear?	☐	☐
2 Wait within them when going right if your exit is not clear?	☐	☐
3 Wait within them if there is oncoming traffic stopping you turning right but your exit is clear?	☐	☐

Answers on page 101

Pedestrians have certain rights of way at pedestrian crossings.

7

On approaching a zebra crossing, drivers will notice four features. Name them

1 ____________________

____

2 ____________________

____

3 ____________________

____

4 ____________________

____

8

Are these statements about pedestrian crossings true or false?

Tick the correct boxes

	True	False
1 I cannot park or wait on the zig-zag lines on the approach to a zebra crossing.	☐	☐
2 I cannot park or wait on the zig-zag lines on either side of the crossing.	☐	☐
3 I can overtake on the zig-zag lines on the approach to a crossing as long as the other vehicle is travelling slowly.	☐	☐
4 I must give way to a pedestrian once he/she has stepped on to the crossing.	☐	☐

5 If, on approach to a crossing, I intend to slow down or stop, I should use a slowing-down arm signal. ☐ ☐

9

On approaching a pelican crossing, drivers will notice three key features. Name them

1 ______________________________

____

____

____

2 ______________________________

____

____

____

3 ______________________________

____

____

____

10

If you see a pedestrian at a zebra crossing or pelican crossing carrying a white stick, do you think ...

Tick the correct box

1 He/she has difficulty walking? ☐

2 He/she is visually handicapped? ☐

11

The traffic lights at a pelican crossing have the same meaning as ordinary traffic lights, but they do not have a red and amber phase.

1 What do they show instead of the red and amber phase?

Answer______________________________

____

2 What does the light mean?

Answer______________________________

____

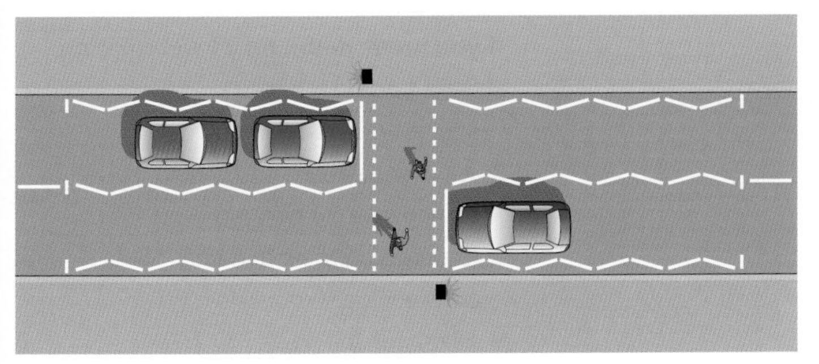

Answers on pages 101–2

12

What sound is usually heard at a pelican crossing when the green man is shown to pedestrians?

Answer________________________________

13

Toucan and puffin crossings are similar to pelican crossings but with one main difference. Name it.

Answer________________________________

14

As well as pedestrians, what other type of road users should you watch for at a toucan crossing?

Answer________________________________

Answers on page 102

A level crossing is where the road crosses at a railway line. It is potentially dangerous and should be approached with caution.

15

Match each traffic sign below with its correct meaning.

1 Level crossing without gates or barriers ☐
2 Level crossing with lights ☐
3 Level crossing with gates or barriers ☐
4 Level crossing without lights ☐

A B C D

KEEP CROSSING CLEAR

GIVE WAY

16

If you break down on a level crossing, should you ...

Tick the appropriate boxes

1 Tell your passengers to wait in the vehicle while you go to get help? ☐
2 Get everybody out and clear of the crossing? ☐
3 Telephone the police? ☐
4 Telephone the signal operator? ☐
5 If there is still time, push your car clear of the crossing? ☐

One-way systems are where all traffic flows in the same direction.

1

Which of these signs means one-way traffic?

A

B

Answer ☐

2

Are these statements about one-way systems true or false?

Tick the correct boxes

	True	False
1 In one-way streets traffic can pass me on both sides.	☐	☐
2 Roundabouts are one-way systems.	☐	☐
3 For normal driving I should stay on the left.	☐	☐
4 I should look out for road markings and get in lane early.	☐	☐

As a rule, the more paint on the road, the more important the message.

3

Road markings are divided into three categories.

Fill in the missing words

1 Those which give i _ _ _ _ _ _ _ _ _ _.

2 Those which give w _ _ _ _ _ _ _.

3 Those which give o _ _ _ _ _.

4

There are two main advantages which road markings have over other traffic signs. Name them.

1 ______________________________

____

2 ______________________________

____

Answers on page 102

5

What do these lines across the road mean?

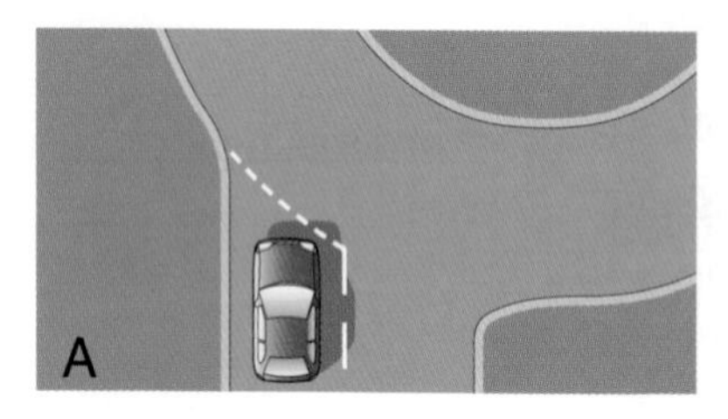

1 Stop and give way

2 Give priority to traffic coming from the immediate right.

3 Give way to traffic coming from the right.

Answer ☐

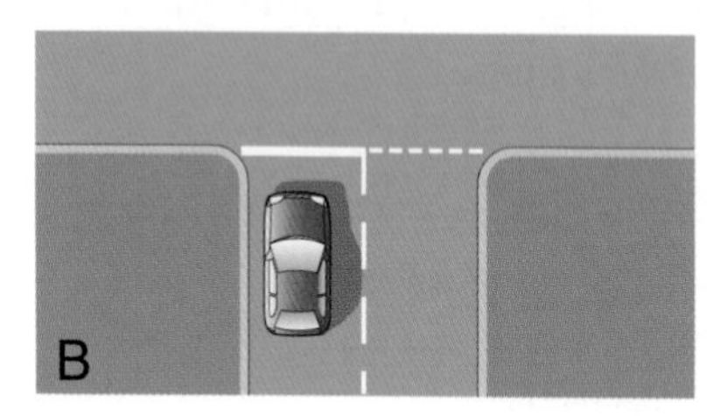

1 Give way to traffic on the major road.

2 Stop at the line and give way to traffic on the major road.

Answer ☐

Answers on page 102

6

Where you see double solid white lines painted along the centre of the road, what does this mean?

Tick any boxes you think are appropriate.

More than one answer may be correct.

1 I must not park or wait on the carriageway. ☐

2 I can park between 7pm and 7am. ☐

3 I must not overtake. ☐

4 I must not cross the white line except to turn right or in circumstances beyond my control. ☐

7

What is the purpose of these hatched markings (chevrons)?

Answer________________________________

____

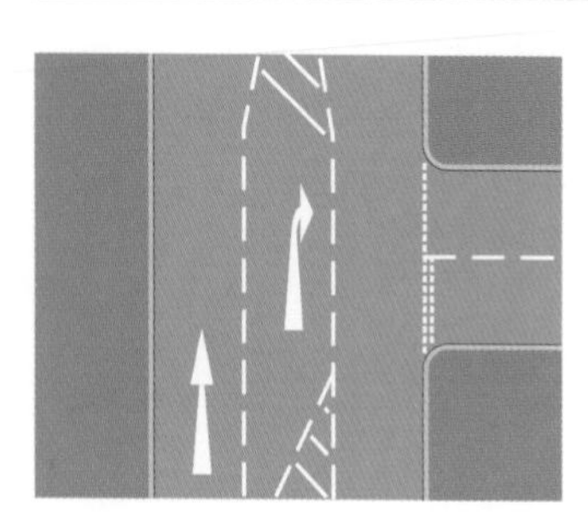

8

What does it mean if the chevrons are edged with a solid white line?

Answer______________________________

____

The shape and colour of a sign will help you understand what it means.

9

Look at the sign shapes below and say whether each gives an order, a warning or information.

1

Answer____________

2

Answer____________

3

Answer____________

10

Complete the sentences

1 A circular sign with a blue background tells you what you m__ __ __ do.

2 A circular sign with a red border tells you what you m__ __ __ n__ __ do.

Answers on pages 102–3

11

What do these signs mean?

GIVE WAY

Answer____________________

____

____

____

STOP

Answer____________________

____

____

____

12

Some junctions have a stop sign, others have a give way sign. *Complete the sentence*

A stop sign is usually placed at a junction where v__ __ __ __ __ is l__ __ __ __ __ __.

13

Information signs are colour-coded.

Match each of the following signs to its colouring.

A White letters on a brown background	☐ Motorway signs
B Black letters on a white background	☐ Primary routes
C Black letters on a white background with a blue border	☐ Other routes
D White letters on a blue background with a white border	☐ Local places
E White letters on a green background, yellow route numbers with a white border	☐ Tourist signs

1

Good observation is vital in today's busy traffic.

Complete the sentence

When using my mirrors I should try to make a mental note of the s__ __ __ __, b__ __ __ __ __ __ __ __ __ and i__ __ __ __ __ __ __ __ __ __ __ of the driver behind.

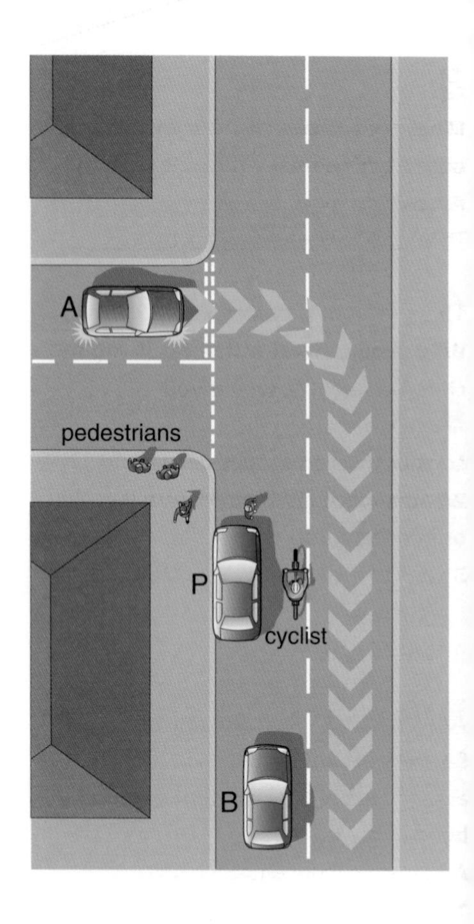

2

Driving in built-up areas is potentially dangerous.

Look at the diagram opposite

1 What action should the driver of car **A** take?

List four options

A ______________________________

B ______________________________

C ______________________________

D ______________________________

2 What action should the driver of car **B** take?

List four options

A ______________________________

B ______________________________

C ______________________________

D ______________________________

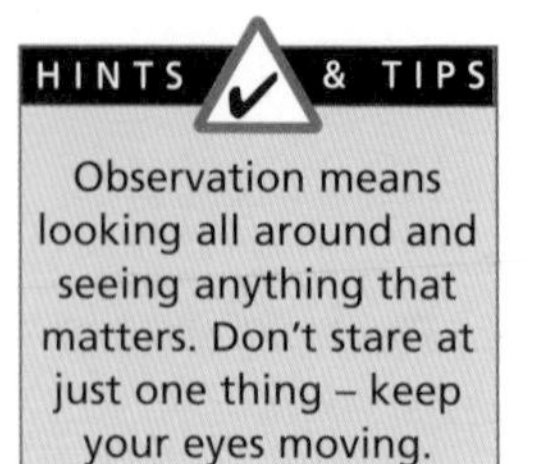

Observation means looking all around and seeing anything that matters. Don't stare at just one thing – keep your eyes moving.

Answers on pages 102–4

3

Motorcyclists are often less visible than other road users.

Complete this well-known phrase

Think once, think twice, think b__ __ __.

4

When you observe traffic following too close behind you, would you

Tick the correct box

1 Speed up to create a bigger gap? ☐

2 Touch your brake lights to warn the following driver? ☐

3 Keep to a safe speed, and keep checking the behaviour and intentions of the following driver? ☐

5

Some hazards are potential, others are actual and there all the time, such as a bend in the road.

A Name five more actual hazards

1 ______________________________

2 ______________________________

3 ______________________________

4 ______________________________

5 ______________________________

B Name five potential hazards, such as a dog off its lead

1 ______________________________

2 ______________________________

3 ______________________________

4 ______________________________

5 ______________________________

6

Modern driving requires full concentration. Are the following statements true or false?

Tick the correct boxes	**True**	**False**
1 Carrying a mobile phone can reduce the stress of a long journey.	☐	☐
2 I must not use a hand-held phone while driving.	☐	☐
3 Conversation on a hands-free phone can still distract my attention.	☐	☐
4 I should pull up in a safe place to make or receive calls.	☐	☐

Answers on page 104

7

When driving, all the following actions have something in common.

What is it?

Reading a map

Eating

Changing a cassette

Listening to loud music

Answer____________________________

____

____

____

One of the features of driving on the open road is taking bends properly.

8

As a rule you should be travelling at the correct s_ _ _ _ _, using the correct g_ _ _ _, and be in the correct p_ _ _ _ _ _ _ _.

9

Should you brake ...

Tick the appropriate box

1 Before you enter the bend? ☐

2 As you enter the bend? ☐

3 While negotiating the bend? ☐

Answers on page 104

10

Which way does force push a car on a bend?

A Inwards or **B** Outwards

Answer ☐

11

What happens to the weight of the car when you use the brakes?

A It is thrown forwards

B It remains even

C It is thrown back

Answer ☐

12

When you approach a bend, what position should you be in?

Complete the sentences

A On a right-hand bend I should keep to the ______________________________

____

B On a left-hand bend I should keep to the______________________________

____

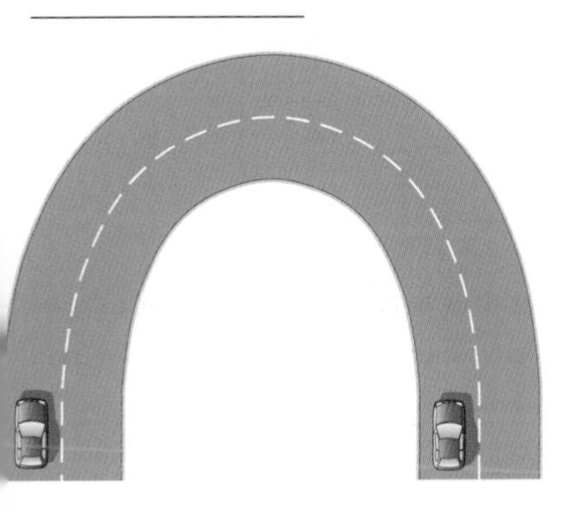

Overtaking is a potentially dangerous manoeuvre.

13

Before overtaking, consider whether it is really n__ __ __ __ __ __ __ __ __.

Fill in the missing word

Always use the safety routine when overtaking.

Put these actions into their correct sequence by putting numbers 1 to 7, as seen in the diagram, in the boxes

☐ Signal ☐ Mirrors ☐ Look
☐ Position ☐ Mirrors ☐ Speed
☐ Manoeuvre

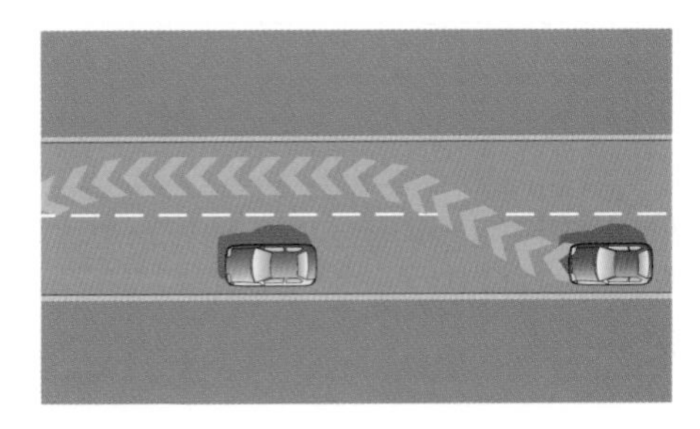

14

What is the minimum amount of clearance you should give a cyclist or motor cyclist?

Answer ______________________________

____

Answers on pages 104–5

15

There are four situations in which you may, with caution, overtake on the left-hand side of the car in front.

Name them

1 ____________________

2 ____________________

3 ____________________

4 ____________________

16

List four places where it would be dangerous to overtake.

1 ____________________

2 ____________________

3 ____________________

4 ____________________

17

Dual carriageways can appear similar to motorways, but there are important differences. Which of the following statements apply to dual carriageways?

Tick the relevant boxes

1 Reflective studs are not used ☐.

2 Cyclists are allowed. ☐

3 The speed limit is always 60mph. ☐

4 You cannot turn right to enter or leave a dual carriageway. ☐

5 Milk floats and slow moving farm vehicles are prohibited. ☐

18

When turning right from a minor road on to a dual carriageway, where would you wait ...

A When there is a wide central reserve?

Answer____________________

B When the central reserve is too narrow for your car?

Answer____________________

19

When travelling at 70mph on a dual carriageway, which lane would you use?

Answer____________________

Answers on pages 105–6

20

What do these signs mean?

A

Answer____________________________

B

Answer____________________________

C

Answer____________________________

21

Which of the signs in Question 20 (see opposite) would you expect to see on a dual carriageway?

Answer____________________________

22

Why is it important to plan your movements especially early when leaving a dual carriageway to the right (see diagram below)?

Answer____________________________

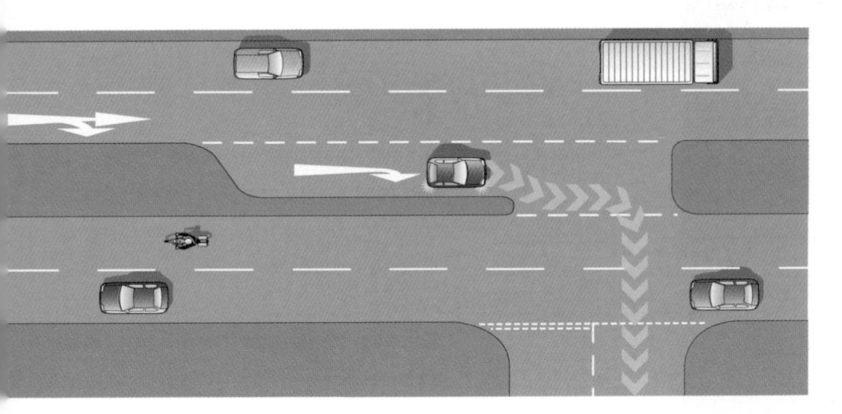

Answers on page 106

1

Cars fitted with automatic transmission select the gear depending on the road speed and the load on the engine. They therefore have no c_ _ _ _ _ _ pedal.

Fill in the missing word

2

The advantages of an automatic car are ...

1 ______________________

____

2 ______________________

____

3

The gear selector has the same function as a manual selector, but what function do each of the following have?

P — Park ______________________

R — Reverse ______________________

N — Neutral ______________________

D — Drive ______________________

3 — 3rd ______________________

2 — 2nd ______________________

1 — 1st ______________________

4

Automatic cars have a device called a kickdown. Is its function ...

Tick the correct box

1 To select a higher gear? ☐

2 To select a lower gear manually? ☐

3 To provide quick accelerations when needed? ☐

5

When driving an automatic car, would you select a lower gear ...

Tick the correct boxes

	True	False
1 To control speed when going down a steep hill?	☐	☐
2 To slow the car down in normal driving?	☐	☐
3 When going uphill?	☐	☐
4 To overtake, in certain circumstances?	☐	☐
5 When manoeuvring?	☐	☐
6 Before stopping?	☐	☐

6

An automatic car has two foot pedals, the foot-brake and the accelerator.

For normal driving, which foot would you use ...

1 For the brake?

Answer______________________

2 For the accelerator?

Answer______________________

Answers on pages 106–7

7

When you are driving an automatic car, using one foot to control both pedals is preferable to using both the left and the right foot. Why?

Answer ____________________

8

Some cars with automatic transmission have a tendency to 'creep'.

Which gears allow the car to creep?

Answer ____________________

9

When driving an automatic car, would you use the handbrake ...

Tick the correct box

1 More than in a manual car? ☐

2 The same? ☐

3 Less? ☐

HINTS & TIPS

Remember – if you haven't got your foot on the brake when you select Drive in an automatic car, the vehicle may begin to move forward

10

In which position should the gear selector be when you are starting the engine?

Answer ____________________

or ____________________

P
R
N
D
3
2
1

11

As you approach a bend, an automatic car will sometimes change up because there is less pressure on the accelerator. What should you do to prevent this happening?

Tick the correct box

1 Slow down before the bend and accelerate gently as you turn. ☐

2 Brake as you go round the bend. ☐

3 Brake and accelerate at the same time. ☐

Answers on page 107

1

There are many myths and misunderstandings surrounding the driving test.

Are the following true or false?

Tick the correct boxes

	True	False
1 The driving test is designed to see whether I can drive around a test route without making any mistakes.	☐	☐
2 The driving test is designed to see whether I can drive safely under various traffic conditions.	☐	☐
3 I do not need to know any of *The Highway Code*.	☐	☐
4 The examiner has a set allocation of passes each week.	☐	☐
5 I may be expected to drive up to the maximum national speed limit, where appropriate.	☐	☐

2

The length of the normal driving test is approximately ...

Tick the correct box

1 60 minutes ☐
2 90 minutes ☐
3 40 minutes ☐

3

If, during the test, you do not understand what the examiner says to you, you would take a guess because you must not talk to him or her.

Is this statement true or false?

Tick the correct box **True** ☐ **False** ☐

4

You may have heard people say that it is easier to pass the driving test in certain parts of the country.

Tick the correct box

	YES	NO
Do you agree with this statement?	☐	☐

5

If you fail your test, you can take it again. Which of the following statements is correct?

Tick the correct box(es)

1 If you fail the test, you can apply straight away for another appointment. ☐
2 If you fail the test you have to wait a month before you can apply for another appointment. ☐
3 You can re-take your test, subject to appointment availability, any time. ☐
4 You have to wait 10 working days before you can re-take the test. ☐

Answers on page 107

6

Before the practical part of your test, the examiner will test your eyesight. This is done by asking you to read a number plate at a distance of ...

Tick the correct box

1 30.5 metres (100 feet) ☐
2 20.5 metres (67 feet) ☐
3 40.5 metres (133 feet) ☐

7

What will happen if you fail your eyesight test?

Answer______________________________

____

8

It is essential that you take both sections of your p_ _ _ _ _ _ _ _ _ _ _ l_ _ _ _ _ _ _ to the test centre. This document must be s_ _ _ _ _ in ink.

Complete the sentence

9

You will also be required to produce another form of identification; this could be a p_ _ _ _ _ _ _ _ , or a photograph signed and authorised by your i_ _ _ _ _ _ _ _ _ _.

Complete the sentence

10

**The examiner will expect you to drive without making any mistakes.
Do you think this statement is true or false?**

Tick the correct box **True** ☐ **False** ☐

11

**Is this statement about what you will be asked to do during the test true or false?
I will be asked to perform four set exercises:**

Tick the correct boxes

	True	False
1 The emergency stop	☐	☐
2 The turn in the road	☐	☐
3 Reversing into a side road on the right or left	☐	☐
4 Reverse parallel parking or reversing into a parking bay	☐	☐

Answers on page 108

12

When reversing, are you allowed to undo your seat belt?

Tick the correct box **Yes** ☐ **No** ☐

13

If you fail your test, what will the examiner do?

1 ______________________________

____

2 ______________________________

____

14

When you have passed your driving test, what are you entitled to do?

1 ______________________________

____

2 ______________________________

____

3 ______________________________

____

15

I have within the last month passed my test.

Can I supervise a learner driver?

Tick the correct box **YES** ☐ **NO** ☐

16

When you pass your test, where should you send your pass certificate?

Answer______________________________

____

17

While you are waiting for your full licence to be sent to you, can you drive legally?

Tick the correct box **YES** ☐ **NO** ☐

18

It is recommended that you take further tuition once you have passed your test, especially on motorway driving.

Complete the sentence

As a learner driver you will not have experienced the special r__ __ __ __ that apply on the motorway and the h__ __ __ s__ __ __ __ of the other traffic.

19

While taking your driving test, you should drive ...

Tick the correct box

1 Especially carefully, keeping about 5mph below the speed limit ☐

2 As you would normally drive with your instructor ☐

3 With confidence, keeping at or just over the speed limit, to show that you can really drive ☐

20

Can you take a driving test if you are deaf?

Tick the correct box **YES** ☐ **NO** ☐

Answers on page 108

The driving test ensures that all drivers reach a minimum standard.

1

Do you think that learning to drive ends with passing the test?

Tick the correct box **YES** ☐ **NO** ☐

2

What knowledge and skills are not necessarily assessed in the present driving test?

List three

1 ____________________

2 ____________________

3 ____________________

3

Which of these statements do you think best describes advanced driving?

Tick the correct box

1 Advanced driving is learning to handle your car to its maximum performance. ☐

2 Advanced driving is learning to drive defensively with courtesy and consideration to others. ☐

3 Advanced driving is learning to drive fast. ☐

4

Some people have difficulty in driving at night.

Which age group would you expect, in general, to experience most difficulties?

Tick the correct box

1 Older people ☐

2 Younger people ☐

5

Once you have passed your driving test, your licence is usually valid until you reach __ __ years of age.

Complete the sentence

6

There are particular circumstances under which you are required to take a driving test again. Name them

Answer____________________

HINTS & TIPS

Driving is a skill you can improve for the rest of your life; consider further training after the test.

Answers on page 109

7

Motorways are designed to enable traffic to travel faster in greater safety. Compared to other roads, are they statistically ...

Tick the correct box

1 Safer? ☐

2 Less safe? ☐

3 No different? ☐

8

Are the following groups allowed on the motorway?

Tick the correct boxes

1 Provisional licence holders ☐

2 Motor cycles over 50cc ☐

3 Pedestrians ☐

4 HGV learner drivers ☐

5 Newly qualified drivers with less than three months' experience ☐

6 Motor cycles under 125cc ☐

7 Cyclists ☐

9

There are some routine checks you should carry out on your car before driving on the motorway.
Name four of them

1 ______________________________

2 ______________________________

3 ______________________________

4 ______________________________

10

On the motorway, if something falls from either your own or another vehicle, should you ...

Tick the correct box

1 Flash your headlights to inform other drivers? ☐

2 Pull over, put your hazard warning lights on and quickly run on to the motorway to collect the object? ☐

3 Pull over on to the hard shoulder, use the emergency telephone to call the police? ☐

4 Flag another motorist down to get help? ☐

Answers on page 109

11

Which colour do you associate with motorway signs?

Tick the correct box

1 Black lettering on a white background ☐
2 White lettering on a green background ☐
3 White lettering on a blue background ☐

12

At night or in poor weather conditions, your headlights will pick out reflective studs. Match the colour of the studs to their function by placing the appropriate letter in the box.

A Amber	Marks the edge of the hard shoulder ☐
B Red	Marks the edge of the central reservation ☐
C Green	Marks the lane lines ☐
D White	Marks exits and entrances ☐

13

Do the broken lines at the end of the acceleration lane mean ...

Tick the correct box

1 The edge of the carriageway? ☐
2 Other traffic should let you in? ☐
3 Give way to traffic already on the carriageway? ☐

14

If you see congestion ahead, is it legal to use your hazard warning lights to warn drivers behind you?

Tick the correct box **YES** ☐ **NO** ☐

15

What is the most common cause of accidents on motorways?

Tick the correct box

1 Vehicles breaking down ☐
2 Drivers falling asleep ☐
3 Drivers travelling too fast, too close to the vehicle in front ☐
4 Fog ☐

16

Are the following statements true or false?

I can use the hard shoulder ...

Tick the correct boxes	True	False
1 To take a short break	☐	☐
2 To stop and read a map	☐	☐
3 To allow the children to stretch their legs	☐	☐
4 To pull over in an emergency	☐	☐
5 To answer a phone call	☐	☐

Answers on pages 109–10

17

In normal driving on the motorway, you should overtake ...

Tick the correct box

1 On the right ☐
2 On the left ☐
3 On either side ☐

Driving at night can cause problems.

18

Which of these statements do you think is correct?

Tick the correct box

1 Street lighting and my car's headlights mean that I can see just as well as in the daylight. Therefore driving at night is just like driving in the daylight. ☐
2 At night I have to rely on my car's headlights and any additional lighting. Therefore I cannot see as far or drive as fast as in the daylight. ☐

19

At dusk and dawn what action should you take to compensate for driving a dark coloured car?

Answer______________________________

____

20

When driving after dark in a built-up area, should you use ...

Tick the correct box

1 Dipped headlights? ☐
2 Side or dim-dipped lights? ☐

21

***The Highway Code* says you should not use your horn in a built-up area between 11.30pm and 7am.**

What is the exception to that rule?

Answer______________________________

____

22

The diagram below illustrates two vehicles parked at night on a two-way road.

Which one is parked correctly?

Tick the correct box

A ☐ B ☐

A

B

Answers on page 110

23

ertain groups of road users are articularly vulnerable at night. lame two of them

1 ______________________

2 ______________________

24

Inder what circumstances would you ise dipped headlights during the day?

Answer______________________

____

nd then complete the sentence

__ __ and b__ s__ __ __.

25

When you are waiting at a junction fter dark, your brake lights might d__ __ __ __ __ the driver behind. t is better to use your h__ __ __ __ __ __ __ __.

Complete the sentences

Certain weather conditions can create hazardous driving conditions in the summer as well as in the winter.

26

Which of the following causes greatest danger to drivers?

Tick the correct box

1 Snow ☐

2 Ice ☐

3 Heavy rain ☐

4 Not being able to see properly ☐

27

In wet weather conditions your tyres can lose their grip. You should allow at least d__ __ __ __ __ the distance between you and the car in front that you allow on a dry road.

Fill in the missing word

28

In very wet conditions there is a danger of a build-up of water between your tyres and the road. This is called a__ __ __ __ __ __ __ __ __ __.

Fill in the missing word

Answers on page 110

29

How can you prevent a build-up of water occurring?

S__ __ __ d__ __ __ __ .

30

How should you deal with floods?

Tick the correct box

1 Drive through as fast as possible to avoid stopping ☐

2 Drive through slowly in 1st gear, slipping the clutch to keep the engine speed high ☐

3 Drive through in the highest gear possible, slipping the clutch to keep the engine speed high ☐

31

Will less tread on your tyres ...

Tick the correct box

1 Increase your braking distance? ☐

2 Decrease your braking distance? ☐

32

When the tyres lose contact with the road, the steering will feel v__ __ __ l__ __ __ __.

Complete the sentence

33

After you have driven through a flood, should you check ...

Tick the correct box

1 Your speedometer? ☐

2 Your brakes? ☐

3 Your oil? ☐

34

There are certain key precautions you should take when driving in fog.

Complete the following sentences

1 S__ __ __ d__ __ __ __.

2 Ensure you are able to s__ __ __ within the distance you can see to be clear.

3 Use your w__ __ __ __ __ __ __ __ __ __ w__ __ __ __ __.

4 Use your d__ __ __ __ __ __ __ __ and your h__ __ __ __ __ __ r__ __ __ w__ __ __ __ __ __ __ __ __ __ __.

35

Under what circumstances should you use your rear fog lights?
When visibility is less than __________ metres/feet.

Fill in the correct number

Answers on page 110

36

Vhen you are following another vehicle n fog, should you ...

ick the correct box

1 Follow closely behind because it will help you see where you are going? ☐

2 Leave plenty of room between you and the vehicle in front? ☐

37

Vhen you are following another vehicle n fog, should you use ...

ick the correct box

1 Main beam headlights? ☐

2 Dipped headlights? ☐

38

xtra precautions are needed when lealing with a junction in fog.

omplete the following sentences

Open your w__ __ __ __ __ __ __ and switch off your a__ __ __ __ s__ __ __ __ __.

L__ __ __ __ __ __ for other vehicles.

Signal e__ __ __ __ __ .

Use your b__ __ __ __ __ __. The light will a__ __ __ __ __ following vehicles.

Use your h__ __ __ if you think it will w__ __ __ other road users.

39

Is the following statement about anti-lock brakes true or false?
Anti-lock brakes will stop me skidding when driving on snow or ice.

Tick the correct box **True** ☐ **False** ☐

40

When driving in snow or ice you should gently test your b__ __ __ __ __ __ from time to time.

Fill in the missing word

41

In order to slow down when driving on snow or ice you should ...

Fill in the missing words

1 Use your brakes g__ __ __ __ __ __ .

2 Get into a l__ __ __ __ __ g__ __ __ earlier than normal.

3 Allow your speed to d__ __ __ and use b__ __ __ __ __ __ gently and early.

42

On snow or ice, braking distances can increase by ...

Tick the correct box

1 10 times ☐

2 5 times ☐

3 20 times ☐

4 15 times ☐

Answers on page 111

43

When going downhill in snow, what would you do to help you slow down?

Answer___________________________________

____

____

44

When cornering in snow or ice, what should you avoid doing?

Answer___________________________________

____

____

45

How can you reduce the risk of wheel spin?

Answer___________________________________

____

____

HINTS & TIPS

If you realise that your car is starting to skid, ease off the brake and accelerator, then steer smoothly in the same direction as the skid.

46

Three important factors cause a skid. Name them.

1 ___________________________________

____

____

2 ___________________________________

____

____

3 ___________________________________

____

____

47

Some everyday driving actions, especially in poor weather, can increase the risk of skidding.

Fill in the missing words

1 S__ __ __ __ __ __ __ down.

2 S__ __ __ __ __ __ __ __ __ up.

3 T__ __ __ __ __ __ __ corners.

4 Driving u__ __ __ __ __ __ and d__ __ __ __ __ __ __ __ __.

Answers on page 111

All vehicles need routine attention and maintenance to keep them in good working order. Neglecting maintenance can be costly and dangerous.

1

With which of these statements do you agree?

Tick the correct box

1 Allowing the fuel gauge to drop too low is bad for the engine. ☐

2 In modern cars the fuel level makes little difference. ☐

2

What do you put into the engine to lubricate the moving parts?

Answer______________________________

____

____

3

How frequently should you check your oil level?

Tick the correct box

1 Once a month ☐

2 Once a year ☐

3 Every time you fill up with fuel ☐

4

The engine is often cooled by a mixture of w_ _ _ _ and a_ _ _ _ f_ _ _ _ _.

Some engines are a_ _ cooled.

Complete the sentence

5

How frequently should you test your brakes?

Tick the correct box

1 Daily ☐

2 Monthly ☐

3 Weekly ☐

4 When I use them ☐

6

Incorrectly adjusted headlamps can cause d_ _ _ _ _ to other road users.

Complete the sentence

7

All headlamps, indicators and brake lights should be kept in good working order. It is also important that they are kept c_ _ _ _ .

Fill in the missing word

Answers on page 111

8

Tyres should be checked for u__ __ __ __ __ wear and tyre walls for b__ __ __ __ __ and c__ __ __.

Complete the sentence

9

The legal requirement for tread depth is not less than ...

Tick the correct box

1 1.4mm ☐
2 1.6mm ☐
3 2mm ☐

10

What should you do if your brakes feel slack or spongy?

Answer__________________________________

____

____

11

Vehicle breakdowns could result from ...

Fill in the missing words

1 N__ __ __ __ __ __ of the vehicle
2 Lack of r__ __ __ __ __ __ c__ __ __ __ __
3 Little or no p__ __ __ __ __ __ __ __ __ __ __ maintenance
4 A__ __ __ __ of the vehicle

Answers on page 111

12

It is advisable to carry a warning triangle.

1 On a straight road how far back should it be placed?

Tick the correct box

50 metres/yards ☐
200 metres/yards ☐
150 metres/yards ☐

2 On a dual carriageway, how far back should it be placed? At least ...

Tick the correct box

200 metres/yards ☐
150 metres/yards ☐
450 metres/yards ☐

13

If you use a warning triangle, is it worth putting your hazard lights on as well?

Tick the correct box **YES** ☐ **NO** ☐

14

If your vehicle breaks down on a motorway, should you ...

Tick the correct box

1 Gently brake, put your hazard lights on and seek assistance? ☐
2 Pull over to the central reservation as far to the right as possible? ☐
3 Pull over safely on to the hard shoulder as far away from the carriageway as possible? ☐

15

If your vehicle has broken down on the motorway, should you tell your passengers to ...

Tick the correct box

1 Stay in the vehicle while you seek assistance? ☐

2 Wait by the car on the hard shoulder but watch for other vehicles? ☐

3 Get out of the vehicle and wait on the embankment away from the hard shoulder? ☐

16

The marker posts at the side of all motorways have a picture of a telephone handset.

How can you tell which way to walk to reach the nearest telephone?

Answer ______________________________

17

When you use the emergency telephone on a motorway, what will the operator ask you?

1 ______________________________

2 ______________________________

3 ______________________________

4 ______________________________

18

Disabled drivers cannot easily get to an emergency telephone. How can they summon help?

1 ______________________________

2 ______________________________

Answers on page 112

19

If you break down when travelling alone, there are three things you are advised NOT to do.

Complete the sentences

1 Do not ask p__ __ __ __ __ __ m__ __ __ __ __ __ __ __ __ for help.

2 Do not accept help from anyone you d__ n__ __ k__ __ __ (except the emergency services or a breakdown service).

3 Do not l__ __ __ __ you vehicle l__ __ __ __ __ than necessary.

20

If I am first or one of the first to arrive at the scene of an accident, should I ...

Tick the correct boxes

	True	False
1 Always move injured people away from vehicles?	☐	☐
2 Tell the ambulance personnel or paramedics what I think is wrong with those injured?	☐	☐
3 Give casualties something warm to drink?	☐	☐
4 Switch off hazard warning lights?	☐	☐
5 Switch off vehicle engines?	☐	☐
6 Inform the police of the accident?	☐	☐

Answers on page 112

21

If you are involved in an accident, what MUST you do?

Answer______________________________

____

____

22

If you are involved in an accident and nobody is injured, do you have to call the police?

Tick the correct box **YES** ☐ **NO** ☐

23

What information do you need to exchange if you are involved in an accident?

1 ______________________________

2 ______________________________

3 ______________________________

4 ______________________________

5 ______________________________

24

If you thought you had a fire in your car's engine, what action would you take?

1 ______________________________

____

____

2 ______________________________

____

____

3 ______________________________

____

____

25

There are three items of emergency equipment it is wise to carry in your car.

Fill in the missing words

1 F_ _ _ _ A_ _ kit.

2 F_ _ _

e_ _ _ _ _ _ _ _ _ _ _.

3 W_ _ _ _ _ _ t_ _ _ _ _ _ _

26

When you rejoin a motorway from the hard shoulder, should you ...

Tick the correct box

1 Signal right and join when there is safe gap? ☐

2 Keep your hazard lights on and drive down the hard shoulder until there is a safe gap? ☐

3 Use the hard shoulder to build up speed and join the carriageway when safe? ☐

27

Fuel combustion causes waste products. One of these is a gas called c_ _ _ _ _ d_ _ _ _ _ _ _.

This is a major cause of the g_ _ _ _ _ _ _ _ _ _ _ effect.

Complete the sentences

28

How much does transport contribute to the production of carbon dioxide in the country (expressed as a percentage of the total production)?

Tick the correct box

1 10 per cent ☐

2 25 per cent ☐

3 50 per cent ☐

4 20 per cent ☐

Answers on page 113

29

The MOT test checks the roadworthiness of a vehicle.

Does it include an exhaust emission test?

Tick the correct box **YES** ☐ **NO** ☐

30

A catalytic convertor stops the emission of carbon dioxide.

Tick the correct box **True** ☐ **False** ☐

31

Which uses up more fuel?

Tick the correct box

1 A car travelling at 50mph ☐

2 A car travelling at 70mph ☐

32

There are some measures car drivers can take to help reduce damage to the environment.

List five

1 ______________________________

2 ______________________________

3 ______________________________

4 ______________________________

5 ______________________________

Before buying a used car it is best to decide what you want the car for and how much you can afford.

33

There are three main sources of supply for used vehicles. You can buy from a d_ _ _ _ _ _, at an a_ _ _ _ _ _ _ or p_ _ _ _ _ _ _ _ _.

Complete the sentence

34

When reading a glowing description of a used car, what should you first consider?

Answer______________________________

Answers on page 113

35

Are these statements about buying a used car through a dealer or at an auction true or false?

Tick the correct boxes **True False**

1 It is often cheaper to buy a car at an auction than through a dealer. ☐ ☐

2 I have the same legal rights when I buy at an auction as when I buy from a dealer. ☐ ☐

3 I should always read the terms and conditions of trade before I buy a car at an auction. ☐ ☐

4 The best way to select a used car dealer is by recommendation. ☐ ☐

36

Cars bought through a dealer often have a warranty.

What should you check?

1 ______________________________

____

____

2 ______________________________

____

____

37

When you test drive a vehicle, you should make sure that it is t_ _ _ _, has a current M_ _ certificate (if applicable) and that all i_ _ _ _ _ _ _ _ requirements are complied with.

Complete the sentence

38

There are some important items that you should check on before you buy a used car.

List three

1 ______________________________

____

____

2 ______________________________

____

____

3 ______________________________

____

____

39

Do you think the following statement is true or false?

It is advisable to have my vehicle examined by a competent and unbiased expert before I buy.

Tick the correct box **True** ☐ **False** ☐

Answers on page 113

Towing a Caravan or Trailer – **Section 16**

Particular difficulties are encountered when towing a caravan or trailer. There are some very good courses which will help you master the skills required.

1

People can underestimate the length of the total combination of car and caravan or trailer.

Is the overall length usually ...

Tick the correct box

1 Twice the length of a normal car? ☐

2 Three times the length of a normal car? ☐

2

What additional fixtures should you attach to your car to help you see more clearly?

1 ______________________________
____
____

Answers on page 114

3

When towing you will need more distance than normal to overtake. Is it ...

Tick the correct box

1 Twice the normal distance? ☐

2 Three times the normal distance? ☐

3 Four times the normal distance? ☐

4

A device called a s_ _ _ _ _ _ _ _ _ _ will make the combination safer to handle.

Fill in the missing word

5

The stability of the caravan will depend on how you load it. Should heavy items be loaded ...

Tick the correct box

1 At the front? ☐

2 At the rear? ☐

3 Over the axle(s)? ☐

6

There are special restrictions for vehicles which are towing.

A What is the speed limit on a dual carriageway?

Tick the correct box

1 50mph ☐

2 60mph ☐

3 70mph ☐

B What is the speed on a single carriageway?

Tick the correct box

1 40mph ☐
2 50mph ☐
3 60mph ☐

7

There are some important checks you should make before starting off.

List four

1 ______________________________
____
2 ______________________________
____
3 ______________________________
____
4 ______________________________
____

8

If you decide to stop to take a break, before allowing anyone to enter the caravan you should lower the j_ _ _ _ _ w_ _ _ _ and c_ _ _ _ _ s_ _ _ _ _ _ _.

Fill in the missing words

Many people now take their car abroad or hire a vehicle when on holiday.

9

Motoring organisations, such as The Automobile Association, can help you plan and organise your trip.
The AA can provide advice on travel and v_ _ _ _ _ _ _ insurance.
They will also help you organise the d_ _ _ _ _ _ _ _ _ that you will need.

Fill in the missing words

10

Before travelling to Europe, you should always ...

Complete the sentences

1 Plan the r_ _ _ _ you wish to take.
2 Know the local m_ _ _ _ _ _ _
r_ _ _ _ _ _ _ _ _ _.

Answers on page 114

11

It is essential that your vehicle should be checked thoroughly.
List four of the routine checks you should make

1 ______________________________

____

____

2 ______________________________

____

____

3 ______________________________

____

____

4 ______________________________

____

____

12

In most European countries you are advised to carry your d_ _ _ _ _ _ _ l_ _ _ _ _ _ _ on you.

Complete the sentence

13

What do the letters IDP stand for?

Answer______________________________

____

____

14

Where might you need an IDP?

Answer______________________________

____

____

15

In most European countries what age do you have to be to drive?

Tick the correct box

1 ☐ 21 **2** ☐ 18 **3** ☐ 16

16

Some European countries can require you to carry additional emergency equipment.
List four of the items you are recommended to carry

1 ______________________________

____

____

2 ______________________________

____

____

3 ______________________________

____

____

4 ______________________________

____

____

Answers on page 114

Answers to Questions

Answers to Questions

Section 1

INTRODUCTION TO LEARNING TO DRIVE

Questions on pages 24–5

A1 A current, signed, full or provisional licence for the category of vehicle that you are driving

A2 examinations
register

A3 21 years old
three years

A4 To the front and rear. It is important not to place them in windows where they could restrict good vision.

A5 True

A6 You should have answered No to all the questions.

A7 Yes. This should be the ambition of every driver.

A8 3, 4

ADJUSTING YOUR DRIVING POSITION

Questions on page 25

A9 **1** handbrake
2 doors
3 seat
4 head restraint
5 mirrors
6 seat belt

INTRODUCTION TO VEHICLE CONTROLS

Questions on pages 25–6

A10 The handbrake E
The driving mirrors D
The gear lever F
The clutch G
The steering wheel A
The foot-brake B
The accelerator C
gas

A11 The foot-brake R
The clutch L
The accelerator R

A12 **1** False. You will need one hand to change gear or use other controls.
2 True
3 False. The best position is quarter to three or ten to two.
4 False. It is safest to feed the wheel through your hands.
5 True
6 True

A13 The direction indicators B
Dipped beam A
Main beam D
Rear fog lamp C
Horn E
Hazard lights F

Section 2

MOVING OFF

Questions on page 27

A1 **A** 1
B 5
C 3
D 2
E 6
F 4
G 7
H 8
I 9

STOPPING (NORMALLY)

Questions on page 28

A2 **A** 1
B 3
C 2
D 4
E 6
F 5
G 8
H 7
I 9

GEAR CHANGING

Questions on pages 29–30

A3 1st gear

A4 5th, or 4th if the car has a 4-speed gear box

A5 Usually 2nd gear, but 1st if you need to go very slowly or 3rd if the corner is sweeping and you can take it safely at a higher speed

A6 engine
vehicle
sound
when

A7 **A** 1
B 3
C 2
D 4
E 5

A8 **1** False. This will cause the engine to labour.
2 False. It is good practice to use the brakes to slow the car down. Using the transmission causes wear and tear which can be very costly. Also, the brakes are more effective.
3 False
4 True
5 False. It is good practice to miss out the unwanted gears and select the gear most appropriate to your road speed.

A9 **1**

A10 **1** Don't
2 Don't
3 Do
4 Do
5 Do
6 Don't
7 Don't
8 Don't

STEERING

Questions on page 31

A11 **A**, except in a few cars fitted with four-wheel steering (in which case al[l] four wheels will move)

A12 **A**

A13 **B**

A14 **B**

ROAD POSITIONING

Questions on page 31

A15 **C** well to the left but not too close to the kerb

A16 **B**. Avoid swerving in and out. It is unnecessary and confuses other drivers.

CLUTCH CONTROL

Questions on page 32

A17 **A**

A18 biting

A19 **1** Yes
2 Yes
3 No
4 Yes
5 No

Section 3

UNCTIONS

Questions on pages 33–5

A1 two or more roads

A2 **A** T-junction
B Y-junction
C Roundabout
D Staggered crossroads
E Crossroads

A3 **1** E
2 C
3 B
4 D
5 A

A4 **A** 1
B 3

A5 **1** Mirrors
2 Signal
3 Position
4 Speed
5 Look

A6 assess
decide
act

A7 **A**

A8 **B**

A9 **D**

A10 **1** mirrors, position
2 signal
3 safe
4 safe distance
5 overtake

CROSSROADS

Questions on page 36

A11 **A 3** Crossroads. Priority for traffic on the major road. Never assume other drivers will give you priority.
B 1 Unmarked crossroads
C 2 Crossroads with give way lines at the end of your road. Give way to traffic on the major road.

ROUNDABOUTS

Questions on pages 36–7

A12 **C**

A13 **1** Left
2 Left
3 Right. Remember to use the MSM routine before signalling left to turn off.

A14 **1** Left
2 Going ahead
3 Right

A15 mirrors
signal
position
speed
look

A16 **2**

Section 4

PARKING (ON THE ROAD)
Questions on pages 38–9

A1 **1** safe
2 considerate
3 legal
A2 Cars 1, 2, 3, 6
A3 **1** False
2 False
3 True
4 True
A4 Any of the following:
at a bus stop
at a school entrance
opposite a junction
on a bend
on the brow of a hill
on a Clearway
on a motorway
at night facing oncoming traffic
in a residents' parking zone.

Section 5

PASSING STATIONARY VEHICLES AND OBSTRUCTIONS

Questions on page 40
A1 Vehicle 2
A2 Vehicle 2, even though the obstruction is on the right. Where safe, when travelling downhill be prepared to give priority to vehicles (especially heavy vehicles) that are coming uphill.

MEETING AND CROSSING THE PATH OF OTHER VEHICLES
Questions on pages 41

A3 **1** True
2 False. Always consider whether it is safe. Are there dangers the other driver cannot see? Remember, flashing headlamps has the same meaning as sounding the horn. It is a warning: 'I am here!' Sometimes it is taken to mean: 'I am here and I am letting you pass.'
3 True
A4 **1** Yes
2 Yes
3 No
4 Yes
5 Yes
6 Yes
7 Yes

Section 6

STOPPING IN AN EMERGENCY

Questions on pages 42–3

A1 **1** True
2 True
3 True
4 False. Looking in the mirror should not be necessary. You should know what is behind you.
5 False
6 True
7 True

A2 False. An emergency stop will be conducted randomly on only some tests. You must always know how to stop safely in an emergency.

A3 pump
1 maximum
2 lock
3 quickly

A4 steer
brake
pump
pressure
1 False. Other elements beyond braking can cause skidding e.g. acceleration or going too fast into a bend.
2 False. Although you may stop in a shorter distance, you still need to leave the correct distance to allow yourself time to react and vehicles behind you time to stop.

STOPPING DISTANCES

Questions on pages 43

A5 **1** No
2 Yes
3 Yes
4 No

A6 ½ second

A7 **1** 23 metres/75 feet
2 15 metres/50 feet
3 96 metres/315 feet

A8 longer
more

A9 breaks
two-second

Section 7

MOVING OFF AT AN ANGLE

Question on page 44

A1 **1** False. You should check your mirrors and blindspot before moving out. Keep alert for other traffic as you pull out and stop if necessary.
2 True
3 False. Move out slowly and carefully.
4 True. The closer you are, the greater the angle.
5 True. As you move out, you are likely to move on to the right-hand side of the road and into conflict with oncoming vehicles.
6 False. You should signal only if it helps or warns other road users. Signalling gives you no right to pull out.

MOVING OFF UPHILL

Question on page 44

A2 **1** True
2 False. Using the accelerator pedal will not move the car forwards.
3 False. As your feet will be using the clutch pedal and the accelerator pedal you need to use the handbrake to stop the car rolling back.
4 True
5 True
6 True
7 True

MOVING OFF DOWNHILL

Question on page 45

A3 **1** True
2 False. Almost certainly you will need to use the foot-brake.
3 False. It is often better to move off in 2nd gear.
4 True. This will stop the car rolling forwards.
5 True
6 False. You will need to have your foot on the foot-brake to stop the car rolling forwards.

APPROACHING JUNCTIONS UPHILL AND DOWNHILL

Question on page 46

A4 The following statements are correct: 1, 4, 5, 6, 7

Section 8

REVERSING

Questions on pages 47–8

A1 safe
convenient
law

A2 **1** False
2 False
3 True
4 True

A3 **A**

A4 **1, 4**

A5 Car A: to the left
Car B: to the right

A6 observation

REVERSING INTO A SIDE ROAD ON THE LEFT

Questions on pages 48–9

A7 **3**

A8 **1** True
2 False
3 True

A9 **4**

A10 **C**

A11 Left

A12 The front of the car will swing out to the right

A13 **1** True
2 False
3 True

A14 pedestrians
road users
stop

REVERSING INTO A SIDE ROAD ON THE RIGHT

Questions on pages 49–50

A15 True

A16 **B**

A17 **2**

A18 True. You may need to place your left hand at 12 o'clock and lower your right hand.

A19 True

A20 **2**

A21 **B**

TURNING IN THE ROAD

Questions on pages 51–2

A22 **A**

A23 slowly
briskly

A24 False, but you should try to complete the manoeuvre in as few moves as possible.

A25 **2, 3, 4**

A26 all round

A27 **1** Right
2 Steer briskly left
3 Left
4 Steer briskly right
5 Right

A28 **1** Left
2 Over your right shoulder to where the car is going

REVERSE PARALLEL PARKING

Questions on pages 52–4

A29 **2**

A30 **C**, in line with the rear of the parked vehicle

A31 **2**

A32 **1** To the left
2 The nearside headlamp of the vehicle towards which you are reversing
3 Clipping the rear offside of the lead car
4 Take off the left lock
5 Steer to the right and then take off the right lock as you get straight

A33 **1** False
2 False
3 True. You will be expected to be able to complete the exercise within approximately two car lengths.

A34 All round, particularly for pedestrians and oncoming vehicles

A35 **C**. The other bay widths are reduced by parked vehicles. This may make opening doors a squeeze.

A36 Allows you to make best use of the area in front of the bay. Gives you a better view when driving out of the space

A37 close
directions
pedestrians

Section 9

TRAFFIC LIGHTS AND YELLOW BOX JUNCTIONS

Questions on pages 55–6

A1 **1** red
2 red and amber
3 green
4 amber
5 red

A2 **1** green
2 red and amber
3 amber
4 red

A3 **1** False
2 True
3 True
4 False. Pedestrians who are already crossing have priority.

A4 **2**

A5 **1** Lane A or B
2 Lane C
3 Lane A

A6 **1** No. If your exit is blocked you should not enter a yellow box junction.
2 No. If your exit is blocked you should not enter a yellow box junction.
3 Yes

PEDESTRIAN CROSSINGS

Questions on pages 56–8

A7 **1** Zig-zag lines
2 Flashing yellow beacons on both sides of the road
3 Black and white stripes on the crossing
4 A give way line

A8 **1** True
2 True. You must not park or wait on the zig-zag lines on either side of the crossing.
3 False. You must not overtake on the zig-zag lines on approach to the crossing.
4 True
5 True. A slowing down arm signal should be used. It helps pedestrians understand what you intend to do. They cannot see your brake lights.

A9 **1** Traffic lights
2 Zig-zag lines
3 A white stop line

A10 **2** A white stick means the pedestrian is visually handicapped. A white stick with two reflector bands means the pedestrian may be deaf as well as visually handicapped.

A11 **1** Flashing amber
2 You must give way to pedestrians on the crossing, but if it is clear you may go on.

A12 A bleeping tone. This sounds when the red light shows to drivers and helps visually handicapped pedestrians know when it is safe to cross.

A13 There is no flashing amber light sequence. The light sequence is the same as normal traffic lights.

A14 cyclists

LEVEL CROSSINGS

Questions on page 58

A15 **A** 3
B 1
C 2
D 4

A16 **2**
4
5

Section 10

ONE-WAY SYSTEMS

Questions on page 59

A1 **A** is the correct sign for a one-way street.
B tells you 'Ahead only'.

A2 **1** True
2 True
3 True
4 True

ROAD MARKINGS

Questions on pages 59–61

A3 information
warnings
orders

A4 **1** They can be seen when other signs may be hidden
2 They give a continuing message

A5 **A** 2
B 2

A6 **1, 4**

A7 They are used to separate potentially dangerous streams of traffic.

A8 You must not enter the hatched area.

TRAFFIC SIGNS

Questions on pages 61

A9 **1** Warning
2 Order
3 Information

A10 **1** must
2 must not

A11 **1** You must give way to traffic on the major road. Delay your entry until it is safe to join the major road.
2 You must stop (even if the road is clear). Wait until you can enter the new road safely.

A12 vision is limited

A13 Motorway signs D
Primary routes E
Other routes B
Local places C
Tourist signs A

Section 11

ROAD OBSERVATION

Questions on pages 62–4

A1 speed
behaviour
intentions

A2 **1** Observe that the view into the new road is restricted.
The driver should ...
Move forward slowly, to get a better view.
Note the pedestrian who may walk in front of or behind car **A**.
Note the pedestrian waiting to cross.
Allow the cyclist to pass.
Once in position to see car **B**, stop and give way.
2 Observe that the parked car restricts the view into and out of the side road.
The driver should ...

Slow down on approach to parked car **P**.
Take up position to gain a better view and be more visible to car A and the pedestrian.
Slow down in case the pedestrian walks out from behind the parked car **P**.
Consider signal to pass parked car **P**.
Look carefully into minor road. Note the actions of car **A**. Be prepared to stop.

A3 bike

A4 **3**, but touching the brakes may encourage the driver to drop back

A5 **A**
1 Junctions
2 Hump-back bridges
3 Concealed entrances
4 Dead ground
5 Narrow lanes

B
1 Children playing
2 Horses
3 Pedestrians
4 Especially elderly and young cyclists
5 Other vehicles

A6 **1** True. The ability to advise those at your destination of delays can help to reduce the worry of late arrivals
2 True
3 True
4 True

A7 All are distracting and upset concentration, and should not be carried out while driving.

DEALING WITH BENDS

Questions on pages 64–5

A8 speed
gear
position

A9 **1**

A10 **B**

A11 **A**

A12 **A** On a right-hand bend keep to the left. This will help to improve your view.
B On a left-hand bend keep to the centre of the lane. Do not move to the centre of the road to get a better view. A vehicle travelling in the opposite direction may be taking the bend wide.

OVERTAKING

Questions on pages 65–6

A13 necessary
1 Mirrors
2 Position
3 Speed
4 Look
5 Mirrors
6 Signal
7 Manoeuvre

A14 About the width of a small car, more in windy or poor weather conditions

A15 **1** The vehicle in front is signalling and positioned to turn right
2 You are using the correct lane to turn left at a junction
3 Traffic is moving slowly in queues and the traffic on the right is moving more slowly than you are
4 You are in a one-way street

A16 **1** On approach to a junction
2 The brow of a hill
3 The approach to a bend
4 Where there is dead ground.
NB These are examples. Be guided by *The Highway Code*.

DUAL CARRIAGEWAYS

Questions on pages 66–7

A17 **2** Statements 1, 3, 4 and 5 do not apply:
1 Reflective studs are used on some dual carriageways.
3 The speed limit is subject to local conditions and may vary from 40mph up to the national speed limit.
4 You can turn right on to and off dual carriageways unlike motorways, where all traffic enters and leaves on the left.
5 You may find slow moving vehicles sometimes displaying a flashing amber light.

A18 **A** You would cross over the first carriageway then wait in the gap in the central reservation. Be careful, if you are towing or if your vehicle is long, that you do not cause other road users to change course or slow down.

B You would wait until there is a gap in the traffic long enough for you safely to clear the first carriageway and emerge into the second.

A19 The speed limit applies to all lanes. Use the first lane to travel in and the second for overtaking.

A20 **A** Dual carriageway ends
B Road narrows on both sides
C Two-way traffic straight ahead

A21 **A** and **C**

A22 Traffic is moving much faster, and one or more lanes will have to be crossed.

Section 12

DRIVING AN AUTOMATIC CAR

Questions on pages 68–9

A1 Clutch

A2 **1** Driving is easier
2 There is more time to concentrate on the road

A3 Park – Locks the transmission. This should be selected only when the vehicle is stationary.
Reverse – Enables the car to go backwards, as in a manual car.
Neutral – Has the same function as in a manual car. The engine is not in contact with the driving wheels.
Drive – Is used for driving forwards. It automatically selects the most appropriate gear.
3rd – Has the same function as manual gears
2nd – Has the same function as manual gears
1st – Has the same function as manual gears

A4 **3**

A5 **1** Yes
2 No
3 Yes, if you needed extra control
4 You would probably use kickdown, but possibly in certain circumstances you would manually select a lower gear
5 Yes, maybe using 1st gear
6 No. Use the brakes

A6 **1** The right foot
2 The right foot

A7 It stops you trying to control the brake and accelerator at the same time. It encourages early release of the accelerator and progressive braking.

A8 Drive, reverse, all forward gears.

A9 **1** You should apply the handbrake every time you stop. Otherwise you have to keep your foot on the foot-brake.

A10 Park (P) or Neutral (N)

A11 **1**

Section 13

THE DRIVING TEST

Questions on pages 70–2

A1 **1** False
2 True
3 False
4 False
5 True

A2 **3**

A3 False. If you did not hear clearly or did not understand what the examiner said, you should ask him or her to repeat the instruction. If you have any problem with your hearing, it is advisable to tell the examiner at the start of the test.

A4 No. The standard test does not vary. The test result should be the same wherever it is taken.

A5 **1, 4**

Answers to Questions

A6 **2**

A7 The test will not proceed. You have failed not only the eyesight section, but the whole test. Remember, if you wear glasses or contact lenses, to wear them for the eyesight test and for the rest of the driving test.

A8 provisional licence
signed

A9 passport
instructor

A10 False. You can make some minor errors and still reach the required standard.

A11 False. Only about one third of test candidates will be asked to complete an emergency stop. You will be asked to do two out of the three reversing manoeuvres.

A12 Yes, but remember to do it up again when you have completed the exercise.

A13 **1** Give you a verbal explanation of the main reasons for failure
2 Write out a form for you to take away showing you your main errors

A14 **1** Drive unsupervised
2 Drive on a motorway
3 Drive without L-plates

A15 No. You must have had at least three years' driving experience (and be over 21 years of age).

A16 To the DVLA, Swansea

A17 Yes. It is a good idea to keep a note of your driver number and the date you passed your test.

A18 rules
high speed

A19 **2** The examiner will expect you to drive normally. You should abide by all speed limits and drive according to road and traffic conditions.

A20 Yes. The examiner will be skilled in giving instructions and directions to deaf candidates.

Section 14

BEYOND THE TEST

Questions on page 73

A1 No

A2 **1** Bad weather driving
2 Night-time driving
3 Motorway driving
4 Skid control ... and more

A3 **2**

A4 **1**, although people of any age can find it difficult to drive at night

A5 70

A6 There are certain serious driving offences which carry the penalty of disqualification. In order to regain a full licence, the disqualified driver has to apply for a provisional licence and take an extended test. If, because of certain illnesses, you have been unable to drive for 10 years, you will be required to take the test again in order to gain a full licence.
For new drivers: the accumulation of six or more penalty points within two years of passing the test will mean reverting to a provisional licence and re-sitting the test.

MOTORWAY DRIVING

Questions on pages 74–6

A7 **1**

A8 **1** No
2 Yes
3 No
4 Yes
5 Yes
6 Yes
7 No

A9 **1** Oil
2 Water
3 Fuel
4 Tyre pressures
These are just some of the checks; for more information, refer to your car's manual.

A10 **3** You should never attempt to retrieve anything from the carriageway.

A11 **3**

A12 **B** Amber
A Red
D Green
C White

A13 **3**

A14 Yes

A15 **3**

A16 **1** False
2 False
3 False
4 True
5 False

A17 **1**, except when traffic is moving slowly in queues and the queue on the right is travelling more slowly

SAFE NIGHT DRIVING

Questions on pages 76–7

A18 **2**

A19 Switch on earlier, switch off later.

A20 **1**. It helps others to see you.

A21 If you are stationary, to avoid danger from a moving vehicle.

A22 **A**. Always park with the flow of traffic. You will show red reflectors to vehicles travelling in your direction.

A23 **1** Pedestrians
2 Cyclists
3 Motor cyclists
} two of these

A24 In poor weather conditions – see and be seen

A25 dazzle
handbrake

ALL-WEATHER DRIVING

Questions on pages 77–80

A26 4

A27 double

A28 aquaplaning

A29 Slow down
Allow time for the tread patterns to disperse the water.

A30 **2**

A31 **1**

A32 very light

A33 **2**

A34 **1** Slow down
2 stop
3 windscreen wipers
4 demister, heated rear windscreen

A35 100 metres/328 feet

A36 **2**

A37 **2**

A38 **1** windows, audio system. Listen
2 early
3 brakes, alert
4 horn, warn

A39 False, because your tyres are not in contact with the road

A40 brakes

A41 **1** gently
2 lower gear
3 drop, brakes

A42 **1**

A43 If possible, control your speed before reaching the hill. Select a low gear early.

A44 Using your brakes

A45 Avoid harsh acceleration

A46 **1** The driver
2 The vehicle
3 The road conditions

A47 **1** Slowing
2 Speeding
3 Turning
4 uphill, downhill

Section 15

VEHICLE CARE

Questions on pages 81–2

A1 **1**

A2 Oil

A3 **3**

A4 Water, anti-freeze, air

A5 **1**

A6 dazzle

A7 clean

A8 uneven, bulges, cuts

A9 **2**

A10 Get them checked as quickly as possible

BREAKDOWNS, ACCIDENTS AND EMERGENCIES

Questions on pages 82–5

A11 **1** Neglect
2 routine checks
3 preventative
4 abuse

A12 **1** 50 metres/yards
2 At least 150 metres/yards

A13 Yes. Try to give as much warning as possible.

A14 **3**

A15 **3**

A16 Under the drawing of the handset is an arrow which points to the nearest telephone.

A17 **1** The emergency number (painted on the box)
2 Vehicle details (make, registration mark, colour)
3 Membership details of your motoring organisation
4 Details of the fault

A18 **1** By displaying a Help pennant
2 By using a mobile telephone

A19 **1** passing motorists
2 do not know
3 leave, longer

A20 **1** False. Do not move injured people unless they are in danger.
2 False. Tell them the facts, not what you think is wrong.
3 False. Do not give those injured anything to eat or drink. Keep them warm and reassure them.
4 False. Keep hazard lights on to warn other drivers.
5 True. Switch off engines. Put out cigarettes.
6 True, in the case of injury.

A21 Stop

A22 No

A23 **1** The other driver's name, address and contact number
2 The registration numbers of all vehicles involved
3 The make of the other car
4 The other driver's insurance details
5 If the driver is not the owner, the owner's details.

A24 **1** Pull up quickly
2 Get all passengers out
3 Call assistance

A25 **1** First aid
2 Fire extinguisher
3 Warning triangle

A26 **3**

THE MOTOR CAR AND THE ENVIRONMENT

Questions on pages 85–6

A27 carbon dioxide, greenhouse

A28 **4**

A29 Yes

A30 False. A catalytic convertor reduces the level of carbon monoxide, nitrogen oxide and hydrocarbons by up to 90 per cent. Carbon dioxide is still produced.

A31 **2**

A32 Nine measures are listed here:
1 Make sure your vehicle is in good condition and regularly serviced.
2 Make sure tyres are correctly inflated. Under-inflated tyres waste fuel.
3 Push the choke in as soon as possible when starting from cold.
4 Avoid harsh braking.
5 Buy a fuel-efficient vehicle.
6 Use the most appropriate gear.
7 Use your accelerator sensibly and avoid harsh acceleration.
8 Use unleaded fuel.
9 Dispose of waste oil, old batteries and used tyres sensibly.

BUYING A USED CAR

Questions on pages 86–7

A33 dealer, auction, privately

A34 Why is it being sold?

A35 **1** True
2 False
3 True
4 True

A36 **1** What is covered
2 The length of the agreement

A37 taxed, MOT, insurance

A38 Four items to check are listed here:
1 Mileage
2 Has it been involved in any accidents?
3 Number of owners
4 Is there any hire purchase or finance agreement outstanding?

A39 True. The AA offer a national inspection scheme.

Answers to Questions

Section 16

TOWING A CARAVAN OR TRAILER

Questions on pages 88–9

A1 **1**

A2 Exterior towing mirrors, to give you a good view

A3 **2**

A4 stabilizer

A5 **3**

A6 **A** 2
B 2

A7 Seven checks are listed here:
1 Is the caravan or trailer loaded correctly?
2 Is it correctly hitched up to your vehicle?
3 Are the lights and indicators working properly?
4 Is the braking system working correctly?
5 Is the jockey wheel assembly fully retracted?
6 Are tyre pressures correct?
7 Are all windows, doors and roof lights closed?

A8 jockey wheel, corner steadies

DRIVING IN EUROPE

Questions on pages 89–90

A9 vehicle, documents

A10 **1** route
2 motoring regulations

A11 Here are five routine checks:
1 Tyres, including spare. Always carry a spare tyre.
2 Tool kit and jack.
3 Lamps and brake lights.
4 Fit deflectors to your headlamps to prevent dazzle to other drivers approaching on the left.
5 Check you have an extra exterior mirror on the left.

A12 driving licence

A13 International Driving Permit

A14 Some non-EU countries

A15 **2**

A16 Five items are listed here:
1 Spare lamps and bulbs
2 Warning triangle
3 First aid kit
4 Fire extinguisher
5 Emergency windscreen

Part 3 Understanding the Theory behind the test

Contents Page

Section 1
Alertness

The first section in the Theory Test questions is headed ALERTNESS. Alertness is a short section and is a good place to start.

- Alertness means being wide awake and concentrating on what you are doing – driving – not being distracted by mobile phones or loud music.
- Alertness means looking out for hazards.
- Alertness means noticing all road signs and road markings, and acting on the instructions and information they give.

Are you fit to drive?

'Fit' can mean:

- Did you have any alcoholic drinks before you set out?
- Are you under the influence of illegal substances (drugs)?
- Are you feeling groggy or unwell?
- Are you taking prescription medicine that could affect your ability to control the car?
- Are you too tired to drive?

It's unwise to set out on a journey if you're not well, on the basis of 'I'll see how I go – I'll probably be all right':

- Your reactions are likely to be slower.
- You may be unable to judge distances properly.
- Your actions may be less well co-ordinated than usual and it's not legal.

If you are tired, open the window for a few moments to let in some fresh air. If you drive when you are too tired, you risk falling asleep at the wheel – an all too common cause of serious accidents. Driving for long stretches on a motorway at night can be especially dangerous. If you sense that you are losing your concentration, then take a break at a motorway service station. Plan your journey ahead, giving yourself plenty of time for rest stops – at least every couple of hours.

Tackling the questions

Look at the questions in the Alertness section. You'll see that the Alertness questions are all about these

- anticipation
- observation
- signalling
- reversing
- using your mirrors
- concentration
- getting distracted
- feeling sleepy
- using mobile phones

DID YOU KNOW?

The main causes of distraction are:

- Loud music in the car
- Passengers (usually children)
- Events happening outside (such as accidents)
- Using a mobile phone

Now test yourself on the questions about Alertness

Section 2
Attitude

The government road safety organisations believe that the ATTITUDE of learner drivers is extremely important for road safety.

Attitude means
- Your frame of mind when you get in the car
- How you react when you meet hazards on the road
- How you behave towards other drivers

Attitude is a very important part of being a good driver. Your attitude when you are driving plays a big part in ensuring your safety and that of other road users.

Do you aim to be a careful and safe driver or a fast and skilful driver? If you don't want to end up as another road accident statistic, then carefully and safely is the way to go.

Remember that a car is not an offensive weapon, and often people don't realise what a potentially lethal machine they are in control of when they get behind the wheel. You only have to think about this to understand the importance of your attitude when driving.

You'll see that questions in this section are concerned with encouraging you to be a careful and safe driver, and cover:
- Tailgating
- Consideration for other road users, including pedestrians, buses, slow-moving vehicles and horse riders
- Driving at the right speed for the conditions
- When to flash headlights
- The right place, time and way to overtake

And remembering a few dos and don'ts will help you achieve the right attitude for driving and make passing this section of the test much easier.

Good drivers do
- drive at the right speed and for the road and traffic conditions
- observe speed limits
- overtake only when it is safe to do so
- park in correct and safe places
- wait patiently if the driver in front is a learner or elderly or hesitant
- look out for vulnerable road users such as cyclists, pedestrians and children
- concentrate on their driving at all times
- plan their journey so that they have plenty of time to get to their destination

Good drivers don't
- allow themselves to become involved in road rage
- break speed limits
- drive too fast, particularly in wet, foggy or icy weather
- accelerate or brake too harshly
- overtake and 'cut in', forcing others to brake sharply
- put pressure on other drivers by driving too close behind them (this is called 'tailgating'), flashing headlights or gesturing
- allow their attention to be distracted by passengers, mobile phones or loud music, or what is happening on the road, such as staring at an accident

Tailgating

Driving excessively close behind another vehicle is known as tailgating – and it's dangerous! The car in front may stop suddenly (to avoid hitting a child or animal that has dashed out into the road, for example); when this happens the car following runs the risk of crashing into it.

You should always leave enough space between your vehicle and the one in front, so that you can stop safely if the driver in front suddenly slows down or stops.

Rear-end shunts account for a large percentage of all accidents on the road. In these situations, the driver of the car behind is almost always judged to be the guilty party.

So tailgating is potentially expensive as well as dangerous.

Another time when drivers are tempted to tailgate is when attempting to pass a large, slow-moving vehicle. However, keeping well back will improve your view of the road ahead, so that you're better able to judge when it's safe to overtake and the driver of the large vehicle will also be able to see you.

Useful tip

If you are being followed too closely by another driver you should slow down and increase the distance between your vehicle and the one in front. If you slow down or have to stop suddenly, the driver behind may crash into you, but you will have increased your stopping distance and will not be pushed into the vehicle in front of you.

Always remember

- Expect the unexpected, and make provision for the potential errors of other drivers – everyone makes mistakes sometimes.
- Don't create unnecessary stress for other drivers by showing your frustration in an aggressive manner.

If you are driving at the right speed for the road and weather conditions and a driver behind tries to overtake, you should pull back a bit from the vehicle in front so that if the driver behind insists on overtaking, there is less risk of an accident.

Do not try to stop the car behind from overtaking. Do not move into the middle of the road or move up close to the car in front. These actions could be very dangerous.

You should not give confusing signals such as indicating left or waving the other driver on.

Now test yourself on the questions about Attitude

Section 3
Safety and Your Vehicle

When you go through this section you will notice that the questions are a bit of a mixture. They cover a number of topics about SAFETY, including:

- Understanding the controls of your vehicle
- What the car's warning lights tell you
- Tyres – correct inflation, pressures and tread depths
- When to use hazard warning lights
- Passenger safety
- The environment
- Security and crime prevention

Many of the questions in this section are to do with 'legal requirements' and rules regarding parking your car and using lights. Look up all the sections in *The Highway Code* that deal with parking rules. Find out the rules for red routes, white lines and zigzag lines as well as yellow lines.

Seat belts
If any of your passengers are young people under 14, you are responsible for making sure that they wear seat belts. You are responsible for them by law, even if you are still a learner driver yourself.

Tips for this section

Learn *The Highway Code* and you will be able to answer most of the questions in this section. In particular make sure you know the rules regarding seat belts, tyres, and when to use your lights, including your hazard warning lights.

A confusing question

One of the most confusing questions in this section asks what kind of driving results in high fuel consumption. The answer, of course, is **bad** driving – especially harsh braking and acceleration. This means you will use more fuel than you should and therefore cause more damage to the environment than is necessary.

BUT many people read the word 'high' as meaning 'good' – as in a level of driving skill – and so pick the wrong answer.

Don't let it be you…

Now test yourself on the questions about Safety and Your Vehicle

Section 4
Safety Margins

Experienced drivers are usually better than new or learner drivers at leaving good SAFETY MARGINS. Learner drivers find it harder to keep their vehicle at a safe distance from the one in front. Therefore the questions in this section cover
- safe stopping distances

and
- safe separation distances (these are the same as safety margins)

What is a safety margin?
A safety margin is the space that you need to leave between your vehicle and the one in front so that you will not crash into it if it slows downs or stops suddenly. They are also called 'separation distances' and are an important part of anticipating road and traffic hazards. When you are learning to drive, you can feel pressured to speed up by drivers behind you.

Don't let other drivers make you cut down on your safety margins. Stay a safe distance behind the vehicle in front. Then you will have time to anticipate and react to hazards.

The two-second rule
In traffic that's moving at normal speed, allow at least a two-second gap between you and the vehicle in front.

Stopping distances
Many people who are taking their Theory Test get confused about this. You will notice that some of the questions ask for your overall stopping distance and others ask for your braking distance. These are different.

Overall stopping distance or stopping distance is not the same as braking distance. Stopping distance is made up of thinking distance + braking distance.

In other words, the time it takes to notice that there's a hazard ahead plus the time it takes to brake to deal with it.

Thinking distance
Thinking distance is sometimes called reaction time or reaction distance. If you are driving at 30mph, your thinking distance will be 30 feet (9 metres). That means your vehicle will travel 30 feet (9 metres) before you start braking.

The link between stopping distance and safety margins
You should always leave enough space between your vehicle and the one in front. If the other driver has to slow down suddenly or stop without warning, you need to be able to stop safely. The space is your safety margin.

Safety margins for other vehicles
Long vehicles and motorcycles need more room to stop – in other words, you must leave a bigger safety margin when following a long vehicle or motorbike. When driving behind a long vehicle, pull back to increase your separation distance and your safety margin so that you get a better view of the road ahead – there could be hazards developing and if you are too close he will be unable to see you in his rear view mirror. Strong winds can blow

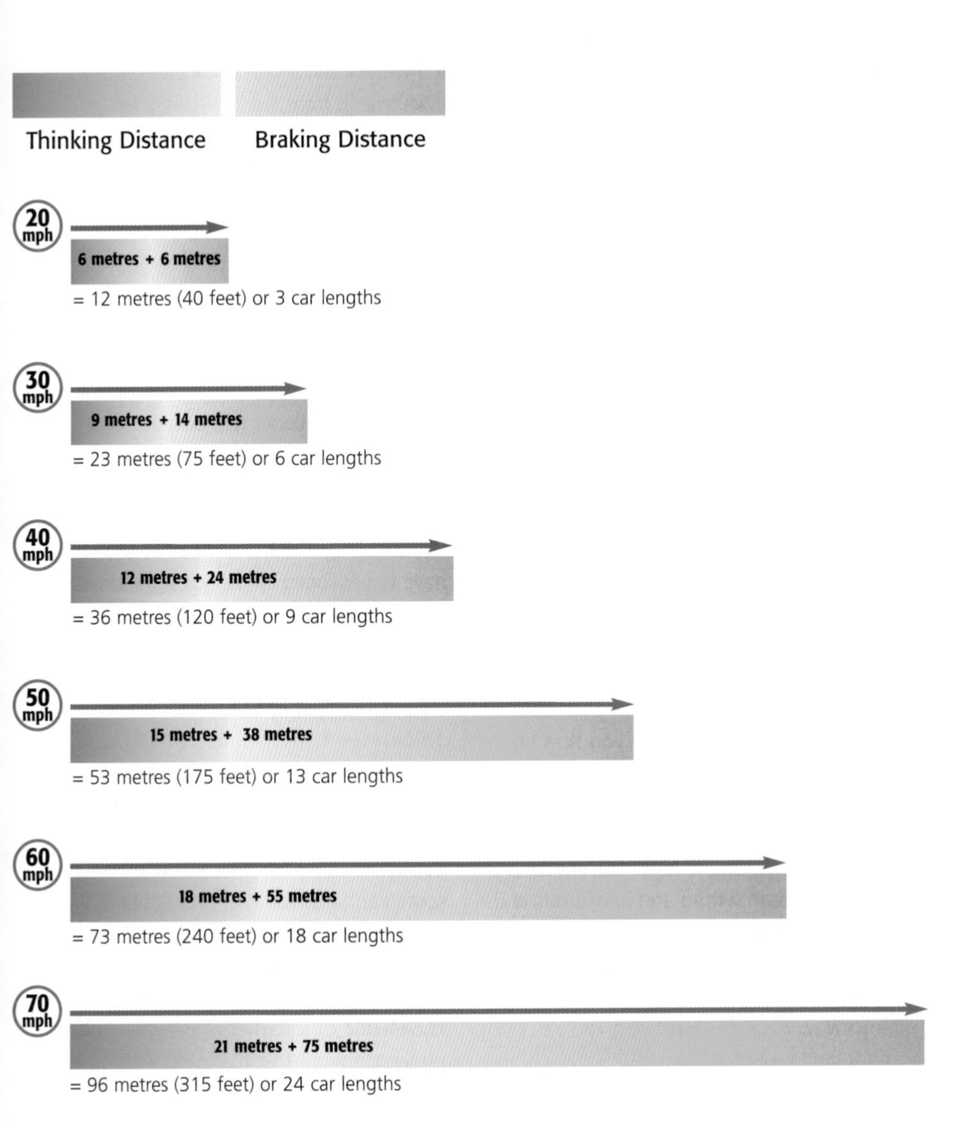
Thinking Distance
Braking Distance
20 mph
6 metres + 6 metres
= 12 metres (40 feet) or 3 car lengths
30 mph
9 metres + 14 metres
= 23 metres (75 feet) or 6 car lengths
40 mph
12 metres + 24 metres
= 36 metres (120 feet) or 9 car lengths
50 mph
15 metres + 38 metres
= 53 metres (175 feet) or 13 car lengths
60 mph
18 metres + 55 metres
= 73 metres (240 feet) or 18 car lengths
70 mph
21 metres + 75 metres
= 96 metres (315 feet) or 24 car lengths

lorries and motorbikes off course. So leave a bigger safety margin.

Different conditions and safety margins

You may find that one or more questions in your Theory Test might be about driving in 'different conditions'. These questions aim to make sure you know what adjustments you should make to your driving when either road conditions are different from normal, for example, when parts of the road are closed off for roadworks or weather conditions affect your driving.

Road works

You should always take extra care when you see a sign warning you that there are road works ahead. Remember, road works are a hazard and you have to anticipate them.

If you see the driver in front of you slowing down, take this as a sign that you should do the same – even if you can't see a hazard ahead. You still need to keep a safe distance from him. Harassing the driver in front by 'tailgating' is both wrong and dangerous and so is overtaking to fill the gap. It's especially important that you know what to do when you see a sign for road works ahead on a motorway.

- There may be a lower speed limit than normal – keep to it.
- Use your mirrors and indicators, and get into the correct lane in plenty of time.
- Don't overtake the queue and then force your way in at the last minute (this is an example of showing an inconsiderate attitude to other road users).
- Always keep a safe distance from the vehicle in front.

Weather conditions

In bad weather (often called 'adverse' weather), you need to increase your safety margins.

When it's raining you need to leave at least twice as much distance between you and the vehicle in front. When there's ice on the road leave an even bigger gap because your stopping distance increases tenfold.

It's amazing how often drivers go too fast in bad weather. In adverse weather motorways have lower speed limits, but some drivers don't take any notice of them.

When it's icy you should multiply your two-second gap by ten.

Questions that look alike

There are a number of questions about anti-lock brakes in this section. Lots of questions look the same. Some are easy and some are hard. Some of them appear to be the same but they are not.

The questions test two things – your knowledge of the rules of the road and your understanding of words to do with driving.

Now test yourself on the questions about Safety Margins

Section 5
Hazard Awareness

How often does a motorist protest that the accident happened before they had time to realise the person they hit was there? Some accidents will inevitably happen, but part of your instructor's job while teaching you to drive is to help you learn to anticipate problems before they happen.

What is the difference between Hazard Awareness and Hazard Perception?

- Hazard Awareness and Hazard Perception mean the same thing.
- Hazard Perception is the name for the part of the Theory Test that uses video clips. This test is about spotting developing hazards. One of the key skills of good driving, this is called anticipation.
- Anticipating hazards means looking out for them in advance and taking action now.
- Hazard Awareness is about being alert whenever you are driving.

That is why some of the questions in the HAZARD AWARENESS section deal with things that might make you less alert. For example feeling tired, feeling ill, taking medicines prescribed by your doctor or drinking alcohol.

Other questions in Hazard Awareness cover noticing road and traffic signs as well as road markings, what to do at traffic lights and when to slow down for hazards ahead.

Why are young male drivers more at risk?

New drivers have a greater than average chance of being involved in accidents. Statistics show that young male drivers have the most accidents.

- Maybe it's because when they first get their licence they want to show off to other drivers.
- Some people think that driving much too fast will earn them 'respect' from their friends.
- Some people think that they are such good drivers that the rules of the road should not apply to them.

Whatever the reason – drivers who don't watch out for hazards are at risk of being involved in an accident. The problem has a lot to do with people's attitude to driving. You'll find more about this aspect of driving in the Attitude part of the Theory Test.

We've already said that young drivers often don't learn to anticipate hazards until they are older and more experienced. The Hazard Perception test aims to 'fill the gap' in hazard perception for young drivers and other new drivers by making sure they have some proper training to make up for their lack of experience.

This should make them safer drivers when they start out on the road alone.

Looking for clues to hazards developing on the road

As you get more driving experience you will start to learn about the times and places where you are most likely to meet hazards. Think about some of these examples.

Rush hour

You know that people take more risks when driving in the rush hour. Maybe they have to drop their children off at school before going to work. Maybe they are late for a business meeting. So you have to be prepared for bad driving, such as other drivers pulling out in front of you.

Dustbin day

Drivers in a hurry may get frustrated if they are held up in traffic because of a hazard such as a dustcart. They may accelerate and pull out to overtake even though they cannot see clearly ahead. You should not blindly follow the lead of another driver. Check for yourself that there are no hazards ahead.

Schoolchildren

Young children are often not very good at judging how far away a car is from them, and may run into the road unexpectedly. Always be on the lookout for hazards near a school entrance.

Parked cars

Imagine you are driving on a quiet one-way street with cars parked down each side of the road. You wouldn't expect to meet any vehicles coming the other way – but what about children playing? They might run out into the road after a football. It would be difficult to see them because of the parked cars, until they were in the road in front of you.

More examples of hazards

So, what kinds of hazards are we talking about? And what should you do about them?

Road markings and road signs sometimes highlight likely hazards for you.

The list below gives some of the hazards you should look out for when driving along a busy street in town.

After each hazard there are some ideas about what you should be looking out for, and what to do next.

- You see a bus which has stopped in a lay-by ahead.

There may be some pedestrians hidden by the bus who are trying to cross the road, or the bus may signal to pull out. Be ready to slow down and stop.

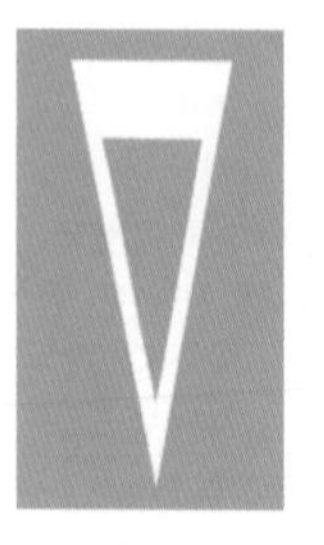

- You see a white triangle painted on the road surface ahead.

This is a hazard warning sign. It tells you that there is a 'Give Way' junction just ahead. Slow down and be ready to stop.

- You see a sign for a roundabout on the road ahead.

Anticipate that other drivers may need to change lane, and be ready to leave them enough room.

- You come to some road works where the traffic is controlled by temporary traffic lights.

Watch out for drivers speeding to get through before the lights change.

- You look in your rear view mirror and see an emergency vehicle with flashing lights coming up behind you.

An emergency vehicle wants to pass, so get ready to pull over when it's safe.

- You see a small child standing with an adult near the edge of the pavement.

Check if the child is safely holding the adult's hand. Be ready to stop safely if the child suddenly steps into the road.

- You notice dustbins or rubbish bags put out on the pavement.

The dustcart could be around the next corner, or the bin men could be crossing the road with bags of rubbish. Be ready to slow down and stop if necessary.

- You hear a siren.

Look all around to find out where the emergency vehicle is. You may have to pull over to let it pass.

You will find out more about the different types of hazards you may encounter, including what to look for when driving on narrow country roads, or in bad (adverse) weather conditions, in the Vehicle Handling section of this book.

Always expect the unexpected
Don't forget that not all hazards can be anticipated. There are bound to be some you haven't expected.

Red flashing warning lights
Level crossings, ambulance stations, fire stations and swing bridges all have red lights that flash on and off to warn you when you must stop.

Observation

Another word for taking in information through our eyes is observation. Observation is one of the three key skills needed in hazard perception. The three skills are

- observation
- anticipation
- planning

An easy way to remember this is **O A P** for

Observe
Anticipate
Plan

Talk to yourself!

It's a good idea to 'talk to yourself' when you're learning to drive – and even after you've passed your test. Talk about all the things you see that could be potential hazards. Your driving instructor might suggest this as a way of making you concentrate and notice hazards ahead.

Even if you don't talk out loud, you can do a 'running commentary' in your head on everything you see around you as you drive.

For example, you might say to yourself – 'I am following a cyclist and the traffic lights ahead are red. *When the lights change I will allow him/her plenty of time and room to move off.*'
or
'The dual carriageway ahead is starting to look very busy. There is a sign showing that the right lane is closing in 800 yards. *I must get ready to check my mirrors and, if safe to do so, drop back to allow other vehicles to move into the left-hand lane ahead of me.*'

Note: Don't forget the mirrors! This way, you will notice more hazards, and you will learn to make more sense of the information that your eyes are taking in.

Learn your road signs!
Notice the information at the bottom of the first page of traffic signs in *The Highway Code*. It explains that you won't find every road sign shown here.

You can buy a copy of *Know Your Traffic Signs* from a bookshop to see some of the extra signs that are not in *The Highway Code*.

Note: In Wales, some road signs include the Welsh spelling as well as the English, and in Scotland, some signs are written using Gaelic spelling. You'll also see some 'old-style' road signs around, which are slightly different too.

Scanning the road

Learner drivers tend to look straight ahead of their car and may not notice all the hazards that might be building up on both sides. You will spot more hazards when driving if you train yourself to scan the road.

- Practise looking up and ahead as far as possible.
- Use all your mirrors to look out for hazards too.
- Don't forget that you have 'blind spots' when driving – work out where they are and find safe ways of checking all round for hazards.
- Ask your driving instructor to help you with all of this.

How is learning to scan the road going to help me pass my Theory Test?

- The idea of the Hazard Perception element of the test is to encourage you to get some real experience of driving before you take the Theory Test.
- If you meet real hazards on the road and learn how to anticipate them, you'll learn how to pass the Hazard Perception element of the test.
- In the video test you may not be able to look all around you as you would when driving a car; but the clips will be as realistic as possible in giving you a wide 'view' of the road ahead.

Observation questions

Study some of the pictures in the Hazard Awareness section.

They include photographs of scenes such as

- a cyclist at traffic lights, seen from the viewpoint of a driver in a car behind the cyclist

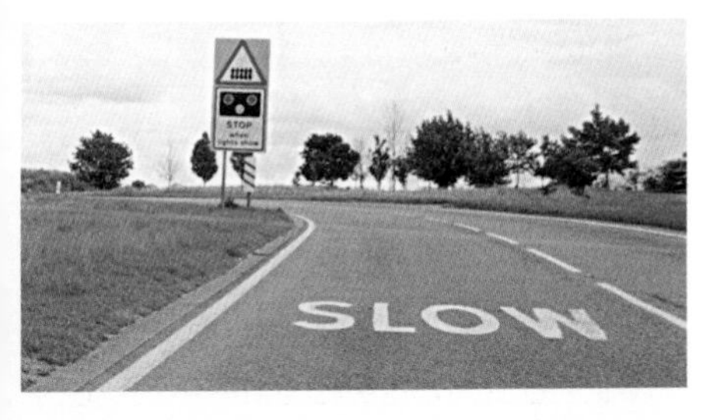

- what you see as a driver when you are approaching a level crossing

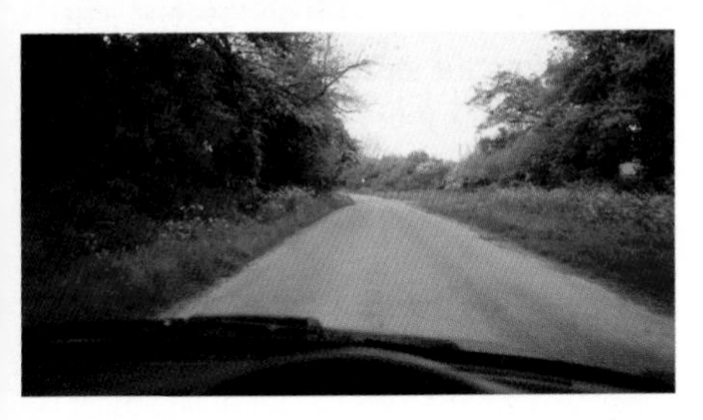

- what you see when coming up to a 'blind bend'

- a view of the road ahead with traffic building up where one lane is closing.

Look out for situations like these when you are out driving with your instructor, and use the practice to improve your hazard awareness.

As well as photographs, there are pictures of road and traffic signs.

What do these signs mean?

What actions should you take when you see these signs?

- If you are not sure, look them up in *The Highway Code*.

- Think about why the square yellow sign with the two children is in the Vehicle Markings section and not with the rest of the road signs.

Now test yourself on the questions about Hazard Awareness

Section 6
Vulnerable Road Users

Today's new vehicles are becoming safer all the time for the driver inside the car, but sadly this is not always the case for the pedestrian or cyclist outside. Many road users who are not driving cars have nothing to protect them if they are in an accident with a motor vehicle.

The questions in the VULNERABLE ROAD USERS section deal with the following:
- why different types of road users are vulnerable
- what you as a driver must do to keep them safe

Who are vulnerable road users?
The following are all vulnerable road users and you must drive with extra care when you are near vulnerable road users.
- pedestrians
- children
- elderly people
- people with disabilities
- cyclists
- motorcycle riders
- horse riders
- learner drivers and new drivers
- animals being herded along the road

Cyclists
Give cyclists plenty of room. Remember to keep well back from cyclists when you are coming up to a junction or a roundabout because you cannot be sure what they are going to do. On the roundabout they may go in any direction – left, right or straight ahead. They are allowed to stay in the left lane and signal right if they are going to continue round. Leave them enough room to cross in front of you if they need to. Turn to the section headed Vulnerable Road Users in the Theory Test questions to see some pictures of this. You must also give way to cyclists at toucan crossings and in cycle lanes (see the rules for cyclists set out in *The Highway Code*).

Look out for cyclists!
- It can be hard to see cyclists in busy town traffic.
- It can also be hard to see them coming when you are waiting to turn out at a junction. They can be hidden by other vehicles.

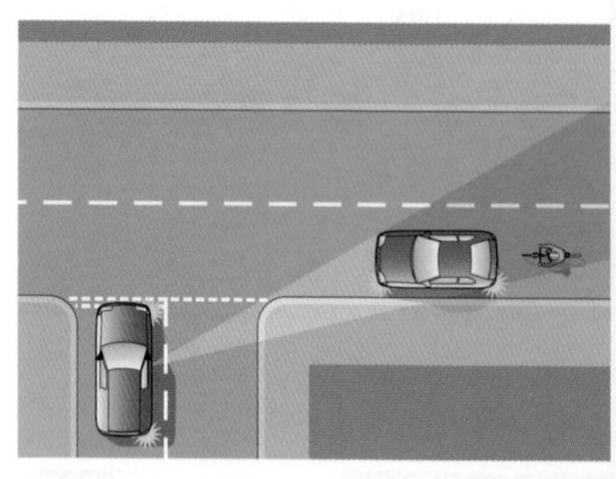

Always be on the lookout for cyclists. Especially, check your mirror to make sure you do not trap a cyclist on your left when you are turning left into a side road. Check your blind spots for cyclists, too.

Controlling your vehicle near cyclists
When you are following a cyclist, you must be able to drive as slowly as they do, and keep your vehicle under control. Only overtake

when you can allow them plenty of room, and it is safe to do so.

Cycle lanes
Cycle lanes are reserved for cyclists. Car drivers should not use them.

A cycle lane is marked by a white line on the road. A solid white line means you must not drive or park in the cycle lane during the hours it is in use.
A broken white line means that you should drive or park in it only if there is no alternative. You should not park there at any time when there are waiting restrictions.

When you overtake a cyclist, a motorcyclist or a horse rider, give them at least as much room as you would give a car.

Cyclists and motorcycle riders

Cyclists and motorcycle riders are more at risk than car drivers because

- they are more affected by strong winds, or by turbulence caused by other vehicles
- they are more affected by an uneven road surface, and they may have to move out suddenly to avoid a pot-hole
- car drivers often cannot see them

Pedestrians

Pedestrians most at risk include elderly people and children. Elderly people and others who cannot move easily may be slower to cross roads – you must give them plenty of time. Children don't have a sense of danger on the road; they can't tell how close a car is, or how fast it is going. They may run out into the road without looking. Or they may step out behind you when you are reversing – you may not see them because they are small.

People who are unable to see and/or hear

A blind person will usually carry a white stick to alert you to their presence. If the stick has a red band, this means that the person is also deaf, so will have no warning of an approaching car either visually or from engine noise.

When to give way to pedestrians

At any pedestrian crossing, if a pedestrian has started to cross, wait until they have reached the other side. Do not harass them by revving your engine or edging forward.

At a crossing with lights (pelican, toucan or puffin crossings), pedestrians have priority once they have started to cross even if, when on a pelican crossing, the amber lights start flashing.

Once a pedestrian has stepped on to a zebra crossing, you must stop and wait for them to cross.

Note: It is courteous to stop at a zebra crossing if a pedestrian is waiting to cross.

When you take your Practical Driving Test, you must stop for any pedestrians who are waiting on the pavement at a zebra crossing even if they haven't stepped on to the crossing yet. However, you must not wave to them to cross.

If you want to turn left into a side road and pedestrians have already started to cross the side road on foot, wait for them to finish crossing. People on foot have priority over car drivers.

DID YOU KNOW?
If a car hits a pedestrian at 40mph, the pedestrian will probably be killed.
Even at 30mph, 50% of pedestrians hit by cars will be killed.
At 20mph, pedestrians have a better chance of surviving. This is why you will find 20mph limits and other things to slow traffic in some residential streets and near school entrances.

Other types of vulnerable road users

Be prepared to slow down for animals, learner drivers, and other more unusual hazards such as people walking along the road in organised groups (for example, on a demonstration, or a sponsored walk). There are rules in *The Highway Code* that walkers must follow. But even if they break the rules, make sure you keep to them.

Animals

Drive slowly past horses or other animals. Allow them plenty of space on the road. Don't frighten them by sounding your horn or revving your engine.

If you see a flock of sheep or a herd of cattle blocking the road, you must

- stop
- switch off your engine
- and wait until they have left the road

People riding horses on the road are often children, so you need to take extra care; when you see two riders abreast, it may well be that the one on the outside is shielding a less experienced rider.

Traffic signs

Look up the Traffic Signs and Vehicle Markings sections in *The Highway Code* and find the following signs

- pedestrians walking in the road ahead (no pavement)
- cycle lane and pedestrian route
- advance warning of school crossing patrol ahead
- school crossing patrol
- elderly or disabled people crossing
- sign on back of school bus or coach

Now test yourself on the questions about Vulnerable Road Users

Section 7
Other Types of Vehicle

We have already come across some of the other types of vehicle that share the road with you and your car including motorbikes and bicycles. The questions in this part of the Theory Test are mostly about long vehicles such as lorries. However, you also need to know what to do about

- buses
- caravans
- trams
- tractors and other farm vehicles
- special vehicles for disabled drivers (powered invalid carriages)
- slow vehicles such as road gritters
- motorway repair vehicles

Important points to remember about these types of vehicle

- Many of them can only move very slowly.
- They cannot easily stop or change direction.

The driver's field of vision may be restricted – this means that car drivers have to allow them plenty of room.

Motorcycles

- Motorcycles are easily blown off course by strong winds. If you see a motorcyclist overtaking a high-sided vehicle such as a lorry, keep well back. The lorry may shield the motorcyclist from the wind as it is overtaking, but then a sudden gust could blow the motorcyclist off course.
- It can be hard to see a motorcyclist when you are waiting at a junction. Always look out for them.
- If you see a motorcyclist looking over their shoulder, it could mean that they will soon give a signal to turn right. This applies to cyclists too. Keep back to give them plenty of room.
- Motorcyclists and cyclists sometimes have to swerve to avoid hazards such as bumps in the road, patches of ice and drain covers. As before – give them plenty of room.

Long vehicles

- Like cyclists, long vehicles coming up to roundabouts may stay in the left lane even if they intend to turn right. This is because they need lots of room to manoeuvre. Keep well back so they have room to turn.
- Take great care when overtaking long or high-sided vehicles. Before you pull out to overtake, make sure you have a clear view of the road ahead.
- A long vehicle that needs to turn left off a major road into a minor road may prepare to do so by moving out towards the centre of the road, or by moving across to the other side.

If you're following them

- Give way, and don't try to overtake – on the right or the left.
- You might need to slow down and stop while the driver of the long vehicle makes the turn.

Buses and trams

- Always give way to buses when they signal to pull out.
- Always give way to trams as they cannot steer to avoid you.
- Don't try to overtake a tram.

Trams are **quiet** vehicles – you cannot rely on approaching engine noise to warn you that a tram is coming.

Take extra care when you see this sign, because trams are sometimes allowed to go when car drivers are not.

Tractors and slow-moving vehicles

- Always be patient if you are following a slow vehicle.

Drivers of slow vehicles will usually try to find a safe place to pull in to let the traffic go past. In the meantime you should keep well back, so that you can see the road ahead. Allow a safe distance in case they slow down or stop.

Slow vehicles are not allowed on motorways because they cannot keep up with the fast-moving traffic. Vehicles not allowed on motorways include

- motorcycles under 50cc
- bicycles
- tractors and other farm vehicles
- powered invalid carriages

Now test yourself on the questions about Other Types of Vehicle

Section 8 Vehicle Handling

The questions in this section test how much you know about controlling your vehicle on different road surfaces and in different weather.

Your control is affected by

- the road surface – is it rough or smooth? Are there any holes or bumps? Are there any 'traffic-calming measures', such as humps or chicanes?
- the weather conditions – you have to drive in different ways when there is fog, snow, ice or heavy rain.

Other questions in this section cover driving on country roads – on narrow and one-way roads, humpback bridges, steep hills, fords. Other questions need practical knowledge, for example, on engine braking, brake fade, and coasting your vehicle – use the Glossary.

This section also has some questions on overtaking and parking.

Road surface

The condition of the road surface can affect the way your vehicle handles. Your vehicle handles better on a smooth surface than on a surface that is damaged, bumpy or full of holes. If you have to drive on an uneven surface, keep your speed down so that you have full control of your vehicle, even if your steering wheel is jolted.

Take care also where there are tramlines on the road. The layout of the road affects the way your vehicle handles.

You may have to adjust your driving for traffic calming measures, such as traffic humps (sometimes called 'sleeping policemen') and chicanes. These are double bends that have been put into the road layout to slow the traffic down. The sign before the chicane tells you who has priority.

Traffic calming measures are often used in residential areas or near school entrances to make it safer for pedestrians.

Weather conditions

Bad weather (adverse weather) such as heavy rain, ice or snow affects the way your vehicle handles. If you drive too fast in adverse weather, your tyres may lose their grip on the road when you try to brake. This means the car may skid or 'aquaplane'. Aquaplaning means sliding out of control on a wet surface.

Driving in snow

In snow, the best advice is do not drive at all unless you really have to make a journey. If you have to drive in snowy conditions, leave extra time for your journey and keep to the main roads. You can fit snow chains to your tyres to increase their grip in deep snow.

Driving in fog

In fog your field of vision can be down to a few metres. Your vehicle is fitted with fog lights to help you see and be seen in fog. But you must know how and when to use them. Look up the three rules about fog lights in *The Highway Code*. You'll see that the key points to remember are:

- Don't dazzle other road users with your fog lights.
- Switch them off as soon as you can see better (as soon as the fog starts to clear).

> **Remember the two-second rule**
> You should double the two-second gap to four seconds when driving in rain, and increase the gap by as much as ten times when there is ice on the road.

Country driving

If you have had most of your driving lessons in a town, you need to know how to drive on narrow country roads. Some are only wide enough for one vehicle ('single-track'), and some are on very steep hills.

Your control of the gears, clutch and brakes will be important if you have to follow a tractor very slowly up a hill. On a steep downward slope you have to make sure your vehicle does not 'run away'.

On country roads you might find humpback bridges and fords. The signs below warn you of these hazards.

- Find out what you must do first after you have driven through a ford.

Technical knowledge

We have already mentioned engine braking. Understanding how engine braking works is part of good vehicle handling.

Note: If you press the footbrake constantly on a long hill, you may get brake fade. If you're not sure, check what that means in the Glossary at the back of this book.

Use the gears to control your vehicle on a downhill slope (or 'gradient'). If you put the vehicle in 'neutral', or drive with the clutch down (called coasting), your vehicle will increase speed beyond what is safe and will not be under proper control.

10%

This sign warns you of a steep hill downwards.

- Coasting is wrong and dangerous – you should not be tempted to do it to save fuel.

Remember that if there is sudden heavy rain after a dry hot spell, the road surface can get very slippery.

Now test yourself on the questions about Vehicle Handling

Section 9

Motorway Rules

Learner drivers aren't allowed on motorways, so you can't get experience of what it's like to drive on them until you've passed your test. However, you do need to know all about MOTORWAY RULES before taking your Practical Test, and your Theory Test will most likely include a question about motorways.

As soon as you pass your driving test you will be legally allowed to drive on motorways. You need to know all the motorway rules in advance, so that you are confident and ready to cope with motorway driving when you pass your test.

There are some major roads and dual carriageways that learners can drive on which are very much like motorways. You may drive on some of these fast roads during your driving test, so that your examiner can see how well you cope with hazards at higher speeds.

When driving on these fast roads you will need some of the very same skills that you will need for motorway driving – for example, using lanes properly, knowing when it is safe to overtake, and controlling your vehicle at speed.

If you are learning to drive with a driving school, you will have the chance to book a motorway lesson with your instructor after you have passed your test. It makes sense to take up this offer before you drive on a motorway alone for the first time.

Motorways and other roads

- On a motorway traffic is moving at high speed all the time.
- All lanes are in use.
- No stopping is allowed on a motorway – traffic only slows or comes to a stop because of accidents or other types of hold-up.
- Some road users are not allowed on motorways. These include
  - pedestrians, cyclists and learner drivers
  - horses and other animals
  - motorcycles under 50cc
  - slow-moving vehicles, tractors and farm vehicles and invalid carriages
- You always enter and leave a motorway on the left, via a slip road.
- To the left of the inside lane (left-hand lane) on a motorway is the hard shoulder. You can only drive on this in an emergency.
- Special signs and signals are used on motorways. These include signs above the road on overhead gantries, signs on the central reservation, and amber and red flashing lights.

Checks before your journey

Be extra careful about doing all your regular checks before you set out on a motorway journey. You cannot stop on the motorway to fix small problems, and no one wants to break down in the middle of fast traffic.

Always check

- oil and coolant levels, screen wash container
- tyres and tyre pressures
- fuel gauge
- that all mirrors and windows are free of dirt and grease
- that the horn works

Many of these checks are legally necessary, as well as important for your safety.

How to move on to the motorway

- Join the motorway by building up your speed on the slip road to match the speed of traffic in the left lane of the motorway.
- Use MSM (Mirrors – Signal – Manoeuvre) and move into the flow of traffic when it is safe to do so.

Changing lanes and overtaking

Driving on a motorway needs all the skills you have learned about anticipation and forward planning.

You should

- make good use of all mirrors, and check your blind spots
- signal to move out in plenty of time
- look out for hazards ahead in the lane you want to move to
- not go ahead if it will force another vehicle to brake or swerve
- keep a safe distance from the vehicle in front

Take a break

When you drive on motorways you will sometimes see signs that say 'Tiredness can kill – take a break!' This is very good advice. Motorways are monotonous – boring to drive, with long stretches of road that look the same for miles. A major cause of accidents is drivers falling asleep at the wheel. Plan your journey so that you have time to get out, stretch your legs and have a drink or snack.

The rules you need to know

- Keep to the left-hand lane unless you are overtaking and move back to the left lane as soon as it is safe to do so. Sometimes you need to stay in the centre lane for a time – for example, when a line of lorries is travelling up a hill in the left lane. Stay in the centre lane until you have passed the hazard, then signal left and return to the left lane.
- NEVER
  reverse
  park
  walk
  drive in the wrong direction on the motorway.
- Don't exceed the speed limit. This is normally 70mph, but lower speed limits may be signed when the road is busy, or in bad weather.
- Keep to the correct separation distance (see Safety Margins).
- Don't overtake on the left.
  If traffic is moving slowly in all three lanes you may find that the lane on the left is moving faster than the one to its right for a short time. Or the left lane may be signed for traffic turning off at the next junction only. But these are exceptions to the rule.
- If luggage falls from your vehicle, do not get out to pick it up. Stop at the next emergency phone and tell the police. Posts on the edge of the motorway show the way to the nearest emergency phone. You should use these phones rather than your mobile phone, because the emergency phone connects directly to the police and tells them exactly where you are calling from on the motorway.
- Don't stop on the hard shoulder except in an emergency. The hard shoulder is an extremely dangerous place, as many as one in eight road deaths happen there.

Traffic signs and road markings

Light signals

In *The Highway Code* you'll find the light signals only seen on motorways. Signs above the roadway or on the central reservation are activated as needed to warn of accidents, lane closures or weather conditions. Overhead gantries display arrows or red crosses showing which lanes are open or closed to traffic and which lanes to move to

when motorways merge or diverge. They may also show temporary speed limits.

Direction signs

Direction signs on motorways are blue and those on other major roads are green – other direction signs are white with black print.

Reflective studs

It's useful to know the colours of studs on a motorway; this can help in working out which part of the road you're on if it's dark or foggy. White studs mark lanes or the centre of the road and red studs mark the left edge of the carriageway.

Amber studs are used alongside the central reservation and green studs mark the entry to a slip road.
Note: these markings are also found on some dual carriageways.

Using the hard shoulder

- Stop as far to the left as possible and, if you can, near an emergency phone.
- Emergency phones are situated 1 mile apart and have blue and white marker posts every 100 metres. An arrow on the posts points the direction of the nearest phone.

- If you are using a mobile phone you can identify your location from the number on the post.
- Switch on your hazard warning lights.
- Use the left-hand door to get out of the vehicle, and make sure your passengers do too.
- Get everyone away from the road – if possible, behind the barrier or up the bank.
- Leave animals in the vehicle unless they aren't safe there.
- Phone the police with full details of where you are, then go back and wait in a safe place near your vehicle.

Now test yourself on the questions about Motorway Rules

Section 10
Rules of the Road

'Rules of the Road' is a good way to describe what is in *The Highway Code*.

The questions that come under this heading in the Theory Test include several on road signs and road markings. There are many more road sign questions in the section on Road and Traffic Signs. Several of the topics listed in this section have already come up.

Other questions in this section cover

- speed limits
- overtaking
- parking
- lanes and roundabouts
- clearways
- box junctions
- crossroads
- pedestrian crossings
- towing caravans and trailers

Speed limits

Driving too fast for the road, traffic or weather conditions causes accidents. Make sure that you keep below the speed limit shown on the signs for the road that you are on.

30mph in a built-up area

50mph on a long, twisty country road

or as low as 20mph in a residential area with speed humps or traffic calming measures

> The national speed limit for cars on a dual carriageway is 70mph.
> This is also the maximum speed for motorway driving.

National speed limit

When you leave a built-up area you will usually see this sign.

- This sign tells you that the national speed limit for this type of road applies here.
- The national speed limit for cars on a normal road (single carriageway outside a built-up area) is 60mph. So on this road you must drive below 60mph even if it is straight and empty.

Street lights usually mean that a 30mph limit applies, unless there are signs showing other limits.

The right speed for the conditions

If it is raining or there is snow and ice on the road or if you are driving in a high wind you will have to drive more slowly than the maximum speed limit. This will keep you and other road users safe.

- Remember – you have to double the time you allow for stopping and braking in wet weather. Allow even more time in snow and ice.
- You need to be extra careful when driving in fog.

The right speed for your vehicle

Some other vehicles have lower speed limits than cars. You can find out more about speed limits from the table in *The Highway Code*.

Parking rules

There are some general rules about parking that all drivers should know.

- Whenever you can, you should use off-street car parks, or parking bays. These are marked out with white lines on the road.
- Never park where your vehicle could be a danger to other road users.

Look for special signs that tell you that you cannot park there at certain times of the day or that only certain people may park in that place. Examples include signs showing bus lanes, cycle lanes, residents' parking zones and roads edged with red or yellow lines.

Orange or blue badges are given to people with disabilities. Do not park in a space reserved for a disabled driver, even if that is the only place left to park. A disabled driver may need to park there. You will break the law if you park in that space.

Parking at night

- If you park at night on a road that has a speed limit higher than 30mph, you must switch on your parking lights. You must switch on your parking lights even if you have parked in a lay-by on this type of road.
- When parking at night, always park facing in the same direction as the traffic flow.
- If your vehicle has a trailer, you must switch on parking lights, even if the road has a 30mph speed limit.

Where not to park

You are not permitted to park

- on the pavement
- at a bus stop
- in front of someone's drive
- opposite a traffic island
- near a school entrance
- on a pedestrian crossing (or inside the zigzag lines either side of it)
- near a junction
- on a clearway
- on a motorway

Now test yourself on the questions about Rules of the Road

Section 11

Road and Traffic Signs

When you look up the chapter on ROAD AND TRAFFIC SIGNS in the Theory Test questions you will see that it takes up a lot of pages. This is because most of the questions have a picture of a road sign or marking. You will also see that a lot of questions ask 'What does this sign mean?'

But however differently the questions are worded, it all comes down to how well you know *The Highway Code*. You can try to learn as much of *The Highway Code* as possible, but there are other ways you can get to know the road signs.

As you walk or drive around, look at the road signs you see in the street, and the different markings painted on the road surface.

On foot

Look at the signs and signals that all road users must obey, whether they are in a car or walking. For example, when you use a pedestrian crossing, check what kind of crossing it is (such as a pelican, toucan or zebra crossing).

Check whether you know the following

- What are the rules for pedestrians and drivers coming up to the crossing?
- What kinds of crossings are controlled by traffic lights?
- What is different about a zebra crossing?

During your driving lessons
If you are having a driving lesson look well ahead so that you see all the signs that tell you what to do next. Obey them in good time.

During your test
When you take your test the examiner will tell you when to move off, when to make a turn and when to carry out one of the set manoeuvres. The examiner will expect you to watch out for lane markings on the road, and signs giving directions, and to decide how to react to these yourself.

Signs
If you see several signs all on the same post, it can be confusing. The general rule is to start at the top and read down the post. The sign at the top tells you about the first hazard you have to look out for.

If you are a passenger in a car on a motorway, look at the motorway signs, because you need to know them, even though you can't drive on a motorway yet yourself.

Check that you can answer the following:
What colour are the signs at the side of the motorway?
What do the light signals above the road tell you?
What signs tell you that you are coming to an exit?

Shapes of signs
Road and traffic signs come in three main shapes. Get to know them. You must learn what the signs mean.

Circles
Signs in circles tell you to do (blue) or not do (red) something – they give orders.

Triangles
Signs in triangles tell you of a hazard ahead – they give warnings.

Rectangles
Signs in rectangles tell you about where you are or where you are going – they give information.

There is only one sign which is octagonal – that is, it has eight sides. This is the sign for STOP. The eight-sided shape makes the sign stand out.

Now test yourself on the questions about Road and Traffic Signs

Section 12
Documents

This is quite a short section in the Theory Test questions. It is also different from the other sections, because it does not deal with either your driving skills or knowledge of *The Highway Code*.

It covers all the paperwork and the laws that you need to know about when you start learning to drive.

In this section there are questions about
- driving licences
- insurance
- MOT certificate
- Vehicle Excise Duty (tax disc)
- Vehicle Registration Document (log book)

This section also covers who can supervise a learner driverand changes you must tell the licensing authority about

Driving licence

If you are learning to drive, you need a provisional licence.
- You must have a valid licence to drive legally.
- All licences now have two parts – a photo card and a paper document.
- Your signature appears on both parts of the licence.
- Take good care of your provisional licence. If you lose it by mistake, you can get another one but you will have to pay a fee, and wait for the new licence to come.
- When you pass your test you can apply for a full licence.

Insurance

You must have a valid insurance certificate that covers you at least for third party liability. If you are learning with a driving school, you are covered by their insurance while you are in the driving school car. When you are in your own or anybody else's car, you must have insurance. Third party insurance cover usually comes as 'Third Party, Fire and Theft'. It is a basic insurance policy that will pay for repairs to another person's car and allows you to claim on the other driver's insurance if you are in an accident that was not your fault. If you have comprehensive insurance, the policy will pay for repairs to your vehicle even when the accident was your fault.

MOT certificate

Cars and motorcycles must have their first MOT test three years after they are new and first registered. After that, they must have an MOT test every year.

The MOT test checks that your vehicle

- is roadworthy – that is, all the parts work properly and the vehicle is safe to drive
- keeps to the legal limits for exhaust emissions – that is, the level of poisons in the gas that comes from the exhaust

If your vehicle is more than three years old you must not drive it without a valid MOT certificate – unless you are on your way to get an MOT and you have booked it in advance.

Vehicle Excise Duty (tax disc)

Your vehicle must have an up-to-date tax disc on the windscreen. The disc shows that you have paid Vehicle Excise Duty up to the date on the disc (you can pay for 6 or 12 months at a time). If you don't renew your tax disc within a month of the old one expiring you will be automatically fined. If you are not going to renew your tax disc (if you don't use your vehicle or keep it on a public road) you must inform the DVLA by completing a Statutory Off Road Vehicle Notification (SORN).

Vehicle Excise Duty is the tax that the government charges you to drive your vehicle on the roads. It is also sometimes called road tax. When you get your tax disc, you must show proof that your vehicle is insured, and that it has a valid MOT if required.

Vehicle Registration Document/Certificate

The Vehicle Registration Document/Certificate has all the important details about you and your vehicle, such as the make and model of the vehicle. It also has your name and address as the registered keeper of the vehicle. It is a record of the vehicle's history and is sometimes called 'the log book'.

DVLA

The Driver and Vehicle Licensing Agency is known as the DVLA. You must tell the DVLA if you are going to keep your car off road and are not renewing your tax disc, when you buy or sell a car and if you change your name or your address.

This is because your details go on to the Vehicle Registration Document/Certificate and you are legally responsible for the vehicle (car tax, parking fines, etc) until you have notified the DVLA that it is off road or you have sold it.

Supervising a learner driver

As a learner driver you cannot drive on your own. If you are not with your driving instructor, you must be supervised by a person who is at least 21 years old, has a full licence for the kind of car you drive and has had that licence for at least three years. Note that if a person has a licence to drive an automatic car only, they cannot supervise a learner in a manual car.

Now test yourself on the questions about Documents

Section 13
Accidents

The questions in this section are about helping anyone who is hurt in a road accident. Some people think they might do more harm than good if they try to help. But if you have a basic knowledge of first aid you won't panic and if you are first on the scene at an accident, you could even save a life. Look up Accidents and First Aid in *The Highway Code*.

The Theory Test questions in this section cover

- what to do when warning lights come on in your vehicle
- what to do if you break down
- safety equipment to carry with you
- when to use hazard warning lights
- what to do – and what not to do – at the scene of an accident
- what to do in tunnels

Basic first aid

What to do at an accident scene

- Check that you are not putting yourself in danger before you go to help somebody else. You may need to warn other drivers of the accident.
- Check all vehicle engines are switched off.
- Make sure no one is smoking.
- Move people who are not injured to a safe place. If the accident has happened on a motorway, if possible get uninjured people away from the hard shoulder, behind the barrier or on to the bank.
- Call the emergency services. You will need to tell them exactly where you are, and how many vehicles are involved in the accident. On motorways, use the emergency phone which connects directly to the police and tells them exactly where you are.
- Do not move injured people – unless there is a risk of fire or of an explosion.
- Give essential first aid to injured people (see below).
- Stay there until the emergency services arrive.

The ABC of first aid

This tells you what three things to check for when you go to help an injured person

A is for Airway
B is for Breathing
C is for Circulation

Airway

If an injured person is breathing, but unconscious, if possible place them in the recovery position. If they are not breathing, first make sure there is nothing in their mouth that might be blocking the airway.

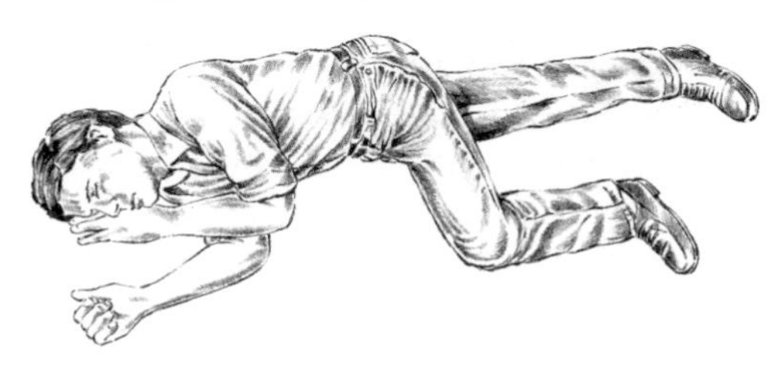

Breathing

If you have checked the airway and they are still not breathing, then give first aid as follows

- lift their chin
- carefully tilt their head back to open their airway

- pinch their nose and blow into their mouth until their chest rises

Repeat this every 4 seconds until the person can breathe alone, or until help arrives.

Circulation

'Circulation' here means 'bleeding'. If a person is bleeding, press firmly on the wound for up to 10 minutes, until the bleeding slows or stops. You can raise an injured arm or leg to reduce the bleeding – as long as the limb is not broken. If you carry a first aid kit use a sterile dressing over the wound.

Other ways to help

- Do speak in a calm way to the injured person.
- Do try to keep them warm and as comfortable as possible.
- Do not give them anything to drink.
- Do not give them a cigarette.
- Don't let injured people wander into the road.

The AA's advice on safety if you break down

If you are on a non-motorway road

- Try to get your vehicle off the main road. At least, get it right to the side of the road or on to the verge.
- If the vehicle is in a place where it might be hit by another vehicle, get any passengers out and to a safer place.
- Switch on the hazard warning lights to warn other drivers.
- If you have a red warning triangle, place it at least 45 metres behind your car to warn other traffic (but don't use it on a motorway).
- If you are a member of a motoring organisation such as the AA, call them and tell them where you are and what has happened. Wait with your vehicle until the patrol arrives.

If you are on a motorway

- If possible, leave the motorway at the next exit. If you can't get that far, drive on to the hard shoulder. Stop far over to the left, and switch on your hazard warning lights.
- Get everyone out of the vehicle, using the nearside doors (but leave pets in the vehicle). Get them to sit on the bank, well away from the traffic.
- Use the nearest orange emergency phone to call the emergency services and tell them where you are and what has happened (for your safety, face the oncoming traffic while you are on the phone).
- Go back to your vehicle and wait on the bank near by until help arrives.
- Do not cross the motorway on foot or try to do repairs yourself – even changing a wheel. This is too dangerous on a motorway.

DID YOU KNOW?
Before driving into a tunnel you should tune into a local radio station and listen to the traffic reports in case there are any accidents or problems in the tunnel.

Now test yourself on the questions about Accidents

Section 14

Vehicle Loading

This last section, called VEHICLE LOADING, is the shortest of all. It covers a mixture of the following

- how to load your vehicle safely
- using a roof rack
- towing caravans and trailers
- child restraints and safety locks

When you have passed your test you can tow a trailer, if the combined weight of the vehicle and trailer is less than 3,500kg. So you need to know the rules about towing.

Towing

When you get your first full driving licence, check it to see how much you are allowed to tow. Do not tow any trailer that comes to more than that weight. The weight of a trailer should be no more than 85% of the weight of the car that is to pull it. But it is best to stay well below that top weight, because towing a trailer will affect the way your vehicle handles. When you are towing, you need to allow more room when overtaking and more time to brake and stop.

When you are turning at a roundabout or junction you will need to think about where you are on the road.

When towing a heavy load, you might need to blow your tyres up to more than the normal pressures. Check your vehicle's handbook for advice. Remember to change back to the normal tyre pressures when you finish your journey.

Roof racks

If you attach a roof rack to your car, it will make a difference to the way in which your vehicle handles. Any load that is carried on a roof rack must be tied down securely.

- The roof rack makes your vehicle taller, so more vulnerable to strong winds.
- You will increase your fuel consumption.
- You need to change the way you drive to allow for the extra weight.

To find out more, look up the parts of *The Highway Code* that deal with Loads and Towing.

Loading a trailer

If the weight of the load is arranged properly, this should cut down the risk of losing control, swerving and snaking.

- Try to spread the weight evenly when you load your trailer. Do not put more weight towards the front, or the back, or to one side.
- It is against the law to have a load that is sticking out in a dangerous way.
- Don't forget that if you park a vehicle with a trailer overnight, it must have lights.

A vehicle towing a trailer

- must not go over a maximum speed limit of 60mph
- must not use the right (outside) lane on a motorway

If you are going to buy a trailer, make sure it fits your car's tow bar. Tow bars must keep to EU regulations, and must have electric sockets to connect to the lights on the trailer.

Snaking

'Snaking' means moving from side to side. A caravan will snake if it is not properly attached or loaded, or if the car pulling it is going too fast.

If you are towing a caravan or trailer and it starts to snake

- slow down – stop pressing the accelerator (do not brake suddenly)
- get back in control of the steering
- then brake gently

You are responsible for passengers in your vehicle

There are also questions in the Vehicle Loading section about the safety of passengers. As the driver, you are responsible for making sure your vehicle is not overloaded – and this applies to people and animals as well as to luggage. Remember that all passengers must wear a seat belt (unless they have a medical certificate saying they should not wear one) and that all children under the age of 14 must wear a seat belt or be strapped into a child seat or other 'restraint' suitable for their age. (See the section on Child Restraints in *The Highway Code*).

Children

Children must not sit in the space behind the back seat of a hatchback car, and no passengers should sit in a caravan while it is being towed.

Pets

Pets should be kept under careful control. You might keep them and you safe with a special harness, or if they are kept behind a screen in a hatchback which would stop them being thrown forward in the event of an accident.

Now test yourself on the questions about Vehicle Loading

Part 4 Theory Test Questions

Contents	Page

1 Before you make a U-turn in the road, you should

Mark one answer

- [ ] A. give an arm signal as well as using your indicators
- [ ] B. signal so that other drivers can slow down for you
- [ ] C. look over your shoulder for a final check
- [ ] D. select a higher gear than normal

2 As you approach this bridge you should

Mark three answers

- [ ] A. move into the middle of the road to get a better view
- [ ] B. slow down
- [ ] C. get over the bridge as quickly as possible
- [ ] D. consider using your horn
- [ ] E. find another route
- [ ] F. beware of pedestrians

3 When following a large vehicle you should keep well back because this

Mark one answer

- [ ] A. allows you to corner more quickly
- [ ] B. helps the large vehicle to stop more easily
- [ ] C. allows the driver to see you in the mirrors
- [ ] D. helps you to keep out of the wind

4 In which of these situations should you avoid overtaking?

Mark one answer

- [ ] A. Just after a bend
- [ ] B. In a one-way street
- [ ] C. On a 30mph road
- [ ] D. Approaching a dip in the road

5 This road marking warns

Mark one answer

- [ ] A. drivers to use the hard shoulder
- [ ] B. overtaking drivers there is a bend to the left
- [ ] C. overtaking drivers to move back to the left
- [ ] D. drivers that it is safe to overtake

6 Your mobile phone rings while you are travelling. You should

Mark one answer

- [ ] A. stop immediately
- [ ] B. answer it immediately
- [ ] C. pull up in a suitable place
- [ ] D. pull up at the nearest kerb

7 Why are these yellow lines painted across the road?

Mark one answer

- [ ] **A.** To help you choose the correct lane
- [ ] **B.** To help you keep the correct separation distance
- [ ] **C.** To make you aware of your speed
- [ ] **D.** To tell you the distance to the roundabout

8 You are approaching traffic lights that have been on green for some time. You should

Mark one answer

- [ ] **A.** accelerate hard
- [ ] **B.** maintain your speed
- [ ] **C.** be ready to stop
- [ ] **D.** brake hard

9 Which of the following should you do before stopping?

Mark one answer

- [ ] **A.** Sound the horn
- [ ] **B.** Use the mirrors
- [ ] **C.** Select a higher gear
- [ ] **D.** Flash your headlights

10 What does the term 'blind spot' mean for a driver?

Mark one answer

- [ ] **A.** An area covered by your right-hand mirror
- [ ] **B.** An area not covered by your headlights
- [ ] **C.** An area covered by your left-hand mirror
- [ ] **D.** An area not covered by your mirrors

11 Objects hanging from your interior mirror may

Mark two answers

- [ ] **A.** restrict your view
- [ ] **B.** improve your driving
- [ ] **C.** distract your attention
- [ ] **D.** help your concentration

12 Which of the following may cause loss of concentration on a long journey?

Mark four answers

- [ ] **A.** Loud music
- [ ] **B.** Arguing with a passenger
- [ ] **C.** Using a mobile phone
- [ ] **D.** Putting in a cassette tape
- [ ] **E.** Stopping regularly to rest
- [ ] **F.** Pulling up to tune the radio

13 On a long motorway journey boredom can cause you to feel sleepy. You should

Mark two answers

- [ ] **A.** leave the motorway and find a safe place to stop
- [ ] **B.** keep looking around at the surrounding landscape
- [ ] **C.** drive faster to complete your journey sooner
- [ ] **D.** ensure a supply of fresh air into your vehicle
- [ ] **E.** stop on the hard shoulder for a rest

14 **You are driving at dusk. You should switch your lights on**

Mark two answers

- [ ] **A.** even when street lights are not lit
- [ ] **B.** so others can see you
- [ ] **C.** only when others have done so
- [ ] **D.** only when street lights are lit

15 **You are most likely to lose concentration when driving if you**

Mark two answers

- [ ] **A.** use a mobile phone
- [ ] **B.** listen to very loud music
- [ ] **C.** switch on the heated rear window
- [ ] **D.** look at the door mirrors

16 **Which FOUR are most likely to cause you to lose concentration while you are driving?**

Mark four answers

- [ ] **A.** Using a mobile phone
- [ ] **B.** Talking into a microphone
- [ ] **C.** Tuning your car radio
- [ ] **D.** Looking at a map
- [ ] **E.** Checking the mirrors
- [ ] **F.** Using the demisters

17 **Your vehicle is fitted with a hands-free phone system. Using this equipment whilst driving**

Mark one answer

- [ ] **A.** is quite safe as long as you slow down
- [ ] **B.** could distract your attention from the road
- [ ] **C.** is recommended by *The Highway Code*
- [ ] **D.** could be very good for road safety

18 **Using a hands-free phone is likely to**

Mark one answer

- [ ] **A.** improve your safety
- [ ] **B.** increase your concentration
- [ ] **C.** reduce your view
- [ ] **D.** divert your attention

19 **You should ONLY use a mobile phone when**

Mark one answer

- [ ] **A.** receiving a call
- [ ] **B.** suitably parked
- [ ] **C.** driving at less than 30mph
- [ ] **D.** driving an automatic vehicle

20 **Using a mobile phone while you are driving**

Mark one answer

- [ ] **A.** is acceptable in a vehicle with power steering
- [ ] **B.** will reduce your field of vision
- [ ] **C.** could distract your attention from the road
- [ ] **D.** will affect your vehicle's electronic systems

21 What is the safest way to use a mobile phone in your vehicle?

Mark one answer

- [ ] **A.** Use hands-free equipment
- [ ] **B.** Find a suitable place to stop
- [ ] **C.** Drive slowly on a quiet road
- [ ] **D.** Direct your call through the operator

22 You are driving on a wet road. You have to stop your vehicle in an emergency. You should

Mark one answer

- [ ] **A.** apply the handbrake and footbrake together
- [ ] **B.** keep both hands on the wheel
- [ ] **C.** select reverse gear
- [ ] **D.** give an arm signal

23 When you are moving off from behind a parked car you should

Mark three answers

- [ ] **A.** look round before you move off
- [ ] **B.** use all the mirrors on the vehicle
- [ ] **C.** look round after moving off
- [ ] **D.** use the exterior mirrors only
- [ ] **E.** give a signal if necessary
- [ ] **F.** give a signal after moving off

24 You are travelling along this narrow country road. When passing the cyclist you should go

Mark one answer

- [ ] **A.** slowly, sounding the horn as you pass
- [ ] **B.** quickly, leaving plenty of room
- [ ] **C.** slowly, leaving plenty of room
- [ ] **D.** quickly, sounding the horn as you pass

25 Your vehicle is fitted with a hand-held telephone. To use the telephone you should

Mark one answer

- [ ] **A.** reduce your speed
- [ ] **B.** find a safe place to stop
- [ ] **C.** steer the vehicle with one hand
- [ ] **D.** be particularly careful at junctions

26 To answer a call on your mobile phone while travelling you should

Mark one answer

- [ ] **A.** reduce your speed wherever you are
- [ ] **B.** stop in a proper and convenient place
- [ ] **C.** keep the call time to a minimum
- [ ] **D.** slow down and allow others to overtake

27 **Your mobile phone rings while you are on the motorway. Before answering you should**

Mark one answer
- A. reduce your speed to 30mph
- B. pull up on the hard shoulder
- C. move into the left-hand lane
- D. stop in a safe place

28 **You are turning right onto a dual carriageway. What should you do before emerging?**

Mark one answer
- A. Stop, apply the handbrake and then select a low gear
- B. Position your vehicle well to the left of the side road
- C. Check that the central reservation is wide enough for your vehicle
- D. Make sure that you leave enough room for a vehicle behind

29 **You lose your way on a busy road. What is the best action to take?**

Mark one answer
- A. Stop at traffic lights and ask pedestrians
- B. Shout to other drivers to ask them the way
- C. Turn into a side road, stop and check a map
- D. Check a map, and keep going with the traffic flow

30 **You are waiting to emerge from a junction. The windscreen pillar is restricting your view. What should you be particularly aware of?**

Mark one answer
- A. Lorries
- B. Buses
- C. Motorcyclists
- D. Coaches

31 **When emerging from junctions which is most likely to obstruct your view?**

Mark one answer
- A. Windscreen pillars
- B. Steering wheel
- C. Interior mirror
- D. Windscreen wipers

32 **Windscreen pillars can obstruct your view. You should take particular care when**

Mark one answer
- A. driving on a motorway
- B. driving on a dual carriageway
- C. approaching a one-way street
- D. approaching bends and junctions

33 **You cannot see clearly behind when reversing. What should you do?**

Mark one answer
- A. Open your window to look behind
- B. Open the door and look behind
- C. Look in the nearside mirror
- D. Ask someone to guide you

34 When you see a hazard ahead you should use the mirrors. Why is this?

Mark one answer

- [ ] **A.** Because you will need to accelerate out of danger
- [ ] **B.** To assess how your actions will affect following traffic
- [ ] **C.** Because you will need to brake sharply to a stop
- [ ] **D.** To check what is happening on the road ahead

35 You are waiting to turn right at the end of a road. Your view is obstructed by parked vehicles. What should you do?

Mark one answer

- [ ] **A.** Stop and then move forward slowly and carefully for a proper view
- [ ] **B.** Move quickly to where you can see so you only block traffic from one direction
- [ ] **C.** Wait for a pedestrian to let you know when it is safe for you to emerge
- [ ] **D.** Turn your vehicle around immediately and find another junction to use

36 Your vehicle is fitted with a navigation system. How should you avoid letting this distract you while driving?

Mark one answer

- [ ] **A.** Keep going and input your destination into the system
- [ ] **B.** Keep going as the system will adjust to your route
- [ ] **C.** Stop immediately to view and use the system
- [ ] **D.** Stop in a safe place before using the system

37 Using a mobile phone when driving is illegal. The chance of you having an accident while using one is

Mark one answer

- [ ] **A.** two times higher
- [ ] **B.** four times higher
- [ ] **C.** six times higher
- [ ] **D.** ten times higher

38 You are driving on a motorway and want to use your mobile phone. What should you do?

Mark one answer

- [ ] **A.** Try to find a safe place on the hard shoulder
- [ ] **B.** Leave the motorway and stop in a safe place
- [ ] **C.** Use the next exit and pull up on the slip road
- [ ] **D.** Move to the left lane and reduce your speed

39 Using a mobile phone when driving is illegal. Your chances of having an accident increase by

Mark one answer

- [ ] **A.** two times
- [ ] **B.** four times
- [ ] **C.** eight times
- [ ] **D.** twelve times

40 **At a pelican crossing the flashing amber light means you MUST**

Mark one answer
- [ ] **A.** stop and wait for the green light
- [ ] **B.** stop and wait for the red light
- [ ] **C.** give way to pedestrians waiting to cross
- [ ] **D.** give way to pedestrians already on the crossing

41 **You should never wave people across at pedestrian crossings because**

Mark one answer
- [ ] **A.** there may be another vehicle coming
- [ ] **B.** they may not be looking
- [ ] **C.** it is safer for you to carry on
- [ ] **D.** they may not be ready to cross

42 **At a puffin crossing, which colour follows the green signal?**

Mark one answer
- [ ] **A.** Steady red
- [ ] **B.** Flashing amber
- [ ] **C.** Steady amber
- [ ] **D.** Flashing green

43 **The conditions are good and dry. You could use the 'two-second rule'**

Mark one answer
- [ ] **A.** before restarting the engine after it has stalled
- [ ] **B.** to keep a safe gap from the vehicle in front
- [ ] **C.** before using the 'Mirror-Signal-Manoeuvre' routine
- [ ] **D.** when emerging on wet roads

44 **'Tailgating' means**

Mark one answer
- [ ] **A.** using the rear door of a hatchback car
- [ ] **B.** reversing into a parking space
- [ ] **C.** following another vehicle too closely
- [ ] **D.** driving with rear fog lights on

45 **Following this vehicle too closely is unwise because**

Mark one answer
- [ ] **A.** your brakes will overheat
- [ ] **B.** your view ahead is increased
- [ ] **C.** your engine will overheat
- [ ] **D.** your view ahead is reduced

46 **You are following a vehicle on a wet road. You should leave a time gap of at least**

Mark one answer
- [ ] **A.** one second
- [ ] **B.** two seconds
- [ ] **C.** three seconds
- [ ] **D.** four seconds

47 **You are in a line of traffic. The driver behind you is following very closely. What action should you take?**

Mark one answer
- [ ] **A.** Ignore the following driver and continue to travel within the speed limit
- [ ] **B.** Slow down, gradually increasing the gap between you and the vehicle in front
- [ ] **C.** Signal left and wave the following driver past
- [ ] **D.** Move over to a position just left of the centre line of the road

48 **A long, heavily laden lorry is taking a long time to overtake you. What should you do?**

Mark one answer

- [ ] **A.** Speed up
- [ ] **B.** Slow down
- [ ] **C.** Hold your speed
- [ ] **D.** Change direction

49 **Which of the following vehicles will use blue flashing beacons?**

Mark three answers

- [ ] **A.** Motorway maintenance
- [ ] **B.** Bomb disposal
- [ ] **C.** Blood transfusion
- [ ] **D.** Police patrol
- [ ] **E.** Breakdown recovery

50 **Which THREE of these emergency services might have blue flashing beacons?**

Mark three answers

- [ ] **A.** Coastguard
- [ ] **B.** Bomb disposal
- [ ] **C.** Gritting lorries
- [ ] **D.** Animal ambulances
- [ ] **E.** Mountain rescue
- [ ] **F.** Doctors' cars

51 **When being followed by an ambulance showing a flashing blue beacon you should**

Mark one answer

- [ ] **A.** pull over as soon as safely possible to let it pass
- [ ] **B.** accelerate hard to get away from it
- [ ] **C.** maintain your speed and course
- [ ] **D.** brake harshly and immediately stop in the road

52 **What type of emergency vehicle is fitted with a green flashing beacon?**

Mark one answer

- [ ] **A.** Fire engine
- [ ] **B.** Road gritter
- [ ] **C.** Ambulance
- [ ] **D.** Doctor's car

53 **A flashing green beacon on a vehicle means**

Mark one answer

- [ ] **A.** police on non-urgent duties
- [ ] **B.** doctor on an emergency call
- [ ] **C.** road safety patrol operating
- [ ] **D.** gritting in progress

54 **A vehicle has a flashing green beacon. What does this mean?**

Mark one answer

- [ ] **A.** A doctor is answering an emergency call
- [ ] **B.** The vehicle is slow moving
- [ ] **C.** It is a motorway police patrol vehicle
- [ ] **D.** The vehicle is carrying hazardous chemicals

55 **Diamond-shaped signs give instructions to**

30

Mark one answer

- [ ] **A.** tram drivers
- [ ] **B.** bus drivers
- [ ] **C.** lorry drivers
- [ ] **D.** taxi drivers

56 **On a road where trams operate, which of these vehicles will be most at risk from the tram rails?**

Mark one answer

- [ ] **A.** Cars
- [ ] **B.** Cycles
- [ ] **C.** Buses
- [ ] **D.** Lorries

57 **What should you use your horn for?**

Mark one answer

- [ ] **A.** To alert others to your presence
- [ ] **B.** To allow you right of way
- [ ] **C.** To greet other road users
- [ ] **D.** To signal your annoyance

58 **You are in a one-way street and want to turn right. You should position yourself**

Mark one answer

- [ ] **A.** in the right-hand lane
- [ ] **B.** in the left-hand lane
- [ ] **C.** in either lane, depending on the traffic
- [ ] **D.** just left of the centre line

59 **You wish to turn right ahead. Why should you take up the correct position in good time?**

Mark one answer

- [ ] **A.** To allow other drivers to pull out in front of you
- [ ] **B.** To give a better view into the road that you're joining
- [ ] **C.** To help other road users know what you intend to do
- [ ] **D.** To allow drivers to pass you on the right

60 **At which type of crossing are cyclists allowed to ride across with pedestrians?**

Mark one answer

- [ ] **A.** Toucan
- [ ] **B.** Puffin
- [ ] **C.** Pelican
- [ ] **D.** Zebra

61 **A bus has stopped at a bus stop ahead of you. Its right-hand indicator is flashing. You should**

Mark one answer

- [ ] **A.** flash your headlights and slow down
- [ ] **B.** slow down and give way if it is safe to do so
- [ ] **C.** sound your horn and keep going
- [ ] **D.** slow down and then sound your horn

62 **You are travelling at the legal speed limit. A vehicle comes up quickly behind, flashing its headlights. You should**

Mark one answer

- [ ] **A.** accelerate to make a gap behind you
- [ ] **B.** touch the brakes sharply to show your brake lights
- [ ] **C.** maintain your speed to prevent the vehicle from overtaking
- [ ] **D.** allow the vehicle to overtake

63 **You should ONLY flash your headlights to other road users**

Mark one answer

- [ ] **A.** to show that you are giving way
- [ ] **B.** to show that you are about to turn
- [ ] **C.** to tell them that you have right of way
- [ ] **D.** to let them know that you are there

64

You are approaching unmarked crossroads. How should you deal with this type of junction?

Mark one answer

- [ ] **A.** Accelerate and keep to the middle
- [ ] **B.** Slow down and keep to the right
- [ ] **C.** Accelerate looking to the left
- [ ] **D.** Slow down and look both ways

65

You are approaching a pelican crossing. The amber light is flashing. You must

Mark one answer

- [ ] **A.** give way to pedestrians who are crossing
- [ ] **B.** encourage pedestrians to cross
- [ ] **C.** not move until the green light appears
- [ ] **D.** stop even if the crossing is clear

66

At puffin crossings, which light will not show to a driver?

Mark one answer

- [ ] **A.** Flashing amber
- [ ] **B.** Red
- [ ] **C.** Steady amber
- [ ] **D.** Green

67

You should leave at least a two-second gap between your vehicle and the one in front when conditions are

Mark one answer

- [ ] **A.** wet
- [ ] **B.** good
- [ ] **C.** damp
- [ ] **D.** foggy

68

You are driving on a clear night. There is a steady stream of oncoming traffic. The national speed limit applies. Which lights should you use?

Mark one answer

- [ ] **A.** Full beam headlights
- [ ] **B.** Sidelights
- [ ] **C.** Dipped headlights
- [ ] **D.** Fog lights

69

You are driving behind a large goods vehicle. It signals left but steers to the right. You should

Mark one answer

- [ ] **A.** slow down and let the vehicle turn
- [ ] **B.** drive on, keeping to the left
- [ ] **C.** overtake on the right of it
- [ ] **D.** hold your speed and sound your horn

70

You are driving along this road. The red van cuts in close in front of you. What should you do?

Mark one answer

- [ ] **A.** Accelerate to get closer to the red van
- [ ] **B.** Give a long blast on the horn
- [ ] **C.** Drop back to leave the correct separation distance
- [ ] **D.** Flash your headlights several times

71 **You are waiting in a traffic queue at night. To avoid dazzling following drivers you should**

Mark one answer

- [ ] **A.** apply the handbrake only
- [ ] **B.** apply the footbrake only
- [ ] **C.** switch off your headlights
- [ ] **D.** use both the handbrake and footbrake

72 **You are driving in traffic at the speed limit for the road. The driver behind is trying to overtake. You should**

Mark one answer

- [ ] **A.** move closer to the car ahead, so the driver behind has no room to overtake
- [ ] **B.** wave the driver behind to overtake when it is safe
- [ ] **C.** keep a steady course and allow the driver behind to overtake
- [ ] **D.** accelerate to get away from the driver behind

73 **You are driving at night on an unlit road behind another vehicle. You should**

Mark one answer

- [ ] **A.** flash your headlights
- [ ] **B.** use dipped beam headlights
- [ ] **C.** switch off your headlights
- [ ] **D.** use full beam headlights

74 **A bus lane on your left shows no times of operation. This means it is**

BUS
LANE

Mark one answer

- [ ] **A.** not in operation at all
- [ ] **B.** only in operation at peak times
- [ ] **C.** in operation 24 hours a day
- [ ] **D.** only in operation in daylight hours

75 **You are driving along a country road. A horse and rider are approaching. What should you do?**

Mark two answers

- [ ] **A.** Increase your speed
- [ ] **B.** Sound your horn
- [ ] **C.** Flash your headlights
- [ ] **D.** Drive slowly past
- [ ] **E.** Give plenty of room
- [ ] **F.** Rev your engine

76 A person herding sheep asks you to stop. You should

Mark one answer

- [ ] **A.** ignore them as they have no authority
- [ ] **B.** stop and switch off your engine
- [ ] **C.** continue on but drive slowly
- [ ] **D.** try and get past quickly

77 When overtaking a horse and rider you should

Mark one answer

- [ ] **A.** sound your horn as a warning
- [ ] **B.** go past as quickly as possible
- [ ] **C.** flash your headlights as a warning
- [ ] **D.** go past slowly and carefully

78 You are approaching a zebra crossing. Pedestrians are waiting to cross. You should

Mark one answer

- [ ] **A.** give way to the elderly and infirm only
- [ ] **B.** slow down and prepare to stop
- [ ] **C.** use your headlights to indicate they can cross
- [ ] **D.** wave at them to cross the road

79 You are driving a slow-moving vehicle on a narrow winding road. You should

Mark one answer

- [ ] **A.** keep well out to stop vehicles overtaking dangerously
- [ ] **B.** wave following vehicles past you if you think they can overtake quickly
- [ ] **C.** pull in safely when you can, to let following vehicles overtake
- [ ] **D.** give a left signal when it is safe for vehicles to overtake you

80 You have a loose filler cap on your diesel fuel tank. This will

Mark two answers

- [ ] **A.** waste fuel and money
- [ ] **B.** make roads slippery for other road users
- [ ] **C.** improve your vehicle's fuel consumption
- [ ] **D.** increase the level of exhaust emissions

81 To avoid spillage after refuelling, you should make sure that

Mark one answer

- [ ] **A.** your tank is only three-quarters full
- [ ] **B.** you have used a locking filler cap
- [ ] **C.** you check your fuel gauge is working
- [ ] **D.** your filler cap is securely fastened

82 A vehicle pulls out in front of you at a junction. What should you do?

Mark one answer

- [ ] **A.** Swerve past it and sound your horn
- [ ] **B.** Flash your headlights and drive up close behind
- [ ] **C.** Slow down and be ready to stop
- [ ] **D.** Accelerate past it immediately

83 You stop for pedestrians waiting to cross at a zebra crossing. They do not start to cross. What should you do?

Mark one answer

- [ ] **A.** Be patient and wait
- [ ] **B.** Sound your horn
- [ ] **C.** Carry on
- [ ] **D.** Wave them to cross

84 **You are following this lorry. You should keep well back from it to**

Mark one answer

- [ ] **A.** give you a good view of the road ahead
- [ ] **B.** stop following traffic from rushing through the junction
- [ ] **C.** prevent traffic behind you from overtaking
- [ ] **D.** allow you to hurry through the traffic lights if they change

85 **You are approaching a red light at a puffin crossing. Pedestrians are on the crossing. The red light will stay on until**

Mark one answer

- [ ] **A.** you start to edge forward on to the crossing
- [ ] **B.** the pedestrians have reached a safe position
- [ ] **C.** the pedestrians are clear of the front of your vehicle
- [ ] **D.** a driver from the opposite direction reaches the crossing

86 **Which instrument panel warning light would show that headlights are on full beam?**

Mark one answer

- [ ] **A.**
- [ ] **B.**
- [ ] **C.**
- [ ] **D.**

87 **If your vehicle uses diesel fuel, take extra care when refuelling. Diesel fuel when spilt is**

Mark one answer

- [ ] **A.** sticky
- [ ] **B.** odourless
- [ ] **C.** clear
- [ ] **D.** slippery

88 **What style of driving causes increased risk to everyone?**

Mark one answer

- [ ] **A.** Considerate
- [ ] **B.** Defensive
- [ ] **C.** Competitive
- [ ] **D.** Responsible

89 Which of these, if allowed to get low, could cause an accident?

Mark one answer

- A. Anti-freeze level
- B. Brake fluid level
- C. Battery water level
- D. Radiator coolant level

90 Which TWO are badly affected if the tyres are under-inflated?

Mark two answers

- A. Braking
- B. Steering
- C. Changing gear
- D. Parking

91 Motor vehicles can harm the environment. This has resulted in

Mark three answers

- A. air pollution
- B. damage to buildings
- C. less risk to health
- D. improved public transport
- E. less use of electrical vehicles
- F. using up of natural resources

92 Excessive or uneven tyre wear can be caused by faults in which THREE of the following?

Mark three answers

- A. The gearbox
- B. The braking system
- C. The accelerator
- D. The exhaust system
- E. Wheel alignment
- F. The suspension

93 You must NOT sound your horn

Mark one answer

- A. between 10pm and 6am in a built-up area
- B. at any time in a built-up area
- C. between 11.30pm and 7am in a built-up area
- D. between 11.30pm and 6am on any road

94 The pictured vehicle is 'environmentally friendly' because it

Mark three answers

- A. reduces noise pollution
- B. uses diesel fuel
- C. uses electricity
- D. uses unleaded fuel
- E. reduces parking spaces
- F. reduces town traffic

95 Supertrams or Light Rapid Transit (LRT) systems are environmentally friendly because

Mark one answer

- A. they use diesel power
- B. they use quieter roads
- C. they use electric power
- D. they do not operate during rush hour

96 'Red routes' in major cities have been introduced to

Mark one answer

- A. raise the speed limits
- B. help the traffic flow
- C. provide better parking
- D. allow lorries to load more freely

97 Road humps, chicanes and narrowings are

Mark one answer

- A. always at major road works
- B. used to increase traffic speed
- C. at toll-bridge approaches only
- D. traffic calming measures

98 The purpose of a catalytic converter is to reduce

Mark one answer

- A. fuel consumption
- B. the risk of fire
- C. toxic exhaust gases
- D. engine wear

99 Catalytic converters are fitted to make the

Mark one answer

- A. engine produce more power
- B. exhaust system easier to replace
- C. engine run quietly
- D. exhaust fumes cleaner

100 It is essential that tyre pressures are checked regularly. When should this be done?

Mark one answer

- A. After any lengthy journey
- B. After travelling at high speed
- C. When tyres are hot
- D. When tyres are cold

101 When should you NOT use your horn in a built-up area?

Mark one answer

- A. Between 8pm and 8am
- B. Between 9pm and dawn
- C. Between dusk and 8am
- D. Between 11.30pm and 7am

102 You will use more fuel if your tyres are

Mark one answer

- A. under-inflated
- B. of different makes
- C. over-inflated
- D. new and hardly used

103 How should you dispose of a used battery?

Mark two answers

- A. Take it to a local authority site
- B. Put it in the dustbin
- C. Break it up into pieces
- D. Leave it on waste land
- E. Take it to a garage
- F. Burn it on a fire

104 What is most likely to cause high fuel consumption?

Mark one answer

- A. Poor steering control
- B. Accelerating around bends
- C. Staying in high gears
- D. Harsh braking and accelerating

105 The fluid level in your battery is low. What should you top it up with?

Mark one answer

- A. Battery acid
- B. Distilled water
- C. Engine oil
- D. Engine coolant

106 You need to top up your battery. What level should you fill to?

Mark one answer

- A. The top of the battery
- B. Half-way up the battery
- C. Just below the cell plates
- D. Just above the cell plates

107 You have too much oil in your engine. What could this cause?

Mark one answer

- A. Low oil pressure
- B. Engine overheating
- C. Chain wear
- D. Oil leaks

108 **You are parking on a two-way road at night. The speed limit is 40mph. You should park on the**

Mark one answer

- A. left with parking lights on
- B. left with no lights on
- C. right with parking lights on
- D. right with dipped headlights on

109 **You are parked on the road at night. Where must you use parking lights?**

Mark one answer

- A. Where there are continuous white lines in the middle of the road
- B. Where the speed limit exceeds 30mph
- C. Where you are facing oncoming traffic
- D. Where you are near a bus stop

110 **Which FOUR of these must be in good working order for your car to be roadworthy?**

Mark four answers

- A. The temperature gauge
- B. The speedometer
- C. The windscreen washers
- D. The windscreen wipers
- E. The oil warning light
- F. The horn

111 **New petrol-engined cars must be fitted with catalytic converters. The reason for this is to**

Mark one answer

- A. control exhaust noise levels
- B. prolong the life of the exhaust system
- C. allow the exhaust system to be recycled
- D. reduce harmful exhaust emissions

112 **What can cause heavy steering?**

Mark one answer

- A. Driving on ice
- B. Badly worn brakes
- C. Over-inflated tyres
- D. Under-inflated tyres

113 **Driving with under-inflated tyres can affect**

Mark two answers

- A. engine temperature
- B. fuel consumption
- C. braking
- D. oil pressure

114 **Excessive or uneven tyre wear can be caused by faults in the**

Mark two answers

- A. gearbox
- B. braking system
- C. suspension
- D. exhaust system

115 **The main cause of brake fade is**

Mark one answer

- A. the brakes overheating
- B. air in the brake fluid
- C. oil on the brakes
- D. the brakes out of adjustment

116 **Your anti-lock brakes warning light stays on. You should**

Mark one answer

- A. check the brake fluid level
- B. check the footbrake free play
- C. check that the handbrake is released
- D. have the brakes checked immediately

117 **While driving, this warning light on your dashboard comes on. It means**

Mark one answer

- A. a fault in the braking system
- B. the engine oil is low
- C. a rear light has failed
- D. your seat belt is not fastened

118 It is important to wear suitable shoes when you are driving. Why is this?

Mark one answer

- A. To prevent wear on the pedals
- B. To maintain control of the pedals
- C. To enable you to adjust your seat
- D. To enable you to walk for assistance if you break down

119 The most important reason for having a properly adjusted head restraint is to

Mark one answer

- A. make you more comfortable
- B. help you to avoid neck injury
- C. help you to relax
- D. help you to maintain your driving position

120 What will reduce the risk of neck injury resulting from a collision?

Mark one answer

- A. An air-sprung seat
- B. Anti-lock brakes
- C. A collapsible steering wheel
- D. A properly adjusted head restraint

121 You are driving the children of a friend home from school. They are both under 14 years old. Who is responsible for making sure they wear a seat belt or approved child restraint where required?

Mark one answer

- A. An adult passenger
- B. The children
- C. You, the driver
- D. Your friend

122 Car passengers MUST wear a seat belt/restraint if one is available, unless they are

Mark one answer

- A. under 14 years old
- B. under 1.5 metres (5 feet) in height
- C. sitting in the rear seat
- D. exempt for medical reasons

123 You are testing your suspension. You notice that your vehicle keeps bouncing when you press down on the front wing. What does this mean?

Mark one answer

- A. Worn tyres
- B. Tyres under-inflated
- C. Steering wheel not located centrally
- D. Worn shock absorbers

124 A roof rack fitted to your car will

Mark one answer

- A. reduce fuel consumption
- B. improve the road handling
- C. make your car go faster
- D. increase fuel consumption

125 It is illegal to drive with tyres that

Mark one answer

- A. have been bought second-hand
- B. have a large deep cut in the side wall
- C. are of different makes
- D. are of different tread patterns

126 The legal minimum depth of tread for car tyres over three quarters of the breadth is

Mark one answer

- A. 1mm
- B. 1.6mm
- C. 2.5mm
- D. 4mm

127 You are carrying two 13-year-old children and their parents in your car. Who is responsible for seeing that the children wear seat belts?

Mark one answer

- A. The children's parents
- B. You, the driver
- C. The front-seat passenger
- D. The children

128 **When a roof rack is not in use it should be removed. Why is this?**

Mark one answer

- A. It will affect the suspension
- B. It is illegal
- C. It will affect your braking
- D. It will waste fuel

129 **How can you, as a driver, help the environment?**

Mark three answers

- A. By reducing your speed
- B. By gentle acceleration
- C. By using leaded fuel
- D. By driving faster
- E. By harsh acceleration
- F. By servicing your vehicle properly

130 **To help the environment, you can avoid wasting fuel by**

Mark three answers

- A. having your vehicle properly serviced
- B. making sure your tyres are correctly inflated
- C. not over-revving in the lower gears
- D. driving at higher speeds where possible
- E. keeping an empty roof rack properly fitted
- F. servicing your vehicle less regularly

131 **To reduce the volume of traffic on the roads you could**

Mark three answers

- A. use public transport more often
- B. share a car when possible
- C. walk or cycle on short journeys
- D. travel by car at all times
- E. use a car with a smaller engine
- F. drive in a bus lane

132 **Which THREE of the following are most likely to waste fuel?**

Mark three answers

- A. Reducing your speed
- B. Carrying unnecessary weight
- C. Using the wrong grade of fuel
- D. Under-inflated tyres
- E. Using different brands of fuel
- F. A fitted, empty roof rack

133 **Which THREE things can you, as a road user, do to help the environment?**

Mark three answers

- A. Cycle when possible
- B. Drive on under-inflated tyres
- C. Use the choke for as long as possible on a cold engine
- D. Have your vehicle properly tuned and serviced
- E. Watch the traffic and plan ahead
- F. Brake as late as possible without skidding

134 **As a driver you can cause more damage to the environment by**

Mark two answers

- A. choosing a fuel-efficient vehicle
- B. making a lot of short journeys
- C. driving in as high a gear as possible
- D. accelerating as quickly as possible
- E. having your vehicle regularly serviced

135 **To help protect the environment you should NOT**

Mark one answer

- A. remove your roof rack when unloaded
- B. use your car for very short journeys
- C. walk, cycle or use public transport
- D. empty the boot of unnecessary weight

136 **Which THREE does the law require you to keep in good condition?**

Mark three answers

- A. Gears
- B. Transmission
- C. Headlights
- D. Windscreen
- E. Seat belts

137 **Driving at 70mph uses more fuel than driving at 50mph by up to**

Mark one answer

- A. 10%
- B. 30%
- C. 75%
- D. 100%

138 **Your vehicle pulls to one side when braking. You should**

Mark one answer

- A. change the tyres around
- B. consult your garage as soon as possible
- C. pump the pedal when braking
- D. use your handbrake at the same time

139 **As a driver, you can help reduce pollution levels in town centres by**

Mark one answer

- A. driving more quickly
- B. over-revving in a low gear
- C. walking or cycling
- D. driving short journeys

140 **Unbalanced wheels on a car may cause**

Mark one answer

- A. the steering to pull to one side
- B. the steering to vibrate
- C. the brakes to fail
- D. the tyres to deflate

141 **Turning the steering wheel while your car is stationary can cause damage to the**

Mark two answers

- A. gearbox
- B. engine
- C. brakes
- D. steering
- E. tyres

142 **How can you reduce the chances of your car being broken into when leaving it unattended?**

Mark one answer

- A. Take all valuables with you
- B. Park near a taxi rank
- C. Place any valuables on the floor
- D. Park near a fire station

143 **You have to leave valuables in your car. It would be safer to**

Mark one answer

- A. put them in a carrier bag
- B. park near a school entrance
- C. lock them out of sight
- D. park near a bus stop

144 **How could you deter theft from your car when leaving it unattended?**

Mark one answer

- A. Leave valuables in a carrier bag
- B. Lock valuables out of sight
- C. Put valuables on the seats
- D. Leave valuables on the floor

145 **Which of the following may help to deter a thief from stealing your car?**

Mark one answer

- A. Always keeping the headlights on
- B. Fitting reflective glass windows
- C. Always keeping the interior light on
- D. Etching the car number on the windows

146 How can you help to prevent your car radio being stolen?

Mark one answer
- A. Park in an unlit area
- B. Hide the radio with a blanket
- C. Park near a busy junction
- D. Install a security-coded radio

147 Which of the following should not be kept in your vehicle?

Mark one answer
- A. A first aid kit
- B. A road atlas
- C. The tax disc
- D. The vehicle documents

148 What should you do when leaving your vehicle?

Mark one answer
- A. Put valuable documents under the seats
- B. Remove all valuables
- C. Cover valuables with a blanket
- D. Leave the interior light on

149 You are parking your car. You have some valuables which you are unable to take with you. What should you do?

Mark one answer
- A. Park near a police station
- B. Put them under the driver's seat
- C. Lock them out of sight
- D. Park in an unlit side road

150 Which of these is most likely to deter the theft of your vehicle?

Mark one answer
- A. An immobiliser
- B. Tinted windows
- C. Locking wheel nuts
- D. A sun screen

151 Wherever possible, which one of the following should you do when parking at night?

Mark one answer
- A. Park in a quiet car park
- B. Park in a well-lit area
- C. Park facing against the flow of traffic
- D. Park next to a busy junction

152 When parking and leaving your car you should

Mark one answer
- A. park under a shady tree
- B. remove the tax disc
- C. park in a quiet road
- D. engage the steering lock

153 When leaving your vehicle parked and unattended you should

Mark one answer
- A. park near a busy junction
- B. park in a housing estate
- C. remove the key and lock it
- D. leave the left indicator on

154 How can you lessen the risk of your vehicle being broken into at night?

Mark one answer
- A. Leave it in a well-lit area
- B. Park in a quiet side road
- C. Don't engage the steering lock
- D. Park in a poorly-lit area

155 To help keep your car secure you could join a

Mark one answer
- A. vehicle breakdown organisation
- B. vehicle watch scheme
- C. advanced driver's scheme
- D. car maintenance class

156 Which TWO of the following will improve fuel consumption?

Mark two answers

- A. Reducing your road speed
- B. Planning well ahead
- C. Late and harsh braking
- D. Driving in lower gears
- E. Short journeys with a cold engine
- F. Rapid acceleration

157 You service your own vehicle. How should you get rid of the old engine oil?

Mark one answer

- A. Take it to a local authority site
- B. Pour it down a drain
- C. Tip it into a hole in the ground
- D. Put it into your dustbin

158 On a vehicle, where would you find a catalytic converter?

Mark one answer

- A. In the fuel tank
- B. In the air filter
- C. On the cooling system
- D. On the exhaust system

159 Why do MOT tests include a strict exhaust emission test?

Mark one answer

- A. To recover the cost of expensive garage equipment
- B. To help protect the environment against pollution
- C. To discover which fuel supplier is used the most
- D. To make sure diesel and petrol engines emit the same fumes

160 To reduce the damage your vehicle causes to the environment you should

Mark three answers

- A. use narrow side streets
- B. avoid harsh acceleration
- C. brake in good time
- D. anticipate well ahead
- E. use busy routes

161 Your vehicle has a catalytic converter. Its purpose is to reduce

Mark one answer

- A. exhaust noise
- B. fuel consumption
- C. exhaust emissions
- D. engine noise

162 A properly serviced vehicle will give

Mark two answers

- A. lower insurance premiums
- B. you a refund on your road tax
- C. better fuel economy
- D. cleaner exhaust emissions

163 You enter a road where there are road humps. What should you do?

Mark one answer

- A. Maintain a reduced speed throughout
- B. Accelerate quickly between each one
- C. Always keep to the maximum legal speed
- D. Drive slowly at school times only

164 When should you especially check the engine oil level?

Mark one answer

- A. Before a long journey
- B. When the engine is hot
- C. Early in the morning
- D. Every 6,000 miles

165 You are having difficulty finding a parking space in a busy town. You can see there is space on the zigzag lines of a zebra crossing. Can you park there?

Mark one answer

- A. No, unless you stay with your car
- B. Yes, in order to drop off a passenger
- C. Yes, if you do not block people from crossing
- D. No, not in any circumstances

166 When leaving your car unattended for a few minutes you should

Mark one answer

- A. leave the engine running
- B. switch the engine off but leave the key in
- C. lock it and remove the key
- D. park near a traffic warden

167 When parking and leaving your car for a few minutes you should

Mark one answer

- A. leave it unlocked
- B. lock it and remove the key
- C. leave the hazard warning lights on
- D. leave the interior light on

168 When leaving your car to help keep it secure you should

Mark one answer

- A. leave the hazard warning lights on
- B. lock it and remove the key
- C. park on a one-way street
- D. park in a residential area

169 When leaving your vehicle where should you park if possible?

Mark one answer

- A. Opposite a traffic island
- B. In a secure car park
- C. On a bend
- D. At or near a taxi rank

170 You are leaving your vehicle parked on a road. When may you leave the engine running?

Mark one answer

- A. If you will be parking for less than 5 minutes
- B. If the battery is flat
- C. When in a 20mph zone
- D. Never on any occasion

171 In which THREE places would parking your vehicle cause danger or obstruction to other road users?

Mark three answers

- A. In front of a property entrance
- B. At or near a bus stop
- C. On your driveway
- D. In a marked parking space
- E. On the approach to a level crossing

172 In which THREE places would parking cause an obstruction to others?

Mark three answers

- A. Near the brow of a hill
- B. In a lay-by
- C. Where the kerb is raised
- D. Where the kerb has been lowered for wheelchairs
- E. At or near a bus stop

173 You are away from home and have to park your vehicle overnight. Where should you leave it?

Mark one answer

- [ ] **A.** Opposite another parked vehicle
- [ ] **B.** In a quiet road
- [ ] **C.** Opposite a traffic island
- [ ] **D.** In a secure car park

174 Before starting a journey it is wise to plan your route. How can you do this?

Mark one answer

- [ ] **A.** Look at a map
- [ ] **B.** Contact your local garage
- [ ] **C.** Look in your vehicle handbook
- [ ] **D.** Check your vehicle registration document

175 It can help to plan your route before starting a journey. You can do this by contacting

Mark one answer **NI**

- [ ] **A.** your local filling station
- [ ] **B.** a motoring organisation
- [ ] **C.** the Driver Vehicle Licensing Agency
- [ ] **D.** your vehicle manufacturer

176 How can you plan your route before starting a long journey?

Mark one answer

- [ ] **A.** Check your vehicle's workshop manual
- [ ] **B.** Ask your local garage
- [ ] **C.** Use a route planner on the internet
- [ ] **D.** Consult your travel agents

177 Planning your route before setting out can be helpful. How can you do this?

Mark one answer

- [ ] **A.** Look in a motoring magazine
- [ ] **B.** Only visit places you know
- [ ] **C.** Try to travel at busy times
- [ ] **D.** Print or write down the route

178 Why is it a good idea to plan your journey to avoid busy times?

Mark one answer

- [ ] **A.** You will have an easier journey
- [ ] **B.** You will have a more stressful journey
- [ ] **C.** Your journey time will be longer
- [ ] **D.** It will cause more traffic congestion

179 Planning your journey to avoid busy times has a number of advantages. One of these is

Mark one answer

- [ ] **A.** your journey will take longer
- [ ] **B.** you will have a more pleasant journey
- [ ] **C.** you will cause more pollution
- [ ] **D.** your stress level will be greater

180 It is a good idea to plan your journey to avoid busy times. This is because

Mark one answer

- [ ] **A.** your vehicle will use more fuel
- [ ] **B.** you will see less road works
- [ ] **C.** it will help to ease congestion
- [ ] **D.** you will travel a much shorter distance

181 By avoiding busy times when travelling

Mark one answer

- [ ] **A.** you are more likely to be held up
- [ ] **B.** your journey time will be longer
- [ ] **C.** you will travel a much shorter distance
- [ ] **D.** you are less likely to be delayed

182 It can help to plan your route before starting a journey. Why should you also plan an alternative route?

Mark one answer

- [ ] **A.** Your original route may be blocked
- [ ] **B.** Your maps may have different scales
- [ ] **C.** You may find you have to pay a congestion charge
- [ ] **D.** Because you may get held up by a tractor

183 You will find that driving smoothly can

Mark one answer

- A. reduce journey times by about 15%
- B. increase fuel consumption by about 15%
- C. reduce fuel consumption by about 15%
- D. increase journey times by about 15%

184 You can save fuel when conditions allow by

Mark one answer

- A. using lower gears as often as possible
- B. accelerating sharply in each gear
- C. using each gear in turn
- D. missing out some gears

185 As well as planning your route before starting a journey, you should also plan an alternative route. Why is this?

Mark one answer

- A. To let another driver overtake
- B. Your first route may be blocked
- C. To avoid a railway level crossing
- D. In case you have to avoid emergency vehicles

186 Who of these will not have to pay Congestion Charges in London?

Mark one answer

- A. A van driver making deliveries
- B. A rider of a two-wheeled vehicle
- C. A car driver whose vehicle is more than 1000 cc
- D. A driver who just wants to park in the area

187 You are making an appointment and will have to travel a long distance. You should

Mark one answer

- A. allow plenty of time for your journey
- B. plan to go at busy times
- C. avoid all national speed limit roads
- D. prevent other drivers from overtaking

188 You are checking your trailer tyres. What is the legal minimum tread depth over the central three quarters of its breadth?

Mark one answer

- A. 1mm
- B. 1.6mm
- C. 2mm
- D. 2.6mm

189 How can driving in an Eco-safe manner help protect the environment?

Mark one answer

- A. Through the legal enforcement of speed regulations
- B. By increasing the number of cars on the road
- C. Through increased fuel bills
- D. By reducing exhaust emissions

190 What does Eco-safe driving achieve?

Mark one answer

- A. Increased fuel consumption
- B. Improved road safety
- C. Damage to the environment
- D. Increased exhaust emissions

191 How can missing out some gear changes save fuel?

Mark one answer

- A. By reducing the amount of time you are accelerating
- B. Because there is less need to use the footbrake
- C. By controlling the amount of steering
- D. Because coasting is kept to a minimum

192 Fuel consumption is at its highest when you are

Mark one answer

- A. braking
- B. coasting
- C. accelerating
- D. steering

193 Missing out some gears saves fuel by reducing the amount of time you spend

Mark one answer

- A. braking
- B. coasting
- C. steering
- D. accelerating

194 Rapid acceleration and heavy braking can lead to

Mark one answer

- A. reduced pollution
- B. increased fuel consumption
- C. reduced exhaust emissions
- D. increased road safety

195 What percentage of all emissions does road transport account for?

Mark one answer

- A. 10%
- B. 20%
- C. 30%
- D. 40%

196 Car passengers MUST wear a seat belt if one is available, unless they are

Mark one answer

- A. in a vehicle fitted with air bags
- B. travelling within a congestion charging zone
- C. sitting in the rear seat
- D. exempt for medical reasons

197 You are carrying a 5-year-old child in the back seat of your car. They are under 1.35 metres (4 feet 5 inches) in height. A correct child restraint is NOT available. They MUST

Mark one answer

- A. sit behind the passenger seat
- B. use an adult seat belt
- C. share a belt with an adult
- D. sit between two other children

198 You are carrying a child using a rear-facing baby seat. You want to put it on the front passenger seat. What MUST you do before setting off?

Mark one answer

- A. Deactivate all front and rear airbags
- B. Make sure any front passenger airbag is deactivated
- C. Make sure all the child safety locks are off
- D. Recline the front passenger seat

199 You are carrying an 11-year-old child in the back seat of your car. They are under 1.35 metres (4 feet 5 inches) in height. You MUST make sure that

Mark one answer

- A. they sit between two belted people
- B. they can fasten their own seat belt
- C. a suitable child restraint is available
- D. they can see clearly out of the front window

200 You are parked at the side of the road. You will be waiting for some time for a passenger. What should you do?

Mark one answer

- A. Switch off the engine
- B. Apply the steering lock
- C. Switch off the radio
- D. Use your headlights

201 You are using a rear-facing baby seat. You want to put it on the front passenger seat which is protected by a frontal airbag. What MUST you do before setting off?

Mark one answer

- A. Deactivate the airbag
- B. Turn the seat to face sideways
- C. Ask a passenger to hold the baby
- D. Put the child in an adult seat belt

202 You are carrying a 5-year-old child in the back seat of your car. They are under 1.35 metres (4 feet 5 inches) in height. They MUST use an adult seat belt ONLY if

Mark one answer

- A. a correct child restraint is not available
- B. it is a lap type belt
- C. they sit between two adults
- D. it can be shared with another child

203 Braking distances on ice can be

Mark one answer

- [ ] **A.** twice the normal distance
- [ ] **B.** five times the normal distance
- [ ] **C.** seven times the normal distance
- [ ] **D.** ten times the normal distance

204 Freezing conditions will affect the distance it takes you to come to a stop. You should expect stopping distances to increase by up to

Mark one answer

- [ ] **A.** two times
- [ ] **B.** three times
- [ ] **C.** five times
- [ ] **D.** ten times

205 In very hot weather the road surface can become soft. Which TWO of the following will be most affected?

Mark two answers

- [ ] **A.** The suspension
- [ ] **B.** The grip of the tyres
- [ ] **C.** The braking
- [ ] **D.** The exhaust

206 Where are you most likely to be affected by a side wind?

Mark one answer

- [ ] **A.** On a narrow country lane
- [ ] **B.** On an open stretch of road
- [ ] **C.** On a busy stretch of road
- [ ] **D.** On a long, straight road

207 In windy conditions you need to take extra care when

Mark one answer

- [ ] **A.** using the brakes
- [ ] **B.** making a hill start
- [ ] **C.** turning into a narrow road
- [ ] **D.** passing pedal cyclists

208 In good conditions, what is the typical stopping distance at 70mph?

Mark one answer

- [ ] **A.** 53 metres (175 feet)
- [ ] **B.** 60 metres (197 feet)
- [ ] **C.** 73 metres (240 feet)
- [ ] **D.** 96 metres (315 feet)

209 What is the shortest overall stopping distance on a dry road at 60mph?

Mark one answer

- [ ] **A.** 53 metres (175 feet)
- [ ] **B.** 58 metres (190 feet)
- [ ] **C.** 73 metres (240 feet)
- [ ] **D.** 96 metres (315 feet)

210 You are following a vehicle at a safe distance on a wet road. Another driver overtakes you and pulls into the gap you have left. What should you do?

Mark one answer

- [ ] **A.** Flash your headlights as a warning
- [ ] **B.** Try to overtake safely as soon as you can
- [ ] **C.** Drop back to regain a safe distance
- [ ] **D.** Stay close to the other vehicle until it moves on

211 When approaching a right-hand bend you should keep well to the left. Why is this?

Mark one answer

- [ ] **A.** To improve your view of the road
- [ ] **B.** To overcome the effect of the road's slope
- [ ] **C.** To let faster traffic from behind overtake
- [ ] **D.** To be positioned safely if you skid

212 **You have just gone through deep water. To dry off the brakes you should**

Mark one answer

- ☐ **A.** accelerate and keep to a high speed for a short time
- ☐ **B.** go slowly while gently applying the brakes
- ☐ **C.** avoid using the brakes at all for a few miles
- ☐ **D.** stop for at least an hour to allow them time to dry

213 **You are on a fast, open road in good conditions. For safety, the distance between you and the vehicle in front should be**

Mark one answer

- ☐ **A.** a two-second time gap
- ☐ **B.** one car length
- ☐ **C.** 2 metres (6 feet 6 inches)
- ☐ **D.** two car lengths

214 **What is the most common cause of skidding?**

Mark one answer

- ☐ **A.** Worn tyres
- ☐ **B.** Driver error
- ☐ **C.** Other vehicles
- ☐ **D.** Pedestrians

215 **You are driving on an icy road. How can you avoid wheelspin?**

Mark one answer

- ☐ **A.** Drive at a slow speed in as high a gear as possible
- ☐ **B.** Use the handbrake if the wheels start to slip
- ☐ **C.** Brake gently and repeatedly
- ☐ **D.** Drive in a low gear at all times

216 **Skidding is mainly caused by**

Mark one answer

- ☐ **A.** the weather
- ☐ **B.** the driver
- ☐ **C.** the vehicle
- ☐ **D.** the road

217 **You are driving in freezing conditions. What should you do when approaching a sharp bend?**

Mark two answers

- ☐ **A.** Slow down before you reach the bend
- ☐ **B.** Gently apply your handbrake
- ☐ **C.** Firmly use your footbrake
- ☐ **D.** Coast into the bend
- ☐ **E.** Avoid sudden steering movements

218 **You are turning left on a slippery road. The back of your vehicle slides to the right. You should**

Mark one answer

- ☐ **A.** brake firmly and not turn the steering wheel
- ☐ **B.** steer carefully to the left
- ☐ **C.** steer carefully to the right
- ☐ **D.** brake firmly and steer to the left

219 You are braking on a wet road. Your vehicle begins to skid. It does not have anti-lock brakes. What is the FIRST thing you should do?

Mark one answer **NI**

- [ ] **A.** Quickly pull up the handbrake
- [ ] **B.** Release the footbrake fully
- [ ] **C.** Push harder on the brake pedal
- [ ] **D.** Gently use the accelerator

220 Travelling for long distances in neutral (known as coasting)

Mark one answer

- [ ] **A.** improves the driver's control
- [ ] **B.** makes steering easier
- [ ] **C.** reduces the driver's control
- [ ] **D.** uses more fuel

221 Before starting a journey in freezing weather you should clear ice and snow from your vehicle's

Mark four answers

- [ ] **A.** aerial
- [ ] **B.** windows
- [ ] **C.** bumper
- [ ] **D.** lights
- [ ] **E.** mirrors
- [ ] **F.** number plates

222 You are trying to move off on snow. You should use

Mark one answer

- [ ] **A.** the lowest gear you can
- [ ] **B.** the highest gear you can
- [ ] **C.** a high engine speed
- [ ] **D.** the handbrake and footbrake together

223 When driving in falling snow you should

Mark one answer

- [ ] **A.** brake firmly and quickly
- [ ] **B.** be ready to steer sharply
- [ ] **C.** use sidelights only
- [ ] **D.** brake gently in plenty of time

224 The main benefit of having four-wheel drive is to improve

Mark one answer

- [ ] **A.** road holding
- [ ] **B.** fuel consumption
- [ ] **C.** stopping distances
- [ ] **D.** passenger comfort

225 You are about to go down a steep hill. To control the speed of your vehicle you should

Mark one answer

- [ ] **A.** select a high gear and use the brakes carefully
- [ ] **B.** select a high gear and use the brakes firmly
- [ ] **C.** select a low gear and use the brakes carefully
- [ ] **D.** select a low gear and avoid using the brakes

226 How can you use your vehicle's engine as a brake?

Mark one answer

- [ ] **A.** By changing to a lower gear
- [ ] **B.** By selecting reverse gear
- [ ] **C.** By changing to a higher gear
- [ ] **D.** By selecting neutral gear

227 You wish to park facing DOWNHILL. Which TWO of the following should you do?

Mark two answers

- [ ] **A.** Turn the steering wheel towards the kerb
- [ ] **B.** Park close to the bumper of another car
- [ ] **C.** Park with two wheels on the kerb
- [ ] **D.** Put the handbrake on firmly
- [ ] **E.** Turn the steering wheel away from the kerb

228 **You are driving in a built-up area. You approach a speed hump. You should**

Mark one answer
- A. move across to the left-hand side of the road
- B. wait for any pedestrians to cross
- C. slow your vehicle right down
- D. stop and check both pavements

229 **You are on a long, downhill slope. What should you do to help control the speed of your vehicle?**

Mark one answer
- A. Select neutral
- B. Select a lower gear
- C. Grip the handbrake firmly
- D. Apply the parking brake gently

230 **Your vehicle is fitted with anti-lock brakes. To stop quickly in an emergency you should**

Mark one answer
- A. brake firmly and pump the brake pedal on and off
- B. brake rapidly and firmly without releasing the brake pedal
- C. brake gently and pump the brake pedal on and off
- D. brake rapidly once, and immediately release the brake pedal

231 **Anti-lock brakes prevent wheels from locking. This means the tyres are less likely to**

Mark one answer
- A. aquaplane
- B. skid
- C. puncture
- D. wear

232 **Anti-lock brakes reduce the chances of a skid occurring particularly when**

Mark one answer
- A. driving down steep hills
- B. braking during normal driving
- C. braking in an emergency
- D. driving on good road surfaces

233 **Anti-lock brakes are most effective when you**

Mark one answer
- A. keep pumping the footbrake to prevent skidding
- B. brake normally, but grip the steering wheel tightly
- C. brake promptly and firmly until you have slowed down
- D. apply the handbrake to reduce the stopping distance

234 **Your car is fitted with anti-lock brakes. You need to stop in an emergency. You should**

Mark one answer
- A. brake normally and avoid turning the steering wheel
- B. press the brake pedal promptly and firmly until you have stopped
- C. keep pushing and releasing the footbrake quickly to prevent skidding
- D. apply the handbrake to reduce the stopping distance

235 **Vehicles fitted with anti-lock brakes**

Mark one answer
- A. are impossible to skid
- B. can be steered while you are braking
- C. accelerate much faster
- D. are not fitted with a handbrake

236 Anti-lock brakes may not work as effectively if the road surface is

Mark two answers

- A. dry
- B. loose
- C. wet
- D. good
- E. firm

237 Anti-lock brakes are of most use when you are

Mark one answer

- A. braking gently
- B. driving on worn tyres
- C. braking excessively
- D. driving normally

238 Driving a vehicle fitted with anti-lock brakes allows you to

Mark one answer

- A. brake harder because it is impossible to skid
- B. drive at higher speeds
- C. steer and brake at the same time
- D. pay less attention to the road ahead

239 Anti-lock brakes can greatly assist with

Mark one answer

- A. a higher cruising speed
- B. steering control when braking
- C. control when accelerating
- D. motorway driving

240 When would an anti-lock braking system start to work?

Mark one answer

- A. After the parking brake has been applied
- B. Whenever pressure on the brake pedal is applied
- C. Just as the wheels are about to lock
- D. When the normal braking system fails to operate

241 You are driving a vehicle fitted with anti-lock brakes. You need to stop in an emergency. You should apply the footbrake

Mark one answer

- A. slowly and gently
- B. slowly but firmly
- C. rapidly and gently
- D. rapidly and firmly

242 Your vehicle has anti-lock brakes, but they may not always prevent skidding. This is most likely to happen when driving

Mark two answers

- A. in foggy conditions
- B. on surface water
- C. on loose road surfaces
- D. on dry tarmac
- E. at night on unlit roads

243 Anti-lock brakes will take effect when

Mark one answer

- A. you do not brake quickly enough
- B. maximum brake pressure has been applied
- C. you have not seen a hazard ahead
- D. speeding on slippery road surfaces

244 When driving in fog, which of the following are correct?

Mark three answers

- A. Use dipped headlights
- B. Use headlights on full beam
- C. Allow more time for your journey
- D. Keep close to the car in front
- E. Slow down
- F. Use sidelights only

245 You are driving along a country road. You see this sign. AFTER dealing safely with the hazard you should always

Ford

Mark one answer

- [ ] **A.** check your tyre pressures
- [ ] **B.** switch on your hazard warning lights
- [ ] **C.** accelerate briskly
- [ ] **D.** test your brakes

246 You are driving in heavy rain. Your steering suddenly becomes very light. You should

Mark one answer

- [ ] **A.** steer towards the side of the road
- [ ] **B.** apply gentle acceleration
- [ ] **C.** brake firmly to reduce speed
- [ ] **D.** ease off the accelerator

247 How can you tell when you are driving over black ice?

Mark one answer

- [ ] **A.** It is easier to brake
- [ ] **B.** The noise from your tyres sounds louder
- [ ] **C.** You will see tyre tracks on the road
- [ ] **D.** Your steering feels light

248 The roads are icy. You should drive slowly

Mark one answer

- [ ] **A.** in the highest gear possible
- [ ] **B.** in the lowest gear possible
- [ ] **C.** with the handbrake partly on
- [ ] **D.** with your left foot on the brake

249 You are driving along a wet road. How can you tell if your vehicle is aquaplaning?

Mark one answer

- [ ] **A.** The engine will stall
- [ ] **B.** The engine noise will increase
- [ ] **C.** The steering will feel very heavy
- [ ] **D.** The steering will feel very light

250 How can you tell if you are driving on ice?

Mark two answers

- [ ] **A.** The tyres make a rumbling noise
- [ ] **B.** The tyres make hardly any noise
- [ ] **C.** The steering becomes heavier
- [ ] **D.** The steering becomes lighter

251 You are driving along a wet road. How can you tell if your vehicle's tyres are losing their grip on the surface?

Mark one answer

- [ ] **A.** The engine will stall
- [ ] **B.** The steering will feel very heavy
- [ ] **C.** The engine noise will increase
- [ ] **D.** The steering will feel very light

252 **You are travelling at 50mph on a good, dry road. What is your shortest overall stopping distance?**

Mark one answer

- A. 36 metres (120 feet)
- B. 53 metres (175 feet)
- C. 75 metres (245 feet)
- D. 96 metres (315 feet)

253 **Your overall stopping distance will be much longer when driving**

Mark one answer

- A. in the rain
- B. in fog
- C. at night
- D. in strong winds

254 **You have driven through a flood. What is the first thing you should do?**

Mark one answer

- A. Stop and check the tyres
- B. Stop and dry the brakes
- C. Check your exhaust
- D. Test your brakes

255 **You are on a good, dry road surface. Your vehicle has good brakes and tyres. What is the BRAKING distance at 50mph?**

Mark one answer

- A. 38 metres (125 feet)
- B. 14 metres (46 feet)
- C. 24 metres (79 feet)
- D. 55 metres (180 feet)

256 **You are on a good, dry road surface and your vehicle has good brakes and tyres. What is the typical overall STOPPING distance at 40mph?**

Mark one answer

- A. 23 metres (75 feet)
- B. 36 metres (120 feet)
- C. 53 metres (175 feet)
- D. 96 metres (315 feet)

257 **You are on a wet motorway with surface spray. You should use**

Mark one answer

- A. hazard flashers
- B. dipped headlights
- C. rear fog lights
- D. sidelights

258 **You see this sign on the rear of a slow-moving lorry that you want to pass. It is travelling in the middle lane of a three-lane motorway. You should**

Mark one answer

- [ ] **A.** cautiously approach the lorry then pass on either side
- [ ] **B.** follow the lorry until you can leave the motorway
- [ ] **C.** wait on the hard shoulder until the lorry has stopped
- [ ] **D.** approach with care and keep to the left of the lorry

259 **Where would you expect to see these markers?**

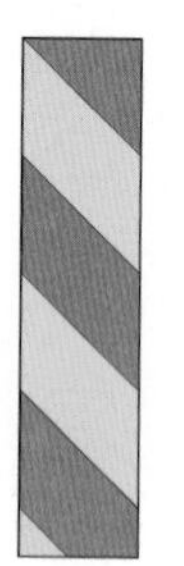

Mark two answers

- [ ] **A.** On a motorway sign
- [ ] **B.** At the entrance to a narrow bridge
- [ ] **C.** On a large goods vehicle
- [ ] **D.** On a builder's skip placed on the road

260 **What does this signal from a police officer mean to oncoming traffic?**

Mark one answer

- [ ] **A.** Go ahead
- [ ] **B.** Stop
- [ ] **C.** Turn left
- [ ] **D.** Turn right

261 **What is the main hazard shown in this picture?**

Mark one answer

- [ ] **A.** Vehicles turning right
- [ ] **B.** Vehicles doing U-turns
- [ ] **C.** The cyclist crossing the road
- [ ] **D.** Parked cars around the corner

262 Which road user has caused a hazard?

ark one answer

- [ ] **A.** The parked car (arrowed A)
- [ ] **B.** The pedestrian waiting to cross (arrowed B)
- [ ] **C.** The moving car (arrowed C)
- [ ] **D.** The car turning (arrowed D)

263 What should the driver of the car approaching the crossing do?

ark one answer

- [ ] **A.** Continue at the same speed
- [ ] **B.** Sound the horn
- [ ] **C.** Drive through quickly
- [ ] **D.** Slow down and get ready to stop

264 What THREE things should the driver of the grey car (arrowed) be especially aware of?

Mark three answers

- [ ] **A.** Pedestrians stepping out between cars
- [ ] **B.** Other cars behind the grey car
- [ ] **C.** Doors opening on parked cars
- [ ] **D.** The bumpy road surface
- [ ] **E.** Cars leaving parking spaces
- [ ] **F.** Empty parking spaces

265 You think the driver of the vehicle in front has forgotten to cancel their right indicator. You should

Mark one answer

- [ ] **A.** flash your lights to alert the driver
- [ ] **B.** sound your horn before overtaking
- [ ] **C.** overtake on the left if there is room
- [ ] **D.** stay behind and not overtake

266 **What is the main hazard the driver of the red car (arrowed) should be aware of?**

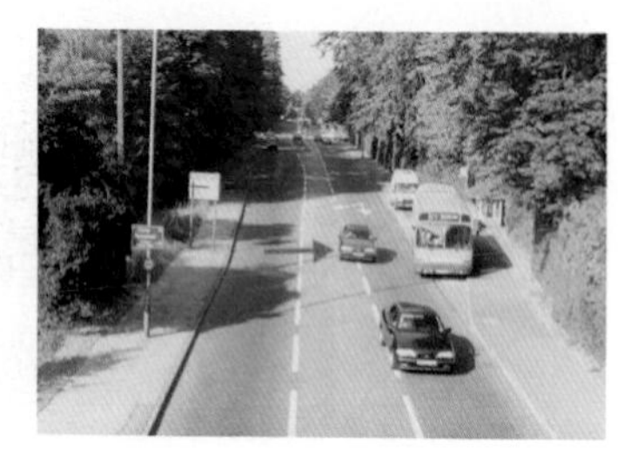

Mark one answer

- [ ] **A.** Glare from the sun may affect the driver's vision
- [ ] **B.** The black car may stop suddenly
- [ ] **C.** The bus may move out into the road
- [ ] **D.** Oncoming vehicles will assume the driver is turning right

267 **In heavy motorway traffic you are being followed closely by the vehicle behind. How can you lower the risk of an accident?**

Mark one answer

- [ ] **A.** Increase your distance from the vehicle in front
- [ ] **B.** Tap your foot on the brake pedal sharply
- [ ] **C.** Switch on your hazard lights
- [ ] **D.** Move on to the hard shoulder and stop

268 **You see this sign ahead. You should expect the road to**

Mark one answer

- [ ] **A.** go steeply uphill
- [ ] **B.** go steeply downhill
- [ ] **C.** bend sharply to the left
- [ ] **D.** bend sharply to the right

269 **You are approaching this cyclist. You should**

Mark one answer

- [ ] **A.** overtake before the cyclist gets to the junction
- [ ] **B.** flash your headlights at the cyclist
- [ ] **C.** slow down and allow the cyclist to turn
- [ ] **D.** overtake the cyclist on the left-hand side

270 Why must you take extra care when turning right at this junction?

Mark one answer

- [ ] **A.** Road surface is poor
- [ ] **B.** Footpaths are narrow
- [ ] **C.** Road markings are faint
- [ ] **D.** There is reduced visibility

271 This yellow sign on a vehicle indicates this is

Mark one answer

- [ ] **A.** a broken-down vehicle
- [ ] **B.** a school bus
- [ ] **C.** an ice-cream van
- [ ] **D.** a private ambulance

272 When approaching this bridge you should give way to

Mark one answer

- [ ] **A.** bicycles
- [ ] **B.** buses
- [ ] **C.** motorcycles
- [ ] **D.** cars

273 What type of vehicle could you expect to meet in the middle of the road?

Mark one answer

- [ ] **A.** Lorry
- [ ] **B.** Bicycle
- [ ] **C.** Car
- [ ] **D.** Motorcycle

274 At this blind junction you must stop

Mark one answer

- [ ] A. behind the line, then edge forward to see clearly
- [ ] B. beyond the line at a point where you can see clearly
- [ ] C. only if there is traffic on the main road
- [ ] D. only if you are turning to the right

275 A driver pulls out of a side road in front of you. You have to brake hard. You should

Mark one answer

- [ ] A. ignore the error and stay calm
- [ ] B. flash your lights to show your annoyance
- [ ] C. sound your horn to show your annoyance
- [ ] D. overtake as soon as possible

276 An elderly person's driving ability could be affected because they may be unable to

Mark one answer

- [ ] A. obtain car insurance
- [ ] B. understand road signs
- [ ] C. react very quickly
- [ ] D. give signals correctly

277 You have just passed these warning lights. What hazard would you expect to see next?

Mark one answer

- [ ] A. A level crossing with no barrier
- [ ] B. An ambulance station
- [ ] C. A school crossing patrol
- [ ] D. An opening bridge

278 Why should you be especially cautious when going past this stationary bus?

Mark two answers

- [ ] A. There is traffic approaching in the distance
- [ ] B. The driver may open the door
- [ ] C. It may suddenly move off
- [ ] D. People may cross the road in front of it
- [ ] E. There are bicycles parked on the pavement

279 In areas where there are 'traffic calming' measures you should

Mark one answer

- [ ] A. travel at a reduced speed
- [ ] B. always travel at the speed limit
- [ ] C. position in the centre of the road
- [ ] D. only slow down if pedestrians are near

280 You are planning a long journey. Do you need to plan rest stops?

Mark one answer

- [ ] **A.** Yes, you should plan to stop every half an hour
- [ ] **B.** Yes, regular stops help concentration
- [ ] **C.** No, you will be less tired if you get there as soon as possible
- [ ] **D.** No, only fuel stops will be needed

281 A driver does something that upsets you. You should

Mark one answer

- [ ] **A.** try not to react
- [ ] **B.** let them know how you feel
- [ ] **C.** flash your headlights several times
- [ ] **D.** sound your horn

282 The red lights are flashing. What should you do when approaching this level crossing?

Mark one answer

- [ ] **A.** Go through quickly
- [ ] **B.** Go through carefully
- [ ] **C.** Stop before the barrier
- [ ] **D.** Switch on hazard warning lights

283 What TWO main hazards should you be aware of when going along this street?

Mark two answers

- [ ] **A.** Glare from the sun
- [ ] **B.** Car doors opening suddenly
- [ ] **C.** Lack of road markings
- [ ] **D.** The headlights on parked cars being switched on
- [ ] **E.** Large goods vehicles
- [ ] **F.** Children running out from between vehicles

284 What is the main hazard you should be aware of when following this cyclist?

Mark one answer

- [ ] **A.** The cyclist may move to the left and dismount
- [ ] **B.** The cyclist may swerve out into the road
- [ ] **C.** The contents of the cyclist's carrier may fall on to the road
- [ ] **D.** The cyclist may wish to turn right at the end of the road

285 When approaching this hazard why should you slow down?

Mark two answers

- [ ] **A.** Because of the bend
- [ ] **B.** Because it's hard to see to the right
- [ ] **C.** Because of approaching traffic
- [ ] **D.** Because of animals crossing
- [ ] **E.** Because of the level crossing

286 A driver's behaviour has upset you. It may help if you

Mark one answer

- [ ] **A.** stop and take a break
- [ ] **B.** shout abusive language
- [ ] **C.** gesture to them with your hand
- [ ] **D.** follow their car, flashing your headlights

287 You are on a dual carriageway. Ahead you see a vehicle with an amber flashing light. What will this be?

Mark one answer

- [ ] **A.** An ambulance
- [ ] **B.** A fire engine
- [ ] **C.** A doctor on call
- [ ] **D.** A disabled person's vehicle

288 You are approaching crossroads. The traffic lights have failed. What shoul you do?

Mark one answer

- [ ] **A.** Brake and stop only for large vehicles
- [ ] **B.** Brake sharply to a stop before looking
- [ ] **C.** Be prepared to brake sharply to a stop
- [ ] **D.** Be prepared to stop for any traffic

289 Why are place names painted on the road surface?

Mark one answer

- [ ] **A.** To restrict the flow of traffic
- [ ] **B.** To warn you of oncoming traffic
- [ ] **C.** To enable you to change lanes early
- [ ] **D.** To prevent you changing lanes

290 What should the driver of the red ca (arrowed) do?

Mark one answer

- [ ] **A.** Wave the pedestrians who are waiting to cross
- [ ] **B.** Wait for the pedestrian in the road to cross
- [ ] **C.** Quickly drive behind the pedestrian in the road
- [ ] **D.** Tell the pedestrian in the road she should not have crossed

291

You are following a slower-moving vehicle on a narrow country road. There is a junction just ahead on the right. What should you do?

Mark one answer

- [ ] **A.** Overtake after checking your mirrors and signalling
- [ ] **B.** Stay behind until you are past the junction
- [ ] **C.** Accelerate quickly to pass before the junction
- [ ] **D.** Slow down and prepare to overtake on the left

292

What should you do as you approach this overhead bridge?

Mark one answer

- [ ] **A.** Move out to the centre of the road before going through
- [ ] **B.** Find another route, this is only for high vehicles
- [ ] **C.** Be prepared to give way to large vehicles in the middle of the road
- [ ] **D.** Move across to the right-hand side before going through

293

Why are mirrors often slightly curved (convex)?

Mark one answer

- [ ] **A.** They give a wider field of vision
- [ ] **B.** They totally cover blind spots
- [ ] **C.** They make it easier to judge the speed of following traffic
- [ ] **D.** They make following traffic look bigger

294

What does the solid white line at the side of the road indicate?

Mark one answer

- [ ] **A.** Traffic lights ahead
- [ ] **B.** Edge of the carriageway
- [ ] **C.** Footpath on the left
- [ ] **D.** Cycle path

295

You are driving towards this level crossing. What would be the first warning of an approaching train?

Mark one answer

- [ ] **A.** Both half barriers down
- [ ] **B.** A steady amber light
- [ ] **C.** One half barrier down
- [ ] **D.** Twin flashing red lights

296

You are driving along this motorway. It is raining. When following this lorry you should

Mark two answers

- [ ] **A.** allow at least a two-second gap
- [ ] **B.** move left and drive on the hard shoulder
- [ ] **C.** allow at least a four-second gap
- [ ] **D.** be aware of spray reducing your vision
- [ ] **E.** move right and stay in the right-hand lane

297

You are behind this cyclist. When the traffic lights change, what should you do?

Mark one answer

- [ ] **A.** Try to move off before the cyclist
- [ ] **B.** Allow the cyclist time and room
- [ ] **C.** Turn right but give the cyclist room
- [ ] **D.** Tap your horn and drive through first

298

You are driving towards this left-hand bend. What dangers should you be aware of?

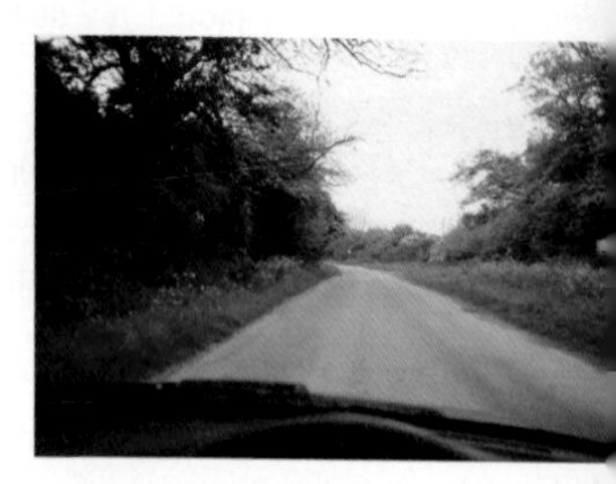

Mark one answer

- [ ] **A.** A vehicle overtaking you
- [ ] **B.** No white lines in the centre of the road
- [ ] **C.** No sign to warn you of the bend
- [ ] **D.** Pedestrians walking towards you

299

While driving, you see this sign ahead. You should

Mark one answer

- [ ] **A.** stop at the sign
- [ ] **B.** slow, but continue around the bend
- [ ] **C.** slow to a crawl and continue
- [ ] **D.** stop and look for open farm gates

300 Why should the junction on the left be kept clear?

Mark one answer

- [ ] **A.** To allow vehicles to enter and emerge
- [ ] **B.** To allow the bus to reverse
- [ ] **C.** To allow vehicles to make a U-turn
- [ ] **D.** To allow vehicles to park

301 When the traffic lights change to green the white car should

Mark one answer

- [ ] **A.** wait for the cyclist to pull away
- [ ] **B.** move off quickly and turn in front of the cyclist
- [ ] **C.** move close up to the cyclist to beat the lights
- [ ] **D.** sound the horn to warn the cyclist

302 You intend to turn left at the traffic lights. Just before turning you should

Mark one answer

- [ ] **A.** check your right mirror
- [ ] **B.** move close up to the white car
- [ ] **C.** straddle the lanes
- [ ] **D.** check for bicycles on your left

303 You should reduce your speed when drving along this road because

Mark one answer

- [ ] **A.** there is a staggered junction ahead
- [ ] **B.** there is a low bridge ahead
- [ ] **C.** there is a change in the road surface
- [ ] **D.** the road ahead narrows

304 You are driving at 60mph. As you approach this hazard you should

Mark one answer

- A. maintain your speed
- B. reduce your speed
- C. take the next right turn
- D. take the next left turn

305 The traffic ahead of you in the left-hand lane is slowing. You should

Mark two answers

- A. be wary of cars on your right cutting in
- B. accelerate past the vehicles in the left-hand lane
- C. pull up on the left-hand verge
- D. move across and continue in the right-hand lane
- E. slow down, keeping a safe separation distance

306 What might you expect to happen in this situation?

Mark one answer

- A. Traffic will move into the right-hand lane
- B. Traffic speed will increase
- C. Traffic will move into the left-hand lane
- D. Traffic will not need to change position

307 You are driving on a road with several lanes. You see these signs above the lanes. What do they mean?

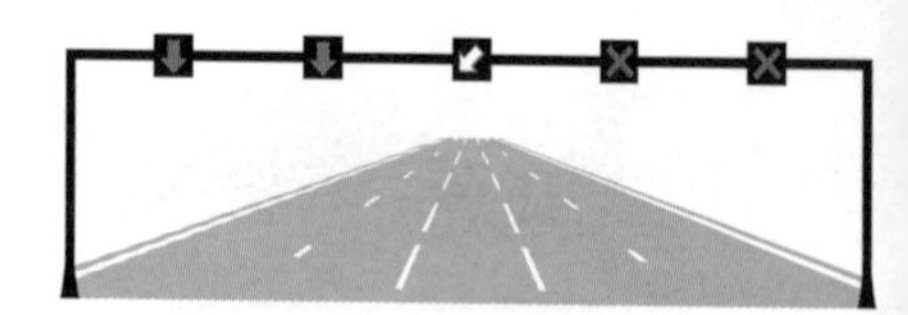

Mark one answer

- A. The two right lanes are open
- B. The two left lanes are open
- C. Traffic in the left lanes should stop
- D. Traffic in the right lanes should stop

308 As a provisional licence holder, you must not drive a motor car

Mark two answers

- A. at more than 40mph
- B. on your own
- C. on the motorway
- D. under the age of 18 years at night
- E. with passengers in the rear seats

309 After passing your driving test, you suffer from ill health. This affects your driving. You MUST

Mark one answer

- A. inform your local police station
- B. avoid using motorways
- C. always drive accompanied
- D. inform the licensing authority

310 You are invited to a pub lunch. You know that you will have to drive in the evening. What is your best course of action?

Mark one answer

- A. Avoid mixing your alcoholic drinks
- B. Not drink any alcohol at all
- C. Have some milk before drinking alcohol
- D. Eat a hot meal with your alcoholic drinks

311 You have been convicted of driving whilst unfit through drink or drugs. You will find this is likely to cause the cost of one of the following to rise considerably. Which one?

Mark one answer

- A. Road fund licence
- B. Insurance premiums
- C. Vehicle test certificate
- D. Driving licence

312 What advice should you give to a driver who has had a few alcoholic drinks at a party?

Mark one answer

- A. Have a strong cup of coffee and then drive home
- B. Drive home carefully and slowly
- C. Go home by public transport
- D. Wait a short while and then drive home

313 You have been taking medicine for a few days which made you feel drowsy. Today you feel better but still need to take the medicine. You should only drive

Mark one answer

- A. if your journey is necessary
- B. at night on quiet roads
- C. if someone goes with you
- D. after checking with your doctor

314 **You are about to return home from holiday when you become ill. A doctor prescribes drugs which are likely to affect your driving. You should**

Mark one answer

- [ ] A. drive only if someone is with you
- [ ] B. avoid driving on motorways
- [ ] C. not drive yourself
- [ ] D. never drive at more than 30mph

315 **During periods of illness your ability to drive may be impaired. You MUST**

Mark two answers

- [ ] A. see your doctor each time before you drive
- [ ] B. only take smaller doses of any medicines
- [ ] C. be medically fit to drive
- [ ] D. not drive after taking certain medicines
- [ ] E. take all your medicines with you when you drive

316 **You feel drowsy when driving. You should**

Mark two answers

- [ ] A. stop and rest as soon as possible
- [ ] B. turn the heater up to keep you warm and comfortable
- [ ] C. make sure you have a good supply of fresh air
- [ ] D. continue with your journey but drive more slowly
- [ ] E. close the car windows to help you concentrate

317 **You are driving along a motorway and become tired. You should**

Mark two answers

- [ ] A. stop at the next service area and rest
- [ ] B. leave the motorway at the next exit and rest
- [ ] C. increase your speed and turn up the radio volume
- [ ] D. close all your windows and set heating to warm
- [ ] E. pull up on the hard shoulder and change drivers

318 **You are taking drugs that are likely to affect your driving. What should you do?**

Mark one answer

- [ ] A. Seek medical advice before driving
- [ ] B. Limit your driving to essential journeys
- [ ] C. Only drive if accompanied by a full licence-holder
- [ ] D. Drive only for short distances

319 **You are about to drive home. You feel very tired and have a severe headache. You should**

Mark one answer

- [ ] A. wait until you are fit and well before driving
- [ ] B. drive home, but take a tablet for headaches
- [ ] C. drive home if you can stay awake for the journey
- [ ] D. wait for a short time, then drive home slowly

320 If you are feeling tired it is best to stop as soon as you can. Until then you should

Mark one answer

- A. increase your speed to find a stopping place quickly
- B. ensure a supply of fresh air
- C. gently tap the steering wheel
- D. keep changing speed to improve concentration

321 If your motorway journey seems boring and you feel drowsy while driving, you should

Mark one answer

- A. open a window and drive to the next service area
- B. stop on the hard shoulder for a sleep
- C. speed up to arrive at your destination sooner
- D. slow down and let other drivers overtake

322 Driving long distances can be tiring. You can prevent this by

Mark three answers

- A. stopping every so often for a walk
- B. opening a window for some fresh air
- C. ensuring plenty of refreshment breaks
- D. completing the journey without stopping
- E. eating a large meal before driving

323 You go to a social event and need to drive a short time after. What precaution should you take?

Mark one answer

- A. Avoid drinking alcohol on an empty stomach
- B. Drink plenty of coffee after drinking alcohol
- C. Avoid drinking alcohol completely
- D. Drink plenty of milk before drinking alcohol

324 You take some cough medicine given to you by a friend. What should you do before driving?

Mark one answer

- A. Ask your friend if taking the medicine affected their driving
- B. Drink some strong coffee one hour before driving
- C. Check the label to see if the medicine will affect your driving
- D. Drive a short distance to see if the medicine is affecting your driving

325 You take the wrong route and find you are on a one-way street. You should

Mark one answer

- A. reverse out of the road
- B. turn round in a side road
- C. continue to the end of the road
- D. reverse into a driveway

326 Which THREE are likely to make you lose concentration while driving?

Mark three answers

- [ ] **A.** Looking at road maps
- [ ] **B.** Listening to loud music
- [ ] **C.** Using your windscreen washers
- [ ] **D.** Looking in your wing mirror
- [ ] **E.** Using a mobile phone

327 You are driving along this road. The driver on the left is reversing from a driveway. You should

Mark one answer

- [ ] **A.** move to the opposite side of the road
- [ ] **B.** drive through as you have priority
- [ ] **C.** sound your horn and be prepared to stop
- [ ] **D.** speed up and drive through quickly

328 You have been involved in an argument before starting your journey. This has made you feel angry. You should

Mark one answer

- [ ] **A.** start to drive, but open a window
- [ ] **B.** drive slower than normal and turn your radio on
- [ ] **C.** have an alcoholic drink to help you relax before driving
- [ ] **D.** calm down before you start to drive

329 You start to feel tired while driving. What should you do?

Mark one answer

- [ ] **A.** Increase your speed slightly
- [ ] **B.** Decrease your speed slightly
- [ ] **C.** Find a less busy route
- [ ] **D.** Pull over at a safe place to rest

330 You are driving on this dual carriageway. Why may you need to slow down?

Mark one answer

- [ ] **A.** There is a broken white line in the centre
- [ ] **B.** There are solid white lines either side
- [ ] **C.** There are road works ahead of you
- [ ] **D.** There are no footpaths

331 You have just been overtaken by this motorcyclist who is cutting in sharply. You should

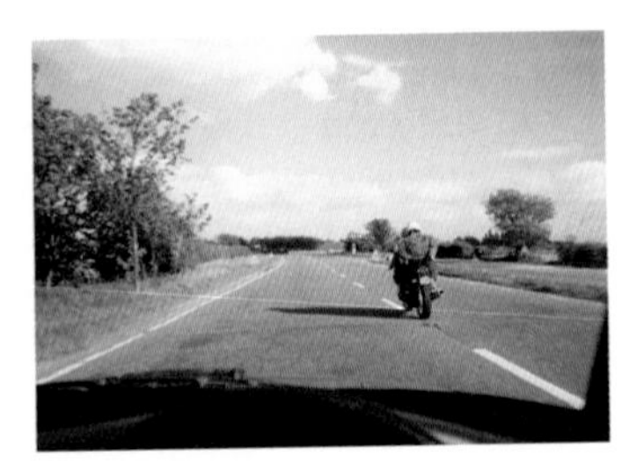

Mark one answer

- [ ] **A.** sound the horn
- [ ] **B.** brake firmly
- [ ] **C.** keep a safe gap
- [ ] **D.** flash your lights

332 You are about to drive home. You cannot find the glasses you need to wear. You should

Mark one answer

- [ ] **A.** drive home slowly, keeping to quiet roads
- [ ] **B.** borrow a friend's glasses and use those
- [ ] **C.** drive home at night, so that the lights will help you
- [ ] **D.** find a way of getting home without driving

333 Which THREE result from drinking alcohol?

Mark three answers

- [ ] **A.** Less control
- [ ] **B.** A false sense of confidence
- [ ] **C.** Faster reactions
- [ ] **D.** Poor judgement of speed
- [ ] **E.** Greater awareness of danger

334 Which THREE of these are likely effects of drinking alcohol?

Mark three answers

- [ ] **A.** Reduced co-ordination
- [ ] **B.** Increased confidence
- [ ] **C.** Poor judgement
- [ ] **D.** Increased concentration
- [ ] **E.** Faster reactions
- [ ] **F.** Colour blindness

335 How does alcohol affect you?

Mark one answer

- [ ] **A.** It speeds up your reactions
- [ ] **B.** It increases your awareness
- [ ] **C.** It improves your co-ordination
- [ ] **D.** It reduces your concentration

336 Your doctor has given you a course of medicine. Why should you ask how it will affect you?

Mark one answer

- [ ] **A.** Drugs make you a better driver by quickening your reactions
- [ ] **B.** You will have to let your insurance company know about the medicine
- [ ] **C.** Some types of medicine can cause your reactions to slow down
- [ ] **D.** The medicine you take may affect your hearing

337 You are not sure if your cough medicine will affect you. What TWO things should you do?

Mark two answers

- [ ] **A.** Ask your doctor
- [ ] **B.** Check the medicine label
- [ ] **C.** Drive if you feel alright
- [ ] **D.** Ask a friend or relative for advice

338 You are on a motorway. You feel tired. You should

Mark one answer

- [ ] **A.** carry on but go slowly
- [ ] **B.** leave the motorway at the next exit
- [ ] **C.** complete your journey as quickly as possible
- [ ] **D.** stop on the hard shoulder

339 You find that you need glasses to read vehicle number plates at the required distance. When MUST you wear them?

Mark one answer

- [ ] **A.** Only in bad weather conditions
- [ ] **B.** At all times when driving
- [ ] **C.** Only when you think it necessary
- [ ] **D.** Only in bad light or at night time

340 Which TWO things would help to keep you alert during a long journey?

Mark two answers

- [ ] **A.** Finishing your journey as fast as you can
- [ ] **B.** Keeping off the motorways and using country roads
- [ ] **C.** Making sure that you get plenty of fresh air
- [ ] **D.** Making regular stops for refreshments

341 Which of the following types of glasses should NOT be worn when driving at night?

Mark one answer

- [ ] **A.** Half-moon
- [ ] **B.** Round
- [ ] **C.** Bi-focal
- [ ] **D.** Tinted

342 Drinking any amount of alcohol is likely to

Mark three answers

- [ ] **A.** slow down your reactions to hazards
- [ ] **B.** increase the speed of your reactions
- [ ] **C.** worsen your judgement of speed
- [ ] **D.** improve your awareness of danger
- [ ] **E.** give a false sense of confidence

343 What else can seriously affect your concentration, other than alcoholic drinks?

Mark three answers

- [ ] **A.** Drugs
- [ ] **B.** Tiredness
- [ ] **C.** Tinted windows
- [ ] **D.** Contact lenses
- [ ] **E.** Loud music

344 As a driver you find that your eyesight has become very poor. Your optician says they cannot help you. The law says that you should tell

Mark one answer

- [ ] **A.** the licensing authority
- [ ] **B.** your own doctor
- [ ] **C.** the local police station
- [ ] **D.** another optician

345 For which of these may you use hazard warning lights?

Mark one answer

- [ ] A. When driving on a motorway to warn traffic behind of a hazard ahead
- [ ] B. When you are double parked on a two-way road
- [ ] C. When your direction indicators are not working
- [ ] D. When warning oncoming traffic that you intend to stop

346 When should you use hazard warning lights?

Mark one answer

- [ ] A. When you are double parked on a two-way road
- [ ] B. When your direction indicators are not working
- [ ] C. When warning oncoming traffic that you intend to stop
- [ ] D. When your vehicle has broken down and is causing an obstruction

347 You want to turn left at this junction. The view of the main road is restricted. What should you do?

Mark one answer

- [ ] A. Stay well back and wait to see if something comes
- [ ] B. Build up your speed so that you can emerge quickly
- [ ] C. Stop and apply the handbrake even if the road is clear
- [ ] D. Approach slowly and edge out until you can see more clearly

348 You are driving on a motorway. The traffic ahead is braking sharply because of an accident. How could you warn traffic behind you?

Mark one answer

- [ ] A. Briefly use the hazard warning lights
- [ ] B. Switch on the hazard warning lights continuously
- [ ] C. Briefly use the rear fog lights
- [ ] D. Switch on the headlights continuously

349 **When may you use hazard warning lights?**

Mark one answer

- [ ] **A.** To park alongside another car
- [ ] **B.** To park on double yellow lines
- [ ] **C.** When you are being towed
- [ ] **D.** When you have broken down

350 **Hazard warning lights should be used when vehicles are**

Mark one answer

- [ ] **A.** broken down and causing an obstruction
- [ ] **B.** faulty and moving slowly
- [ ] **C.** being towed along a road
- [ ] **D.** reversing into a side road

351 **Some two-way roads are divided into three lanes. Why are these particularly dangerous?**

Mark one answer

- [ ] **A.** Traffic in both directions can use the middle lane to overtake
- [ ] **B.** Traffic can travel faster in poor weather conditions
- [ ] **C.** Traffic can overtake on the left
- [ ] **D.** Traffic uses the middle lane for emergencies only

352 **To avoid an accident when entering a contraflow system, you should**

Mark three answers

- [ ] **A.** reduce speed in good time
- [ ] **B.** switch lanes any time to make progress
- [ ] **C.** choose an appropriate lane early
- [ ] **D.** keep the correct separation distance
- [ ] **E.** increase speed to pass through quickly
- [ ] **F.** follow other motorists closely to avoid long queues

353 **When driving a car fitted with automatic transmission what would you use 'kick down' for?**

Mark one answer

- [ ] **A.** Cruise control
- [ ] **B.** Quick acceleration
- [ ] **C.** Slow braking
- [ ] **D.** Fuel economy

354 **You are waiting to emerge at a junction. Your view is restricted by parked vehicles. What can help you to see traffic on the road you are joining?**

Mark one answer

- [ ] **A.** Looking for traffic behind you
- [ ] **B.** Reflections of traffic in shop windows
- [ ] **C.** Making eye contact with other road users
- [ ] **D.** Checking for traffic in your interior mirror

355 **Overtaking is a major cause of collisions. In which THREE of these situations should you NOT overtake?**

Mark three answers

- [ ] **A.** If you are turning left shortly afterwards
- [ ] **B.** When you are in a one-way street
- [ ] **C.** When you are approaching a junction
- [ ] **D.** If you are travelling up a long hill
- [ ] **E.** When your view ahead is blocked

356 **It is an offence to drive under the influence of illegal drugs. Many of the effects are unpredictable. The direct effects of some drugs can last for up to**

Mark one answer

- [ ] **A.** 24 hours
- [ ] **B.** 48 hours
- [ ] **C.** 72 hours
- [ ] **D.** 96 hours

357 Which sign means that there may be people walking along the road?

Mark one answer

- [ ] A.

- [ ] B.

- [ ] C.

- [ ] D.

358 You are turning left at a junction. Pedestrians have started to cross the road. You should

Mark one answer

- [ ] A. go on, giving them plenty of room
- [ ] B. stop and wave at them to cross
- [ ] C. blow your horn and proceed
- [ ] D. give way to them

359 You are turning left from a main road into a side road. People are already crossing the road into which you are turning. You should

Mark one answer

- [ ] A. continue, as it is your right of way
- [ ] B. signal to them to continue crossing
- [ ] C. wait and allow them to cross
- [ ] D. sound your horn to warn them of your presence

360 You are at a road junction, turning into a minor road. There are pedestrians crossing the minor road. You should

Mark one answer

- [ ] A. stop and wave the pedestrians across
- [ ] B. sound your horn to let the pedestrians know that you are there
- [ ] C. give way to the pedestrians who are already crossing
- [ ] D. carry on; the pedestrians should give way to you

361 You are turning left into a side road. What hazards should you be especially aware of?

Mark one answer

- A. One-way street
- B. Pedestrians
- C. Traffic congestion
- D. Parked vehicles

362 You intend to turn right into a side road. Just before turning you should check for motorcyclists who might be

Mark one answer

- A. overtaking on your left
- B. following you closely
- C. emerging from the side road
- D. overtaking on your right

363 A toucan crossing is different from other crossings because

Mark one answer

- A. moped riders can use it
- B. it is controlled by a traffic warden
- C. it is controlled by two flashing lights
- D. cyclists can use it

364 At toucan crossings

Mark one answer

- A. you only stop if someone is waiting to cross
- B. cyclists are not permitted
- C. there is a continuously flashing amber beacon
- D. pedestrians and cyclists may cross

365 What does this sign tell you?

Mark one answer

- A. No cycling
- B. Cycle route ahead
- C. Cycle parking only
- D. End of cycle route

366 How will a school crossing patrol signal you to stop?

Mark one answer

- A. By pointing to children on the opposite pavement
- B. By displaying a red light
- C. By displaying a stop sign
- D. By giving you an arm signal

367 Where would you see this sign?

Mark one answer

- A. In the window of a car taking children to school
- B. At the side of the road
- C. At playground areas
- D. On the rear of a school bus or coach

368 Which sign tells you that pedestrians may be walking in the road as there is no pavement?

Mark one answer

- [ ] A. 
- [ ] B. 
- [ ] C. 
- [ ] D.

369 What does this sign mean?

Mark one answer

- [ ] A. No route for pedestrians and cyclists
- [ ] B. A route for pedestrians only
- [ ] C. A route for cyclists only
- [ ] D. A route for pedestrians and cyclists

370 You see a pedestrian with a white stick and red band. This means that the person is

Mark one answer

- [ ] A. physically disabled
- [ ] B. deaf only
- [ ] C. blind only
- [ ] D. deaf and blind

371 What action would you take when elderly people are crossing the road?

Mark one answer

- [ ] A. Wave them across so they know that you have seen them
- [ ] B. Be patient and allow them to cross in their own time
- [ ] C. Rev the engine to let them know that you are waiting
- [ ] D. Tap the horn in case they are hard of hearing

372 You see two elderly pedestrians about to cross the road ahead. You should

Mark one answer

- [ ] A. expect them to wait for you to pass
- [ ] B. speed up to get past them quickly
- [ ] C. stop and wave them across the road
- [ ] D. be careful, they may misjudge your speed

373 What does this sign mean?

Mark one answer

- [ ] A. Contraflow pedal cycle lane
- [ ] B. With-flow pedal cycle lane
- [ ] C. Pedal cycles and buses only
- [ ] D. No pedal cycles or buses

374

You are coming up to a roundabout. A cyclist is signalling to turn right. What should you do?

Mark one answer

- [ ] **A.** Overtake on the right
- [ ] **B.** Give a horn warning
- [ ] **C.** Signal the cyclist to move across
- [ ] **D.** Give the cyclist plenty of room

375

You are approaching this roundabout and see the cyclist signal right. Why is the cyclist keeping to the left?

Mark one answer

- [ ] **A.** It is a quicker route for the cyclist
- [ ] **B.** The cyclist is going to turn left instead
- [ ] **C.** The cyclist thinks *The Highway Code* does not apply to bicycles
- [ ] **D.** The cyclist is slower and more vulnerable

376

When you are overtaking a cyclist you should leave as much room as you would give to a car. What is the main reason for this?

Mark one answer

- [ ] **A.** The cyclist might change lanes
- [ ] **B.** The cyclist might get off the bike
- [ ] **C.** The cyclist might swerve
- [ ] **D.** The cyclist might have to make a right turn

377

Which TWO should you allow extra room when overtaking?

Mark two answers

- [ ] **A.** Motorcycles
- [ ] **B.** Tractors
- [ ] **C.** Bicycles
- [ ] **D.** Road-sweeping vehicles

378

Why should you look particularly for motorcyclists and cyclists at junctions?

Mark one answer

- [ ] **A.** They may want to turn into the side road
- [ ] **B.** They may slow down to let you turn
- [ ] **C.** They are harder to see
- [ ] **D.** They might not see you turn

379

You are waiting to come out of a side road. Why should you watch carefully for motorcycles?

Mark one answer

- [ ] **A.** Motorcycles are usually faster than cars
- [ ] **B.** Police patrols often use motorcycles
- [ ] **C.** Motorcycles are small and hard to see
- [ ] **D.** Motorcycles have right of way

380

In daylight, an approaching motorcyclist is using a dipped headlight. Why?

Mark one answer

- [ ] **A.** So that the rider can be seen more easily
- [ ] **B.** To stop the battery overcharging
- [ ] **C.** To improve the rider's vision
- [ ] **D.** The rider is inviting you to proceed

381 Motorcyclists should wear bright clothing mainly because

Mark one answer

- [ ] **A.** they must do so by law
- [ ] **B.** it helps keep them cool in summer
- [ ] **C.** the colours are popular
- [ ] **D.** drivers often do not see them

382 There is a slow-moving motorcyclist ahead of you. You are unsure what the rider is going to do. You should

Mark one answer

- [ ] **A.** pass on the left
- [ ] **B.** pass on the right
- [ ] **C.** stay behind
- [ ] **D.** move closer

383 Motorcyclists will often look round over their right shoulder just before turning right. This is because

Mark one answer

- [ ] **A.** they need to listen for following traffic
- [ ] **B.** motorcycles do not have mirrors
- [ ] **C.** looking around helps them balance as they turn
- [ ] **D.** they need to check for traffic in their blind area

384 At road junctions which of the following are most vulnerable?

Mark three answers

- [ ] **A.** Cyclists
- [ ] **B.** Motorcyclists
- [ ] **C.** Pedestrians
- [ ] **D.** Car drivers
- [ ] **E.** Lorry drivers

385 Motorcyclists are particularly vulnerable

Mark one answer

- [ ] **A.** when moving off
- [ ] **B.** on dual carriageways
- [ ] **C.** when approaching junctions
- [ ] **D.** on motorways

386 An injured motorcyclist is lying unconscious in the road. You should

Mark one answer

- [ ] **A.** remove the safety helmet
- [ ] **B.** seek medical assistance
- [ ] **C.** move the person off the road
- [ ] **D.** remove the leather jacket

387 You notice horse riders in front. What should you do FIRST?

Mark one answer

- [ ] **A.** Pull out to the middle of the road
- [ ] **B.** Slow down and be ready to stop
- [ ] **C.** Accelerate around them
- [ ] **D.** Signal right

388
You are approaching a roundabout. There are horses just ahead of you. You should

Mark two answers

- A. be prepared to stop
- B. treat them like any other vehicle
- C. give them plenty of room
- D. accelerate past as quickly as possible
- E. sound your horn as a warning

389
Which THREE should you do when passing sheep on a road?

Mark three answers

- A. Allow plenty of room
- B. Go very slowly
- C. Pass quickly but quietly
- D. Be ready to stop
- E. Briefly sound your horn

390
At night you see a pedestrian wearing reflective clothing and carrying a bright red light. What does this mean?

Mark one answer

- A. You are approaching road works
- B. You are approaching an organised walk
- C. You are approaching a slow-moving vehicle
- D. You are approaching an accident black spot

391
As you approach a pelican crossing the lights change to green. Elderly people are half-way across. You should

Mark one answer

- A. wave them to cross as quickly as they can
- B. rev your engine to make them hurry
- C. flash your lights in case they have not heard you
- D. wait because they will take longer to cross

392
There are flashing amber lights under a school warning sign. What action should you take?

Mark one answer

- A. Reduce speed until you are clear of the area
- B. Keep up your speed and sound the horn
- C. Increase your speed to clear the area quickly
- D. Wait at the lights until they change to green

393 **You are approaching this crossing. You should**

Mark one answer

- A. prepare to slow down and stop
- B. stop and wave the pedestrians across
- C. speed up and pass by quickly
- D. continue unless the pedestrians step out

394 **You see a pedestrian with a dog. The dog has a yellow or burgundy coat. This especially warns you that the pedestrian is**

Mark one answer

- A. elderly
- B. dog training
- C. colour blind
- D. deaf

395 **These road markings must be kept clear to allow**

Mark one answer

- A. schoolchildren to be dropped off
- B. for teachers to park
- C. schoolchildren to be picked up
- D. a clear view of the crossing area

396 **You must not stop on these road markings because you may obstruct**

Mark one answer

- A. children's view of the crossing area
- B. teachers' access to the school
- C. delivery vehicles' access to the school
- D. emergency vehicles' access to the school

397 **The left-hand pavement is closed due to street repairs. What should you do?**

Mark one answer

- A. Watch out for pedestrians walking in the road
- B. Use your right-hand mirror more often
- C. Speed up to get past the road works quicker
- D. Position close to the left-hand kerb

398 **Where would you see this sign?**

Mark one answer

- A. Near a school crossing
- B. At a playground entrance
- C. On a school bus
- D. At a 'pedestrians only' area

399 **You are following a motorcyclist on an uneven road. You should**

Mark one answer

- [ ] **A.** allow less room so you can be seen in their mirrors
- [ ] **B.** overtake immediately
- [ ] **C.** allow extra room in case they swerve to avoid potholes
- [ ] **D.** allow the same room as normal because road surfaces do not affect motorcyclists

400 **You are following two cyclists. They approach a roundabout in the left-hand lane. In which direction should you expect the cyclists to go?**

Mark one answer

- [ ] **A.** Left
- [ ] **B.** Right
- [ ] **C.** Any direction
- [ ] **D.** Straight ahead

401 **You are travelling behind a moped. You want to turn left just ahead. You should**

Mark one answer

- [ ] **A.** overtake the moped before the junction
- [ ] **B.** pull alongside the moped and stay level until just before the junction
- [ ] **C.** sound your horn as a warning and pull in front of the moped
- [ ] **D.** stay behind until the moped has passed the junction

402 **Which THREE of the following are hazards motorcyclists present in queues of traffic?**

Mark three answers

- [ ] **A.** Cutting in just in front of you
- [ ] **B.** Riding in single file
- [ ] **C.** Passing very close to you
- [ ] **D.** Riding with their headlight on dipped beam
- [ ] **E.** Filtering between the lanes

403 **You see a horse rider as you approach a roundabout. They are signalling right but keeping well to the left. You should**

Mark one answer

- [ ] **A.** proceed as normal
- [ ] **B.** keep close to them
- [ ] **C.** cut in front of them
- [ ] **D.** stay well back

404 **How would you react to drivers who appear to be inexperienced?**

Mark one answer

- [ ] **A.** Sound your horn to warn them of your presence
- [ ] **B.** Be patient and prepare for them to react more slowly
- [ ] **C.** Flash your headlights to indicate that it is safe for them to proceed
- [ ] **D.** Overtake them as soon as possible

405 You are following a learner driver who stalls at a junction. You should

Mark one answer

- A. be patient as you expect them to make mistakes
- B. stay very close behind and flash your headlights
- C. start to rev your engine if they take too long to restart
- D. immediately steer around them and drive on

406 You are on a country road. What should you expect to see coming towards you on YOUR side of the road?

Mark one answer

- A. Motorcycles
- B. Bicycles
- C. Pedestrians
- D. Horse riders

407 You are turning left into a side road. Pedestrians are crossing the road near the junction. You must

Mark one answer

- A. wave them on
- B. sound your horn
- C. switch on your hazard lights
- D. wait for them to cross

408 You are following a car driven by an elderly driver. You should

Mark one answer

- A. expect the driver to drive badly
- B. flash your lights and overtake
- C. be aware that the driver's reactions may not be as fast as yours
- D. stay very close behind but be careful

409 You are following a cyclist. You wish to turn left just ahead. You should

Mark one answer

- A. overtake the cyclist before the junction
- B. pull alongside the cyclist and stay level until after the junction
- C. hold back until the cyclist has passed the junction
- D. go around the cyclist on the junction

410 A horse rider is in the left-hand lane approaching a roundabout. You should expect the rider to

Mark one answer

- A. go in any direction
- B. turn right
- C. turn left
- D. go ahead

411 You have just passed your test. How can you decrease your risk of accidents on the motorway?

Mark one answer
- [ ] **A.** By keeping up with the car in front
- [ ] **B.** By never going over 40mph
- [ ] **C.** By staying only in the left-hand lane
- [ ] **D.** By taking further training

412 Powered vehicles used by disabled people are small and hard to see. How do they give early warning when on a dual carriageway?

Mark one answer
- [ ] **A.** They will have a flashing red light
- [ ] **B.** They will have a flashing green light
- [ ] **C.** They will have a flashing blue light
- [ ] **D.** They will have a flashing amber light

413 You should never attempt to overtake a cyclist

Mark one answer
- [ ] **A.** just before you turn left
- [ ] **B.** on a left-hand bend
- [ ] **C.** on a one-way street
- [ ] **D.** on a dual carriageway

414 Ahead of you there is a moving vehicle with a flashing amber beacon. This means it is

Mark one answer
- [ ] **A.** slow moving
- [ ] **B.** broken down
- [ ] **C.** a doctor's car
- [ ] **D.** a school crossing patrol

415 You want to reverse into a side road. You are not sure that the area behind your car is clear. What should you do?

Mark one answer
- [ ] **A.** Look through the rear window only
- [ ] **B.** Get out and check
- [ ] **C.** Check the mirrors only
- [ ] **D.** Carry on, assuming it is clear

416 You are about to reverse into a side road. A pedestrian wishes to cross behind you. You should

Mark one answer
- [ ] **A.** wave to the pedestrian to stop
- [ ] **B.** give way to the pedestrian
- [ ] **C.** wave to the pedestrian to cross
- [ ] **D.** reverse before the pedestrian starts to cross

417 Who is especially in danger of not being seen as you reverse your car?

Mark one answer
- [ ] **A.** Motorcyclists
- [ ] **B.** Car drivers
- [ ] **C.** Cyclists
- [ ] **D.** Children

418 You are reversing around a corner when you notice a pedestrian walking behind you. What should you do?

Mark one answer
- [ ] **A.** Slow down and wave the pedestrian across
- [ ] **B.** Continue reversing and steer round the pedestrian
- [ ] **C.** Stop and give way
- [ ] **D.** Continue reversing and sound your horn

419 You want to turn right from a junction but your view is restricted by parked vehicles. What should you do?

Mark one answer

- [ ] **A.** Move out quickly, but be prepared to stop
- [ ] **B.** Sound your horn and pull out if there is no reply
- [ ] **C.** Stop, then move slowly forward until you have a clear view
- [ ] **D.** Stop, get out and look along the main road to check

420 You are at the front of a queue of traffic waiting to turn right into a side road. Why is it important to check your right mirror just before turning?

Mark one answer

- [ ] **A.** To look for pedestrians about to cross
- [ ] **B.** To check for overtaking vehicles
- [ ] **C.** To make sure the side road is clear
- [ ] **D.** To check for emerging traffic

421 What must a driver do at a pelican crossing when the amber light is flashing?

Mark one answer

- [ ] **A.** Signal the pedestrian to cross
- [ ] **B.** Always wait for the green light before proceeding
- [ ] **C.** Give way to any pedestrians on the crossing
- [ ] **D.** Wait for the red-and-amber light before proceeding

422 You have stopped at a pelican crossing. A disabled person is crossing slowly in front of you. The lights have now changed to green. You should

Mark two answers

- [ ] **A.** allow the person to cross
- [ ] **B.** drive in front of the person
- [ ] **C.** drive behind the person
- [ ] **D.** sound your horn
- [ ] **E.** be patient
- [ ] **F.** edge forward slowly

423 You are driving past parked cars. You notice a bicycle wheel sticking out between them. What should you do?

Mark one answer

- [ ] **A.** Accelerate past quickly and sound your horn
- [ ] **B.** Slow down and wave the cyclist across
- [ ] **C.** Brake sharply and flash your headlights
- [ ] **D.** Slow down and be prepared to stop for a cyclist

424

You are driving past a line of parked cars. You notice a ball bouncing out into the road ahead. What should you do?

Mark one answer

- ☐ **A.** Continue driving at the same speed and sound your horn
- ☐ **B.** Continue driving at the same speed and flash your headlights
- ☐ **C.** Slow down and be prepared to stop for children
- ☐ **D.** Stop and wave the children across to fetch their ball

425

You want to turn right from a main road into a side road. Just before turning you should

Mark one answer

- ☐ **A.** cancel your right-turn signal
- ☐ **B.** select first gear
- ☐ **C.** check for traffic overtaking on your right
- ☐ **D.** stop and set the handbrake

426

You are driving in slow-moving queues of traffic. Just before changing lane you should

Mark one answer

- ☐ **A.** sound the horn
- ☐ **B.** look for motorcyclists filtering through the traffic
- ☐ **C.** give a 'slowing down' arm signal
- ☐ **D.** change down to first gear

427

You are driving in town. There is a bus at the bus stop on the other side o the road. Why should you be careful?

Mark one answer

- ☐ **A.** The bus may have broken down
- ☐ **B.** Pedestrians may come from behind the bus
- ☐ **C.** The bus may move off suddenly
- ☐ **D.** The bus may remain stationary

428

How should you overtake horse riders?

Mark one answer

- ☐ **A.** Drive up close and overtake as soon as possibl
- ☐ **B.** Speed is not important but allow plenty of room
- ☐ **C.** Use your horn just once to warn them
- ☐ **D.** Drive slowly and leave plenty of room

429

A friend wants to help you learn to drive. They must be

Mark one answer

- ☐ **A.** over 21 and have held a full licence for at least two years
- ☐ **B.** over 18 and hold an advanced driver's certificate
- ☐ **C.** over 18 and have fully comprehensive insurance
- ☐ **D.** over 21 and have held a full licence for at least three years

430

You are dazzled at night by a vehicle behind you. You should

Mark one answer

- ☐ **A.** set your mirror to anti-dazzle
- ☐ **B.** set your mirror to dazzle the other driver
- ☐ **C.** brake sharply to a stop
- ☐ **D.** switch your rear lights on and off

431 You have a collision whilst your car is moving. What is the first thing you must do?

Mark one answer

- [ ] **A.** Stop only if there are injured people
- [ ] **B.** Call the emergency services
- [ ] **C.** Stop at the scene of the accident
- [ ] **D.** Call your insurance company

432 Yellow zigzag lines on the road outside schools mean

SCHOOL KEEP CLEAR

Mark one answer

- [ ] **A.** sound your horn to alert other road users
- [ ] **B.** stop to allow children to cross
- [ ] **C.** you must not wait or park on these lines
- [ ] **D.** you must not drive over these lines

433 What do these road markings outside a school mean?

SCHOOL KEEP CLEAR

Mark one answer

- [ ] **A.** You may park here if you are a teacher
- [ ] **B.** Sound your horn before parking
- [ ] **C.** When parking, use your hazard warning lights
- [ ] **D.** You must not wait or park your vehicle here

434 You are driving on a main road. You intend to turn right into a side road. Just before turning you should

Mark one answer

- [ ] **A.** adjust your interior mirror
- [ ] **B.** flash your headlamps
- [ ] **C.** steer over to the left
- [ ] **D.** check for traffic overtaking on your right

435 Why should you allow extra room when overtaking a motorcyclist on a windy day?

Mark one answer

- [ ] **A.** The rider may turn off suddenly to get out of the wind
- [ ] **B.** The rider may be blown across in front of you
- [ ] **C.** The rider may stop suddenly
- [ ] **D.** The rider may be travelling faster than normal

436 Which age group of drivers is most likely to be involved in a road accident?

Mark one answer

- [ ] **A.** 17–25-year-olds
- [ ] **B.** 36–45-year-olds
- [ ] **C.** 46–55-year-olds
- [ ] **D.** over 55-year-olds

437 You are driving towards a zebra crossing. A person in a wheelchair is waiting to cross. What should you do?

Mark one answer

- [ ] **A.** Continue on your way
- [ ] **B.** Wave to the person to cross
- [ ] **C.** Wave to the person to wait
- [ ] **D.** Be prepared to stop

438 Where in particular should you look out for motorcyclists?

Mark one answer

- [ ] **A.** In a filling station
- [ ] **B.** At a road junction
- [ ] **C.** Near a service area
- [ ] **D.** When entering a car park

439 Where should you take particular care to look out for motorcyclists and cyclists?

Mark one answer

- [ ] **A.** On dual carriageways
- [ ] **B.** At junctions
- [ ] **C.** At zebra crossings
- [ ] **D.** On one-way streets

440 The road outside this school is marked with yellow zigzag lines. What do these lines mean?

Mark one answer

- [ ] **A.** You may park on the lines when dropping off schoolchildren
- [ ] **B.** You may park on the lines when picking schoolchildren up
- [ ] **C.** You must not wait or park your vehicle here at all
- [ ] **D.** You must stay with your vehicle if you park here

441 Some junctions controlled by traffic lights have a marked area between two stop lines. What is this for?

Mark one answer

- [ ] **A.** To allow taxis to position in front of other traffic
- [ ] **B.** To allow people with disabilities to cross the road
- [ ] **C.** To allow cyclists and pedestrians to cross the road together
- [ ] **D.** To allow cyclists to position in front of other traffic

442 At some traffic lights there are advance stop lines and a marked area. What are these for?

Mark one answer

- [ ] **A.** To allow cyclists to position in front of other traffic
- [ ] **B.** To let pedestrians cross when the lights change
- [ ] **C.** To prevent traffic from jumping the lights
- [ ] **D.** To let passengers get off a bus which is queuing

443

You are about to overtake a slow-moving motorcyclist. Which one of these signs would make you take special care?

Mark one answer

- [ ] A. 
- [ ] B. 
- [ ] C. 
- [ ] D. 

444

You are waiting to emerge left from a minor road. A large vehicle is approaching from the right. You have time to turn, but you should wait. Why?

Mark one answer

- [ ] **A.** The large vehicle can easily hide an overtaking vehicle
- [ ] **B.** The large vehicle can turn suddenly
- [ ] **C.** The large vehicle is difficult to steer in a straight line
- [ ] **D.** The large vehicle can easily hide vehicles from the left

445

You are following a long vehicle. It approaches a crossroads and signals left, but moves out to the right. You should

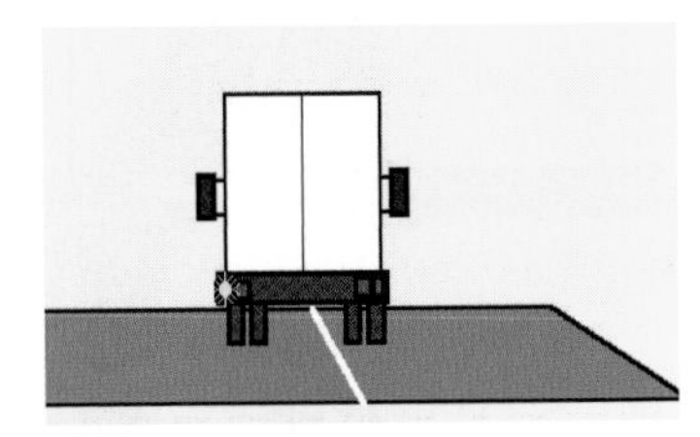

Mark one answer

- [ ] **A.** get closer in order to pass it quickly
- [ ] **B.** stay well back and give it room
- [ ] **C.** assume the signal is wrong and it is really turning right
- [ ] **D.** overtake as it starts to slow down

446

You are following a long vehicle approaching a crossroads. The driver signals right but moves close to the left-hand kerb. What should you do?

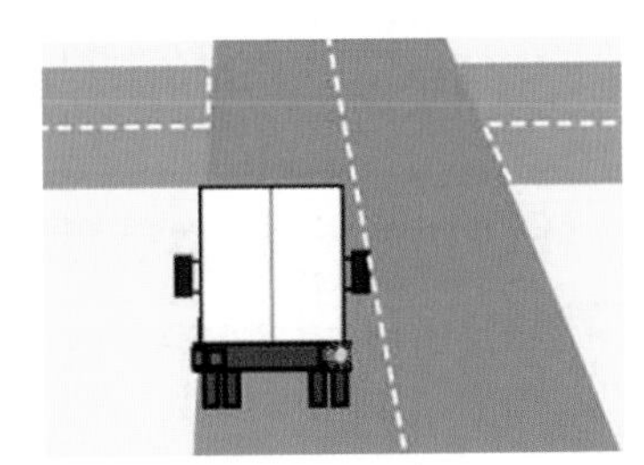

Mark one answer

- [ ] **A.** Warn the driver of the wrong signal
- [ ] **B.** Wait behind the long vehicle
- [ ] **C.** Report the driver to the police
- [ ] **D.** Overtake on the right-hand side

447 **You are approaching a mini-roundabout. The long vehicle in front is signalling left but positioned over to the right. You should**

Mark one answer
- [ ] **A.** sound your horn
- [ ] **B.** overtake on the left
- [ ] **C.** follow the same course as the lorry
- [ ] **D.** keep well back

448 **Before overtaking a large vehicle you should keep well back. Why is this?**

Mark one answer
- [ ] **A.** To give acceleration space to overtake quickly on blind bends
- [ ] **B.** To get the best view of the road ahead
- [ ] **C.** To leave a gap in case the vehicle stops and rolls back
- [ ] **D.** To offer other drivers a safe gap if they want to overtake you

449 **Why is passing a lorry more risky than passing a car?**

Mark one answer
- [ ] **A.** Lorries are longer than cars
- [ ] **B.** Lorries may suddenly pull up
- [ ] **C.** The brakes of lorries are not as good
- [ ] **D.** Lorries climb hills more slowly

450 **You are travelling behind a bus that pulls up at a bus stop. What should you do?**

Mark two answers
- [ ] **A.** Accelerate past the bus sounding your horn
- [ ] **B.** Watch carefully for pedestrians
- [ ] **C.** Be ready to give way to the bus
- [ ] **D.** Pull in closely behind the bus

451 **When you approach a bus signalling to move off from a bus stop you should**

Mark one answer
- [ ] **A.** get past before it moves
- [ ] **B.** allow it to pull away, if it is safe to do so
- [ ] **C.** flash your headlights as you approach
- [ ] **D.** signal left and wave the bus on

452 Which of these is LEAST likely to be affected by crosswinds?

Mark one answer

- ☐ **A.** Cyclists
- ☐ **B.** Motorcyclists
- ☐ **C.** High-sided vehicles
- ☐ **D.** Cars

453 You are following a large lorry on a wet road. Spray makes it difficult to see. You should

Mark one answer

- ☐ **A.** drop back until you can see better
- ☐ **B.** put your headlights on full beam
- ☐ **C.** keep close to the lorry, away from the spray
- ☐ **D.** speed up and overtake quickly

454 What should you do as you approach this lorry?

Mark one answer

- ☐ **A.** Slow down and be prepared to wait
- ☐ **B.** Make the lorry wait for you
- ☐ **C.** Flash your lights at the lorry
- ☐ **D.** Move to the right-hand side of the road

455 You are following a large articulated vehicle. It is going to turn left into a narrow road. What action should you take?

Mark one answer

- ☐ **A.** Move out and overtake on the right
- ☐ **B.** Pass on the left as the vehicle moves out
- ☐ **C.** Be prepared to stop behind
- ☐ **D.** Overtake quickly before the lorry moves out

456 You keep well back while waiting to overtake a large vehicle. A car fills the gap. You should

Mark one answer

- ☐ **A.** sound your horn
- ☐ **B.** drop back further
- ☐ **C.** flash your headlights
- ☐ **D.** start to overtake

457 You are following a large vehicle approaching crossroads. The driver signals to turn left. What should you do?

Mark one answer

- ☐ **A.** Overtake if you can leave plenty of room
- ☐ **B.** Overtake only if there are no oncoming vehicles
- ☐ **C.** Do not overtake until the vehicle begins to turn
- ☐ **D.** Do not overtake when at or approaching a junction

458 **You are following a long lorry. The driver signals to turn left into a narrow road. What should you do?**

Mark one answer

- A. Overtake on the left before the lorry reaches the junction
- B. Overtake on the right as soon as the lorry slows down
- C. Do not overtake unless you can see there is no oncoming traffic
- D. Do not overtake, stay well back and be prepared to stop

459 **You wish to overtake a long, slow-moving vehicle on a busy road. You should**

Mark one answer

- A. follow it closely and keep moving out to see the road ahead
- B. flash your headlights for the oncoming traffic to give way
- C. stay behind until the driver waves you past
- D. keep well back until you can see that it is clear

460 **It is very windy. You are behind a motorcyclist who is overtaking a high-sided vehicle. What should you do?**

Mark one answer

- A. Overtake the motorcyclist immediately
- B. Keep well back
- C. Stay level with the motorcyclist
- D. Keep close to the motorcyclist

461 **It is very windy. You are about to overtake a motorcyclist. You should**

Mark one answer

- A. overtake slowly
- B. allow extra room
- C. sound your horn
- D. keep close as you pass

462 **You are towing a caravan. Which is the safest type of rear-view mirror to use?**

Mark one answer

- A. Interior wide-angle mirror
- B. Extended-arm side mirrors
- C. Ordinary door mirrors
- D. Ordinary interior mirror

463 **You are driving in town. Ahead of you a bus is at a bus stop. Which TWO of the following should you do?**

Mark two answers

- A. Be prepared to give way if the bus suddenly moves off
- B. Continue at the same speed but sound your horn as a warning
- C. Watch carefully for the sudden appearance of pedestrians
- D. Pass the bus as quickly as you possibly can

464 You are driving in heavy traffic on a wet road. Spray makes it difficult to be seen. You should use your

Mark two answers

- [ ] **A.** full beam headlights
- [ ] **B.** rear fog lights if visibility is less than 100 metres (328 feet)
- [ ] **C.** rear fog lights if visibility is more than 100 metres (328 feet)
- [ ] **D.** dipped headlights
- [ ] **E.** sidelights only

465 You are driving along this road. What should you be prepared to do?

Mark one answer

- [ ] **A.** Sound your horn and continue
- [ ] **B.** Slow down and give way
- [ ] **C.** Report the driver to the police
- [ ] **D.** Squeeze through the gap

466 As a driver why should you be more careful where trams operate?

Mark one answer

- [ ] **A.** Because they do not have a horn
- [ ] **B.** Because they do not stop for cars
- [ ] **C.** Because they do not have lights
- [ ] **D.** Because they cannot steer to avoid you

467 It is a very windy day and you are about to overtake a cyclist. What should you do?

Mark one answer

- [ ] **A.** Overtake very closely
- [ ] **B.** Keep close as you pass
- [ ] **C.** Sound your horn repeatedly
- [ ] **D.** Allow extra room

468 Powered vehicles, such as wheelchairs or scooters, used by disabled people have a maximum speed of

Mark one answer

- [ ] **A.** 8mph
- [ ] **B.** 12mph
- [ ] **C.** 16mph
- [ ] **D.** 20mph

469 In front of you is a powered vehicle (powered wheelchair) driven by a disabled person. These vehicles have a maximum speed of

Mark one answer

- [ ] **A.** 8mph
- [ ] **B.** 18mph
- [ ] **C.** 28mph
- [ ] **D.** 38mph

470 In which THREE of these situations may you overtake another vehicle on the left?

Mark three answers

- A. When you are in a one-way street
- B. When approaching a motorway slip road where you will be turning off
- C. When the vehicle in front is signalling to turn right
- D. When a slower vehicle is travelling in the right-hand lane of a dual carriageway
- E. In slow-moving traffic queues when traffic in the right-hand lane is moving more slowly

471 You are travelling in very heavy rain. Your overall stopping distance is likely to be

Mark one answer

- A. doubled
- B. halved
- C. up to ten times greater
- D. no different

472 Which TWO of the following are correct? When overtaking at night you should

Mark two answers

- A. wait until a bend so that you can see the oncoming headlights
- B. sound your horn twice before moving out
- C. be careful because you can see less
- D. beware of bends in the road ahead
- E. put headlights on full beam

473 When may you wait in a box junction?

Mark one answer

- A. When you are stationary in a queue of traffic
- B. When approaching a pelican crossing
- C. When approaching a zebra crossing
- D. When oncoming traffic prevents you turning right

474 Which of these plates normally appear with this road sign?

Mark one answer

- A. Humps for ½ mile
- B. Hump Bridge
- C. Low Bridge
- D. Soft Verge

475 Areas reserved for trams may have

Mark three answers

- A. metal studs around them
- B. white line markings
- C. zigzag markings
- D. a different coloured surface
- E. yellow hatch markings
- F. a different surface texture

476 Traffic calming measures are used to

Mark one answer

- A. stop road rage
- B. help overtaking
- C. slow traffic down
- D. help parking

477 Why should you always reduce your speed when travelling in fog?

Mark one answer

- A. The brakes do not work as well
- B. You will be dazzled by other headlights
- C. The engine will take longer to warm up
- D. It is more difficult to see events ahead

478 You are on a motorway in fog. The left-hand edge of the motorway can be identified by reflective studs. What colour are they?

Mark one answer

- A. Green
- B. Amber
- C. Red
- D. White

479 A rumble device is designed to

Mark two answers

- A. give directions
- B. prevent cattle escaping
- C. alert you to low tyre pressure
- D. alert you to a hazard
- E. encourage you to reduce speed

480 You are on a narrow road at night. A slower-moving vehicle ahead has been signalling right for some time. What should you do?

Mark one answer

- A. Overtake on the left
- B. Flash your headlights before overtaking
- C. Signal right and sound your horn
- D. Wait for the signal to be cancelled before overtaking

481 After this hazard you should test your brakes. Why is this?

Ford

Mark one answer

- A. You will be on a slippery road
- B. Your brakes will be soaking wet
- C. You will be going down a long hill
- D. You will have just crossed a long bridge

482 You have to make a journey in foggy conditions. You should

Mark one answer

- [ ] **A.** follow other vehicles' tail-lights closely
- [ ] **B.** avoid using dipped headlights
- [ ] **C.** leave plenty of time for your journey
- [ ] **D.** keep two seconds behind other vehicles

483 You see a vehicle coming towards you on a single-track road. You should

Mark one answer

- [ ] **A.** go back to the main road
- [ ] **B.** do an emergency stop
- [ ] **C.** stop at a passing place
- [ ] **D.** put on your hazard warning lights

484 You are overtaking a car at night. You must be sure that

Mark one answer

- [ ] **A.** you flash your headlights before overtaking
- [ ] **B.** you select a higher gear
- [ ] **C.** you have switched your lights to full beam before overtaking
- [ ] **D.** you do not dazzle other road users

485 You are on a road which has speed humps. A driver in front is travelling slower than you. You should

Mark one answer

- [ ] **A.** sound your horn
- [ ] **B.** overtake as soon as you can
- [ ] **C.** flash your headlights
- [ ] **D.** slow down and stay behind

486 You are following other vehicles in fog with your lights on. How else can you reduce the chances of being involved in an accident?

Mark one answer

- [ ] **A.** Keep close to the vehicle in front
- [ ] **B.** Use your main beam instead of dipped headlights
- [ ] **C.** Keep together with the faster vehicles
- [ ] **D.** Reduce your speed and increase the gap

487 You see these markings on the road. Why are they there?

Mark one answer

- [ ] **A.** To show a safe distance between vehicles
- [ ] **B.** To keep the area clear of traffic
- [ ] **C.** To make you aware of your speed
- [ ] **D.** To warn you to change direction

488 When MUST you use dipped headlights during the day?

Mark one answer

- [ ] **A.** All the time
- [ ] **B.** Along narrow streets
- [ ] **C.** In poor visibility
- [ ] **D.** When parking

89 **What are TWO main reasons why coasting downhill is wrong?**

k two answers

- **A.** Fuel consumption will be higher
- **B.** The vehicle will get faster
- **C.** It puts more wear and tear on the tyres
- **D.** You have less braking and steering control
- **E.** It damages the engine

90 **Hills can affect the performance of your vehicle. Which TWO apply when driving up steep hills?**

k two answers

- **A.** Higher gears will pull better
- **B.** You will slow down sooner
- **C.** Overtaking will be easier
- **D.** The engine will work harder
- **E.** The steering will feel heavier

91 **Why is travelling in neutral for long distances (known as coasting) wrong?**

k one answer

- **A.** It will cause the car to skid
- **B.** It will make the engine stall
- **C.** The engine will run faster
- **D.** There is no engine braking

92 **You are driving on the motorway in windy conditions. When passing high-sided vehicles you should**

k one answer

- **A.** increase your speed
- **B.** be wary of a sudden gust
- **C.** drive alongside very closely
- **D.** expect normal conditions

493 **To correct a rear-wheel skid you should**

Mark one answer

- ☐ **A.** not steer at all
- ☐ **B.** steer away from it
- ☐ **C.** steer into it
- ☐ **D.** apply your handbrake

494 **You have to make a journey in fog. What are the TWO most important things you should do before you set out?**

Mark two answers

- ☐ **A.** Top up the radiator with antifreeze
- ☐ **B.** Make sure that you have a warning triangle in the vehicle
- ☐ **C.** Check that your lights are working
- ☐ **D.** Check the battery
- ☐ **E.** Make sure that the windows are clean

495 **You are driving in fog. Why should you keep well back from the vehicle in front?**

Mark one answer

- ☐ **A.** In case it changes direction suddenly
- ☐ **B.** In case its fog lights dazzle you
- ☐ **C.** In case it stops suddenly
- ☐ **D.** In case its brake lights dazzle you

496 **You should switch your rear fog lights on when visibility drops below**

Mark one answer

- ☐ **A.** your overall stopping distance
- ☐ **B.** ten car lengths
- ☐ **C.** 200 metres (656 feet)
- ☐ **D.** 100 metres (328 feet)

497 Whilst driving, the fog clears and you can see more clearly. You must remember to

Mark one answer

- A. switch off the fog lights
- B. reduce your speed
- C. switch off the demister
- D. close any open windows

498 You have to park on the road in fog. You should

Mark one answer

- A. leave sidelights on
- B. leave dipped headlights and fog lights on
- C. leave dipped headlights on
- D. leave main beam headlights on

499 On a foggy day you unavoidably have to park your car on the road. You should

Mark one answer

- A. leave your headlights on
- B. leave your fog lights on
- C. leave your sidelights on
- D. leave your hazard lights on

500 You are travelling at night. You are dazzled by headlights coming towards you. You should

Mark one answer

- A. pull down your sun visor
- B. slow down or stop
- C. switch on your main beam headlights
- D. put your hand over your eyes

501 Which FOUR of the following may apply when dealing with this hazard?

Ford

Mark four answers

- A. It could be more difficult in winter
- B. Use a low gear and drive slowly
- C. Use a high gear to prevent wheelspin
- D. Test your brakes afterwards
- E. Always switch on fog lamps
- F. There may be a depth gauge

502 Front fog lights may be used ONLY if

Mark one answer

- A. visibility is seriously reduced
- B. they are fitted above the bumper
- C. they are not as bright as the headlights
- D. an audible warning device is used

503 Front fog lights may be used ONLY if

Mark one answer

- A. your headlights are not working
- B. they are operated with rear fog lights
- C. they were fitted by the vehicle manufacturer
- D. visibility is seriously reduced

504 You are driving with your front fog lights switched on. Earlier fog has now cleared. What should you do?

Mark one answer

- [ ] **A.** Leave them on if other drivers have their lights on
- [ ] **B.** Switch them off as long as visibility remains good
- [ ] **C.** Flash them to warn oncoming traffic that it is foggy
- [ ] **D.** Drive with them on instead of your headlights

505 Front fog lights should be used ONLY when

Mark one answer

- [ ] **A.** travelling in very light rain
- [ ] **B.** visibility is seriously reduced
- [ ] **C.** daylight is fading
- [ ] **D.** driving after midnight

506 Why is it dangerous to leave rear fog lights on when they are not needed?

Mark two answers

- [ ] **A.** Brake lights are less clear
- [ ] **B.** Following drivers can be dazzled
- [ ] **C.** Electrical systems could be overloaded
- [ ] **D.** Direction indicators may not work properly
- [ ] **E.** The battery could fail

507 You are driving on a clear dry night with your rear fog lights switched on. This may

Mark two answers

- [ ] **A.** reduce glare from the road surface
- [ ] **B.** make other drivers think you are braking
- [ ] **C.** give a better view of the road ahead
- [ ] **D.** dazzle following drivers
- [ ] **E.** help your indicators to be seen more clearly

508 You have just driven out of fog. Visibility is now good. You MUST

Mark one answer

- [ ] **A.** switch off all your fog lights
- [ ] **B.** keep your rear fog lights on
- [ ] **C.** keep your front fog lights on
- [ ] **D.** leave fog lights on in case fog returns

509 You forget to switch off your rear fog lights when the fog has cleared. This may

Mark three answers

- [ ] **A.** dazzle other road users
- [ ] **B.** reduce battery life
- [ ] **C.** cause brake lights to be less clear
- [ ] **D.** be breaking the law
- [ ] **E.** seriously affect engine power

510 You have been driving in thick fog which has now cleared. You must switch OFF your rear fog lights because

Mark one answer

- [ ] **A.** they use a lot of power from the battery
- [ ] **B.** they make your brake lights less clear
- [ ] **C.** they will cause dazzle in your rear-view mirrors
- [ ] **D.** they may not be properly adjusted

511 Front fog lights should be used

Mark one answer

- [ ] **A.** when visibility is reduced to 100 metres (328 feet)
- [ ] **B.** as a warning to oncoming traffic
- [ ] **C.** when driving during the hours of darkness
- [ ] **D.** in any conditions and at any time

512 Using rear fog lights in clear daylight will

Mark one answer

- [ ] **A.** be useful when towing a trailer
- [ ] **B.** give extra protection
- [ ] **C.** dazzle other drivers
- [ ] **D.** make following drivers keep back

513 Using front fog lights in clear daylight will

Mark one answer

- [ ] **A.** flatten the battery
- [ ] **B.** dazzle other drivers
- [ ] **C.** improve your visibility
- [ ] **D.** increase your awareness

514 You may use front fog lights with headlights ONLY when visibility is reduced to less than

Mark one answer

- [ ] **A.** 100 metres (328 feet)
- [ ] **B.** 200 metres (656 feet)
- [ ] **C.** 300 metres (984 feet)
- [ ] **D.** 400 metres (1,312 feet)

515 You may drive with front fog lights switched on

Mark one answer

- [ ] **A.** when visibility is less than 100 metres (328 feet)
- [ ] **B.** at any time to be noticed
- [ ] **C.** instead of headlights on high-speed roads
- [ ] **D.** when dazzled by the lights of oncoming vehicles

516 Chains can be fitted to your wheels to help prevent

Mark one answer

- [ ] **A.** damage to the road surface
- [ ] **B.** wear to the tyres
- [ ] **C.** skidding in deep snow
- [ ] **D.** the brakes locking

517 Holding the clutch pedal down or rolling in neutral for too long while driving will

Mark one answer

- [ ] **A.** use more fuel
- [ ] **B.** cause the engine to overheat
- [ ] **C.** reduce your control
- [ ] **D.** improve tyre wear

518 How can you use the engine of your vehicle to control your speed?

Mark one answer

- [ ] **A.** By changing to a lower gear
- [ ] **B.** By selecting reverse gear
- [ ] **C.** By changing to a higher gear
- [ ] **D.** By selecting neutral

519 You are driving down a steep hill. Why could keeping the clutch down or rolling in neutral for too long be dangerous?

Mark one answer

- [ ] **A.** Fuel consumption will be higher
- [ ] **B.** Your vehicle will pick up speed
- [ ] **C.** It will damage the engine
- [ ] **D.** It will wear tyres out more quickly

520 Why could keeping the clutch down or selecting neutral for long periods of time be dangerous?

Mark one answer

- [ ] **A.** Fuel spillage will occur
- [ ] **B.** Engine damage may be caused
- [ ] **C.** You will have less steering and braking control
- [ ] **D.** It will wear tyres out more quickly

521 You are driving on an icy road. What distance should you drive from the car in front?

Mark one answer

- [ ] **A.** four times the normal distance
- [ ] **B.** six times the normal distance
- [ ] **C.** eight times the normal distance
- [ ] **D.** ten times the normal distance

522 You are on a well-lit motorway at night. You must

Mark one answer

- [ ] **A.** use only your sidelights
- [ ] **B.** always use your headlights
- [ ] **C.** always use rear fog lights
- [ ] **D.** use headlights only in bad weather

523 You are on a motorway at night with other vehicles just ahead of you. Which lights should you have on?

Mark one answer

- [ ] **A.** Front fog lights
- [ ] **B.** Main beam headlights
- [ ] **C.** Sidelights only
- [ ] **D.** Dipped headlights

524 Which THREE of the following will affect your stopping distance?

Mark three answers

- [ ] **A.** How fast you are going
- [ ] **B.** The tyres on your vehicle
- [ ] **C.** The time of day
- [ ] **D.** The weather
- [ ] **E.** The street lighting

525 You are on a motorway at night. You MUST have your headlights switched on unless

Mark one answer

- [ ] **A.** there are vehicles close in front of you
- [ ] **B.** you are travelling below 50mph
- [ ] **C.** the motorway is lit
- [ ] **D.** your vehicle is broken down on the hard shoulder

526 You will feel the effects of engine braking when you

Mark one answer

- A. only use the handbrake
- B. only use neutral
- C. change to a lower gear
- D. change to a higher gear

527 Daytime visibility is poor but not seriously reduced. You should switch on

Mark one answer

- A. headlights and fog lights
- B. front fog lights
- C. dipped headlights
- D. rear fog lights

528 Why are vehicles fitted with rear fog lights?

Mark one answer

- A. To be seen when driving at high speed
- B. To use if broken down in a dangerous position
- C. To make them more visible in thick fog
- D. To warn drivers following closely to drop back

529 While you are driving in fog, it becomes necessary to use front fog lights. You should

Mark one answer

- A. only turn them on in heavy traffic conditions
- B. remember not to use them on motorways
- C. only use them on dual carriageways
- D. remember to switch them off as visibility improves

530 When snow is falling heavily you should

Mark one answer

- A. only drive with your hazard lights on
- B. not drive unless you have a mobile phone
- C. only drive when your journey is short
- D. not drive unless it is essential

531 You are driving down a long steep hill. You suddenly notice your brakes are not working as well as normal. What is the usual cause of this?

Mark one answer

- A. The brakes overheating
- B. Air in the brake fluid
- C. Oil on the brakes
- D. Badly adjusted brakes

532 The road is wet. Why might a motorcyclist steer round drain covers on a bend?

Mark one answer

- A. To avoid puncturing the tyres on the edge of the drain covers
- B. To prevent the motorcycle sliding on the metal drain covers
- C. To help judge the bend using the drain covers as marker points
- D. To avoid splashing pedestrians on the pavement

533 **Which FOUR of these must NOT use motorways?**

Mark four answers

- **A.** Learner car drivers
- **B.** Motorcycles over 50cc
- **C.** Double-deck buses
- **D.** Farm tractors
- **E.** Horse riders
- **F.** Cyclists

534 **Which FOUR of these must NOT use motorways?**

Mark four answers

- **A.** Learner car drivers
- **B.** Motorcycles over 50cc
- **C.** Double-deck buses
- **D.** Farm tractors
- **E.** Learner motorcyclists
- **F.** Cyclists

535 **Immediately after joining a motorway you should normally**

Mark one answer

- **A.** try to overtake
- **B.** re-adjust your mirrors
- **C.** position your vehicle in the centre lane
- **D.** keep in the left-hand lane

536 **When joining a motorway you must always**

Mark one answer

- **A.** use the hard shoulder
- **B.** stop at the end of the acceleration lane
- **C.** come to a stop before joining the motorway
- **D.** give way to traffic already on the motorway

537 **What is the national speed limit for cars and motorcycles in the centre lane of a three-lane motorway?**

Mark one answer

- **A.** 40mph
- **B.** 50mph
- **C.** 60mph
- **D.** 70mph

538 **What is the national speed limit on motorways for cars and motorcycles?**

Mark one answer

- **A.** 30mph
- **B.** 50mph
- **C.** 60mph
- **D.** 70mph

539 **The left-hand lane on a three-lane motorway is for use by**

Mark one answer

- **A.** any vehicle
- **B.** large vehicles only
- **C.** emergency vehicles only
- **D.** slow vehicles only

540 **What is the right-hand lane used for on a three-lane motorway?**

Mark one answer

- **A.** Emergency vehicles only
- **B.** Overtaking
- **C.** Vehicles towing trailers
- **D.** Coaches only

541 Which of these IS NOT allowed to travel in the right-hand lane of a three-lane motorway?

Mark one answer

- [ ] **A.** A small delivery van
- [ ] **B.** A motorcycle
- [ ] **C.** A vehicle towing a trailer
- [ ] **D.** A motorcycle and sidecar

542 You are travelling on a motorway. You decide you need a rest. You should

Mark two answers

- [ ] **A.** stop on the hard shoulder
- [ ] **B.** go to a service area
- [ ] **C.** park on the slip road
- [ ] **D.** park on the central reservation
- [ ] **E.** leave at the next exit

543 You break down on a motorway. You need to call for help. Why may it be better to use an emergency roadside telephone rather than a mobile phone?

Mark one answer

- [ ] **A.** It connects you to a local garage
- [ ] **B.** Using a mobile phone will distract other drivers
- [ ] **C.** It allows easy location by the emergency services
- [ ] **D.** Mobile phones do not work on motorways

544 What should you use the hard shoulder of a motorway for?

Mark one answer

- [ ] **A.** Stopping in an emergency
- [ ] **B.** Leaving the motorway
- [ ] **C.** Stopping when you are tired
- [ ] **D.** Joining the motorway

545 After a breakdown you need to rejoin the main carriageway of a motorway from the hard shoulder. You should

Mark one answer

- [ ] **A.** move out onto the carriageway then build up your speed
- [ ] **B.** move out onto the carriageway using your hazard lights
- [ ] **C.** gain speed on the hard shoulder before moving out onto the carriageway
- [ ] **D.** wait on the hard shoulder until someone flashes their headlights at you

546 A crawler lane on a motorway is found

Mark one answer

- [ ] **A.** on a steep gradient
- [ ] **B.** before a service area
- [ ] **C.** before a junction
- [ ] **D.** along the hard shoulder

Crawler lane

547 You are on a motorway. There are red flashing lights above every lane. You must

Mark one answer

- A. pull on to the hard shoulder
- B. slow down and watch for further signals
- C. leave at the next exit
- D. stop and wait

548 You are in the right-hand lane on a motorway. You see these overhead signs. This means

Mark one answer

- A. move to the left and reduce your speed to 50mph
- B. there are road works 50 metres (55 yards) ahead
- C. use the hard shoulder until you have passed the hazard
- D. leave the motorway at the next exit

549 What do these motorway signs show?

Mark one answer

- A. They are countdown markers to a bridge
- B. They are distance markers to the next telephone
- C. They are countdown markers to the next exit
- D. They warn of a police control ahead

550 On a motorway the amber reflective studs can be found between

Mark one answer

- A. the hard shoulder and the carriageway
- B. the acceleration lane and the carriageway
- C. the central reservation and the carriageway
- D. each pair of the lanes

551 What colour are the reflective studs between the lanes on a motorway?

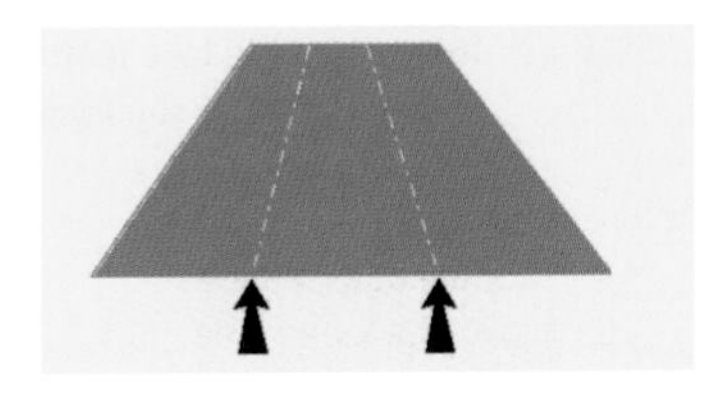

Mark one answer

- A. Green
- B. Amber
- C. White
- D. Red

552 What colour are the reflective studs between a motorway and its slip road?

Mark one answer

- A. Amber
- B. White
- C. Green
- D. Red

553 You are allowed to stop on a motorway when you

Mark one answer

- A. need to walk and get fresh air
- B. wish to pick up hitchhikers
- C. are told to do so by flashing red lights
- D. need to use a mobile telephone

554 **You have broken down on a motorway. To find the nearest emergency telephone you should always walk**

Mark one answer

- [ ] **A.** with the traffic flow
- [ ] **B.** facing oncoming traffic
- [ ] **C.** in the direction shown on the marker posts
- [ ] **D.** in the direction of the nearest exit

555 **You are travelling along the left-hand lane of a three-lane motorway. Traffic is joining from a slip road. You should**

Mark one answer

- [ ] **A.** race the other vehicles
- [ ] **B.** move to another lane
- [ ] **C.** maintain a steady speed
- [ ] **D.** switch on your hazard flashers

556 **You are joining a motorway. Why is it important to make full use of the slip road?**

Mark one answer

- [ ] **A.** Because there is space available to turn round if you need to
- [ ] **B.** To allow you direct access to the overtaking lanes
- [ ] **C.** To build up a speed similar to traffic on the motorway
- [ ] **D.** Because you can continue on the hard shoulder

557 **How should you use the emergency telephone on a motorway?**

Mark one answer

- [ ] **A.** Stay close to the carriageway
- [ ] **B.** Face the oncoming traffic
- [ ] **C.** Keep your back to the traffic
- [ ] **D.** Stand on the hard shoulder

558 **You are on a motorway. What colour are the reflective studs on the left of the carriageway?**

Mark one answer

- [ ] **A.** Green
- [ ] **B.** Red
- [ ] **C.** White
- [ ] **D.** Amber

559 **On a three-lane motorway which lane should you normally use?**

Mark one answer

- [ ] **A.** Left
- [ ] **B.** Right
- [ ] **C.** Centre
- [ ] **D.** Either the right or centre

560 **A basic rule when on motorways is**

Mark one answer

- [ ] **A.** use the lane that has least traffic
- [ ] **B.** keep to the left-hand lane unless overtaking
- [ ] **C.** overtake on the side that is clearest
- [ ] **D.** try to keep above 50mph to prevent congestion

561 When going through a contraflow system on a motorway you should

Mark one answer

- [ ] **A.** ensure that you do not exceed 30mph
- [ ] **B.** keep a good distance from the vehicle ahead
- [ ] **C.** switch lanes to keep the traffic flowing
- [ ] **D.** stay close to the vehicle ahead to reduce queues

562 You are on a three-lane motorway. There are red reflective studs on your left and white ones to your right. Where are you?

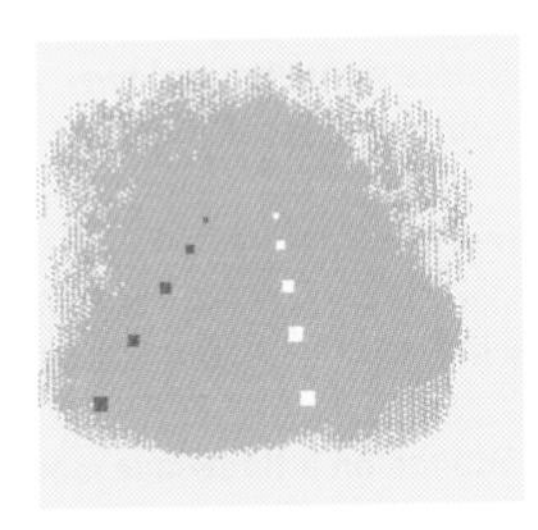

Mark one answer

- [ ] **A.** In the right-hand lane
- [ ] **B.** In the middle lane
- [ ] **C.** On the hard shoulder
- [ ] **D.** In the left-hand lane

563 When should you stop on a motorway?

Mark three answers

- [ ] **A.** If you have to read a map
- [ ] **B.** When you are tired and need a rest
- [ ] **C.** If red lights show above every lane
- [ ] **D.** When told to by the police
- [ ] **E.** If your mobile phone rings
- [ ] **F.** When signalled by a Highways Agency Traffic Officer

564 You are approaching road works on a motorway. What should you do?

Mark one answer

- [ ] **A.** Speed up to clear the area quickly
- [ ] **B.** Always use the hard shoulder
- [ ] **C.** Obey all speed limits
- [ ] **D.** Stay very close to the vehicle in front

565 On motorways you should never overtake on the left unless

Mark one answer

- [ ] **A.** you can see well ahead that the hard shoulder is clear
- [ ] **B.** the traffic in the right-hand lane is signalling right
- [ ] **C.** you warn drivers behind by signalling left
- [ ] **D.** there is a queue of slow-moving traffic to your right that is moving more slowly than you are

566 You are towing a trailer on a motorway. What is your maximum speed limit?

Mark one answer

- [ ] **A.** 40mph
- [ ] **B.** 50mph
- [ ] **C.** 60mph
- [ ] **D.** 70mph

567 The left-hand lane of a motorway should be used for

Mark one answer

- [ ] **A.** breakdowns and emergencies only
- [ ] **B.** overtaking slower traffic in the other lanes
- [ ] **C.** slow vehicles only
- [ ] **D.** normal driving

568 You are driving on a motorway. You have to slow down quickly due to a hazard. You should

Mark one answer

- [ ] **A.** switch on your hazard lights
- [ ] **B.** switch on your headlights
- [ ] **C.** sound your horn
- [ ] **D.** flash your headlights

569 You get a puncture on the motorway. You manage to get your vehicle on to the hard shoulder. You should

Mark one answer

- [ ] **A.** change the wheel yourself immediately
- [ ] **B.** use the emergency telephone and call for assistance
- [ ] **C.** try to wave down another vehicle for help
- [ ] **D.** only change the wheel if you have a passenger to help you

570 You are driving on a motorway. By mistake, you go past the exit that you wanted to take. You should

Mark one answer

- [ ] **A.** carefully reverse on the hard shoulder
- [ ] **B.** carry on to the next exit
- [ ] **C.** carefully reverse in the left-hand lane
- [ ] **D.** make a U-turn at the next gap in the central reservation

571 Your vehicle breaks down on the hard shoulder of a motorway. You decide to use your mobile phone to call for help. You should

Mark one answer

- [ ] **A.** stand at the rear of the vehicle while making the call
- [ ] **B.** try to repair the vehicle yourself
- [ ] **C.** get out of the vehicle by the right-hand door
- [ ] **D.** check your location from the marker posts on the left

572 You are travelling on a motorway. Unless signs show a lower speed limit you must NOT exceed

Mark one answer **NI**

- [ ] **A.** 50mph
- [ ] **B.** 60mph
- [ ] **C.** 70mph
- [ ] **D.** 80mph

573 You are on a three-lane motorway towing a trailer. You may use the right-hand lane when

Mark one answer **NI**

- [ ] **A.** there are lane closures
- [ ] **B.** there is slow-moving traffic
- [ ] **C.** you can maintain a high speed
- [ ] **D.** large vehicles are in the left and centre lanes

574 You are on a motorway. There is a contraflow system ahead. What would you expect to find?

Mark one answer

- [ ] **A.** Temporary traffic lights
- [ ] **B.** Lower speed limits
- [ ] **C.** Wider lanes than normal
- [ ] **D.** Speed humps

575 You are driving at 70mph on a three-lane motorway. There is no traffic ahead. Which lane should you use?

Mark one answer

- [ ] **A.** Any lane
- [ ] **B.** Middle lane
- [ ] **C.** Right lane
- [ ] **D.** Left lane

576 Your vehicle has broken down on a motorway. You are not able to stop on the hard shoulder. What should you do?

Mark one answer

- [ ] **A.** Switch on your hazard warning lights
- [ ] **B.** Stop following traffic and ask for help
- [ ] **C.** Attempt to repair your vehicle quickly
- [ ] **D.** Stand behind your vehicle to warn others

577 Why is it particularly important to carry out a check on your vehicle before making a long motorway journey?

Mark one answer

- [ ] **A.** You will have to do more harsh braking on motorways
- [ ] **B.** Motorway service stations do not deal with breakdowns
- [ ] **C.** The road surface will wear down the tyres faster
- [ ] **D.** Continuous high speeds may increase the risk of your vehicle breaking down

578 For what reason may you use the right-hand lane of a motorway?

Mark one answer

- [ ] **A.** For keeping out of the way of lorries
- [ ] **B.** For travelling at more than 70mph
- [ ] **C.** For turning right
- [ ] **D.** For overtaking other vehicles

579 On a motorway you may ONLY stop on the hard shoulder

Mark one answer

- [ ] **A.** in an emergency
- [ ] **B.** if you feel tired and need to rest
- [ ] **C.** if you accidentally go past the exit that you wanted to take
- [ ] **D.** to pick up a hitchhiker

580 You are driving on a motorway. The car ahead shows its hazard lights for a short time. This tells you that

Mark one answer

- A. the driver wants you to overtake
- B. the other car is going to change lanes
- C. traffic ahead is slowing or stopping suddenly
- D. there is a police speed check ahead

581 Motorway emergency telephones are usually linked to the police. In some areas they are now linked to

Mark one answer

- A. the local ambulance service
- B. an Highways Agency control centre
- C. the local fire brigade
- D. a breakdown service control centre

582 You are intending to leave the motorway at the next exit. Before you reach the exit you should normally position your vehicle

Mark one answer

- A. in the middle lane
- B. in the left-hand lane
- C. on the hard shoulder
- D. in any lane

583 As a provisional licence holder you should not drive a car

Mark one answer

- A. over 30mph
- B. at night
- C. on the motorway
- D. with passengers in rear seats

584 Motorway emergency telephones are usually linked to the police. In some areas they are now linked to

Mark one answer NI

- A. the Highways Agency Control Centre
- B. the Driver Vehicle Licensing Agency
- C. the Driving Standards Agency
- D. the local Vehicle Registration Office

585 An Emergency Refuge Area is an area

Mark one answer

- A. on a motorway for use in cases of emergency or breakdown
- B. for use if you think you will be involved in a road rage incident
- C. on a motorway for a police patrol to park and watch traffic
- D. for construction and road workers to store emergency equipment

586 What is an Emergency Refuge Area on a motorway for?

Mark one answer

- A. An area to park in when you want to use a mobile phone
- B. To use in cases of emergency or breakdown
- C. For an emergency recovery vehicle to park in a contraflow system
- D. To drive in when there is queuing traffic ahead

587 Highways Agency Traffic Officers

Mark one answer NI

- A. will not be able to assist at a breakdown or emergency
- B. are not able to stop and direct anyone on a motorway
- C. will tow a broken down vehicle and its passengers home
- D. are able to stop and direct anyone on a motorway

588 **You are on a motorway. A red cross is displayed above the hard shoulder. What does this mean?**

Mark one answer NI

- [ ] **A.** Pull up in this lane to answer your mobile phone
- [ ] **B.** Use this lane as a running lane
- [ ] **C.** This lane can be used if you need a rest
- [ ] **D.** You should not travel in this lane

589 **You are on a motorway in an Active Traffic Management (ATM) area. A mandatory speed limit is displayed above the hard shoulder. What does this mean?**

Mark one answer NI

- [ ] **A.** You should not travel in this lane
- [ ] **B.** The hard shoulder can be used as a running lane
- [ ] **C.** You can park on the hard shoulder if you feel tired
- [ ] **D.** You can pull up in this lane to answer a mobile phone

590 **The aim of an Active Traffic Management scheme on a motorway is to**

Mark one answer NI

- [ ] **A.** prevent overtaking
- [ ] **B.** reduce rest stops
- [ ] **C.** prevent tailgating
- [ ] **D.** reduce congestion

591 **You are in an Active Traffic Management area on a motorway. When the Actively Managed mode is operating**

Mark one answer NI

- [ ] **A.** speed limits are only advisory
- [ ] **B.** the national speed limit will apply
- [ ] **C.** the speed limit is always 30mph
- [ ] **D.** all speed limit signals are set

592 **You are on a three-lane motorway. A red cross is shown above the hard shoulder and mandatory speed limits above all other lanes. This means**

Mark one answer NI

- [ ] **A.** the hard shoulder can be used as a rest area if you feel tired
- [ ] **B.** the hard shoulder is for emergency or breakdown use only
- [ ] **C.** the hard shoulder can be used as a normal running lane
- [ ] **D.** the hard shoulder has a speed limit of 50mph

593 **You are travelling on a motorway. A red cross is shown above the hard shoulder. What does this mean?**

Mark one answer NI

- A. Use this lane as a rest area
- B. Use this as a normal running lane
- C. Do not use this lane to travel in
- D. National speed limit applies in this lane

594 **You are on a three-lane motorway and see this sign. It means you can use**

Mark one answer NI

- A. any lane except the hard shoulder
- B. the hard shoulder only
- C. the three right hand lanes only
- D. all the lanes including the hard shoulder

595 **Why can it be an advantage for traffic speed to stay constant over a longer distance?**

Mark one answer

- A. You will do more stop-start driving
- B. You will use far more fuel
- C. You will be able to use more direct routes
- D. Your overall journey time will normally improve

596 **You should not normally travel on the hard shoulder of a motorway. When can you use it?**

Mark one answer NI

- A. When taking the next exit
- B. When traffic is stopped
- C. When signs direct you to
- D. When traffic is slow moving

597 **On a motorway what is used to reduce traffic bunching?**

Mark one answer

- A. Variable speed limits
- B. Contraflow systems
- C. National speed limits
- D. Lane closures

598 **When may you stop on a motorway?**

Mark one answer

- A. If you have to read a map
- B. When you are tired and need a rest
- C. If your mobile phone rings
- D. In an emergency or breakdown

599 What is the meaning of this sign?

Mark one answer

- A. Local speed limit applies
- B. No waiting on the carriageway
- C. National speed limit applies
- D. No entry to vehicular traffic

600 What is the national speed limit on a single carriageway road for cars and motorcycles?

Mark one answer

- A. 30mph
- B. 50mph
- C. 60mph
- D. 70mph

601 What is the national speed limit for cars and motorcycles on a dual carriageway?

Mark one answer

- A. 30mph
- B. 50mph
- C. 60mph
- D. 70mph

602 There are no speed limit signs on the road. How is a 30mph limit indicated?

Mark one answer

- A. By hazard warning lines
- B. By street lighting
- C. By pedestrian islands
- D. By double or single yellow lines

603 Where you see street lights but no speed limit signs the limit is usually

Mark one answer

- A. 30mph
- B. 40mph
- C. 50mph
- D. 60mph

604 What does this sign mean?

Mark one answer

- A. Minimum speed 30mph
- B. End of maximum speed
- C. End of minimum speed
- D. Maximum speed 30mph

605 There is a tractor ahead of you. You wish to overtake but you are NOT sure if it is safe to do so. You should

Mark one answer

- A. follow another overtaking vehicle through
- B. sound your horn to the slow vehicle to pull over
- C. speed through but flash your lights to oncoming traffic
- D. not overtake if you are in doubt

606 Which three of the following are most likely to take an unusual course at roundabouts?

Mark three answers

- A. Horse riders
- B. Milk floats
- C. Delivery vans
- D. Long vehicles
- E. Estate cars
- F. Cyclists

607 In which TWO places should you NOT park?

Mark two answers

- A. Near a school entrance
- B. Near a police station
- C. In a side road
- D. At a bus stop
- E. In a one-way street

608 On a clearway you must not stop

Mark one answer

- A. at any time
- B. when it is busy
- C. in the rush hour
- D. during daylight hours

609 What is the meaning of this sign?

Mark one answer

- A. No entry
- B. Waiting restrictions
- C. National speed limit
- D. School crossing patrol

610 You can park on the right-hand side of a road at night

Mark one answer

- A. in a one-way street
- B. with your sidelights on
- C. more than 10 metres (32 feet) from a junction
- D. under a lamppost

611 On a three-lane dual carriageway the right-hand lane can be used for

Mark one answer

- A. overtaking only, never turning right
- B. overtaking or turning right
- C. fast-moving traffic only
- D. turning right only, never overtaking

612 You are approaching a busy junction. There are several lanes with road markings. At the last moment you realise that you are in the wrong lane. You should

Mark one answer

- [ ] **A.** continue in that lane
- [ ] **B.** force your way across
- [ ] **C.** stop until the area has cleared
- [ ] **D.** use clear arm signals to cut across

613 Where may you overtake on a one-way street?

Mark one answer

- [ ] **A.** Only on the left-hand side
- [ ] **B.** Overtaking is not allowed
- [ ] **C.** Only on the right-hand side
- [ ] **D.** Either on the right or the left

614 When going straight ahead at a roundabout you should

Mark one answer

- [ ] **A.** indicate left before leaving the roundabout
- [ ] **B.** not indicate at any time
- [ ] **C.** indicate right when approaching the roundabout
- [ ] **D.** indicate left when approaching the roundabout

615 Which vehicle might have to use a different course to normal at roundabouts?

Mark one answer

- [ ] **A.** Sports car
- [ ] **B.** Van
- [ ] **C.** Estate car
- [ ] **D.** Long vehicle

616 You are going straight ahead at a roundabout. How should you signal?

Mark one answer

- [ ] **A.** Signal right on the approach and then left to leave the roundabout
- [ ] **B.** Signal left as you leave the roundabout
- [ ] **C.** Signal left on the approach to the roundabout and keep the signal on until you leave
- [ ] **D.** Signal left just after you pass the exit before the one you will take

617 You may only enter a box junction when

Mark one answer

- [ ] **A.** there are less than two vehicles in front of you
- [ ] **B.** the traffic lights show green
- [ ] **C.** your exit road is clear
- [ ] **D.** you need to turn left

618 You may wait in a yellow box junction when

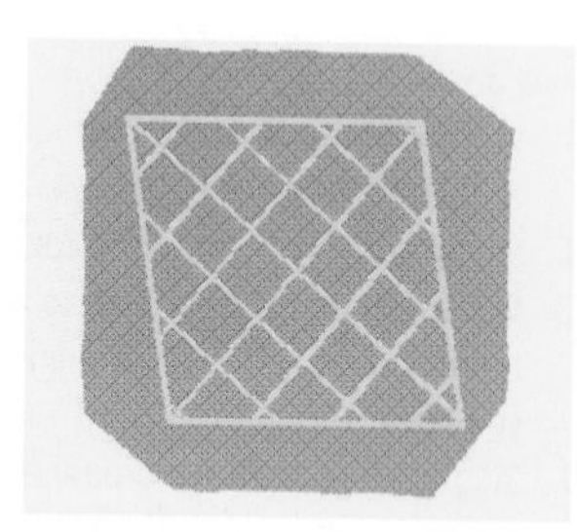

Mark one answer

- A. oncoming traffic is preventing you from turning right
- B. you are in a queue of traffic turning left
- C. you are in a queue of traffic to go ahead
- D. you are on a roundabout

619 You MUST stop when signalled to do so by which THREE of these?

Mark three answers

- A. A police officer
- B. A pedestrian
- C. A school crossing patrol
- D. A bus driver
- E. A red traffic light

620 You will see these red and white markers when approaching

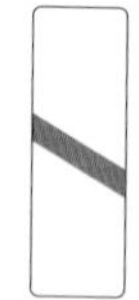

Mark one answer

- A. the end of a motorway
- B. a concealed level crossing
- C. a concealed speed limit sign
- D. the end of a dual carriageway

621 Someone is waiting to cross at a zebra crossing. They are standing on the pavement. You should normally

Mark one answer

- A. go on quickly before they step on to the crossing
- B. stop before you reach the zigzag lines and let them cross
- C. stop, let them cross, wait patiently
- D. ignore them as they are still on the pavement

622 At toucan crossings, apart from pedestrians you should be aware of

Mark one answer

- A. emergency vehicles emerging
- B. buses pulling out
- C. trams crossing in front
- D. cyclists riding across

623 Who can use a toucan crossing?

Mark two answers

- [ ] A. Trains
- [ ] B. Cyclists
- [ ] C. Buses
- [ ] D. Pedestrians
- [ ] E. Trams

624 At a pelican crossing, what does a flashing amber light mean?

Mark one answer

- [ ] A. You must not move off until the lights stop flashing
- [ ] B. You must give way to pedestrians still on the crossing
- [ ] C. You can move off, even if pedestrians are still on the crossing
- [ ] D. You must stop because the lights are about to change to red

625 You are waiting at a pelican crossing. The red light changes to flashing amber. This means you must

Mark one answer

- [ ] A. wait for pedestrians on the crossing to clear
- [ ] B. move off immediately without any hesitation
- [ ] C. wait for the green light before moving off
- [ ] D. get ready and go when the continuous amber light shows

626 You are travelling on a well-lit road at night in a built-up area. By using dipped headlights you will be able to

Mark one answer

- [ ] A. see further along the road
- [ ] B. go at a much faster speed
- [ ] C. switch to main beam quickly
- [ ] D. be easily seen by others

627 When can you park on the left opposite these road markings?

Mark one answer

- [ ] A. If the line nearest to you is broken
- [ ] B. When there are no yellow lines
- [ ] C. To pick up or set down passengers
- [ ] D. During daylight hours only

628 You are intending to turn right at a crossroads. An oncoming driver is also turning right. It will normally be safer to

Mark one answer

- [ ] A. keep the other vehicle to your RIGHT and turn behind it (offside to offside)
- [ ] B. keep the other vehicle to your LEFT and turn in front of it (nearside to nearside)
- [ ] C. carry on and turn at the next junction instead
- [ ] D. hold back and wait for the other driver to turn first

629 You are on a road that has no traffic signs. There are street lights. What is the speed limit?

Mark one answer

- [ ] A. 20mph
- [ ] B. 30mph
- [ ] C. 40mph
- [ ] D. 60mph

630 **You are going along a street with parked vehicles on the left-hand side. For which THREE reasons should you keep your speed down?**

Mark three answers
- [ ] **A.** So that oncoming traffic can see you more clearly
- [ ] **B.** You may set off car alarms
- [ ] **C.** Vehicles may be pulling out
- [ ] **D.** Drivers' doors may open
- [ ] **E.** Children may run out from between the vehicles

631 **You meet an obstruction on your side of the road. You should**

Mark one answer
- [ ] **A.** carry on, you have priority
- [ ] **B.** give way to oncoming traffic
- [ ] **C.** wave oncoming vehicles through
- [ ] **D.** accelerate to get past first

632 **You are on a two-lane dual carriageway. For which TWO of the following would you use the right-hand lane?**

Mark two answers
- [ ] **A.** Turning right
- [ ] **B.** Normal progress
- [ ] **C.** Staying at the minimum allowed speed
- [ ] **D.** Constant high speed
- [ ] **E.** Overtaking slower traffic
- [ ] **F.** Mending punctures

633 **Who has priority at an unmarked crossroads?**

Mark one answer
- [ ] **A.** The larger vehicle
- [ ] **B.** No one has priority
- [ ] **C.** The faster vehicle
- [ ] **D.** The smaller vehicle

634 **What is the nearest you may park to a junction?**

Mark one answer **NI**
- [ ] **A.** 10 metres (32 feet)
- [ ] **B.** 12 metres (39 feet)
- [ ] **C.** 15 metres (49 feet)
- [ ] **D.** 20 metres (66 feet)

635 **In which THREE places must you NOT park?**

Mark three answers **NI**
- [ ] **A.** Near the brow of a hill
- [ ] **B.** At or near a bus stop
- [ ] **C.** Where there is no pavement
- [ ] **D.** Within 10 metres (32 feet) of a junction
- [ ] **E.** On a 40mph road

636 **You are waiting at a level crossing. A train has passed but the lights keep flashing. You must**

Mark one answer
- [ ] **A.** carry on waiting
- [ ] **B.** phone the signal operator
- [ ] **C.** edge over the stop line and look for trains
- [ ] **D.** park and investigate

637 You park at night on a road with a 40mph speed limit. You should park

Mark one answer

- [ ] **A.** facing the traffic
- [ ] **B.** with parking lights on
- [ ] **C.** with dipped headlights on
- [ ] **D.** near a street light

638 The dual carriageway you are turning right on to has a very narrow central reservation. What should you do?

Mark one answer

- [ ] **A.** Proceed to the central reservation and wait
- [ ] **B.** Wait until the road is clear in both directions
- [ ] **C.** Stop in the first lane so that other vehicles give way
- [ ] **D.** Emerge slightly to show your intentions

639 At a crossroads there are no signs or road markings. Two vehicles approach. Which has priority?

Mark one answer

- [ ] **A.** Neither of the vehicles
- [ ] **B.** The vehicle travelling the fastest
- [ ] **C.** Oncoming vehicles turning right
- [ ] **D.** Vehicles approaching from the right

640 What does this sign tell you?

Mark one answer

- [ ] **A.** That it is a no-through road
- [ ] **B.** End of traffic calming zone
- [ ] **C.** Free parking zone ends
- [ ] **D.** No waiting zone ends

641 You are entering an area of road works. There is a temporary speed limit displayed. You should

Mark one answer

- [ ] **A.** not exceed the speed limit
- [ ] **B.** obey the limit only during rush hour
- [ ] **C.** ignore the displayed limit
- [ ] **D.** obey the limit except at night

642 You may drive over a footpath

Mark one answer

- [ ] **A.** to overtake slow-moving traffic
- [ ] **B.** when the pavement is very wide
- [ ] **C.** if no pedestrians are near
- [ ] **D.** to get into a property

643 **A single-carriageway road has this sign. What is the maximum permitted speed for a car towing a trailer?**

Mark one answer

- A. 30mph
- B. 40mph
- C. 50mph
- D. 60mph

644 **You are towing a small caravan on a dual carriageway. You must not exceed**

Mark one answer

- A. 50mph
- B. 40mph
- C. 70mph
- D. 60mph

645 **You want to park and you see this sign. On the days and times shown you should**

Mark one answer

- A. park in a bay and not pay
- B. park on yellow lines and pay
- C. park on yellow lines and not pay
- D. park in a bay and pay

Meter
ZONE
Mon - Fri
8.30 am - 6.30 pm
Saturday
8.30 am - 1.30 pm

646 **As a car driver which THREE lanes are you NOT normally allowed to use?**

Mark three answers

- A. Crawler lane
- B. Bus lane
- C. Overtaking lane
- D. Acceleration lane
- E. Cycle lane
- F. Tram lane

647 **You are driving along a road that has a cycle lane. The lane is marked by a solid white line. This means that during its period of operation**

Mark one answer

- A. the lane may be used for parking your car
- B. you may drive in that lane at any time
- C. the lane may be used when necessary
- D. you must not drive in that lane

648 **A cycle lane is marked by a solid white line. You must not drive or park in it**

Mark one answer

- A. at any time
- B. during the rush hour
- C. if a cyclist is using it
- D. during its period of operation

649 **While driving, you intend to turn left into a minor road. On the approach you should**

Mark one answer

- A. keep just left of the middle of the road
- B. keep in the middle of the road
- C. swing out wide just before turning
- D. keep well to the left of the road

650 **You are waiting at a level crossing. The red warning lights continue to flash after a train has passed by. What should you do?**

Mark one answer

- A. Get out and investigate
- B. Telephone the signal operator
- C. Continue to wait
- D. Drive across carefully

651 **You are driving over a level crossing. The warning lights come on and a bell rings. What should you do?**

Mark one answer

- A. Get everyone out of the vehicle immediately
- B. Stop and reverse back to clear the crossing
- C. Keep going and clear the crossing
- D. Stop immediately and use your hazard warning lights

652 **You are on a busy main road and find that you are travelling in the wrong direction. What should you do?**

Mark one answer

- A. Turn into a side road on the right and reverse into the main road
- B. Make a U-turn in the main road
- C. Make a 'three-point' turn in the main road
- D. Turn round in a side road

653 **You may remove your seat belt when carrying out a manoeuvre that involves**

Mark one answer

- A. reversing
- B. a hill start
- C. an emergency stop
- D. driving slowly

654 **You must not reverse**

Mark one answer

- A. for longer than necessary
- B. for more than a car's length
- C. into a side road
- D. in a built-up area

655 **You are parked in a busy high street. What is the safest way to turn your vehicle around so you can go the opposite way?**

Mark one answer

- A. Find a quiet side road to turn round in
- B. Drive into a side road and reverse into the main road
- C. Get someone to stop the traffic
- D. Do a U-turn

656 When you are NOT sure that it is safe to reverse your vehicle you should

Mark one answer

- [ ] **A.** use your horn
- [ ] **B.** rev your engine
- [ ] **C.** get out and check
- [ ] **D.** reverse slowly

657 When may you reverse from a side road into a main road?

Mark one answer

- [ ] **A.** Only if both roads are clear of traffic
- [ ] **B.** Not at any time
- [ ] **C.** At any time
- [ ] **D.** Only if the main road is clear of traffic

658 You want to turn right at a box junction. There is oncoming traffic. You should

Mark one answer

- [ ] **A.** wait in the box junction if your exit is clear
- [ ] **B.** wait before the junction until it is clear of all traffic
- [ ] **C.** drive on, you cannot turn right at a box junction
- [ ] **D.** drive slowly into the box junction when signalled by oncoming traffic

659 You are reversing your vehicle into a side road. When would the greatest hazard to passing traffic occur?

Mark one answer

- [ ] **A.** After you've completed the manoeuvre
- [ ] **B.** Just before you actually begin to manoeuvre
- [ ] **C.** After you've entered the side road
- [ ] **D.** When the front of your vehicle swings out

660 You are driving on a road that has a cycle lane. The lane is marked by a broken white line. This means that

Mark two answers

- [ ] **A.** you should not drive in the lane unless it is unavoidable
- [ ] **B.** you should not park in the lane unless it is unavoidable
- [ ] **C.** cyclists can travel in both directions in that lane
- [ ] **D.** the lane must be used by motorcyclists in heavy traffic

661 Where is the safest place to park your vehicle at night?

Mark one answer

- [ ] **A.** In a garage
- [ ] **B.** On a busy road
- [ ] **C.** In a quiet car park
- [ ] **D.** Near a red route

662 To help keep your vehicle secure at night where should you park?

Mark one answer

- [ ] **A.** Near a police station
- [ ] **B.** In a quiet road
- [ ] **C.** On a red route
- [ ] **D.** In a well-lit area

663

You are in the right-hand lane of a dual carriageway. You see signs showing that the right-hand lane is closed 800 yards ahead. You should

GET IN LANE

800 yards

Mark one answer

- [ ] **A.** keep in that lane until you reach the queue
- [ ] **B.** move to the left immediately
- [ ] **C.** wait and see which lane is moving faster
- [ ] **D.** move to the left in good time

664

You are driving on an urban clearway. You may stop only to

Mark one answer

- [ ] **A.** set down and pick up passengers
- [ ] **B.** use a mobile telephone
- [ ] **C.** ask for directions
- [ ] **D.** load or unload goods

665

You are looking for somewhere to park your vehicle. The area is full EXCEPT for spaces marked 'disabled use'. You can

Mark one answer

- [ ] **A.** use these spaces when elsewhere is full
- [ ] **B.** park if you stay with your vehicle
- [ ] **C.** use these spaces, disabled or not
- [ ] **D.** not park there unless permitted

666

Your vehicle is parked on the road at night. When must you use sidelights?

Mark one answer

- [ ] **A.** Where there are continuous white lines in the middle of the road
- [ ] **B.** Where the speed limit exceeds 30mph
- [ ] **C.** Where you are facing oncoming traffic
- [ ] **D.** Where you are near a bus stop

667

On which THREE occasions MUST you stop your vehicle?

Mark three answers

- [ ] **A.** When in an accident where damage or injury is caused
- [ ] **B.** At a red traffic light
- [ ] **C.** When signalled to do so by a police officer
- [ ] **D.** At a junction with double broken white lines
- [ ] **E.** At a pelican crossing when the amber light is flashing and no pedestrians are crossing

668

You are on a road that is only wide enough for one vehicle. There is a car coming towards you. What should you do?

Mark one answer

- [ ] **A.** Pull into a passing place on your right
- [ ] **B.** Force the other driver to reverse
- [ ] **C.** Pull into a passing place if your vehicle is wider
- [ ] **D.** Pull into a passing place on your left

669 **What MUST you have to park in a disabled space?**

Mark one answer

- A. An orange or blue badge
- B. A wheelchair
- C. An advanced driver certificate
- D. A modified vehicle

670 **You are driving at night with full beam headlights on. A vehicle is overtaking you. You should dip your lights**

Mark one answer

- A. some time after the vehicle has passed you
- B. before the vehicle starts to pass you
- C. only if the other driver dips their headlights
- D. as soon as the vehicle passes you

671 **When may you drive a motor car in this bus lane?**

Mark one answer

- A. Outside its hours of operation
- B. To get to the front of a traffic queue
- C. You may not use it at any time
- D. To overtake slow-moving traffic

672 **Signals are normally given by direction indicators and**

Mark one answer

- A. brake lights
- B. sidelights
- C. fog lights
- D. interior lights

673 **You are travelling on a motorway. You MUST stop when signalled to do so by which of these?**

Mark one answer NI

- A. Flashing amber lights above your lane
- B. A Highways Agency Traffic Officer
- C. Pedestrians on the hard shoulder
- D. A driver who has broken down

674 **At a busy unmarked crossroads, which of the following has priority?**

Mark one answer

- A. Vehicles going straight ahead
- B. Vehicles turning right
- C. None of the vehicles
- D. The vehicles that arrived first

675 You MUST obey signs giving orders. These signs are mostly in

Mark one answer

- A. green rectangles
- B. red triangles
- C. blue rectangles
- D. red circles

676 Traffic signs giving orders are generally which shape?

Mark one answer

- A. 
- B. 
- C. 
- D.

677 Which type of sign tells you NOT to do something?

Mark one answer

- A. 
- B. 
- C.
- D.

678 What does this sign mean?

Mark one answer

- A. Maximum speed limit with traffic calming
- B. Minimum speed limit with traffic calming
- C. '20 cars only' parking zone
- D. Only 20 cars allowed at any one time

20
ZONE
symbol
Place Name

679 Which sign means no motor vehicles are allowed?

Mark one answer

- A. 
- B. 
- C. 
- D.

680 Which of these signs means no motor vehicles?

Mark one answer

- A. 
- B. 
- C. 
- D.

681 What does this sign mean?

Mark one answer
- [ ] **A.** New speed limit 20mph
- [ ] **B.** No vehicles over 30 tonnes
- [ ] **C.** Minimum speed limit 30mph
- [ ] **D.** End of 20mph zone

682 What does this sign mean?

Mark one answer
- [ ] **A.** No overtaking
- [ ] **B.** No motor vehicles
- [ ] **C.** Clearway (no stopping)
- [ ] **D.** Cars and motorcycles only

683 What does this sign mean?

Mark one answer
- [ ] **A.** No parking
- [ ] **B.** No road markings
- [ ] **C.** No through road
- [ ] **D.** No entry

684 What does this sign mean?

Mark one answer
- [ ] **A.** Bend to the right
- [ ] **B.** Road on the right closed
- [ ] **C.** No traffic from the right
- [ ] **D.** No right turn

685 Which sign means 'no entry'?

Mark one answer
- [ ] **A.**

- [ ] **B.**

- [ ] **C.**

- [ ] **D.**

686 What does this sign mean?

Mark one answer
- [ ] **A.** Route for trams only
- [ ] **B.** Route for buses only
- [ ] **C.** Parking for buses only
- [ ] **D.** Parking for trams only

687 Which type of vehicle does this sign apply to?

Mark one answer

- [ ] **A.** Wide vehicles
- [ ] **B.** Long vehicles
- [ ] **C.** High vehicles
- [ ] **D.** Heavy vehicles

688 Which sign means NO motor vehicles allowed?

Mark one answer

- [ ] **A.** 
- [ ] **B.** 
- [ ] **C.** 
- [ ] **D.**

689 What does this sign mean?

Mark one answer

- [ ] **A.** You have priority
- [ ] **B.** No motor vehicles
- [ ] **C.** Two-way traffic
- [ ] **D.** No overtaking

690 What does this sign mean?

Mark one answer

- [ ] **A.** Keep in one lane
- [ ] **B.** Give way to oncoming traffic
- [ ] **C.** Do not overtake
- [ ] **D.** Form two lanes

691 Which sign means no overtaking?

Mark one answer

- [ ] **A.** 
- [ ] **B.** 
- [ ] **C.** 
- [ ] **D.**

692 What does this sign mean?

Mark one answer

- [ ] **A.** Waiting restrictions apply
- [ ] **B.** Waiting permitted
- [ ] **C.** National speed limit applies
- [ ] **D.** Clearway (no stopping)

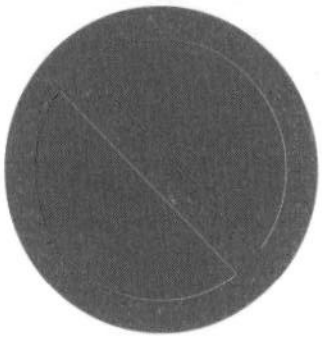

693 What does this sign mean?

Mark one answer

- [ ] A. End of restricted speed area
- [ ] B. End of restricted parking area
- [ ] C. End of clearway
- [ ] D. End of cycle route

Zone
ENDS

694 Which sign means 'no stopping'?

Mark one answer

- [ ] A.
- [ ] B.
- [ ] C.
- [ ] D.

695 What does this sign mean?

Mark one answer

- [ ] A. Roundabout
- [ ] B. Crossroads
- [ ] C. No stopping
- [ ] D. No entry

696 You see this sign ahead. It means

Mark one answer

- [ ] A. national speed limit applies
- [ ] B. waiting restrictions apply
- [ ] C. no stopping
- [ ] D. no entry

697 What does this sign mean?

Mark one answer

- [ ] A. Distance to parking place ahead
- [ ] B. Distance to public telephone ahead
- [ ] C. Distance to public house ahead
- [ ] D. Distance to passing place ahead

P
1 mile

698 What does this sign mean?

P

Mark one answer

- [ ] A. Vehicles may not park on the verge or footway
- [ ] B. Vehicles may park on the left-hand side of the road only
- [ ] C. Vehicles may park fully on the verge or footway
- [ ] D. Vehicles may park on the right-hand side of the road only

699 What does this traffic sign mean?

Mark one answer

- [ ] **A.** No overtaking allowed
- [ ] **B.** Give priority to oncoming traffic
- [ ] **C.** Two-way traffic
- [ ] **D.** One-way traffic only

700 What is the meaning of this traffic sign?

Mark one answer

- [ ] **A.** End of two-way road
- [ ] **B.** Give priority to vehicles coming towards you
- [ ] **C.** You have priority over vehicles coming towards you
- [ ] **D.** Bus lane ahead

701 What MUST you do when you see this sign?

Mark one answer

- [ ] **A.** Stop, only if traffic is approaching
- [ ] **B.** Stop, even if the road is clear
- [ ] **C.** Stop, only if children are waiting to cross
- [ ] **D.** Stop, only if a red light is showing

STOP

702 What does this sign mean?

Mark one answer

- [ ] **A.** No overtaking
- [ ] **B.** You are entering a one-way street
- [ ] **C.** Two-way traffic ahead
- [ ] **D.** You have priority over vehicles from the opposite direction

703 What shape is a STOP sign at a junction?

Mark one answer

- [ ] **A.**
- [ ] **B.**
- [ ] **C.**
- [ ] **D.**

704 At a junction you see this sign partly covered by snow. What does it mean?

Mark one answer

- [ ] **A.** Crossroads
- [ ] **B.** Give way
- [ ] **C.** Stop
- [ ] **D.** Turn right

705 Which shape is used for a 'give way' sign?

Mark one answer

- [ ] A.
- [ ] B.
- [ ] C.
- [ ] D.

706 What does this sign mean?

Mark one answer

- [ ] A. Service area 30 miles ahead
- [ ] B. Maximum speed 30mph
- [ ] C. Minimum speed 30mph
- [ ] D. Lay-by 30 miles ahead

707 Which of these signs means turn left ahead?

Mark one answer

- [ ] A.
- [ ] B.
- [ ] C.
- [ ] D.

708 What does this sign mean?

Mark one answer

- [ ] A. Buses turning
- [ ] B. Ring road
- [ ] C. Mini-roundabout
- [ ] D. Keep right

709 What does this sign mean?

Mark one answer

- [ ] A. Give way to oncoming vehicles
- [ ] B. Approaching traffic passes you on both sides
- [ ] C. Turn off at the next available junction
- [ ] D. Pass either side to get to the same destination

710 What does this sign mean?

Mark one answer

- [ ] A. Route for trams
- [ ] B. Give way to trams
- [ ] C. Route for buses
- [ ] D. Give way to buses

711 What does a circular traffic sign with a blue background do?

Mark one answer

- [ ] **A.** Give warning of a motorway ahead
- [ ] **B.** Give directions to a car park
- [ ] **C.** Give motorway information
- [ ] **D.** Give an instruction

712 Which of these signs means that you are entering a one-way street?

Mark one answer

- [ ] **A.** 
- [ ] **B.** 
- [ ] **C.** 
- [ ] **D.**

713 Where would you see a contraflow bus and cycle lane?

Mark one answer

- [ ] **A.** On a dual carriageway
- [ ] **B.** On a roundabout
- [ ] **C.** On an urban motorway
- [ ] **D.** On a one-way street

714 What does this sign mean?

Mark one answer

- [ ] **A.** Bus station on the right
- [ ] **B.** Contraflow bus lane
- [ ] **C.** With-flow bus lane
- [ ] **D.** Give way to buses

715 What does this sign mean?

local
taxi

Mark one answer

- [ ] **A.** With-flow bus and cycle lane
- [ ] **B.** Contraflow bus and cycle lane
- [ ] **C.** No buses and cycles allowed
- [ ] **D.** No waiting for buses and cycles

716 What does a sign with a brown background show?

Mark one answer

- [ ] **A.** Tourist directions
- [ ] **B.** Primary roads
- [ ] **C.** Motorway routes
- [ ] **D.** Minor routes

717 This sign means

Mark one answer

- [ ] **A.** tourist attraction
- [ ] **B.** beware of trains
- [ ] **C.** level crossing
- [ ] **D.** beware of trams

718 What are triangular signs for?

Mark one answer

- [ ] **A.** To give warnings
- [ ] **B.** To give information
- [ ] **C.** To give orders
- [ ] **D.** To give directions

719 What does this sign mean?

Mark one answer

- [ ] **A.** Turn left ahead
- [ ] **B.** T-junction
- [ ] **C.** No through road
- [ ] **D.** Give way

720 What does this sign mean?

Mark one answer

- [ ] **A.** Multi-exit roundabout
- [ ] **B.** Risk of ice
- [ ] **C.** Six roads converge
- [ ] **D.** Place of historical interest

721 What does this sign mean?

Mark one answer

- [ ] **A.** Crossroads
- [ ] **B.** Level crossing with gate
- [ ] **C.** Level crossing without gate
- [ ] **D.** Ahead only

722 What does this sign mean?

Mark one answer

- [ ] **A.** Ring road
- [ ] **B.** Mini-roundabout
- [ ] **C.** No vehicles
- [ ] **D.** Roundabout

723 Which FOUR of these would be indicated by a triangular road sign?

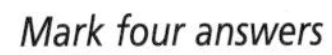

Mark four answers

- A. Road narrows
- B. Ahead only
- C. Low bridge
- D. Minimum speed
- E. Children crossing
- F. T-junction

724 What does this sign mean?

Mark one answer

- A. Cyclists must dismount
- B. Cycles are not allowed
- C. Cycle route ahead
- D. Cycle in single file

725 Which sign means that pedestrians may be walking along the road?

Mark one answer

A.

B.

C.

D.

726 Which of these signs warn you of a pedestrian crossing?

Mark one answer

A.

B.

C.

D.

727 What does this sign mean?

Mark one answer

- A. No footpath ahead
- B. Pedestrians only ahead
- C. Pedestrian crossing ahead
- D. School crossing ahead

728 What does this sign mean?

Mark one answer

- A. School crossing patrol
- B. No pedestrians allowed
- C. Pedestrian zone – no vehicles
- D. Pedestrian crossing ahead

729 Which of these signs means there is a double bend ahead?

Mark one answer

- [ ] A. 
- [ ] B. 
- [ ] C. 
- [ ] D.

730 What does this sign mean?

Mark one answer

- [ ] A. Wait at the barriers
- [ ] B. Wait at the crossroads
- [ ] C. Give way to trams
- [ ] D. Give way to farm vehicles

731 What does this sign mean?

Mark one answer

- [ ] A. Humpback bridge
- [ ] B. Humps in the road
- [ ] C. Entrance to tunnel
- [ ] D. Soft verges

732 What does this sign mean?

Mark one answer

- [ ] A. Low bridge ahead
- [ ] B. Tunnel ahead
- [ ] C. Ancient monument ahead
- [ ] D. Accident black spot ahead

733 What does this sign mean?

Mark one answer

- [ ] A. Two-way traffic straight ahead
- [ ] B. Two-way traffic crosses a one-way road
- [ ] C. Two-way traffic over a bridge
- [ ] D. Two-way traffic crosses a two-way road

734 Which sign means 'two-way traffic crosses a one-way road'?

Mark one answer

- [ ] A. 
- [ ] B. 
- [ ] C. 
- [ ] D.

735 Which of these signs means the end of a dual carriageway?

Mark one answer

- [ ] A.
- [ ] B.
- [ ] C.
- [ ] D.

736 What does this sign mean?

Mark one answer

- [ ] A. End of dual carriageway
- [ ] B. Tall bridge
- [ ] C. Road narrows
- [ ] D. End of narrow bridge

737 What does this sign mean?

Mark one answer

- [ ] A. Two-way traffic ahead across a one-way road
- [ ] B. Traffic approaching you has priority
- [ ] C. Two-way traffic straight ahead
- [ ] D. Motorway contraflow system ahead

738 What does this sign mean?

Mark one answer

- [ ] A. Crosswinds
- [ ] B. Road noise
- [ ] C. Airport
- [ ] D. Adverse camber

739 What does this traffic sign mean?

Mark one answer

- [ ] A. Slippery road ahead
- [ ] B. Tyres liable to punctures ahead
- [ ] C. Danger ahead
- [ ] D. Service area ahead

740 You are about to overtake when you see this sign. You should

Mark one answer

- [ ] A. overtake the other driver as quickly as possible
- [ ] B. move to the right to get a better view
- [ ] C. switch your headlights on before overtaking
- [ ] D. hold back until you can see clearly ahead

Hidden dip

741 What does this sign mean?

Mark one answer

- [ ] **A.** Level crossing with gate or barrier
- [ ] **B.** Gated road ahead
- [ ] **C.** Level crossing without gate or barrier
- [ ] **D.** Cattle grid ahead

742 What does this sign mean?

Mark one answer

- [ ] **A.** No trams ahead
- [ ] **B.** Oncoming trams
- [ ] **C.** Trams crossing ahead
- [ ] **D.** Trams only

743 What does this sign mean?

Mark one answer

- [ ] **A.** Adverse camber
- [ ] **B.** Steep hill downwards
- [ ] **C.** Uneven road
- [ ] **D.** Steep hill upwards

744 What does this sign mean?

Mark one answer

- [ ] **A.** Uneven road surface
- [ ] **B.** Bridge over the road
- [ ] **C.** Road ahead ends
- [ ] **D.** Water across the road

745 What does this sign mean?

Mark one answer

- [ ] **A.** Humpback bridge
- [ ] **B.** Traffic calming hump
- [ ] **C.** Low bridge
- [ ] **D.** Uneven road

746 What does this sign mean?

Mark one answer

- [ ] **A.** Turn left for parking area
- [ ] **B.** No through road on the left
- [ ] **C.** No entry for traffic turning left
- [ ] **D.** Turn left for ferry terminal

747 What does this sign mean?

Mark one answer

- A. T-junction
- B. No through road
- C. Telephone box ahead
- D. Toilet ahead

748 Which sign means 'no through road'?

Mark one answer

- A. 
- B. 
- C. 
- D.

749 Which of the following signs informs you that you are coming to a 'no through road'?

Mark one answer

- A. 
- B. 
- C. 
- D.

750 What does this sign mean?

P+

Mark one answer

- A. Direction to park-and-ride car park
- B. No parking for buses or coaches
- C. Directions to bus and coach park
- D. Parking area for cars and coaches

751 You are in a tunnel and you see this sign. What does it mean?

Mark one answer

- A. Direction to emergency pedestrian exit
- B. Beware of pedestrians, no footpath ahead
- C. No access for pedestrians
- D. Beware of pedestrians crossing ahead

752 Which is the sign for a ring road?

Mark one answer

- A. 
- B. 
- C.  R
- D.

753 At a railway level crossing the red light signal continues to flash after a train has gone by. What should you do?

Mark one answer

- [ ] **A.** Phone the signal operator
- [ ] **B.** Alert drivers behind you
- [ ] **C.** Wait
- [ ] **D.** Proceed with caution

754 At a junction you see this signal. It means

Mark one answer

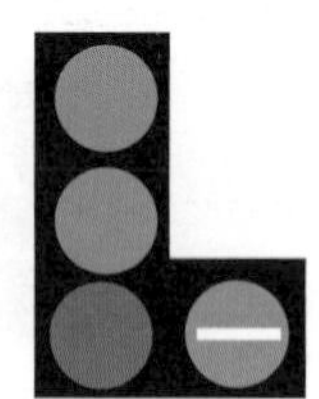

- [ ] **A.** cars must stop
- [ ] **B.** trams must stop
- [ ] **C.** both trams and cars must stop
- [ ] **D.** both trams and cars can continue

755 What does this sign mean?

Mark one answer

- [ ] **A.** The right-hand lane ahead is narrow
- [ ] **B.** Right-hand lane for buses only
- [ ] **C.** Right-hand lane for turning right
- [ ] **D.** The right-hand lane is closed

756 What does this sign mean?

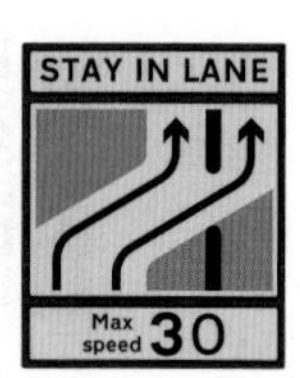

Mark one answer

- [ ] **A.** Change to the left lane
- [ ] **B.** Leave at the next exit
- [ ] **C.** Contraflow system
- [ ] **D.** One-way street

757 What does this sign mean?

Mark one answer

- [ ] **A.** Leave motorway at next exit
- [ ] **B.** Lane for heavy and slow vehicles
- [ ] **C.** All lorries use the hard shoulder
- [ ] **D.** Rest area for lorries

758 You are approaching a red traffic light. The signal will change from red to

Mark one answer

- [ ] **A.** red and amber, then green
- [ ] **B.** green, then amber
- [ ] **C.** amber, then green
- [ ] **D.** green and amber, then green

759 A red traffic light means

Mark one answer

- [ ] **A.** you should stop unless turning left
- [ ] **B.** stop, if you are able to brake safely
- [ ] **C.** you must stop and wait behind the stop line
- [ ] **D.** proceed with caution

760 At traffic lights, amber on its own means

Mark one answer

- [ ] **A.** prepare to go
- [ ] **B.** go if the way is clear
- [ ] **C.** go if no pedestrians are crossing
- [ ] **D.** stop at the stop line

761 You are approaching traffic lights. Red and amber are showing. This means

Mark one answer

- [ ] **A.** pass the lights if the road is clear
- [ ] **B.** there is a fault with the lights – take care
- [ ] **C.** wait for the green light before you cross the stop line
- [ ] **D.** the lights are about to change to red

762 You are at a junction controlled by traffic lights. When should you NOT proceed at green?

Mark one answer

- [ ] **A.** When pedestrians are waiting to cross
- [ ] **B.** When your exit from the junction is blocked
- [ ] **C.** When you think the lights may be about to change
- [ ] **D.** When you intend to turn right

763 You are in the left-hand lane at traffic lights. You are waiting to turn left. At which of these traffic lights must you NOT move on?

Mark one answer

- [ ] **A.**
- [ ] **B.**
- [ ] **C.**
- [ ] **D.**

764 What does this sign mean?

Mark one answer

- [ ] A. Traffic lights out of order
- [ ] B. Amber signal out of order
- [ ] C. Temporary traffic lights ahead
- [ ] D. New traffic lights ahead

765 When traffic lights are out of order, who has priority?

Mark one answer

- [ ] A. Traffic going straight on
- [ ] B. Traffic turning right
- [ ] C. Nobody
- [ ] D. Traffic turning left

766 These flashing red lights mean STOP. In which THREE of the following places could you find them?

Mark three answers

- [ ] A. Pelican crossings
- [ ] B. Lifting bridges
- [ ] C. Zebra crossings
- [ ] D. Level crossings
- [ ] E. Motorway exits
- [ ] F. Fire stations

767 What do these zigzag lines at pedestrian crossings mean?

Mark one answer

- [ ] A. No parking at any time
- [ ] B. Parking allowed only for a short time
- [ ] C. Slow down to 20mph
- [ ] D. Sounding horns is not allowed

768 When may you cross a double solid white line in the middle of the road?

Mark one answer

- [ ] A. To pass traffic that is queuing back at a junction
- [ ] B. To pass a car signalling to turn left ahead
- [ ] C. To pass a road maintenance vehicle travelling at 10mph or less
- [ ] D. To pass a vehicle that is towing a trailer

769 What does this road marking mean?

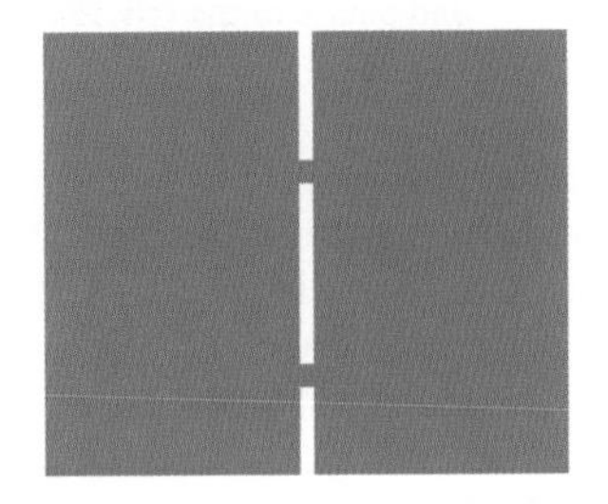

Mark one answer

- [ ] **A.** Do not cross the line
- [ ] **B.** No stopping allowed
- [ ] **C.** You are approaching a hazard
- [ ] **D.** No overtaking allowed

770 This marking appears on the road just before a

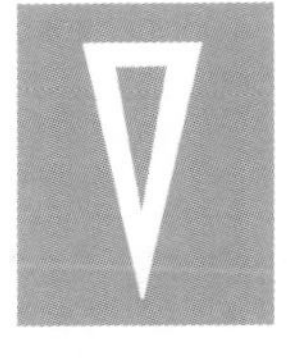

Mark one answer

- [ ] **A.** 'no entry' sign
- [ ] **B.** 'give way' sign
- [ ] **C.** 'stop' sign
- [ ] **D.** 'no through road' sign

771 Where would you see this road marking?

Mark one answer

- [ ] **A.** At traffic lights
- [ ] **B.** On road humps
- [ ] **C.** Near a level crossing
- [ ] **D.** At a box junction

772 Which is a hazard warning line?

Mark one answer

- [ ] **A.**

- [ ] **B.**

- [ ] **C.**

- [ ] **D.**

773 At this junction there is a stop sign with a solid white line on the road surface. Why is there a stop sign here?

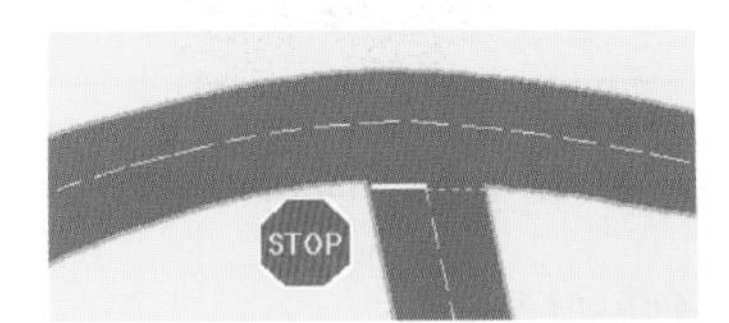

Mark one answer

- [ ] **A.** Speed on the major road is de-restricted
- [ ] **B.** It is a busy junction
- [ ] **C.** Visibility along the major road is restricted
- [ ] **D.** There are hazard warning lines in the centre of the road

774 **You see this line across the road at the entrance to a roundabout. What does it mean?**

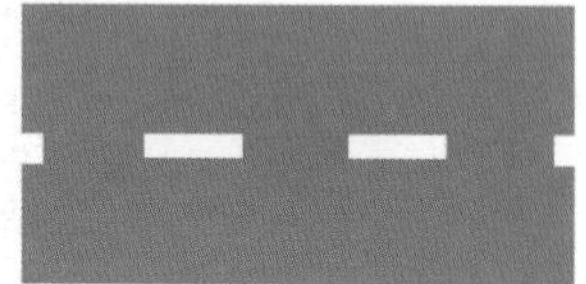

Mark one answer

- [ ] **A.** Give way to traffic from the right
- [ ] **B.** Traffic from the left has right of way
- [ ] **C.** You have right of way
- [ ] **D.** Stop at the line

775 **Where would you find these road markings?**

Mark one answer

- [ ] **A.** At a railway crossing
- [ ] **B.** At a junction
- [ ] **C.** On a motorway
- [ ] **D.** On a pedestrian crossing

776 **How will a police officer in a patrol vehicle normally get you to stop?**

Mark one answer

- [ ] **A.** Flash the headlights, indicate left and point to the left
- [ ] **B.** Wait until you stop, then approach you
- [ ] **C.** Use the siren, overtake, cut in front and stop
- [ ] **D.** Pull alongside you, use the siren and wave you to stop

777 **There is a police car following you. The police officer flashes the headlights and points to the left. What should you do?**

Mark one answer

- [ ] **A.** Turn left at the next junction
- [ ] **B.** Pull up on the left
- [ ] **C.** Stop immediately
- [ ] **D.** Move over to the left

778 **You approach a junction. The traffic lights are not working. A police officer gives this signal. You should**

Mark one answer

- [ ] **A.** turn left only
- [ ] **B.** turn right only
- [ ] **C.** stop level with the officer's arm
- [ ] **D.** stop at the stop line

779 **The driver of the car in front is giving this arm signal. What does it mean?**

Mark one answer

- [ ] **A.** The driver is slowing down
- [ ] **B.** The driver intends to turn right
- [ ] **C.** The driver wishes to overtake
- [ ] **D.** The driver intends to turn left

780 Where would you see these road markings?

Mark one answer

- A. At a level crossing
- B. On a motorway slip road
- C. At a pedestrian crossing
- D. On a single-track road

781 When may you NOT overtake on the left?

Mark one answer

- A. On a free-flowing motorway or dual carriageway
- B. When the traffic is moving slowly in queues
- C. On a one-way street
- D. When the car in front is signalling to turn right

782 What does this motorway sign mean?

Mark one answer

- A. Change to the lane on your left
- B. Leave the motorway at the next exit
- C. Change to the opposite carriageway
- D. Pull up on the hard shoulder

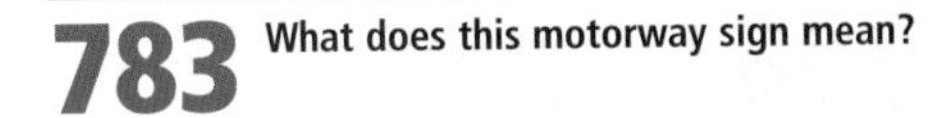

783 What does this motorway sign mean?

Mark one answer

- A. Temporary minimum speed 50mph
- B. No services for 50 miles
- C. Obstruction 50 metres (164 feet) ahead
- D. Temporary maximum speed 50mph

784 What does this sign mean?

Mark one answer

- A. Through traffic to use left lane
- B. Right-hand lane T-junction only
- C. Right-hand lane closed ahead
- D. 11 tonne weight limit

785 On a motorway this sign means

Mark one answer

- A. move over on to the hard shoulder
- B. overtaking on the left only
- C. leave the motorway at the next exit
- D. move to the lane on your left

786 What does '25' mean on this motorway sign?

Mark one answer
- [ ] A. The distance to the nearest town
- [ ] B. The route number of the road
- [ ] C. The number of the next junction
- [ ] D. The speed limit on the slip road

787 The right-hand lane of a three-lane motorway is

Mark one answer
- [ ] A. for lorries only
- [ ] B. an overtaking lane
- [ ] C. the right-turn lane
- [ ] D. an acceleration lane

788 Where can you find reflective amber studs on a motorway?

Mark one answer
- [ ] A. Separating the slip road from the motorway
- [ ] B. On the left-hand edge of the road
- [ ] C. On the right-hand edge of the road
- [ ] D. Separating the lanes

789 Where on a motorway would you find green reflective studs?

Mark one answer
- [ ] A. Separating driving lanes
- [ ] B. Between the hard shoulder and the carriageway
- [ ] C. At slip road entrances and exits
- [ ] D. Between the carriageway and the central reservation

790 You are travelling along a motorway. You see this sign. You should

Mark one answer
- [ ] A. leave the motorway at the next exit
- [ ] B. turn left immediately
- [ ] C. change lane
- [ ] D. move on to the hard shoulder

791 What does this sign mean?

Mark one answer
- [ ] A. No motor vehicles
- [ ] B. End of motorway
- [ ] C. No through road
- [ ] D. End of bus lane

792 Which of these signs means that the national speed limit applies?

Mark one answer

- A.
- B.
- C.
- D.

793 What is the maximum speed on a single carriageway road?

Mark one answer

- A. 50mph
- B. 60mph
- C. 40mph
- D. 70mph

794 What does this sign mean?

End

Mark one answer

- A. End of motorway
- B. End of restriction
- C. Lane ends ahead
- D. Free recovery ends

795 This sign is advising you to

Mark one answer

- A. follow the route diversion
- B. follow the signs to the picnic area
- C. give way to pedestrians
- D. give way to cyclists

796 Why would this temporary speed limit sign be shown?

Mark one answer

50
¾ mile ahead

- A. To warn of the end of the motorway
- B. To warn you of a low bridge
- C. To warn you of a junction ahead
- D. To warn of road works ahead

797 This traffic sign means there is

Mark one answer

- A. a compulsory maximum speed limit
- B. an advisory maximum speed limit
- C. a compulsory minimum speed limit
- D. an advised separation distance

798 You see this sign at a crossroads. You should

Mark one answer

- [ ] **A.** maintain the same speed
- [ ] **B.** carry on with great care
- [ ] **C.** find another route
- [ ] **D.** telephone the police

799 You are signalling to turn right in busy traffic. How would you confirm your intention safely?

Mark one answer

- [ ] **A.** Sound the horn
- [ ] **B.** Give an arm signal
- [ ] **C.** Flash your headlights
- [ ] **D.** Position over the centre line

800 What does this sign mean?

Mark one answer

- [ ] **A.** Motorcycles only
- [ ] **B.** No cars
- [ ] **C.** Cars only
- [ ] **D.** No motorcycles

801 You are on a motorway. You see this sign on a lorry that has stopped in the right-hand lane. You should

Mark one answer

- [ ] **A.** move into the right-hand lane
- [ ] **B.** stop behind the flashing lights
- [ ] **C.** pass the lorry on the left
- [ ] **D.** leave the motorway at the next exit

802 You are on a motorway. Red flashing lights appear above your lane only. What should you do?

Mark one answer

- [ ] **A.** Continue in that lane and look for further information
- [ ] **B.** Move into another lane in good time
- [ ] **C.** Pull on to the hard shoulder
- [ ] **D.** Stop and wait for an instruction to proceed

803 A red traffic light means

Mark one answer

- [ ] **A.** you must stop behind the white stop line
- [ ] **B.** you may go straight on if there is no other traffic
- [ ] **C.** you may turn left if it is safe to do so
- [ ] **D.** you must slow down and prepare to stop if traffic has started to cross

804 The driver of this car is giving an arm signal. What are they about to do?

Mark one answer

- [ ] **A.** Turn to the right
- [ ] **B.** Turn to the left
- [ ] **C.** Go straight ahead
- [ ] **D.** Let pedestrians cross

805 Which arm signal tells you that the car you are following is going to turn left?

Mark one answer

- [ ] **A.**

- [ ] **B.**

- [ ] **C.**

- [ ] **D.**

806 When may you sound the horn?

Mark one answer

- [ ] **A.** To give you right of way
- [ ] **B.** To attract a friend's attention
- [ ] **C.** To warn others of your presence
- [ ] **D.** To make slower drivers move over

807 You must not use your horn when you are stationary

Mark one answer

- [ ] **A.** unless a moving vehicle may cause you danger
- [ ] **B.** at any time whatsoever
- [ ] **C.** unless it is used only briefly
- [ ] **D.** except for signalling that you have just arrived

808 What does this sign mean?

Mark one answer

- [ ] **A.** You can park on the days and times shown
- [ ] **B.** No parking on the days and times shown
- [ ] **C.** No parking at all from Monday to Friday
- [ ] **D.** End of the urban clearway restrictions

809 What does this sign mean?

Mark one answer

- [ ] **A.** Quayside or river bank
- [ ] **B.** Steep hill downwards
- [ ] **C.** Uneven road surface
- [ ] **D.** Road liable to flooding

810 You see this amber traffic light ahead. Which light or lights will come on next?

Mark one answer

- [ ] **A.** Red alone
- [ ] **B.** Red and amber together
- [ ] **C.** Green and amber together
- [ ] **D.** Green alone

811 This broken white line painted in the centre of the road means

Mark one answer

- [ ] **A.** oncoming vehicles have priority over you
- [ ] **B.** you should give priority to oncoming vehicles
- [ ] **C.** there is a hazard ahead of you
- [ ] **D.** the area is a national speed limit zone

812 Which sign means you have priority over oncoming vehicles?

Mark one answer

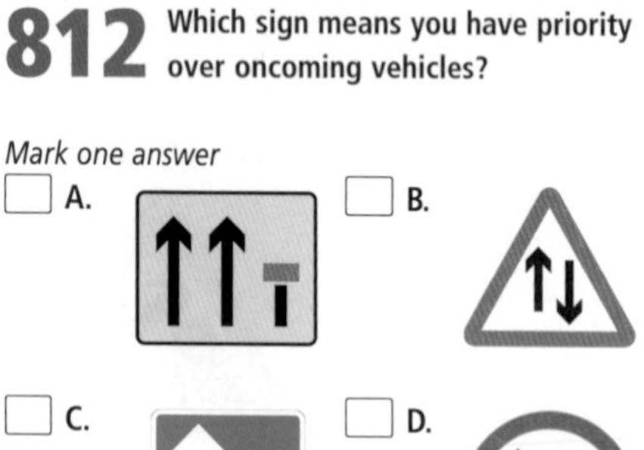

- [ ] **A.**
- [ ] **B.**
- [ ] **C.**
- [ ] **D.**

813 You see this signal overhead on the motorway. What does it mean?

Mark one answer

- [ ] **A.** Leave the motorway at the next exit
- [ ] **B.** All vehicles use the hard shoulder
- [ ] **C.** Sharp bend to the left ahead
- [ ] **D.** Stop, all lanes ahead closed

814 A white line like this along the centre of the road is a

Mark one answer

- [ ] **A.** bus lane marking
- [ ] **B.** hazard warning
- [ ] **C.** give way marking
- [ ] **D.** lane marking

815 What is the purpose of these yellow criss-cross lines on the road?

Mark one answer

- [ ] **A.** To make you more aware of the traffic lights
- [ ] **B.** To guide you into position as you turn
- [ ] **C.** To prevent the junction becoming blocked
- [ ] **D.** To show you where to stop when the lights change

816 What is the reason for the yellow criss-cross lines painted on the road here?

Mark one answer

- [ ] **A.** To mark out an area for trams only
- [ ] **B.** To prevent queuing traffic from blocking the junction on the left
- [ ] **C.** To mark the entrance lane to a car park
- [ ] **D.** To warn you of the tram lines crossing the road

817 What is the reason for the area marked in red and white along the centre of this road?

Mark one answer

- [ ] **A.** It is to separate traffic flowing in opposite directions
- [ ] **B.** It marks an area to be used by overtaking motorcyclists
- [ ] **C.** It is a temporary marking to warn of the road works
- [ ] **D.** It is separating the two sides of the dual carriageway

818 Other drivers may sometimes flash their headlights at you. In which situation are they allowed to do this?

Mark one answer

- [ ] **A.** To warn of a radar speed trap ahead
- [ ] **B.** To show that they are giving way to you
- [ ] **C.** To warn you of their presence
- [ ] **D.** To let you know there is a fault with your vehicle

819

You are approaching a zebra crossing where pedestrians are waiting. Which arm signal might you give?

Mark one answer

- [ ] A.
- [ ] B.
- [ ] C.
- [ ] D.

820

The white line along the side of the road

Mark one answer

- [ ] A. shows the edge of the carriageway
- [ ] B. shows the approach to a hazard
- [ ] C. means no parking
- [ ] D. means no overtaking

821

You see this white arrow on the road ahead. It means

Mark one answer

- [ ] A. entrance on the left
- [ ] B. all vehicles turn left
- [ ] C. keep left of the hatched markings
- [ ] D. road bending to the left

822

How should you give an arm signal t turn left?

Mark one answer

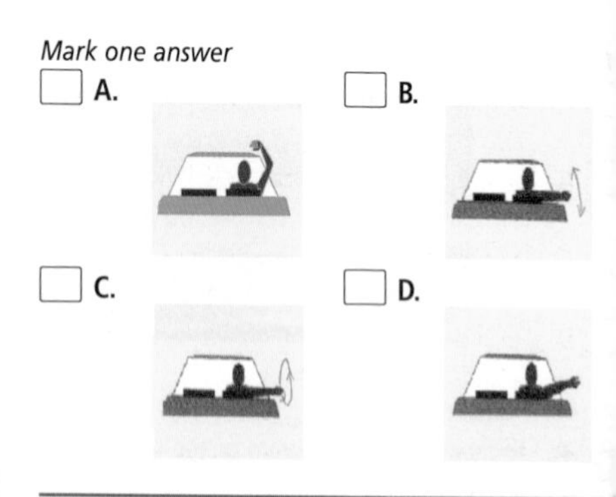

- [ ] A.
- [ ] B.
- [ ] C.
- [ ] D.

823

You are waiting at a T-junction. A vehicl is coming from the right with the left signal flashing. What should you do?

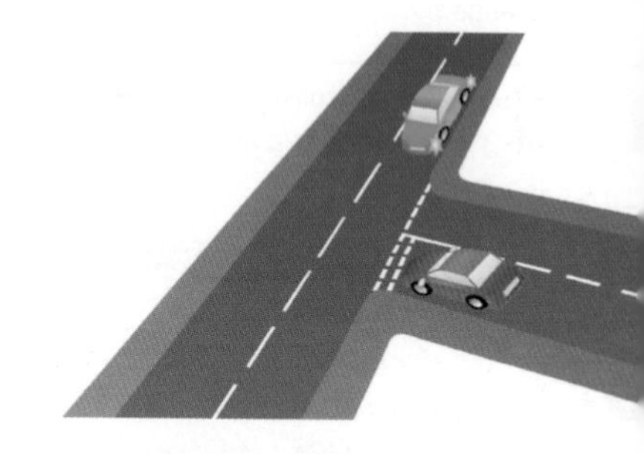

Mark one answer

- [ ] A. Move out and accelerate hard
- [ ] B. Wait until the vehicle starts to turn in
- [ ] C. Pull out before the vehicle reaches the junction
- [ ] D. Move out slowly

824 **When may you use hazard warning lights when driving?**

Mark one answer

- [ ] **A.** Instead of sounding the horn in a built-up area between 11.30pm and 7am
- [ ] **B.** On a motorway or unrestricted dual carriageway, to warn of a hazard ahead
- [ ] **C.** On rural routes, after a warning sign of animals
- [ ] **D.** On the approach to toucan crossings where cyclists are waiting to cross

825 **You are driving on a motorway. There is a slow-moving vehicle ahead. On the back you see this sign. You should**

Mark one answer

- [ ] **A.** pass on the right
- [ ] **B.** pass on the left
- [ ] **C.** leave at the next exit
- [ ] **D.** drive no further

826 **In some narrow residential streets you may find a speed limit of**

Mark one answer

- [ ] **A.** 20mph
- [ ] **B.** 25mph
- [ ] **C.** 35mph
- [ ] **D.** 40mph

827 **You should NOT normally stop on these markings near schools**

SCHOOL KEEP CLEAR

Mark one answer

- [ ] **A.** except when picking up children
- [ ] **B.** under any circumstances
- [ ] **C.** unless there is nowhere else available
- [ ] **D.** except to set down children

828 **Why should you make sure that your indicators are cancelled after turning?**

Mark one answer

- [ ] **A.** To avoid flattening the battery
- [ ] **B.** To avoid misleading other road users
- [ ] **C.** To avoid dazzling other road users
- [ ] **D.** To avoid damage to the indicator relay

829 **You are driving in busy traffic. You want to pull up on the left just after a junction on the left. When should you signal?**

Mark one answer

- [ ] **A.** As you are passing or just after the junction
- [ ] **B.** Just before you reach the junction
- [ ] **C.** Well before you reach the junction
- [ ] **D.** It would be better not to signal at all

830 An MOT certificate is normally valid for

Mark one answer

- A. three years after the date it was issued
- B. 10,000 miles
- C. one year after the date it was issued
- D. 30,000 miles

831 A cover note is a document issued before you receive your

Mark one answer

- A. driving licence
- B. insurance certificate
- C. registration document
- D. MOT certificate

832 A police officer asks to see your documents. You do not have them with you. You may produce them at a police station within

Mark one answer

- A. 5 days
- B. 7 days
- C. 14 days
- D. 21 days

833 You have just passed your practical test. You do not hold a full licence in another category. Within two years you get six penalty points on your licence. What will you have to do?

Mark two answers

- A. Retake only your theory test
- B. Retake your theory and practical tests
- C. Retake only your practical test
- D. Reapply for your full licence immediately
- E. Reapply for your provisional licence

834 To drive on the road learners MUST

Mark one answer

- A. have NO penalty points on their licence
- B. have taken professional instruction
- C. have a signed, valid provisional licence
- D. apply for a driving test within 12 months

835 Before driving anyone else's motor vehicle you should make sure that

Mark one answer

- A. the vehicle owner has third party insurance cover
- B. your own vehicle has insurance cover
- C. the vehicle is insured for your use
- D. the owner has left the insurance documents in the vehicle

836 Your car needs an MOT certificate. If you drive without one this could invalidate your

Mark one answer

- A. vehicle service record
- B. insurance
- C. road tax disc
- D. vehicle registration document

837 When is it legal to drive a car over three years old without an MOT certificate?

Mark one answer **NI**

- A. Up to seven days after the old certificate has run out
- B. When driving to an MOT centre to arrange an appointment
- C. Just after buying a second-hand car with no MOT
- D. When driving to an appointment at an MOT centre

838 To supervise a learner driver you must

Mark two answers

- [ ] **A.** have held a full licence for at least 3 years
- [ ] **B.** be at least 21 years old
- [ ] **C.** be an approved driving instructor
- [ ] **D.** hold an advanced driving certificate

839 How old must you be to supervise a learner driver?

Mark one answer

- [ ] **A.** 18 years old
- [ ] **B.** 19 years old
- [ ] **C.** 20 years old
- [ ] **D.** 21 years old

840 A newly qualified driver must

Mark one answer

- [ ] **A.** display green 'L' plates
- [ ] **B.** not exceed 40mph for 12 months
- [ ] **C.** be accompanied on a motorway
- [ ] **D.** have valid motor insurance

841 You have third party insurance. What does this cover?

Mark three answers

- [ ] **A.** Damage to your own vehicle
- [ ] **B.** Damage to your vehicle by fire
- [ ] **C.** Injury to another person
- [ ] **D.** Damage to someone's property
- [ ] **E.** Damage to other vehicles
- [ ] **F.** Injury to yourself

842 For which TWO of these must you show your motor insurance certificate?

Mark two answers

- [ ] **A.** When you are taking your driving test
- [ ] **B.** When buying or selling a vehicle
- [ ] **C.** When a police officer asks you for it
- [ ] **D.** When you are taxing your vehicle
- [ ] **E.** When having an MOT inspection

843 Vehicle excise duty is often called 'Road Tax' or 'The Tax Disc'. You must

Mark one answer

- [ ] **A.** keep it with your registration document
- [ ] **B.** display it clearly on your vehicle
- [ ] **C.** keep it concealed safely in your vehicle
- [ ] **D.** carry it on you at all times

844 Motor cars must first have an MOT test certificate when they are

NI

Mark one answer

- [ ] **A.** one year old
- [ ] **B.** three years old
- [ ] **C.** five years old
- [ ] **D.** seven years old

845 Your vehicle needs a current MOT certificate. You do not have one. Until you do have one you will not be able to renew your

Mark one answer

- [ ] **A.** driving licence
- [ ] **B.** vehicle insurance
- [ ] **C.** road tax disc
- [ ] **D.** vehicle registration document

846 Which THREE pieces of information are found on a vehicle registration document?

Mark three answers

- [ ] **A.** Registered keeper
- [ ] **B.** Make of the vehicle
- [ ] **C.** Service history details
- [ ] **D.** Date of the MOT
- [ ] **E.** Type of insurance cover
- [ ] **F.** Engine size

847 You have a duty to contact the licensing authority when

Mark three answers

- A. you go abroad on holiday
- B. you change your vehicle
- C. you change your name
- D. your job status is changed
- E. your permanent address changes
- F. your job involves travelling abroad

848 You must notify the licensing authority when

Mark three answers

- A. your health affects your driving
- B. your eyesight does not meet a set standard
- C. you intend lending your vehicle
- D. your vehicle requires an MOT certificate
- E. you change your vehicle

849 Your vehicle is insured third party only. This covers

Mark two answers

- A. damage to your vehicle
- B. damage to other vehicles
- C. injury to yourself
- D. injury to others
- E. all damage and injury

850 Your motor insurance policy has an excess of £100. What does this mean?

Mark one answer

- A. The insurance company will pay the first £100 of any claim
- B. You will be paid £100 if you do not have an accident
- C. Your vehicle is insured for a value of £100 if it is stolen
- D. You will have to pay the first £100 of any claim

851 When you apply to renew your vehicle excise licence (tax disc) you must produc

Mark one answer

- A. a valid insurance certificate
- B. the old tax disc
- C. the vehicle handbook
- D. a valid driving licence

852 What is the legal minimum insurance cove you must have to drive on public roads?

Mark one answer

- A. Third party, fire and theft
- B. Comprehensive
- C. Third party only
- D. Personal injury cover

853 Which THREE of the following do you need before you can drive legally?

Mark three answers

- A. A valid driving licence with signature
- B. A valid tax disc displayed on your vehicle
- C. A vehicle service record
- D. Proper insurance cover
- E. Breakdown cover
- F. A vehicle handbook

854 The cost of your insurance may reduce if you

Mark one answer **NI**

- A. are under 25 years old
- B. do not wear glasses
- C. pass the driving test first time
- D. take the Pass Plus scheme

855 Which of the following may reduce the cost of your insurance?

Mark one answer **NI**

- A. Having a valid MOT certificate
- B. Taking a Pass Plus course
- C. Driving a powerful car
- D. Having penalty points on your licence

356 **The Pass Plus scheme has been created for new drivers. What is its main purpose?**

NI

lark one answer

- A. To allow you to drive faster
- B. To allow you to carry passengers
- C. To improve your basic skills
- D. To let you drive on motorways

357 **How long will a Statutory Off Road Notification (SORN) last for?**

lark one answer

- A. 12 months
- B. 24 months
- C. 3 years
- D. 10 years

358 **What is a Statutory Off Road Notification (SORN) declaration?**

NI

lark one answer

- A. A notification to tell VOSA that a vehicle does not have a current MOT
- B. Information kept by the police about the owner of the vehicle
- C. A notification to tell DVLA that a vehicle is not being used on the road
- D. Information held by insurance companies to check the vehicle is insured

359 **A Statutory Off Road Notification (SORN) declaration is**

NI

Mark one answer

- A. to tell DVLA that your vehicle is being used on the road but the MOT has expired
- B. to tell DVLA that you no longer own the vehicle
- C. to tell DVLA that your vehicle is not being used on the road
- D. to tell DVLA that you are buying a personal number plate

860 **You claim on your insurance to have your car repaired. Your policy has an excess of £100. What does this mean?**

Mark one answer

- A. The insurance company will pay the first £100 of any claim
- B. You will be paid £100 if you do not claim within one year
- C. Your vehicle is insured for a value of £100 if it is stolen
- D. You will have to pay the first £100 of the cost of repair to your car

861 **A Statutory Off Road Notification (SORN) is valid**

Mark one answer

- A. for as long as the vehicle has an MOT
- B. for 12 months only
- C. only if the vehicle is more than 3 years old
- D. provided the vehicle is insured

862 **A Statutory Off Road Notification (SORN) will last**

Mark one answer

- A. for the life of the vehicle
- B. for as long as you own the vehicle
- C. for 12 months only
- D. until the vehicle warranty expires

863 **What is the maximum specified fine for driving without insurance?**

NI

Mark one answer

- A. £50
- B. £500
- C. £1,000
- D. £5,000

864 **When should you update your Vehicle Registration Certificate (V5C)?**

Mark one answer

- A. When you pass your driving test
- B. When you move house
- C. When your vehicle needs an MOT
- D. When you have an accident

865 **Who is legally responsible for ensuring that a Vehicle Registration Certificate (V5C) is updated?**

Mark one answer

- A. The registered vehicle keeper
- B. The vehicle manufacturer
- C. Your insurance company
- D. The licensing authority

866 **The Pass Plus scheme is designed to**

Mark one answer NI

- A. give you a discount on your MOT
- B. improve your basic driving skills
- C. increase your mechanical knowledge
- D. allow you to drive anyone else's vehicle

867 **By taking part in the Pass Plus scheme you will**

Mark one answer NI

- A. never get any points on your licence
- B. be able to service your own car
- C. allow you to drive anyone else's vehicle
- D. improve your basic driving skills

868 **The Pass Plus scheme is aimed at all newly qualified drivers. It enables them to**

Mark one answer NI

- A. widen their driving experience
- B. supervise a learner driver
- C. increase their insurance premiums
- D. avoid mechanical breakdowns

869 **New drivers can take further training after passing the practical test. A Pass Plus course will help to**

Mark two answers NI

- A. improve your basic skills
- B. widen your experience
- C. increase your insurance premiums
- D. get cheaper road tax

870 **The Pass Plus scheme is operated by DSA for newly qualified drivers. It is intended to**

Mark one answer NI

- A. improve your basic skills
- B. reduce the cost of your driving licence
- C. prevent you from paying congestion charges
- D. allow you to supervise a learner driver

871 At the scene of an accident you should

Mark one answer

- A. not put yourself at risk
- B. go to those casualties who are screaming
- C. pull everybody out of their vehicles
- D. leave vehicle engines switched on

872 You are the first to arrive at the scene of an accident. Which FOUR of these should you do?

Mark four answers

- A. Leave as soon as another motorist arrives
- B. Switch off the vehicle engine(s)
- C. Move uninjured people away from the vehicle(s)
- D. Call the emergency services
- E. Warn other traffic

873 An accident has just happened. An injured person is lying in a busy road. What is the FIRST thing you should do to help?

Mark one answer

- A. Treat the person for shock
- B. Warn other traffic
- C. Place them in the recovery position
- D. Make sure the injured person is kept warm

874 You are the first person to arrive at an accident where people are badly injured. Which THREE should you do?

Mark three answers

- A. Switch on your own hazard warning lights
- B. Make sure that someone telephones for an ambulance
- C. Try and get people who are injured to drink something
- D. Move the people who are injured clear of their vehicles
- E. Get people who are not injured clear of the scene

875 You arrive at the scene of a motorcycle accident. The rider is injured. When should the helmet be removed?

Mark one answer

- A. Only when it is essential
- B. Always straight away
- C. Only when the motorcyclist asks
- D. Always, unless they are in shock

876 You arrive at a serious motorcycle accident. The motorcyclist is unconscious and bleeding. Your main priorities should be to

Mark three answers

- A. try to stop the bleeding
- B. make a list of witnesses
- C. check the casualty's breathing
- D. take the numbers of the vehicles involved
- E. sweep up any loose debris
- F. check the casualty's airways

877 You arrive at an accident. A motorcyclist is unconscious. Your FIRST priority is the casualty's

Mark one answer

- A. breathing
- B. bleeding
- C. broken bones
- D. bruising

878 At an accident a casualty is unconscious. Which THREE of the following should you check urgently?

Mark three answers

- A. Circulation
- B. Airway
- C. Shock
- D. Breathing
- E. Broken bones

879 **You arrive at the scene of an accident. It has just happened and someone is unconscious. Which of the following should be given urgent priority to help them?**

Mark three answers

- [ ] **A.** Clear the airway and keep it open
- [ ] **B.** Try to get them to drink water
- [ ] **C.** Check that they are breathing
- [ ] **D.** Look for any witnesses
- [ ] **E.** Stop any heavy bleeding
- [ ] **F.** Take the numbers of vehicles involved

880 **At an accident someone is unconscious. Your main priorities should be to**

Mark three answers

- [ ] **A.** sweep up the broken glass
- [ ] **B.** take the names of witnesses
- [ ] **C.** count the number of vehicles involved
- [ ] **D.** check the airway is clear
- [ ] **E.** make sure they are breathing
- [ ] **F.** stop any heavy bleeding

881 **You have stopped at the scene of an accident to give help. Which THREE things should you do?**

Mark three answers

- [ ] **A.** Keep injured people warm and comfortable
- [ ] **B.** Keep injured people calm by talking to them reassuringly
- [ ] **C.** Keep injured people on the move by walking them around
- [ ] **D.** Give injured people a warm drink
- [ ] **E.** Make sure that injured people are not left alone

882 **You arrive at the scene of an accident. It has just happened and someone is injured. Which THREE of the following should be given urgent priority?**

Mark three answers

- [ ] **A.** Stop any severe bleeding
- [ ] **B.** Get them a warm drink
- [ ] **C.** Check that their breathing is OK
- [ ] **D.** Take numbers of vehicles involved
- [ ] **E.** Look for witnesses
- [ ] **F.** Clear their airway and keep it open

883 **At an accident a casualty has stopped breathing. You should**

Mark two answers

- [ ] **A.** remove anything that is blocking the mouth
- [ ] **B.** keep the head tilted forwards as far as possible
- [ ] **C.** raise the legs to help with circulation
- [ ] **D.** try to give the casualty something to drink
- [ ] **E.** tilt the head back gently to clear the airway

884 **You are at the scene of an accident. Someone is suffering from shock. You should**

Mark four answers

- [ ] **A.** reassure them constantly
- [ ] **B.** offer them a cigarette
- [ ] **C.** keep them warm
- [ ] **D.** avoid moving them if possible
- [ ] **E.** avoid leaving them alone
- [ ] **F.** give them a warm drink

885 **Which of the following should you NOT do at the scene of an accident?**

Mark one answer

- [ ] **A.** Warn other traffic by switching on your hazard warning lights
- [ ] **B.** Call the emergency services immediately
- [ ] **C.** Offer someone a cigarette to calm them down
- [ ] **D.** Ask drivers to switch off their engines

886 **There has been an accident. The driver is suffering from shock. You should**

Mark two answers

- [ ] **A.** give them a drink
- [ ] **B.** reassure them
- [ ] **C.** not leave them alone
- [ ] **D.** offer them a cigarette
- [ ] **E.** ask who caused the accident

887 **You have to treat someone for shock at the scene of an accident. You should**

Mark one answer

- [ ] **A.** reassure them constantly
- [ ] **B.** walk them around to calm them down
- [ ] **C.** give them something cold to drink
- [ ] **D.** cool them down as soon as possible

888 **You arrive at the scene of a motorcycle accident. No other vehicle is involved. The rider is unconscious, lying in the middle of the road. The first thing you should do is**

Mark one answer

- [ ] **A.** move the rider out of the road
- [ ] **B.** warn other traffic
- [ ] **C.** clear the road of debris
- [ ] **D.** give the rider reassurance

889 **At an accident a small child is not breathing. When giving mouth to mouth you should breathe**

Mark one answer

- [ ] **A.** sharply
- [ ] **B.** gently
- [ ] **C.** heavily
- [ ] **D.** rapidly

890 **To start mouth to mouth on a casualty you should**

Mark three answers

- [ ] **A.** tilt their head forward
- [ ] **B.** clear the airway
- [ ] **C.** turn them on their side
- [ ] **D.** tilt their head back gently
- [ ] **E.** pinch the nostrils together
- [ ] **F.** put their arms across their chest

891 **When you are giving mouth to mouth you should only stop when**

Mark one answer

- [ ] **A.** you think the casualty is dead
- [ ] **B.** the casualty can breathe without help
- [ ] **C.** the casualty has turned blue
- [ ] **D.** you think the ambulance is coming

892 **You arrive at the scene of an accident. There has been an engine fire and someone's hands and arms have been burnt. You should NOT**

Mark one answer

- [ ] **A.** douse the burn thoroughly with cool liquid
- [ ] **B.** lay the casualty down
- [ ] **C.** remove anything sticking to the burn
- [ ] **D.** reassure them constantly

893 **You arrive at an accident where someone is suffering from severe burns. You should**

Mark one answer

- [ ] **A.** apply lotions to the injury
- [ ] **B.** burst any blisters
- [ ] **C.** remove anything stuck to the burns
- [ ] **D.** douse the burns with cool liquid

894 You arrive at the scene of an accident. A pedestrian has a severe bleeding wound on their leg, although it is not broken. What should you do?

Mark two answers
- [ ] A. Dab the wound to stop bleeding
- [ ] B. Keep both legs flat on the ground
- [ ] C. Apply firm pressure to the wound
- [ ] D. Raise the leg to lessen bleeding
- [ ] E. Fetch them a warm drink

895 You arrive at the scene of a crash. Someone is bleeding badly from an arm wound. There is nothing embedded in it. What should you do?

Mark one answer
- [ ] A. Apply pressure over the wound and keep the arm down
- [ ] B. Dab the wound
- [ ] C. Get them a drink
- [ ] D. Apply pressure over the wound and raise the arm

896 At an accident a casualty is unconscious but still breathing. You should only move them if

Mark one answer
- [ ] A. an ambulance is on its way
- [ ] B. bystanders advise you to
- [ ] C. there is further danger
- [ ] D. bystanders will help you to

897 At an accident you suspect a casualty has back injuries. The area is safe. You should

Mark one answer
- [ ] A. offer them a drink
- [ ] B. not move them
- [ ] C. raise their legs
- [ ] D. offer them a cigarette

898 At an accident it is important to look after the casualty. When the area is safe, you should

Mark one answer
- [ ] A. get them out of the vehicle
- [ ] B. give them a drink
- [ ] C. give them something to eat
- [ ] D. keep them in the vehicle

899 A tanker is involved in an accident. Which sign would show that the tanker is carrying dangerous goods?

Mark one answer
- [ ] A. LONG VEHICLE
- [ ] B. 2YE 1089
- [ ] C.
- [ ] D.

900 The police may ask you to produce which three of these documents following an accident?

Mark three answers
- [ ] A. Vehicle registration document
- [ ] B. Driving licence
- [ ] C. Theory test certificate
- [ ] D. Insurance certificate
- [ ] E. MOT test certificate
- [ ] F. Road tax disc

901 You see a car on the hard shoulder of a motorway with a HELP pennant displayed. This means the driver is most likely to be

Mark one answer
- [ ] A. a disabled person
- [ ] B. first aid trained
- [ ] C. a foreign visitor
- [ ] D. a rescue patrol person

902 On the motorway the hard shoulder should be used

Mark one answer

- A. to answer a mobile phone
- B. when an emergency arises
- C. for a short rest when tired
- D. to check a road atlas

903 For which TWO should you use hazard warning lights?

Mark two answers

- A. When you slow down quickly on a motorway because of a hazard ahead
- B. When you have broken down
- C. When you wish to stop on double yellow lines
- D. When you need to park on the pavement

904 When are you allowed to use hazard warning lights?

Mark one answer

- A. When stopped and temporarily obstructing traffic
- B. When travelling during darkness without headlights
- C. When parked for shopping on double yellow lines
- D. When travelling slowly because you are lost

905 You are on a motorway. A large box falls on to the road from a lorry. The lorry does not stop. You should

Mark one answer

- A. go to the next emergency telephone and inform the police
- B. catch up with the lorry and try to get the driver's attention
- C. stop close to the box until the police arrive
- D. pull over to the hard shoulder, then remove the box

906 There has been an accident. A motorcyclist is lying injured and unconscious. Unless it is essential, why should you usually not attempt to remove their helmet?

Mark one answer

- A. Because they may not want you to
- B. This could result in more serious injury
- C. They will get too cold if you do this
- D. Because you could scratch the helmet

907 After an accident, someone is unconscious in their vehicle. When should you call the emergency services?

Mark one answer

- A. Only as a last resort
- B. As soon as possible
- C. After you have woken them up
- D. After checking for broken bones

908 An accident casualty has an injured arm. They can move it freely, but it is bleeding. Why should you get them to keep it in a raised position?

Mark one answer

- A. Because it will ease the pain
- B. It will help them to be seen more easily
- C. To stop them touching other people
- D. It will help to reduce the bleeding

909 You are going through a congested tunnel and have to stop. What should you do?

Mark one answer

- A. Pull up very close to the vehicle in front to save space
- B. Ignore any message signs as they are never up to date
- C. Keep a safe distance from the vehicle in front
- D. Make a U-turn and find another route

910 **You are going through a tunnel. What should you look out for that warns of accidents or congestion?**

Mark one answer

- [ ] **A.** Hazard warning lines
- [ ] **B.** Other drivers flashing their lights
- [ ] **C.** Variable message signs
- [ ] **D.** Areas marked with hatch markings

911 **You are going through a tunnel. What systems are provided to warn of any accidents or congestion?**

Mark one answer

- [ ] **A.** Double white centre lines
- [ ] **B.** Variable message signs
- [ ] **C.** Chevron 'distance markers'
- [ ] **D.** Rumble strips

912 **While driving, a warning light on your vehicle's instrument panel comes on. You should**

Mark one answer

- [ ] **A.** continue if the engine sounds alright
- [ ] **B.** hope that it is just a temporary electrical fault
- [ ] **C.** deal with the problem when there is more time
- [ ] **D.** check out the problem quickly and safely

913 **You have broken down on a two-way road. You have a warning triangle. You should place the warning triangle at least how far from your vehicle?**

Mark one answer

- [ ] **A.** 5 metres (16 feet)
- [ ] **B.** 25 metres (82 feet)
- [ ] **C.** 45 metres (147 feet)
- [ ] **D.** 100 metres (328 feet)

914 **You break down on a level crossing. The lights have not yet begun to flash. Which THREE things should you do?**

Mark three answers

- [ ] **A.** Telephone the signal operator
- [ ] **B.** Leave your vehicle and get everyone clear
- [ ] **C.** Walk down the track and signal the next train
- [ ] **D.** Move the vehicle if a signal operator tells you to
- [ ] **E.** Tell drivers behind what has happened

915 **Your vehicle has broken down on an automatic railway level crossing. What should you do FIRST?**

Mark one answer

- [ ] **A.** Get everyone out of the vehicle and clear of the crossing
- [ ] **B.** Phone the signal operator so that trains can be stopped
- [ ] **C.** Walk along the track to give warning to any approaching trains
- [ ] **D.** Try to push the vehicle clear of the crossing as soon as possible

916 **Your tyre bursts while you are driving. Which TWO things should you do?**

Mark two answers

- [ ] **A.** Pull on the handbrake
- [ ] **B.** Brake as quickly as possible
- [ ] **C.** Pull up slowly at the side of the road
- [ ] **D.** Hold the steering wheel firmly to keep control
- [ ] **E.** Continue on at a normal speed

917 **Which TWO things should you do when a front tyre bursts?**

Mark two answers

- [ ] **A.** Apply the handbrake to stop the vehicle
- [ ] **B.** Brake firmly and quickly
- [ ] **C.** Let the vehicle roll to a stop
- [ ] **D.** Hold the steering wheel lightly
- [ ] **E.** Grip the steering wheel firmly

918 **Your vehicle has a puncture on a motorway. What should you do?**

Mark one answer

- [ ] **A.** Drive slowly to the next service area to get assistance
- [ ] **B.** Pull up on the hard shoulder. Change the wheel as quickly as possible
- [ ] **C.** Pull up on the hard shoulder. Use the emergency phone to get assistance
- [ ] **D.** Switch on your hazard lights. Stop in your lane

919 **Which of these items should you carry in your vehicle for use in the event of an accident?**

Mark three answers

- [ ] **A.** Road map
- [ ] **B.** Can of petrol
- [ ] **C.** Jump leads
- [ ] **D.** Fire extinguisher
- [ ] **E.** First aid kit
- [ ] **F.** Warning triangle

920 **You are in an accident on a two-way road. You have a warning triangle with you. At what distance before the obstruction should you place the warning triangle?**

Mark one answer

- [ ] **A.** 25 metres (82 feet)
- [ ] **B.** 45 metres (147 feet)
- [ ] **C.** 100 metres (328 feet)
- [ ] **D.** 150 metres (492 feet)

921 **You have broken down on a two-way road. You have a warning triangle. It should be displayed**

Mark one answer

- [ ] **A.** on the roof of your vehicle
- [ ] **B.** at least 150 metres (492 feet) behind your vehicle
- [ ] **C.** at least 45 metres (147 feet) behind your vehicle
- [ ] **D.** just behind your vehicle

922 **You have stalled in the middle of a level crossing and cannot restart the engine. The warning bell starts to ring. You should**

Mark one answer

- [ ] **A.** get out and clear of the crossing
- [ ] **B.** run down the track to warn the signal operator
- [ ] **C.** carry on trying to restart the engine
- [ ] **D.** push the vehicle clear of the crossing

923 **You are on the motorway. Luggage falls from your vehicle. What should you do?**

Mark one answer

- [ ] **A.** Stop at the next emergency telephone and contact the police
- [ ] **B.** Stop on the motorway and put on hazard lights while you pick it up
- [ ] **C.** Walk back up the motorway to pick it up
- [ ] **D.** Pull up on the hard shoulder and wave traffic down

924 **You are on a motorway. When can you use hazard warning lights?**

Mark two answers

- [ ] A. When a vehicle is following too closely
- [ ] B. When you slow down quickly because of danger ahead
- [ ] C. When you are towing another vehicle
- [ ] D. When driving on the hard shoulder
- [ ] E. When you have broken down on the hard shoulder

925 **You are involved in an accident with another vehicle. Someone is injured. Your vehicle is damaged. Which FOUR of the following should you find out?**

Mark four answers

- [ ] A. Whether the driver owns the other vehicle involved
- [ ] B. The other driver's name, address and telephone number
- [ ] C. The make and registration number of the other vehicle
- [ ] D. The occupation of the other driver
- [ ] E. The details of the other driver's vehicle insurance
- [ ] F. Whether the other driver is licensed to drive

926 **You have broken down on a motorway. When you use the emergency telephone you will be asked**

Mark three answers

- [ ] A. for the number on the telephone that you are using
- [ ] B. for your driving licence details
- [ ] C. for the name of your vehicle insurance company
- [ ] D. for details of yourself and your vehicle
- [ ] E. whether you belong to a motoring organisation

927 **You lose control of your car and damage a garden wall. No one is around. What must you do?**

Mark one answer **NI**

- [ ] A. Report the accident to the police within 24 hours
- [ ] B. Go back to tell the house owner the next da
- [ ] C. Report the accident to your insurance company when you get home
- [ ] D. Find someone in the area to tell them about it immediately

928 **Your engine catches fire. What should you do first?**

Mark one answer

- [ ] A. Lift the bonnet and disconnect the battery
- [ ] B. Lift the bonnet and warn other traffic
- [ ] C. Call a breakdown service
- [ ] D. Call the fire brigade

929 **Before driving through a tunnel what should you do?**

Mark one answer

- [ ] A. Switch your radio off
- [ ] B. Remove any sunglasses
- [ ] C. Close your sunroof
- [ ] D. Switch on windscreen wipers

930 **You are driving through a tunnel and the traffic is flowing normally. What should you do?**

Mark one answer

- [ ] A. Use parking lights
- [ ] B. Use front spot lights
- [ ] C. Use dipped headlights
- [ ] D. Use rear fog lights

931 **When approaching a tunnel it is good advice to**

Mark one answer

- [ ] A. put on your sunglasses
- [ ] B. check tyre pressures
- [ ] C. change to a lower gear
- [ ] D. tune your radio to a local channel

932 You are driving through a tunnel. Your vehicle breaks down. What should you do?

Mark one answer
- A. Switch on hazard warning lights
- B. Remain in your vehicle
- C. Wait for the police to find you
- D. Rely on CCTV cameras seeing you

933 Your vehicle breaks down in a tunnel. What should you do?

Mark one answer
- A. Stay in your vehicle and wait for the police
- B. Stand in the lane behind your vehicle to warn others
- C. Stand in front of your vehicle to warn oncoming drivers
- D. Switch on hazard lights then go and call for help immediately

934 You have an accident while driving through a tunnel. You are not injured but your vehicle CANNOT be driven. What should you do first?

Mark one answer
- A. Rely on other drivers phoning for the police
- B. Switch off the engine and switch on hazard lights
- C. Take the names of witnesses and other drivers
- D. Sweep up any debris that is in the road

935 When driving through a tunnel you should

Mark one answer
- A. Look out for variable message signs
- B. Use your air conditioning system
- C. Switch on your rear fog lights
- D. Always use your windscreen wipers

936 What TWO safeguards could you take against fire risk to your vehicle?

Mark two answers
- A. Keep water levels above maximum
- B. Carry a fire extinguisher
- C. Avoid driving with a full tank of petrol
- D. Use unleaded petrol
- E. Check out any strong smell of petrol
- F. Use low octane fuel

937 Your vehicle catches fire while driving through a tunnel. It is still driveable. What should you do?

Mark one answer
- A. Leave it where it is with the engine running
- B. Pull up, then walk to an emergency telephone point
- C. Park it away from the carriageway
- D. Drive it out of the tunnel if you can do so

938 You are driving through a tunnel. Your vehicle catches fire. What should you do?

Mark one answer
- A. Continue through the tunnel if you can
- B. Turn your vehicle around immediately
- C. Reverse out of the tunnel
- D. Carry out an emergency stop

939 You are in a tunnel. Your vehicle is on fire and you CANNOT drive it. What should you do?

Mark two answers
- A. Stay in the vehicle and close the windows
- B. Switch on hazard warning lights
- C. Leave the engine running
- D. Try and put out the fire
- E. Switch off all of your lights
- F. Wait for other people to phone for help

940 You are driving through a tunnel. There has been an accident and the car in front is on fire and blocking the road. What should you do?

Mark one answer
- [ ] A. Overtake and continue as quickly as you can
- [ ] B. Lock all the doors and windows
- [ ] C. Switch on hazard warning lights
- [ ] D. Stop, then reverse out of the tunnel

941 You are at an incident where a casualty is unconscious. Their breathing should be checked. This should be done for at least

Mark one answer
- [ ] A. 2 seconds
- [ ] B. 10 seconds
- [ ] C. 1 minute
- [ ] D. 2 minutes

942 Following a collision someone has suffered a burn. The burn needs to be cooled. What is the shortest time it should be cooled for?

Mark one answer
- [ ] A. 5 minutes
- [ ] B. 10 minutes
- [ ] C. 15 minutes
- [ ] D. 20 minutes

943 After a collision someone has suffered a burn. The burn needs to be cooled. What is the shortest time it should be cooled for?

Mark one answer
- [ ] A. 30 seconds
- [ ] B. 60 seconds
- [ ] C. 5 minutes
- [ ] D. 10 minutes

944 A casualty is not breathing normally. Chest compressions should be given. At what rate?

Mark one answer
- [ ] A. 50 per minute
- [ ] B. 100 per minute
- [ ] C. 200 per minute
- [ ] D. 250 per minute

945 A casualty is not breathing. To maintain circulation compressions should be given. What is the correct depth to press?

Mark one answer
- [ ] A. 1 to 2 centimetres
- [ ] B. 4 to 5 centimetres
- [ ] C. 10 to 15 centimetres
- [ ] D. 15 to 20 centimetres

946 A person has been injured. They may be suffering from shock. What are the warning signs to look for?

Mark one answer
- [ ] A. Flushed complexion
- [ ] B. Warm dry skin
- [ ] C. Slow pulse
- [ ] D. Pale grey skin

947 You suspect that an injured person may be suffering from shock. What are the warning signs to look for?

Mark one answer
- [ ] A. Warm dry skin
- [ ] B. Sweating
- [ ] C. Slow pulse
- [ ] D. Skin rash

948 A person is injured and lying on their back. They are unconscious but breathing normally. What treatment should be given?

Mark one answer
- [ ] A. Try to get them to drink water
- [ ] B. Raise their legs above head height
- [ ] C. Place them in the recovery position
- [ ] D. Leave them in the position found

949 An injured person has been placed in the recovery position. They are unconscious but breathing normally. What else should be done?

Mark one answer
- [ ] A. Press firmly between the shoulders
- [ ] B. Place their arms by their side
- [ ] C. Give them a hot sweet drink
- [ ] D. Check the airway is clear

950 You are towing a small trailer on a busy three-lane motorway. All the lanes are open. You must

Mark two answers

- A. not exceed 60mph
- B. not overtake
- C. have a stabiliser fitted
- D. use only the left and centre lanes

951 Any load that is carried on a roof rack should be

Mark one answer

- A. securely fastened when driving
- B. loaded towards the rear of the vehicle
- C. visible in your exterior mirror
- D. covered with plastic sheeting

952 You are planning to tow a caravan. Which of these will mostly help to aid the vehicle handling?

Mark one answer

- A. A jockey wheel fitted to the tow bar
- B. Power steering fitted to the towing vehicle
- C. Anti-lock brakes fitted to the towing vehicle
- D. A stabiliser fitted to the tow bar

953 If a trailer swerves or snakes when you are towing it you should

Mark one answer

- A. ease off the accelerator and reduce your speed
- B. let go of the steering wheel and let it correct itself
- C. brake hard and hold the pedal down
- D. increase your speed as quickly as possible

954 How can you stop a caravan snaking from side to side?

Mark one answer

- A. Turn the steering wheel slowly to each side
- B. Accelerate to increase your speed
- C. Stop as quickly as you can
- D. Slow down very gradually

955 On which TWO occasions might you inflate your tyres to more than the recommended normal pressure?

Mark two answers

- A. When the roads are slippery
- B. When driving fast for a long distance
- C. When the tyre tread is worn below 2mm
- D. When carrying a heavy load
- E. When the weather is cold
- F. When the vehicle is fitted with anti-lock brakes

956 A heavy load on your roof rack will

Mark one answer

- A. improve the road holding
- B. reduce the stopping distance
- C. make the steering lighter
- D. reduce stability

957 Are passengers allowed to ride in a caravan that is being towed?

Mark one answer

- A. Yes, if they are over 14
- B. No, not at any time
- C. Only if all the seats in the towing vehicle are full
- D. Only if a stabiliser is fitted

958 **You are towing a caravan along a motorway. The caravan begins to swerve from side to side. What should you do?**

Mark one answer

- [ ] **A.** Ease off the accelerator slowly
- [ ] **B.** Steer sharply from side to side
- [ ] **C.** Do an emergency stop
- [ ] **D.** Speed up very quickly

959 **A trailer must stay securely hitched up to the towing vehicle. What additional safety device can be fitted to the trailer braking system?**

Mark one answer

- [ ] **A.** Stabiliser
- [ ] **B.** Jockey wheel
- [ ] **C.** Corner steadies
- [ ] **D.** Breakaway cable

960 **Overloading your vehicle can seriously affect the**

Mark two answers

- [ ] **A.** gearbox
- [ ] **B.** steering
- [ ] **C.** handling
- [ ] **D.** battery life
- [ ] **E.** journey time

961 **Who is responsible for making sure that a vehicle is not overloaded?**

Mark one answer

- [ ] **A.** The driver of the vehicle
- [ ] **B.** The owner of the items being carried
- [ ] **C.** The person who loaded the vehicle
- [ ] **D.** The licensing authority

962 **You are carrying a child in your car. They are under three years of age. Which of these is a suitable restraint?**

Mark one answer

- [ ] **A.** A child seat
- [ ] **B.** An adult holding a child
- [ ] **C.** An adult seat belt
- [ ] **D.** An adult lap belt

963 **Why would you fit a stabiliser before towing a caravan?**

Mark one answer

- [ ] **A.** It will help with stability when driving in crosswinds
- [ ] **B.** It will allow heavy items to be loaded behind the axle
- [ ] **C.** It will help you to raise and lower the jockey wheel
- [ ] **D.** It will allow you to tow without the breakaway cable

964 **You wish to tow a trailer. Where would you find the maximum noseweight of your vehicle's tow ball?**

Mark one answer

- [ ] **A.** In the vehicle handbook
- [ ] **B.** In The Highway Code
- [ ] **C.** In your vehicle registration certificate
- [ ] **D.** In your licence documents

Part 5
Glossary

Accelerate
To make the vehicle move faster by pressing the right-hand pedal.

Advanced stop lines
A marked area on the road at traffic lights, which permits cyclists or buses to wait in front of other traffic.

Adverse weather
Bad weather that makes driving difficult or dangerous.

Alert
Quick to notice possible hazards.

Anticipation
Looking out for hazards and taking action before a problem starts.

Anti-lock brakes
Brakes that stop the wheels locking so that you are less likely to skid on a slippery road.

Aquaplane
To slide out of control on a wet road surface.

Articulated vehicle
A long vehicle that is divided into two or more sections joined by cables.

Attitude
The way you think or feel, which affects the way you drive. Especially, whether you are patient and polite, or impatient and aggressive.

Automatic
A vehicle with gears that change by themselves as you speed up or slow down.

Awareness
Taking notice of the road and traffic conditions around you at all times.

Black ice
An invisible film of ice that forms over the road surface, creating very dangerous driving conditions.

Blind spot
The section of road behind you which you cannot see in your mirrors. You 'cover' your blind spot by looking over your shoulder before moving off or overtaking.

Brake fade
Loss of power to the brakes when you have been using them for a long time without taking your foot off the brake pedal. For example, when driving down a steep hill. The brakes will overheat and not work properly.

Braking distance
The distance you must allow to slow the vehicle in order to come to a stop.

Brow
The highest point of a hill.

Built-up area
A town, or place with lots of buildings.

Carriageway
One side of a road or motorway. A 'dual carriageway' has two lanes on each side of a central reservation.

Catalytic converter
A piece of equipment fitted in the exhaust system that changes harmful gases into less harmful ones.

Chicane
A sharp double bend that has been put into a road to make traffic slow down.

Child restraint
A child seat or special seat belt for children. It keeps them safe and stops them moving around in the car.

Clearway
A road where no stopping is allowed at any time. The sign for a clearway is a red cross in a red circle on a blue background.

Coasting
Driving a vehicle without using any of the gears. That is, with your foot on the clutch pedal and the car in neutral.

Commentary driving
Talking to yourself about what you see on the road ahead and what action you are going to take – an aid to concentration.

Comprehensive insurance
A motor insurance policy that pays for repairs even if you cause an accident.

Concentration
Keeping all your attention on your driving.

Conditions
How good or bad the road surface is, volume of traffic on the road, and what the weather is like.

Congestion
Heavy traffic that makes it difficult to get to where you want to go.

Consideration
Thinking about other road users and not just yourself. For example, letting another driver go first at a junction, or stopping at a zebra crossing to let pedestrians cross over.

Contraflow
When traffic on a motorway follows signs to move to the opposite carriageway for a short distance because of roadworks. (During a contraflow, there is traffic driving in both directions on the same side of the motorway.)

Coolant
Liquid in the radiator that removes heat from the engine.

Defensive driving
Driving safely without taking risks, looking out for hazards and thinking for others.

Disqualified
Stopped from doing something (eg driving) by law, because you have broken the law.

Distraction
Anything that stops you concentrating on your driving, such as chatting to passengers or on your mobile phone.

Document
An official paper or card, eg your driving licence.

Dual carriageway
One side of a road or motorway, with two lanes on each side of a central reservation.

Engine braking – see also gears
Using the low gears to keep your speed down. For example, when you are driving down a steep hill and you want to stop the vehicle running away. Using the gears instead of braking will help to prevent brake fade.

Environment
The world around us and the air we breathe.

Exceed
Go higher than an upper limit.

Exhaust emissions
Gases that come out of the exhaust pipe to form part of the outside air.

Field of vision
How far you can see in front and around you when you are driving.

Filler cap
Provides access to the vehicle's fuel tank, for filling up with petrol or diesel.

Fog lights
Extra bright rear (and sometimes front) lights which may be switched on in conditions of very poor visibility.You must remember to switch them off when visibility improves, as they can dazzle and distract other drivers.

Ford
A place in a stream or river which is shallow enough to drive across with care.

Four-wheel drive (4WD)
On a conventional vehicle, steering and engine speed affect just two 'drive' wheels. On 4WD, they affect all four wheels, ensuring optimum grip on loose ground.

Frustration
Feeling annoyed because you cannot drive as fast as you want to because of other drivers or heavy traffic.

Fuel consumption
The amount of fuel (petrol or diesel) that your vehicle uses. Different vehicles have different rates of consumption. Increased fuel consumption means using more fuel. Decreased fuel consumption means using less fuel.

Fuel gauge
A display or dial on the instrument panel that tells you how much fuel (petrol or diesel) you have left.

Gantry
An overhead platform like a high narrow bridge that displays electric signs on a motorway.

Gears
Control the speed of the engine in relation to the vehicle's speed. May be hand operated (manual) or automatically controlled. In a low gear (such as first or second) the engine runs more slowly. In a high gear (such as fourth or fifth), it runs more quickly. Putting the car into a lower gear as you drive can create the effect of engine braking – forcing the engine to run more slowly.

Handling
How well your vehicle moves or responds when you steer or brake.

Harass
To drive in away that makes other road users afraid.

Hard shoulder
The single lane to the left of the inside lane on a motorway, which is for emergency use only. You should not drive on the hard shoulder except in an emergency, or when there are signs telling you to use the hard shoulder because of roadworks.

Harsh braking (or harsh acceleration)
Using the brake or accelerator too hard so as to cause wear on the engine.

Hazard warning lights
Flashing amber lights which you should use only when you have broken down. On a motorway you can use them to warn other drivers behind of a hazard ahead.

High-sided vehicle
A van or truck with tall sides, or a tall trailer such as a caravan or horse-box, that is at risk of being blown off-course in strong winds.

Impatient
Not wanting to wait for pedestrians and other road users.

Inflate
To blow up – to put air in your tyres until they are at the right pressures.

Instrument panel
The car's electrical controls and gauges, set behind the steering wheel. Also called the dashboard.

Intimidate
To make someone feel afraid.

Involved
Being part of something. For example, being one of the drivers in an accident.

Jump leads
A pair of thick electric cables with clips at either end. You use it to charge a flat battery by connecting it to the live battery in another vehicle.

Junction
A place where two or more roads join.

Liability
Being legally responsible.

Manoeuvre
Using the controls to make your car move in a particular direction. For example turning, reversing or parking.

Manual
By hand. In a car that is a 'manual' or has manual gears, you have to change the gears yourself.

Maximum
The largest possible; 'maximum speed' is the highest speed allowed.

Minimum
The smallest possible.

Mirrors
Modern cars have a minimum of three rear view mirrors: one in the centre of the windscreen, and one on each front door. Additional mirrors may be required on longer vehicles, or when towing a high trailer such as a caravan. Some mirrors may be curved (convex or concave) to increase the field of vision. The mirror on the windscreen can be turned to anti-dazzle position, if glare from headlights behind creates a distraction.

Mobility
The ability to move around easily.

Monotonous
Boring. For example, a long stretch of motorway with no variety and nothing interesting to see.

MOT

The test that proves your car is safe to drive. Your MOT certificate is one of the important documents for your vehicle.

Motorway

A fast road that has two or more lanes on each side and a hard shoulder. Drivers must join or leave it on the left, via a motorway junction. Many kinds of slower vehicles – such as bicycles – are not allowed on motorways.

Multiple-choice questions

Questions with several possible answers where you have to try to choose the right one.

Observation

The ability to notice important information, such as hazards developing ahead.

Obstruct

To get in the way of another road user.

Octagonal

Having eight sides.

Oil level

The amount of oil needed for the engine to run effectively.The oil level should be checked as part of your regular maintenance routine, and the oil replaced as necessary.

Pedestrian

A person walking.

Pegasus crossing

An unusual kind of crossing. It has a button high up for horse riders to push (Pegasus was a flying horse in Greek legend).

Pelican crossing

A crossing with traffic lights that pedestrians can use by pushing a button. Cars must give way to pedestrians on the crossing while the amber light is flashing. You must give pedestrians enough time to get to the other side of the road.

Perception

Seeing or noticing (as in Hazard Perception).

Peripheral vision

The area around the edges of your field of vision.

Positive attitude

Being sensible and obeying the law when you drive.

Priority

The vehicle or other road user that is allowed by law to go first is the one that has priority.

Provisional licence

A first driving licence. all learner drivers must get one before they start having lessons.

Puffin crossing

A type of pedestrian crossing that does not have a flashing amber light phase.

Reaction time

The amount of time it takes you to see a hazard and decide what to do about it.

Red route

You see these in London and some other cities. Double red lines at the edge of the road tell you that you must not stop or park there at any time. Single red lines have notices with times when you must not stop or park. Some red routes have marked bays for either parking or loading at certain times.

Red warning triangle

An item of safety equipment to carry in your car in case you break down. You can place the triangle 45m behind your car on the same side of the road. It warns traffic that your vehicle is causing an obstruction. (Do not use these on motorways.)

Residential areas

Areas of housing where people live. The speed limit is 30mph or sometimes 20mph.

Road hump

A low bump built across the road to slow vehicles down. Also called 'sleeping policemen'.

Rumble strips

Raised strips across the road near a roundabout or junction that change the sound the tyres make on the road surface, warning drivers to slow down. They are also used on motorways to separate the main carriageway from the hard shoulder.

Safety margin
The amount of space you need to leave between your vehicle and the one in front so that you are not in danger of crashing into it if the driver slows down suddenly or stops. Safety margins have to be longer in wet or icy conditions.

Separation distance
The amount of space you need to leave between your vehicle and the one in front so that you are not in danger of crashing into it if the driver slows down suddenly or stops. The separation distance must be longer in wet or icy conditions.

Security coded radio
To deter thieves, a radio or CD unit which requires a security code (or pin number) to operate it.

Single carriageway
Generally, a road with one lane in each direction.

Skid
When the tyres fail to grip the surface of the road, the subsequent loss of control of the vehicle's movement is called a skid. Usually caused by harsh or fierce braking, steering or acceleration.

Snaking
Moving from side to side. This sometimes happens with caravans or trailers when you drive too fast, or they are not properly loaded.

Staggered junction
Where you drive cross another road. Instead of going straight across, you have to go a bit to the right or left.

Steering
Control of the direction of the vehicle. May be affected by road surface conditions: when the steering wheel turns very easily, steering is 'light', and when you have to pull hard on the wheel it is described as 'heavy'.

Sterile
Clean and free from bacteria.

Stopping distance
The time it takes for you to stop your vehicle – made up of 'thinking distance' and 'braking distance'.

Supervisor
Someone who sits in the passenger seat with a learner driver. They must be over 21 and have held a full driving licence for at least three years.

Tailgating
Driving too closely behind another vehicle – either to harass the driver in front or to help you in thick fog.

Tax disc
The disc you display on your windscreen to show that you have taxed your car (see Vehicle Excise Duty, below).

Thinking distance
The time it takes you to notice something and take the right action. You need to add thinking distance to your braking distance to make up your total stopping distance.

Third party insurance
An insurance policy that insures you against any claim by passengers or other persons for damage or injury to their person or property.

Toucan crossing
A type of pedestrian crossing that does not have a flashing amber light phase, and cyclists are allowed to ride across.

Tow
To pull something behind your vehicle. It could be a caravan or trailer.

Traffic calming measures
Speed humps, chicanes and other devices placed in roads to slow traffic down.

Tram
A public transport vehicle which moves along the streets on fixed rails, usually electrically powered by overhead lines.

Tread depth
The depth of the grooves in a car's tyres that help them grip the road surface. The grooves must all be at least 1.6mm deep.

Turbulence
Strong movement of air. For example, when a large vehicle passes a much smaller one.

wo-second rule

In normal driving, the ideal minimum distance between you and the vehicle in front can be timed using the 'two-second' rule. As the vehicle in front passes a fixed object (such as a signpost), say to yourself 'Only a fool breaks the two second rule'. It takes two seconds to say it. If you have passed the same object before you finish, you are too close – pull back.

yre pressures

The amount of air which must be pumped into a tyre in order for it to be correctly blown up.

ehicle Excise Duty

The tax you pay for your vehicle so that you may drive it on public roads.

Vehicle Registration Document

A record of details about a vehicle and its owner.

Vehicle watch scheme

A system for identifying vehicles that may have been stolen.

Vulnerable

At risk of harm or injury.

Waiting restrictions

Times when you may not park or load your vehicle in a particular area.

Wheel balancing

To ensure smooth rotation at all speeds, wheels need to be 'balanced' correctly. This is a procedure done at a garage or tyre centre, when each wheel is removed for testing. Balancing may involve minor adjustment with the addition of small weights, to avoid wheel wobble.

Wheel spin

When the vehicle's wheels spin round out of control with no grip on the road surface.

Zebra crossing

A pedestrian crossing without traffic lights. It has an orange light, and is marked by black and white stripes on the road. Drivers must stop for pedestrians to cross.

Part 6 The Answers to the Theory Test Questions

ALERTNESS – SECTION 1

1 C	2 BDF	3 C	4 D	5 C	6 C	7 C	8 C	9 B
10 D	11 AC	12 ABCD	13 AD	14 AB	15 AB	16 ABCD	17 B	18 D
19 B	20 C	21 B	22 B	23 ABE	24 C	25 B	26 B	27 D
28 C	29 C	30 C	31 A	32 D	33 D	34 B	35 A	36 D
37 B	38 B	39 B						

ATTITUDE – SECTION 2

40 D	41 A	42 C	43 B	44 C	45 D	46 D	47 B	48 B
49 BCD	50 ABE	51 A	52 D	53 B	54 A	55 A	56 B	57 A
58 A	59 C	60 A	61 B	62 D	63 D	64 D	65 A	66 A
67 B	68 C	69 A	70 C	71 A	72 C	73 B	74 C	75 DE
76 B	77 D	78 B	79 C	80 AB	81 D	82 C	83 A	84 A
85 B	86 A	87 D	88 C					

SAFETY AND YOUR VEHICLE – SECTION 3

89 B	90 AB	91 ABF	92 BEF	93 C	94 ACF	95 C	96 B	97 D
98 C	99 D	100 D	101 D	102 A	103 AE	104 D	105 B	106 D
107 D	108 A	109 B	110 BCDF	111 D	112 D	113 BC	114 BC	115 A
116 D	117 A	118 B	119 B	120 D	121 C	122 D	123 D	124 D
125 B	126 B	127 B	128 D	129 ABF	130 ABC	131 ABC	132 BDF	133 ADE
134 BD	135 B	136 CDE	137 B	138 B	139 C	140 B	141 DE	142 A
143 C	144 B	145 D	146 D	147 D	148 B	149 C	150 A	151 B
152 D	153 C	154 A	155 B	156 AB	157 A	158 D	159 B	160 BCD
161 C	162 CD	163 A	164 A	165 D	166 C	167 B	168 B	169 B
170 D	171 ABE	172 ADE	173 D	174 A	175 B	176 C	177 D	178 A
179 B	180 C	181 D	182 A	183 C	184 D	185 B	186 B	187 A
188 B	189 D	190 B	191 A	192 C	193 D	194 B	195 B	196 D
197 B	198 B	199 C	200 A	201 A	202 A			

SAFETY MARGINS – SECTION 4

203 D	204 D	205 BC	206 B	207 D	208 D	209 C	210 C	211 A
212 B	213 A	214 B	215 A	216 B	217 AE	218 C	219 B	220 C
221 BDEF	222 B	223 D	224 A	225 C	226 A	227 AD	228 C	229 B
230 B	231 B	232 C	233 C	234 B	235 B	236 BC	237 C	238 C
239 B	240 C	241 D	242 BC	243 B	244 ACE	245 D	246 D	247 D
248 A	249 D	250 BD	251 D	252 B	253 A	254 D	255 A	256 B
257 B								

Answers to Questions

HAZARD AWARENESS – SECTION 5

258 D	259 CD	260 B	261 C	262 A	263 D	264 ACE	265 D	266 C
267 A	268 C	269 C	270 D	271 B	272 B	273 A	274 A	275 A
276 C	277 C	278 CD	279 A	280 B	281 A	282 C	283 BF	284 B
285 AE	286 A	287 D	288 D	289 C	290 B	291 B	292 C	293 A
294 B	295 B	296 CD	297 B	298 D	299 B	300 A	301 A	302 D
303 A	304 B	305 AE	306 C	307 B	308 BC	309 D	310 B	311 B
312 C	313 D	314 C	315 CD	316 AC	317 AB	318 A	319 A	320 B
321 A	322 ABC	323 C	324 C	325 C	326 ABE	327 C	328 D	329 D
330 C	331 C	332 D	333 ABD	334 ABC	335 D	336 C	337 AB	338 B
339 B	340 CD	341 D	342 ACE	343 ABE	344 A	345 A	346 D	347 D
348 A	349 D	350 A	351 A	352 ACD	353 B	354 B	355 ACE	356 C

VULNERABLE ROAD USERS – SECTION 6

357 D	358 D	359 C	360 C	361 B	362 D	363 D	364 D	365 B
366 C	367 D	368 A	369 D	370 D	371 B	372 D	373 B	374 D
375 D	376 C	377 AC	378 C	379 C	380 A	381 D	382 C	383 D
384 ABC	385 C	386 B	387 B	388 AC	389 ABD	390 B	391 D	392 A
393 A	394 D	395 D	396 A	397 A	398 C	399 C	400 C	401 D
402 ACE	403 D	404 B	405 A	406 C	407 D	408 C	409 C	410 A
411 D	412 D	413 A	414 A	415 B	416 B	417 D	418 C	419 C
420 B	421 C	422 AE	423 D	424 C	425 C	426 B	427 B	428 D
429 D	430 A	431 C	432 C	433 D	434 D	435 B	436 A	437 D
438 B	439 B	440 C	441 D	442 A				

OTHER TYPES OF VEHICLE – SECTION 7

443 A	444 A	445 B	446 B	447 D	448 B	449 A	450 BC	451 B
452 D	453 A	454 A	455 C	456 B	457 D	458 D	459 D	460 B
461 B	462 B	463 AC	464 BD	465 B	466 D	467 D	468 A	469 A

VEHICLE HANDLING – SECTION 8

470 ACE	471 A	472 CD	473 D	474 A	475 BDF	476 C	477 D	478 C
479 DE	480 D	481 B	482 C	483 C	484 D	485 D	486 D	487 C
488 C	489 BD	490 BD	491 D	492 B	493 C	494 CE	495 C	496 D
497 A	498 A	499 C	500 B	501 ABDF	502 A	503 D	504 B	505 B
506 AB	507 BD	508 A	509 ACD	510 B	511 A	512 C	513 B	514 A
515 A	516 C	517 C	518 A	519 B	520 C	521 D	522 B	523 D
524 ABD	525 D	526 C	527 C	528 C	529 D	530 D	531 A	532 B

MOTORWAY RULES – SECTION 9

533 ADEF	534 ADEF	535 D	536 D	537 D	538 D	539 A	540 B	541 C
542 BE	543 C	544 A	545 C	546 A	547 D	548 A	549 C	550 C
551 C	552 C	553 C	554 C	555 B	556 C	557 B	558 B	559 A
560 B	561 B	562 D	563 CDF	564 C	565 D	566 C	567 D	568 A
569 B	570 B	571 D	572 C	573 A	574 B	575 D	576 A	577 D
578 D	579 A	580 C	581 B	582 B	583 C	584 A	585 A	586 B
587 D	588 D	589 B	590 D	591 D	592 B	593 C	594 D	595 D
596 C	597 A	598 D						

RULES OF THE ROAD – SECTION 10

599 C	600 C	601 D	602 B	603 A	604 C	605 D	606 ADF	607 AD
608 A	609 B	610 A	611 B	612 A	613 D	614 A	615 D	616 D
617 C	618 A	619 ACE	620 B	621 C	622 D	623 BD	624 B	625 A
626 D	627 C	628 A	629 B	630 CDE	631 B	632 AE	633 B	634 A
635 ABD	636 A	637 B	638 B	639 A	640 D	641 A	642 D	643 C
644 D	645 D	646 BEF	647 D	648 D	649 D	650 C	651 C	652 D
653 A	654 A	655 A	656 C	657 B	658 A	659 D	660 AB	661 A
662 D	663 D	664 A	665 D	666 B	667 ABC	668 D	669 A	670 D
671 A	672 A	673 B	674 C					

ROAD AND TRAFFIC SIGNS – SECTION 11

675 D	676 D	677 A	678 A	679 B	680 A	681 D	682 B	683 D
684 D	685 D	686 A	687 C	688 B	689 D	690 C	691 B	692 A
693 B	694 B	695 C	696 C	697 A	698 C	699 B	700 C	701 B
702 D	703 D	704 C	705 D	706 C	707 B	708 C	709 D	710 A
711 D	712 B	713 D	714 B	715 A	716 A	717 A	718 A	719 B
720 B	721 A	722 D	723 ACEF	724 C	725 A	726 A	727 C	728 D
729 B	730 C	731 B	732 B	733 B	734 B	735 D	736 A	737 C
738 A	739 C	740 D	741 A	742 C	743 B	744 D	745 A	746 B
747 B	748 C	749 C	750 A	751 A	752 C	753 C	754 B	755 D
756 C	757 B	758 A	759 C	760 D	761 C	762 B	763 A	764 A
765 C	766 BDF	767 A	768 C	769 C	770 B	771 B	772 A	773 C
774 A	775 B	776 A	777 B	778 D	779 D	780 B	781 A	782 A
783 D	784 C	785 D	786 C	787 B	788 C	789 C	790 A	791 B
792 D	793 B	794 B	795 A	796 D	797 A	798 B	799 B	800 D
801 C	802 B	803 A	804 B	805 A	806 C	807 A	808 B	809 A
810 A	811 C	812 C	813 A	814 B	815 C	816 B	817 A	818 C
819 A	820 A	821 C	822 C	823 B	824 B	825 B	826 A	827 B
828 B	829 A							

Answers to Questions

DOCUMENTS – SECTION 12

830 C	831 B	832 B	833 BE	834 C	835 C	836 B	837 D	838 AB
839 D	840 D	841 CDE	842 CD	843 B	844 B	845 C	846 ABF	847 BCE
848 ABE	849 BD	850 D	851 A	852 C	853 ABD	854 D	855 B	856 C
857 A	858 C	859 C	860 D	861 B	862 C	863 D	864 B	865 A
866 B	867 D	868 A	869 AB	870 A				

ACCIDENTS – SECTION 13

871 A	872 BCDE	873 B	874 ABE	875 A	876 ACF	877 A	878 ABD	879 ACE
880 DEF	881 ABE	882 ACF	883 AE	884 ACDE	885 C	886 BC	887 A	888 B
889 B	890 BDE	891 B	892 C	893 D	894 CD	895 D	896 C	897 B
898 D	899 B	900 BDE	901 A	902 B	903 AB	904 A	905 A	906 B
907 B	908 D	909 C	910 C	911 B	912 D	913 C	914 ABD	915 A
916 CD	917 CE	918 C	919 DEF	920 B	921 C	922 A	923 A	924 BE
925 ABCE	926 ADE	927 A	928 D	929 B	930 C	931 D	932 A	933 D
934 B	935 A	936 BE	937 D	938 A	939 BD	940 C	941 B	942 B
943 D	944 B	945 B	946 D	947 B	948 C	949 D		

VEHICLE LOADING – SECTION 14

950 AD	951 A	952 D	953 A	954 D	955 BD	956 D	957 B	958 A
959 D	960 BC	961 A	962 A	963 A	964 A			

Part 7 The Highway Code

Contents Page

Introduction

This Highway Code applies to England, Scotland and Wales. ***The Highway Code*** is essential reading for everyone.

The most vulnerable road users are pedestrians, particularly children, older or disabled people, cyclists, motorcyclists and horse riders. It is important that all road users are aware of The Code and are considerate towards each other. This applies to pedestrians as much as to drivers and riders.

Many of the rules in the Code are legal requirements, and if you disobey these rules you are committing a criminal offence. You may be fined, given penalty points on your licence or be disqualified from driving. In the most serious cases you may be sent to prison. Such rules are identified by the use of the words **'MUST/MUST NOT'**. In addition, the rule includes an abbreviated reference to the legislation which creates the offence. An explanation of the abbreviations is given in Annexe 4 – The road user and the law.

Although failure to comply with the other rules of the Code will not, in itself, cause a person to be prosecuted, ***The Highway Code*** may be used in evidence in any court proceedings under the Traffic Acts (see Annexe 4 – The road user and the law) to establish liability. This includes rules which use advisory wording such as 'should/should not' or 'do/do not'.

Knowing and applying the rules contained in ***The Highway Code*** could significantly reduce road casualties. Cutting the number of deaths and injuries that occur on our roads every day is a responsibility we all share. ***The Highway Code*** can help us discharge that responsibility. Further information on driving/riding techniques can be found in 'The Official DSA Guide to Driving – the essential skills' and 'The Official DSA Guide to Riding – the essential skills'.

Rules for pedestrians

General guidance

1. Pavements (including any path along the side of a road) should be used if provided. Where possible, avoid being next to the kerb with your back to the traffic. If you have to step into the road, look both ways first. Always show due care and consideration for others.

2. If there is no pavement keep to the right-hand side of the road so that you can see oncoming traffic. You should take extra care and

- be prepared to walk in single file, especially on narrow roads or in poor light
- keep close to the side of the road.

It may be safer to cross the road well before a sharp right-hand bend so that oncoming traffic has a better chance of seeing you. Cross back after the bend.

3. Help other road users to see you. Wear or carry something light-coloured, bright or fluorescent in poor daylight conditions. When it is dark, use reflective materials (e.g. armbands, sashes, waistcoats, jackets, footwear), which can be seen by drivers using headlights up to three times as far away as non-reflective materials.

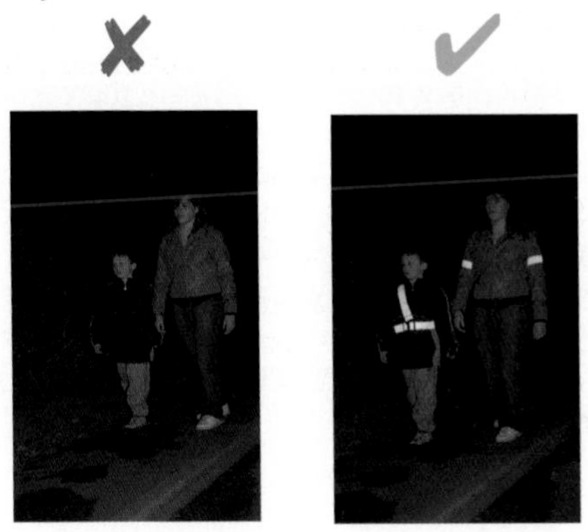

Help yourself to be seen

4. Young children should not be out alone on the pavement or road (see Rule 7). When taking children out, keep between them and the traffic and hold their hands firmly. Strap very young children into push-chairs or use reins. When pushing a young child in a buggy, do not push the buggy into the road when checking to see if it is clear to cross, particularly from between parked vehicles.

5. Organised walks. Large groups of people walking together should use a pavement if available; if one is not, they should keep to the left. Look-outs should be positioned at the front and back of the group, and they should wear fluorescent clothes in daylight and reflective clothes in the dark. At night, the look-out in front should show a white light and the one at the back a red light. People on the outside of large groups should also carry lights and wear reflective clothing.

6. Motorways. Pedestrians **MUST NOT** be on motorways or slip roads except in an emergency (see Rules 271 and 275).

Laws RTRA sect 17, MT(E&W)R 1982 as amended, reg 15(1)(b) & MT(S)R reg 13

Crossing the road

7. The Green Cross Code. The advice given below on crossing the road is for all pedestrians. Children should be taught the Code and should not be allowed out alone until they can understand and use it properly. The age when they can do this is different for each child. Many children cannot judge how fast vehicles are going or how far away they are. Children learn by example, so parents and carers should always use the Code in full when out with their children. They are responsible for deciding at what age children can use it safely by themselves.

a. First find a safe place to cross and where there is space to reach the pavement on the other side. Where there is a crossing nearby, use it. It is safer to cross using a subway, a footbridge, an island, a zebra, pelican, toucan or puffin crossing, or where there is a crossing point controlled by a police officer, a school crossing patrol or a traffic warden. Otherwise choose a place where you can see clearly in all directions. Try to avoid crossing between parked cars (see Rule 14), on a blind bend, or close to the brow of a hill. Move to a space where drivers and riders can see you clearly. Do not cross the road diagonally.

Look all around and listen for traffic before crossing

b. Stop just before you get to the kerb, where you can see if anything is coming. Do not get too close to the traffic. If there's no pavement, keep back from the edge of the road but make sure you can still see approaching traffic.

c. Look all around for traffic and listen. Traffic could come from any direction. Listen as well, because you can sometimes hear traffic before you see it.

d. If traffic is coming, let it pass. Look all around again and listen. Do not cross until there is a safe gap in the traffic and you are certain that there is plenty of time. Remember, even if traffic is a long way off, it may be approaching very quickly.

e. When it is safe, go straight across the road – do not run. Keep looking and listening for traffic while you cross, in case there is any traffic you did not see, or in case other traffic appears suddenly. Look out for cyclists and motorcyclists travelling between lanes of traffic. Do not walk diagonally across the road.

8. At a junction. When crossing the road, look out for traffic turning into the road, especially from behind you. If you have started crossing and traffic wants to turn into the road, you have priority and they should give way (see Rule 170).

9. Pedestrian Safety Barriers. Where there are barriers, cross the road only at the gaps provided for pedestrians. Do not climb over the barriers or walk between them and the road.

10. Tactile paving. Raised surfaces that can be felt underfoot provide warning and guidance to blind or partially sighted people. The most common surfaces are a series of raised studs, which are used at crossing points with a dropped kerb, or a series of rounded raised bars which are used at level crossings, at the top and bottom of steps and at some other hazards.

11. One-way streets. Check which way the traffic is moving. Do not cross until it is safe to do so without stopping. Bus and cycle lanes may operate in the opposite direction to the rest of the traffic.

12. Bus and cycle lanes. Take care when crossing these lanes as traffic may be moving faster than in the other lanes, or against the flow of traffic.

13. Routes shared with cyclists. Some cycle tracks run alongside footpaths or pavements, using a segregating feature to separate cyclists from people on foot. Segregated routes may also incorporate short lengths of tactile paving to help visually impaired people stay on the correct side. On the pedestrian side this will comprise a series of flat-topped bars running across the direction of travel (ladder pattern). On the cyclist side the same bars are orientated in the direction of travel (tramline pattern). Not all routes which are shared with cyclists are segregated. Take extra care where this is so (see Rule 62).

14. Parked vehicles. If you have to cross between parked vehicles, use the outside edges of the vehicles as if they were the kerb. Stop there and make sure you can see all around and that the traffic can see you. Make sure there is a gap between any parked vehicles on the other side, so you can reach the pavement. Never cross the road in front of, or behind, any vehicle with its engine running, especially a large vehicle, as the driver may not be able to see you.

15. Reversing vehicles. Never cross behind a vehicle which is reversing, showing white reversing lights or sounding a warning.

16. Moving vehicles. You **MUST NOT** get onto or hold onto a moving vehicle.

Law RTA 1988 sect 26

17. At night. Wear something reflective to make it easier for others to see you (see Rule 3). If there is no pedestrian crossing nearby, cross the road near a street light so that traffic can see you more easily.

Crossings

18. At all crossings. When using any type of crossing you should

- always check that the traffic has stopped before you start to cross or push a pram onto a crossing
- always cross between the studs or over the zebra markings. Do not cross at the side of the crossing or on the zig-zag lines, as it can be dangerous.

You **MUST NOT** loiter on any type of crossing.

Laws ZPPPCRGD reg 19 & RTRA sect 25(5)

19. Zebra crossings. Give traffic plenty of time to see you and to stop before you start to cross. Vehicles will need more time when the road is slippery. Wait until traffic has stopped from both directions or the road is clear before crossing. Remember that traffic does not have to stop until someone has moved onto the crossing. Keep looking both ways, and listening, in case a driver or rider has not seen you and attempts to overtake a vehicle that has stopped.

Zebra crossings have flashing beacons

20. Where there is an island in the middle of a zebra crossing, wait on the island and follow Rule 19 before you cross the second half of the road – it is a separate crossing.

Zebra crossings with a central island are two separate crossings

21. At traffic lights. There may be special signals for pedestrians. You should only start to cross the road when the green figure shows. If you have started to cross the road and the green figure goes out, you should still have time to reach the other side, but do not delay. If no pedestrian signals have been provided, watch carefully and do not cross until the traffic lights are red and the traffic has stopped. Keep looking and check for traffic that may be turning the corner. Remember that traffic lights may let traffic move in some lanes while traffic in other lanes has stopped.

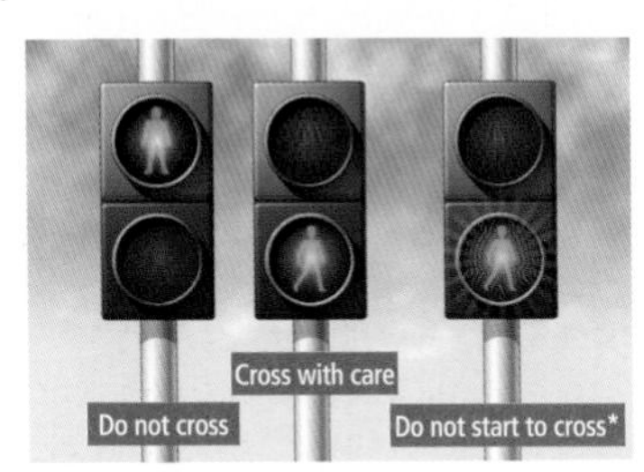

At traffic lights, puffin and pelican crossings
*At pelican crossings only

22. Pelican crossings. These are signal-controlled crossings operated by pedestrians. Push the control button to activate the traffic signals. When the red figure shows, do not cross. When a steady green figure shows, check the traffic has stopped then cross with care. When the green figure begins to flash you should not start to cross. If you have already started you should have time to finish crossing safely.

23. Puffin crossings differ from pelican crossings as the red and green figures are above the control box on your side of the road and there is no flashing green figure phase. Press the button and wait for the green figure to show.

24. When the road is congested, traffic on your side of the road may be forced to stop even though their lights are green. Traffic may still be moving on the other side of the road, so press the button and wait for the signal to cross.

25. Toucan crossings are light-controlled crossings which allow cyclists and pedestrians to share crossing space and cross at the same time. They are push-button operated. Pedestrians and cyclists will see the green signal together. Cyclists are permitted to ride across.

Toucan crossings can be used by both cyclists and pedestrians

26. At some crossings there is a bleeping sound or voice signal to indicate to blind or partially sighted people when the steady green figure is showing, and there may be a tactile signal to help deafblind people.

27. Equestrian crossings are for horse riders. They have pavement barriers, wider crossing spaces, horse and rider figures in the light panels and either two sets of controls (one higher), or just one higher control panel.

Equestrian crossings are used by horse riders
There is often a parallel crossing

28. 'Staggered' pelican or puffin crossings. When the crossings on each side of the central refuge are not in line they are two separate crossings. On reaching the central island, press the button again and wait for a steady green figure.

Staggered crossings (with an island in the middle)
are two separate crossings

29. Crossings controlled by an authorised person. Do not cross the road unless you are signalled to do so by a police officer, traffic warden or school crossing patrol. Always cross in front of them.

30. Where there are no controlled crossing points available it is advisable to cross where there is an island in the middle of the road. Use the Green Cross Code (see Rule 7) to cross to the island and then stop and use it again to cross the second half of the road.

Situations needing extra care

31. Emergency vehicles. If an ambulance, fire engine, police or other emergency vehicle approaches using flashing blue lights, headlights and/or sirens, keep off the road.

32. Buses. Get on or off a bus only when it has stopped to allow you to do so. Watch out for cyclists when you are getting off. Never cross the road directly behind or in front of a bus. Wait until it has moved off and you can see clearly in both directions.

33. Tramways. These may run through pedestrian areas. Their path will be marked out by shallow kerbs, changes in the paving or other road surface, white lines or yellow dots. Cross at designated crossings where provided. Elsewhere treat trams as you would other road vehicles and look both ways along the track before crossing. Do not walk along the track as trams may come up behind you. Trams move quietly and cannot steer to avoid you.

34. Railway level crossings. You **MUST NOT** cross or pass a stop line when the red lights show, (including a red pedestrian figure). Also do not cross if an alarm is sounding or the barriers are being lowered. The tone of the alarm may change if another train is approaching. If there are no lights, alarms or barriers, stop, look both ways and listen before crossing. A tactile surface comprising rounded bars running across the direction of pedestrian travel may be installed on the footpath approaching a level crossing to warn visually impaired people of its presence. The tactile surface should extend across the full width of the footway and should be located at an appropriate distance from the barrier or projected line of the barrier.

Law TSRGD, reg 52

35. Street and pavement repairs. A pavement may be closed temporarily because it is not safe to use. Take extra care if you are directed to walk in or to cross the road.

Rules for users of powered wheelchairs and powered mobility scooters

(Called Invalid Carriages in law)

36. There is one class of manual wheelchair (called a Class 1 invalid carriage) and two classes of powered wheelchairs and powered mobility scooters. Manual wheelchairs and Class 2 vehicles are those with an upper speed limit of 4mph (6km/h) and are designed to be used on pavements. Class 3 vehicles are those with an upper speed limit of 8mph (12km/h) and are equipped to be used on the road as well as the pavement.

37. When you are on the road you should obey the guidance and rules for other vehicles; when on the pavement you should follow the guidance and rules for pedestrians.

On pavements

38. Pavements are safer than roads and should be used when available. You should give pedestrians priority and show consideration for other pavement users, particularly those with a hearing or visual impairment who may not be aware that you are there.

39. Powered wheelchairs and scooters **MUST NOT** travel faster than 4mph (6km/h) on pavements or in pedestrian areas. You may need to reduce your speed to adjust to other pavement users who may not be able to move out of your way quickly enough or where the pavement is too narrow.
Law UICHR 1988 reg 4

40. When moving off the pavement onto the road, you should take special care. Before moving off, always look round and make sure it's safe to join the traffic. Always try to use dropped kerbs when moving off the pavement, even if this means travelling further to locate one. If you have to climb or descend a kerb, always approach it at right angles and don't try to negotiate a kerb higher than the vehicle manufacturer's recommendations.

On the road

41. You should take care when travelling on the road as you may be travelling more slowly than other traffic (your machine is restricted to 8mph (12km/h) and may be less visible).

42. When on the road, Class 3 vehicles should travel in the direction of the traffic. Class 2 users should always use the pavement when it is available. When there is no pavement, you should use caution when on the road. Class 2 users should, where possible, travel in the direction of the traffic. If you are travelling at night when lights **MUST** be used, you should travel in the direction of the traffic to avoid confusing other road users.

Law UICHR 1988 reg 9

43. You **MUST** follow the same rules about using lights, indicators and horns as for other road vehicles, if your vehicle is fitted with them. At night, lights **MUST** be used. Be aware that other road users may not see you and you should make yourself more visible – even in the daytime and also at dusk – by, for instance, wearing a reflective jacket or reflective strips on the back of the vehicle.

Law UICHR 1988 reg 9

44. Take extra care at road junctions. When going straight ahead, check to make sure there are no vehicles about to cross your path from the left, the right, or overtaking you and turning left. There are several options for dealing with right turns, especially turning from a major road. If moving into the middle of the road is difficult or dangerous, you can

- stop on the left-hand side of the road and wait for a safe gap in the traffic
- negotiate the turn as a pedestrian, i.e. travel along the pavement and cross the road between pavements where it is safe to do so. Class 3 users should switch the vehicle to the lower speed limit when on pavements.

If the junction is too hazardous, it may be worth considering an alternative route. Similarly, when negotiating major roundabouts (i.e. with two or more lanes) it may be safer for you to use the pavement or find a route which avoids the roundabout altogether.

45. All normal parking restrictions should be observed. Your vehicle should not be left unattended if it causes an obstruction to other pedestrians – especially those in wheelchairs. Parking concessions provided under the Blue Badge scheme (see Further reading) will apply to those vehicles displaying a valid badge.

46. These vehicles **MUST NOT** be used on motorways (see Rule 253). They should not be used on unrestricted dual carriageways where the speed limit exceeds 50mph (80km/h) but if they are used on these dual carriageways, they **MUST** have a flashing amber beacon.
A flashing amber beacon should be used on all other dual carriageways (see Rule 220).

Laws RTRA sect 17(2) & (3), & RVLR reg 17(1) & 26

Rules about animals

Horse-Drawn Vehicles

47. Horse-drawn vehicles used on the highway should be operated and maintained in accordance with standards set out in the Department for Transport's Code of Practice for Horse-Drawn Vehicles. This Code lays down the requirements for a road driving assessment and includes a comprehensive list of safety checks to ensure that a carriage and its fittings are safe and in good working order. The standards set out in the Road Driving Assessment may be required to be met by a Local Authority if an operator wishes to obtain a local authority licence to operate a passenger-carrying service (see Further reading).

48. Safety equipment and clothing. All horse-drawn vehicles should have two red rear reflectors. It is safer not to drive at night but if you do, a light showing white to the front and red to the rear **MUST** be fitted.
Law RVLR 1989 reg 4

Horse riders

49. Safety equipment. Children under the age of 14 **MUST** wear a helmet which complies with the Regulations. It **MUST** be fastened securely. Other riders should also follow these requirements. These requirements do not apply to a child who is a follower of the Sikh religion while wearing a turban.
Laws H(PHYR) Act 1990, sect 1 & H(PHYR) Regulations 1992, reg 3

50. Other clothing. You should wear
- boots or shoes with hard soles and heels
- light-coloured or fluorescent clothing in daylight
- reflective clothing if you have to ride at night or in poor visibility.

Help yourself to be seen

51. At night. It is safer not to ride on the road at night or in poor visibility, but if you do, make sure you wear reflective clothing and your horse has reflective bands above the fetlock joints. A light which shows white to the front and red to the rear should be fitted, with a band, to the rider's right arm and/or leg/riding boot. If you are leading a horse at night, carry a light in your right hand, showing white to the front and red to the rear, and wear reflective clothing on both you and your horse. It is strongly recommended that a fluorescent/reflective tail guard is also worn by your horse.

Riding

52. Before you take a horse on to a road, you should

- ensure all tack fits well and is in good condition
- make sure you can control the horse.

Always ride with other, less nervous horses if you think that your horse will be nervous of traffic. Never ride a horse without both a saddle and bridle.

53. Before riding off or turning, look behind you to make sure it is safe, then give a clear arm signal.
When riding on the road you should

- keep to the left
- keep both hands on the reins unless you are signalling
- keep both feet in the stirrups
- not carry another person
- not carry anything which might affect your balance or get tangled up with the reins
- keep a horse you are leading to your left
- move in the direction of the traffic flow in a one-way street
- never ride more than two abreast, and ride in single file on narrow or busy roads and when riding round bends.

54. You **MUST NOT** take a horse onto a footpath or pavement, and you should not take a horse onto a cycle track. Use a bridleway where possible. Equestrian crossings may be provided for horse riders to cross the road and you should use these where available (see Rule 27). You should dismount at level crossings where a 'horse rider dismount' sign is displayed.

Laws HA 1835 sect 72, R(S)A 1984, sect 129(5)

55. Avoid roundabouts wherever possible. If you use them you should
- keep to the left and watch out for vehicles crossing your path to leave or join the roundabout
- signal right when riding across exits to show you are not leaving
- signal left just before you leave the roundabout.

Other animals

56. Dogs. Do not let a dog out on the road on its own. Keep it on a short lead when walking on the pavement, road or path shared with cyclists or horse riders.

57. When in a vehicle make sure dogs or other animals are suitably restrained so they cannot distract you while you are driving or injure you, or themselves, if you stop quickly. A seat belt harness, pet carrier, dog cage or dog guard are ways of restraining animals in cars.

58. Animals being herded. These should be kept under control at all times. You should, if possible, send another person along the road in front to warn other road users, especially at a bend or the brow of a hill. It is safer not to move animals after dark, but if you do, then wear reflective clothing and ensure that lights are carried (white at the front and red at the rear of the herd).

Rules for cyclists

These rules are in addition to those in the following sections, which apply to all vehicles (except the Motorway section). See also Annexe 1 – You and your bicycle.

59. Clothing. You should wear

- a cycle helmet which conforms to current regulations, is the correct size and securely fastened
- appropriate clothes for cycling. Avoid clothes that may get tangled in the chain, or in a wheel or may obscure your lights
- light-coloured or fluorescent clothing which helps other road users to see you in daylight and poor light
- reflective clothing and/or accessories (belt, arm or ankle bands) in the dark.

Help yourself to be seen

60. At night your cycle **MUST** have white front and red rear lights lit. It **MUST** also be fitted with a red rear reflector (and amber pedal reflectors, if manufactured after 1/10/85). White front reflectors and spoke reflectors will also help you to be seen. Flashing lights are permitted but it is recommended that cyclists who are riding in areas without street lighting use a steady front lamp.

Law RVLR regs 13, 18 & 24

61. Cycle Routes and Other Facilities. Use cycle routes, advanced stop lines, cycle boxes and toucan crossings unless at the time it is unsafe to do so. Use of these facilities is not compulsory and will depend on your experience and skills, but they can make your journey safer.

62. Cycle Tracks. These are normally located away from the road, but may occasionally be found alongside footpaths or pavements. Cyclists and pedestrians may be segregated or they may share the same space (unsegregated). When using segregated tracks you **MUST** keep to the side intended for cyclists as the pedestrian side remains a pavement or footpath. Take care when passing pedestrians, especially children, older or disabled people, and allow them plenty of room. Always be prepared to slow down and stop if necessary. Take care near road junctions as you may have difficulty seeing other road users, who might not notice you.

Law HA 1835 sect 72

63. Cycle Lanes. These are marked by a white line (which may be broken) along the carriageway (see Rule 140). Keep within the lane when practicable. When leaving a cycle lane check before pulling out that it is safe to do so and signal your intention clearly to other road users. Use of cycle lanes is not compulsory and will depend on your experience and skills, but they can make your journey safer.

64. You **MUST NOT** cycle on a pavement.

Laws HA 1835 sect 72 & R(S)A 1984, sect 129

65. Bus Lanes. Most bus lanes may be used by cyclists as indicated on signs. Watch out for people getting on or off a bus. Be very careful when overtaking a bus or leaving a bus lane as you will be entering a busier traffic flow. Do not pass between the kerb and a bus when it is at a stop.

66. You should

- keep both hands on the handlebars except when signalling or changing gear
- keep both feet on the pedals
- never ride more than two abreast, and ride in single file on narrow or busy roads and when riding round bends
- not ride close behind another vehicle
- not carry anything which will affect your balance or may get tangled up with your wheels or chain
- be considerate of other road users, particularly blind and partially sighted pedestrians. Let them know you are there when necessary, for example, by ringing your bell if you have one. It is recommended that a bell be fitted.

67. You should

- look all around before moving away from the kerb, turning or manoeuvring, to make sure it is safe to do so. Give a clear signal to show other road users what you intend to do (see Signals to other road users)
- look well ahead for obstructions in the road, such as drains, pot-holes and parked vehicles so that you do not have to swerve suddenly to avoid them. Leave plenty of room when passing parked vehicles and watch out for doors being opened or pedestrians stepping into your path
- be aware of traffic coming up behind you
- take extra care near road humps, narrowings and other traffic calming features
- take care when overtaking (see Rules 162–169).

68. You **MUST NOT**

- carry a passenger unless your cycle has been built or adapted to carry one
- hold onto a moving vehicle or trailer
- ride in a dangerous, careless or inconsiderate manner
- ride when under the influence of drink or drugs, including medicine.

Law RTA 1988 sects 24, 26, 28, 29 & 30 as amended by RTA 1991

69. You **MUST** obey all traffic signs and traffic light signals.

Laws RTA 1988 sect 36 & TSRGD reg 10(1)

70. When parking your cycle

- find a conspicuous location where it can be seen by passers-by
- use cycle stands or other cycle parking facilities wherever possible
- do not leave it where it would cause an obstruction or hazard to other road users
- secure it well so that it will not fall over and become an obstruction or hazard.

71. You **MUST NOT** cross the stop line when the traffic lights are red. Some junctions have an advanced stop line to enable you to wait and position yourself ahead of other traffic (see Rule 178).

Laws RTA 1988 sect 36 & TSRGD regs 10 & 36(1)

Road junctions

72. On the left. When approaching a junction on the left, watch out for vehicles turning in front of you, out of or into the side road. Just before you turn, check for undertaking cyclists or motorcyclists. Do not ride on the inside of vehicles signalling or slowing down to turn left.

73. Pay particular attention to long vehicles which need a lot of room to manoeuvre at corners. Be aware that drivers may not see you. They may have to move over to the right before turning left. Wait until they have completed the manoeuvre because the rear wheels come very close to the kerb while turning. Do not be tempted to ride in the space between them and the kerb.

74. On the right. If you are turning right, check the traffic to ensure it is safe, then signal and move to the centre of the road. Wait until there is a safe gap in the oncoming traffic and give a final look before completing the turn. It may be safer to wait on the left until there is a safe gap or to dismount and push your cycle across the road.

75. Dual carriageways. Remember that traffic on most dual carriageways moves quickly. When crossing wait for a safe gap and cross each carriageway in turn. Take extra care when crossing slip roads.

Roundabouts

76. Full details about the correct procedure at roundabouts are contained in Rules 184–190. Roundabouts can be hazardous and should be approached with care.

77. You may feel safer walking your cycle round on the pavement or verge. If you decide to ride round keeping to the left-hand lane you should

- be aware that drivers may not easily see you
- take extra care when cycling across exits. You may need to signal right to show you are not leaving the roundabout
- watch out for vehicles crossing your path to leave or join the roundabout.

78. Give plenty of room to long vehicles on the roundabout as they need more space to manoeuvre. Do not ride in the space they need to get round the roundabout. It may be safer to wait until they have cleared the roundabout.

Crossing the road

79. Do not ride across equestrian crossings, as they are for horse riders only. Do not ride across a pelican, puffin or zebra crossing. Dismount and wheel your cycle across.

80. Toucan crossings. These are light-controlled crossings which allow cyclists and pedestrians to share crossing space and cross at the same time. They are push-button operated. Pedestrians and cyclists will see the green signal together. Cyclists are permitted to ride across.

81. Cycle-only crossings. Cycle tracks on opposite sides of the road may be linked by signalled crossings. You may ride across but you **MUST NOT** cross until the green cycle symbol is showing.

Law TSRGD regs 33(2) & 36(1)

82. Level crossings/Tramways. Take extra care when crossing the tracks (see Rule 306). You should dismount at level crossings where a 'cyclist dismount' sign is displayed.

Rules for motorcyclists

These Rules are in addition to those in the following sections which apply to all vehicles. For motorcycle licence requirements see Annexe 2.

General

83. On all journeys, the rider and pillion passenger on a motorcycle, scooter or moped **MUST** wear a protective helmet. This does not apply to a follower of the Sikh religion while wearing a turban. Helmets **MUST** comply with the Regulations and they **MUST** be fastened securely. Riders and passengers of motor tricycles and quadricycles, also called quadbikes, should also wear a protective helmet. Before each journey check that your helmet visor is clean and in good condition.

Laws RTA 1988 sects 16 & 17 & MC(PH)R as amended reg 4

84. It is also advisable to wear eye protectors, which **MUST** comply with the Regulations. Scratched or poorly fitting eye protectors can limit your view when riding, particularly in bright sunshine and the hours of darkness. Consider wearing ear protection. Strong boots, gloves and suitable clothing may help to protect you if you are involved in a collision.

Laws RTA sect 18 & MC(EP)R as amended reg 4

85. You **MUST NOT** carry more than one pillion passenger who **MUST** sit astride the machine on a proper seat. They should face forward with both feet on the footrests. You **MUST NOT** carry a pillion passenger unless your motorcycle is designed to do so. Provisional licence holders **MUST NOT** carry a pillion passenger.

Laws RTA 1988 sect 23, MV(DL)R 1999 reg 16(6) & CUR 1986 reg 102

86. Daylight riding. Make yourself as visible as possible from the side as well as the front and rear. You could wear a light or brightly coloured helmet and fluorescent clothing or strips. Dipped headlights, even in good daylight, may also make you more conspicuous. However, be aware that other vehicle drivers may still not have seen you, or judged your distance or speed correctly, especially at junctions.

Help yourself to be seen

87. Riding in the dark. Wear reflective clothing or strips to improve your visibility in the dark. These reflect light from the headlamps of other vehicles, making you visible from a longer distance. See Rules 113–116 for lighting requirements.

88. Manoeuvring. You should be aware of what is behind and to the sides before manoeuvring. Look behind you; use mirrors if they are fitted. When in traffic queues look out for pedestrians crossing between vehicles and vehicles emerging from junctions or changing lanes. Position yourself so that drivers in front can see you in their mirrors. Additionally, when filtering in slow-moving traffic, take care and keep your speed low.
Remember: Observation – Signal – Manoeuvre.

Rules for drivers and motorcyclists

89. Vehicle condition. You **MUST** ensure your vehicle and trailer comply with the full requirements of the Road Vehicles (Construction and Use) Regulations and Road Vehicles Lighting Regulations (see Annexe 4 – The road user and the law).

Fitness to drive

90. Make sure that you are fit to drive. You **MUST** report to the Driver and Vehicle Licensing Agency (DVLA) any health condition likely to affect your driving.
Law RTA 1988 sect 94

91. Driving when you are tired greatly increases your risk of collision. To minimise this risk

- make sure you are fit to drive. Do not begin a journey if you are tired. Get a good night's sleep before embarking on a long journey
- avoid undertaking long journeys between midnight and 6am, when natural alertness is at a minimum
- plan your journey to take sufficient breaks. A minimum break of at least 15 minutes after every two hours of driving is recommended
- if you feel at all sleepy, stop in a safe place. Do not stop on the hard shoulder of a motorway
- the most effective ways to counter sleepiness are to drink, for example, two cups of caffeinated coffee and to take a short nap (at least 15 minutes).

92. Vision. You **MUST** be able to read a vehicle number plate, in good daylight, from a distance of 20 metres (or 20.5 metres where the old style number plate is used). If you need to wear glasses (or contact lenses) to do this, you **MUST** wear them at all times while driving. The police have the power to require a driver to undertake an eyesight test.
Laws RTA 1988 sect 96 & MV(DL)R reg 40 & sch 8

93. Slow down, and if necessary stop, if you are dazzled by bright sunlight.

94. At night or in poor visibility, do not use tinted glasses, lenses or visors if they restrict your vision.

Alcohol and drugs

95. Do not drink and drive as it will seriously affect your judgement and abilities. You **MUST NOT** drive with a breath alcohol level higher than 35 microgrammes/100 millilitres of breath or a blood alcohol level of more than 80 milligrammes/100 millilitres of blood. Alcohol will

- give a false sense of confidence
- reduce co-ordination and slow down reactions
- affect judgement of speed, distance and risk
- reduce your driving ability, even if you're below the legal limit
- take time to leave your body; you may be unfit to drive in the evening after drinking at lunchtime, or in the morning after drinking the previous evening.

The best solution is not to drink at all when planning to drive because any amount of alcohol affects your ability to drive safely. If you are going to drink, arrange another means of transport.

Law RTA 1988 sects 4, 5 & 11(2)

96. You **MUST NOT** drive under the influence of drugs or medicine. Check the instructions or ask your doctor or pharmacist. Using illegal drugs is highly dangerous. Never take them if you intend to drive; the effects are unpredictable, but can be even more severe than alcohol and may result in fatal or serious road crashes.

Law RTA 1988 sect 4

97. Before setting off. You should ensure that

- you have planned your route and allowed sufficient time
- clothing and footwear do not prevent you using the controls in the correct manner
- you know where all the controls are and how to use them before you need them. Not all vehicles are the same; do not wait until it is too late to find out
- your mirrors and seat are adjusted correctly to ensure comfort, full control and maximum vision
- head restraints are properly adjusted to reduce the risk of neck and spine injuries in the event of a collision
- you have sufficient fuel before commencing your journey, especially if it includes motorway driving. It can be dangerous to lose power when driving in traffic
- ensure your vehicle is legal and roadworthy
- switch off your mobile phone.

Make sure head restraints are properly adjusted

98. Vehicle towing and loading. As a driver

- you **MUST NOT** tow more than your licence permits. If you passed a car test after 1 January 1997 you are restricted on the weight of trailer you can tow
- you **MUST NOT** overload your vehicle or trailer. You should not tow a weight greater than that recommended by the manufacturer of your vehicle
- you **MUST** secure your load and it **MUST NOT** stick out dangerously. Make sure any heavy or sharp objects and any animals are secured safely. If there is a collision, they might hit someone inside the vehicle and cause serious injury
- you should properly distribute the weight in your caravan or trailer with heavy items mainly over the axle(s) and ensure a downward load on the tow ball. Manufacturer's recommended weight and tow ball load should not be exceeded. This should avoid the possibility of swerving or snaking and going out of control. If this does happen, ease off the accelerator and reduce speed gently to regain control
- carrying a load or pulling a trailer may require you to adjust the headlights.

In the event of a breakdown, be aware that towing a vehicle on a tow rope is potentially dangerous. You should consider professional recovery.

Laws CUR reg 100 & MV(DL)R reg 43

Seat belts and child restraints

99. You **MUST** wear a seat belt in cars, vans and other goods vehicles if one is fitted (see table below). Adults, and children aged 14 years and over, **MUST** use a seat belt or child restraint, where fitted, when seated in minibuses, buses and coaches. Exemptions are allowed for the holders of medical exemption certificates and those making deliveries or collections in goods vehicles when travelling less than 50 metres (approx 162 feet).

Laws RTA 1988 sects 14 & 15, MV(WSB)R, MV(WSBCFS)R & MV(WSB)(A)R

Seat Belt Requirements.

This table summarises the main legal requirements for wearing seat belts in cars, vans and other goods vehicles

	Front seat	Rear seat	Who is responsible?
Driver	Seat belt **MUST** be worn if fitted		**Driver**
Child under 3 years of age	Correct child restraint **MUST** be used	Correct child restraint **MUST** be used. If one is not available in a taxi, may travel unrestrained.	**Driver**
Child from 3rd birthday up to 1.35 metres (approx 4ft 5ins) in height (or 12th birthday, whichever they reach first)	Correct child restraint **MUST** be used	Correct child restraint **MUST** be used where seat belts fitted. **MUST** use adult belt if correct child restraint is not available in a licensed taxi or private hire vehicle, or for reasons of unexpected necessity over a short distance, or if two occupied restraints prevent fitment of a third.	**Driver**
Child over 1.35 metres (approx 4ft 5ins) in height or 12 or 13 years	Adult seat belt **MUST** be worn if available	Adult seat belt **MUST** be worn if available	**Driver**
Adult passengers aged 14 and over	Seat belt **MUST** be worn if available	Seat belt **MUST** be worn if available	**Passenger**

100. The driver **MUST** ensure that all children under 14 years of age in cars, vans and other goods vehicles wear seat belts or sit in an approved child restraint where required (see table opposite). If a child is under 1.35 metres (approx 4 feet 5 ins) tall, a baby seat, child seat, booster seat or booster cushion **MUST** be used suitable for the child's weight and fitted to the manufacturer's instructions.
Laws RTA 1988 sects 14 & 15, MV(WSB)R, MV(WSBCFS)R & MV(WSB)(A)R

Make sure that a child uses a suitable restraint which is correctly adjusted

101. A rear-facing baby seat **MUST NOT** be fitted into a seat protected by an active frontal airbag, as in a crash it can cause serious injury or death to the child.
Laws RTA 1988 sects 14 & 15, MV(WSB)R, MV(WSBCFS)R & MV(WSB)(A)R

102. Children in cars, vans and other goods vehicles. Drivers who are carrying children in cars, vans and other goods vehicles should also ensure that

- children should get into the vehicle through the door nearest the kerb
- child restraints are properly fitted to manufacturer's instructions
- children do not sit behind the rear seats in an estate car or hatchback, unless a special child seat has been fitted
- the child safety door locks, where fitted, are used when children are in the vehicle
- children are kept under control.

General rules, techniques and advice for all drivers and riders

This section should be read by all drivers, motorcyclists, cyclists and horse riders. The rules in ***The Highway Code*** do not give you the right of way in any circumstance, but they advise you when you should give way to others. Always give way if it can help to avoid an incident.

Signals

103. Signals warn and inform other road users, including pedestrians (see Signals to other road users), of your intended actions. You should always

- give clear signals in plenty of time, having checked it is not misleading to signal at that time
- use them to advise other road users before changing course or direction, stopping or moving off
- cancel them after use
- make sure your signals will not confuse others. If, for instance, you want to stop after a side road, do not signal until you are passing the road. If you signal earlier it may give the impression that you intend to turn into the road. Your brake lights will warn traffic behind you that you are slowing down
- use an arm signal to emphasise or reinforce your signal if necessary. Remember that signalling does not give you priority.

104. You should also

- watch out for signals given by other road users and proceed only when you are satisfied that it is safe
- be aware that an indicator on another vehicle may not have been cancelled.

105. You **MUST** obey signals given by police officers, traffic officers, traffic wardens (see Signals by authorised persons) and signs used by school crossing patrols.

Laws RTRA sect 28, RTA 1988 sect 35, TMA 2004 sect 6, & FTWO art 3

106. Police stopping procedures. If the police want to stop your vehicle they will, where possible, attract your attention by

- flashing blue lights, headlights or sounding their siren or horn, usually from behind
- directing you to pull over to the side by pointing and/or using the left indicator.

You **MUST** then pull over and stop as soon as it is safe to do so. Then switch off your engine.

Law RTA 1988 sect 163

Other stopping procedures

107. Vehicle & Operator Services Agency Officers have powers to stop vehicles on all roads, including motorways and trunk roads, in England and Wales. They will attract your attention by flashing amber lights

- either from the front requesting you to follow them to a safe place to stop
- or from behind directing you to pull over to the side by pointing and/or using the left indicator.

It is an offence not to comply with their directions. You **MUST** obey any signals given (see Signals by authorised persons).

Laws RTA 1988, sect 67, & PRA 2002, sect 41 & sched 5(8)

108. Highways Agency Traffic Officers have powers to stop vehicles on most motorways and some 'A' class roads, in England only. If HA traffic officers in uniform want to stop your vehicle on safety grounds (e.g. an insecure load) they will, where possible, attract your attention by

- flashing amber lights, usually from behind
- directing you to pull over to the side by pointing and/or using the left indicator.

You **MUST** then pull over and stop as soon as it is safe to do so. Then switch off your engine. It is an offence not to comply with their directions (see Signals by authorised persons).

Law RTA1988, sects 35 & 163 as amended by TMA 2004, sect 6

Traffic light signals and traffic signs

109. You **MUST** obey all traffic light signals (see Light signals controlling traffic) and traffic signs giving orders, including temporary signals & signs (see Signs giving orders, Warning signs and Direction signs). Make sure you know, understand and act on all other traffic and information signs and road markings (see Signs giving orders, Warning signs, Direction signs, Information signs, Road markings and Vehicle markings).

Laws RTA 1988 sect 36 & TSRGD regs 10, 15, 16, 25, 26, 27, 28, 29, 36, 38 & 40

110. Flashing headlights. Only flash your headlights to let other road users know that you are there. Do not flash your headlights to convey any other message or intimidate other road users.

111. Never assume that flashing headlights is a signal inviting you to proceed. Use your own judgement and proceed carefully.

112. The horn. Use only while your vehicle is moving and you need to warn other road users of your presence. Never sound your horn aggressively. You **MUST NOT** use your horn

- while stationary on the road
- when driving in a built-up area between the hours of 11.30pm and 7am

except when another road user poses a danger.

Law CUR reg 99

Lighting requirements

113. You **MUST**

- ensure all sidelights and rear registration plate lights are lit between sunset and sunrise
- use headlights at night, except on a road which has lit street lighting. These roads are generally restricted to a speed limit of 30mph (48km/h) unless otherwise specified
- use headlights when visibility is seriously reduced (see Rule 226).

Night (the hours of darkness) is defined as the period between half an hour after sunset and half an hour before sunrise).

Laws RVLR regs 3, 24, & 25, (In Scotland – RTRA 1984 sect 82 (as amended by NRSWA, para 59 of sched 8))

114. You **MUST NOT**

- use any lights in a way that would dazzle or cause discomfort to other road users, including pedestrians, cyclists and horse riders
- use front or rear fog lights unless visibility is seriously reduced. You **MUST** switch them off when visibility improves to avoid dazzling other road users (see Rule 226).

In stationary queues of traffic, drivers should apply the parking brake and, once the following traffic has stopped, take their foot off the footbrake to deactivate the vehicle brake lights. This will minimise glare to road users behind until the traffic moves again.

Law RVLR reg 27

115. You should also

- use dipped headlights, or dim-dip if fitted, at night in built-up areas and in dull daytime weather, to ensure that you can be seen
- keep your headlights dipped when overtaking until you are level with the other vehicle and then change to main beam if necessary, unless this would dazzle oncoming road users
- slow down, and if necessary stop, if you are dazzled by oncoming headlights.

116. Hazard warning lights. These may be used when your vehicle is stationary, to warn that it is temporarily obstructing traffic. Never use them as an excuse for dangerous or illegal parking. You **MUST NOT** use hazard warning lights while driving or being towed unless you are on a motorway or unrestricted dual carriageway and you need to warn drivers behind you of a hazard or obstruction ahead. Only use them for long enough to ensure that your warning has been observed.
Law RVLR reg 27

Control of the vehicle

Braking

117. In normal circumstances. The safest way to brake is to do so early and lightly. Brake more firmly as you begin to stop. Ease the pressure off just before the vehicle comes to rest to avoid a jerky stop.

118. In an emergency. Brake immediately. Try to avoid braking so harshly that you lock your wheels. Locked wheels can lead to loss of control.

119. Skids. Skidding is usually caused by the driver braking, accelerating or steering too harshly or driving too fast for the road conditions. If skidding occurs, remove the cause by releasing the brake pedal fully or easing off the accelerator. Turn the steering wheel in the direction of the skid. For example, if the rear of the vehicle skids to the right, steer immediately to the right to recover.

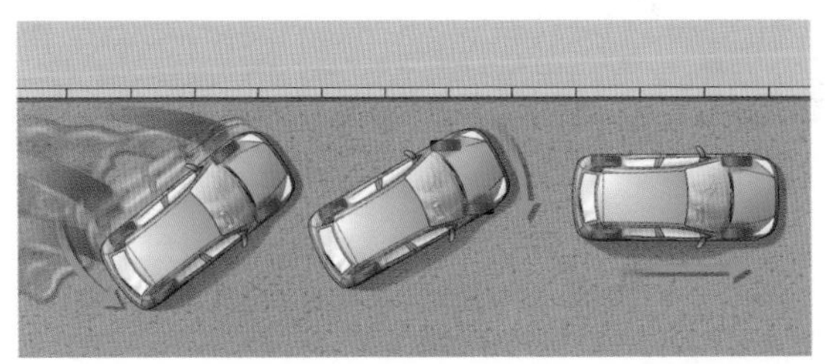

Rear of the car skids to the right. Driver steers to the right.

120. ABS. If your vehicle is fitted with anti-lock brakes, you should follow the advice given in the vehicle handbook. However, in the case of an emergency, apply the footbrake firmly; do not release the pressure until the vehicle has slowed to the desired speed. The ABS should ensure that steering control will be retained, but do not assume that a vehicle with ABS will stop in a shorter distance.

121. Brakes affected by water. If you have driven through deep water your brakes may be less effective. Test them at the first safe opportunity by pushing gently on the brake pedal to make sure that they work. If they are not fully effective, gently apply light pressure while driving slowly. This will help to dry them out.

122. Coasting. This term describes a vehicle travelling in neutral or with the clutch pressed down. It can reduce driver control because

- engine braking is eliminated
- vehicle speed downhill will increase quickly
- increased use of the footbrake can reduce its effectiveness
- steering response will be affected, particularly on bends and corners
- it may be more difficult to select the appropriate gear when needed.

The Driver and the Environment

123. You **MUST NOT** leave a parked vehicle unattended with the engine running or leave a vehicle engine running unnecessarily while that vehicle is stationary on a public road. Generally, if the vehicle is stationary and is likely to remain so for more than a couple of minutes, you should apply the parking brake and switch off the engine to reduce emissions and noise pollution. However it is permissible to leave the engine running if the vehicle is stationary in traffic or for diagnosing faults.

Law CUR regs 98 & 107

Speed limits

124. You **MUST NOT** exceed the maximum speed limits for the road and for your vehicle (see the table opposite). The presence of street lights generally means that there is a 30mph (48km/h) speed limit unless otherwise specified.

Law RTRA sects 81, 86, 89 & sch 6

125. The speed limit is the absolute maximum and does not mean it is safe to drive at that speed irrespective of conditions. Driving at speeds too fast for the road and traffic conditions is dangerous. You should always reduce your speed when

- the road layout or condition presents hazards, such as bends
- sharing the road with pedestrians, cyclists and horse riders, particularly children, and motorcyclists
- weather conditions make it safer to do so
- driving at night as it is more difficult to see other road users.

Speed Limits

Types of vehicle	Built up areas* MPH (km/h)	Single carriageways MPH (km/h)	Dual carriageways MPH (km/h)	Motorways MPH (km/h)
 **Cars & motorcycles** (including car derived vans up to 2 tonnes maximum laden weight)	30 (48)	60 (96)	70 (112)	70 (112)
 **Cars towing caravans or trailers** (including car derived vans and motorcycles)	30 (48)	50 (80)	60 (96)	60 (96)
 **Buses, coaches and minibuses** (not exceeding 12 metres (39 feet) in overall length)	30 (48)	50 (80)	60 (96)	70 (112)
Goods vehicles (not exceeding 7.5 tonnes maximum laden weight)	30 (48)	50 (80)	60 (96)	70† (112)
 **Goods vehicles** (exceeding 7.5 tonnes maximum laden weight)	30 (48)	40 (64)	50 (80)	60 (96)

* The 30mph (48km/h) limit usually applies to all traffic on all roads with street lighting unless signs show otherwise.
† 60mph (96km/h) if articulated or towing a trailer.

126. Stopping Distances. Drive at a speed that will allow you to stop well within the distance you can see to be clear. You should

- leave enough space between you and the vehicle in front so that you can pull up safely if it suddenly slows down or stops. The safe rule is never to get closer than the overall stopping distance (see Typical Stopping Distances diagram, opposite)
- allow at least a two-second gap between you and the vehicle in front on roads carrying faster-moving traffic and in tunnels where visibility is reduced. The gap should be at least doubled on wet roads and increased still further on icy roads
- remember, large vehicles and motorcycles need a greater distance to stop. If driving a large vehicle in a tunnel, you should allow a four-second gap between you and the vehicle in front.

If you have to stop in a tunnel, leave at least a 5-metre (16 feet) gap between you and the vehicle in front.

Use a fixed point to help measure a two-second gap

Typical Stopping distances

The distances below are a general guide. The distance will depend on your attention (thinking distance), the road surface, the weather and the condition of your vehicle at the time.

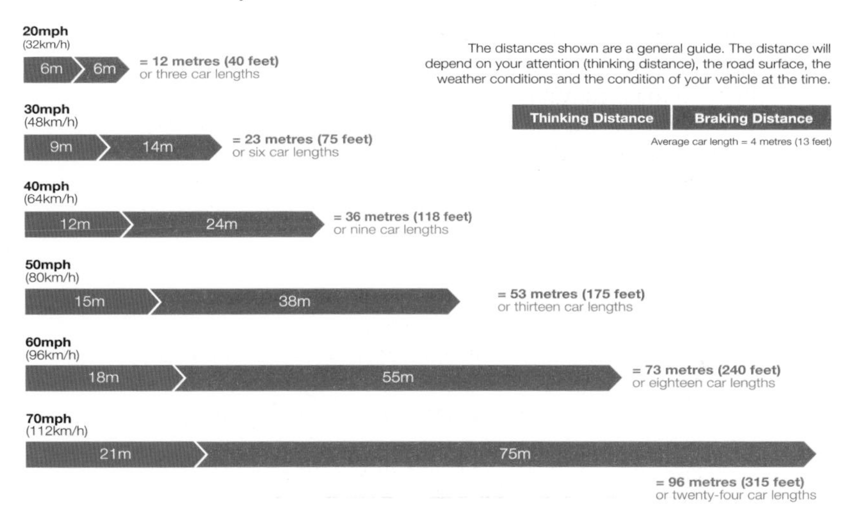

Lines and lane markings on the road

Diagrams of all lines are shown in Road markings.

127. A broken white line. This marks the centre of the road. When this line lengthens and the gaps shorten, it means that there is a hazard ahead. Do not cross it unless you can see the road is clear and wish to overtake or turn off.

128. Double white lines where the line nearest to you is broken. This means you may cross the lines to overtake if it is safe, provided you can complete the manoeuvre before reaching a solid white line on your side. White direction arrows on the road indicate that you need to get back onto your side of the road.

129. Double white lines where the line nearest you is solid. This means you **MUST NOT** cross or straddle it unless it is safe and you need to enter adjoining premises or a side road. You may cross the line if necessary, provided the road is clear, to pass a stationary vehicle, or overtake a pedal cycle, horse or road maintenance vehicle, if they are travelling at 10mph (16km/h) or less.

Laws RTA 1988 sect 36 & TSRGD regs 10 & 26

130. Areas of white diagonal stripes or chevrons painted on the road. These are to separate traffic lanes or to protect traffic turning right.

- If the area is bordered by a broken white line, you should not enter the area unless it is necessary and you can see that it is safe to do so.
- If the area is marked with chevrons and bordered by solid white lines you **MUST NOT** enter it except in an emergency.

Laws MT(E&W)R regs 5, 9, 10 & 16, MT(S)R regs 4, 8, 9 & 14, RTA sect 36 & TSRGD 10(1)

131. Lane dividers. These are short, broken white lines which are used on wide carriageways to divide them into lanes. You should keep between them.

132. Reflective road studs may be used with white lines.

- White studs mark the lanes or the middle of the road.
- Red studs mark the left edge of the road.
- Amber studs mark the central reservation of a dual carriageway or motorway.
- Green studs mark the edge of the main carriageway at lay-bys and slip roads.
- Green/yellow studs indicate temporary adjustments to lane layouts, e.g. where road works are taking place.

Reflective road studs mark the lanes and edges of the carriageway

Multi-lane carriageways

Lane discipline

133. If you need to change lane, first use your mirrors and if necessary take a quick sideways glance to make sure you will not force another road user to change course or speed. When it is safe to do so, signal to indicate your intentions to other road users and when clear, move over.

134. You should follow the signs and road markings and get into the lane as directed. In congested road conditions do not change lanes unnecessarily. Merging in turn is recommended but only if safe and appropriate when vehicles are travelling at a very low speed, e.g. when approaching roadworks or a road traffic incident. It is not recommended at high speed.

Single carriageway

135. Where a single carriageway has three lanes and the road markings or signs do not give priority to traffic in either direction

- use the middle lane only for overtaking or turning right. Remember, you have no more right to use the middle lane than a driver coming from the opposite direction
- do not use the right-hand lane.

136. Where a single carriageway has four or more lanes, use only the lanes that signs or markings indicate.

Dual carriageways

A dual carriageway is a road which has a central reservation to separate the carriageways.

137. On a two-lane dual carriageway you should stay in the left-hand lane. Use the right-hand lane for overtaking or turning right. After overtaking, move back to the left-hand lane when it is safe to do so.

138. On a three-lane dual carriageway, you may use the middle lane or the right-hand lane to overtake but return to the middle and then the left-hand lane when it is safe.

139. Climbing and crawler lanes. These are provided on some hills. Use this lane if you are driving a slow-moving vehicle or if there are vehicles behind you wishing to overtake. Be aware of the signs and road markings which indicate the lane is about to end.

140. Cycle lanes. These are shown by road markings and signs. You **MUST NOT** drive or park in a cycle lane marked by a solid white line during its times of operation. Do not drive or park in a cycle lane marked by a broken white line unless it is unavoidable. You **MUST NOT** park in any cycle lane whilst waiting restrictions apply.
Law RTRA sects 5 & 8

141. Bus lanes. These are shown by road markings and signs that indicate which (if any) other vehicles are permitted to use the bus lane. Unless otherwise indicated, you should not drive in a bus lane during its period of operation. You may enter a bus lane to stop, to load or unload where this is not prohibited.

142. High-occupancy vehicle lanes and other designated vehicle lanes. Lanes may be restricted for use by particular types of vehicle; these restrictions may apply some or all of the time. The operating times and vehicle types will be indicated on the accompanying traffic signs. You **MUST NOT** drive in such lanes during their times of operation unless signs indicate that your vehicle is permitted (see Information signs).

Vehicles permitted to use designated lanes may or may not include cycles, buses, taxis, licensed private hire vehicles, motorcycles, heavy goods vehicles (HGVs) and high-occupancy vehicles (HOVs).
Where HOV lanes are in operation, they **MUST** ONLY be used by

- vehicles containing at least the minimum number of people indicated on the traffic signs
- any other vehicles, such as buses and motorcycles, as indicated on signs prior to the start of the lane, irrespective of the number of occupants.

Laws RTRA sects 5 & 8, & RTA 1988, sect 36

143. One-way streets. Traffic **MUST** travel in the direction indicated by signs. Buses and/or cycles may have a contraflow lane. Choose the correct lane for your exit as soon as you can. Do not change lanes suddenly. Unless road signs or markings indicate otherwise, you should use

- the left-hand lane when going left
- the right-hand lane when going right
- the most appropriate lane when going straight ahead. Remember – traffic could be passing on both sides.

Laws RTA 1988 sect 36 & RTRA sects 5 & 8

General advice

144. You **MUST NOT**
- drive dangerously
- drive without due care and attention
- drive without reasonable consideration for other road users.

Law RTA 1988 sects 2 & 3 as amended by RTA 1991

145. You **MUST NOT** drive on or over a pavement, footpath or bridleway except to gain lawful access to property, or in the case of an emergency.

Laws HA 1835 sect 72 & RTA 1988 sect 34

146. Adapt your driving to the appropriate type and condition of road you are on. In particular
- do not treat speed limits as a target. It is often not appropriate or safe to drive at the maximum speed limit
- take the road and traffic conditions into account. Be prepared for unexpected or difficult situations, for example, the road being blocked beyond a blind bend. Be prepared to adjust your speed as a precaution
- where there are junctions, be prepared for road users emerging
- in side roads and country lanes look out for unmarked junctions where nobody has priority
- be prepared to stop at traffic control systems, roadworks, pedestrian crossings or traffic lights as necessary
- try to anticipate what pedestrians and cyclists might do. If pedestrians, particularly children, are looking the other way, they may step out into the road without seeing you.

147. Be considerate. Be careful of and considerate towards all types of road users, especially those requiring extra care (see Rule 204). You should
- try to be understanding if other road users cause problems; they may be inexperienced or not know the area well
- be patient; remember that anyone can make a mistake
- not allow yourself to become agitated or involved if someone is behaving badly on the road. This will only make the situation worse. Pull over, calm down and, when you feel relaxed, continue your journey
- slow down and hold back if a road user pulls out into your path at a junction. Allow them to get clear. Do not over-react by driving too close behind to intimidate them
- do not throw anything out of a vehicle, for example, cigarette ends, cans, paper or carrier bags. This can endanger other road users, particularly motorcyclists and cyclists.

148. Safe driving and riding needs concentration. Avoid distractions when driving or riding such as

- loud music (this may mask other sounds)
- trying to read maps
- inserting a cassette or CD or tuning a radio
- arguing with your passengers or other road users
- eating and drinking
- smoking.

You **MUST NOT** smoke in public transport vehicles or in vehicles used for work purposes in certain prescribed circumstances. Separate regulations apply to England, Wales and Scotland.

Laws TSf(EV) regs 2007, TSfP(W) regs 2007 & TPSCP(S) regs 2006

Mobile phones and in-vehicle technology

149. You **MUST** exercise proper control of your vehicle at all times. You **MUST NOT** use a hand-held mobile phone, or similar device, when driving or when supervising a learner driver, except to call 999 or 112 in a genuine emergency when it is unsafe or impractical to stop. Never use a hand-held microphone when driving. Using hands-free equipment is also likely to distract your attention from the road. It is far safer not to use any telephone while you are driving or riding – find a safe place to stop first or use the voicemail facility and listen to messages later.

Laws RTA 1988 sects 2 & 3 & CUR regs 104 & 110

150. There is a danger of driver distraction being caused by in-vehicle systems such as satellite navigation systems, congestion warning systems, PCs, multi-media, etc. You **MUST** exercise proper control of your vehicle at all times. Do not rely on driver assistance systems such as cruise control or lane departure warnings. They are available to assist but you should not reduce your concentration levels. Do not be distracted by maps or screen-based information (such as navigation or vehicle management systems) while driving or riding. If necessary find a safe place to stop.

Laws RTA 1988 sects 2 & 3 & CUR reg 104

151. In slow-moving traffic. You should

- reduce the distance between you and the vehicle ahead to maintain traffic flow
- never get so close to the vehicle in front that you cannot stop safely
- leave enough space to be able to manoeuvre if the vehicle in front breaks down or an emergency vehicle needs to get past
- not change lanes to the left to overtake
- allow access into and from side roads, as blocking these will add to congestion
- be aware of cyclists and motorcyclists who may be passing on either side.

Do not block access to a side road

Driving in built-up areas

152. Residential streets. You should drive slowly and carefully on streets where there are likely to be pedestrians, cyclists and parked cars. In some areas a 20mph (32km/h) maximum speed limit may be in force. Look out for

- vehicles emerging from junctions or driveways
- vehicles moving off
- car doors opening
- pedestrians
- children running out from between parked cars
- cyclists and motorcyclists.

153. Traffic-calming measures. On some roads there are features such as road humps, chicanes and narrowings which are intended to slow you down. When you approach these features reduce your speed. Allow cyclists and motorcyclists room to pass through them. Maintain a reduced speed along the whole of the stretch of road within the calming measures. Give way to oncoming road users if directed to do so by signs. You should not overtake other moving road users while in these areas.

Chicanes may be used to slow traffic down

Country roads

154. Take extra care on country roads and reduce your speed at approaches to bends, which can be sharper than they appear, and at junctions and turnings, which may be partially hidden. Be prepared for pedestrians, horse riders, cyclists, slow-moving farm vehicles or mud on the road surface. Make sure you can stop within the distance you can see to be clear. You should also reduce your speed where country roads enter villages.

155. Single-track roads. These are only wide enough for one vehicle. They may have special passing places. If you see a vehicle coming towards you, or the driver behind wants to overtake, pull into a passing place on your left, or wait opposite a passing place on your right. Give way to vehicles coming uphill whenever you can. If necessary, reverse until you reach a passing place to let the other vehicle pass. Slow down when passing pedestrians, cyclists and horse riders.

156. Do not park in passing places.

Vehicles prohibited from using roads and pavements

157. Certain motorised vehicles do not meet the construction and technical requirements for road vehicles and are generally not intended, not suitable and not legal for road, pavement, footpath, cycle path or bridleway use. These include most types of miniature motorcycles, also called mini motos, and motorised scooters, also called go peds, which are powered by electric or internal combustion engines. These types of vehicle **MUST NOT** be used on roads, pavements, footpaths or bridleways.

Laws RTA 1988 sects 34, 41a, 42, 47, 63 & 66, HA 1835, sect 72, & R(S)A sect 129

158. Certain models of motorcycles, motor tricycles and quadricycles, also called quad bikes, are suitable only for off-road use and do not meet legal standards for use on roads. Vehicles that do not meet these standards **MUST NOT** be used on roads. They **MUST NOT** be used on pavements, footpaths, cycle paths or bridleways either. You **MUST** make sure that any motorcycle, motor tricycle, quadricycle or any other motor vehicle meets legal standards and is properly registered, taxed and insured before using it on the roads. Even when registered, taxed and insured for the road, vehicles **MUST NOT** be used on pavements.

Laws RTA 1988 sects 34, 41a, 42, 47, 63, 66 & 156, HA 1835, sect 72, R(S)A sect 129, & VERA Sects 1, 29, 31A, & 43A

Using the Road

General rules

159. Before moving off you should

- use all mirrors to check the road is clear
- look round to check the blind spots (the areas you are unable to see in the mirrors)
- signal if necessary before moving out
- look round for a final check.

Move off only when it is safe to do so.

Check the blind spot before moving off

160. Once moving you should

- keep to the left, unless road signs or markings indicate otherwise. The exceptions are when you want to overtake, turn right or pass parked vehicles or pedestrians in the road
- keep well to the left on right-hand bends. This will improve your view of the road and help avoid the risk of colliding with traffic approaching from the opposite direction
- drive with both hands on the wheel where possible. This will help you to remain in full control of the vehicle at all times
- be aware of other road users, especially cycles and motorcycles who may be filtering through the traffic. These are more difficult to see than larger vehicles and their riders are particularly vulnerable. Give them plenty of room, especially if you are driving a long vehicle or towing a trailer
- select a lower gear before you reach a long downhill slope. This will help to control your speed
- when towing, remember the extra length will affect overtaking and manoeuvring. The extra weight will also affect the braking and acceleration.

161. Mirrors. All mirrors should be used effectively throughout your journey. You should

- use your mirrors frequently so that you always know what is behind and to each side of you
- use them in good time before you signal or change direction or speed
- be aware that mirrors do not cover all areas and there will be blind spots. You will need to look round and check.

Remember: Mirrors – Signal – Manoeuvre

Overtaking

162. Before overtaking you should make sure

- the road is sufficiently clear ahead
- road users are not beginning to overtake you
- there is a suitable gap in front of the road user you plan to overtake.

163. Overtake only when it is safe and legal to do so. You should

- not get too close to the vehicle you intend to overtake
- use your mirrors, signal when it is safe to do so, take a quick sideways glance if necessary into the blind spot area and then start to move out
- not assume that you can simply follow a vehicle ahead which is overtaking; there may only be enough room for one vehicle
- move quickly past the vehicle you are overtaking, once you have started to overtake. Allow plenty of room. Move back to the left as soon as you can but do not cut in
- take extra care at night and in poor visibility when it is harder to judge speed and distance
- give way to oncoming vehicles before passing parked vehicles or other obstructions on your side of the road
- only overtake on the left if the vehicle in front is signalling to turn right, and there is room to do so
- stay in your lane if traffic is moving slowly in queues. If the queue on your right is moving more slowly than you are, you may pass on the left
- give motorcyclists, cyclists and horse riders at least as much room as you would when overtaking a car (see Rules 211–215).

Remember: Mirrors – Signal – Manoeuvre

Give vulnerable road users at least as much space as you would a car

164. Large vehicles. Overtaking these is more difficult. You should

- drop back. This will increase your ability to see ahead and should allow the driver of the large vehicle to see you in their mirrors. Getting too close to large vehicles, including agricultural vehicles such as a tractor with a trailer or other fixed equipment, will obscure your view of the road ahead and there may be another slow-moving vehicle in front
- make sure that you have enough room to complete your overtaking manoeuvre before committing yourself. It takes longer to pass a large vehicle. If in doubt do not overtake
- not assume you can follow a vehicle ahead which is overtaking a long vehicle. If a problem develops, they may abort overtaking and pull back in.

Do not cut in too quickly

165. You **MUST NOT** overtake

- if you would have to cross or straddle double white lines with a solid line nearest to you (but see Rule129)
- if you would have to enter an area designed to divide traffic, if it is surrounded by a solid white line
- the nearest vehicle to a pedestrian crossing, especially when it has stopped to let pedestrians cross
- if you would have to enter a lane reserved for buses, trams or cycles during its hours of operation
- after a 'No Overtaking' sign and until you pass a sign cancelling the restriction.

Laws RTA 1988 sect 36, TSRGD regs 10, 22, 23 & 24, ZPPPCRGD reg 24

166. DO NOT overtake if there is any doubt, or where you cannot see far enough ahead to be sure it is safe. For example, when you are approaching

- a corner or bend
- a hump bridge
- the brow of a hill.

167. DO NOT overtake where you might come into conflict with other road users. For example

- approaching or at a road junction on either side of the road
- where the road narrows
- when approaching a school crossing patrol
- between the kerb and a bus or tram when it is at a stop
- where traffic is queuing at junctions or roadworks
- when you would force another road user to swerve or slow down
- at a level crossing
- when a road user is indicating right, even if you believe the signal should have been cancelled. Do not take a risk; wait for the signal to be cancelled
- stay behind if you are following a cyclist approaching a roundabout or junction, and you intend to turn left
- when a tram is standing at a kerbside tram stop and there is no clearly marked passing lane for other traffic.

168. Being overtaken. If a driver is trying to overtake you, maintain a steady course and speed, slowing down if necessary to let the vehicle pass. Never obstruct drivers who wish to pass. Speeding up or driving unpredictably while someone is overtaking you is dangerous. Drop back to maintain a two-second gap if someone overtakes and pulls into the gap in front of you.

169. Do not hold up a long queue of traffic, especially if you are driving a large or slow-moving vehicle. Check your mirrors frequently, and if necessary, pull in where it is safe and let traffic pass.

Road junctions

170. Take extra care at junctions. You should

- watch out for cyclists, motorcyclists, powered wheelchairs/mobility scooters and pedestrians as they are not always easy to see. Be aware that they may not have seen or heard you if you are approaching from behind
- watch out for pedestrians crossing a road into which you are turning. If they have started to cross they have priority, so give way
- watch out for long vehicles which may be turning at a junction ahead; they may have to use the whole width of the road to make the turn (see Rule 221)
- watch out for horse riders who may take a different line on the road from that which you would expect
- not assume, when waiting at a junction, that a vehicle coming from the right and signalling left will actually turn. Wait and make sure
- look all around before emerging. Do not cross or join a road until there is a gap large enough for you to do so safely.

Give way to pedestrians who have started to cross

171. You **MUST** stop behind the line at a junction with a 'Stop' sign and a solid white line across the road. Wait for a safe gap in the traffic before you move off.

Laws RTA 1988 sect 36 & TSRGD regs 10 & 16

172. The approach to a junction may have a 'Give Way' sign or a triangle marked on the road. You **MUST** give way to traffic on the main road when emerging from a junction with broken white lines across the road.

Laws RTA 1988 sect 36 & TSRGD regs 10(1),16(1) & 25

173. Dual carriageways. When crossing or turning right, first assess whether the central reservation is deep enough to protect the full length of your vehicle.

- If it is, then you should treat each half of the carriageway as a separate road. Wait in the central reservation until there is a safe gap in the traffic on the second half of the road.
- If the central reservation is too shallow for the length of your vehicle, wait until you can cross both carriageways in one go.

Assess your vehicle's length and do not obstruct traffic

174. Box junctions. These have criss-cross yellow lines painted on the road (see Road markings). You **MUST NOT** enter the box until your exit road or lane is clear. However, you may enter the box and wait when you want to turn right, and are only stopped from doing so by oncoming traffic, or by other vehicles waiting to turn right. At signalled roundabouts you **MUST NOT** enter the box unless you can cross over it completely without stopping.

Law TSRGD regs 10(1) & 29(2)

Enter a box junction only if your exit road is clear

Junctions controlled by traffic lights

175. You **MUST** stop behind the white 'Stop' line across your side of the road unless the light is green. If the amber light appears you may go on only if you have already crossed the stop line or are so close to it that to stop might cause a collision.

Laws RTA 1988 sect 36 & TSRGD regs 10 & 36

176. You **MUST NOT** move forward over the white line when the red light is showing. Only go forward when the traffic lights are green if there is room for you to clear the junction safely or you are taking up a position to turn right. If the traffic lights are not working, treat the situation as you would an unmarked junction and proceed with great care.

Laws RTA 1988 sect 36 & TSRGD regs 10 & 36

177. Green filter arrow. This indicates a filter lane only. Do not enter that lane unless you want to go in the direction of the arrow. You may proceed in the direction of the green arrow when it, or the full green light shows. Give other traffic, especially cyclists, time and room to move into the correct lane.

178. Advanced stop lines. Some signal-controlled junctions have advanced stop lines to allow cycles to be positioned ahead of other traffic. Motorists, including motorcyclists, **MUST** stop at the first white line reached if the lights are amber or red and should avoid blocking the way or encroaching on the marked area at other times, e.g. if the junction ahead is blocked. If your vehicle has proceeded over the first white line at the time that the signal goes red, you **MUST** stop at the second white line, even if your vehicle is in the marked area. Allow cyclists time and space to move off when the green signal shows.
Laws RTA 1988 sect 36 & TSRGD regs 10, 36(1) & 43(2)

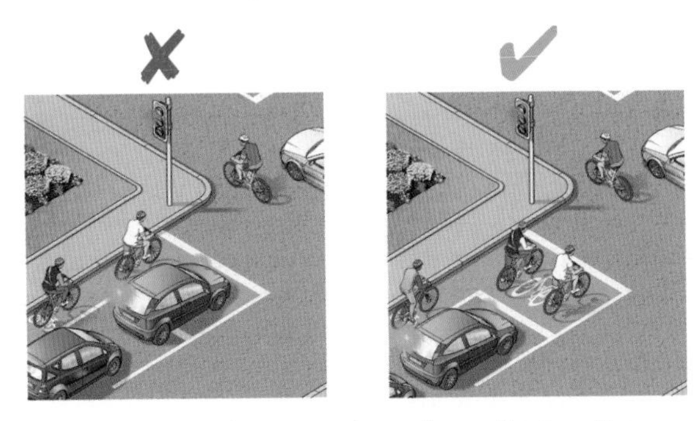

Do not unnecessarily encroach on the cyclists' waiting area

Turning right

179. Well before you turn right you should

- use your mirrors to make sure you know the position and movement of traffic behind you
- give a right-turn signal
- take up a position just left of the middle of the road or in the space marked for traffic turning right
- leave room for other vehicles to pass on the left, if possible.

180. Wait until there is a safe gap between you and any oncoming vehicle. Watch out for cyclists, motorcyclists, pedestrians and other road users. Check your mirrors and blind spot again to make sure you are not being overtaken, then make the turn. Do not cut the corner. Take great care when turning into a main road; you will need to watch for traffic in both directions and wait for a safe gap.
Remember: Mirrors – Signal – Manoeuvre

Position your vehicle correctly to avoid obstructing traffic

181. When turning right at crossroads where an oncoming vehicle is also turning right, there is a choice of two methods

- turn right side to right side; keep the other vehicle on your right and turn behind it. This is generally the safer method as you have a clear view of any approaching traffic when completing your turn
- left side to left side, turning in front of each other. This can block your view of oncoming vehicles, so take extra care. Cyclists and motorcyclists in particular may be hidden from your view. Road layout, markings or how the other vehicle is positioned can determine which course should be taken.

Left – Turning right side to right side.
Right – Turning left side to left side.

Turning left

182. Use your mirrors and give a left-turn signal well before you turn left. Do not overtake just before you turn left and watch out for traffic coming up on your left before you make the turn, especially if driving a large vehicle. Cyclists, motorcyclists and other road users in particular may be hidden from your view.

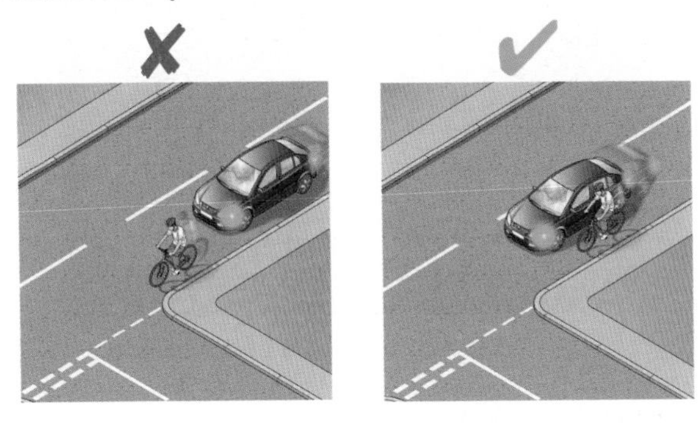

Do not cut in on cyclists

183. When turning

- keep as close to the left as is safe and practicable
- give way to any vehicles using a bus lane, cycle lane or tramway from either direction.

Roundabouts

184. On approaching a roundabout take notice and act on all the information available to you, including traffic signs, traffic lights and lane markings which direct you into the correct lane. You should

- use **Mirrors – Signal – Manoeuvre** at all stages
- decide as early as possible which exit you need to take
- give an appropriate signal (see Rule 186). Time your signals so as not to confuse other road users
- get into the correct lane
- adjust your speed and position to fit in with traffic conditions
- be aware of the speed and position of all the road users around you.

185. When reaching the roundabout you should

- give priority to traffic approaching from your right, unless directed otherwise by signs, road markings or traffic lights
- check whether road markings allow you to enter the roundabout without giving way. If so, proceed, but still look to the right before joining

- watch out for all other road users already on the roundabout; be aware they may not be signalling correctly or at all
- look forward before moving off to make sure traffic in front has moved off.

Follow the correct procedure at roundabouts

186. Signals and position. When taking the first exit, unless signs or markings indicate otherwise

- signal left and approach in the left-hand lane
- keep to the left on the roundabout and continue signalling left to leave.

When taking an exit to the right or going full circle, unless signs or markings indicate otherwise

- signal right and approach in the right-hand lane
- keep to the right on the roundabout until you need to change lanes to exit the roundabout
- signal left after you have passed the exit before the one you want.

When taking any intermediate exit, unless signs or markings indicate otherwise

- select the appropriate lane on approach to and on the roundabout
- you should not normally need to signal on approach
- stay in this lane until you need to alter course to exit the roundabout
- signal left after you have passed the exit before the one you want.

When there are more than three lanes at the entrance to a roundabout, use the most appropriate lane on approach and through it.

187. In all cases watch out for and give plenty of room to

- pedestrians who may be crossing the approach and exit roads
- traffic crossing in front of you on the roundabout, especially vehicles intending to leave by the next exit
- traffic which may be straddling lanes or positioned incorrectly
- motorcyclists
- cyclists and horse riders who may stay in the left-hand lane and signal right if they intend to continue round the roundabout. Allow them to do so
- long vehicles (including those towing trailers). These might have to take a different course or straddle lanes either approaching or on the roundabout because of their length. Watch out for their signals.

188. Mini-roundabouts. Approach these in the same way as normal roundabouts. All vehicles **MUST** pass round the central markings except large vehicles which are physically incapable of doing so. Remember, there is less space to manoeuvre and less time to signal. Avoid making U-turns at mini-roundabouts. Beware of others doing this.

Laws RTA 1988 sect 36 & TSRGD regs 10(1) & 16(1)

189. At double mini-roundabouts treat each roundabout separately and give way to traffic from the right.

190. Multiple roundabouts. At some complex junctions, there may be a series of mini-roundabouts at each intersection. Treat each mini-roundabout separately and follow the normal rules.

Treat each roundabout separately

Pedestrian crossings

191. You **MUST NOT** park on a crossing or in the area covered by the zig-zag lines. You **MUST NOT** overtake the moving vehicle nearest the crossing or the vehicle nearest the crossing which has stopped to give way to pedestrians.

Laws ZPPPCRGD regs 18, 20 & 24, RTRA sect 25(5) & TSRGD regs 10, 27 & 28

192. In queuing traffic, you should keep the crossing clear.

Keep the crossing clear

193. You should take extra care where the view of either side of the crossing is blocked by queuing traffic or incorrectly parked vehicles. Pedestrians may be crossing between stationary vehicles.

194. Allow pedestrians plenty of time to cross and do not harass them by revving your engine or edging forward.

195. Zebra crossings. As you approach a zebra crossing

- look out for pedestrians waiting to cross and be ready to slow down or stop to let them cross
- you **MUST** give way when a pedestrian has moved onto a crossing
- allow more time for stopping on wet or icy roads
- do not wave or use your horn to invite pedestrians across; this could be dangerous if another vehicle is approaching
- be aware of pedestrians approaching from the side of the crossing.

A zebra crossing with a central island is two separate crossings (see Rule 20).

Law ZPPPCRGD reg 25

Signal-controlled crossings

196. Pelican crossings. These are signal-controlled crossings where flashing amber follows the red 'Stop' light. You **MUST** stop when the red light shows. When the amber light is flashing, you **MUST** give way to any pedestrians on the crossing. If the amber light is flashing and there are no pedestrians on the crossing, you may proceed with caution.
Laws ZPPPCRGD regs 23 & 26 & RTRA sect 25(5)

Allow pedestrians to cross when the amber light is flashing

197. Pelican crossings which go straight across the road are one crossing, even when there is a central island. You **MUST** wait for pedestrians who are crossing from the other side of the island.
Laws ZPPPCRGD reg 26 & RTRA sect 25(5)

198. Give way to anyone still crossing after the signal for vehicles has changed to green. This advice applies to all crossings.

199. Toucan, puffin and equestrian crossings. These are similar to pelican crossings, but there is no flashing amber phase; the light sequence for traffic at these three crossings is the same as at traffic lights. If the signal-controlled crossing is not working, proceed with extreme caution.

Reversing

200. Choose an appropriate place to manoeuvre. If you need to turn your vehicle around, wait until you find a safe place. Try not to reverse or turn round in a busy road; find a quiet side road or drive round a block of side streets.

201. Do not reverse from a side road into a main road. When using a driveway, reverse in and drive out if you can.

202. Look carefully before you start reversing. You should

- use all your mirrors
- check the 'blind spot' behind you (the part of the road you cannot see easily in the mirrors)
- check there are no pedestrians (particularly children), cyclists, other road users or obstructions in the road behind you.

Reverse slowly while

- checking all around
- looking mainly through the rear window
- being aware that the front of your vehicle will swing out as you turn.

Get someone to guide you if you cannot see clearly.

Check all round when reversing

203. You **MUST NOT** reverse your vehicle further than necessary.
Law CUR reg 106

Road users requiring extra care

204. The most vulnerable road users are pedestrians, cyclists, motorcyclists and horse riders. It is particularly important to be aware of children, older and disabled people, and learner and inexperienced drivers and riders.

Pedestrians

205. There is a risk of pedestrians, especially children, stepping unexpectedly into the road. You should drive with the safety of children in mind at a speed suitable for the conditions.

206. Drive carefully and slowly when

- in crowded shopping streets, Home Zones and Quiet Lanes (see Rule 218) or residential areas
- driving past bus and tram stops; pedestrians may emerge suddenly into the road
- passing parked vehicles, especially ice cream vans; children are more interested in ice cream than traffic and may run into the road unexpectedly
- needing to cross a pavement or cycle track; for example, to reach or leave a driveway. Give way to pedestrians and cyclists on the pavement
- reversing into a side road; look all around the vehicle and give way to any pedestrians who may be crossing the road
- turning at road junctions; give way to pedestrians who are already crossing the road into which you are turning
- the pavement is closed due to street repairs and pedestrians are directed to use the road
- approaching pedestrians on narrow rural roads without a footway or footpath. Always slow down and be prepared to stop if necessary, giving them plenty of room as you drive past.

Watch out for children in busy areas

207. Particularly vulnerable pedestrians. These include

- children and older pedestrians who may not be able to judge your speed and could step into the road in front of you. At 40mph (64km/h) your vehicle will probably kill any pedestrians it hits. At 20mph (32km/h) there is only a 1 in 20 chance of the pedestrian being killed. So kill your speed
- older pedestrians who may need more time to cross the road. Be patient and allow them to cross in their own time. Do not hurry them by revving your engine or edging forward
- people with disabilities. People with hearing impairments may not be aware of your vehicle approaching. Those with walking difficulties require more time
- blind or partially sighted people, who may be carrying a white cane or using a guide dog. They may not be able to see you approaching
- deafblind people who may be carrying a white cane with a red band or using a dog with a red and white harness. They may not see or hear instructions or signals.

208. Near schools. Drive slowly and be particularly aware of young cyclists and pedestrians. In some places, there may be a flashing amber signal below the 'School' warning sign which tells you that there may be children crossing the road ahead. Drive very slowly until you are clear of the area.

209. Drive carefully and slowly when passing a stationary bus showing a 'School Bus' sign (see Vehicle markings) as children may be getting on or off.

210. You **MUST** stop when a school crossing patrol shows a 'Stop for children' sign (see pages Signals by authorised persons and Signs giving orders).
Law RTRA sect 28

Motorcyclists and cyclists

211. It is often difficult to see motorcyclists and cyclists, especially when they are coming up from behind, coming out of junctions, at roundabouts, overtaking you or filtering through traffic. Always look out for them before you emerge from a junction; they could be approaching faster than you think. When turning right across a line of slow-moving or stationary traffic, look out for cyclists or motorcyclists on the inside of the traffic you are crossing. Be especially careful when turning, and when changing direction or lane. Be sure to check mirrors and blind spots carefully.

Look out for motorcyclists and cyclists at junctions

212. When passing motorcyclists and cyclists, give them plenty of room (see Rules162–167). If they look over their shoulder it could mean that they intend to pull out, turn right or change direction. Give them time and space to do so.

213. Motorcyclists and cyclists may suddenly need to avoid uneven road surfaces and obstacles such as drain covers or oily, wet or icy patches on the road. Give them plenty of room and pay particular attention to any sudden change of direction they may have to make.

Other road users

214. Animals. When passing animals, drive slowly. Give them plenty of room and be ready to stop. Do not scare animals by sounding your horn, revving your engine or accelerating rapidly once you have passed them. Look out for animals being led, driven or ridden on the road and take extra care. Keep your speed down at bends and on narrow country roads. If a road is blocked by a herd of animals, stop and switch off your engine until they have left the road. Watch out for animals on unfenced roads.

215. Horse riders and horse-drawn vehicles. Be particularly careful of horse riders and horse-drawn vehicles especially when overtaking. Always pass wide and slowly. Horse riders are often children, so take extra care and remember riders may ride in double file when escorting a young or inexperienced horse or rider. Look out for horse riders' and horse drivers' signals and heed a request to slow down or stop. Take great care and treat all horses as a potential hazard; they can be unpredictable, despite the efforts of their rider/driver.

216. Older drivers. Their reactions may be slower than other drivers. Make allowance for this.

217. Learners and inexperienced drivers. They may not be so skilful at anticipating and responding to events. Be particularly patient with learner drivers and young drivers. Drivers who have recently passed their test may display a 'new driver' plate or sticker (see Annexe 8 – Safety code for new drivers).

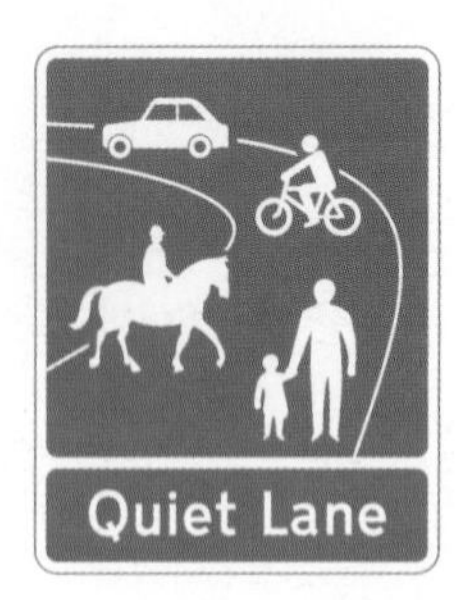

218. Home Zones and Quiet Lanes. These are places where people could be using the whole of the road for a range of activities such as children playing or for a community event. You should drive slowly and carefully and be prepared to stop to allow people extra time to make space for you to pass them in safety.

Other vehicles

219. Emergency and Incident Support vehicles. You should look and listen for ambulances, fire engines, police, doctors or other emergency vehicles using flashing blue, red or green lights and sirens or flashing headlights, or Highways Agency Traffic Officer and Incident Support vehicles using flashing amber lights. When one approaches do not panic. Consider the route of such a vehicle and take appropriate action to let it pass, while complying with all traffic signs. If necessary, pull to the side of the road and stop, but try to avoid stopping before the brow of a hill, a bend or narrow section of road. Do not endanger yourself, other road users or pedestrians and avoid mounting the kerb. Do not brake harshly on approach to a junction or roundabout, as a following vehicle may not have the same view as you.

220. Powered vehicles used by disabled people. These small vehicles travel at a maximum speed of 8mph (12km/h). On a dual carriageway where the speed limit exceeds 50mph (80km/h) they **MUST** have a flashing amber beacon, but on other roads you may not have that advance warning (see Rules 36–46 inclusive).

Law RVLR reg 17(1) & 26

221. Large vehicles. These may need extra road space to turn or to deal with a hazard that you are not able to see. If you are following a large vehicle, such as a bus or articulated lorry, be aware that the driver may not be able to see you in the mirrors. Be prepared to stop and wait if it needs room or time to turn.

Large vehicles need extra room

222. Large vehicles can block your view. Your ability to see and to plan ahead will be improved if you pull back to increase your separation distance. Be patient, as larger vehicles are subject to lower speed limits than cars and motorcycles. Many large vehicles may be fitted with speed limiting devices which will restrict speed to 56mph (90km/h) even on a motorway.

223. Buses, coaches and trams. Give priority to these vehicles when you can do so safely, especially when they signal to pull away from stops. Look out for people getting off a bus or tram and crossing the road.

224. Electric vehicles. Be careful of electric vehicles such as milk floats and trams. Trams move quickly but silently and cannot steer to avoid you.

225. Vehicles with flashing amber beacons. These warn of a slow-moving or stationary vehicle (such as a Traffic Officer vehicle, salt spreader, snow plough or recovery vehicle) or abnormal loads, so approach with caution. On unrestricted dual carriageways, motor vehicles first used on or after 1 January 1947 with a maximum speed of 25mph (40km/h) or less (such as tractors) **MUST** use a flashing amber beacon (also see Rule 220).

Law RVLR 1989, reg 17

Driving in adverse weather conditions

226. You **MUST** use headlights when visibility is seriously reduced, generally when you cannot see for more than 100 metres (328 feet). You may also use front or rear fog lights but you **MUST** switch them off when visibility improves (see Rule 236).

Law RVLR regs 25 & 27

227. Wet weather. In wet weather, stopping distances will be at least double those required for stopping on dry roads (see Rule 126). This is because your tyres have less grip on the road. In wet weather

- you should keep well back from the vehicle in front. This will increase your ability to see and plan ahead
- if the steering becomes unresponsive, it probably means that water is preventing the tyres from gripping the road. Ease off the accelerator and slow down gradually
- the rain and spray from vehicles may make it difficult to see and be seen
- be aware of the dangers of spilt diesel that will make the surface very slippery (see Annexe 6)
- take extra care around pedestrians, cyclists, motorcyclists and horse riders.

Icy and snowy weather

228. In winter check the local weather forecast for warnings of icy or snowy weather. **DO NOT** drive in these conditions unless your journey is essential. If it is, take great care and allow more time for your journey. Take an emergency kit of de-icer and ice scraper, torch, warm clothing and boots, first aid kit, jump leads and a shovel, together with a warm drink and emergency food in case you get stuck or your vehicle breaks down.

229. Before you set off

- you **MUST** be able to see, so clear all snow and ice from all your windows
- you **MUST** ensure that lights are clean and number plates are clearly visible and legible
- make sure the mirrors are clear and the windows are demisted thoroughly
- remove all snow that might fall off into the path of other road users
- check your planned route is clear of delays and that no further snowfalls or severe weather are predicted.

Laws CUR reg 30, RVLR reg 23, VERA sect 43 & RV(DRM)R reg 11

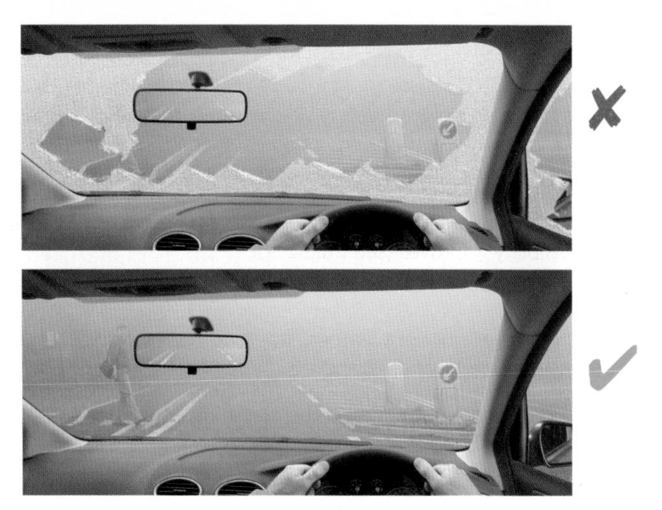

Make sure your windscreen is completely clear

230. When driving in icy or snowy weather

- drive with care, even if the roads have been treated
- keep well back from the road user in front as stopping distances can be ten times greater than on dry roads
- take care when overtaking vehicles spreading salt or other de-icer, particularly if you are riding a motorcycle or cycle
- watch out for snowploughs which may throw out snow on either side. Do not overtake them unless the lane you intend to use has been cleared
- be prepared for the road conditions to change over relatively short distances
- listen to travel bulletins and take note of variable message signs that may provide information about weather, road and traffic conditions ahead.

231. Drive extremely carefully when the roads are icy. Avoid sudden actions as these could cause loss of control. You should

- drive at a slow speed in as high a gear as possible; accelerate and brake very gently
- drive particularly slowly on bends where loss of control is more likely. Brake progressively on the straight before you reach a bend. Having slowed down, steer smoothly round the bend, avoiding sudden actions
- check your grip on the road surface when there is snow or ice by choosing a safe place to brake gently. If the steering feels unresponsive this may indicate ice and your vehicle losing its grip on the road. When travelling on ice, tyres make virtually no noise.

Windy weather

232. High-sided vehicles are most affected by windy weather, but strong gusts can also blow a car, cyclist, motorcyclist or horse rider off course. This can happen on open stretches of road exposed to strong crosswinds, or when passing bridges or gaps in hedges.

233. In very windy weather your vehicle may be affected by turbulence created by large vehicles. Motorcyclists are particularly affected, so keep well back from them when they are overtaking a high-sided vehicle.

Fog

234. Before entering fog check your mirrors then slow down. If the word 'Fog' is shown on a roadside signal but the road is clear, be prepared for a bank of fog or drifting patchy fog ahead. Even if it seems to be clearing, you can suddenly find yourself in thick fog.

235. When driving in fog you should

- use your lights as required (see Rule 226)
- keep a safe distance behind the vehicle in front. Rear lights can give a false sense of security
- be able to pull up well within the distance you can see clearly. This is particularly important on motorways and dual carriageways, as vehicles are travelling faster
- use your windscreen wipers and demisters
- beware of other drivers not using headlights
- not accelerate to get away from a vehicle which is too close behind you
- check your mirrors before you slow down. Then use your brakes so that your brake lights warn drivers behind you that you are slowing down
- stop in the correct position at a junction with limited visibility and listen for traffic. When you are sure it is safe to emerge, do so positively and do not hesitate in a position that puts you directly in the path of approaching vehicles.

236. You **MUST NOT** use front or rear fog lights unless visibility is seriously reduced (see Rule 226) as they dazzle other road users and can obscure your brake lights. You **MUST** switch them off when visibility improves.
Law RVLR regs 25 & 27

Hot weather

237. Keep your vehicle well ventilated to avoid drowsiness. Be aware that the road surface may become soft or if it rains after a dry spell it may become slippery. These conditions could affect your steering and braking. If you are dazzled by bright sunlight, slow down and if necessary, stop.

Waiting and parking

238. You **MUST NOT** wait or park on yellow lines during the times of operation shown on nearby time plates (or zone entry signs if in a Controlled Parking Zone) – see Information signs and Road markings. Double yellow lines indicate a prohibition of waiting at any time even if there are no upright signs. You **MUST NOT** wait or park, or stop to set down and pick up passengers, on school entrance markings (see Road markings) when upright signs indicate a prohibition of stopping.

Law RTRA sects 5 & 8

Parking

239. Use off-street parking areas, or bays marked out with white lines on the road as parking places, wherever possible. If you have to stop on the roadside

- do not park facing against the traffic flow
- stop as close as you can to the side
- do not stop too close to a vehicle displaying a Blue Badge: remember, the occupant may need more room to get in or out
- you **MUST** switch off the engine, headlights and fog lights
- you **MUST** apply the handbrake before leaving the vehicle
- you **MUST** ensure you do not hit anyone when you open your door. Check for cyclists or other traffic
- it is safer for your passengers (especially children) to get out of the vehicle on the side next to the kerb
- put all valuables out of sight and make sure your vehicle is secure
- lock your vehicle.

Laws CUR reg 98, 105 & 107, RVLR reg 27 & RTA 1988 sect 42

Check before opening your door

240. You **MUST NOT** stop or park on
- the carriageway or the hard shoulder of a motorway except in an emergency (see Rule 270)
- a pedestrian crossing, including the area marked by the zig-zag lines (see Rule 191)
- a clearway (see Traffic signs)
- taxi bays as indicated by upright signs and markings
- an Urban Clearway within its hours of operation, even when a broken white line is on your side of the road, except to pick up or set down passengers (see Traffic signs)
- a road marked with double white lines, except to pick up or set down passengers
- a tram or cycle lane during its period of operation
- a cycle track
- red lines, in the case of specially designated 'red routes', unless otherwise indicated by signs.

Any vehicle may enter a bus lane to stop, load or unload where this is not prohibited (see Rule 141).

Laws MT(E&W)R regs 7 & 9, MT(S)R regs 6 & 8, ZPPPCRGD regs 18 & 20, RTRA sects 5, 6 & 8, TSRGD regs 10, 26 & 27, RTA 1988 sects 21(1) & 36

241. You **MUST NOT** park in parking spaces reserved for specific users, such as Blue Badge holders, residents or motorcycles, unless entitled to do so.

Laws CSDPA sect 21 & RTRA sects 5 & 8

242. You **MUST NOT** leave your vehicle or trailer in a dangerous position or where it causes any unnecessary obstruction of the road.

Laws RTA 1988, sect 22 & CUR reg 103

243. DO NOT stop or park
- near a school entrance
- anywhere you would prevent access for Emergency Services
- at or near a bus or tram stop or taxi rank
- on the approach to a level crossing/tramway crossing
- opposite or within 10 metres (32 feet) of a junction, except in an authorised parking space
- near the brow of a hill or hump bridge
- opposite a traffic island or (if this would cause an obstruction) another parked vehicle
- where you would force other traffic to enter a tram lane
- where the kerb has been lowered to help wheelchair users and powered mobility vehicles

- in front of an entrance to a property
- on a bend
- where you would obstruct cyclists' use of cycle facilities

except when forced to do so by stationary traffic.

244. You **MUST NOT** park partially or wholly on the pavement in London, and should not do so elsewhere unless signs permit it. Parking on the pavement can obstruct and seriously inconvenience pedestrians, people in wheelchairs or with visual impairments and people with prams or pushchairs.

Law GL(GP)A sect 15

245. Controlled Parking Zones. The zone entry signs indicate the times when the waiting restrictions within the zone are in force. Parking may be allowed in some places at other times. Otherwise parking will be within separately signed and marked bays.

246. Goods vehicles. Vehicles with a maximum laden weight of over 7.5 tonnes (including any trailer) **MUST NOT** be parked on a verge, pavement or any land situated between carriageways, without police permission. The only exception is when parking is essential for loading and unloading, in which case the vehicle **MUST NOT** be left unattended.

Law RTA 1988 sect 19

247. Loading and unloading. Do not load or unload where there are yellow markings on the kerb and upright signs advise restrictions are in place (see Road markings). This may be permitted where parking is otherwise restricted. On red routes, specially marked and signed bays indicate where and when loading and unloading is permitted.

Law RTRA sects 5 & 8

Parking at night

248. You **MUST NOT** park on a road at night facing against the direction of the traffic flow unless in a recognised parking space.

Laws CUR reg 101 & RVLR reg 24

249. All vehicles **MUST** display parking lights when parked on a road or a lay-by on a road with a speed limit greater than 30mph (48km/h).

Law RVLR reg 24

250. Cars, goods vehicles not exceeding 1525kg unladen weight, invalid carriages, motorcycles and pedal cycles may be parked without lights on a road (or lay-by) with a speed limit of 30mph (48km/h) or less if they are

- at least 10 metres (32 feet) away from any junction, close to the kerb and facing in the direction of the traffic flow
- in a recognised parking place or lay-by.

Other vehicles and trailers, and all vehicles with projecting loads, **MUST NOT** be left on a road at night without lights.

Laws RVLR reg 24 & CUR reg 82(7)

251. Parking in fog. It is especially dangerous to park on the road in fog. If it is unavoidable, leave your parking lights or sidelights on.

252. Parking on hills. If you park on a hill you should

- park close to the kerb and apply the handbrake firmly
- select a forward gear and turn your steering wheel away from the kerb when facing uphill
- select reverse gear and turn your steering wheel towards the kerb when facing downhill
- use 'park' if your car has an automatic gearbox.

Turn your wheels away from the kerb when parking facing uphill.

Turn your wheels towards the kerb when parking facing downhill.

Decriminalised Parking Enforcement (DPE)

DPE is becoming increasingly common as more authorities take on this role. The local traffic authority assumes responsibility for enforcing many parking contraventions in place of the police. Further details on DPE may be found at the following websites:

www.parking-appeals.gov.uk (outside London)

www.parkingandtrafficappeals.gov.uk (inside London)

Motorways

Many other Rules apply to motorway driving, either wholly or in part: Rules 46, 57, 83–126, 130–134, 139, 144, 146–151, 160, 161, 219, 221–222, 225, 226–237, 274–278, 280, and 281–290.

General

253. Prohibited vehicles. Motorways **MUST NOT** be used by pedestrians, holders of provisional motorcycle or car licences, riders of motorcycles under 50cc, cyclists, horse riders, certain slow-moving vehicles and those carrying oversized loads (except by special permission), agricultural vehicles and powered wheelchairs/powered mobility scooters (see Rules 36–46 incl)

Laws HA 1980 sects 16, 17 & sch 4, MT(E&W)R regs 3(d), 4 & 11, MT(E&W)(A)R, R(S)A sects 7, 8 & sch 3, RTRA sects 17(2) & (3), & MT(S)R reg 10

254. Traffic on motorways usually travels faster than on other roads, so you have less time to react. It is especially important to use your mirrors earlier and look much further ahead than you would on other roads.

Motorway signals

255. Motorway signals (see Motorway signals) are used to warn you of a danger ahead. For example, there may be an incident, fog, a spillage or road workers on the carriageway which you may not immediately be able to see.

256. Signals situated on the central reservation apply to all lanes. On very busy stretches, signals may be overhead with a separate signal for each lane.

257. Amber flashing lights. These warn of a hazard ahead. The signal may show a temporary maximum speed limit, lanes that are closed or a message such as ‘Fog’. Adjust your speed and look out for the danger until you pass a signal which is not flashing or one that gives the ‘All clear’ sign and you are sure it is safe to increase your speed.

258. Red flashing lights. If red lights on the overhead signals flash above your lane and a red ‘X’ is showing, you **MUST NOT** go beyond the signal in that lane. If red lights flash on a signal in the central reservation or at the side of the road, you **MUST NOT** go beyond the signal in any lane.

Laws RTA 1988 sect 36 & TSRGD regs 10 & 38

Driving on the motorway

Joining the motorway.

259. When you join the motorway you will normally approach it from a road on the left (a slip road) or from an adjoining motorway. You should

- give priority to traffic already on the motorway
- check the traffic on the motorway and match your speed to fit safely into the traffic flow in the left-hand lane
- not cross solid white lines that separate lanes or use the hard shoulder
- stay on the slip road if it continues as an extra lane on the motorway
- remain in the left-hand lane long enough to adjust to the speed of traffic before considering overtaking.

On the motorway

260. When you can see well ahead and the road conditions are good, you should

- drive at a steady cruising speed which you and your vehicle can handle safely and is within the speed limit (see Rule 124)
- keep a safe distance from the vehicle in front and increase the gap on wet or icy roads, or in fog (see Rules 126 and 235).

261. You **MUST NOT** exceed 70mph (112km/h), or the maximum speed limit permitted for your vehicle (see Rule 124). If a lower speed limit is in force, either permanently or temporarily, at roadworks for example, you **MUST NOT** exceed the lower limit. On some motorways, mandatory motorway signals (which display the speed within a red ring) are used to vary the maximum speed limit to improve traffic flow. You **MUST NOT** exceed this speed limit.

Law RTRA sects 17, 86, 89 & sch 6

262. The monotony of driving on a motorway can make you feel sleepy. To minimise the risk, follow the advice in Rule 91.

263. You **MUST NOT** reverse, cross the central reservation, or drive against the traffic flow. If you have missed your exit, or have taken the wrong route, carry on to the next exit.

Laws MT(E&W)R regs 6, 8 & 10 & MT(S)R regs 4, 5, 7 & 9

Lane discipline

264. You should always drive in the left-hand lane when the road ahead is clear. If you are overtaking a number of slower-moving vehicles, you should return to the left-hand lane as soon as you are safely past. Slow-moving or speed-restricted vehicles should always remain in the left-hand lane of the carriageway unless overtaking. You **MUST NOT** drive on the hard shoulder except in an emergency or if directed to do so by the police, HA traffic officers in uniform or by signs.

Laws MT(E&W)R regs 5, 9 & 16(1)(a), MT(S)R regs 4, 8 & 14(1)(a), and RTA 1988, sects 35 & 186, as amended by TMA 2004 sect 6

265. The right-hand lane of a motorway with three or more lanes **MUST NOT** be used (except in prescribed circumstances) if you are driving

- any vehicle drawing a trailer
- a goods vehicle with a maximum laden weight exceeding 3.5 tonnes but not exceeding 7.5 tonnes, which is required to be fitted with a speed limiter
- a goods vehicle with a maximum laden weight exceeding 7.5 tonnes
- a passenger vehicle with a maximum laden weight exceeding 7.5 tonnes constructed or adapted to carry more than eight seated passengers in addition to the driver
- a passenger vehicle with a maximum laden weight not exceeding 7.5 tonnes which is constructed or adapted to carry more than eight seated passengers in addition to the driver, which is required to be fitted with a speed limiter.

Laws MT(E&W)R reg 12, MT(E&W)AR (2004), MT(S)R reg 11 & MT(S)AR (2004)

266. Approaching a junction. Look well ahead for signals or signs. Direction signs may be placed over the road. If you need to change lanes, do so in good time. At some junctions a lane may lead directly off the motorway. Only get in that lane if you wish to go in the direction indicated on the overhead signs.

Overtaking

267. Do not overtake unless you are sure it is safe and legal to do so. Overtake only on the right. You should

- check your mirrors
- take time to judge the speeds correctly
- make sure that the lane you will be joining is sufficiently clear ahead and behind
- take a quick sideways glance into the blind spot area to verify the position of a vehicle that may have disappeared from your view in the mirror
- remember that traffic may be coming up behind you very quickly. Check all your mirrors carefully. Look out for motorcyclists. When it is safe to do so, signal in plenty of time, then move out
- ensure you do not cut in on the vehicle you have overtaken
- be especially careful at night and in poor visibility when it is harder to judge speed and distance.

268. Do not overtake on the left or move to a lane on your left to overtake. In congested conditions, where adjacent lanes of traffic are moving at similar speeds, traffic in left-hand lanes may sometimes be moving faster than traffic to the right. In these conditions you may keep up with the traffic in your lane even if this means passing traffic in the lane to your right. Do not weave in and out of lanes to overtake.

269. Hard shoulder. You **MUST NOT** use the hard shoulder for overtaking. In areas where an Active Traffic Management (ATM) Scheme is in force, the hard shoulder may be used as a running lane. You will know when you can use this because a speed limit sign will be shown above all open lanes, including the hard shoulder. A red cross or blank sign above the hard shoulder means that you **MUST NOT** drive on the hard shoulder except in an emergency or breakdown. Emergency refuge areas have also been built into these areas for use in cases of emergency or breakdown.

Laws MT(E&W)R regs 5, 5A & 9, MT(S)R regs 4 & 8

Overhead gantry showing red cross over hard shoulder

Stopping

270. You **MUST NOT** stop on the carriageway, hard shoulder, slip road, central reservation or verge except in an emergency, or when told to do so by the police, HA traffic officers in uniform, an emergency sign or by flashing red light signals. Do not stop on the hard shoulder to either make or receive mobile phone calls.

Laws MT(E&W)R regs 5A, 7, 9, 10 & 16, MT(S)R regs 6(1), 8, 9 & 14, PRA 2002 sect 41 & sched 5(8), & RTA 1988 sects 35 & 163 as amended by TMA 2004, sect 6

271. You **MUST NOT** pick up or set down anyone, or walk on a motorway, except in an emergency.

Laws RTRA sect 17 & MT(E&W)R reg 15

Leaving the motorway

272. Unless signs indicate that a lane leads directly off the motorway, you will normally leave the motorway by a slip road on your left. You should

- watch for the signs letting you know you are getting near your exit
- move into the left-hand lane well before reaching your exit
- signal left in good time and reduce your speed on the slip road as necessary.

273. On leaving the motorway or using a link road between motorways, your speed may be higher than you realise – 50mph (80km/h) may feel like 30mph (48km/h). Check your speedometer and adjust your speed accordingly. Some slip-roads and link roads have sharp bends, so you will need to slow down.

Breakdowns and incidents

Breakdowns

274. If your vehicle breaks down, think first of all other road users and

- get your vehicle off the road if possible
- warn other traffic by using your hazard warning lights if your vehicle is causing an obstruction
- help other road users see you by wearing light-coloured or fluorescent clothing in daylight and reflective clothing at night or in poor visibility
- put a warning triangle on the road at least 45 metres (147 feet) behind your broken-down vehicle on the same side of the road, or use other permitted warning devices if you have them. Always take great care when placing or retrieving them, but never use them on motorways
- if possible, keep your sidelights on if it is dark or visibility is poor
- do not stand (or let anybody else stand) between your vehicle and oncoming traffic
- at night or in poor visibility do not stand where you will prevent other road users seeing your lights.

Additional rules for the motorway

275. If your vehicle develops a problem, leave the motorway at the next exit or pull into a service area. If you cannot do so, you should

- pull on to the hard shoulder and stop as far to the left as possible, with your wheels turned to the left
- try to stop near an emergency telephone (situated at approximately one-mile (1.6km) intervals along the hard shoulder)
- leave the vehicle by the left-hand door and ensure your passengers do the same. You **MUST** leave any animals in the vehicle or, in an emergency, keep them under proper control on the verge. Never attempt to place a warning triangle on a motorway
- do not put yourself in danger by attempting even simple repairs
- ensure that passengers keep away from the carriageway and hard shoulder, and that children are kept under control
- walk to an emergency telephone on your side of the carriageway (follow the arrows on the posts at the back of the hard shoulder) – the telephone is free of charge and connects directly to the Highways Agency or the police. Use these in preference to a mobile phone (see Rule 283). Always face the traffic when you speak on the phone
- give full details to the Highways Agency or the police; also inform them if you are a vulnerable motorist such as disabled, older or travelling alone
- return and wait near your vehicle (well away from the carriageway and hard shoulder)
- if you feel at risk from another person, return to your vehicle by a left-hand door and lock all doors. Leave your vehicle again as soon as you feel this danger has passed.

Laws MT(E&W)R reg 14 & MT(S)R reg 12

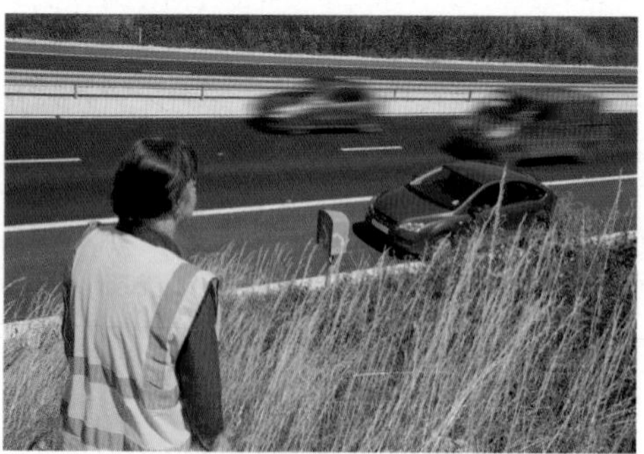

Keep well back from the hard shoulder

276. Before you rejoin the carriageway after a breakdown, build up speed on the hard shoulder and watch for a safe gap in the traffic. Be aware that other vehicles may be stationary on the hard shoulder.

277. If you cannot get your vehicle onto the hard shoulder
- do not attempt to place any warning device on the carriageway
- switch on your hazard warning lights
- leave your vehicle only when you can safely get clear of the carriageway.

Disabled drivers

278. If you have a disability which prevents you from following the above advice you should
- stay in your vehicle
- switch on your hazard warning lights
- display a 'Help' pennant or, if you have a car or mobile telephone, contact the emergency services and be prepared to advise them of your location.

Obstructions

279. If anything falls from your vehicle (or any other vehicle) on to the road, stop and retrieve it only if it is safe to do so.

280. Motorways. On a motorway do not try to remove the obstruction yourself. Stop at the next emergency telephone and call the Highways Agency or the police.

Incidents

281. Warning signs or flashing lights. If you see or hear emergency or incident support vehicles in the distance, be aware there may be an incident ahead (see Rule 219). Police Officers and Highways Agency Traffic Officers may be required to work in the carriageway, for example dealing with debris, collisions or conducting rolling road blocks. Police officers will use rear-facing flashing red and blue lights and HA Traffic Officers will use rear-facing flashing red and amber lights in these situations. Watch out for such signals, slow down and be prepared to stop. You **MUST** follow any directions given by Police officers or Traffic officers as to whether you can safely pass the incident or blockage.

Laws RTA1988, sects 35 & 163, and as amended by TMA 2004, sect 6

282. When passing the scene of an incident or crash do not be distracted or slow down unnecessarily (for example if an incident is on the other side of a dual carriageway). This may cause a collision or traffic congestion, but see Rule 283.

283. If you are involved in a crash or stop to give assistance

- use your hazard warning lights to warn other traffic
- ask drivers to switch off their engines and stop smoking
- arrange for the emergency services to be called immediately with full details of the incident location and any casualties (on a motorway, use the emergency telephone which allows easy location by the emergency services. If you use a mobile phone, first make sure you have identified your location from the marker posts on the side of the hard shoulder)
- move uninjured people away from the vehicles to safety; on a motorway this should, if possible, be well away from the traffic, the hard shoulder and the central reservation
- do not move injured people from their vehicles unless they are in immediate danger from fire or explosion
- do not remove a motorcyclist's helmet unless it is essential to do so
- be prepared to give first aid as shown in Annexe 7, First aid on the road
- stay at the scene until emergency services arrive.

If you are involved in any other medical emergency on the motorway you should contact the emergency services in the same way.

Incidents involving dangerous goods

284. Vehicles carrying dangerous goods in packages will be marked with plain orange reflective plates. Road tankers and vehicles carrying tank containers of dangerous goods will have hazard warning plates (see Vehicle markings).

285. If an incident involves a vehicle containing dangerous goods, follow the advice in Rule 283 and, in particular

- switch off engines and **DO NOT SMOKE**
- keep well away from the vehicle and do not be tempted to try to rescue casualties as you yourself could become one
- call the emergency services and give as much information as possible about the labels and markings on the vehicle. **DO NOT** use a mobile phone close to a vehicle carrying flammable loads.

Documentation

286. If you are involved in a collision which causes damage or injury to any other person, vehicle, animal or property, you **MUST**

- stop
- give your own and the vehicle owner's name and address, and the registration number of the vehicle, to anyone having reasonable grounds for requiring them
- if you do not give your name and address at the time of the collision, report it to the police as soon as reasonably practicable, and in any case within 24 hours.

Law RTA 1988 sect 170

287. If another person is injured and you do not produce your insurance certificate at the time of the crash to a police officer or to anyone having reasonable grounds to request it, you **MUST**

- report it to the police as soon as possible and in any case within 24 hours
- produce your insurance certificate for the police within seven days.

Law RTA 1988 sect 170

Roadworks

288. When the 'Road Works Ahead' sign is displayed, you will need to be more watchful and look for additional signs providing more specific instructions. Observe all signs – they are there for your safety and the safety of road workers.

- You **MUST NOT** exceed any temporary maximum speed limit.
- Use your mirrors and get into the correct lane for your vehicle in good time and as signs direct.
- Do not switch lanes to overtake queuing traffic.
- Take extra care near cyclists and motorcyclists as they are vulnerable to skidding on grit, mud or other debris at roadworks.
- Where lanes are restricted due to roadworks, merge in turn (see Rule 134).
- Do not drive through an area marked off by traffic cones.
- Watch out for traffic entering or leaving the works area, but do not be distracted by what is going on there. Concentrate on the road ahead, not the roadworks.
- Bear in mind that the road ahead may be obstructed by the works or by slow moving or stationary traffic.
- Keep a safe distance – there could be queues in front.

To obtain further information about roadworks see Other information.

Law RTRA sect 16

Additional rules for high-speed roads

289. Take special care on motorways and other high-speed dual carriageways.

- One or more lanes may be closed to traffic and a lower speed limit may apply.
- Works vehicles that are slow moving or stationary with a large 'Keep Left' or 'Keep Right' sign on the back are sometimes used to close lanes for repairs, and a flashing light arrow may also be used to make the works vehicle more conspicuous from a distance and give earlier warning to drivers that they need to move over to the next lane.
- Check mirrors, slow down and change lanes if necessary.
- Keep a safe distance from the vehicle in front (see Rule 126).

290. Contraflow systems mean that you may be travelling in a narrower lane than normal and with no permanent barrier between you and oncoming traffic. The hard shoulder may be used for traffic, but be aware that there may be broken-down vehicles ahead of you. Keep a good distance from the vehicle ahead and observe any temporary speed limits.

Level crossings

291. A level crossing is where a road crosses a railway or tramway line. Approach and cross it with care. Never drive onto a crossing until the road is clear on the other side and do not get too close to the car in front. Never stop or park on, or near a crossing.

292. Overhead electric lines. It is dangerous to touch overhead electric lines. You **MUST** obey the safe height warning road signs and you should not continue forward onto the railway if your vehicle touches any height barrier or bells. The clearance available is usually 5 metres (16 feet 6 inches) but may be lower.

Laws RTA 1988 sect 36, TSRGD 2002 reg 17(5)

293. Controlled Crossings. Most crossings have traffic light signals with a steady amber light, twin flashing red stop lights (see Light signals controlling traffic and Warning signs) and an audible alarm for pedestrians. They may have full, half or no barriers.

- You **MUST** always obey the flashing red stop lights.
- You **MUST** stop behind the white line across the road.
- Keep going if you have already crossed the white line when the amber light comes on.
- Do not reverse onto or over a controlled crossing.
- You **MUST** wait if a train goes by and the red lights continue to flash. This means another train will be passing soon.
- Only cross when the lights go off and barriers open.
- Never zig-zag around half-barriers, they lower automatically because a train is approaching.
- At crossings where there are no barriers, a train is approaching when the lights show.

Laws RTA 1988 sect 36 & TSRGD regs 10 & 40

Stop when the traffic lights show

294. Railway telephones. If you are driving a large or slow-moving vehicle, a long, low vehicle with a risk of grounding, or herding animals, a train could arrive before you are clear of the crossing. You **MUST** obey any sign instructing you to use the railway telephone to obtain permission to cross. You **MUST** also telephone when clear of the crossing if requested to do so.

Laws RTA 1988 sect 36 & TSRGD regs 10 & 16(1)

295. Crossings without traffic lights. Vehicles should stop and wait at the barrier or gate when it begins to close and not cross until the barrier or gate opens.

296. User-operated gates or barriers. Some crossings have 'Stop' signs and small red and green lights. You **MUST NOT** cross when the red light is showing, only cross if the green light is on. If crossing with a vehicle, you should

- open the gates or barriers on both sides of the crossing
- check that the green light is still on and cross quickly
- close the gates or barriers when you are clear of the crossing.

Laws RTA 1988 sect 36 & TSRGD regs 10 & 52(2)

297. If there are no lights, follow the procedure in Rule 295. Stop, look both ways and listen before you cross. If there is a railway telephone, always use it to contact the signal operator to make sure it is safe to cross. Inform the signal operator again when you are clear of the crossing.

298. Open crossings. These have no gates, barriers, attendant or traffic lights but will have a 'Give Way' sign. You should look both ways, listen and make sure there is no train coming before you cross.

299. Incidents and breakdowns. If your vehicle breaks down, or if you have an incident on a crossing you should

- get everyone out of the vehicle and clear of the crossing immediately
- use a railway telephone if available to tell the signal operator. Follow the instructions you are given
- move the vehicle clear of the crossing if there is time before a train arrives. If the alarm sounds, or the amber light comes on, leave the vehicle and get clear of the crossing immediately.

Tramways

300. You **MUST NOT** enter a road, lane or other route reserved for trams. Take extra care where trams run along the road. You should avoid driving directly on top of the rails and should take care where trams leave the main carriageway to enter the reserved route, to ensure you do not follow them. The width taken up by trams is often shown by tram lanes marked by white lines, yellow dots or by a different type of road surface. Diamond-shaped signs and white light signals give instructions to tram drivers only.

Law RTRA sects 5 & 8

301. Take extra care where the track crosses from one side of the road to the other and where the road narrows and the tracks come close to the kerb. Tram drivers usually have their own traffic signals and may be permitted to move when you are not. Always give way to trams. Do not try to race or overtake them or pass them on the inside, unless they are at tram stops or stopped by tram signals and there is a designated tram lane for you to pass.

302. You **MUST NOT** park your vehicle where it would get in the way of trams or where it would force other drivers to do so. Do not stop on any part of a tram track, except in a designated bay where this has been provided alongside and clear of the track. When doing so, ensure that all parts of your vehicle are outside the delineated tram path. Remember that a tram cannot steer round an obstruction.

Law RTRA sects 5 & 8

303. Tram stops. Where the tram stops at a platform, either in the middle or at the side of the road, you **MUST** follow the route shown by the road signs and markings. At stops without platforms you **MUST NOT** drive between a tram and the left-hand kerb when a tram has stopped to pick up passengers. If there is no alternative route signed, do not overtake the tram – wait until it moves off.

Law RTRA sects 5 & 8

304. Look out for pedestrians, especially children, running to catch a tram approaching a stop.

305. Always give priority to trams, especially when they signal to pull away from stops, unless it would be unsafe to do so. Remember that they may be carrying large numbers of standing passengers who could be injured if the tram had to make an emergency stop. Look out for people getting off a bus or tram and crossing the road.

306. All road users, but particularly cyclists and motorcyclists, should take extra care when driving or riding close to or crossing the tracks, especially if the rails are wet. You should take particular care when crossing the rails at shallow angles, on bends and at junctions. It is safest to cross the tracks directly at right angles. Other road users should be aware that cyclists and motorcyclists may need more space to cross the tracks safely.

307. Overhead electric lines. Tramway overhead wires are normally 5.8 metres above any carriageway, but can be lower. You should ensure that you have sufficient clearance between the wire and your vehicle (including any load you are carrying) before driving under an overhead wire. Drivers of vehicles with extending cranes, booms, tipping apparatus or other types of variable height equipment should ensure that the equipment is fully lowered. Where overhead wires are set lower than 5.8 metres (19 feet), these will be indicated by height clearance markings – similar to 'low bridge' signs. The height clearances on these plates should be carefully noted and observed. If you are in any doubt as to whether your vehicle will pass safely under the wires, you should always contact the local police or the tramway operator. Never take a chance as this can be extremely hazardous.

Light signals controlling traffic

Traffic Light Signals

RED means 'Stop'. Wait behind the stop line on the carriageway

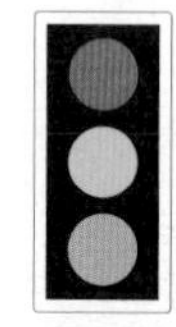

RED AND AMBER also means 'Stop'. Do not pass through or start until GREEN shows

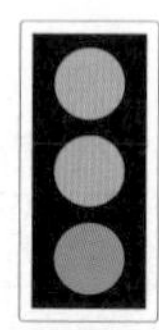

GREEN means you may go on if the way is clear. Take special care if you intend to turn left or right and give way to pedestrians who are crossing

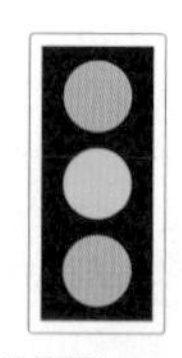

AMBER means 'Stop' at the stop line. You may go on only if the AMBER appears after you have crossed the stop line or are so close to it that to pull up might cause an accident

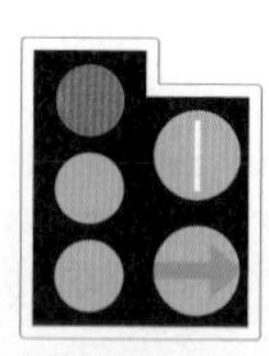

A GREEN ARROW may be provided in addition to the full green signal if movement in a certain direction is allowed before or after the full green phase. If the way is clear you may go but only in the direction shown by the arrow. You may do this whatever other lights may be showing. White light signals may be provided for trams

Flashing red lights

Alternately flashing red lights mean YOU MUST STOP

At level crossings, lifting bridges, airfields, fire stations, etc.

Motorway signals

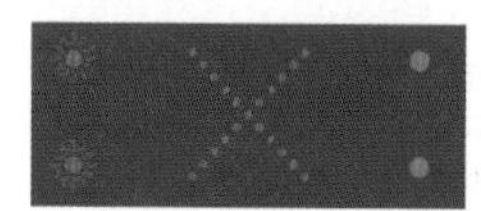

You **MUST NOT** proceed further in this lane

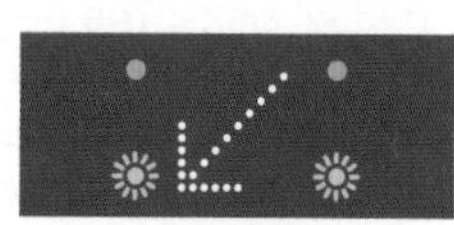

Change lane

Reduced visibility ahead

Lane ahead closed

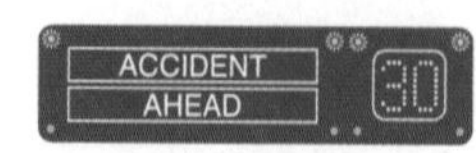

Temporary maximum speed advised and information message

Leave motorway at next exit

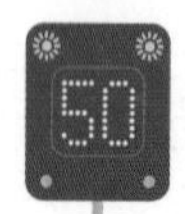

Temporary maximum speed advised

End of restriction

Lane control signals

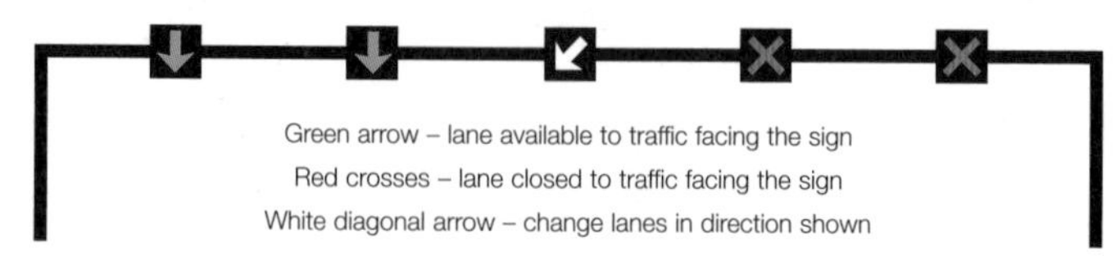

Green arrow – lane available to traffic facing the sign

Red crosses – lane closed to traffic facing the sign

White diagonal arrow – change lanes in direction shown

Signals to other road users

Direction indicator signals

I intend to move out to the right or turn right

I intend to move in to the left or turn left or stop on the left

Brake light signals

 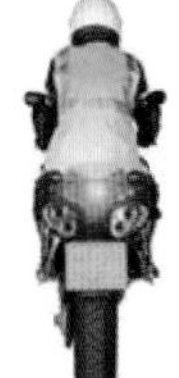

I am applying the brakes

Reversing light signals

I intend to reverse

These signals should not be used except for the purposes described.

Arm signals

For use when direction indicator signals are not used, or when necessary to reinforce direction indicator signals and stop lights. ***Also for use by pedal cyclists and those in charge of horses.***

I intend to move in to the left or turn left

I intend to move out to the right or turn right

I intend to slow down or stop

Signals by authorised persons

Police officers

Stop

Traffic approaching from the front

Traffic approaching from both front and behind

Traffic approaching from behind

To beckon traffic on

From the side

From the front

From behind*

Arm signals to persons controlling traffic

I want to go straight on

I want to turn left; use either hand

I want to turn right

* In Wales, bilingual signs appear on emergency services vehicles and clothing

Vehicle and Operator Services Agency and Highways Agency Traffic Officers

Highways Agency Traffic Officer

VOSA Traffic Officer

These officers now have new powers to stop/direct vehicles and will be using hand signals and light signals similar to those used by police. You **MUST** obey any signals given (see Rules 107 and 108).

School Crossing Patrols

Not ready to cross pedestrians

Barrier to stop pedestrians crossing

Ready to cross pedestrians, vehicles must be prepared to stop

All vehicles must stop

Traffic signs

Signs giving orders

Signs with red circles are mostly prohibitive.
Plates below signs qualify their message.

Entry to 20mph zone

End of 20mph zone

Maximum speed

National speed limit applies

School crossing patrol

Stop and give way

Give way to traffic on major road

Manually operated temporary STOP and GO signs

No entry for vehicular traffic

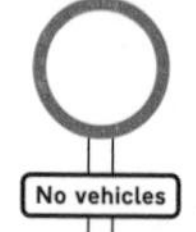

No vehicles except bicycles being pushed

No cycling

No motor vehicles

No buses (over 8 passenger seats)

No overtaking

No towed caravans

No vehicles carrying explosives

No vehicle or combination of vehicles over length shown

No vehicles over height shown

No vehicles over width shown

Give priority to vehicles from opposite direction

No right turn

No left turn

No U-turns

No goods vehicles over maximum gross weight shown (in tonnes) except for loading and unloading

Note: Although *The Highway Code* shows many of the signs commonly in use, a comprehensive explanation of our signing system is given in the Department's booklet *Know Your Traffic Signs*, which is on sale at booksellers. The booklet also illustrates and explains the vast majority of signs the road user is likely to encounter. The signs illustrated in *The Highway Code* are not all drawn to the same scale. In Wales, bilingual versions of some signs are used including Welsh and English versions of place names. Some older designs of signs may still be seen on the roads.

No vehicles over maximum gross weight shown (in tonnes)

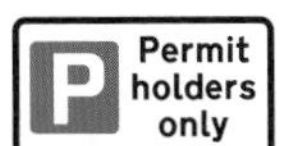

Parking restricted to permit holders

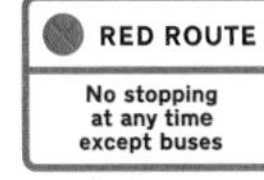

No stopping during period indicated except for buses

No stopping during times shown except for as long as necessary to set down or pick up passengers

No waiting

No stopping (Clearway)

Signs with blue circles but no red border mostly give positive instruction.

Ahead only

Turn left ahead (right if symbol reversed)

Turn left (right if symbol reversed)

Keep left (right if symbol reversed)

Vehicles may pass either side to reach same destination

Mini-roundabout (roundabout circulation – give way to vehicles from the immediate right)

Route to be used by pedal cycles only

Segregated pedal cycle and pedestrian route

Minimum speed

End of minimum speed

Buses and cycles only

Trams only

Pedestrian crossing point over tramway

One-way traffic (note: compare circular 'Ahead only' sign)

With-flow bus and cycle lane

Contraflow bus lane

With-flow pedal cycle lane

Warning signs

Mostly triangular

Distance to 'STOP' line ahead

Dual carriageway ends

Road narrows on right (left if symbol reversed)

Road narrows on both sides

Distance to 'Give Way' line ahead

Crossroads

Junction on bend ahead

T-junction with priority over vehicles from the right

Staggered junction

Traffic merging from left ahead

The priority through route is indicated by the broader line.

Double bend first to left (symbol may be reversed)

Bend to right (or left if symbol reversed)

Roundabout

Uneven road

Plate below some signs

Two-way traffic crosses one-way road

Two-way traffic straight ahead

Opening or swing bridge ahead

Low-flying aircraft or sudden aircraft noise

Falling or fallen rocks

Traffic signals not in use

Traffic signals

Slippery road

Steep hill downwards

Steep hill upwards

Gradients may be shown as a ratio i.e. 20% = 1:5

Tunnel ahead

Trams crossing ahead

Level crossing with barrier or gate ahead

Level crossing without barrier or gate ahead

Level crossing without barrier

Warning signs – continued

School crossing patrol ahead (some signs have amber lights which flash when crossings are in use)

Frail (or blind or disabled if shown) pedestrians likely to cross road ahead

Pedestrians in road ahead

Zebra crossing

Overhead electric cable; plate indicates maximum height of vehicles which can pass safely

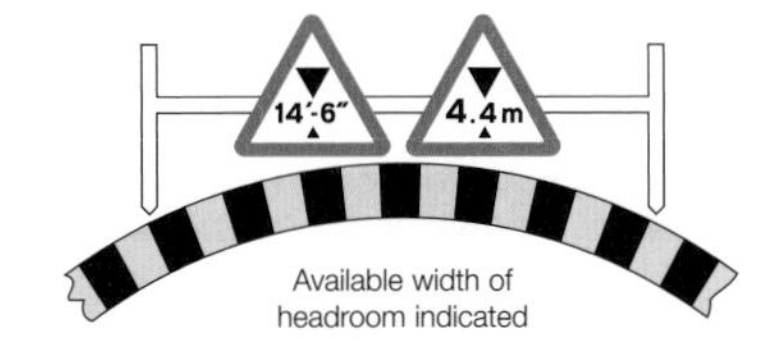

Available width of headroom indicated

Sharp deviation of route to left (or right if chevrons reversed)

Light signals ahead at level crossing, airfield or bridge

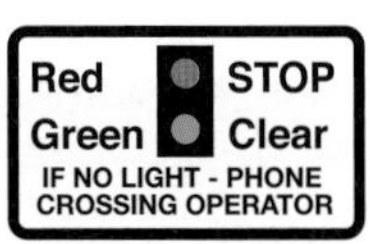

Miniature warning lights at level crossings

Cattle

Wild animals

Wild horses or ponies

Accompanied horses or ponies

Cycle route ahead

Risk of ice

Traffic queues likely ahead

Distance over which road humps extend

Other danger; plate indicates nature of danger

Soft verges

Side winds

Hump bridge

Worded warning sign

Quayside or river bank

Risk of grounding

Direction signs

Mostly rectangular

Signs on motorways – blue backgrounds

At a junction leading directly into a motorway (junction number may be shown on a black background)

On approaches to junctions (junction number on black background)

Route confirmatory sign after junction

Downward pointing arrows mean 'Get in lane'
The left-hand lane leads to a different destination from the other lanes.

The panel with the inclined arrow indicates the destinations which can be reached by leaving the motorway at the next junction

Signs on primary routes - green backgrounds

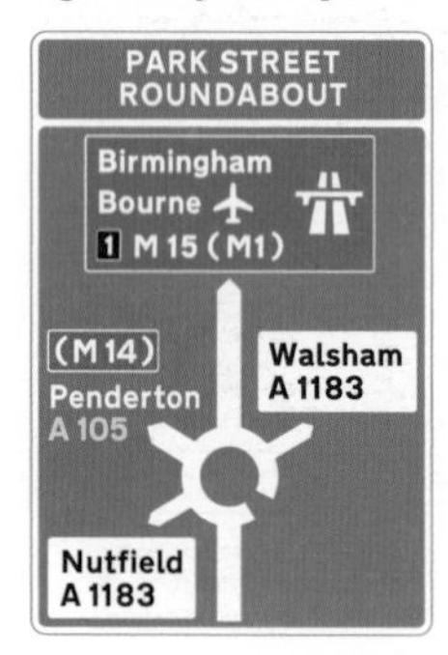

On approaches to junctions

At the junction

Route confirmatory sign after junction

On approaches to junctions

On approach to a junction in Wales (bilingual)

Blue panels indicate that the motorway starts at the junction ahead.
Motorways shown in brackets can also be reached along the route indicated.
White panels indicate local or non-primary routes leading from the junction ahead.
Brown panels show the route to tourist attractions.
The name of the junction may be shown at the top of the sign.
The aircraft symbol indicates the route to an airport.
A symbol may be included to warn of a hazard or restriction along that route.

Green background signs – continued

Primary route forming part of a ring road

Signs on non-primary and local routes - black borders

On approaches to junctions

Market Walborough B 486 7

At the junction

Direction to toilets with access for the disabled

Green panels indicate that the primary route starts at the junction ahead.
Route numbers on a blue background show the direction to a motorway.
Route numbers on a green background show the direction to a primary route.

Other direction signs

Picnic site

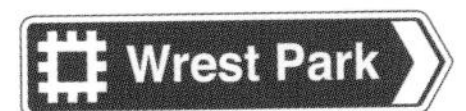

Ancient monument in the care of English Heritage

Direction to a car park

Tourist attraction

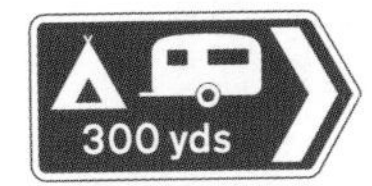

Direction to camping and caravan site

Advisory route for lorries

Route for pedal cycles forming part of a network

Recommended route for pedal cycles to place shown

Route for pedestrians

Symbols showing emergency diversion route for motorway and other main road traffic

Diversion route

Information signs

All rectangular

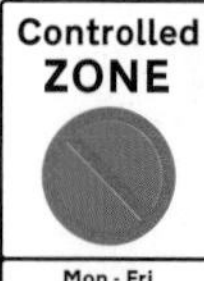

Entrance to controlled parking zone

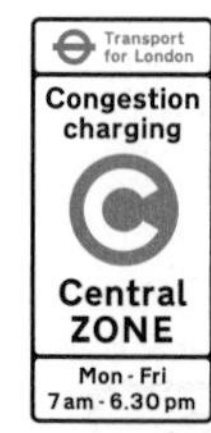

Entrance to congestion charging zone

End of controlled parking zone

Advance warning of restriction or prohibition ahead

Parking place for solo motorcycles

With-flow bus lane ahead which pedal cycles and taxis may also use

Lane designated for use by high occupancy vehicles (HOV) - see rule 142

Vehicles permitted to use an HOV lane ahead

End of motorway

Start of motorway and point from which motorway regulations apply

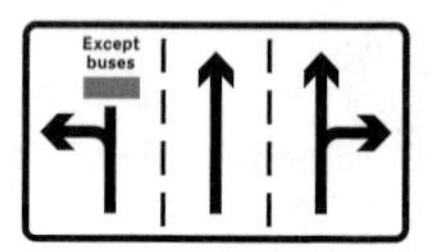

Appropriate traffic lanes at junction ahead

Traffic on the main carriageway coming from right has priority over joining traffic

Additional traffic joining from left ahead. Traffic on main carriageway has priority over joining traffic from right hand lane of slip road

Traffic in right hand lane of slip road joining the main carriageway has prority over left hand lane

'Countdown' markers at exit from motorway (each bar represents 100 yards to the exit). Green-backed markers may be used on primary routes and white-backed markers with black bars on other routes. At approaches to concealed level crossings white-backed markers with red bars may be used. Although these will be erected at equal distances the bars do not represent 100 yard intervals.

Motorway service area sign showing the operator's name

Information signs – continued

Traffic has priority over oncoming vehicles

Hospital ahead with Accident and Emergency facilities

Tourist information point

No through road for vehicles

Recommended route for pedal cycles

Home Zone Entry

Area in which cameras are used to enforce traffic regulations

Bus lane on road at junction ahead

Roadworks signs

Road works

Loose chippings

Temporary hazard at roadworks

Temporary lane closure (the number and position of arrows and red bars may be varied according to lanes open and closed)

Slow-moving or stationary works vehicle blocking a traffic lane. Pass in the direction shown by the arrow.

Mandatory speed limit ahead

Roadworks 1 mile ahead

End of roadworks and any temporary restrictions including speed limits

Signs used on the back of slow-moving or stationary vehicles warning of a lane closed ahead by a works vehicle. There are no cones on the road.

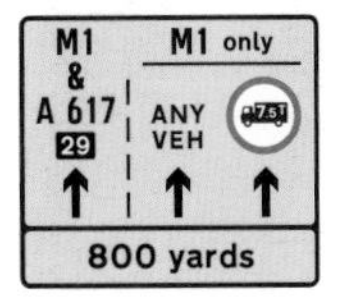

Lane restrictions at roadworks ahead

One lane crossover at contraflow roadworks

Road markings

Across the carriageway

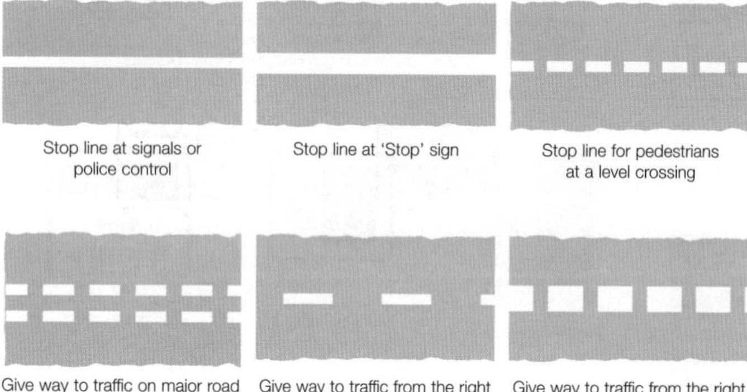

Stop line at signals or police control

Stop line at 'Stop' sign

Stop line for pedestrians at a level crossing

Give way to traffic on major road (can also be used at mini roundabouts)

Give way to traffic from the right at a roundabout

Give way to traffic from the right at a mini-roundabout

Along the carriageway

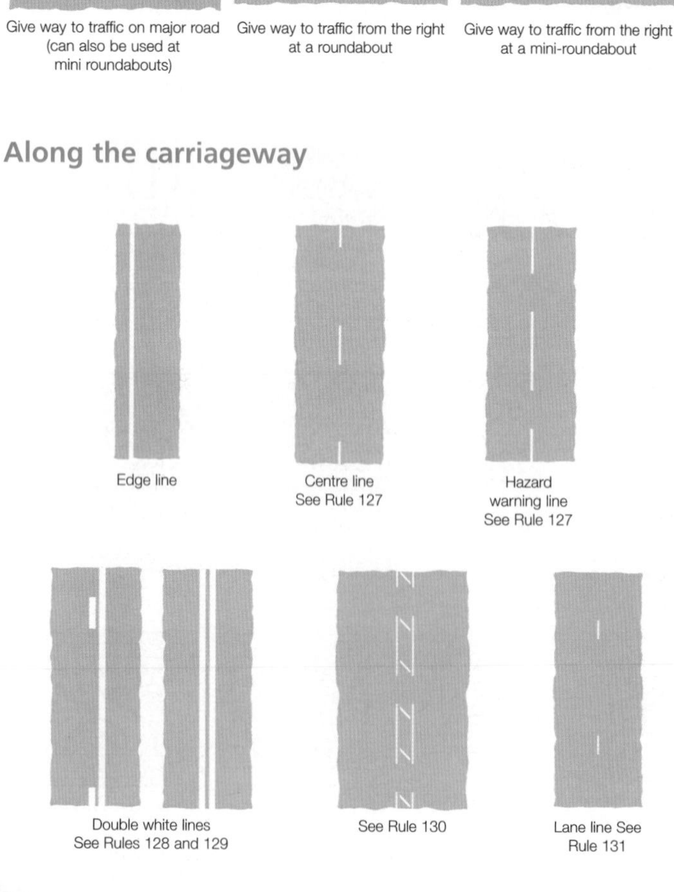

Edge line

Centre line See Rule 127

Hazard warning line See Rule 127

Double white lines See Rules 128 and 129

See Rule 130

Lane line See Rule 131

Along the edge of the carriageway

Waiting restrictions

Waiting restrictions indicated by yellow lines apply to the carriageway, pavement and verge. You may stop to load or unload (unless there are also loading restrictions as described below) or while passengers board or alight. Double yellow lines mean no waiting at any time, unless there are signs that specifically indicate seasonal restrictions. The times at which the restrictions apply for other road markings are shown on nearby plates or on entry signs to controlled parking zones. If no days are shown on the signs, the restrictions are in force every day including Sundays and Bank Holidays. White bay markings and upright signs (see below) indicate where parking is allowed.

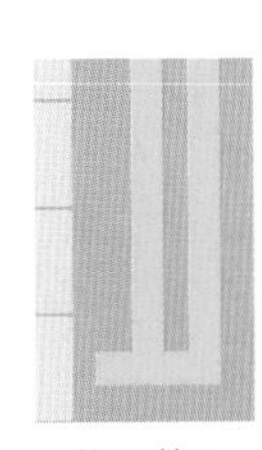

No waiting
at any time

No waiting
during times
shown on sign

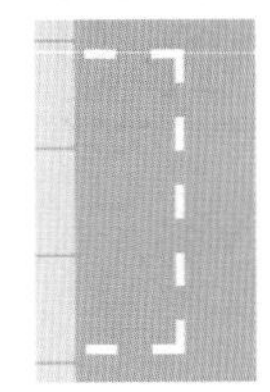

Waiting is limited to the
duration specified during the
days and times shown

Red Route stopping controls

Red lines are used on some roads instead of yellow lines. In London the double and single red lines used on Red Routes indicate that stopping to park, load/unload or to board and alight from a vehicle (except for a licensed taxi or if you hold a Blue Badge) is prohibited. The red lines apply to the carriageway, pavement and verge. The times that the red line prohibitions apply are shown on nearby signs, but the double red line ALWAYS means no stopping at any time. On Red Routes you may stop to park, load/unload in specially marked boxes and adjacent signs specify the times and purposes and duration allowed. A box MARKED IN RED indicates that it may only be available for the purpose specified for part of the day (e.g. between busy peak periods). A box MARKED IN WHITE means that it is available throughout the day.

RED AND SINGLE YELLOW LINES CAN ONLY GIVE A GUIDE TO THE RESTRICTIONS AND CONTROLS IN FORCE AND SIGNS, NEARBY OR AT A ZONE ENTRY, MUST BE CONSULTED.

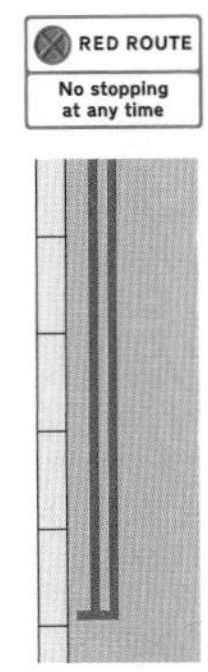

No stopping
at any time

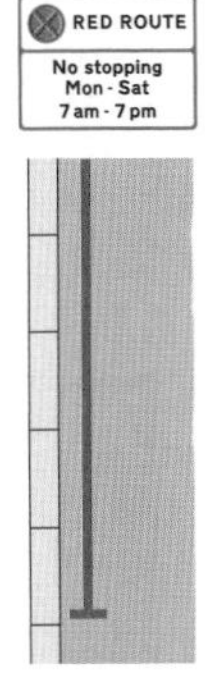

No stopping
during times
shown on sign

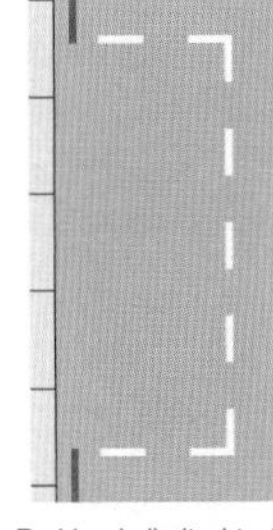

Parking is limited to the
duration specified during
the days and times shown

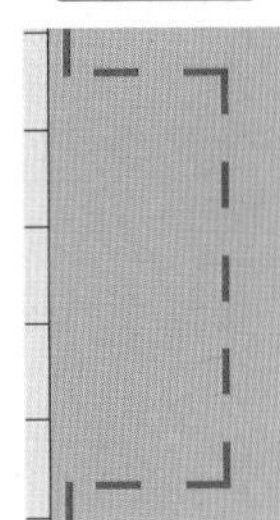

Only loading may take
place at the times shown
for up to a maximum
duration of 20 mins

On the kerb or at the edge of the carriageway

Loading restrictions on roads other than Red Routes

Yellow marks on the kerb or at the edge of the carriageway indicate that loading or unloading is prohibited at the times shown on the nearby black and white plates. You may stop while passengers board or alight. If no days are indicated on the signs the restrictions are in force every day including Sundays and Bank Holidays.

ALWAYS CHECK THE TIMES SHOWN ON THE PLATES.

Lengths of road reserved for vehicles loading and unloading are indicated by a white 'bay' marking with the words 'Loading Only' and a sign with the white on blue 'trolley' symbol. This sign also shows whether loading and unloading is restricted to goods vehicles and the times at which the bay can be used. If no times or days are shown it may be used at any time. Vehicles may not park here if they are not loading or unloading.

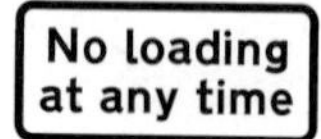

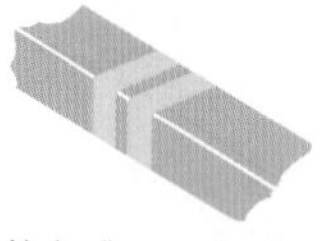

No loading or unloading at any time

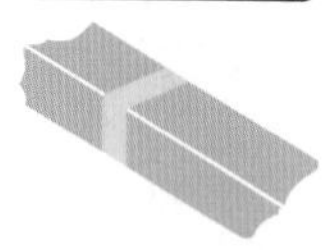

No loading or unloading at the times shown

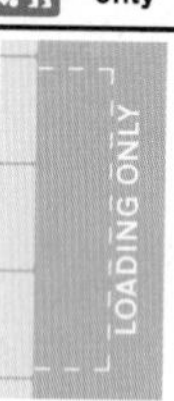

Loading bay

Other road markings

Keep entrance clear of stationary vehicles, even if picking up or setting down children

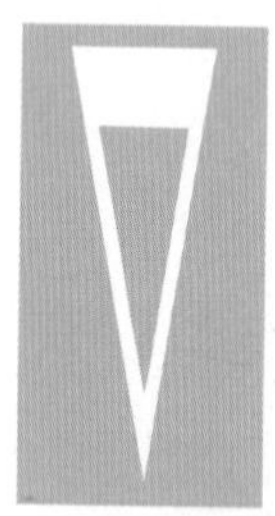

Warning of 'Give Way' just ahead

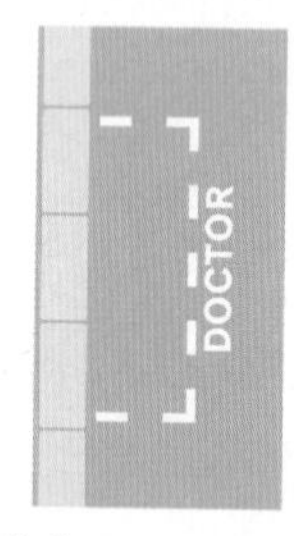

Parking space reserved for vehicles named

See Rule 243

See Rule 141

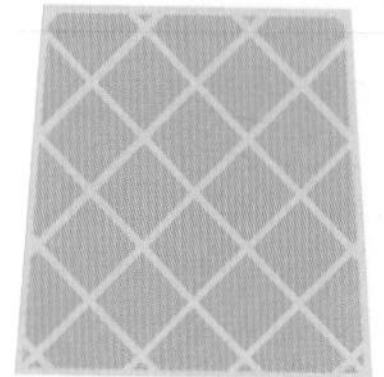

Box junction - See Rule 174

Do not block that part of the carriageway indicated

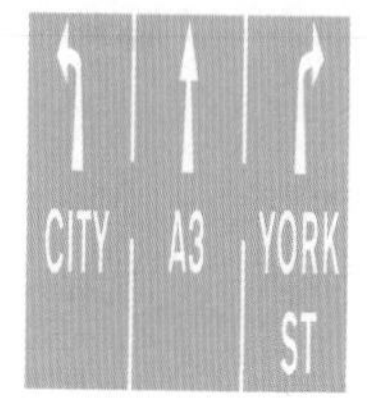

Indication of traffic lanes

Vehicle markings

Large goods vehicle rear markings

Motor vehicles over 7500 kilograms maximum gross weight and trailers over 3500 kilograms maximum gross weight

The vertical markings are also required to be fitted to builders' skips placed in the road, commercial vehicles or combinations longer than 13 metres (optional on combinations between 11 and 13 metres)

Hazard warning plates

Certain tank vehicles carrying dangerous goods must display hazard information panels

The panel illustrated is for flammable liquid. Diamond symbols indicating other risks include:

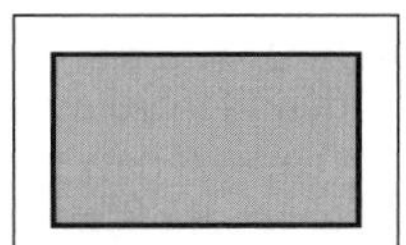

The above panel will be displayed by vehicles carrying certain dangerous goods in packages

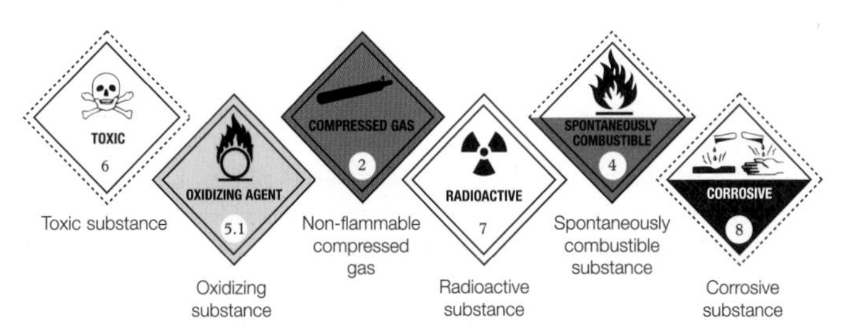

Toxic substance

Oxidizing substance

Non-flammable compressed gas

Radioactive substance

Spontaneously combustible substance

Corrosive substance

Projection markers

Both required when load or equipment (eg crane jib) overhangs front or rear by more than two metres

Other

School bus
(displayed in front or rear window of bus or coach)

Annexes

1. You and your bicycle

Make sure that you feel confident of your ability to ride safely on the road. Be sure that

- you choose the right size and type of cycle for comfort and safety
- lights and reflectors are kept clean and in good working order
- tyres are in good condition and inflated to the pressure shown on the tyre
- gears are working correctly
- the chain is properly adjusted and oiled
- the saddle and handlebars are adjusted to the correct height.

It is recommended that you fit a bell to your cycle.

You **MUST**

- ensure your brakes are efficient
- at night, use lit front and rear lights and have a red rear reflector.

Laws PCUR regs 6 & 10 & RVLR reg 18

Cycle training can help both children and adults, especially those adults returning to cycling to develop the skills needed to cycle safely on today's roads. A new national cycle training standard has been developed which the Government is promoting and making funding available for delivery in schools.

All cyclists should consider the benefits of undertaking cycle training. For information, contact your local authority.

2. Motorcycle licence requirements

If you have a provisional motorcycle licence, you **MUST** satisfactorily complete a Compulsory Basic Training (CBT) course. You can then ride on the public road, with L plates (in Wales either D plates, L plates or both can be used), for up to two years. To obtain your full motorcycle licence you **MUST** pass a motorcycle theory test and then a practical test.

Law MV(DL)R regs 16 & 68

If you have a full car licence you may ride motorcycles up to 125cc and 11kW power output, with L plates (and/or D plates in Wales), on public roads, but you **MUST** first satisfactorily complete a CBT course if you have not already done so.

Law MV(DL)R reg 43

If you have a full moped licence and wish to obtain full motorcycle entitlement, you will be required to take a motorcycle theory test if you did not take a separate theory test when you obtained your moped licence. You **MUST** then pass a practical motorcycle test. Note that if CBT was completed for the full moped licence there is no need to repeat it, but if the moped test was taken before 1/12/90 CBT will need to be completed before riding a motorcycle as a learner.
Law MV(DL)R regs 42(1) & 69(1)

Light motorcycle licence (A1): you take a test on a motorcycle of between 75 and 125cc. If you pass you may ride a motorcycle up to 125cc with power output up to 11kW.

Standard motorcycle licence (A): if your test vehicle is between 120 and 125cc and capable of more than 100km/h you will be given a standard (A) licence. You will then be restricted to motorcycles of up to 25kW for two years. After two years you may ride any size machine.

Direct or Accelerated Access enables riders over the age of 21, or those who reach 21 before their two-year restriction ends, to ride larger motorcycles sooner. To obtain a licence to do so they are required to
- have successfully completed a CBT course
- pass a theory test, if they are required to do so
- pass a practical test on a machine with power output of at least 35kW.

To practise, they can ride larger motorcycles, with L plates (and/or D plates in Wales), on public roads, but only when accompanied by an approved instructor on another motorcycle in radio contact.

You **MUST NOT** carry a pillion passenger or pull a trailer until you have passed your test.
Law MV(DL)R reg 16

Moped licence requirements

A moped **MUST** have an engine capacity not exceeding 50cc, not weigh more than 250kg and be designed to have a maximum speed not exceeding 31mph (50km/h). From June 2003 all EC Type Approved mopeds have been restricted to 28mph (45km/h).

Law RTA 1988 (as amended) sect 108

To ride a moped, learners **MUST**

- be 16 or over
- have a provisional moped licence
- complete CBT training.

You **MUST** first pass the theory test for motorcycles and then the moped practical test to obtain your full moped licence. If you passed your driving test before 1 February 2001 you are qualified to ride a moped without L plates (and/or D plates in Wales), although it is recommended that you complete CBT before riding on the road. If you passed your driving test after this date you **MUST** complete CBT before riding a moped on the road.

Laws RTA 1988 sects 97(e) & 101 & MV(DL)R regs 38(4) & 43

Note. For motorcycle and moped riders wishing to upgrade, the following give exemption from taking the motorcycle theory test

- full A1 motorcycle licence
- full moped licence, if gained after 1 July 1996.

Law MV(DL)R reg 42

3. Motor vehicle documentation and learner driver requirements

Documents

Driving licence. You **MUST** have a valid driving licence for the category of motor vehicle you are driving. You **MUST** inform the Driver and Vehicle Licensing Agency (DVLA) if you change your name and/or address.

Law RTA 1988 sects 87 & 99(4)

Holders of non-European Community licences who are now resident in the UK may only drive on that licence for a maximum of 12 months from the date they become resident in this country. To ensure continuous driving entitlement

- a British provisional licence should be obtained and a driving test(s) passed before the 12-month period elapses, or
- in the case of a driver who holds a licence from a country which has been designated in law for licence exchange purposes, the driver should exchange the licence for a British one.

MOT. Cars and motorcycles **MUST** normally pass an MOT test three years from the date of the first registration and every year after that. You **MUST NOT** drive a motor vehicle without an MOT certificate when it should have one. Exceptionally, you may drive to a pre-arranged test appointment or to a garage for repairs required for the test. Driving an unroadworthy motor vehicle may invalidate your insurance.
Law RTA 1988 sects 45, 47, 49 & 53

Insurance. To use a motor vehicle on the road, you **MUST** have a valid insurance policy. This **MUST** at least cover you for injury or damage to a third party while using that motor vehicle. Before driving any motor vehicle, make sure that it has this cover for your use or that your own insurance provides adequate cover. You **MUST NOT** drive a motor vehicle without insurance. Also, be aware that even if a road traffic incident is not your fault, you may still be held liable by insurance companies.
Law RTA 1988 sect 143

Uninsured drivers can now be automatically detected by roadside cameras. Further to the penalties for uninsured driving listed in Annexe 5, Penalties, an offender's vehicle can now be seized by the Police, taken away and crushed.
Law RTA 1988, sects 165a & 165b

The types of cover available are indicated below:

Third-Party insurance – this is often the cheapest form of insurance, and is the minimum cover required by law. It covers anyone you might injure or whose property you might damage. It does not cover damage to your own motor vehicle or injury to yourself.

Third-Party, Fire and Theft insurance – similar to third-party, but also covers you against your motor vehicle being stolen, or damaged by fire.

Comprehensive insurance – this is the most expensive but the best insurance. Apart from covering other persons and property against injury or damage, it also covers damage to your own motor vehicle, up to the market value of that vehicle, and personal injury to yourself.

Registration certificate. Registration certificates (also called harmonised registration certificates) are issued for all motor vehicles used on the road, describing them (make, model, etc) and giving details of the registered keeper. You **MUST** notify the Driver and Vehicle Licensing Agency in Swansea as soon as possible when you buy or sell a motor vehicle, or if you change your name or address.

For registration certificates issued after 27 March 1997, the buyer and seller are responsible for completing the registration certificates. The seller is responsible for forwarding them to DVLA. The procedures are explained on the back of the registration certificates.
Law RV(R&L)R regs 21, 22, 23 & 24

Vehicle Excise Duty (VED). All motor vehicles used or kept on public roads **MUST** display a valid Vehicle Excise Duty disc (tax disc) displayed at all times. Even motor vehicles exempt from duty **MUST** display a tax disc at all times.
Law VERA sects 29 and 33

Statutory Off-Road Notification (SORN). This is a notification to the DVLA that a motor vehicle is not being used on the road. If you are the vehicle keeper and want to keep a motor vehicle untaxed and off the public road you **MUST** declare SORN – it is an offence not to do so. You then won't have to pay any road tax for that vehicle for a period of 12 months. You need to send a further declaration after that period if the vehicle is still off the public road. The SORN will end if you sell the vehicle and the new owner will become immediately responsible.
Law RV(RL)R 2002, reg 26 sched 4

Production of documents. You **MUST** be able to produce your driving licence and counterpart, a valid insurance certificate and (if appropriate) a valid MOT certificate, when requested by a police officer. If you cannot do this you may be asked to take them to a police station within seven days.
Law RTA 1988 sects 164 & 165

Learner drivers

Learners driving a car **MUST** hold a valid provisional licence. They **MUST** be supervised by someone at least 21 years old who holds a full EC/EEA licence for that type of car (automatic or manual) and has held one for at least three years.
Laws MV(DL)R reg 16 & RTA 1988 sect 87

Vehicles. Any vehicle driven by a learner **MUST** display red L plates. In Wales, either red D plates, red L plates, or both, can be used. Plates **MUST** conform to legal specifications and **MUST** be clearly visible to others from in front of the vehicle and from behind. Plates should be removed or covered when not being driven by a learner (except on driving school vehicles).
Law MV(DL)R reg 16 & sched 4

You **MUST** pass the theory test (if one is required) and then a practical driving test for the category of vehicle you wish to drive before driving unaccompanied.
Law MV(DL)R reg 40

4. The road user and the law

Road traffic law

The following list can be found abbreviated throughout The Code. It is not intended to be a comprehensive guide, but a guide to some of the important points of law. For the precise wording of the law, please refer to the various Acts and Regulations (as amended) indicated in The Code. Abbreviations are listed on the following page.

Most of the provisions apply on all roads throughout Great Britain, although there are some exceptions. The definition of a road in England and Wales is 'any highway and any other road to which the public has access and includes bridges over which a road passes' (RTA 1988 sect 192(1)). In Scotland, there is a similar definition which is extended to include any way over which the public have a right of passage (R(S)A 1984 sect 151(1)).

It is important to note that references to 'road' therefore generally include footpaths, bridleways and cycle tracks, and many roadways and driveways on private land (including many car parks). In most cases, the law will apply to them and there may be additional rules for particular paths or ways. Some serious driving offences, including drink-driving offences, also apply to all public places, for example public car parks.

Chronically Sick & Disabled Persons Act 1970	CSDPA
Functions of Traffic Wardens Order 1970	FTWO
Greater London (General Powers) Act 1974	GL(GP)A
Highway Act 1835 or 1980 (as indicated)	HA
Horses (Protective Headgear for Young Riders) Act 1990	H(PHYR)A
Horses (Protective Headgear for Young Riders) Regulations 1992	H(PHYR)R
Motor Cycles (Eye Protectors) Regulations 1999	MC(EP)R
Motor Cycles (Protective Helmets) Regulations 1980	MC(PH)R
Motorways Traffic (England & Wales) Regulations 1982	MT(E&W)R
Motorways Traffic (England & Wales) Amended Regulations	MT(E&W)(A)R
Motorways Traffic (Scotland) Regulations 1995	MT(S)R
Motor Vehicles (Driving Licences) Regulations 1999	MV(DL)R
Motor Vehicles (Wearing of Seat Belts) Regulations 1993	MV(WSB)R
Motor Vehicles (Wearing of Seat Belts) (Amendment) Regulations 2006	MV(WSB)(A)R
Motor Vehicles (Wearing of Seat Belts by Children in Front Seats) Regulations 1993	MV(WSBCFS)R
New Roads and Streetworks Act 1991	NRSWA
Pedal Cycles (Construction & Use) Regulations 1983	PCUR
Powers of Criminal Courts (Sentencing) Act 2000	PCC(S)A
Police Reform Act 2002	PRA
Prohibition of Smoking in Certain Premises (Scotland) Regulations 2006 (SI no 90)	PSCP(S)R*
Public Passenger Vehicles Act 1981	PPVA
Road Safety Act 2006	RSA
Road Traffic Act 1984, 1988 or 1991 (as indicated)	RTA
Road Traffic (New Drivers) Act 1995	RT(ND)A
Road Traffic Offenders Act 1988	RTOA
Road Traffic Regulation Act 1984	RTRA
Road Vehicles (Construction & Use) Regulations 1986	CUR
Road Vehicles (Display of Registration Marks) Regulations 2001	RV(DRM)R
Road Vehicles Lighting Regulations 1989	RVLR
Road Vehicles (Registration & Licensing) Regulations 2002	RV(R&L)R
Roads (Scotland) Act 1984	R(S)A
Traffic Management Act 2004	TMA
Traffic Signs Regulations & General Directions 2002	TSRGD
Use of Invalid Carriages on Highways Regulations 1988	UICHR
Vehicle Excise and Registration Act 1994	VERA
Zebra, Pelican and Puffin Pedestrian Crossings Regulations and General Directions 1997	ZPPPCRGD

Acts and regulations from 1988 can be viewed on the Office of Public Sector Information website (www.opsi.gov.uk). Acts and regulations prior to 1988 are only available in their original print format which may be obtained from The Stationery Office as detailed inside the back cover.

*Specific legislation applies to smoking in vehicles which constitute workplaces. For information, visit
www.smokefreeengland.co.uk
www.clearingtheairscotland.com
www.smokingbanwales.co.uk

5. Penalties

Parliament sets the maximum penalties for road traffic offences. The seriousness of the offence is reflected in the maximum penalty. It is for the courts to decide what sentence to impose according to circumstances.

The penalty table on the next page indicates some of the main offences, and the associated penalties. There is a wide range of other more specific offences which, for the sake of simplicity, are not shown here. The penalty points and disqualification system is described below.

Penalty points and disqualification

The penalty point system is intended to deter drivers and motorcyclists from following unsafe motoring practices. Certain non-motoring offences, e.g. failure to rectify vehicle defects, can also attract penalty points. The court **MUST** order points to be endorsed on the licence according to the fixed number or the range set by Parliament. The accumulation of penalty points acts as a warning to drivers and motorcyclists that they risk disqualification if further offences are committed.

Law RTOA sects 44 & 45

A driver or motorcyclist who accumulates 12 or more penalty points within a three-year period **MUST** be disqualified. This will be for a minimum period of six months, or longer if the driver or motorcyclist has previously been disqualified.

Law RTOA sect 35

For every offence which carries penalty points the court has a discretionary power to order the licence holder to be disqualified. This may be for any period the court thinks fit, but will usually be between a week and a few months.

In the case of serious offences, such as dangerous driving and drink-driving, the court **MUST** order disqualification. The minimum period is 12 months, but for repeat offenders or where the alcohol level is high, it may be longer. For example, a second drink-drive offence in the space of 10 years will result in a minimum of three years' disqualification.

Law RTOA sect 34

Penalty Table

Offence	Maximum Penalties			
	Imprisonment	Fine	Disqualification	Penalty Points
*Causing death by dangerous driving	14 years	Unlimited	Obligatory – 2 years minimum	3–11 (if exceptionally not disqualified)
*Dangerous driving	2 years	Unlimited	Obligatory	3–11 (if exceptionally not disqualified)
*Causing death by careless driving under the influence of drink or drugs	14 years	Unlimited	Obligatory - 2 years minimum	3–11 (if exceptionally not disqualified)
Careless and inconsiderate driving	-	£5,000	Discretionary	3–9
Driving while unfit through drink or drugs or with excess alcohol; or failing to provide a specimen for analysis	6 months	£5,000	Obligatory	3–11 (if exceptionally not disqualified)
Failing to stop after an accident or failing to report an accident	6 months	£5,000	Discretionary	5–10
Driving when disqualified	6 months (12 months in Scotland)	£5,000	Discretionary	6
Driving after refusal or revocation of licence on medical grounds	6 months	£5,000	Discretionary	3–6
Driving without insurance	-	£5,000	Discretionary	6–8
Using a vehicle in a dangerous condition	-	LGV £5,000 PCV £5,000 Other £2,500	Obligatory for 2 offences in 3 yrs – 6 mths min. Otherwise Discretionary in each case	3 in each case
Driving otherwise than in accordance with a licence	-	£1,000	Discretionary	3–6
Speeding	-	£1,000 (£2,500 for motorway offences)	Discretionary	3–6 or 3 (fixed penalty)
Traffic light offences	-	£1,000	Discretionary	3
No MOT certificate	-	£1,000	-	-
Seat belt offences	-	£500	-	-
Dangerous cycling	-	£2,500	-	-
Careless cycling	-	£1,000	-	-
Cycling on pavement	-	£500	-	-
Failing to identify driver of a vehicle	-	£1,000	Discretionary	6

*Where a court disqualifies a person on conviction for one of these offences, it must order an extended retest. The courts also have discretion to order a retest for any other offence which carries penalty points, an extended retest where disqualification is obligatory, and an ordinary test where disqualification is not obligatory.

Furthermore, in some serious cases, the court **MUST** (in addition to imposing a fixed period of disqualification) order the offender to be disqualified until they pass a driving test. In other cases the court has a discretionary power to order such disqualification. The test may be an ordinary length test or an extended test according to the nature of the offence.
Law RTOA sect 36

New drivers. Special rules as set out below apply for a period of two years from the date of passing their first driving test, to drivers and motorcyclists from

- the UK, EU/EEA, the Isle of Man, the Channel Islands or Gibraltar who passed their first driving test in any of those countries
- other foreign countries who have to pass a UK driving test to gain a UK licence, in which case the UK driving test is treated as their first driving test; and
- other foreign countries who (without needing a test) exchanged their licence for a UK licence and subsequently passed a UK driving test to drive another type of vehicle, in which case the UK driving test is treated as their first driving test. For example a driver who exchanges a foreign licence (car) for a UK licence (car) and who later passes a test to drive another type of vehicle (e.g. an HGV) will be subject to the special rules.

Where a person subject to the special rules accumulates six or more penalty points before the end of the two-year period (including any points acquired before passing the test) their licence will be revoked automatically. To regain the licence they **MUST** reapply for a provisional licence and may drive only as a learner until they pass a further driving test (also see Annexe 8 – Safety code for new drivers.)
Law RT(ND)A

Note. This applies even if they pay for offences by fixed penalty. Drivers in the first group (UK, EU/EEA etc.) who already have a full licence for one type of vehicle are not affected by the special rules if they later pass a test to drive another type of vehicle.

Other consequences of offending

Where an offence is punishable by imprisonment then the vehicle used to commit the offence may be confiscated.
Law PCC(S)A, sect 143

In addition to the penalties a court may decide to impose, the cost of insurance is likely to rise considerably following conviction for a serious driving offence. This is because insurance companies consider such drivers are more likely to be involved in a collision.

Drivers disqualified for drinking and driving twice within 10 years, or once if they are over two and a half times the legal limit, or those who refused to give a specimen, also have to satisfy the Driver and Vehicle Licensing Agency's Medical Branch that they do not have an alcohol problem and are otherwise fit to drive before their licence is returned at the end of their period of disqualification. Persistent misuse of drugs or alcohol may lead to the withdrawal of a driving licence.

6. Vehicle maintenance, safety and security

Vehicle maintenance

Take special care that lights, brakes, steering, exhaust system, seat belts, demisters, wipers and washers are all working. Also

- lights, indicators, reflectors, and number plates **MUST** be kept clean and clear
- windscreens and windows **MUST** be kept clean and free from obstructions to vision
- lights **MUST** be properly adjusted to prevent dazzling other road users. Extra attention needs to be paid to this if the vehicle is heavily loaded
- exhaust emissions **MUST NOT** exceed prescribed levels
- ensure your seat, seat belt, head restraint and mirrors are adjusted correctly before you drive
- ensure that items of luggage are securely stowed.

Laws RVLR 1989 regs 23 & 27 & CUR 1986, regs 30 & 61

Warning displays

Make sure that you understand the meaning of all warning displays on the vehicle instrument panel. Do not ignore warning signs, they could indicate a dangerous fault developing.

- When you turn the ignition key, warning lights will be illuminated but will go out when the engine starts (except the handbrake warning light). If they do not, or if they come on while you are driving, stop and investigate the problem, as you could have a serious fault.
- If the charge warning light comes on while you are driving, it may mean that the battery isn't charging. This should also be checked as soon as possible to avoid loss of power to lights and other electrical systems.

Window tints

You **MUST NOT** use a vehicle with excessively dark tinting applied to the windscreen, or to the glass in any front window to either side of the driver. Window tinting applied during manufacture complies with the Visual Light Transmittance (VLT) standards. There are no VLT limits for rear windscreens or rear passenger windows.

Laws RTA 1988 sect 42 & CUR reg 32

Tyres

Tyres **MUST** be correctly inflated to the vehicle manufacturer's specification for the load being carried. Always refer to the vehicle's handbook or data. Tyres should also be free from certain cuts and other defects.

Cars, light vans and light trailers **MUST** have a tread depth of at least 1.6 mm across the central three-quarters of the breadth of the tread and around the entire circumference.

Motorcycles, large vehicles and passenger-carrying vehicles **MUST** have a tread depth of at least 1 mm across three-quarters of the breadth of the tread and in a continuous band around the entire circumference.

Mopeds should have visible tread.

Be aware that some vehicle defects can attract penalty points.

Law CUR reg 27

If a tyre bursts while you are driving, try to keep control of your vehicle. Grip the steering wheel firmly and allow the vehicle to roll to a stop at the side of the road.

If you have a flat tyre, stop as soon as it is safe to do so. Only change the tyre if you can do so without putting yourself or others at risk – otherwise call a breakdown service.

Tyre pressures

Check weekly. Do this before your journey, when tyres are cold. Warm or hot tyres may give a misleading reading.

Your brakes and steering will be adversely affected by under-inflated or over-inflated tyres. Excessive or uneven tyre wear may be caused by faults in the braking or suspension systems, or wheels which are out of alignment. Have these faults corrected as soon as possible.

Fluid levels

Check the fluid levels in your vehicle at least weekly. Low brake fluid may result in brake failure and a crash. Make sure you recognise the low fluid warning lights if your vehicle has them fitted.

Before winter

Ensure that the battery is well maintained and that there are appropriate anti-freeze agents in your radiator and windscreen bottle.

Other problems

If your vehicle

- pulls to one side when braking, it is most likely to be a brake fault or incorrectly inflated tyres. Consult a garage or mechanic immediately

- continues to bounce after pushing down on the front or rear, its shock absorbers are worn. Worn shock absorbers can seriously affect the operation of a vehicle and should be replaced
- smells of anything unusual such as burning rubber, petrol or an electrical fault; investigate immediately. Do not risk a fire.

Overheated engines or fire

Most engines are water-cooled. If your engine overheats you should wait until it has cooled naturally. Only then remove the coolant filler cap and add water or other coolant.

If your vehicle catches fire, get the occupants out of the vehicle quickly and to a safe place. Do not attempt to extinguish a fire in the engine compartment, as opening the bonnet will make the fire flare. Call the fire brigade.

Petrol stations/fuel tank/fuel leaks

Ensure that, when filling up your vehicle's tank or any fuel cans you are carrying, you do not spill fuel on the forecourt. Any spilled fuel should be immediately reported to the petrol station attendant. Diesel spillage is dangerous to other road users, particularly motorcyclists, as it will significantly reduce the level of grip between the tyres and road surface. Double-check for fuel leaks and make sure that

- you do not overfill your fuel tank
- the fuel cap is fastened securely
- the seal in the cap is not torn, perished or missing
- there is no visual damage to the cap or the fuel tank

Emergency fuel caps, if fitted, should form a good seal.

Never smoke, or use a mobile phone, on the forecourt of petrol stations as these are major fire risks and could cause an explosion.

Vehicle security

When you leave your vehicle you should

- remove the ignition key and engage the steering lock
- lock the car, even if you only leave it for a few minutes
- close the windows completely
- never leave children or pets in an unventilated car
- take all contents with you, or lock them in the boot. Remember, for all a thief knows a carrier bag may contain valuables
- never leave vehicle documents in the car.

For extra security fit an anti-theft device such as an alarm or immobiliser. If you are buying a new car it is a good idea to check the level of built-in security features. Consider having your registration number etched on all your car windows. This is a cheap and effective deterrent to professional thieves.

7. First Aid on the road

In the event of an incident, you can do a number of things to help, even if you have had no training.

1. Deal with danger

Further collisions and fire are the main dangers following a crash. Approach any vehicle involved with care. Switch off all engines and, if possible, warn other traffic. Stop anyone from smoking.

2. Get help

Try to get the assistance of bystanders. Get someone to call the appropriate emergency services as soon as possible. They will need to know the exact location of the incident and the number of vehicles involved.

3. Help those involved

DO NOT move casualties still in vehicles unless further danger is threatened. **DO NOT** remove a motorcyclist's helmet unless it is essential. Remember the casualty may be suffering from shock. **DO NOT** give them anything to eat or drink. **DO** try to make them warm and as comfortable as you can, but avoid unnecessary movement. **DO** give reassurance confidently and try not to leave them alone or let them wander into the path of other traffic.

4. Provide emergency care

Remember the letters **D R A B C:**

D – Danger – check that you are not in danger.

R – Response – try to get a response by asking questions and gently shaking their shoulders.

A – Airway – the airway should be clear and kept open. Place one hand on the forehead, two fingers under the chin and gently tilt the head back.

B – Breathing – normal breathing should be established. Once the airway is open check breathing for up to 10 seconds.

C – Compressions – if they are not breathing normally compressions should be administered to maintain circulation; place two hands in the centre of the chest and press down 4–5cms at a rate of 100/minute. You may only need one hand for a child. Give 30 chest compressions. Then tilt the head back gently, pinch the casualty's nostrils together and place your mouth over theirs. Give two breaths, each lasting one second (use gentle breaths for a small child).

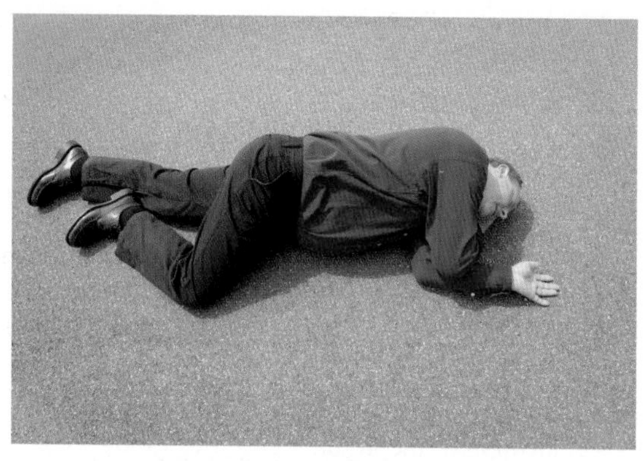

If the casualty is unconscious and breathing, place them in the recovery position until medical help arrives

Bleeding. First check for anything that may be in the wound, such as glass. If there is nothing embedded apply firm pressure over the wound. Take care not to press on the object – build up padding on either side of it. Fasten a pad to the wound with a bandage or length of cloth. Use the cleanest material available. If a limb is bleeding, but not broken, raise it above the level of the heart to reduce the flow of blood. Any restriction of blood circulation for more than a short time could cause long-term injuries.

Burns. Try to cool the burn by dousing it with clean, cold water or similar non-toxic liquid for at least 10 minutes. Do not try to remove anything sticking to the burn.

5. Be prepared

Always carry a first aid kit. You could save a life by learning emergency aid and first aid from a qualified organisation, such as the local ambulance services, the St John Ambulance Association and Brigade, St Andrew's Ambulance Association, the British Red Cross or any suitable qualified body (see Useful websites for contact details).

8. Safety code for new drivers

Once you have passed the driving test you will be able to drive on your own. This will provide you with lots of opportunities but you need to remain safe. Even though you have shown you have the skills you need to drive safely, many newly qualified drivers lack experience. You need to continue to develop your skills, especially anticipating other road users' behaviour to avoid having a collision. As many as one new driver in five has some kind of collision in their first year of driving. This code provides advice to help you get through the first twelve months after passing the driving test, when you are most vulnerable, as safely as possible.

- Many of the worst collisions happen at night. Between midnight and 6am is a time of high risk for new drivers. Avoid driving then unless it's really necessary.
- If you are driving with passengers, you are responsible for their safety. Don't let them distract you or encourage you to take risks. Tell your passengers that you need to concentrate if you are to get to your destination safely.
- Never show off or try to compete with other drivers, particularly if they are driving badly.
- Don't drive if you have consumed any alcohol or taken drugs. Even over-the-counter medicines can affect your ability to drive safely – read the label to see if they may affect your driving.
- Make sure everyone in the car is wearing a seat belt throughout the journey.
- Keep your speed down – many serious collisions happen because the driver loses control, particularly on bends.
- Most new drivers have no experience of driving high-powered or sporty cars. Unless you have learnt to drive in such a vehicle you need to get plenty of experience driving on your own before driving a more powerful car.
- Driving while uninsured is an offence. See Annexe 3 for information on types of insurance cover.

REMEMBER that under the New Drivers Act you will have your licence revoked if you get six penalty points on your licence within two years of passing your first driving test. You will need to pass both the theory and practical tests again to get back your full licence.

You could consider taking further training such as Pass Plus, which could also save you money on your insurance, as well as helping you reduce your risk of being involved in a collision. There are three ways to find out more:

- internet – www.passplus.org.uk
- telephone – DSA head office on 0115 901 2633
- Email – passplus@dsa.gsi.gov.uk

Other information

Metric conversions

The conversions given throughout *The Highway Code* are rounded but a detailed conversion chart is shown below.

Miles	Kilometres	Miles	Kilometres
1.00	1.61	40.00	64.37
5.00	8.05	45.00	72.42
10.00	16.09	50.00	80.47
15.00	24.14	55.00	88.51
20.00	32.19	60.00	96.56
25.00	40.23	65.00	104.60
30.00	48.28	70.00	112.65
35.00	56.33		

Useful websites

www.sja.org.uk (St John Ambulance Association and Brigade)
www.firstaid.org.uk (St Andrew's Ambulance Association)
www.redcross.org.uk (The British Red Cross)
www.dft.gov.uk
www.direct.gov.uk
www.transportoffice.gov.uk
www.highways.gov.uk/traffic info
www.direct.gov.uk/highway code
www.larsoa.org.uk
www.collisionreporting.gov.uk
www.askthe.police.uk
www.secureyourmotor.gov.uk
www.parking-appeals.gov.uk (outside London)
www.parkingandtrafficappeals.gov.uk (inside London)

Further reading

Best practice

Further information about good driving and riding practice can be found in The Driving Standards Agency books *The Official DSA Guide to Driving – the essential skills* and *The Official DSA Guide to Riding – the essential skills*. Information specifically for drivers of large vehicles can be found in *The Official DSA Guide to Driving Goods Vehicles* and *The Official DSA Guide to Driving Buses and Coaches.*

The Blue Badge Scheme

Information on this scheme can be found on the Department for Transport Website: www.dft.gov.uk

Code of Practice for Horse-Drawn Vehicles

The Code of Practice is available from the Department for Transport, Transport Technology and Standards Division 6, 2nd Floor, Great Minster House, 76 Marsham Street, London SW1P 4DR.
Tel: 0207 944 2078

Roadworks

A leaflet giving further information on driving through roadworks can be obtained from Highways Agency Publications, tel: 0870 1226 236, quoting reference number HA113/04. For general Highways Agency information, tel: 08457 504030 or email ha_info@highways.gsi.gov.uk

Index

References are to rule numbers, except those numbers in *bold italics*, which refer to the annexes

AA